2/-

THE INTERNATIONAL
ANARCHY, 1904—1914

By the same Author

THE CONTRIBUTION OF
ANCIENT GREECE TO MODERN LIFE

PLATO AND HIS DIALOGUES

AFTER TWO THOUSAND YEARS
A MODERN SYMPOSIUM

THE MEANING OF GOOD

JUSTICE AND LIBERTY
A POLITICAL DIALOGUE

RELIGION AND IMMORTALITY

RELIGION: A CRITICISM AND A FORECAST

THE GREEK VIEW OF LIFE

THE MAGIC FLUTE
A FANTASIA IN PROSE AND VERSE

LETTERS FROM JOHN CHINAMAN

APPEARANCES
BEING NOTES ON TRAVEL

AN ESSAY ON THE CIVILIZATIONS OF
INDIA, CHINA AND JAPAN

REVOLUTION AND REACTION IN MODERN FRANCE, 1789–1871

THE EUROPEAN ANARCHY

WAR: ITS NATURE, CAUSE AND CURE

CAUSES OF INTERNATIONAL WAR

THE CHOICE BEFORE US

ETC,

THE INTERNATIONAL ANARCHY, 1904-1914

BY

G. LOWES DICKINSON

NEW EDITION

WITH A FOREWORD BY

SIR ARTHUR SALTER

LONDON: GEORGE ALLEN & UNWIN LTD.
RUSKIN HOUSE, 40 MUSEUM STREET, W.C 1

FIRST PUBLISHED IN 1926
CHEAP EDITION 1937

PRINTED IN GREAT BRITAIN BY
KIMBLE & BRADFORD, LONDON, W.I.

FOREWORD TO THE POPULAR EDITION

By Sir Arthur Salter

Lowes Dickinson was by nature a poet and a philosopher. His *Goethe, The Magic Flute*, his poems, and the felicitous idealisation of the Chinese outlook on life in his *Letters from John Chinaman* indicate what would, in a happier age, have been the sphere of his work and interest. He was impelled to the study of politics and public affairs, not because these were for him of intrinsically equal value, but because they deal with the conditions upon which all higher values are dependent. In particular, in the latter years of his life his mind was occupied with the menace of another war which would be destructive of all civilisation. And more and more the core of his convictions was expressed in a single theme. War results from the juxtaposition of independent states, armed and sovereign, neither recognising nor willing to establish any superior authority; and will be inevitable while that fundamental cause remains.

I well remember the impression made on me by Lowes Dickinson's *European Anarchy* of 1916 in which he first advanced the theme he was to develop more fully in the present book ten years later. I had read and re-read the history of the previous half-century. But I had read, as most people then read, and many do now, without any real understanding of the inner springs of action. As dispute and crisis succeeded each other, we searched for the immediate causes, allotted blame or praise to the several negotiators—and took for granted everything that was below the surface. Or occasionally, at the best, we would penetrate a little deeper and realise that there were enduring conflicts of economic interest or political ambition, of which more trivial occasions of dispute were in some part the temporary and superficial expression. Few of us, however, penetrated to the deeper truth. We did not realise that, necessary as it was that separate sovereign

States should show a magnanimous wisdom and restraint in their economic policies and a moderation in their political aspirations, this by itself could never be enough; for, however much the causes of conflict might be so reduced, they could never be eliminated, and unless there was some method of settlement beyond negotiation based upon the known competitive strength behind the negotiators, sooner or later this strength would be brought to a trial in warfare. State virtue can no more by itself be relied on as a means of avoiding violence than personal virtue could be without the strong framework for all our interacting interests of an enforceable system of law. Some optimists have indeed imagined a time in which the virtues of good citizenship will have so developed that the State can be safely allowed to " fade away." But the most sanguine of them have only conceived of this as possible after civic virtue has been long trained in a system of law enforced by the State, never as a prior alternative. In international affairs we have not yet reached that first stage; we have only made a first effort in the establishment of the League of Nations, and its present weakness is not due to the fact that the conflicting ambitions of sovereign States have been so reduced that a controlling authority is not needed. On the contrary, it is due to the fact that they are so powerful that they are reluctant to tolerate it. And it is just as true in international affairs as in the relations of men within a nation, that anarchy inevitably results in violence.

No one perhaps perceived this truth at once so soon and so vividly as Lowes Dickinson, or has so richly supported it by historical illustration and persuasive argument. *The International Anarchy*, in which he develops his theme most fully, deserves to be both a classic and a best-seller. It depicts, as in a Greek drama, the tragic evolution of European politics from 1870 to 1914, the statesmen being no more than " little puppets, knocking away with lilliputian hammers the last stays that restrained the launch of that great death-ship, war."

His theme is stated briefly in an introduction and still more briefly in a few concluding paragraphs. Within this setting the main part of the book describes the evolution of the relations between the four protagonists, France, Germany, Russia, and Great Britain, and his chapter headings indicate—on a constantly enlarging time-scale—the tragic sequence of political events, the Triple Alliance and Bismarck's secret treaties, the Triple Entente, Morocco and the Conference of Algeciras, the Annexation of Bosnia, Agadir, Tripoli, the Bagdad Railway, Persia, The Far East, The Balkan Wars, " The Last Year," The Hague Conferences, Armaments, and " The Last Three Weeks."

At first sight, therefore, his book is one more volume in the library of research into the origins of the war.   If it were only that, or mainly that, it would have long been superseded, for immense stores of new evidence have become available since he wrote.   Its value remains, however, because while the rest of the library deals with the action of individuals the whole meaning and purpose of his book is to indicate the underlying forces of which they were the victims.   His actual account of political events is accurate and unbiased, and is based on a full and meticulous examination of all the sources available at the time.   The picture presented is a true one, and all the new information that is now in our possession has only added further detail, without changing the main outline and design. Never has the general picture been more vividly, or more faithfully, presented; and all later experience only shows more conclusively that his interpretation is the true one.

His book therefore remains of abiding interest and importance.   I am glad that while it is now being published in a popular form the integrity of the text to which a classic is entitled is being preserved.   Mr. Frank Hardie has added a few valuable footnotes as to a few crucial developments since 1926, but what Dickinson wrote is left in its entirety without omission, amendment, or supplement.

What is the picture of Europe before the war which is presented in this vivid account of this half-century of modern history?   Let me attempt to give it in miniature in words I have used elsewhere, and may with permission repeat here.[1]

We see five great countries, Germany, Austria-Hungary, France, Russia, and Great Britain, as the protagonists on the European, indeed, on the world arena.   Just outside this first rank is a sixth country, Italy, not yet quite a Great Power. From the other hemisphere there is an occasional impact from the United States, and half-way through the period a new

[1] *Economic Policies and Peace.*   Merthens Lecture, 1936.   The Hogarth Press.

country, Japan, begins to emerge as a no longer negligible factor in the calculations of the " Big Five." The rest of the world lives, for the most part, subject to the will or grace of these five. South America, indeed, is apart, under the protection of the Monroe doctrine. But Asia is subject to rule or exploitation through rival spheres of influence. Africa is partitioned. In Europe the present Poland is in fragments between three of the Great Powers, Czechoslovakia a part of two of them, the Baltic States a part of another; the Balkans, though looked on as a tinder-box which might start an unwelcome conflagration which would spread to the greater Powers, might as truly have been described as an arena in which these Powers tried out their strength. Other countries maintain a precarious independence with the help of the jealousies or, more rarely, a collective guarantee of the stronger Powers. Dominating the fate of the whole Continent, and in large measure the world, is a never-ending, extremely complicated, almost unintelligible " power game " of the great five. They are perpetually attempting, by methods obviously very dangerous, objectives which by comparison with the risks seem almost worthless. Indeed, as we watch them it becomes more and more clear that the main purpose in achieving any particular objective is less its intrinsic value than the demonstration it will afford of the successful country's power, the additional " prestige " it will give as a help to its next attempt. It is a dangerous game, and every one of the five realises that, if it is strong enough to fight one of the others, it cannot alone fight a combination. Each of them, therefore, is engaged in a feverish search for allies, preferably so combined that it will be the strongest in its own group and the group as a whole stronger than any opposing one. It is a competition carried on feverishly, secretly, unscrupulously. The running is made by Napoleon III in France and by Germany under the greatest master in the art, Bismarck, whose success drives those threatened by it along the same path, till under his less skilful successors they have their chance. All are drawn into the game, Germany the leader, Great Britain the last and most reluctant. But none dare stand out. Even an invincible navy and a country and empire most of which is inaccessible except by sea does not exempt us; the Low Countries are too near; the North-West Frontier too vulnerable to a dominant land Power.   All five act on certain assumptions, regarded as so certain as never to be questioned and scarcely even mentioned. Recurrent wars are regarded as inevitable, and are the legitimate and indispensable instruments of national policy.   They must not be undertaken lightly and never, if it can be avoided, except when diplomacy has created a situation in which victory may be expected.   The principal object in diplomacy is therefore to establish such a relation to the other principal countries (whether by joining combinations, or preventing their formation, or occupying a " balancing " attitude to them) as will enable national objectives to be obtained without war.   The " prestige " of a government is the measure of the success it has achieved in this purpose and its instrument for future success. In negotiations on specific questions, success is usually desired and failure feared because of their effect upon this prestige.   It follows that, in the most dangerous crises, the issues of war and peace turn more upon prestige than upon the merits of the actual dispute or the value of the tangible prize.   War may therefore be risked on what seems the most trivial occasion, for everyone feels that one surrender will make the next more likely, and there is no end to such a process—except a later war, under less advantageous conditions.   Prestige is thus not mainly a matter of ministers', or even national, vanity, though both enter into it and may be a substantial factor at some stages; it is essentially the measure of a country's potential ability to enforce a national policy, whether in the defence of existing rights or the acquisition of new ones.   It is the only instrument for this purpose apart from war itself.   Prestige, in a word, is potential victory in war, and may give actual victory without war.   War will therefore be risked to increase it or to avoid losing it.   And yet nearly all the governments at nearly all times desire to avoid war.   Some are more reluctant than others (and that is a handicap in negotiations as serious as the known weakness of their armaments); some will actually desire a war at a particular moment, but usually even then only in order to snatch victory when the moment is favourable, to prevent having to fight under less advantageous conditions later.   Diplomacy thus becomes an ever more dangerous game of bluff, each country desiring to secure its objectives and increase its prestige through the fear of others that it is ready to fight for them.   To watch the interchanges of the five Powers in the years before 1914 is like watching five conjurers trying to keep a number of balls in the air; the slightest slip—or the interruption of an outsider—will bring them all down.   Year after year skill averts disaster, but with every success it becomes more certain that failure must come some time—must come soon.   A gunboat off Morocco—not quite; a murder at Sarajevo—crash.

Under such conditions, the goal of victory is success itself and not the tangible prizes.   The danger of war cannot be measured by considering the nature of these prizes.   The " causes of war " in the ordinary sense, divergences of tangible interest, are quite secondary—almost irrelevant—at least quite remote from the actual point of danger.   Now and then—in the negotiations for a sphere of influence in Persia, for example—there may be a discernible economic advantage, and a group of special interests may egg on their government.   But in the worst crises, such as Sarajevo, any such element is remote.   In some cases hereditary hatreds and remembered grievances may play a part.   But again they are a secondary factor.   Great Britain moves in a few years from contemplating an alliance with Germany to forming an entente with France.   To Germany, Russia is first a secret ally and then a potential foe.   Nor are any general political sympathies of importance; a Liberal parliament shows distaste for an entente with the Czar, but this does not affect policy.   Everything is subordinated, and necessarily subordinated, to the quest for power.

" The economic necessities," says Spender, " which in previous ages were supposed to have driven nations to war had been largely removed by modern conditions.   International finance was more and more operating across national boundaries, raw material was accessible to all, doors were open to immigration, tariffs were moderate, there was free exchange of goods over a vast area.   Economically and materially . . . the nations had nothing to gain by war or conquest, but this did not affect the belief of the dominant Powers that military ascendancy and acquisition of territory were marks of national greatness, and periodical trials of strength a necessary part of the historical process."

With all this in mind, I think it is impossible to dispute that the diagnosis of Mr. Lowes Dickinson was right.   " International anarchy " was the fundamental cause of the last war.   There was no system which did for the competing and conflicting ambitions that extend beyond national frontiers what national government did for those within them; that is, establish and modify as need arises, a framework of law; settle disputes that arise by a judicial or arbitral process; and prevent a resort to violence in breach of the law by the use or prospect of collective force. Where human activities interact, they will sometimes conflict; where governments are associated with the conflicts they will be dangerous. If there is no other method of securing settlement except the one party's fear of the other's armed power, each will seek that power—and the " prestige " which means the known ability to use power. This search will be competitive; and, in a world with several great Powers, each will fear the others and none can be secure against a combination of the rest. This means that every dispute is essentially a trial of strength, and the most trivial may be as dangerous as one in which great interests are involved. Fear becomes the first motive in seeking the power which inspires it in others. " Prestige," being the only available instrument with which to secure national objectives without war itself, is the chief goal of diplomacy; it is essentially a function of anarchy.

The conclusion that follows is clear. No removal of either economic or political causes of war can, by itself, put an end to wars. If we succeeded beyond all reasonable hope in removing economic causes of conflict and dispute, there would still be a competitive scramble for power and prestige of the kind which led to the late war. More is required. International anarchy is the cause of war; and international government, therefore, the indispensable condition of preventing it. That is Lowes Dickinson's theme, the truth of which is confirmed not only by the events which he narrates, but by all that has happened since.

ALL SOULS COLLEGE
    OXFORD
     August 1937

PREFACE

HISTORY may be written in many ways and with many objects. It is no part of my present purpose to discuss the merits or demerits of these ; but I think it will be useful to state, at the outset, what my own object is in this book. I have written, consciously and deliberately, to point a moral. I believe, with most instructed people, that modern war, with all the resources of science at its disposal, has become incompatible with the continuance of civilisation. If this be true, it is a mistake to look back upon the course of history and say : There has always been war, and yet civilisation, has survived. At the best, what has survived is a poor thing compared to what might have been, had there been no war. But even such poor survival cannot be counted upon in the future. We are therefore faced with a problem which has never before presented itself to mankind.

I do not think there will be much serious questioning of this conclusion. The obstacle that keeps people passive or indifferent in the face of it is rather a fatalistic scepticism. They think that war is inevitable, and therefore refuse to face the facts about it. It may, indeed, be inevitable; but it cannot be pronounced so until its causes have been more carefully analysed than they have yet been. This book is intended as a contribution to that analysis. My thesis is, that whenever and wherever the anarchy of armed States exists, war does become inevitable. That was the condition in ancient Greece, in Republican Rome, in Mediæval Italy, and in Europe for several centuries after its emergence from the feudal chaos. That chaos also involved war. But such war is not properly to be called either civil or international; and with that particular condition we are not now concerned. International war, in our own age as in the others referred to, is a clash between sovereign armed States. It arises in consequence of the international anarchy.

The general conditions of that anarchy I have described in my first chapter. In those that follow I have made a detailed analysis of their operation in the particular case that led up to the recent war. This case, of course, differed in innumerable details from others ; but in essence it was the same. The anarchy of armed States always has produced war, and always must.

I am writing history, then, with a purpose and a moral. But I am not, therefore, assuming the liberty to write it untruly. I have done my best to be fair and accurate throughout ; and I do not think that a candid reader will accuse me of wilful misrepresentation. The objection is more likely to be taken that we do not yet know the facts sufficiently to write trustworthy history of a period so recent. There is some truth in this, but not a truth that affects my argument. We do not know all the facts, and we never can know them all. But we know enough to see clearly the main lines upon which the catastrophe developed. Further facts that may be revealed will not alter these, though they may fill in gaps, correct details, and round off the picture. But the picture will not be substantially changed ; it will only be painted in harder, firmer forms, and with a greater wealth of circumstance.

Further, we have already a mass of authentic material, such as has never before been available so soon after the occurrence of the events. In the first place, the chief of the defeated nations, desirous to refute the charge that it was solely responsible for the war, is in the course of publishing the whole of its diplomatic documents since 1870. A flood of light is thus thrown, not only on the policy of Germany, but on that of all the other Great Powers. This material has not, indeed, at the time of my writing, been brought down beyond the year 1909, nor completely so far as that. But it has been read to the end by a distinguished historian, Professor Brandenburg, who has written an account, based upon it, which will not, I think, be accused of partiality, and which, at any rate, assures us that nothing very startling or novel is likely to be revealed in the later volumes. No other State has yet embarked upon a similar work. But the Austrian historian, Professor Pribram, has had access to the documents at Vienna, and, upon their authority, has written a full account of the origin and successive renewals of the Triple Alliance.

So far, our light falls from the side of the Central Powers, though it illuminates also the policies of the Entente. But, in addition, the Bolshevist Government has published a number of dispatches which passed between the statesmen of England, Russia, and France in the years 1907 to 1914; and also five volumes of those exchanged in the years 1911 to 1914 between Isvolski, then Russian Ambassador in Paris, and his Government. From both these sources further light is thrown on the policy of the Entente Powers during those critical years. If we are unable to supplement these works by the complete documents of the Entente, that is because those Powers have not thought fit to publish their material. The British Government has announced that they will give theirs to the world, under the editorship of two distinguished scholars; but I have heard nothing of similar intentions in France and in Italy. If, during the interval, the policies of the Entente have less than justice done to them, that will be their own fault for maintaining secrecy. Those who do not publish cannot complain if they are suspected of having something to conceal.

Finally, we have, for the last three weeks before the final catastrophe, the published dispatches of all the Powers concerned. Whether these are complete and untampered with may be doubted. We know that the Russian and the French documents, at any rate, were doctored.[1] But, taking it all in all, it is possible now to have a pretty complete picture of what happened in those critical weeks.

These documents are, and always will be, the best authorities obtainable. They are good, just because they were not written for publication, but represent the real thoughts and intentions, at the time, of the Governments concerned. They have, of course, to be read with care, and with due account taken of any bias likely, under the circumstances, to distort them. A dispatch, for example, of a German to a Russian, or vice versa, after 1907, must be scanned more critically than one from an Englishman to a Frenchman. But when all is said, these dispatches give us a better opportunity of coming close to the truth than is often vouchsafed to historians. Nor is this conclusion impugned by

[1] See list of books under Romberg, and an article by August Bach in *Die Kriegsschuldfrage*, May 1924.

the view, sometimes put forward, that the real forces determining events move outside the region of Foreign Offices.
For such forces only become operative by and through
Governments, and, if influential at all, are reflected in the
policy of Governments. Nothing, therefore, of their influence
upon reality is neglected if we concentrate upon the acts and
the private and undoctored words of the statesmen who were
actually conducting events.

After the dispatches come the texts of treaties. Europe,
before the war, was tied up in a net of these, mostly secret;
and of the principal of them (perhaps not of all) the texts
are now published. We thus know, better than any but a
small circle of men knew before the war, how the States were
really bound to and against one another. These treaties are
analysed somewhat elaborately in the course of the chapters
that follow.

Besides dispatches and treaties we have memoirs and
histories. Of the former there is already a good store, and it
will no doubt be constantly increasing. They are often more
interesting than dispatches; but they must be read with
greater caution, except where they contain, as they sometimes do, contemporary documents. For the authors may
have reasons for concealing or perverting the truth; and
even where there is no such intention, memory, years after
the events, may play them false.

Of histories, biographies, and the like, the flood is already
overwhelming. I have read in these abundantly, but I make
no pretence to have read exhaustively. The lifetime, even of
a young man, would hardly suffice for that. But at any rate,
I have spared no pains to make myself acquainted with the
facts; and I feel convinced that the corrections and additions
which will be required as time goes on will not substantially
alter the picture here presented. The great weights and
pulleys of the huge engine are uncovered; and it is these that
are important.

It would be useless to attempt here a bibliography of the
whole enormous literature.[1] But to assist a reader who
wishes to check my work I have appended a list of the books
and documents I have cited. This list is printed in alpha-
betical order according to the short title commonly used in

---

[1] Cf. my list of books, under *Kriegsschuldfrage*.

the notes, the full title being printed on the opposite side of the page. Where there are English translations I have usually referred to these, for the convenience of English readers. I have taken all the care I could to see that my references are accurate, but errors are almost certain to have crept in, and I should be grateful to any reader who will call my attention to them.

My thanks are due to Mr. G. P. Gooch, Mr. Kingsley Martin, and Mr. L. G. Robinson, who have read my proofs and helped me with suggestions. They are not, of course, in any way responsible for my facts or my arguments.

CONTENTS

CHAPTER I

CHAPTER VI

CHAPTER VII

CHAPTER VIII

CHAPTER IX

CHAPTER X

CHAPTER XI

CONTENTS

CHAPTER XVII

THE INTERNATIONAL ANARCHY
1904-1914

CHAPTER I

THE INTERNATIONAL ANARCHY

I. The General Situation

THE special subject of this book is the series of events and situations which led up to the Great War. But that subject is regarded from a certain point of view, and it is the point of view that is important. The distinguished French writer, M. Romain Rolland, published during the war a little book called *Above the Battle*. When the battle is raging such appeals do not meet with much response. But after the battle they must be heard, if any real attempt is to be made to escape from similar calamities in future. In the pages that follow the reader is invited to forget that he is an Englishman and to remember that he is a man ; for it is the future of mankind that is at stake.

If we look back over the course of history we find war to be a normal part of its process; and historians are so hypnotised by that fact that they commonly consider, not the fundamental conditions which make war inevitable, but the superficial occasions out of which this or that war happened to arise. These occasions, of course, vary indefinitely in detail ; but underneath them all lies a general situation which makes it certain that war will come, though it is always doubtful by what particular circumstances or at what precise date it may be precipitated. It is this general situation which is the real theme of this book, although it has seemed timely to take as an illustration the particular events that led up to the last and worst catastrophe. The general situation, then, must first be made clear to the reader. It results from the juxtaposition of a number of States, independent and armed. That was the condition of civilisation in the three periods of European history that are most studied—ancient Greece, Renaissance Italy, and modern Europe ; and under that condition war is not an accident. It springs inevitably from the facts which we shall now proceed to analyse and illustrate, choosing our illustrations from recent times.

II. The Balance of Power

It matters little, in this analysis, at what point we begin, for all the points are connected ; so that, metaphorically, we shall be describing a circle, and shall complete the same figure wherever we start. For convenience we will begin with the fact that States are armed. That they should be so seems to men so much a matter of course that it is difficult to find anyone who will take seriously the idea that they need not be. But why are they armed ? The usual reply is, for defence. The rejoinder lies close at hand that, in that case, there is no need for any of them to be armed, since none of them has offensive purposes. But, in fact, each believes or fears that some other has such purposes. There thus develops the theory known as the " balance of power." States pursuing contrary aims will, it is urged, nevertheless not go to war if they are confronted by forces equal to their own. In that case, it is supposed, they will prefer to find some peaceful way of settling their differences. The balance may be " complicated," in the sense that there may be several weights pulling against one another, or " simple," in the sense that there may be only two. The latter was the case during the years preceding the Great War ; and a few sentences of M. Nelidoff, then Russian Ambassador at Paris, written in 1909, may serve as an illustration of what such a balance is held to mean. After referring to a recent diplomatic victory of Germany, he proceeds :

" The two Western Powers, together with Russia, must now pay their attention to the systematic development of their forces in order to be able, once they are in a position not to fear a challenge of the Triple Alliance—and in this case Italy would separate herself from the Triple Alliance—to set up on their part demands which would restore the political

balance which has now been displaced in favour of Germany
and Austria. The experience of the last five years has shown
us that a policy of this sort need not necessarily lead to war.
During the Morocco crisis the close unity of the Dual Alliance
in conjunction with England brought the German attempts
to a standstill. Also in the present case the supremacy of the
one side has been attained without the shedding of blood.
It is merely necessary to establish a close agreement between
the Powers, and to be firmly determined not to admit further
provocations on the part of the Triple Alliance, disposing at
the same time of sufficiently strong forces which would enable
us to offer resistance. This is the direction which the Cabinet
of Paris and also, apparently, that of London wish to give
to their policy, in the firm conviction that Russian policy is
also directed towards this end, since the shifting of the European
balance of power closely concerns Russia." [1]

That was the attitude, five years before the war broke out,
of one of the two groups into which Europe was divided.
That of the other group is thus described by an Austrian
statesman. It was, he says, the conviction of Germany and
Austria that Russia was working methodically for war, and
that " the only possibility to avoid a European conflict lay in
redressing the balance of power between the Triple Alliance
and the Triple Entente, to the advantage of the Middle
European Group." [2]

These passages, it will be observed, both describe the same
situation, but viewed from opposite standpoints. The balance
is conceived as substantially equal, but as oscillating now to
one side, now to the other, though never far enough to make
it worth while for either side to proceed to actual war. Under
such circumstances advantages will be attained now by this
party, now by the other, but there will not " necessarily " be
war. What Nelidoff desires is a permanent superiority of
the Triple Entente, so that the solutions reached would be
its solutions, not those of the other side. But, and equally,
the opposite result is desired by the Triple Alliance. Each
group aims at being sufficiently stronger than the other to
dictate rather than accept results. Thus both increase their
armaments ; rivalry, fear, and suspicion increase with these ;
and war, in due time, is produced.

[1] Siebert, p. 266.   [2] Hoyos, p. 83.

The positions thus illustrated bring us at once to the fatal defect of the balance of power. As a distinguished historian has wittily put it, the word " balance " has two meanings. It means, on the one hand, an equality, as of the two sides when an account is balanced, and, on the other hand, an inequality, as when one has a " balance " to one's credit at the bank. The balance of power theory professes the former, but pursues the latter. It is thus, in fact, a perpetual effort to get the better of the balance ; and as this effort is prosecuted on both sides, the ultimate issue is war. All history shows this, for every balance has ended in war. Let us take another example.[1] In the year 1878 the Austrian Minister, Count Andrássy, writes to Count Beust, his Ambassador in London, requesting him to lay before the British Government the Austrian wish to annex Bosnia-Herzegovina. The Russo-Turkish War, he urges, has disturbed the balance of power in favour of Russia and her Slav clients. However much the peace of San Stefano may be modified, from the standpoint of Europe, the fact of the liberation of a great nationality by Russian intervention cannot be undone, and it implies an increase of Slav influence. It is in the interest of Europe to create a counterbalance to this. The counterbalance should be the annexation of Bosnia by Austria-Hungary.[2] This proposal, it will be observed, is a plea for what States call " compensation," that is, the seizure by one State or group of States of some piece of territory to compensate a similar seizure by some other State, and thus restore the balance. It is also a good example of the erroneous calculations which run through history. For, in fact, the newly liberated Bulgaria, instead of becoming a client State of Russia, became, in the next year or two, her enemy ; and the acquisition by Austria-Hungary, thirty years later, of that full sovereignty over Bosnia which she was demanding in 1878 was one of the most marked steps in the series of events which led to the Great War. Such is the comment of actual history on the argument of Andrássy. That argument he concludes as follows : " If Austria-Hungary takes the place of Turkey in Bosnia, a further grouping of the Slavs under Russian protection will

---

[1] German Documents, ii. p. 288.
[2] " Autonomy," under Austrian rule, the solution ultimately adopted, is ruled out in this dispatch.

be ruled out, and a peaceful balance opposed to the prevalence of Russian influence, without any alteration in the relations of the Powers. There is no Power in Europe whose real interest will be touched by this extension of Austrian territory. For our monarchy itself it involves no increase of power, but an act of defence against threatening dangers, an act which is calculated at the same time to safeguard the peace of Europe against any disturbance in the near future, a sacrifice which Austria takes upon herself and the fruits of which will redound to the good of Europe." Whether Count Andrássy believed this statement I am not in a position to say. What followed, in fact, was a long and bloody war to subdue the province, an agitation of the Serbs which reached its climax when the occupation was converted into annexation, and, in a direct line; this cause co-operating with others, the Great War of 1914.

III. Armaments and Counter-armaments

The balance of power means a balance of military and naval forces. Hence the competition of armaments. These are said, by any one State or group of States, to be for defence, but are not believed to be so by the possible or actual opponent ; and thus the formal distinction between defence and offence disappears. Examples abound in diplomatic literature. Thus, an Austrian historian, discussing the situation between Russia and Austria in 1887, writes that if Russia wanted to attack Austria, she had only to threaten her enough to drive her into making an attack first ; if war appeared to be inevitable, Austria would be compelled to attack, and to pass from the political defensive to the military offensive.[1] The same view is implied in a Prussian historian's remark on the Anglo-German naval rivalry : " The firm determination to strike the first blow makes every moment of such a tension dangerous, for it is impossible to calculate whether and when the other Power will hold that the moment has come for that first blow." [2] " Nothing is easier," says another German, " than to construe the conception of attack in any way one likes." [3] These are not aberrations of the German mind ; they are

[1] Sosnosky, ii. pp. 95–6.   [2] Reventlow, ed. 1914, p. 368.
[3] Ger. Docs., vii. p. 27.

deductions from the logic of the situation. " All wars," said
Lord Aberdeen, who was in revolt against the doctrine, " are
called or pretended to be defensive."[1] For offence may always
be interpreted as "really" defence. It was a German
Emperor who said : " In 1870 we did not provoke the war,
but yet we began it offensively, that is, we attacked."[2]   But
equally the Italian Minister, Robilant, promising Italian aid
to Germany in case of a Franco-German war (1886), says :
" Twenty days after mobilisation we shall have 150,000 men
at the north-west frontier for a defensive-offensive war against
France."[3]   It was Bismarck who said to Crispi in 1877, when
an alliance between Germany and Italy was under discussion :
" The alliance must be both offensive and defensive.   Not
because I wish for war, which indeed I should do all in my
power to avoid, but as a natural consequence of prevailing
conditions.   Suppose, for example, that the French assemble
200,000 men at Lyons.   Their intention would be too obvious.
Are we to wait for them to attack us ? "[4]   But it was an
Austrian, Kálnoky, who said, when Italy was joining the Dual
Alliance in 1882 : " In theory one can dispute as to what
provocation is; but in practice this makes little difference. . . .
To establish who has been attacked is always impossible."[5]

Has this view been abandoned after the experience of the
war to end war ?   Not at all.   It is only confirmed, at any
rate in the minds of soldiers.   For in a Report to the Council
of the League of Nations by the Permanent Advisory Commission on Armaments, the representatives of Belgium, Brazil,
Sweden, and France sign the following statement :

" Hitherto aggression could be defined as mobilisation, or
the violation of a frontier.   This double test has lost its value.

" Mobilisation, which consisted until quite recently of a
few comparatively simple operations (calling up reserves,
purchases or requisitions and establishment of war industries
after the calling up of the men), has become infinitely more
complicated and more difficult both to discover in its origin
and to follow in its development.   In future, mobilisation will
apply not merely to the army, but to the whole country before
the outbreak of hostilities (collection of stocks of raw material

---

[1] Morley's *Gladstone*, Popular Ed., i. p. 365.
[2] Ger. Docs., iii. p. 123.   [3] Ib., iv. p. 208.
[4] Crispi, ii. p. 59.   [5] Ger. Docs., iii. p. 232.

and munitions of war, industrial mobilisation, establishment or increased output of industries). All these measures (which give evidence of an intention to go to war) may lead to discussion and conflicting interpretations, thus securing decisive advantages for the aggressor unless action be taken.

" The violation of a frontier by ' armed forces ' will not necessarily be, in future, such an obvious act of violence as it has hitherto been. The expression ' armed forces ' has now become somewhat indefinite, as certain States possess police forces and irregular troops which may or may not be legally constituted, but which have a definite military value. Frontiers themselves are not easy to define, since the treaties of 1919–20 have created neutral zones, since political and military frontiers no longer necessarily coincide, and since air forces take no account of either. Moreover, the passage of the frontier by the troops of another country does not always mean that the latter country is the aggressor. Particularly in the case of small States, the object of such action may be to establish an initial position which shall be as advantageous as possible for the defending country, and to do so before the adversary has had time to mass his superior forces. A military offensive of as rapid a character as possible may therefore be a means, and perhaps the only means, whereby the weaker party can defend himself against the stronger. It is also conceivable that a small nation might be compelled to make use of its air forces in order to forestall the superior forces of the enemy and take what advantage was possible from such action.

" Finally, the hostilities between two naval Powers generally begin upon sea by the capture of merchant vessels or other acts of violence—very possibly on the high seas outside territorial waters. The same applies to air operations, which may take place without any violation of the air frontiers of States.

" These few considerations illustrate some of the difficulties inherent in any attempt to define the expression ' cases of aggression,' and raise doubts as to the possibility of accurately defining this expression a priori in a treaty from the military point of view, especially as the question is often invested with a political character." [1]

---

[1] League of Nations. Report of the Temporary Mixed Commission for the Reduction of Armaments. Geneva, August 30th, 1923.

If a military definition of aggression is thus ruled out, is a political definition possible ? It may be claimed that one really watertight has been given in the protocol drawn up by the League of Nations in 1924,[1] and the acceptance of such a definition by the States of the world would be the greatest advance in international practice which has yet been made. At the moment of writing the fate of this treaty still hangs in the balance. But whatever that fate may be, in the preceding centuries there has been no possibility of deciding, by a test that cannot be disputed, which State is the aggressor in a war and which the defender.

Under such conditions there can be no real possibility of a permanent limitation of armaments. Statesmen have sometimes played with the idea, and perhaps sincerely. But the situation of itself defeats them. An interesting example of this fact occurred in 1870.[2] The French Government, which

---

[1] The Definition is given in Article 10, which runs as follows :

ARTICLE 10.

Every State which resorts to war in violation of the undertakings contained in the Covenant or in the present Protocol is an aggressor. Violation of the rules laid down for a demilitarised zone shall be held equivalent to resort to war.

In the event of hostilities having broken out, any State shall be presumed to be an aggressor, unless a decision of the Council, which must be taken unanimously, shall otherwise declare :

(1) If it has refused to submit the dispute to the procedure of pacific settlement provided by Articles 13 and 15 of the Covenant as amplified by the present Protocol, or to comply with a judicial sentence or arbitral award or with a unanimous recommendation of the Council, or has disregarded a unanimous report of the Council, a judicial sentence or an arbitral award recognising that the dispute between it and the other belligerent State arises out of a matter which by international law is solely within the domestic jurisdiction of the latter State ; nevertheless, in the last case the State shall only be presumed to be an aggressor if it has not previously submitted the question to the Council or the Assembly, in accordance with Article 11 of the Covenant.

(2) If it has violated provisional measures enjoined by the Council for the period while the proceedings are in progress as contemplated by Article 7 of the present Protocol.

Apart from the cases dealt with in paragraphs 1 and 2 of the present Article, if the Council does not at once succeed in determining the aggressor, it shall be bound to enjoin upon the belligerents an armistice, and shall fix the terms, acting, if need be, by a two-thirds majority and shall supervise its execution.

Any belligerent which has refused to accept the armistice or has violated its terms shall be deemed an aggressor.

The Council shall call upon the signatory States to apply forthwith against the aggressor the sanctions provided by Article 11 of the present Protocol, and any signatory State thus called upon shall thereupon be entitled to exercise the rights of a belligerent.

[2] Newton, *Lord Lyons*, chap. vii.

had just adopted the democratic reform of 1868, had approached the British Government asking them to "give advice" to Prussia on the subject of disarmament. Lord Stanley, then Foreign Secretary, had declined. But in 1870 Mr. Gladstone was in power, and his Foreign Minister, Lord Clarendon, took the matter up. Summing up the situation, Lord Newton writes: "Mutatis mutandis, there was a curious similarity between the language used at Paris and Berlin respectively. The French proclaimed that they would not go to war with the Prussians provided the latter did nothing objectionable. The Prussians replied that they did not want to go to war with France, provided they were allowed to do as they pleased, and both asserted that the maintenance of peace depended upon England, which they explained by affirming that England had only to declare that she would join against whichever Power broke the peace ; the real meaning of this being that at Paris it was expected that England should announce beforehand that she would side with France in case of war, while at Berlin it meant she should announce beforehand that she would side with Prussia." France, it would seem, at this time really desired to reduce her Army, in order to conciliate the peasants and to retain their support against the Socialists. But also she was determined not to witness the unification of Germany without armed resistance. Bismarck, on the other hand, intended to achieve that unification, which of course would give a great access of strength to Germany. Thus behind this question, as always, was the balance of power ; and the proposal for a reduction of armaments broke down. England was acting as the honest broker. But now note. In the course of the discussion Bismarck remarked to the British negotiator : " It is all very well for you, living on an island where no one can attack you, to preach disarmament, but put yourself into our skin. You would then think and act differently. What would you say if we were to observe that your Navy was too large, that you did not require so many ironclads, that you lavished too large a portion of the taxation of the country in building ships, which in the peaceful disposition of Europe were not required ? If we recommended you to diminish your naval armament ? " " To this home thrust," Lord Newton continues, " the Ambassador made the somewhat unconvincing reply that, as evidence of our pacific disposition, we had just sold an ironclad to the Prussian Government, and were ready to sell others—a reply which was received with irreverent merriment." He goes on : " Lord Clarendon's language rather conveyed the impression that England stood upon a moral pinnacle which entitled her to admonish other nations as to the errors of their ways ; but the claim was vitiated by the fact that she maintained, and intended to maintain, a Navy of overwhelming strength, while, if her military power was even more insignificant than it is at the present day, the cost of the British Army amounted to much more than the cost of the Prussian Army, and therefore the less said about unproductive expenditure the better. . . . It might be added that England was quite ready at all times to supply to an unlimited amount ironclads, rifles, and munitions of war to any foreign customer, however depraved. And yet we are pained and surprised when anyone suggests that we are occasionally hypocritical."

As to Bismarck, who, whatever may be thought of him, was not hypocritical, his view is given succintly in a conversation with Crispi, held in 1877 : " This question," he said, " was gone into with the Emperor Napoleon before 1870, and after long discussion it was proved beyond doubt that the principle of disarmament can never succeed in practice. There are no words in the dictionary that accurately define the limits of disarmament and armament. Military institutions differ in every State, and even when you have succeeded in placing the armies on a peaceful footing you will not be able to affirm that the conditions of offence and defence are equal with all the nations which have participated in disarmament. Let us leave this question to the Society of Friends." [1] It is not the only question which the Society could solve if men would listen to them ; but only on condition that they could persuade States to cease pursuing the purposes which in fact they do pursue. If armaments were really, as is always pretended, merely for defence in all countries, there would be no difficulty in all-round disarmament, for that would make attack impossible. Such an idea, however, has not yet penetrated the minds either of statesmen or of their peoples ; and it is still less likely to penetrate those

[1] Crispi, ii. p. 37.

of soldiers, whose whole training and interest is bound up
with the perpetuation of war. For, as Lord Salisbury once
remarked : " If you believe the doctors, nothing is wholesome ;
if you believe the theologians, nothing is innocent ; if you
believe the soldiers, nothing is safe." [1]

IV. The Motives of Aggression

It is not, however, only inertia, habit, and professional
interest which stands in the way of disarmament.   It is something else. Always some State, and usually many States,
desire something that is only to be had by war. In other
words, their real purposes are offensive, as well as defensive.
This is a complicated matter, for such purposes are seldom
avowed and, though pursued, are pursued conditionally.
The formula runs : " We don't want to fight, but by jingo if
we do," or less epigrammatically : " We don't want a war,
but if a war should come—as of course it will come sooner or
later—then we shall take so-and-so, which we have long
wanted." For—and this is the cardinal point of the whole
situation—every strong and expanding State wants to seize
territory, and this it can only seize by force. That is why
every war, whatever its origin, whatever the professions of
the combatants, has ended, if there was victory at all, in
annexations. According to the professions of statesmen, all
wars are defensive. According to the facts of peace-treaties,
all are offensive. Let us illustrate this point by a few examples,
though that should be superfluous, since all history is its
illustration.

We may admit, to begin with, that some offensive wars
are usually regarded with sympathy, even by those who are
opposed in general to war. They are what are called wars
for liberation. In the long course of history States and
Empires have conquered and reduced under their authority
large numbers of unwilling and recalcitrant peoples. These
have seldom acquiesced permanently in such a position.
Italy under the Spanish and Austrians, the Balkan States
under the Turks, Ireland under the English, are familiar
examples of this fact. Such wars for liberty are not usually
regarded with reprobation, and might even, without undue

[1] *Salisbury*, ii. p. 153.

fatalism, be considered "inevitable." They show how war breeds war, and converts into a kind of virtue what, from a larger point of view, is the greatest of crimes. But such wars to gain liberty, proceeding from wars to destroy it, do but bring into greater distinctness the normal fact, that the root of war is acquisitiveness. If it were otherwise, there need not be wars for liberty, for liberty would be granted freely— a thing which has seldom, or never, been done in the course of history, though prudent States have sometimes granted to their discontented subjects a large measure of autonomy. On the other hand, it is seldom, or never, that a nation, once it has gained its liberty, has not set out upon a career of conquest. The view of statesmen and nations is that they will not make offensive war. Nevertheless, when they do make war, they act in the same way as if it had been offensive, by annexing all that they safely and profitably can.

This annexation has various motives and justifications. In the case of Empires with frontiers bordering on unsettled and warlike tribes, conquests are made for the sake of security and internal peace. It is thus that the ancient Roman Empire was led on from step to step; thus the Russian Empire; and thus the British Empire of India. In this process Empires may meet and conflict, as did Macedonia and Persia, Rome and Carthage, Britain and Russia. In such cases we get, in its simplest form, the competition for power between rival States. By these extensions of Empire, States become involved in the need to acquire fresh military and naval resources. A Sea-Power, like Great Britain, looks out for naval stations, which she has in fact secured all over the world, and which she grudges to any other State that may be her rival at sea. A continental and military Power aims at new soldiers to conscribe. Thus the Roman Empire, in its later days, was defended more by its foreign than by its Italian subjects; and modern France seizes African territory as much for the sake of raising black troops for war in Europe as for the sake of economic advantage. M. Caillaux, one of the most moderate of expansionists, avows this quite frankly. "Colonial expansion," he writes, "became the complement and buttress of the general policy of French Governments. It gave France the material power, the weight necessary for her affirmations of Right in Europe."[1] The phrase "affirmations of Right" may be noted in passing. It is the common cant of States; whether sincere or no, it is hardly worth while to inquire. But the important point is the affirmation of policy. France now conscribes her natives throughout Africa; she claims the right, apparently granted her during the discussions on the Treaty of Peace, to transfer such troops, even from mandated territories, to Europe, in spite of a clause in the Covenant of the League of Nations which appears to prohibit such a claim.[2] A far-seeing historian might feel grave doubts whether these black forces may not before long overwhelm Europe, as the bar-barians once overwhelmed the Roman Empire. But that possibility does not trouble France. She thinks, as all States always think, exclusively of herself, and by herself she means her power.

Similar considerations impel landlocked States to make war in order to reach the sea. They need not, indeed, do this, and they need not suffer from not doing it. Switzerland is a case in point. But commonly, if they have the chance, they want to do it; and they are often impelled to do it by the fact that their neighbours exploit the situation to force trade into channels favourable to themselves. This for many years was the grievance of Serbia against Austria. It is also, in part, the cause of the long effort of Russia to secure an ice-free harbour, either on the east, which brought her into competition with Japan, or on the west, which involved the series of wars that have turned upon the possession of Con-stantinople. The military and economic motives here coalesce, for the port is required at once for trade and for war.

These kind of reasons for aggressive expansion have a realistic justification. The objects, that is, are intelligible, granted the anarchy of international relations and the desire of States to exploit their neighbours to their own advantage. But behind these causes of war, which we may call realities, there lies something less amenable to rational discussion. That something is the passion, possessing always some indi-viduals and capable of seizing, at times and in places, whole masses of men, for size and power as a good and desirable thing for its own sake. It is not useful to argue about this

[1] *Agadir*, p. 6. See below, Chapter VII.   [2] See Baker, chap. xxiv.

passion, for it is independent of reasons ; so that, if these
are given at all, they are given by way of dialectics, to push
the opponent if possible, by hook or by crook, out of the way.
The feeling in question may therefore be called mystical,
if by that word we describe a position for which no reasoned
defence can be made ; and it must be admitted that the
greater part of human conduct is of that kind.   In literature
and journalism this blind impulse is often signified by the
Greek word " pan."   Men speak of " pan-Slavism," " pan-
Germanism," " pan-Americanism," and if we do not use in
that sense the word " pan-Anglicanism," we have the simpler
phrase with the same meaning—" all red."   Red, it may be
remarked in passing, is not only the colour in which the
British Empire is painted ; it is also the colour of blood.
The kind of excitement symbolised by such words as these
shows the unreflecting and primitive nature of the mood.
It is in fact the lust for power raised to its highest point
and unrestrained by any sense either of fact or of value.   A
good account of it in its Russian form is given by Isvolski
in his *Memoirs.*[1]   He says there, writing of the middle
seventies :

" Danilevski's book, *Russia and Europe*, was in everybody's
hands.   This book proclaimed in inflammatory terms the
powerful antagonism between Russia and the Occidental
world, and the inferiority of European culture to that of
Russia, based upon the principles dear to the heart of the
Slavophils.   In the field of foreign political relations, Danilevski claimed that Russia should unite all the Slavs, if not
under her sceptre at least under her hegemony ; that Constantinople should become the capital of the Russian Empire,
and at the same time the capital of the future Slavonic
federation.   These results, he maintained, could only be
attained by an armed conflict with the Orient and with the
rest of Europe ; the victory should be gained by the Greco-
Slavs, led by Russia, and should be established by the definite
triumph of its civilisation over that of the Germano-Roman
peoples."[2]   A passion like this may be at times embarrassing
to realistic statesmen, but it may also be of assistance.   Which
it will be depends on whether or no, in their judgment, the
time has come for the war which some, or all, of them are

[1] P. 163.   [2] For other sources, see note 4 to p. 161 of Valentin.

always, for one reason or another, anticipating. Nor is this blind impulse confined to Oriental peoples. It is latent or active in England, in France, in America, and, at the moment of my writing, apparently dominant in Italy. It commandeers history to compel it to its service ; and Italy, Russia, Bulgaria, Greece, or sections of the population of these countries, claim, all of them, or have claimed, a right to Constantinople based upon the past imperial achievements of the people who inhabited, in some time long past, their respective countries. Similarly, no doubt, the new Arabia, if ever it became strong enough, would claim to expand over the old Arab Empire. These ideas work like intoxicants, obscuring all contemporary facts or needs ; and they may become, at a given moment, powerful allies to those ambitions of States which are based on more realistic grounds.

It is not probable, however, that in most cases, or at most times, these violent passions are felt by any except minorities, belonging for the most part to the upper and supposedly educated classes. An interesting passage is worth quoting here from an account by an unusually sane Russian Ambassador of the character of Pan-Slavist fanaticism. The Minister is himself opposed to all advances towards the Mediterranean, and would be willing, he says, to sign a treaty guaranteeing the Turkish Empire for one hundred years. " Ninety per cent. of the Russians," he says, " think as I do ; but unfortunately neither reason nor the majority rule among us. All our leading personalities stand, more or less, under the influence of fanatical minorities, which have written on their banner the unfortunate word ' tradition.' Such is the orthodox movement, cultivated by a few ladies of high rank, with the support of ambitious priests, and urging us in two directions—towards Constantinople and towards the Holy Places ; and such is the Slav propaganda. At the head of both movements are mere nullities. But unfortunately my Government has not the strength to emancipate itself from these. It reckons, and is bound to reckon, that in the case of great events, such as a conflict with Turkey, the extreme parties would raise their voice and sweep away the masses with them." [1] This is very much what happened in 1914. The originators of aggressive policies are usually very

[1] Ger. Docs., xviii., ch. cxviii., pp. 309 seq.

few, but they are supported by others for various reasons of self-interest ; and when the crisis comes even the masses, formerly ignorant and indifferent, are swept away. Yet that, perhaps, less than is imagined or pretended. The people go, rather, like sheep to the slaughter. Their real feeling is hardly known to themselves, and for it is substituted the long and savage drone of an opinion-manufacturing Press.

From these and such-like causes and ideas is derived that urge to expansion, and therefore to aggressive war, which underlies at all times the policies of all States strong enough to pursue it with any hope of success. It may be worth while to illustrate the point further. Bismarck, in 1871, " obligingly remarked " to Count Beust that " one could not conceive of a great Power not making of its faculty for expansion a vital question." [1] Writing of the partition of Poland, Von Sybel says : [2]

" After the most careful consideration we can come to no other conclusion than this, that the resolution to appropriate a frontier province of Poland was the only one which under the circumstances did not lead to evident disaster—the only one, therefore, which was consistent with the duty of the Prussian Government." Dr. Dillon, who knew well Russia and Russian ambitions, says of her policy of expansion : [3] " This duplicity and guile were the principal means employed in peace-time to effect or prepare for that territorial expansion which was a standing postulate of the self-preservation of the Tsardom." And elsewhere : [4] " In this respect there was no essential difference in the treatment applied to the Near, the Middle, and the Far East. The patient was first coaxed and bullied into making a will—in diplomatic language a secret treaty—in favour of Russia, was then forbidden to call in a doctor, and in some cases forced to sip slow poison in lieu of efficacious treatment." Will it be suggested that Dr. Dillon is not an impartial witness ? Let us then take a definite example. Before making war against Turkey, in 1877, Russia had entered into a convention with Roumania, in which that country had promised to facilitate the passage of Russian troops in return for a guarantee of her

---

[1] Hanotaux, p. 297, citing Beust's *Memoirs*, but without reference to page and volume.   Probably ii. p. 267.
[2] II. p. 405, cited Eversley, p. 250.
[3] *Eclipse of Russia*, p. 230.   [4] P. 226.

integrity. The Russian victory was largely gained by Roumanian assistance. But at the Congress of Berlin the Russians proposed to take from Roumania the three northern districts of Bessarabia, giving in exchange some territory in the Dobrudja. In vain did the Roumanians protest. Prince Gortschakoff was adamant. Russia, he maintained, had indeed guaranteed Roumanian territory, but only against Turkey, not against herself. He and Count Schuvaloff even took credit to Russia that she had not asked for more. That was proof, in his view, that the Russian demand was based on " honour," not on ambition and interest. The British protested ; but as they had themselves entered into a private agreement with Russia before the Congress met, they were not in a good position to make their protest effective. The Roumanian delegate complained that the Great Powers, by sacrificing Roumania to Russia, had been enabled to obtain better terms for themselves ; and Lord Beaconsfield was constrained to remark that " in politics ingratitude is often the reward of the greatest services." [1]

That, it may be objected, was in the old days, before the Entente with England. We shall have opportunity enough, in later chapters, to see what Russian ambitions were after the Entente was formed. Meantime, let us recall that in the June of 1914 there appeared in the *Preussisches Jahrbuch* [2] an article by Dr. Paul Mitrofanoff which fell like a bomb into the accumulated materials of war. " The extension southwards," the writer said, " is for Russia an historical, political, and economic necessity, and the foreign Power which stands in the way of this expansion is eo ipso an enemy Power." The enemy was " Germany," and by this time it was a commonplace in Russia that " the road to Constantinople lies over Berlin." It was two years earlier that another famous article appeared in the *Novoe Vremya*, saying that the time-honoured policy of Russia was " founded on the axiom that she needs territorial expansion at the expense of her neighbours." [3]

Russia, perhaps, the reader will not defend. But he may think, with Dr. Dillon, that she and Germany were the only predatory States. This view, if anyone holds it, should have

[1] See De Martens, Ser. II, vol. iii. pp. 354 seq.   [2] P. 392.
[3] Cited Bland, p. 342.

been refuted by the annexations made by the victorious States after the war for liberty ; and if it be not so refuted, argument will serve little purpose.   Let us, however, go back to an earlier date, and take a case where our own country was closely concerned.   In 1793 England decided to enter the war against the French Revolution.   A curious and instructive conversation took place at that time between her representatives and those of her allies, Austria and Prussia.[1] The Prince of Cobourg had issued a manifesto disclaiming any intention of annexing French territory in the coming war.   He proposed now that the three Powers should make a self-denying ordinance to this effect.   The result was reported as follows by Count Staremberg to the Austrian Government.   The proposal of Cobourg, he said, "sounded the tocsin of indignation for all the other personages of the Conference.   Lord Auckland, the British representative, saw in it the sign of treachery on the part of Austria, and his anger was so great that he was on the point of withdrawing. The Duke of York, who was hot with rage, considered himself as tricked by Cobourg.   The Prince of Nassau and his sons followed on the same impulse as their allies.   Cobourg explained that he had thought that the object was to re-establish monarchy in France and order and peace in Europe.   But ' I found that I was mistaken.   I saw that everyone was thinking only of himself, and had much less in view the general interest than that of his own country only.'   Lord Auckland made it clearly understood that the restoration of order did not interest him at all, and announced with much vivacity that the wish of England was to reduce France to a veritable political nullity. . . . ' Each of the Powers in coalition,' he added, ' should seek to make conquests and keep them when made.'   Then, addressing Cobourg, he said : ' Take all the frontier fortresses of France on your side, and obtain a good barrier for Belgium.   As to England, I will frankly say that she wants to make conquests, and she will keep them.' "   The conquests mentioned as desirable were Dunkirk and the colonies of France.

In the preceding illustrations I have had in view those motives for expansion which would commonly be called political

[1] Eversley, p. 164, citing Sorel, *L'Europe et la Révolution Française*, iii. p. 366.

—defence, security, and that passion for power and size which has played so important a part in history. But closely associated with these motives, and particularly in recent years, has been economic need or greed. This has many aspects. The most apparently innocent is that known as "protection," the view, that is, that you benefit your own citizens by shutting out from them the products of foreign countries. We need not here argue this question from the point of view of economic advantage; but it is of interest also in its bearing upon war. This may be slight or important according to circumstances. It may not matter very much to other States what policy Switzerland or Denmark pursues. But it must matter a good deal what policy the British Empire pursues. For if a State acquires by force a quarter of the surface of the globe, containing enormous supplies of raw materials, and then announces to other States that it proposes, so far as it can, to keep these materials as a monopoly for citizens of the Empire, it is inviting a combination against it of all other States on the very plausible ground of their vital interests. Whatever else may be said or thought about the theory of free trade, few, I think, will deny that it is a peace-policy, and few instructed people will deny that its contrary may lead to war. Indeed, if we attend to recent history, we shall find, in example after example, how policies of protection have fostered that friction between States which leads sooner or later to armed conflict. Take, for example, the tariff war between Italy and France in 1890. France at that time determined to employ differential tariffs which were practically prohibitive in order to drive Italy out of the Triple Alliance. So, at any rate, Crispi believed. For in that year we find him writing:[1] "France is going to abolish all her treaties and apply an autonomous tariff to all nations. This contains a threat of war, of an economic war not less terrible than war with the rifle and artillery. We must prepare to retaliate, and I believe we shall be able to do so. . . ." "We should add an economic league to the military and political league already existing, which arrangement, while inoffensive to the autonomy of the three States (of the Triple Alliance) will strengthen them against France."

The whole language of this passage shows that Crispi

[1] *Memoirs*, iii. p. 9.

regarded the tariff war as of the same kind and directed by the same purpose as a war of arms. His thinking is not in terms of economics, but in terms of politics. And it is thus that politicians and statesmen commonly view such questions. Let us take another case, which had a close and direct bearing upon the causation of the Great War. Previous to the treaty of 1894 there had been an acute tariff war between Russia and Germany. Count Witte talks of the " tense situation at this time when mercantile relations between Germany and Russia had practically ceased. . . ." " Dark rumours," he adds, " flew about that my temerity and light-heartedness had dragged Russia to the brink of war with Germany, that the latter's inflexibility would inevitably result in a conflict which was bound to precipitate all of Europe into a sanguinary struggle." [1]   This dispute was ended by the tariff agreement of 1894, which lasted for ten years. At its renewal in 1904 Germany was at an advantage, since Russia was engaged in the war with Japan and the Kaiser was showing his friendship by guaranteeing Russia's rear. For this service, according to Dr. Dillon, " he extorted from the Tsardom a tribute which Stolypin and Witte both assured me was much greater than any war indemnity on record." " I needed," he proceeds, " no one to tell me that this accord would create friction intense enough to start a conflagration. Witte confirmed my view emphatically, repeating, ' It will assuredly lead to war.' He was right. As a matter of fact, before the negotiations for renewal had begun (in 1914) it became one of the main factors in the present struggle." [2]

These examples may serve to illustrate the point that tariffs, in certain cases, may and do become contributory causes of great wars. But they are not the only, nor the most important, economic factors working in that direction. Of recent years particularly, but also at all times throughout history, seizure of territory, a principal motive for war, has been prompted, among other things, by the desire to acquire important raw materials or potential or actual markets. To illustrate this fact from recent history would be almost to rewrite that history. For the colonial expansion of the Great Powers, which has been a principal motive of their policy during the last half-century or more, has been directed as

[1] *Memoirs*, p. 68.   [2] Dillon, pp. 323, 324.

much to economic as to military and political objects. The French are the best example, because their colonial policy has been protectionist as well as militaristic. It will be enough to refer to the single case of Madagascar. British annexations have been enormous, but less offensive to other States because of our policy of free trade. But raw materials do not represent the only advantage which States secure, or think they secure, by seizing territory. They secure also—and this in the modern world is a matter of importance—privileged outlets for their national capital. A good example of this preoccupation is afforded by M. Caillaux's policy with regard to Morocco. M. Caillaux was the Minister who had to handle this question in the crisis of 1911. He was in one sense a free trader, that is, he did not desire to exclude by tariffs the trade of countries other than France. But he was determined that France should have the monopoly of the construction and personnel of railways, harbours, and other public works. "The Germans," he says, "thought of nothing less than having a majority of employés in the railways of an immense section bordering the Atlantic, and in other cases a minority. I do not know whether any French Government could have been found to consent to this. I would not." No one, he says, is more opposed to " economic nationalism " than he is. But to admit German employés in the public services would be "the most humiliating of abdications." [1] All nations, I think, and all statesmen would take the same view, if only because of the risk in case of war. Whence we see once more how the menace of war leads to policies which provoke war. For the more a State claims for itself the monopoly of economic development in the territory it occupies, the more important does it become for other States to seize such territory themselves. On the other hand, if war be ruled out, the question of economic control becomes of subordinate importance. Compromises and adjustments are then possible which are precluded so long as war is a probable or certain event.

The example last adduced involves at once political and economic considerations ; and in fact these are commonly intermingled. Thus, for example, oil, which not long ago was independent of high politics, is now of such importance for war that Governments seek, for that reason alone, to

[1] See Caillaux, especially pp. 88 and 125 seq.

assure themselves of a supply. That is why the British Government has a controlling interest in the Anglo-Persian and in the Burmese oil companies. Apart, however, from the question of war, oil has become a necessity for transport, and States accordingly endeavour to secure their share, or more than their share, of a supply which appears to be limited. Hence the recent acrimonious disputes between the British and American Governments. Hence to some extent —to how great an extent we do not know—the Anglo-French and Anglo-Turkish wrangling over Mosul. A question of this kind need not lead directly and by itself to hostilities ; but handled in the competitive nationalistic way, with armaments at play behind diplomacy, it becomes a very powerful element in the friction which generates war. And when the material in dispute is itself important for the waging of war, when war is regarded as inevitable, and when, therefore, good will is sacrificed to preparing for it, the economic and militaristic motives march hand in hand.[1]

How powerfully these economic causes of war bulk in the minds of realistic statesmen is strikingly illustrated by an episode that occurred in the discussions on the League of Nations at Paris. It arose out of the clause, introduced by the Americans, which safeguards the Monroe doctrine. Europeans, and particularly the French, wanted to know what precisely the doctrine implies. They were afraid it might limit American intervention in Europe under the Covenant. Would America come to the help of any nation involved in a war forbidden by the Covenant, whatever might be the occasion of the war ? " Future wars," said the French delegate, Larnaude, " might not be wars of liberation. They might be economic in origin. The question was therefore whether the United States would come to the help of France in a struggle with a country which happened to be quite as liberal as herself ? "[2] President Wilson, we are informed, " did not ask Larnaude to interpret this utterance." But what lay behind it is sufficiently clear. The French believed that future wars would arise out of economic competition, as they knew that past wars had, and they wished to be quite sure of American aid, even in such a case, supposing they should be fortunate and clever enough to put the enemy technically in the

[1] Cf. Delaisi.   [2] Baker, i. p. 336.

position of " attacking " in the last stage before the outbreak of war.

It should be added that the same kind of mysticism which sweeps away a certain class of minds when they contemplate political expansion, invades them also when they consider economic advantage. Thus a recent French author writes [1] of that industry and commerce which Cobden and Bright regarded as the principal bond of peace, that these can never be divorced from protectionism and are essentially predatory and aggressive institutions which no nation can carry on successfully save to the detriment of its neighbours. This seems to be the extremest point to which political mysticism can be carried. A matter of common-sense management which, by international arrangements, could be adjusted to the mutual interest of all, is treated as a kind of fate in which men are involved, and from which it is idle for them even to attempt to escape. So long and so far as men feel thus—and many men do—so long and so far will trade be a cause of war. But only because we prefer to abandon to passion what should be a matter for expert negotiation based on a calm consideration of mutual economic advantage.

The facts about international relations illustrated in the preceding pages lead to an attitude among statesmen and historians which again reacts on the whole situation ; for it makes every suggestion for radical change appear to be empty idealism protesting idly against ineluctable fact. Thus Lord Salisbury, a very able and experienced statesman, says : " Let those take who have the power, let those keep who can, is practically the only rule of (Russia's) policy ; wherein I am bound to add she does not differ widely from many other civilised States." [2] The Austrian historian, Sosnosky, says : " Questions like that of Serbia must be settled not at the green table, but on the battlefield ; not with the pen, but with the sword ; not with ink, but with blood. Every historical result is, let me repeat it, in the last resort nothing but the bloody reflection of the gleam of victorious bayonets and swords." [3] And Bismarck's remark about " blood and iron " has influenced the mood of thousands of men, not only Germans.

[1] Séché, pp. 58 seq.   [2] *Salisbury*, ii. p. 153.   [3] II. p. 376.

V. Diplomacy

The policies and ideas of statesmen and historians, outlined in the preceding pages, imply in them, as well as in the public opinion which supports them, a morality curiously opposed to all those principles and maxims which are supposed to be valid between individual men. Fraud, indeed, is the natural and necessary ally of force, and men who in private life are scrupulously honest and honourable may descend, in diplomacy, to conduct which they would be the first to reprobate in their personal relations to other individuals. This characteristic of diplomats was noted long ago by observers. The definition of an ambassador as a man who " lies abroad for the good of his country " has become classical. But it may break the monotony of this exposition if I quote from a poet a passage not equally hackneyed. In the seventeenth century Henry Vaughan tells how :

> The darksome statesman, hung with weights of woe
> Like a thick midnight fog, moved there so slow,
> He did not stay nor go ;
> Condemning thoughts, like sad eclipses, scowl
> Upon his soul.
> And crowds of crying witnesses without
> Pursued him with one shout.
> Yet digged the mole, and lest his ways be found,
> Worked under ground,
> Where he did snatch his prey.[1]

Our habitual refusal to look straight at realities in the light of the values we profess to hold makes men regard such words as mere rhetoric. I think them a pretty exact statement of the facts, as an honest and humane man must view them. But if the reader prefers sober prose and a contemporary opinion, I will invite him to consider the following passage, written by a straightforward, honest American, who was injected into a part of the world where intrigue, competition, and fraud were working at their highest tension. This is what Mr. Shuster says in the course of his account of what he rightly calls the *Strangling of Persia* :[2] " One must at times separate a gentleman and diplomat from his official acts performed under orders from his home Govern-

---

[1] From *The World*.   [2] P. 71.

ment, otherwise great confusion and injustice would accrue. Some Governments have a little way of telling those who represent them abroad, and especially in the Orient, to get such-and-such a thing done, and done it must be. Nor would those high Government officials at home care often to hear the painful details of the successful execution of many such orders which are given."

These few and pregnant sentences, interesting in themselves, suggest also the corrective which an English reader is sure to demand if a charge of dishonesty is brought against a class. That corrective I willingly admit. The men may be as honest as men commonly are in other relations of life. But diplomacy, not always in all places, but here or there, now and then, demands dishonesty; and the demand has to be met for the sake of patriotism, prudence, audacity, success, or whatever the immediate need may be. The measure and degree of dishonesty will depend upon circumstances and upon nationality and traditions; and for that reason, among others, generalisations are hazardous. But a few examples culled from a rather wide and miscellaneous study should convince the reader that the charge brought is a true one, not an invention. Let us start with a strong case. Lord Salisbury in 1876-7 is negotiating with the Russians about the Eastern question. Early in the procedure he writes of his fellow diplomat, Ignatieff, " At present all is very smooth between us"; but adds cautiously, being a realist and knowing what diplomacy is, " I am puzzled by the smoothness, and naturally look for a snare." He was right. For at a later stage Ignatieff altered on the official map a frontier line which had been agreed upon, and brought it back to Lord Salisbury, hoping the change would not be noticed. Lord Salisbury observed the fraud, and felt embarrassed how to refer to it. But the event showed he need not have been anxious; for on being tactfully exposed Ignatieff retorted, with a beaming smile and a shrug of the shoulders : " M. le Marquis est si fin—on ne peut lui rien cacher." [1]

Another Russian example. In 1887 M. de Giers, the Russian Foreign Minister, made to the German Ambassador, von Bülow, this categoric statement : " I assure you—you

---

[1] *Life of Salisbury*, ii, pp. 108, 110 ; cf. p. 293, where Gortschakoff tries the same trick.

may cut off my head if it is not the truth—that never, never will the Emperor Alexander lift his arm against the Emperor William, nor against the son or the grandson of the Emperor William." The same year he said : " An alliance with France is an impossibility," for " one does not ally oneself with a piece of rottenness." Again : " A war against Germany is an impossibility for us." [1] Four years later this same Minister is forming an alliance with France against Germany which contemplates war throughout. Did he, nevertheless, mean what he said in 1887 ? Who can say ? I do not know. But an honesty which applies only to the moment in which words are spoken, and which permits the next moment a quite opposite thing to be done from that which has been said, is an honesty too like dishonesty for the distinction to be worth drawing.

The duplicity of Russians will perhaps be readily granted by an English reader ; but he is almost sure to believe and maintain that such things are not done by Englishmen. I make no pretence to generalise as to the comparative virtues or vices of the statesmen of different countries ; but it is an error to suppose that Englishmen are immune from the kind of dishonesty forced upon them by the international situation. We pride ourselves particularly upon our scrupulosity about treaties ; and this view is partly justified by such actions as Mr. Gladstone's in 1871, when he insisted that the Russian breach of the Treaty of Paris should be formally condoned by a conference of the Powers. A similar attempt was made by England, though unsuccessfully, when the Austrians annexed Bosnia in 1908. It is true that in both these cases the most that was attempted was to get a breach formally sanctioned. But this formal scrupulosity is not a universal rule of British diplomacy. Let us take an example from the conduct of Lord Salisbury. In the crisis of 1876-8, in which he played a principal part, what he really wanted was not war with Russia but a partition of Turkey. But he was met by the fact that, in the Treaty of Paris, Great Britain, along with the other Great Powers, had bound herself to respect the " independence and territorial integrity of the Turkish Empire." " That unlucky treaty ! " Lord Salisbury sighs ; and he proceeds : " We might of course snap the

[1] Ger. Docs., v. pp. 301, 307, etc.

bonds of the treaty, throw ourselves into the arms of Russia, and ignore the rest of Europe." His objection to this course is not, it would seem, the breach of the treaty in itself ; that does not seem to have troubled him ; but " such a policy would," he thought, " be attended with very grave risk." [1] A year later, in 1877, he held that Turkey, by rejecting the demands of the Christian Powers, had " freed them from all obligations towards herself in the Treaty of Paris." I do not know what justification he had for this view, for the validity of the Treaty of Paris was not conditional upon Turkey accepting any future demands the Christian Powers might choose to make ; and at the time in question none of them was at war with Turkey.[2] However, that was his opinion, and he proposed " the abandonment of our traditional policy and the substitution for it of a bold initiative in partition." The Cabinet, however, would not hear of this, and the Prime Minister repudiated it as immoral. What Lord Beaconsfield regarded as immoral does not seem likely to have been very moral. On the other hand, Lord Salisbury might naturally have worn, as we are told he did, a " grimly ironic smile " when he reported this verdict. The true ground for the rejection of his policy was probably, as the authoress of the *Life* suggests, that British public opinion at that time would hardly have tolerated it and that it was doubtful whether Austria and France would have consented. Bismarck, on the other hand, might have approved, for he was pressing on England the occupation of Suez and Alexandria, " even at the cost of Turkey." Bismarck, it may be said, was a German and therefore constitutionally dishonest. But it seems relevant to ask how, in this case, Lord Salisbury's attitude differed from his.

On the other hand, Bismarck was, on occasion, as capable as any Englishman of being shocked, and moreover of being shocked by the English. Thus, in the year 1885, when there was danger of war between England and Russia, England was anxious to pass her fleet through the Straits. According to a one-sided declaration which she had made at Berlin in 1878,[3]

[1] *Life*, ii. p. 86.
[2] Ib., p. 134. War was declared between Russia and Turkey on April 24th, and the episode referred to probably occurred on March 23rd (ib., p. 135 note).
[3] See below, p. 64.

she claimed that Turkey had the right to invite her to do this, and she encouraged the invitation by offering to the Porte Egypt and the Suez Canal, a free hand in Bulgaria, and 25 million pounds. Turkey, however, resisted this bribe and insisted on maintaining her neutrality. The British then took up the view that even Turkish neutrality did not forbid them to send their fleet through the Straits. The British Ambassador at Constantinople raised the question "un-officially" in conversation with the Austrian Ambassador : " He endeavoured to show that, in case of a conflict between England and Russia, the closing of the Straits would be very injurious to the former and give all the advantages to the latter," and that therefore to insist on the closure (as guaranteed by the Treaty of Paris, to which England was a party) could not be called on the part of Austria a " strict neutrality." This view, that it is an unneutral act to insist upon the observance of a treaty when such observance would injure a belligerent who wants to break it, might strike a plain man, unaccustomed to diplomacy, as odd. Whether it struck Count Kálnoky as odd I do not know. At any rate he endeavoured to show the British Ambassador the wrongness of his view, pointing out that the violation of the neutrality of Switzerland would have been useful to Germany in 1870, but that the neutrality was nevertheless observed. His Government, he said, would support the Porte with the greatest energy in maintaining its neutrality. Sir Augustus Paget thereupon complained " that he found so little sympathy with England and that even the Press was unfriendly in its attitude." " England," he said pathetically, " had no friend left on the Continent." A brief note of Bismarck's on the episode runs as follows : " In that case, treaties with England are henceforth impossible." [1]

This exclamation of Bismarck's need not, however, be taken too seriously, for, as circumstances change, so do the views of statesmen, about treaties as about other things. Thus, in 1889, Bismarck is in favour of a Russian occupation of Constantinople ; his view being that Russia would be weaker, not stronger, in consequence. Crispi, with whom he was conversing, mentioned the treaty between England and Italy, which guaranteed the status quo. "That is not

---

[1] Ger. Docs., iv. p. 116 ; cf. vii. p. 25.

enough," Bismarck replied. " England might easily find a
way of evading the fulfilment of her promises. She must
be compromised, and thus there will be four of us when once
we have got England to join." [1] In this connexion it is
interesting to cite the following words of the great master in
diplomacy : " In the case of every international treaty the
first thing to ask is, ' Who is being cheated here ? ' " [2]

The truth is that statesmen commonly think a treaty to be
binding so long as it is convenient, and only so long. But,
naturally, what is convenient to one State is not necessarily
convenient to another. The Turkish Empire and its maintenance supplies continual examples. Thus in 1882 the
French Ambassador, Baron de Courcel, writes home from
Berlin that Germany desires to get a footing in Egypt, and
that therefore, " relying on the treaties," she wishes to prevent
England and France from intervening by themselves to
restore order. " In other words," says the ambassador, " she
has restored life to rights which are incontestable in principle
but have become a dead letter, without application, in practice." [3] This raises the interesting point as to when a treaty
may be said to have " become a dead letter " and who is to
be the judge. For example, the treaty of 1839 guaranteeing
Belgium ?

A few years later, in October 1884, when Sir Charles Dilke
was a member of the British Government, it was proposed
by their commissioner, Lord Northbrook, that the Egyptian
Government should issue a loan, the interest to be guaranteed
by the British. Sir Charles Dilke, in a conversation with
Count Herbert Bismarck, said that this operation would be
impossible unless a reduction of interest was allowed. The
obstacle to the reduction was that the International Commission would have had to consent, and of this France was a
member. Sir Charles said that the British must have their
way on that matter, even if it involved war with France.
He admitted that the powers of the Commission were derived
from an international treaty, but, he said, " we are in a
position of unavoidable necessity, and that excuses us if we
don't adhere to the treaties." Mr. Gladstone did not accept
Lord Northbrook's report, and the matter was not proceeded

[1] Crispi, *Memoirs*, iii. p. 253.   [2] Ger. Docs., vii. p. 27.
[3] Bourgeois et Pagès, p. 377.

with.   It is cited here only as an example that British ·states-
men, like others, may be ready to violate treaties when they
think there is sufficient cause, and even at the risk of war.[1]

A more interesting example of the British attitude to
treaties is given by the Belgian guarantee.   Popular support
in England for our participation in the Great War was, it will
hardly be disputed, given, in great part, because Germany had
violated Belgian territory.   But the same question was raised
in 1887, and at that time a very different view appears to
have been taken by those responsible for our policy.   For in
the February of that year there appeared in the *Standard* a
letter signed " Diplomaticus " and a leading article generally
believed to have been semi-official.   The contention in both
was that the duty incumbent on England would be satisfied
if Germany, which it was thought might be the invading
country, were to give guarantees that Belgian territory should
remain intact after the war.   The reason given was that
" for England and Germany to quarrel, it matters not upon
what subject, would be highly injurious to the interests of
both."·   In short, we were then friendly to Germany and at
loggerheads with France.   Does anyone suppose that, if the
contingency in question had then occurred, the British Government would have gone to war, or public opinion have been
seriously outraged because they did not ?   No !   The respect
for treaties has to be reinforced by reasons of another kind
before a country is prepared to take action in their defence.
This may or may not be justifiable ; I do not at present
argue the question.   But those who accept that view would
do better not to profess moral indignation at an act which
under other circumstances they may have to approve, or at
least not to disapprove.[2]

It is not surprising, this being the way in which States
regard treaties, that they should sometimes contradict their
public agreements by secret ones.   A good example of this
is the protocol attached to the " League of the Three Emperors,"
which was entered into in 1881 by Russia, Austria, and Germany.   The first clause of the protocol refers to Bosnia and

---

[1] See Ger. Docs., iv. p. 90, and Cromer's *Modern Egypt*, ii. pp. 304 and
370 seq.
[2] See Sanger and Norton, *England's Guarantee to Belgium and Luxemburg*,
and Dilke in *The Present Position of European Politics*, reprinted from the
Fortnightly Review.

Herzegovina, and runs : " Austria-Hungary reserves the right to annex these provinces at whatever moment she shall deem opportune." This was in direct contradiction to the provisions of the Treaty of Berlin. The fourth clause concerns Bulgaria, and runs : " The three Powers will not oppose the eventual reunion of Bulgaria and Eastern Rumelia within the territorial limits assigned them by the Treaty of Berlin if this question should come up by force of circumstances." This, again, was contrary to the Treaty of Berlin ; but the clause is sufficiently indefinite to leave open the possibility of an agreed modification of that treaty. The union was, in fact, effected in 1885 by the one-sided act of Bulgaria, and the policies of the Powers when faced with this fact are interesting. In the first place, the union was now very distasteful to Russia, who had lost confidence in the Bulgarian Government. Russia accordingly kidnapped Prince Alexander, the then ruler of Bulgaria. Austria supported Serbia in a war against Bulgaria because the Balkan balance of power had been disturbed. England was in a difficult position. Respect for treaties seemed to counsel at least a protest. But then, on this occasion, public opinion approved the breach, because it was prompted by the principle of nationality. On the other hand, we did not want to quarrel with Russia, because the Indian frontier was not safe. Lord Randolph Churchill therefore proposed that we " should adhere in principle to the standpoint taken up, that of national aspirations, since public opinion made that necessary, but in fact let Russia do as she liked." [1]

This is one example of the conflict of policy with treaty obligation. Another is afforded by the treaty of 1877, between Russia and Austria. The third article of that treaty runs as follows :

" If the Government of the Emperor and King is invited to take part in the execution of the treaty of 1856, he shall refuse his co-operation in the case foreseen by the present convention, and without contesting the validity of the said treaty shall declare his neutrality. Similarly, he shall not take active part in any effective action which might be proposed on the basis of Article VIII of the treaty of March 30th of the same year." [2] Here the public obligation made between

[1] See Ger. Docs., iv. p. 139.   [2] Ib. ii. p. 112.

seven Powers to defend the integrity of Turkey is set aside by a private obligation made with one of these Powers. Another case, to which we shall have to refer later, is the secret agreement of Italy with France in 1902, which seems hardly compatible, in " honour " with the continued adherence of that country to the Triple Alliance.[1]

Has anything been altered by the War for Right ? It hardly seems so. For the obligations of the League of Nations, under a covenant publicly signed by over fifty States, are at present held so lightly by certain States that they have formed, contrary to that covenant, secret military agreements with other States, which they refuse to register as the covenant requires. Again, in the recent discussion on the treaty of mutual guarantee at Geneva (1923) it was openly contended that treaties of alliance between a few States should be permitted, because otherwise they would be made in secret, contrary to the Covenant. Most likely that is true ; but it throws an interesting light on international morality as it is still understood and practised. What that morality really is, is pretty well summed up in the following remarks of a German writer, not particularly cynical, but candid, as Englishmen seldom are : " It may be the duty of any State to break a treaty when its vital interests demand it, and the statesman or ruler who is faced with this question will have to calculate whether the moral loss, in reputation and confidence, which results from such a breach is not greater than the immediate practical gain. This question has been answered in different ways at different times. But those who live in glass houses should not throw stones." [2]

VI. National Honour

When this kind of attitude is the one forced upon statesmen by the conditions in which they work, what are we to say about " national honour " ? Honour is one of the words which excite so much passion that it is difficult to discover precisely what the passion is about. An American writer [3] has collected over a hundred instances of the use of the word by politicians, historians, and the like, and some of his examples

[1] See below, p. 94.   [2] Haller, *Die Aera Bülow*, p. 98.
[3] Leo Perla.

are surprising. Thus, according to Maximilian Harden, German "honour" demanded the annexation of Belgium. French "honour" demanded that the question of Morocco should *not* be submitted to an international conference. On the other hand, German "honour" required that it *should*. Japanese "honour" demanded that Japan should predominate in Eastern Asia. Other examples of what honour prescribes are : Breaking a treaty that no longer expresses the actual relations between the Powers (Treitschke). Breaking the American Peace Commission treaties, for these " it would be dishonourable to break, but far more dishonourable to keep " (Roosevelt). Going to war against your ally. Italy did this in the Great War, and d'Annunzio said : " Blessed are the young men who hunger and thirst after honour, for their desire shall be fulfilled." When the Russians in 1914 mobilised against Austria they gave the reason that " Russia is offended in her honour as a Great Power and compelled to take corresponding measures." On this Conrad v. Hoetzendorff remarks : " What the honour of Russia had to do with the Austro-Serbian conflict is not comprehensible ; very strange is the suggestion that Austria-Hungary should not have felt wounded in her honour as a Great Power by the criminal conduct of Şerbia."[1]

Such examples do not leave the observer with a very clear notion of what Governments and nations understand by honour. It may, perhaps, help us in our quest if we note that that sentiment never seems to operate if it is divorced from interest ; a fact which leads to the conjecture that it is only a mask thrown over interest to make it look attractive to generous or scrupulous spirits. In this connexion it will be useful to quote the famous speech made by Mr. Lloyd George in 1911 at the time of the Moroccan crisis. " If," he said, " a situation were to be forced upon us in which peace could only be preserved by the surrender of the great and beneficent position Britain has won by centuries of heroism and achieve- ment, by allowing Britain to be treated, when her interests were vitally affected, as if she were of no account in the Cabinet of Nations, then I say emphatically that peace at that price would be a humiliation intolerable for a great country like ours to endure. National honour is no party question." The

[1] IV. p. 142.

4

transition here from interest to honour might be called classical.
It reveals the whole position. Honour will only be defended
by arms if, and when, it is believed to coincide with interest.
It is, in fact, a word without content, employed to excite or to
sustain emotions. Interest, on the other hand, has a content,
though it may be questionable whether it has one worth
fighting for.[1]

However that may be, there is no doubt that diplomats are
not expected to behave in what is regarded, in private life, as
an honourable way ; nor do they expect such behaviour from
one another. They are, indeed, from the nature of their
employment, constantly in positions where to tell the truth
would be a kind of betrayal. They may be frank with allies ;
they will hardly be frank with potential enemies. A curious
and much-discussed case is that of 1908, when Austria occupied
Bosnia. Previously to this act the Austrian Minister, Aerenthal, came to an agreement with the Russian Minister,
Isvolski, according to which the Austrian occupation was to
be one side of a bargain, the other part being the freedom
of the Straits. But Aerenthal took action independently,
without waiting till Isvolski had secured the consent of the
Powers to the opening of the Straits. This action embittered
Isvolski so much that he is said never to have forgiven Austria,
and to have worked, from that time, for the war which came
in 1914.[2]

Let us take another example of the morals of diplomats.
In 1877 Crispi is endeavouring to persuade Bismarck to make
an alliance with Italy, " in case we should be forced into
war with France and Austria " ; and he tempts him with the
spoils of German Austria.[3]   In the same year he is announcing
to the editors of Austrian journals his friendship for Austria
and the necessity for preserving her Empire.[4]   Further, this
man, who had played a leading part in liberating Italy, urges
on Germany the need of maintaining friendly relations with
Russia in order that Poland may be securely kept under.[5]
Whether this is a breach of " honour " or not I leave to
casuists. It is certainly not the conduct that would generally
be associated with an honourable man.

---

[1] For some further discussion and examples of the use of the word honour,
see the author's *The Choice Before Us*, pp. 151 seq.
[2] For this episode see below, pp. 168 seq.   [3] Crispi, ii. pp. 34 seq.
[4] Ib., ii. p. 82.   [5] Ib., ii. p. 50.

These examples are taken from the actions of foreign statesmen. What about the British ? The annexation of Egypt, following pledge after pledge to evacuate, we commonly regard as an example rather of " muddling through " than of duplicity, though it may be doubted whether we should take so lenient a view if any other State behaved in a similar way. British statesmen, in fact, find themselves in the same dilemmas as statesmen of other countries. Of these, one is the conflict between the secrecy demanded and practised in international policy and candour towards other States and even towards one's own people. A well-known case is that of the premature publication by the *Globe* newspaper of the treaty with Turkey secretly entered into by Beaconsfield before the Congress of Berlin publicly met. Lord Salisbury, challenged on the subject in the House of Lords, said that the report was " wholly unauthentic and not deserving the confidence of your Lordships' House." It was, in fact, mistaken in only one unimportant point. As the author of the *Life of Beaconsfield* puts it : " the Government vented its vexation in somewhat random denials." [1] But the clear-sighted authoress of the *Life of Lord Salisbury* makes the following pregnant remark : " In that perennially disputed dilemma of consistency, where truth and honour are opposed, he (Lord Salisbury) undoubtedly held that honour should have the preference." [2] We come in these words upon yet another sense of that curious word "honour." Whether in fact it is opposed to truth I leave to the reader to decide ; adding only that when Lord Salisbury was informed that a certain politician had expressed his reprobation of this particular falsehood, his comment was : " I am glad that I have been warned. I shall be careful never to entrust him with a secret."

The truth is that even the most naturally honourable men cannot always escape from these dilemmas. Lord Grey of Fallodon seems to be a man by nature and inclination simple and straightforward. But when it came to negotiating a naval agreement between Russia and England in 1914, and secrecy was considered essential, his attitude both to the German Ambassador and to the House of Commons was, to say the least, not candid.[3] It is clear that a condition of anarchy between States, where forces are always ready to break loose

[1] VI. p. 303.   [2] *Life,* ii. p. 263.   [3] See below, p. 406.

and secrecy is therefore essential, is not compatible with
honesty. And if " honour " implies honesty, there are few
statesmen who can be regarded, in their conduct of international affairs, as men of " honour " in any but a Pickwickian
sense.

This view of diplomacy, which I believe to be true, may,
of course, and probably will, be disputed. But its truth is
not essential to my main argument. On the contrary, if it
be denied, then my case is the stronger, not the weaker.
For then it will be clear that the armed anarchy produces
war, even though all the diplomats be archangels. For war
is the continuing fact ; and if it does not arise from the
obliquity of the agents, it must arise from the medium in
which they have to work. The point is put with lucidity by
Mr. Churchill, who has the gift to perceive essential facts.
" When one looks," he says, " at the petty subjects which
have led to wars between great countries and to so many
disputes, it is easy to be misled by the idea that wars
arise out of the machinations of secret diplomacy. But of
course such small matters are only the symptoms of the
dangerous disease, and are only important for that reason.
Behind them lie the interests, the passions, and the destiny
of mighty races of men ; and long antagonisms express themselves in trifles. ' Great commotions,' it was said of old,
' arise out of small things but not concerning small things.'
The old diplomacy did its best to render harmless the small
things ; it could not do more." [1]

What Mr. Churchill calls the " interests, the passions, and
the destiny of mighty nations " I should call their illusions,
their cupidity, and their pride. But if, so far as diplomacy
is concerned, his statement be accepted, the case I am making
is only the more convincing. For it must then be concluded
that the anarchy of armed States defeats the good intentions
of the most admirable of men. Accidents of human weakness,
folly, and crime are ruled out, and the stark fact remains alone
in all its nakedness—the armed anarchy of itself produces war.

Under these conditions it is hardly possible that the relations of States should be determined by anything but a
balance of advantage and power. For that reason those
relations change, like the figures in a kaleidoscope ; and even

[1] I. p. 55.

though they may for a considerable period assume a certain permanence, yet that is no guarantee of perpetuity ; for they are based not on natural sympathy and community of purpose, but on considerations of temporary advantage. A good example of this truth is the relation between England and France. For several centuries these two countries regarded one another as natural enemies, for the simple reason that they were both Great Powers and that they lay on opposite sides of the Channel. Then came the rise of the naval power of Germany, and in a few years she had become the enemy and France the friend. This fact is reflected in our policy all over the world. We may quote in particular the following curious parallelism. In 1885, France and Russia being then our enemies, Lord Randolph Churchill saw wars in the offing, both between France and Germany and between England and Russia. Being anxious to guarantee the Indian Empire against Russia, he suggested, in conversation with Count Wilhelm von Bismarck, that Persia should be jointly guaranteed by England and Germany, and that " the whole settlement in Persia, including the railways, should be in German hands." [1] Twenty years later Russia is the friend and Germany the enemy ; and Sir Edward Grey, under the same preoccupation, arranges that the military, political, and economic control of Persia shall be divided between England and Russia in order to keep out Germany. Incidentally, Lord Randolph was of opinion, in 1885, that " war would do England good, though the majority of the people are not disposed for it." [2] How many people thought that in 1914 ? And how many will be thinking it ten years hence ? But ten years hence, if things go on as they are now going, the enemy may be France and the friend Germany. Plus ça change plus c'est la même chose. One thing, and one thing only, is permanent. To any given nation it is always clear that all the Right is on its own side and all the Wrong on the side of the Power that for the moment is the enemy.

VII. Public Opinion and the Press

The cause of this curious phenomenon I must not attempt to elucidate here. It goes back, very likely, to instincts that

---

[1] Ger. Docs., iv. p. 135. [2] Ib., p. 136.

descend from our animal ancestors. But though I will not attempt to explain, I will briefly illustrate. Of all recent wars there is, I suppose, none that is more generally and more justly condemned than the Crimean. It was at once unnecessary and fruitless ; for the peace that concluded it was torn to pieces in the course of the next decades. But at the time the war was popular ; so much so that it was in the end forced upon a reluctant Government by an impatient public opinion.[1] Yet this opinion was in a state of complete confusion as to why it wanted war. As a recent writer puts it : " The Whigs and Tories were united in demanding immediate war with Russia. But there was no agreement as to its justification or its objects. Some declared that the war would never have come had there been a firm policy in the Cabinet. Others believed that Russia had determined to go to war in any case, and had been preparing the war ever since the time of Peter the Great.[2] One speaker began his speech by stating that the Government had shown no reason why the people of England should go to war ; went on to declare that we were about to enter upon a religious war ' for the Holy Places,' led by that author of all mischief the Pope ; and ended by demanding that England should strike a blow at the heart of Russia and proclaim the re-establishment of the Kingdom of Poland. Other members variously claimed that the war was to avenge the massacre of Sinope, to preserve the balance of power, the independence and integrity of the Sublime Porte, and the rights and the freedom of the Christian minorities in the Ottoman Empire, ' to give liberty to the democracies of Hungary and Poland,' to secure the freedom of the Straits, the honour of the British Empire, the triumph of Right against Might, and civilisation against barbarism." The author comments as follows : " It is a curious picture. In a palace on the Bosphorus sat the Sultan, a fleshy and irascible debauchee, usually intoxicated and always lethargic,

---

[1] Lord Aberdeen having made some rather lukewarm remarks in the House of Lords, suggesting the possibility of making peace, some citizens of London wrote to the Lord Mayor requesting him to summon a public meeting " for the purpose of giving public and marked emphasis to the determination of the country *never* to make peace with Russia." This is a rather extreme example of the " will to victory." (*Aberdeen*, ii. p. 236.)

[2] Compare the common statement, during the late war, that Prussia had been preparing for the war—that particular war !—since the time of Frederick the Great.

surrounded by a group of Mohammedan fanatics of whose plots to supplant him he was dimly aware, and whose ability to rouse the fury of a priest-ridden mob kept him in abject terror and peevish submission. In England were public halls crowded with respectable shopkeepers, evangelical maiden ladies and stolid artisans, enthusiastically proffering their lives and money in the service of this obese little tyrant in a fez whose name they could not pronounce and whose habits of life were as unknown to them as those of a prehistoric monster."[1]

The Crimean War is an extreme case. But the phenomenon is constant. Let friction arise between two States, and let war appear to be in the offing, and great sections of public opinion will always favour war. For example, in the late seventies France was contemplating the annexation of Tunis. It was a rather hazardous operation, although at the Congress of Berlin she had received carte blanche from the Powers to perform it. The biographer of Crispi writes : " The thought of a military expedition was still far off, but a great power, public opinion, had been brought into action which, incited by the Press, ended by determining Government action. A few Parisian journals thought to stem the current, but only brought the reproach of being unpatriotic upon themselves." [2] Again, in 1911, when the crisis about Morocco was acute between Germany and France, M. Jules Cambon, French Ambassador in Berlin, wrote to his Government: " The political parties, and even the Socialists, spurred on by the approach of the elections, begin to chant ' Deutschland über alles.' That is serious, and a German politician of great talent said yesterday that the danger of the present moment was not in the facts, but in the opinion the two countries had of them ; and that public opinion in Germany seemed to him more exasperated than in France. That is an element which makes transactions difficult on both sides."

What *is* this public opinion that thus intervenes sometimes to embarrass, sometimes to support ? No question is more difficult to answer exhaustively. But one thing is pretty clear. The opinion, whatever its deeper roots, is elicited and made effective by a few people who make it their business to evoke it. In that there is nothing to complain of ; it is essential, if government is to rest on popular consent. But

---

[1] Martin, pp. 186, 227.　　　　[2] Crispi, ii. p. 107.

with the increase of the electorate, and its education in the mechanical art of reading, there has come into existence that enormous power which we call the Press. All through the dispatches which record the history of the last fifty years runs, like a continuous thread, this particular influence, creating fear, suspicion, irritation, and the object in all countries of solicitude, pressure, or stark bribery on the part of the harassed Governments. What, then, is the Press? It is an agency whose first object is to make money. To do this it must attract the widest possible public ; and to do that it must appeal to their idleness, their sensations, or their passions—to anything rather than their reason. But for such an appeal nothing is so good as war. I will adduce in evidence a famous journalist, Mr. Kennedy Jones, one of the founders of the *Daily Mail*. He has given us a table of the topics which are the best sellers for a newspaper, and first in order comes war, " which," he tells us, " not only creates a supply of news but a demand for it." [1] " The Crimean War," he adds " gave to *The Times* phenomenal prosperity and prestige, and was an ultimate cause of the creation of the penny daily." The Indian Mutiny enabled the *Standard* to reduce its price to a penny. In the Franco-Prussian War the circulation of the *Daily Telegraph* rose from 50,000 to 150,000. In the Egyptian War it rose to 250,000. In the South African War the circulation of the *Daily Mail* rose from 500,000 to over 1,000,000, while the Great War " brought back *The Times* from twopence to threepence and restored to it all its prestige and prosperity." [2]

It would, no doubt, be rash and improper to infer from these facts that all newspapers are ready at all times to urge war. But the facts do, at any rate, show what pressure there must be in that direction. Examples of this go back a long way, and one or two may be usefully adduced. The occupation of Tunis by the French, as has been mentioned, had been privately assented to by the representatives of the Powers at the Congress of Berlin. But some years later, when it began to be actually engineered, there was great opposition, especially

---

[1] *Fleet Street and Downing Street*, p. 198.
[2] I am not concerned with the question why and under what conditions it may pay the proprietors of a newspaper to raise or to lower their price by a penny. The same cause, it would seem from the above, may produce both effects.

in England. Says a French writer : " The (English) Press began to take fire, and the annoyance of the English Ministers found support in the intemperate manifestations of opinion." He cites *The Times* as saying that it is impossible that the French should seriously think of establishing colonies on the coast of Africa, for that would result in war between France, and England.[1] Later on, in the eighties, the French and the English are quarrelling over the Niger, and the French advance in that direction produced in the English Press " a really extraordinary campaign." [2] In 1898, on the question of Fashoda, " the London Press, by the fury of its invectives, disturbed even British phlegm." [3] And after the British diplomatic victory in that year the *Daily Mail* wrote that the event must be exploited in such a way as to impose upon the French the will of Britain in all parts of the world where the two nations met.[4]

These examples are from the English Press, which is, or was, less rather than more irrational than that of some other nations. In countries where passions are more violent the Press will be more violent too. And when the Serbian states- man Mijatovich tells us that " practically the whole Austro- Hungarian and Serbian Press had been openly at war since 1903, and the hostilities grew in violence every year," [5] we know that one of the causes of the Great War is being exposed.

To an engine of such potency Governments cannot afford to be indifferent. British Governments, so far as is known, confine themselves, at any rate in time of peace, to private representations or to the communication to the newspapers of such facts or views as they desire to have laid before the public.[6] Sometimes the connexion between a minister and a newspaper has been continuous and close. This was the case with Palmerston and the *Morning Post* at the time of the Crimean War.[7] But such evidence as exists seems to show that the British Press hitherto has jealously preserved its independence of Governmental or even of higher influences. A rather interesting example has been recently revealed to us. The authority is the late Kaiser, Wilhelm, not the most

---

[1] Darcy, *L'Afrique*, p. 119.   [2] Ib., p. 241.   [3] Ib., p. 436.
[4] Ib., p. 453.   [5] P. 233.
[6] See, e.g., *Life of Lord Granville*, i p. 67 ; *Diaries of W. S. Blunt, Greville's Memoirs, Life of Delane*, etc.
[7] See Martin ; *passim.*

accurate of men. But the case seems to deserve quotation. In the years 1901–2 *The Times* had been peculiarly active in working up anti-German feeling. But at that time some members of the Government, supported by King Edward, were nibbling at a German alliance. The King sent a trusted envoy to *The Times* to ask them to desist from their campaign. The reply was that the great newspaper was always ready to fulfil His Majesty's wishes, but that on this occasion —this occasion only—it was unable to do so. His Majesty, we are told, " is very deeply disappointed and grieved." [1] Whatever may be thought otherwise of the policy of *The Times*, on this occasion it seems to have been independent even of royal influence.

On the Continent, the relations between Governments and the Press have gone much further than in England. Certain Governments, indeed, appear to be in the habit of bribing not only the Governmental but the Opposition Press, in order to keep opposition within reasonable limits. A curious example of this is the fact, elicited in the French Chamber, that during the war the Government was supplying money to the " Defeatist " organ called the *Bonnet Rouge*. " The Council," we are told, " considered that it was better in the interests of national defence to take under its wing a paper which had influence over a certain part of the population." [2] We may cite also the following passage written by Isvolski in Paris about an anti-Russian campaign in the German Press. " M. Doumergue," the Ambassador says, " has told me that up to now he had not succeeded in establishing the true causes of this concerted campaign of the German Press against us, but that he did not doubt that it had been undertaken with the knowledge and consent of the Berlin Government. According to M. Jules Cambon, the well-informed French Ambassador at Berlin, the most probable hypothesis is that they want to prepare public opinion for new military expenses, either for the renewal of their artillery or for an increase of the fleet." [3] This would be an example of a Government stirring up ill-will abroad for the sake of the reactions upon policy at home. That, perhaps, may not be a very

---

[1] Ger. Docs., xvii. p. 209 note.
[2] Report in *Manchester Guardian*, December 17th, 1924.
[3] *Livre Noir*, ii. p. 243, March 1914.

common occurrence. But we have a good deal of evidence of transactions which to Englishmen may seem strange. It appears to be common on the Continent for foreign Ambassadors to bribe the Press in the interest of their own country. Some examples of this may be here adduced. In 1913, according to Isvolski, the Turkish Ambassador at Paris " has constant relations with the Press, and, in spite of the penury of Turkish finances, states that he has at his disposal considerable sums wherewith to act upon journalists." [1] Again : " It seems that the Turks have promised the French Press five millions, the fourth, or fifth part in bullion. The *Libre Parole* is said to have had 100,000 francs. The sums are distributed by the house of Lenard and Jatislowski on the security of State bonds." [2]

Judging indeed from the evidence available (which must be but a tiny fraction of the whole), it is the practice of many, perhaps of all, Governments to work upon the Press of the countries to which their Ambassadors are accredited. Thus the Italian Ambassador in Constantinople wrote to Sir Charles Dilke in 1888 that " the greater part of the Italian Press was bought up by the Gambetta-Wilson group, in such a way that Italian opinion was directed from Paris by the Italian newspapers as it had already been by the Stefani-Havas agency." [3] In 1904 a German diplomat refers casually to the large sums expended by the French Government on the Italian Press.[4] But particularly interesting to us are the efforts of the Central Powers during the crisis that preceded the Great War. Of this we have plenty of evidence in the German Documents. Thus Count Jagow telegraphs to the German Ambassador in Rome : " Please wire whether Your Excellency requires money to influence the Press, and how much."[5] On the 21st of July 1914 he directs his Ambassador in Vienna to urge the Austrian Government to apply money to this purpose.[6] On the 25th the German Ambassador in Rome reports that his Austrian colleague has received 300,000 francs to expend upon the Press, and asks whether he can count upon 30,000 to 40,000 marks from Berlin for the same purpose.[7] Turning now to Russia, we find Isvolski, when Ambas-

[1] *Livre Noir*, ii. p. 124.   [2] Isvolski, iii. p. 218.
[3] Dilke, *Life*, i. p. 478.   [4] Ger. Docs. xix, p. 36.
[5] Kautsky, No. 47.   [6] Ib., No. 97.
[7] Ib., No. 167.

sador in Paris, peculiarly active in this business. Here, for instance, is an interesting extract from one of his dispatches : " If we are now really decided to broach the question of the Straits, it is especially important to take care to have here ' une bonne Presse.' In this regard, however, I have unfortunately been deprived of my chief instrument, as nothing has come of my constant requests to provide me with a sum for the Press. Naturally I shall do everything in my power, but this is just one of those questions in which public opinion by reason of ancient tradition is inclined to be against us. The Tripoli affair can be taken as an example of how useful it is here to use money for the Press. I know that Tittoni (Italian Ambassador) worked the chief French papers thoroughly and with an especially liberal hand. The results are obvious." [1] The embarrassment here shown owing to lack of money was not permanent. For the next year, July 1912, Isvolski claims that he has corrected certain misunderstandings which were clouding the relations between France and Russia. " This result was obtained by my energetic personal influencing of the principal French newspapers, while similar and naturally even more effectual steps were taken by Poincaré." [2] In October 1912 M. Sazonoff grants another 300,000 francs for this purpose. [3] And it is interesting to note that this was expended, in part, in bribing the French Press to support the military law of 1913, in which Russia had an interest, just as France had an interest in the military development of Russia. [4] In return the Russian Government expects " friendly support in Balkan affairs." [5] In the distribution of the money French statesmen of eminence were concerned. M. Klotz expressed his desire to name the recipients, who should be, he said, " the directors and the Parliamentary reporters." [6] M. Poincaré himself did not disdain to offer his collaboration. " My conversation with M. Poincaré has convinced me that he is inclined to give us his help in the matter before us and to suggest the most suitable plan for distributing the money." Incidentally, the President revealed the fact that large sums were being distributed in Paris and the provinces for purposes directed not only against Russia but

[1] *Is Germany Guilty ?*, ii. p. 107, October 1911.
[2] Siebert, p. 651.   [3] Isvolski, ii. p. 324 ; cf. iii. p. 202.
[4] Ib., iii. p. 204.   [5] Ib., p. 206.   [6] Ib., p. 207.

against the Triple Entente. According to his information, these sums were derived from an international group whose centre was London.[1] M. Tardieu also appears as an intermediary. " There are various ways," says the financial representative of Russia, " of influencing the Press. One of these the Ambassador applies with great assiduity. He sees Hedeman every day, and Tardieu every two days."[2] We have even a note of the way in which one of the cheques was to be distributed.[3] It runs as follows :

La Lanterne ..	..	..	..	42,000 francs
L'Aurore	..	..	..	17,000 francs
L'Evénement ..	..	..	..	11,000 francs
L'Action	..	..	..	9,000 francs
La France	..	..	..	11,000 francs
Le Rappel	..	..	..	7,000 francs
Le Gil Blas	..	..	..	2,000 francs
Paris Journal ..	..	..	..	1,000 francs

This subsidising of the French Press by Russia seems to go back a long way, for we find as early as 1879 M. Waddington referring to French newspapers (the *France* and the *Estafette*) which are in Russian pay.[4]

Enough, perhaps, has been said to illustrate the influence brought to bear upon the Press by representatives of foreign Powers. This, of course, is only one of many influences. But it is one specially relevant to our subject, and it may serve to indicate the more general truth that public opinion is not spontaneous but manufactured. The conditions and limitations of its manufacture we cannot here attempt to disentangle. But we may say with some assurance that it is precisely in the region of foreign affairs that it is most malleable, for it is there that ignorance and indifference are most complete. International situations are created in secrecy behind the scenes by Governments who then, when the crisis comes, represent the facts as they desire to have them seen. The public has no means of effective criticism, for it has no knowledge ; the simple primitive passions are called at once into existence ; young men go off in their thousands and their millions to kill and to die ; and in the end it is found

---

[1] Isvolski, ii. p. 317.   [2] Ib., ii. p. 322.
[3] Ib., iii. p. 351 ; cf. Conrad, iii. p. 72.   [4] Ger. Docs., iii. p. 392.

that the whole pother was about nothing that had anything to do with the real welfare of any real persons. One State rises, another falls ; there is a shift in the balance of power ; a great mass of individuals (the only realities) are injured or ruined, physically or morally, or both ; and the machine, after a brief halt, starts again, to run along the old lines to the old catastrophe. So it will be, and so it must be, until people are ready and able to learn the lesson it is the object of this book to teach.

VIII. Conclusion

This circle of interconnected facts, of which we have given a brief analysis, the reader should carry in his mind throughout the succeeding chapters.   States armed, and therefore a menace to one another ; policies ostensibly defensive, but really just as much offensive ; these policies pursued in the dark by a very few men who, because they act secretly, cannot act honestly ; and this whole complex playing upon primitive passions, arousable at any moment by appropriate appeals from a Press which has no object except to make money out of the weaknesses of men—that is the real situation of the world under the conditions of the international anarchy.

These conditions are commonly regarded as unalterable. Hence the view that war is a fate from which we cannot escape. I will cite in illustration the words of a typical militarist which express, I believe, the real opinion of most soldiers, sailors, politicians, journalists, and plain men. " Possibly in the future great coalitions of Powers will be able to keep the peace for long epochs and to avoid conflict with arms ; but this will not be possible in permanence. The life of man is unbroken combat in every form ; eternal peace, unfortunately, a Utopia in which only philanthropists ignorant of the world believe. A nation which lays down its arms thereby seals its fate." [1]

----

[1] Conrad, i. p. 169.

The application of this doctrine to Austrian conditions led Conrad to be always urging one or other of a series of wars. He names these in one place, as follows :—

(1) War against Italy with minimal precautions against Serbia and Montenegro.

(2) War against Serbia and Montenegro.

(3) War, together with Germany and Roumania, against Russia, with minimal precautions against Serbia and Montenegro.

Those who hold this philosophy also devote their lives to making sure that it shall come true ; for it is impossible to hold any view about life without thereby contributing to its realisation.   The confusion, in the passage quoted, between military conflict and other forms of struggle is patent to anyone who can think.   The same philosophy should conclude that civil war also is an eternal fact, a conclusion to which militarists are usually very much averse.   But this much is certainly true, that until men lay down their arms, and accept the method of peaceable decision of their disputes, war can never cease.   I believe it also to be self-evident that war in future cannot be waged without destroying civilisation.   While, therefore, there is any possibility left of converting men to humanity by showing them whither the path leads on which their feet are set, that effort ought to be made.   I am not optimistic about the fate of my own contribution.   But it is made honestly, and may, perhaps, be one milestone on the narrow road that leads to salvation.

(4) War against Italy, after a previous engagement against Serbia and Montenegro.

(5) War, together with Germany and Roumania, against Russia, after a previous engagement against Serbia and Montenegro.

(6) War against Russia, Serbia, and Montenegro, with an alliance with Germany and Roumania.

This is a rich and varied programme.   Its author adds, almost, one might think with regret, that " war against Germany is not provided for, nor yet against Roumania, owing to the alliances " (ib., ii. p. 85).

CHAPTER II

GENERAL SKETCH, 1870–1914

I. France and Germany

THE analysis of international policy given in the foregoing chapter is, I believe, in its main factors, applicable to all periods of history in which several States have existed side by side and reacted upon one another. It is not, however, essential to a comprehension of the causes of the Great War that this general view should be accepted. A reader, therefore, who has doubts and reservations may dismiss from his mind the general statement, and begin with that account of the relations of the Powers during recent years which is the particular illustration selected in this book. It is here that he will find the nearer causes of the Great War, whether or no he will also admit that these are but one set of variations on a single and persistent theme.

In the present chapter we shall give a general sketch of recent history, starting from that year, 1870, which marks the temporary eclipse of France and the rise of Germany to the leading place in Europe. The first and most direct result of that shift in the kaleidoscope of events was a tension, which proved to be insuperable, between Germany and France. This was due to the annexation of Alsace-Lorraine. Like all such seizures of territory, this was an unjust and unwise act. But it was at least as defensible as most of such appropriations. Alsace and part of Lorraine were occupied by a population of German stock and speech. They had been detached from the German Empire in the course of the last two centuries by the force and fraud of French monarchs. They had been, while in French hands, a constant threat to Germany. Moreover, as we are informed by an historian so learned as Lord Acton, " of all civilised countries France is the one least able to contend with decency that compulsory annexation is a crime. For the most intense desire of almost all Frenchmen has been for the acquisition of territory not their own." [1] Yet this nation resented the loss of two provinces, inhabited in great part by men of different and alien stock, with an intensity peculiar even in the history of those irrational bodies called States. So, at any rate, a student seems to be justified in saying, by such accounts of French opinion as are available. No doubt, in speaking in such a context of the "nation," an historian is really speaking only of those interested in foreign policy, who, in all States, are but a minority of the population. No doubt, also, French policy varied with circumstances, and for many years the aspiration for recovery and revenge seemed an unrealisable dream. But the fact remains that never was any French Government prepared to wipe out the past and resume friendly relations with Germany at the cost of recognising the annexation as an unalterable fact. On this or that particular point the two countries might act in unison, where they had a common adversary; but the deep crevasse remained below the temporary bridges of snow, and Alsace-Lorraine was one of the permanent causes of the Great War.

Subject to that general condition, the relations of France and Germany varied from time to time. The first years after 1870 were full of rumours and alarms. The indemnity imposed by Germany seemed to Frenchmen monstrous, and was so, according to the standards then prevailing, though it was a bagatelle compared to what they were later to impose on her, and was, moreover, as its complete and rapid payment showed, well within the financial capacity of the country. But there were other causes of special anxiety. The continuance of the Republic was uncertain, and a revival of monarchy, such as seemed to be imminent when MacMahon was raised to the Presidency (1873), was generally regarded in Europe as a peril to peace. Moreover, military reorganisation turned France, in the words of a French writer, into a "vast entrenched camp." [2] and Bismarck became suspicious and irritable. Whether at that time he really contemplated a "preventive" war we need not here pretend to determine. Probably no one will ever certainly know. But at any rate

[1] Acton, *Historical Essays and Studies*, p. 254.
[2] *Cambridge Modern History*, vol. xii. p. 96.

he spoke as if he did.   Thus he directed the German Ambassador in Paris, in the autumn of 1873, to say to the French Minister that " no Government, if compelled, contrary to its wish, to recognise a war as inevitable, would be so foolish as to leave the choice of time and place to the adversary and to wait the moment most convenient for him." [1]   The British Government took alarm, and co-operated with the Russians and the Italians to secure peace.[2]   The Queen wrote a personal letter to the German Emperor ; and Bismarck, commenting on this letter and repudiating the suspicion contained in it, remarks that, though he would never advise his master to begin a war merely because, otherwise, an enemy may begin it first, yet " it is not well to give an enemy the assurance that one will, under all circumstances, await his attack." [3]   This suggests that he had hung war as a threat over France rather than actually indended to make it.   At any rate, the immediate danger passed away with the fall of MacMahon and the consolidation of the French Republic, and from that time onwards there can hardly be even a suspicion that Bismarck was intending or desiring war with France.   On the contrary, while steadily maintaining as irrevocable the annexation of Alsace-Lorraine, he was ready and anxious to permit to France any compensation she might need in colonial expansion. Thus, for example, in 1879 : " I think the Tunisian pear is ripe and that it is time for you to pluck it " ; [4] and in 1884 : " What I want is to establish a sort of equilibrium on the sea, and France has a great rôle to play on this side if she will enter into our views." [5]   " Abandon the question of the Rhine and I will assist you to conquer at all other points the satisfactions you desire." [6]   These latter approaches belong to the years when the occupation of Egypt had alienated Great Britain from France, and when Bismarck himself was wrangling with the English over colonial questions.   But such invitations were always regarded with suspicion by the French ; and in 1884 the French Ambassador in Berlin comments upon them as follows.   Bismarck, he reports, had said to him : " I want

---

[1] Ger. Docs., i. p. 221.

[2] v. Eckardstein says that on May 10th, 1875, Prince Gortschakoff and Lord Ampthill called on Bismarck to inform him that if Germany attacked France, Russia and England would side against her (ii. p. 102).

[3] Bismarck, *Gedanken und Erinnerungen*, ii. p. 178, cited Ger. Docs., i. p. 293 note.

[4] Bourgeois et Pagès, p. 365.   [5] Ib., p. 383.   [6] Ib., p. 389.

to arrive at the point at which you will pardon Sedan as you pardoned Waterloo." Whereupon the Ambassador comments to his Government : " If we listen, perhaps one day one of his successors would say to our descendants, ' I want you to pardon a new defeat and a new dismemberment as your fathers pardoned Sedan.' " He proceeds to denounce those " impious souls in France who had tried to justify the treaties of 1815, and thus to quench in our hearts our resentments at those lamentable amputations." [1]   " I think," he goes on, " that in the matter of dismemberment a nation, unless it is prepared to meet with indifference the fate of Poland, ought never to pardon and never to forget." And he concludes : " To pacify the present and reserve the future, such is the programme I have always had before my eyes." [2]   From this attitude of " reserving the future " no French Government, I think, ever departed.[3]

Under these conditions Bismarck could never feel secure, The less so because, if he had to watch France on the west. he had also, and at times with yet more apprehension, to watch Russia on the east. " He desires peace," Crispi reported in 1887, " and much regrets to be obliged to admit that ' two Powers, and two Powers only, France and Russia, are likely to disturb it.' " [4]   To avoid the danger of an alliance between these two Powers was his constant preoccupation. But when he resigned in 1890, his successors were unequal to that task, and the Franco-Russian alliance was formed in the early nineties. This gave to France a new self-confidence ; and in 1896 we find her Minister, Bourgeois, saying to Crispi : " Let me inform you that the eyes of France are still fixed upon the lost provinces, and that nothing, no matter what may happen, will ever make her look elsewhere ; no Frenchman will ever accept the separation of Alsace and Lorraine from France as a definite and inexorable fact ; the French will always make all other questions subordinate to this one." [5]

In 1900, when the English were involved in the Boer War, an attempt seems to have been made at a continental combination against them. The facts, so far as ascertainable, seem to be these. On February 28th, 1900, Count Muravieff,

[1] He is referring to the Saar, a purely German territory, taken from France in 1815.   [2] Bourgeois et Pagès, p. 387.
[3] Grey (i. p. 285) says that before the war " the idea of the revanche had been ' tacitly given up ' " ; but he advances no authority.
[4] Crispi, ii. p 212.   [5] Ib., iii. p. 339.

the Russian Foreign Minister, informed M. Delcassé that the Russian Government thought it desirable to approach the German with the proposal of a joint intervention by the three Powers in the interest of peace. Delcassé, who was sceptical, but did not wish to repel the Russian advance, replied that the proposal must proceed from Berlin. Thereupon the Russian Ambassador approached the German Government, but received the reply that Germany could take no such action so long as she had to fear the hostility of the French, and that a guarantee by the three Powers of their European possessions was a necessary preliminary. This would have meant the recognition by the French of the loss of Alsace-Lorraine. The Russian Ambassador pointed out that fact, and the negotiation ceased. So much appears to be agreed. But now, observe. Within a few days the Russian Chargé d'Affaires in London approached the British Government with the story that Germany was continually endeavouring to persuade Russia and France to intervene on behalf of the Boers, but that Russia so far had steadily refused. The Duke of Devonshire, who reported this to v. Eckardstein, added : " This is another example of the truthfulness of the Russians, who turn everything upside down." A little later the Prince of Wales showed v. Eckardstein a paper in which it was stated that Germany had proposed joint action with France and Russia, holding out the prospect of the acquisition of British territory by Russia in Asia and by France in Africa. Von Eckardstein read this paper with astonishment, and attributed its composition to a French agent, Jules Hansen, who was a " phenomenon of mendacity and perfidy," perpetually employed in the endeavour to separate Germany from England. The Prince appears to have been satisfied that this was the case, and said that in future he should put such communications into the wastepaper-basket. This is the account of a German. The French historians, on the other hand, see in the whole episode a piece of German intrigue. They suggest (without giving evidence) that the original proposition came not from the Russians but from the Germans. With what view ? " Something very bad ! " say the French ; and anyhow, " Could a policy which employed such means be a policy of peace ? " [1]

[1] See Bourgeois et Pagès, pp. 286 seq., and Eckardstein, ii. pp. 167 seq. Cf. also below, p. 57.

Thus it was that although, during the years 1875–1900, the French were usually antagonistic to the British, they were never willing to combine against them with Germany. England was thus able to pursue a policy of " splendid isolation"; and when she abandoned it she turned not to Germany but to France.   Of the provisions of the Anglo-French Entente of 1904 we shall speak later.   It was a consequence, on the one hand, of the diplomatic defeat of France at Fashoda, which led her to feel that she must come to an arrangement with one of her enemies and to decide that she feared, or hated, Germany more than England ;   on the other hand, of the failure of the British Government in their efforts at an alliance with Germany and of their belief that a policy of isolation was no longer tenable.   The result of the Entente was a further recovery of self-confidence in France and a renewed pursuit of her policy of expansion, with a consequent greater readiness to face the chances of war with her eastern neighbour.

II.   Germany and Russia

That this situation was alarming to Germany the reader may be reluctant to admit.   But if so, he forgets that Germany had to consider not only France but Russia, and that her relations with the latter were continually strained.   There were indeed circumstances making for good relations between the two States, such as the old co-operation in arms against Napoleon, the friendly relationship between the Kaiser and the Tsar, and the common interest of both in the maintenance of the monarchic system.   Moreover, in 1870, Russia had done Germany the service (or claimed to have done so) of preventing, by threat of arms, the intervention of Austria against her.   But the Congress of Berlin (1877–8) produced a coolness, for Russia thought that Germany had not adequately returned this service by supporting her claims ;   and in the years that followed there was continual friction between the two States, in spite of the " League of the Three Emperors " (1881–7) and the Reinsurance Treaty (1887–90).[1]

This friction was both accompanied and caused by the bristling of armaments on the frontier.   On the importance of this fact, as affecting the relation between States, we have

[1] See below, Chap. III.

already dealt in our general survey. We will now illustrate
it for this particular case. In 1879 Bismarck writes to the
Kaiser that " the Russian arrangements are such that it needs
only a single word from the Tsar, a signature without motive
and without responsibility, and the war is there ; the army of
the Vistula can invade us." [1] The same year he writes
to the Austrian Ambassador, referring to some remarks of
the Tsar, that these in themselves might not be of importance, but that they gain significance by " the enormous
military preparations which, in spite of financial difficulties,
began immediately after the war, and the threatening movements of the troops on our frontier." " I have no confidence
in Russian assurances, which are contradicted by the facts of
her armaments and her search for an ally." [2] Four years
later we find the same situation. " We have no mistrust,"
says the German Ambassador to the Russian Minister, " of
your sovereign or yourself ; but all proofs of good intentions
and the most beautiful articles of Herr Katkow are of no
avail so long as your cavalry and artillery marches threaten-
ingly upon our frontier. Tout est là ; alter that, and the
diplomatic picture will alter." To this the Minister replies
that these demonstrations are regarded in Russia as an indispensable measure of security. No one wanted war with
Germany, but there was a general anxiety lest Germany
should attack.[3] The case, the reader will observe, is a typical
illustration of one of our main contentions.

That the friction thus engendered and maintained did
not issue in actual war is due, no doubt, to the policy, capacity
and determination of Bismarck. But he was driven to resign
in 1890, and, rightly or wrongly, he regarded the non-renewal
of the Reinsurance Treaty with Russia in that year as a fatal
error on the part of his successor. In any case, his resignation
was followed at once by that Russo-French alliance which it
had been the main object of his policy to prevent. Nevertheless it would not be true to say simply that, from that time
on, the relations between Germany and Russia were continually
hostile. There were indeed dangerous crises. For example,
according to Witte, " several months before the outbreak of
hostilities in the Far East," the Russians " were busy preparing
for what seemed an inevitable war with Germany and Austria-

---

[1] Ger. Docs., iii. p. 29.   [2] Ib., pp. 68 seq.   [3] Ib., p. 296.

Hungary." [1] But there were other factors at play, among them the curious influence exercised by the Kaiser over the Tsar. [2] So that Russian policy, even after the formation of the Franco-Russian Alliance and the Anglo-Russian Entente, was perplexing and sometimes alarming to her friends. Still, on the whole, it must be recognised that, from 1891 onwards, Germany would reasonably regard herself as threatened with war on two fronts, and her policy is only explicable if this fact is remembered.

Among the causes of the friction between Germany and Russia was that between Russia and Austria. The Austro-German alliance dates from 1879 and continued till the outbreak of the Great War. Like all such alliances it was defensive in form. But the constant disputes between Russia and Austria could not fail to involve Germany. These disputes were due to the rivalry of the two Powers in the Balkans, which, after keeping the East in a ferment, on and off, for half a century, finally let loose the war of 1914. Bismarck, during his period of office, played the game of keeping the peace with his usual mastery. But his withdrawal left the cards in less skilful hands, and the annexation of Bosnia by Austria in 1908 proved to be the prelude of 1914. Of these events we shall have to speak in detail in a later chapter.

III. England and Germany

In all this continental turmoil England, it might seem, was not directly interested. She had abandoned, in the sixteenth century, the policy of seizing territory in Europe, and was building up her Empire overseas. But, as is generally recognised (with admiration by Englishmen, with indignation by others), it was her interest to preserve what is called the "balance of power" upon the Continent in order that she might be secure in pursuing her own advantage elsewhere. She had therefore never, if she could help it, allowed a single Power to become too strong in Europe. The single Power which she had usually feared, and with good reason, was France. She did not therefore intervene in the Franco-German War, an abstention which, in the light of more recent events, has sometimes been regretted ; and in spite of her

---

[1] Witte, p. 123.   [2] For this cf. Ger. Docs., v. xix. p. 499.

action in 1875 against the supposed threat of Bismarck to renew the war against France, her relations with Germany, up to the turn of the century, were generally friendly. They were indeed more than that, for again and again there was talk of an actual alliance.

The approaches came, in the first place, from Germany. According to a statement by Count Münster, the earliest was made in 1875, but England was not then " ripe." [1] Again, in 1877, Lord Odo Russell reported to the British Cabinet a conversation with Bismarck on " Europe and Alliances," adding, " How far was he sincere ? There is no doubt that he has often expressed his desire for an English alliance." [2] And Lord Salisbury wrote : " Bismarck has made new propositions for an offensive and defensive alliance, which have happily not been accepted." [3]   At the Congress of Berlin Bismarck startled Lord Beaconsfield by another proposal for an alliance. The English Minister, on reflection, was not unfavourable to the idea. On his return he was visited by Count Münster, who made a formal offer. Lord Beaconsfield, in his account to the Queen, regretted that the earlier proposition (1875) had been rejected, and added that " he was and always had been favourable to the principle of alliance or good understanding with Germany." He referred Count Münster to Lord Salisbury, and in the course of the conversation that ensued it is interesting to note that the German Ambassador expressed fear of a French invasion of Germany via Belgium, and was assured that Britain would never permit it.

As to the proposed alliance, Count Münster reports that Beaconsfield expressed a strong wish for common action with Germany and Austria and for an alliance with both Powers.[4] According to v. Eckardstein, he actually drafted a treaty in 1880, and gave it to Lord Rowton to hand to Bismarck.[5] If this be the case, it would seem that the business was still being pursued up to the time of the change of Government in England. But in the year 1880 Gladstone

---

[1] Eckardstein, i. p. 296. The editors of the German Documents find no evidence in their archives of this approach nor of that of 1876–7 (see iv. p. 3 note).
[2] Gathorne Hardy, *Memoirs of Lord Cranbrook*, ii. p. 15.
[3] *Life*, ii. p. 127.
[4] *Life of Salisbury*, ii. p. 367, and *Life of Disraeli*, vi. p. 486 ; Ger. Docs., iv. p. 12.
[5] Eckardstein, ii. p. 104.

came to power, with his pro-Russian and anti-Turkish policy, and there followed a period of colonial friction with Germany and a consequent approach of Germany to France. The return of the Conservatives to power seems to have brought England and Germany together again, and in the January of 1889 Bismarck made a formal proposal for an alliance between the two countries, pledging either party to assist the other in the eventuality of a French attack.[1] Lord Salisbury appears to have been favourable to such an arrangement, but he dared not bring it before Parliament for fear of incurring a defeat. According to Count Herbert Bismarck, he expressed himself as follows :

" Unfortunately we no longer live in the time of Pitt. Then the aristocracy was in power, and we could pursue an active policy which made England, after the Congress of Vienna, the richest and most respected of European Powers. Now the democracy rules, and has introduced a régime of persons and parties which has made every English Government dependent, unconditionally, on the aura popularis." " This generation," he added, " can only be taught by events." While unable to accede to Bismarck's desire, Lord Salisbury expressed the hope that circumstances might arise which would make it possible for him to pursue the idea. Meantime " we leave it on the table, without saying ' yes ' or ' no ' ; that is, unfortunately, all I can do at present."[2]

During the decade that followed British policy seems to have become even more unpopular than usual in the eyes of the world. This was due, in part, to the Jameson Raid, followed by the South African War ; for public opinion in every State atones for its endorsement of the crimes of its own Government by indignation at those of other Powers. At the end of this period we find, as has been noticed, attempts to combine the Continent against England. In 1899 Russia is suggesting an arrangement with Germany, on the basis that she should give to that Power economic openings in Asia Minor, while Germany should support her in her ambition to control the Straits. Germany, however, thought the compensation inadequate, was reluctant to quarrel with England,

---

[1] Ger. Docs., iv. pp. 399 seq.
[2] Ib., p. 405. Such is the only account of this negotiation at present available. For further light from English sources we must wait for the conclusion of Lord Salisbury's *Life*.

and required the inclusion of France in the arrangement, which would have meant the acceptance of the loss of Alsace-Lorraine. Russia, indeed, insisted that the French Government had become reasonable on that subject, whatever might be the case with French opinion ; but Germany showed some well-founded scepticism. Russia then hinted that if Germany rejected her advances she might make approaches to England ; but that, too, the Germans were not very willing to believe.[1]

The reasons for the breakdown of these attempts at an anti-British combination seem to have been partly the permanent fact that the French could not forget Alsace-Lorraine, partly German mistrust of Russia and unwillingness to quarrel with England. Indeed, in spite of the friction caused by the Jameson Raid and the reaction against it in Germany, the Governments of the two States were still endeavouring to maintain or to re-create friendly relations. One sign of this was the agreement made with regard to the Portuguese colonies in Africa—an agreement so interesting, as an illustration of the principles of diplomacy, that it seems worth while for a moment to dwell upon it.

In the year 1898 Portugal was endeavouring to negotiate a loan with England, and, as security, the revenues of the colonies were under discussion. Germany heard of this and decided to intervene, on that principle of " compensation " which we have seen to be one of the main pillars of diplomacy. Whether the British, before the German intervention, were proposing to combine colonial expansion with business is not clear from the information available. But it seems likely that they intended to secure at any rate Lourenço Marques and the railway thence to Pretoria, in view of that South African War which appears to have been already decided upon, at any rate in the mind of Mr. Chamberlain. The Germans intervened and cried " halves " ; and a long negotiation proceeded which is certainly not characterised by undue moderation on the part of those belated aspirants to colonial empire. In fact, they threatened the British. They said : " If you don't meet us in this matter we shall oppose you at Lisbon, in combination with the French, and quite possibly combine with them against you in our general policy." [2]

[1] See Ger. Docs., v. xiv. chap. xcv.   [2] Ib., xiv. pp. 297, 301.

How seriously the British took these threats does not appear, but they were anxious at this time to be on good terms with Germany, and were, indeed, as we shall see,[1] proposing an alliance. They were ready, therefore, to meet the Germans, and a treaty was negotiated on the following terms : If Portugal should want a loan, both States should participate in it. As security, the customs of North Angola and South Mozambique should be assigned to England, and those of South Angola and North Mozambique to Germany. The port of Lourenço Marques and the railway thence to Pretoria should be earmarked for England ; and in case Portugal should be willing to dispose of her colonies, each Power should take the ports of which the customs had been assigned to them. This was the essence of the public treaty, so-called, though there was apparently no intention of publishing it. To it was added a secret convention of which the principal article was that the two Powers agreed to oppose the intervention of any third Power in the territories in question, " either by way of loan to Portugal on the security of the revenues of those provinces, or by way of acquisition of territory, by grant, cession, lease or otherwise." [2] Such agreements commonly portend the seizure by the Powers concerned of the territories dealt with. But in this case there were complications. The British, no doubt, wanted Lourenço Marques and the railway, but they were not in a hurry about the rest, and most likely they did not relish having to make concessions to the Germans. Moreover, Portugal objected to pledging her colonies for a loan, and was able apparently to get accommodation in France without that sacrifice.[3] The Anglo-German treaty thus came to nothing. But that was not the end. For in the next year, 1899, England renewed with Portugal her ancient treaty of alliance, going back to the seventeenth century. This treaty comprised a guarantee of all Portuguese territory, whether in Europe or outside it.[4] So that we have the curious result that by one agreement, in 1898, England looked forward to the partition of the Portuguese colonies, and by another, in 1899, she guaranteed the same terri-

---

[1] See below, p. 60.
[2] See text in Ger. Docs., xiv. pp. 347 seq.; cf., also Brandenburg, p. 98, Eckardstein, ii. p. 205.
[3] Ger. Docs., xiv. pp. 272, 363.
[4] See text in Blue Book, C. 9088, 1898.

tories against any other Power. Immediately afterwards the South African War broke out and intensified that friction between England and Germany which, though it did not become definite between the Governments before 1901, was to lead up to the Entente with France, the naval rivalry, and all the subsequent history.

The year 1898 was the year of Fashoda and of the acutest crisis in the relations of Great Britain and France ; and presumably it was this situation, as well as the friction with Russia in the East, that led to new proposals for an alliance with Germany. This time the approach was made by the British. In February an interview took place between Chamberlain and the German Ambassador, Count Hatzfeld, at the house of Alfred Rothschild. Chamberlain explained that isolation was becoming more and more disadvantageous to Britain, and suggested an alliance. The discussion was pursued with the German Government, which expressed its doubts about the validity of an alliance which Parliament might repudiate. Chamberlain replied that the proposals might be publicly laid before Parliament. But the German Government objected that this might disturb their relations with Russia. The Germans were determined not to take this risk ; and, in fact, the British proposal was communicated by the Kaiser to the Tsar. In the course of his letter he says : " Now, as my old and trusted friend, I beg you to tell me what you can offer me and will do if I refuse." [1] So that clearly the Germans endeavoured to use the British offer as a means of improving their relations with Russia. The Tsar replied that " it is very difficult for me, if not quite impossible, to answer your question whether it is useful or not for Germany to accept these often-repeated English proposals, as I have not the slightest knowledge of their value. You must, of course, decide what is best and most necessary for your country." He dwelt upon the peaceful and friendly relations of Russia and Germany, but made no further proposition.[2] It is interesting also to note that Chamberlain made it quite clear that if he could not make an arrangement with Germany he would endeavour to make one with France or Russia, and that the Germans dismissed this as an impracticable idea. They were not frightened, then, by the possible alter-

[1] *Kaiser's Letters to the Tsar*, No. 15.   [2] Ger. Docs., xiv. p. 250.

native ; they saw no reason to endanger their relations with Russia ; and they could not rely on an agreement made privately by a Government which would only be in office for a short time. Nor did they believe that, if the proposal were laid before Parliament, as Chamberlain suggested, it would be adopted. For these reasons they did not close with the offer.[1] The British Government, however, did not abandon the idea. Chamberlain endeavoured to convert British opinion, and in the autumn of 1899 made the famous speech in which he said : " We should not remain permanently isolated on the Continent of Europe; and I think that the moment that aspiration was formed it must have appeared evident to everybody that the natural alliance was between ourselves and the great German Empire." A little earlier, as may be remembered, the *Daily Mail* had talked of " rolling France in mud and blood."

, Immediately after this episode came the South African War, and our relations with Germany were strained by the vehement hostility of their Press as well as by certain episodes at sea. It might have been expected, therefore, that the idea of an alliance would be finally dropped ; but, in fact, it was not. The proposal was renewed in 1901. Chamberlain, Lord Lansdowne, and the Duke of Devonshire were its sponsors ; Lord Salisbury was favourable, and so was King Edward. Von Eckardstein reports a conversation with the latter in which he said : " As you know, for years past I have always had the greatest sympathy with Germany, and indeed even to-day I am of opinion that England and Germany would be the most natural allies. Together they might police the world and preserve lasting peace. Of course, Germany requires colonies and economic expansion. She might have plenty of both, for there is place enough for England and Germany in the world." But this readiness, on the part of some members of the Government seems to have been met, on the part of Lord Salisbury, by hesitation, which finally was converted into opposition. The Germans, on their side, were still cool and suspicious. They saw no advantage for themselves in the proposals unless England was prepared to join the Triple Alliance, thus engaging herself, when the casus fœderis arose, to defend Austria and Italy as well as Germany.

[1] See Ger. Docs., xiv. chap. xci., and Fischer.

This might have involved us in war with France over the Mediterranean or over the break-up of Austria. There was, moreover, the suspicion on the side of the Germans that England wanted to involve Germany in war against Russia.[1] The Kaiser states[2] that on being informed of Chamberlain's proposal for an alliance, he immediately inquired, " Against whom ? " and that the answer from London was, " Against Russia." " Chamberlain," he says, " openly spoke about a war to be waged later by England and Germany against Russia." [3] That this would be the probable result of an alliance was also the view of the German Chancellor, von Bülow, who writes in his *Imperial Germany* : [4] " The danger was imminent that if Germany allied herself with England she would have to undertake the rôle against Russia that Japan assumed later single-handed. . . . In the event of a general war we Germans would have had to wage strenuously war on land in two directions, while to England would have fallen the easier task of further extending her colonial empire without much trouble and of profiting by the general weakening of the Continental Powers." Prince Bülow does not say in so many words that the alliance would have been the signal for a European war, but the Kaiser does. " Prince Bülow," he writes, " in full agreement with me, declined politely but firmly to disturb the peace of Europe." Whether the peace would, in fact, have been then disturbed is matter for conjecture. If it had been, the Great War would have come in a different form, and we should have seen England and Germany fighting France and Russia. That this did not happen is due to no inherent preference for France over Germany, in either the Government or the people of England, but to the calculations or miscalculations of statesmen about the balance of power. On such accidents, in the anarchy of international affairs, do the fates of all peoples depend.

The Kaiser states, further, that the question of an alliance

---

[1] Ger. Docs., v. xvii. ch. 109, and Fischer.   [2] *Memoirs*, p. 101.
[3] Ib., p. 304.
[4] P. 34, Eng. trans., ed. 1914. Mr. Asquith (*Genesis of the War*, p. 24) says that " from first to last there was no suggestion or hint that the proposed drawing together of Great Britain and Germany was inspired by or directed to hostility against Russia." Perhaps the English did not say so, and may not have thought so. The question is, what would have been the probable result ?

was raised again in 1905 between Prince Bülow and King Edward, but that the latter then said that "such a thing was not at all necessary in the case of our two countries, seeing that there was no real cause for enmity or strife between them."[1] This, if true, is an interesting fact ; because, on the one hand, the Kaiser, only the year before, had been negotiating the Treaty of Björkoe, which was intended to unite Russia, Germany, and France against England,[2] and, on the other hand, England had already made her Entente with France, which was, to say the least, not favourable to the elimination of "enmity and strife " between England and Germany.

IV. England and Russia

The Entente was, in fact, the sign that England had definitely turned away from Germany and towards France. Chamberlain had already threatened such a result as early as the autumn of 1899,[3] in case the negotiations with Germany should come to nothing ; and again in 1901 he and the Duke of Devonshire had said that some members of the Cabinet were inclining that way, and that they themselves would do the same if an arrangement with Germany were impossible, though regretting the sacrifices they would have to make in Morocco, Persia, and China.[4] It must be added that by 1904 Germany had already become an object of alarm to England in consequence of her naval policy.[5] From the British point of view, if the danger could not be conjured by alliance with Germany, it must be met otherwise ; for, as we know, armaments are always a call for counter-armament, thus producing or increasing the friction that ends in war. By 1904, therefore, England was ready to listen to French proposals, and France, as we have seen, was ready to make them. The result was the Anglo-French Entente, and this carried with it, as a logical consequence, a further understanding with Russia, the ally of France.

Russia, it is true, was, as France had been, what may be called, without much exaggeration, our " hereditary " enemy.

[1] *Memoirs*, p. 112.   [2] See below, p. 115.
[3] Eckardstein, ii. p. 99.   [4] Ib., p. 236.
[5] See below, pp. 381 seq.

The reason of this was our Indian Empire. For Russia was its only strong neighbour, and, in diplomatic practice, a strong neighbour, if not an ally, must be an enemy. It had therefore become a principle of British policy not only to protect the Indian frontier, which involved a continual extension of our influence in the direction of Russia, but also to keep Russia out of the Mediterranean ; a policy which began to seem the more urgent when the cutting of the Suez Canal made that the normal route for reaching India by sea. As Austria and France had the same policy about the Straits, the closing of the Dardanelles to ships of war had become a principal object of the three Powers, and, since 1841, a part of what is sometimes called the " public law " of Europe. It was reaffirmed in the Treaty of Paris (1856), in the Treaty of London (1871), and again in the Treaty of Berlin (1878). But at that time Lord Salisbury was of opinion that " the exclusion of Russia from the Mediter-ranean is not so great a gain to us as the loss resulting from our exclusion from the Black Sea." He was therefore anxious that England should " withdraw from the inter-national guarantee, and reserve to herself the right of going to the Sultan's assistance, with or without his summons, whenever she judged him to be acting under duress." This, he thought, would lead to similar action by other Powers, so that, in fact, the result would have been the removal of all treaty obligations to the free passage of the Straits.[1] This suggestion, however, seemed to the British Government rather extreme. They were willing that Britain should go to the assistance of the Sultan, but not that any other Power should do so. The point seems to have been met by the insertion in the treaty of a one-sided declaration by the British that " the obligations of His Britannic Majesty relating to the closure of the Straits do not go further than an engage-ment with the Sultan to respect in this matter His Majesty's independent determinations in conformity with the spirit of existing treaties." " The distinction," says a distinguished international lawyer, " between engagements towards the Sultan only and those of a general European character seems to have been rather infelicitously chosen as a ground for Lord Salisbury's practical conclusion, for he had himself said at

[1] *Life*, ii. p. 291.

Berlin that if Batoum had not been declared a free and commercial port England would not have been able to engage
herself towards the other European Powers to interdict herself
from entering the Black Sea." [1] But the author goes on to
affirm that " in substance Lord Salisbury was, in our opinion,
right." Whether international lawyers of other countries take
the same view I have not inquired. But it is certain that
the Russian Government did not, for they countered Lord
Salisbury's protocol by another, in the opposite sense, affirming
that the closing of the Straits was a " European principle
binding on the part of all the Powers, in accordance with the
spirit and letter of existing treaties, not only as regards the
Sultan, but also as regards all the Powers signatory to those
transactions." Thus the British point of view was not
adopted by other Powers, and an attempt made in 1885 to
get it accepted by them was, as we have already seen, unsuc-
cessful.[2] The reason, no doubt, was that, in 1878, and, as it
would seem, generally throughout this earlier period, the
Russians were more afraid of the passage of the Dardanelles
by a British fleet than anxious to penetrate them with their
own. For, in the treaty known as the " League of the Three
Emperors " (1881–7), the closure of the Straits was reaffirmed,
and also in the " Reinsurance " treaty between Germany and
Russia (1887–90).

Russian policy, from that time on, continued to oscillate
without much regard to Russian agreements. Thus, in the
course of the negotiations for the treaty of alliance with
France (1891–3), M. de Giers told M. Ribot that Russia
did not want Constantinople and intended to preserve the
status quo.[3] A few years later, according to Count Witte,
she was thinking of seizing the Straits by force and presenting
the Powers with the accomplished fact.[4] After the formation
of the Entente with England British opposition seems to have
weakened, and Sir Edward Grey agreed, in principle, to the
opening of the Straits, if exit and entrance were guaranteed
on equal terms to the warships of all States in time of war.

[1] Westlake, *International Law*, Part I, pp. 195–6, ed. 1904. For
the question of the Straits, see also Ger. Docs., vii. p. 24, and xviii.
chap. cxix.
[2] See above, pp. 27 seq.
[3] Yellow Book, L'Alliance Franco-Russe, 1918.
[4] *Memoirs*, p. 187. Cf. Dillon, p. 242.

He meant, presumably, by international agreement. But of that we shall have to speak later.[1]

The closure of the Straits against Russia was part of the policy of maintaining the Turkish Empire. Hence our defence of that Empire in the Crimean War and in 1876–8. But it was always doubtful whether Turkey could, in fact, be maintained, and its partition had floated before the Powers at many times for many years past. The difficulty was that there was no telling who might profit by the partition, so that a wholesome fear hung about the whole question right up to the Great War. Lord Salisbury himself, as we have seen, as early as the crisis of 1876–8, was half inclined for a partition. "A Government of some kind or other," he wrote, "must be found for all these wretched oppressed multitudes. It cannot be left as a no man's land. But the division of that kind of jetsam is peculiarly difficult. If the Powers quarrel over it the calamities of a gigantic war must be undergone. If they agree, people call it a partition and denounce it as immoral."[2] Later, as we have seen, he proposed to the Cabinet : "The abandonment of England's traditional policy and the substitution for it of a bold initiative in partition."[3] He finally gravitated to preservation, but had the brilliant idea of sending British officers, after the peace was signed, to improve Turkish administration, and thus gradually by a "pacific invasion" appropriate the Empire for Great Britain. As the authoress of the *Life* very aptly remarks : "In its political aspect this proposal did not err on the side of timidity. The collection of the entire revenue of the country by British officers and the control of its application to the expenses of government would have placed

---

[1] See *Livre Noir*, ii. p. 458 (1908). Cf. Siebert, pp. 190, 320, 417. It is odd, in view of these direct references to the question of the Straits in conversations between Sir Edward Grey and the Russian Ambassador, held in the years 1911–12, to find the former stating in 1914 to the German Ambassador that " for more than five years England and Russia had not touched upon the Straits question in their discussions " (*Is Germany Guilty ?*, ii. p. 117). It would seem, from a letter of Holstein's (cited Eckardstein, ii. p. 99), that Chamberlain was thinking, in 1899, of making an agreement with Russia at the price of satisfying her in the question of the Straits.

[2] *Life*, ii. p. 80.

[3] Ib., p. 134. It seems odd, in the face of this, that a writer in the *Cambridge History of British Foreign Policy* should say that Salisbury was " as much opposed as the Prime Minister himself to the dissolution of the Turkish Empire " (iii. p. 109). True the Prime Minister himself was not very clear on the point (*Salisbury's Life*, ii. p. 113).

England in much the same position in Armenia and Mesopotamia and Northern Syria as she was subsequently destined to occupy in Egypt." [1] The British are usually " destined," while other States must seize ; but " destination," judging by results, is even more successful in extending the boundaries of Empire. In this case, however, Lord Salisbury's idea appears to have frightened Sir Stafford Northcote, on financial grounds, and the subsequent advent to power of the Liberals relegated it to the limbo of dreams.

It appears, however, that later on, in the year 1895, Lord Salisbury returned to the idea of a partition. According to the German sources, he made a definite proposal in that sense to the German Ambassador, and afterwards to the Kaiser himself. The Kaiser and his Government thought that partition would involve a European war and declined to consider it. We have no account of this matter from the British side. But it seems that Lord Lansdowne informed the German Ambassador in 1902 that, according to notes left by Lord Salisbury, he had merely raised hypothetically the question of what might happen to the Turkish Empire in case it should collapse. [2]

During the years that followed the Congress of Berlin, British relations with Russia were continually strained, for by a gradual advance she was approaching the frontier of the Indian Empire. It was indeed agreed, in the seventies, that there should be a neutral zone preserved between the frontiers of the two States ; but Russia continued to advance. The Ameer of Afghanistan appealed for subsidies and arms to England, and when Disraeli came into power, in 1874, he determined upon what is called a " forward " policy in that region. The Queen was given the title of Empress of India and Lord Lytton sent out as Viceroy in place of the prudent and pacific Northbrook. There followed an attempt to force

---

[1] *Salisbury's Life*, ii. p. 311.

[2] See Eckardstein, i. p. 212, ii. p. 266 ; Ger. Docs., xvii. p. 84. . In the November of this year it seems that the Empress Frederick unfolded an elaborate scheme of partition to the Kaiser, whereby Russia was to have the Dardanelles and Constantinople ; Austria was to have Albania, Montenegro, Serbia, and so much of Macedonia as would give her free access to Salonica ; Greece was to have all the islands and the Rhodope district ; and France was to have Syria. Possibly this was the plan that floated before Lord Salisbury's mind. If so, it forms an interesting commentary on the origin of the Great War, which was precisely the attack of Austria on that Serbia which this plan would have presented to her (see Ger. Docs.; x. p. 109).

upon the reluctant Ameer a British mission, the murder of
that mission, a war of " punishment " and a policy of annexation, which, however, was reversed when the Liberals came
into power. Another crisis, in 1884–5, followed a further
advance of Russia, and it was at that date, as we have seen,
that the British desired to send their fleet through the Dardanelles. Some fifteen years later, Lord Curzon's accession as
Viceroy was the signal for a new period of alarm, defence,
aggression, or whatever may be the word preferred to represent
the fact that when two Empires come into contact each
becomes the object of fear and cupidity to the other. By
1899 the area of conflict had extended as far as Persia, which
was described by Lord Curzon as " one of those countries
which must inevitably have attracted the attention of Europe,
partly from increasing infirmity, but still more from the
opportunities suggested by their latent but neglected sources
of strength." [1] Lord Curzon accordingly visited the Persian
Gulf in state, accompanied by a flotilla of warships. He
explained to the Arab chiefs how powerful was that sovereign
of Great Britain whose face none of them had ever seen or
would see, how scrupulously he guarded their independence
against other and more aggressive States, and how careful he
was for their welfare and prosperity. " British prestige," the
historian comments, " was enhanced by the journey, which
proclaimed not only to those who saw the squadron and
heard the voice of the Viceroy, but to listeners far away in
Teheran, Petrograd and Berlin, the determination of Great
Britain to defend her position in the Gulf from challenge or
attack." [2] The " position in the Gulf," it is true, was
threatened, or thought to be threatened, at that time,
by Germany rather than by Russia ; for Germany had
embarked upon the enterprise of the Bagdad Railway. But
Russia, being still the potential enemy of England instead of
her cherished friend, as she became a year or two later, might
be expected to take part in the iniquitous enterprise.

Nearer to India was Tibet, nominally under the suzerainty

---

[1] Cited in *Cambridge History of Foreign Policy*, iii. p. 319.

[2] Ib., p. 321. M. Halévy says, with a good deal of truth, that the Franco-
Russian alliance, formed against Germany and finally to lead to war against
her, was at this time rather a combination of Russian and French against
British imperialism. It was not till the years 1904–7 that England made
terms with her two ancient enemies against the new upstart, Germany (see
Revue de Paris, May 15th, 1924, p. 306).

of China, actually, as the British thought, an object of Russian penetration, and in any case showing an unaccountable reluctance to enter into closer relations, political or commercial, with the British Empire. " The time seems to us to have arrived," the enterprising Viceroy wrote, " when we should decline any longer to allow our boundary to be transgressed, our trade to be strangled, and the rights secured to us by treaty denied. It is the most extraordinary anachronism of the twentieth century that there should exist within less than three hundred miles of the borders of British India a State and Government with whom political relations do not exist and with whom it is impossible even to exchange a written communication." [1]   To put an end to this anachronism a military expedition was sent up, a certain number of helpless Tibetans killed, and a treaty agreed upon which seems, in the end, to have left everything very much as it was before, except that " prestige " had been asserted against these frozen, dirty, and very incompetent monks.

Meantime Afghanistan continued to be an object of anxiety. " Russia," says the historian, " was making steady progress and railways were under construction which could only be strategic." [2]   The Indian Government was courteous but firm. It could not believe that Russia was harbouring any aggressive intent ; at the same time, if a strategic railway should be built in Afghanistan in time of peace—well, we should have to increase our forces.

Thus all the usual signs were being hung out which prelude war between two neighbouring Empires ; and the situation was yet further strained by the Russo-Japanese War (1904). For the British were the allies of Japan and bound, under treaty obligations, if France or Germany should enter on the side of Russia, to enter themselves on the side of Japan. Everything seemed to point, as had been the case at almost any time during the last half-century, to war between the two Empires. Yet that war did not come. On the contrary, the Entente with France was followed by one with Russia ; and from that fact alone it is clear that there cannot ever have been any causes of friction between England and Russia which were not capable of friendly adjustment. Yet it

[1] Cited in *Cambridge History of Foreign Policy*, iii. p. 323.
[2] Ib., p. 329.

will hardly, I think, be maintained that they would in fact have been adjusted, unless a new fear had prompted a new friendship. As we have seen, the relations of Russia to Germany had long been strained ; and now, just as France had chosen between her two enemies, making friends with the one in order to be more secure and more effective against the other, so did Russia, in 1907, drop her quarrel with us in order to pursue more safely her quarrel with Germany. The Ententes show that there was no real reason why there should ever have been risk of war between the three Powers concerned, since they could so easily make up their differences. What had been lacking was the desire to make them up. That desire was now induced by a new anxiety.

The relations of England, France, Germany, and Russia have thus been sketched up to the date of the formation of the Ententes. There remain two other Great Powers, Japan and Italy. Of Japan we will not here speak, for she played no direct part in the causation of the war, though she profited by it to achieve her own purposes. Italy in 1882 had joined Germany and Austria to form what had thus become the " Triple " Alliance. This is, at first sight, a curious combination, for Austria was the Power which had long held Lombardy in possession, and on the defeat of which Italian unity had been built. Moreover, large Italian populations were still included in the Austrian Empire. But Italy, like all other States, had no sooner won her liberty than she embarked on the hazardous course of world-politics. From this point of view, her principal enemy seemed to be France ; and it was to counter French expansion in Africa that she joined hands with her old oppressor. The position, however, was difficult, because Austrian and Italian claims conflicted in the Balkans, and were only maintained in equilibrium by a kind of self-denying ordinance. Further, since Italy had a coast so long and so exposed, she was never willing to risk war with England. These difficulties she met by a judicious application of the principles of her great statesman, Machiavelli. While maintaining and even strengthening her position in the Triple Alliance, she entered, at the same time, upon a treaty of amity with France, as will be narrated in the following chapter.

This brief summary of the relations of the Great Powers,

up to the formation of the Entente, will have illustrated, for the reader who is uninformed, the general principles explained in the last chapter. International policy, he will have observed, is a matter of combinations based upon self-interest. Self-interest, in turn, is based both upon fear and upon aggression ; for it both expects attack and intends to profit by it. War is always in prospect ; and in war, though losses are to be feared, gains may be made. The combinations actually formed may be of longer or shorter duration. Thus British hostility to France and Russia was of old date and fairly permanent ; for France was the dangerous neighbour at home, and Russia in the East. But the rise of Germany to the position of a Great Power, after the many years of her invasion and subjection by France, ended by altering the position. For some time the signs pointed to an Anglo-German alliance. But this proved impracticable, partly because, in the earlier phases, England was not (as the Germans neatly put it) " Bündnissreif " (alliable), partly because, in the later years, her intention seemed to be to use Germany as a cat's-paw in a British war against Russia. England, therefore, in the end, by a sudden volte face, turned towards France, and France towards England. This transformation resulted in a similar arrangement with Russia. The " balance of power," which had always been the fetish of British statesmen, became thus both singularly simple and singularly precarious. It made, one may fairly say, by itself, for war. And the history of the following years is but that of the posturings of the combatants, their hesitations and fears, their taking and abandoning of positions, before they are ripe for the great decision. These last movements before the final death-grapple will form the subject of the succeeding chapters.

CHAPTER III

THE TRIPLE ALLIANCE [1]

I. The Austro-German Alliance

" No State," says a German author, " has ever yet entered into a treaty for any other reason than self-interest " ; and he adds : " A statesman who had any other motive would deserve to be hung." [2] Whatever may be thought of the second statement, the first is not likely to be disputed. It will, in any case, be found to be borne out by the facts related in the following chapters.

In the year 1914 the States of Europe were bound together, or separated, by a complex network of treaties, most of which were drawn up in secrecy and kept secret, though many—perhaps not all—have been published since the outbreak of the war. In the present chapter we shall examine the treaties of the Triple Alliance between Germany, Austria, and Italy, and some others that are connected with these. We will begin with the Austro-German Alliance of 1879, which, though it was independent of the Triple Alliance, belonged to the same system.

The Congress of Berlin (1877–8), the resulting treaty, and the friction involved in carrying it out, had strained very

---

[1] The treaties here considered are all contained in Professor Pribram's work, *The Secret Treaties of Austria-Hungary*, which contains, besides the texts, historical introductions, based upon the Austrian archives. My references are to the English translation in two volumes, of which one (which I call vol. i.) contains the texts, the other (which I call vol. ii.) the introductions. Professor Coolidge has usefully added in vol. ii. the texts of the Franco-Italian and Franco-Russian treaties.

On the Austro-German Treaty of 1879 some interesting information is given in the *Memoirs of Sabouroff*, the Russian negotiator (see articles by J. Y. Simpson, on Russo-German relations and the Sabouroff Memoirs, in the *Nineteenth Century* for December 1917 and January 1918).

[2] Haller, p. 101.

seriously the relations between Germany and Russia. Miljutin, the Russian Foreign Minister, was known as a " Deutschhasser " (hater of Germany). There were the usual threatening movements of troops upon the frontier. Finally, in the August of 1879, a letter was sent by the Tsar to the Kaiser, complaining that " the commissioners of France and Italy side, in almost all the questions that arise, with those of Russia, while the Germans seem to have received the order always to support the opinion of the Austrians, which is systematically hostile to us." " The circumstances," the letter concluded, " are becoming too serious for me to be able to conceal from you the fears which preoccupy me, the consequences of which might be disastrous to both our countries." [1]

This letter, called by Germans the " Brief Ohrfeige " (box-on-the-ear letter) Bismarck took very seriously. He regarded it as a threat of war, dwelling particularly upon the recent increases in the Russian army and the movements of troops to the frontier. The Tsar, he said, was no longer to be trusted ; he was worked upon by a party which desired war and which looked to an alliance of Russia both with Austria and with France. A Franco-Russian alliance was always Bismarck's nightmare, and the only way he saw, at this time, to counter it was to anticipate Russia by making a defensive alliance with Austria, thus forming a " balance " which would keep the peace. In this project, however, he met with great reluctance on the part of the then Kaiser. Wilhelm I regarded the plan as a kind of treachery towards his nephew the Tsar ; he did not believe that the danger of war was imminent ; and he insisted that the treaty must at least be really, as well as in form, defensive, and must be made known to the Tsar. After much discussion, and much pressure by Bismarck, the Kaiser gave way on this latter point ; but he insisted that a memorandum should be communicated to the Tsar stating that Germany and Austria were united in the determination to keep the peace ; that they did not regard any of the difficulties arising out of the Treaty of Berlin as a sufficient cause for war ; that they would not take advantage of them to threaten or attack Russia ; and that they had no doubt that Russia reciprocated these sentiments. The text [2] of the treaty, however, was not, at this time, shown to the Tsar,

[1] Ger. Docs., iii. p. 14.   [2] Ib., p. 102, and Pribram, i. p. 23.

and the fact that it was definitely directed against a Russian attack was not communicated.

In the course of the discussion Bismarck professed himself anxious that England should join the alliance,[1] and he instructed Count Münster to approach Disraeli. The English Minister seems to have been favourable to the proposal. " The purpose in the mind of the country," he wrote,[2] " is the maintenance of our Empire and hostility to Russia. Notwithstanding the general depression, a fear of Russia as the Power that will ultimately strike at the root of our Empire is singularly prevalent, and is felt even by those who do not publicly or loudly express it.   I believe that an alliance between the three Powers in question, at this moment, might probably be hailed with something like enthusiasm by the country." Lord Salisbury was more sceptical. He thought indeed that, alliance or no alliance, " it will be very difficult for us not to go to Austria's assistance if she is seriously attacked by Russia—no matter how the attack comes about." But the difficulty of an alliance was that it might injure our relations with France. He proposed to consult the French Government, but this Beaconsfield discouraged ; and on October 15th Salisbury wrote that " there seemed to have been a slight change of mind " and that " Bismarck is not so keen as he was." In fact, Bismarck did not press the matter further, and it is possible that his object in approaching the British Government was to overcome the scruples of the Kaiser by showing that the alliance had England's support. It had, in fact, the support of the Government ; for Lord Salisbury referred to it, in a public speech, as " tidings of great joy." [3]

The Austro-German Treaty was signed October 7th, 1879. Its provisions were that if, " contrary to the hope and against the loyal desire of the two parties," one of them be " attacked " by Russia, the other should come to its assistance with its whole war strength ; that, in case either party were attacked by some State other than Russia, the other party should observe at least a benevolent neutrality ; but that if the attacking party were supported by Russia, then the obligation of armed resistance would arise. The fourth article runs :

[1] Ger. Docs., iii. p. 31.   [2] *Life*, vi. p. 486.
[3] Authorities differ as to the extent of Bismarck's offer to England. Disraeli and Salisbury represent it as a firm offer of alliance. The editors of the German Documents dispute this (see iv. p. 3 note).

" This treaty shall, in conformity with its peaceful character, and to avoid any misinterpretation, be kept secret by
the two high contracting parties, and only communicated
to a third Power upon a joint understanding between
the two parties and according to the terms of a special
agreement.

" The two high contracting parties venture to hope, after
the sentiments expressed by the Emperor Alexander at the
meeting at Alexandovo, that the armaments of Russia will
not in reality prove to be menacing to them, and have, on
that account, no reason for making a communication at
present ; should, however, this hope, contrary to their
expectations, prove to be erroneous, the two high contracting
parties would consider it their loyal obligation to let the
Emperor Alexander know, at least confidentially, that they
must consider an attack on either of them as directed against
both."

The treaty is thus, like most treaties, " defensive " in
form. It remained in force until 1914, and many people
would say that at that date, or earlier, it had become
" offensive." But these terms, as we have seen, mean so
little that the matter hardly deserves discussion. The British
Government, at any rate, welcomed the treaty at its formation,
and the Prime Minister would rather have liked to become a
party to it. In 1887 its terms were revealed to Lord Salisbury,
as well as to Russia and Italy,[1] and in the next year it was
published to the world.[2]

II. The League of the Three Emperors

That Bismarck's policy in making the treaty of 1879 was
really defensive is shown by his continual anxiety to secure himself also by treaty with Russia. His original idea was a " League
of the Three Emperors " (Austria, Germany, and Russia), and
this he had achieved in 1873. This triple agreement was a
little vague in form. It ran : " In case an aggression coming
from a third Power should threaten to compromise European
peace, Their Majesties agree in the first place to come to an
understanding between themselves, without seeking or contracting new alliances, with a view to adopting a common line

---

[1] Ger. Docs., v. p. 281.   [2] Ib., p. 288.

of action." [1]   But that the intention was quite definite is clear
from the military convention made previously between Germany and Russia, which ran : " If one of the two Empires
should be attacked by a European Power, it shall be assisted
in the shortest possible time by an army of two hundred
thousand effective troops." [2]   The motive of the agreement
was said to be to checkmate any attempt of France to disturb
the peace.   The Tsar, we are told, was ready even for an
" offensive and defensive " alliance for this purpose—another
proof that there is really no distinction between these two
terms ; for at the same time it is maintained that the only
object of the agreement is peace, and that no one could possibly
mistake this intention.[3]

But, as we have seen, the Russo-Turkish War of 1878, and
the following events, had alienated Russia from Germany ;
and Bismarck turned to what he regarded as the alternative
policy, alliance with Austria.   But he was still anxious to
have an arrangement also with Russia, and he recurred a year
or so later to the idea of a triple alliance.   In the course of
his discussions with Sabouroff, the Russian negotiator, he put
forward the principles of his policy in words which are worth
reproducing :

" You too often lose sight," he said,[4] " of the importance
of being three on the European chess-board.   That is the
invariable objective of all the Cabinets and of mine above all ;
nobody wishes to be in a minority.   All politics reduces itself
to this formula : Try to be à trois as long as the world is
governed by the unstable equilibrium of five Great Powers."
It would be difficult to express more aptly the guiding ideas
of diplomacy, under the conditions of the European anarchy.
A balance of three against two Bismarck regards as safe ;
in other words, the balance of power really means an over-
balance in one's own favour.   Later combinations, less skilful
on the German side, gave the balance of three to two against,
not for, Germany ; for Italy did not seriously count.   Hence,
at bottom, the Great War.   These casual remarks of a master
of the old diplomacy are much more to the point than the
laborious apologetics of lesser men.

[1] Text in Ger. Docs., i. p. 206.   No period of time is fixed for the agreement.
[2] Ger. Docs., i. p. 203.   [3] Ib., p. 198.
[4] *Nineteenth Century*, December 1917, p. 1119.

The difficulty of the proposed alliance was the strained relation between Austria and Russia. This, however, was outweighed, in the judgment of Sabouroff, by the suspicion that, if Russia were recalcitrant, Bismarck might make an alliance with Austria, and then an agreement with France. This, he said, would be " to the detriment of Russia," as, of course, according to diplomatic principles, it would ; for Russia would then be one against three, or even four. It was not, however, until September 1879 that Sabouroff heard definite rumours of the Austro-German treaty, and not till 1887 that he knew the text. In 1885 Bismarck informed him that " Austria would be very much deceived if she thought that the security resulting from her relations to us was complete. Our interests compel us to prevent her being destroyed, but she is not guaranteed against attack." According to the text of the treaty, that is precisely what she was guaranteed against. The equivocation was possible because the text of the treaty was still secret. As we have seen, it was not till 1887 that it was revealed to the Russian Government, and not till 1888 that it was published.[1]

The Treaty of the Three Emperors was finally signed June 18th, 1881. Its first article runs : " In case one of the High Contracting Parties should find itself at war with a fourth Great Power, the two others shall maintain towards it a benevolent neutrality, and shall devote their efforts to the localisation of the conflict. This stipulation shall apply likewise to a war between one of the three Powers and Turkey, but only in the case where a previous agreement shall have been reached between the three Courts as to the results of the war."

Some comments suggest themselves on this, the main provision.

First, there is no attempt to distinguish aggressive from defensive war. On the other hand, Bismarck was under pledge, by the treaty with Austria, to defend her against " attack " from Russia. But this Russia did not know. Bismarck, no doubt, intended the treaty to be one of defence ;[2] and so did Russia, but only for the time being. The instruc-

---

[1] It was read to Schuvaloff by Bismarck, May 11th, 1887 (see *American Historical Review*, January 1918 p. 335).

[2] See, e.g., *American Historical Review*, January 1918, p. 328.

tions sent to Sabouroff are so illuminating on this point that they are worth citing : " The object of a special arrangement with Germany," the Minister said, " would be to surround the maintenance of peace with solid guarantees, indispensable to the development of our military, naval, and financial strength." [1] That peace is regarded by statesmen as a mere interval during which they may the better prepare for the next war has seldom perhaps been more frankly expressed. Russia, we know, was always aiming ultimately at the Straits and Constantinople, although she was not always prepared to make war for that object.   In December 1883, for example, a memoir by Jomini, of the Russian Foreign Office, states that this was the " sole objective " of Russian policy, and that an essential condition of success is the neutrality of Germany.[2] And it is interesting to note that, in a preliminary stage of the discussions, the Russian Minister had said that his object was to " deprive Great Britain, particularly aggressive at this time, of every ally, in case she should decide to make war upon us."   There are, it would seem, many Englishmen who seriously believe that their country never has been and never would be aggressive.   A study of diplomatic documents would show them how far this view is from being accepted by Continental statesmen.

Meantime, in view of the attitude of England, Russia contented herself with reaffirming the closure of the Straits. But she was, nevertheless, somewhat aggrieved that, under the treaty, she could not count on the benevolent neutrality of her allies, in case of a war with Turkey, unless a new agreement was first arrived at with them.   She wanted, in fact, to be able to make war for the Straits whenever it should seem convenient.   Meantime, she would be supported by Germany and Austria in maintaining the closure.

The League of the Three Emperors was made for three years, and renewed for three years more, from 1884 to 1887. But by the latter year the friction between Russia and Austria had increased to such a point that a further renewal was impracticable.   The friction was due to the events of 1885, which are dealt with elsewhere.[3]   As usual, armaments played a great part in it.   The Russian Ambassador in Vienna

---

[1] *American Historical Review*, u.s., p. 334.
[2] Ib., p. 326.   [3] See above, p. 27.

expressed fears that Austria might start an " aggressive " war, for " the burden of the military armaments is such that nothing is certain." [1] But, as always, the question what was an " aggressive " war remained unsolved. Thus Schuvaloff remarked that " if unexpected complications in the Balkan Peninsula should arise to affect our relations with Austria, a difficulty would present itself, namely, the difficulty of deciding on which side the aggression lay." [2]

As usual under such circumstances, Bismarck began to fear a rapprochement of Russia with France. " Not one voice in France," he said, " has renounced Alsace-Lorraine ; at any moment a Government may be established which will declare war. It may break out in ten days as readily as in ten years ; nothing can be answered for. The war of 1870 was but child's play in comparison with the future war ; on both sides an effort will be made to finish the adversary, to bleed him white, that the vanquished may not be able to rise again, and may never for thirty years dare even to think of the possibility of turning against the conqueror." [3] Bismarck was wrong as to the date at which his prophecy would be fulfilled. But, apart from that, was ever prophecy truer ?

Indeed, even at that time, there was reason for Bismarck's fears ; for talk was going on between Russia and France. Flourens, the French Ambassador, informed the Tsar that France would not attack Germany " unless the latter were strongly engaged elsewhere." The Tsar assured France that an agreement between Russia and Germany was the best guarantee of peace. But what would happen, said the French Minister, if Germany should present a demand for our disarmament ? In such a case the Tsar assured her of his moral support.[4]

These discussions show an approach of the two Powers, but, as yet, no alliance against Germany. Bismarck, as we know, was always determined to prevent such a development, and he endeavoured to do it now by the curious and ingenious device known as the " Reinsurance Treaty " (1887) between Germany and Russia. The effect of this was that whereas, by the Austro-German treaty, Germany was bound to defend Austria against attack by Russia, by the new treaty she

---

American Historical Review, u.s., p. 346.   [2] Ib., p. 335.
[3] Ib., p. 331.   [4] Ib.

would observe a benevolent neutrality if Russia were attacked by Austria. Reciprocally, Russia would observe benevolent neutrality if Germany were attacked by France. The treaty is formally consistent with the Austro-German one, which was indeed, revealed to the Russians while the new treaty was negotiating.[1] Whether it is materially consistent is a question that cannot be answered, in view of the absence of definition as to what attack means. On this point Bismarck showed his usual candour, for he wrote, in the course of the negotiations : " The question what is an aggressive war cannot be defined in a treaty, and the contracting parties must trust one another that, when the case arises, the question will be loyally weighed and decided by the other party." [2] It is, however, clear that Austria would not be likely to agree both with Germany and with Russia as to the meaning of aggression, even if those two Powers should agree with one another.

It should be added that, in this treaty, the closure of the Straits was once more affirmed ; but also that, in an additional protocol, Germany promises " her benevolent neutrality and her moral and diplomatic support," " in case the Emperor of Russia should find himself under the necessity of defending the entrance of the Black Sea in order to safeguard the interests of Russia."

The treaty was kept secret from Austria. How should it not have been ? But it lasted only three years. In 1890, when its renewal was due, Bismarck fell, and Caprivi, who succeeded him, permitted it to lapse. His policy, he said, must be " simple and transparent," and he could not think that the treaty came under that rubric.[3] Moreover, he believed that it did not correspond to the real facts of public opinion in Russia, and he doubted the value of treaties not founded on the genuine expression of national sentiment.[4] There seems, however, to have been another reason for the lapse of the treaty. The young Kaiser Wilhelm II " hoped to win over England to the so-called League of Peace." [5] This may seem an odd idea to a generation nourished on the propaganda of the Great War. But in fact, as we have shown,

[1] Ger. Docs., v. p. 281–2.   [2] Ib., p. 248.
[3] Ib., vii. pp. 29, 35.   [4] Ib., p. 32.
[5] *American Historical Review*, u.s., pp. 345, 349.

Germany at this time, and even later, was, of all the Conti-nental Powers, the one most sympathetic to England, as England was to her.

III. The Triple Alliance

We now come to the Triple Alliance, the texts of which were not published in full until after 1914. This was a new treaty, not a mere accession of Italy to the Austro-German Alliance, which latter remained independently in force. Italy desired to support herself against France by an agree-ment with the Central Powers.[1] The principal reason for this was the occupation by France of Tunis, in 1881, which disturbed the " balance of power " in the Mediterranean and made Italy apprehensive about the future fate of Tripoli. From the Italian point of view, the object was " the preser-vation of peace and the curbing of France's lust for power." [2] " Isolation," said Baron Sonnino, " means annihilation." What " annihilation " means he did not discuss. In the language of statesmen it is apt to mean being weaker than another Power, though who is " annihilated " in that position is not clear. Not, one would suppose, the men and women who really *are* annihilated in war, but that curious abstraction " the State."

Tripoli was the principal concern of the Italians. But, further, they seem to have feared an attack by France on Italy itself, and especially on Rome. The attack on Rome would have been due to clericalism. But also, and not quite consistently, the Italians feared Republican propaganda by the French. " France was a menace not only as a military Power, but to the monarchical interests and to the social order of Italy as well." [3] The proposal for alliance emanated

[1] According to Professor Salvemini, the Italian adherence to the Triple Alliance depended on four points :

(1) The continuance of good relations between England and the Central Powers ; for Italy could never risk war with England.

(2) The threat of France to disturb the status quo in North Africa.

(3) Austria's preservation of the status quo in the Balkans.

(4) Italian fears of French (Catholic) intervention to protect Rome.

Points (1) and (2) were dealt with later in another way, by the agree-ments between England and France, and France and Italy, at the turn of the century ; as to (3) Italy never trusted Austria, and (4) early ceased to be of importance. Thus the pillars of the alliance succumbed, and the way was prepared for Italy's junction with the Entente in 1915 (see Article in the *Cronaca di Genova*, November 1st, 1923).

[2] Pribram, ii. p. 10.   [3] Ib., p. 23.

from Italy, and the Central Powers seem to have been, at first, indifferent or hostile. Bismarck was very rude about Italian policy. He called it " a jackal policy." " Insatiable Italy," he said, " with furtive glance roves restlessly hither and thither, instinctively drawn by the odour of corruption and calamity, always ready to attack anybody from the rear and make off with a bit of plunder." While Italian statesmen complained of Republican propaganda by the French, Bismarck complained of the same thing by the Italians : " Republican propaganda at home, and finally conspiracies with the Internationale in London." [1] And he urged the Austrians to " give them a good fright." This was his first reaction. Later, however, he came round to the idea of an alliance, influenced by the occupation of Egypt and by his dispute with England over colonial policy. He began to fear the possibility of a Franco-Italian rapprochement, and thought it desirable to counter this by attracting Italy to the orbit of the Central Powers.

As to Austria, her position was different from that of Germany, because she was a Mediterranean Power. Her Minister, Haymerle, was therefore anxious, in spite of Bismarck's earlier suggestions, not to quarrel with Italy. " In general," he wrote, " we ought not to divide our political resources or to allow our eyes to be diverted from the chief goal, the permanent blocking of Russia ; these are sufficient reasons for keeping any difference with Italy from the docket as long as possible." " Austria," he said, " coveted no Italian territory," and " Italy is not yet ripe for partition into provincial republics." [2] These indications are interesting as illustrations of the general truth that an alliance between States implies neither confidence nor admiration, but only self-interest. In the present case the latter, in the end, prevailed. For though neither Germany nor Austria thought much of Italy as a military Power, yet in case of a war between Germany and France she could at least, they calculated, keep a French army in check on the Italian frontier, and her Navy might be useful in the Adriatic. These considerations finally carried the day, and after much discussion and many drafts the alliance was concluded.

In the course of the negotiations one or two points were raised which are of special interest to us, in our study of the

---

[1] Pribram, ii. p. 6.   [2] Ib., p. 4.

methods of diplomacy. Thus Kálnoky, the Austrian Minister, made the curious remark that " written agreements no longer harmonise with the diplomatic usage of our times ; and as far as secret treaties are concerned I shall not conceal from you that, in these parliamentary days, I personally regard them with a certain mistrust." [1] Perhaps this was only a polite way of rejecting certain proposals of the Italians ; for all the chief Governments of Europe, parliamentary or not, were up to their necks in secret treaties during the thirty years preceding the war, and the Triple Alliance, in particular, was both concluded in secret and kept secret. More interesting than this piece of insincerity are the curious phrases suggested with regard to " defence " and " offence." Thus a draft by the Austrian statesman Kálnoky distinguishes the case where one of the allies should be " attacked without provocation " from the case where it should be " drawn into war " or " become involved in a war." [2] Whether these latter phrases are intended to signify a kind of intermediary state, a sort of political purgatory, which is neither offence nor defence, but a " muddling into war," or whether they are merely circumlocutions implying offence, does not appear. Presumably the latter. For a later draft of Kálnoky's deals with the case where one of the allied Powers " without being provoked should be engaged in war with a non-signatory State." This seems to contemplate aggressive war. The Italians thereupon suggested the amendment " without direct provocation, should see itself forced to make war." [3] This, however, still left it ambiguous from which side the provocation was to come. For the meaning might be either " without provoking war " or " without being provoked." The former interpretation would make the clause formally defensive, the latter formally offensive. One may be permitted to wonder whether the parties negotiating were endeavouring to cheat one another, or whether, as is so often the case with international treaties, they desired to leave the most important point ambiguous, in the hope of being able to interpret it, each to his own advantage, when the occasion should arise. However this may have been, agreement on the phraseology was at last reached, and on May 20th, 1882, the first treaty of the Triple Alliance was signed.

[1] Pribram, ii. p. 14.   [2] Ib., p. 21.   [3] Ib., p. 32.

The treaty starts with a preamble stating that the parties, " animated by the desire to increase the guarantees of the general peace, to fortify the monarchical principle, and thereby to assure the unimpaired maintenance of the social and political order in their respective States, have agreed to conclude a treaty which, by its essentially conservative and defensive nature, pursues only the aim of forestalling the dangers which might threaten the security of their States and the peace of Europe." The monarchical principle and the social and political order do not at present concern us, though it is interesting to reflect how these entities have actually fared after being " guaranteed " by this treaty for thirty years. What we have to ask is, How did the treaty increase the " guarantees of the general peace " ?

First, the two Central Powers pledged themselves to assist Italy with all their forces if she should be " attacked " by France " without direct provocation on her part." Italy promised to do the same for Germany, if she should be attacked, under the same conditions, by France.

Secondly, if any one, or two, of the parties should be " attacked and engaged in a war with " two or more Great Powers " without direct provocation on their part," the casus fœderis will arise for the other parties, or party.

These two clauses presumably are intended to imply " defensive " war. But the fourth article runs : " In case a Great Power non-signatory to the present treaty should threaten the security of the States of one of the High Contracting Parties, and the threatened party should find itself forced on that account to make war against it, the two others bind themselves to observe towards their ally a benevolent neutrality." In this case, clearly, the war is recognised as not " defensive," since otherwise the obligation of armed assistance would arise, at any rate if the Great Powers were Russia or France. It must therefore be " offensive " war that is contemplated, unless a kind of hybrid intermediary is conceived. Thus the treaty which " is animated by the desire to increase the guarantees of the general peace " does, in fact, contemplate the breaking of the peace by one of the parties to it.

Lastly, " the High Contracting Parties mutually promise secrecy as to the contents and existence of the present treaty." Kálnoky's scruples on that head were thus duly overcome.

In plain language, what does all this amount to ? First, Germany and Austria are pledged to assist Italy if she is " attacked " by France. On the other hand, there is no obligation on Italy to assist Austria if she is " attacked " by Russia. Austria thus gets less out of the treaty than Italy. But she gets something ; for, in an Austro-Russian war, Italy would at least be neutral ; and further, in a war of the two Central Powers against France and Russia combined, she is pledged to armed assistance. Only, however, if it is the Central Powers that are " attacked," a provision which left it free to her to desert them if she should judge them to be the aggressors, as she did in 1914. As to Germany, if she were " attacked " by France, she would receive armed assistance from Italy. And as at that time France was the enemy dreaded by Italy, the latter would no doubt have decided, in case of such a war, that the " attack " had in fact occurred.

There remains one point of special interest to Englishmen. It is stipulated by all the parties that the treaty is not " in any case " directed against England. England was too strong a naval Power for Italy to risk war with her. And this showed already that, if England joined Russia and France, Italy would not be likely to take part in any war against those States.

The treaty of 1882 was concluded for five years, and in July 1886 the question of renewal was raised. The negotiations extended over several months, and when the treaty was renewed it received a very different form ; for circumstances had changed, and Italy's position was stronger than it had been in 1882. In the first place, her military strength was greater, for she had entered with zest into the competition of armaments ; but, also, political conditions favoured her. The relations between Austria and Russia had been further strained by the events of 1885-6 in the Balkans—the union of Bulgaria with Eastern Rumelia, the Serbo-Bulgarian War, and the support of Serbia by Austria. Further, the popularity of Boulanger made Bismarck fear aggression by France. As always, he was haunted by the possibility of a Russo-French alliance, and also, now, of its being joined by Italy, unless she were firmly bound to the Central Powers. On this occasion, therefore, he was determined to have the alliance renewed, and when obstacles were raised by Austria he threatened a separate agreement with Italy.

Italy, on the other hand, and for the same reasons, was in a position to increase her price. She felt, or pretended, dissatisfaction with her position in the alliance, and was determined to secure better terms for the protection of what she called her " just claims " in Tripoli and Morocco. " Just," in this connexion, meant what it usually does mean in international discussions. France had stolen Tunis, and Italy therefore had a " right " to steal Tripoli and to keep a sharp eye on Morocco. Failing an agreement on these lines, Italy, her Minister hinted, might turn to France, and divide with her the mastery of the Mediterranean. In fact, the French Minister, Freycinet, was angling for Italian support. " The Mediterranean," he said, " ought to belong to France and Italy," and the two countries ought to be allied.[1] The method of flirting with one country in order to extort concessions from another is part of the regular mechanism of diplomacy, and is made easy by the fact that alliances rest exclusively on self-interest ; so that a State may and does make an enemy an ally, and an ally an enemy, without any hesitation or scruples, except those prompted by prudence. When that is being done it will be convenient to communicate to the one State the offers of the other ; and that is what the Italian Minister did in this case. He informed the Germans of the French proposals. " It will be interesting," said the Italian Ambassador in Berlin, " to follow closely the further communications of the French Government in Rome and in Berlin, and to circulate them, under pledge of secrecy, between the Chancellor and Count Robilant."[2]

What Italy wanted was a guarantee of the status quo on the coasts and on the islands of the Mediterranean ; this meant (for the present) a guarantee against French aggression on the African and Russian aggression on the Balkan coasts. Germany was quite ready for this, but the Austrians made difficulties. First, they wanted to extend the guarantee to the interior of the Balkans, their interests being concerned with keeping the Russians out and securing in permanence their occupation of Bosnia. On this point, after much haggling, Italy yielded.[3] But, secondly, Italy was determined to secure

---

[1] Ger. Docs., iv. p. 190.   [2] Ib., p. 194.

[3] This concession by Italy turned out unfortunately for Austria in 1914, since it enabled Italy to claim " compensation " for Austrian encroachment on Serbia (see below, Chap. XVI., p. 481).

the help of her allies to keep France out of Tripoli and, when convenient, to put herself in ; and Austria was reluctant to accept such an obligation. In the end it was arranged that Germany, but not Austria, should guarantee Tripoli ; while Italy, but not Germany, should guarantee the Balkans. The result was a change in the form of the treaty, which now included, first, a section common to all three States, reproducing the treaty of 1882 ; secondly, a section binding only Austria and Italy ; thirdly, a section binding only Germany and Italy ; fourthly, a section stating that the two latter agreements, " although distinct, respond none the less to the general spirit of the aforementioned agreement of 1882, because to-day, as then, the three monarchies are aiming essentially at the maintenance of peace."

We have already pointed out that when Governments say they are " aiming at peace " what they really mean is that they do not themselves intend, or at least do not write themselves down as intending, to start the war, which, nevertheless, is " coming," and from which, when it comes, they will, if they can, extract such and such advantages. We may illustrate this general truth from the particular case before us. The first article of the special treaty between Austria and Italy starts by saying that the parties " engage to use their influence to forestall any territorial modification which might be injurious to one or the other of the Powers signatory to the treaty." Modifications which might be beneficial are another matter.. The next paragraph (characteristic and typical) says : " However, if in the course of events the maintenance of the status quo in the Adriatic and in the Ægean Sea should become impossible, and if, whether in consequence of the action of a third Power or otherwise, Austria-Hungary or Italy should find themselves under the necessity of modifying it, by a temporary or permanent occupation on their part, this occupation shall take place only after a previous agreement between the two Powers aforesaid, based upon the principle of a reciprocal compensation for every advantage, territorial or other, which each of them might obtain beyond the present status quo, and giving satisfaction to the interests and well-founded claims of the two parties." In other words, and more briefly, the article says : " We shall see that the territorial status quo is not disturbed to the advantage of any

Power but ourselves ; and if, and when, we choose to disturb it to our own advantage, we will divide the spoils." It will be observed, also, that in this article war is contemplated, even if it be not " provoked," by another Power.

The German-Italian treaty presents an example even more interesting of the principles and practice of diplomacy. First, the two parties state their intention to maintain the status quo in the Ægean and Adriatic, without, however, in this case providing for a division of the spoils when they choose to disturb it. This was because Germany was not then seeking territory in those regions. On the other hand, the third article runs as follows :

" If it were to happen that France should make a move to extend her occupation, or even her protectorate or her sovereignty, under any form whatsoever, in the North African territories, whether of the Vilayet of Tripoli or of the Moroccan Empire, and that, in consequence thereof, Italy, in order to safeguard her position in the Mediterranean, should feel that she must herself undertake action in the said North African territories, or even have recourse to extreme measures in French territory in Europe, the state of war which would thereby ensue between Italy and France would constitute, ipso facto, on the demand of Italy and at the common charge of the two Allies, the casus fœderis with all the effects, etc."

That is to say, if France does anything which looks like extending her African Empire, Italy may go to war with her, either in Africa or in Europe, and Germany on demand will support her. Such a war, presumably, Italy would call " defensive " ; but that view was hardly likely to be taken by France. It may seem surprising that Germany should sign such a treaty ; but Bismarck was quite clear that Germany must intervene in any war between France and Italy, whatever its origin. " The origin of such a war would, in fact, be of no consequence, for Germany could not permit Italy to be annihilated or reduced to a state of dependence by France." [1] Germany, in fact, went even further, for the fourth article of the treaty runs :

" If the fortunes of any war undertaken in common against France should lead Italy to seek for territorial guarantees with respect to France for the security of the frontiers of the

[1] Pribram, ii. p. 52. Cf. Ger. Docs., iv. p. 200.

kingdom and of her maritime position, as well as with a view
to the stability of peace, Germany will present no obstacle
thereto ; and if need be, and in a measure compatible with
circumstances, will apply herself to facilitating the means of
attaining such a purpose." By this article, Bismarck explained,
later, that he meant " to mollify Italy and bind her to the
Central Powers by means of gifts, such as could be made in
the shape of Nice, Corsica, Albania, and territories on the
North African coast." [1]

The reader may now appraise for himself the value of the
statement in the fourth and concluding treaty that " the three
monarchies are aiming essentially at the maintenance of peace."

It may be added, for the interest of Englishmen, that
Article 2 of the German-Italian treaty states that the guarantee
of the status quo " applies in no way to the Egyptian question,
with regard to which the High Contracting Parties preserve
respectively their freedom of action." This probably implies
no hostility to England, whose quarrel at this time was with
France, not with the Central Powers, and who, as we shall
see, at this same moment was entering into a treaty with Austria
and Italy in regard to the Mediterranean. It merely left the
Powers free to take what diplomatic action they might think
fit in Egypt.

The treaty of 1887 was followed by a military convention
of February 1888. This became known at once to the French,
who thereupon broke off the negotiations that were proceeding
for a commercial treaty with Italy. A violent Press campaign
followed, and it was a " miracle " that war did not break out.[2]
But the succession of Rudini to Crispi improved the position,
and the French, like Jupiter in the myth, descended upon
Italy with a shower of golden offers if she would but abandon
the Triple Alliance. But Rudini, though friendly to France,
would not go so far as that. The Triple Alliance continued,
and was buttressed by other engagements. There was, first,
the Reinsurance Treaty with Russia, with which we have
dealt. Then there was the Mediterranean agreement between
England, Italy, and Austria, of which we shall speak later,
and which brought England in as guarantor of the status
quo in the Mediterranean and in North Africa. There was

---

[1] Pribram, ii. p. 80.
[2] Salvemini, in the *Cronaca di Genova*, November 8th, 1923.

also an agreement between Italy and Spain tending to the same purpose. There was a treaty between the Central Powers and Roumania. And, at this time, Serbia could be counted on to join Austria against Russia. The master-craftsman of diplomacy had completed his most complicated machine. As the old Kaiser said : " He was like a rider who juggled on horseback with five balls." But, adds the historian, " there were moments when he himself was frightened at what he had done." [1] The whole structure was, in fact, like all such structures, a house of cards. It was founded on self-interest and mortared by mistrust. None of the allies believed in one another or cared for one another. None of them could be trusted not to fly off into another combination if that could be made to appear more profitable to them. Thus, for example, at the very moment when the treaty of 1887 was waiting for ratification, the Austrian Ambassador at Rome wrote to Kálnoky as follows : " In the case of a war between France and Germany the Italians will probably wait to see how the first battles turn out ; only then will they decide whether to participate actively or to assume a passive attitude. There will probably be much noise and little action." [2] In fact, it will be remembered, when the war did come, both Italy and Roumania sided, in spite of the treaties, against their allies, while England changed sides in 1904.

In 1890 the great juggler was dismissed from office, and with him went the Reinsurance Treaty. His successor, Caprivi, however, was willing and anxious to renew the Triple Alliance. It would lapse in 1892, and already, at the end of 1890, the then Italian Minister, Crispi, raised the question of renewal. He proposed the consolidation of the four treaties of 1887 [1] in one, intending that in this way Germany should make herself responsible, along with Austria, for the Balkans, and Austria, along with Germany, for North Africa. It was upon these questions that the discussions turned. The Central Powers hesitated, until Crispi fell at the beginning of 1891. Rudini succeeded him. He professed loyalty to the Triple Alliance, but also, as always, he desired a rapprochement with France. France was ready, but on conditions. She wanted to know what the terms of the Triple Alliance were, and her Ambassador expressed an incredulity almost rude when the King informed him that it was directed only to the maintenance of peace. It was, moreover, the King explained, so secret that there were only four men in Italy who knew of its terms. Well, said the Ambassador, *I* wouldn't enter a Ministry without knowing the treaties I was bound by! The King expressed a dignified surprise that his word could not be accepted, and the interview ended rather coolly. Shortly afterwards an Italian agent of Rothschild turned up, bringing, with the approval of M. Ribot, the offer of a large loan, if only Italy would state the conditions under which she was pledged to take part in a German war against France. The Italian Minister took a noble line. He was astonished that any Italian subject could consent to be an agent in such a transaction. He had been tempted, he reported to the King, to kick the dirty Jew out of doors. "The proud soul of the Marquis," we are told, "rose against this dirty business." He felt it indeed so strongly that he could not bear to communicate the facts to his Foreign Office.[1]

French policy, in fact, had long been directed towards separating Italy from the Triple Alliance. She had tried bullying, and she had tried, and now tried again, cajoling.[2] The Central Powers grew more and more nervous ; and the negotiation of the Franco-Russian Alliance in 1891 brought matters to a head. The Austrian Minister wanted simple renewal, and, so far as he was concerned, he obtained it. But Italy was able to extort from Germany further concessions. The latter was now pledged to support Italy in Cyrenaica, Tripoli, and also (this is the new point) Tunis. And the obligation becomes more definite ; for Article 9 of the new treaty says : " If, unfortunately, as a result of the mature examination of the situation, Germany and Italy should both recognise that the maintenance of the status quo has become impossible, Germany engages, after a formal and previous agreement, to support Italy in any action in the form of occupation or other taking of guaranty which the latter should undertake in these same regions, with a view to an interest of equilibrium and of legitimate compensation."

[1] Ger. Docs., vii. p. 91.
[2] The French, on several occasions, had offered to let Italy take Tripoli if she would adopt a benevolent attitude towards French ambitions in North Africa (see Salvemini, in *Cronaca di Genova*, October 18th and 25th, 1923).

This new article clearly contemplates war by Italy to seize Tripoli, and pledges Germany to support her. The Italian action, however, was in fact delayed until 1912. With the exceptions referred to, the new treaty was substantially the same as those of 1887 ; only, the four treaties of that year are now grouped in one.

The treaty of 1892 might be renewed or terminated in 1897, but otherwise would continue till 1903. The usual situation recurred. France tempted Italy, and Italy exploited the temptation to put pressure upon her allies. Toward the beginning of 1895 Crispi, as well as Blanc, declared that France " had for years let it be openly known that Italy could have Abyssinia, Tripoli, and Heaven knows what else, if only she would desert the Triple Alliance." [1] Considerations of " honour," Crispi said, had prevented Italy from listening to the siren. But she was now in great distress. She was at war with Abyssinia, while France was striding on in Africa ; and at home there was danger of republicanism and revolution. We must renew the treaty, she said, and the Central Powers must give a firm assent to her acquisition of Tripoli. But the Central Powers were cool, for Italy's need, this time, seemed greater than theirs. They were, apparently, flirting with Russia. There might, the Italians thought, be a renewal of the League of the Three Emperors ; Russia and Austria might partition the Balkans ; and " Italy might come away empty-handed from the division of the spoils." [2] The Austrian Ambassador in Rome wrote of Italy's " desire to have a part in everything, eagerness for new conquests, for a great success, fear of an unexpected coup which might procure this success for someone else and not for them." [3] Then, once more, Crispi fell, and once more Rudini came into power, favourable, as before, to the Triple Alliance, but also desiring friendship with France. He finally decided to renew ; but a dispute arose with regard to the protocol of 1882, which declared that the treaty was not directed against England. This had not been included in the treaties of 1887 and 1891, perhaps because of the Mediterranean Agreements between England, Austria, and Italy. The Italians now wished it included in the main treaty. But the Germans objected, on the ground that it would then become evident that Russia

[1] Pribram, ii. p. 104.   [2] Ib., p. 105.   [3] Ib., p. 106.

and France were the only parties against whom the treaty was aimed. This, of course, was the fact. But in these years there was an approximation between Germany and Russia and an idea of a Continental combination against England, and that perhaps accounts for the German attitude.[1] The discussions on this point were protracted until the date was passed by which the treaty could be modified. It therefore went into action again, automatically and unchanged, for another six years.

The treaty thus prolonged would lapse in 1903, and before that date there began again the usual haggling and wrangling. In 1897 Italy had entered, with Austria, into an agreement about Albania. The status quo was to be maintained if possible ; if not, modifications were to be made only in the direction of autonomy.[2] But also a similar agreement had been made, in the same year, between Austria and Russia, no doubt with the knowledge and approval of Germany. The Italians were alarmed. They thought that the intention was to exclude them altogether from the settlement of Balkan questions. They were also afraid of a Russian aggression in the Straits, which would " reduce Italy to the level of a second-rate Power in the Mediterranean, helplessly wedged in between France and Russia." [3] They therefore pressed their allies to accept a clause declaring that the three Powers pledge themselves to " oppose " the attempt of another Great Power to change the territorial status quo in the Orient,[4] and another to extend the agreement with Austria about Albania to the whole Balkan Peninsula. This proposal was regarded by Austria and Germany as perverting the peaceful intentions of the Alliance.[5] For it would " imply that the Powers of the Triple Alliance were resolved to use armed force in preventing any change in the status quo which did not please them." It is not easy to see what a guarantee of the status quo could mean which was not prepared to use armed force ; but it is idle to pursue the arguments of diplomacy through their tortuous and dishonest lucubrations. The wrangle ended once more in a deadlock, and once more the treaty was prolonged without change (1902).

---

[1] See below, p. 104; and also an article by Professor Salvemini in *Il Lavoro*, November 22nd, 1923.
[2] Pribram, i. p. 197. The agreement was put into writing in 1900.
[3] Ib., ii. p. 121.　　　　[4] Ib., p. 122.　　　　[5] Ib., 125.

IV.   The Franco-Italian Treaties

Meantime, however, Italy had been engaged in separate and secret negotiations with France.   The French, as we have seen, had long been endeavouring, sometimes by bullying, sometimes by bribing, to detach her from the Triple Alliance. In 1898 the tariff war between the two States was ended by a commercial agreement ;   the boundaries of their colonial possessions in the Red Sea were adjusted ;   and in December 1900 an arrangement was reached whereby the French withdrew their opposition to an Italian seizure of Tripoli and the Italians theirs to a French seizure of Morocco.   During 1901–2 negotiations were proceeding for a treaty of alliance, and this was concluded in the latter year.   Italy was thus negotiating simultaneously, and of course secretly, both with her allies and with the enemy against whom her alliance had been formed.   By this treaty of 1902 [1] it was agreed that each of the two Powers might freely develop its sphere of influence, the one in Morocco, the other in Tripoli.   This meant that each would permit the other to annex the territory in question when the time should seem ripe.   In fact, while France began her advance in Morocco in 1904, Italy did not seize Tripoli until 1912.   The former enterprise, however, as we shall have to relate in some detail, was countered by many difficulties, owing to the action of Germany.   This deal, by which Tripoli and Morocco were traded off against one another, was the essence of the treaty.   But there were other provisions, concerning the relations of the Great Powers, which illuminate so clearly the nature of diplomacy that they must be dwelt upon in some detail.   At a certain stage in the negotiations the following formula was proposed :

" In case Italy should be the object of a direct or indirect aggression on the part of one or more Powers, France will maintain a strict neutrality.   The same shall hold good in case Italy, as the result of a direct provocation, should find herself compelled, in defence of her honour or of her security, to take the initiative of a declaration of war.   In that eventuality the Royal Government shall previously communicate its intention to the Government of the Republic, which will

---

[1] See Pribram, ii. App. C, and French Yellow Book. " Les accords Franco-Italiens, 1901–2."

thus be enabled to determine whether there is really a case of direct provocation." Mutatis mutandis, the same obligation was taken by Italy towards France. But then, what did " direct provocation " mean ? The Italian Minister replied by way of example. For instance, he said, it was a case of direct provocation when Bismarck mutilated the famous dispatch before the war of 1870 and when the King of Prussia refused to receive M. Benedetti. On the other hand, it was a case of " indirect provocation " when Prince Hohenzollern became a candidate for the throne of Spain. These examples, presumably, were chosen to please France. At any rate, it is hardly likely that Germany would have admitted their correctness, and historians would certainly differ widely and irreconcilably. But when the French Minister pressed for some more precise definition, he received from his Ambassador the following : " The word ' direct ' has this sense and this meaning, to wit, that the facts capable of being eventually invoked as constituting the provocation must concern the direct relations between the Power provoking and the Power provoked." This resembles the definition of an Ambassador as " one who performs ambassadorial functions." Yet on this undefined and undefinable phrase was to depend the question whether either Power would remain neutral when the other went to war.

This, however, does not exhaust the interest of the negotiations. There was another point. The French were anxious as to the contents of the Triple Alliance, the renewal of which, as we have seen, was proceeding alongside of the transactions we are considering. They were afraid that that Alliance might cover up, under the name " defensive," what would really be " offensive " conduct. The Italian negotiator, Prinetti, was unwilling to show them the text of the treaty, because, as he said, it contained " other points which do not interest or touch " the French. " It was only in the annexes," he said, " that there was anything the latter could object to, and these must be dropped." Now, in fact—

(1) What was contained in the Final Protocol to the treaty as reconstructed in 1891 (the only annex) was a clause expressing the desirability of bringing England in as guarantor precisely of that status quo in Morocco and Tripoli which the Franco-Italian treaty was bargaining away.

(2) To this protocol the Italians attached so much importance that they were pressing Germany to have it included in the text of the treaty.

(3) In the main body of the treaty was that Clause 10 which contemplates war by Germany and Italy if France should " make a move to extend her occupation or her sovereignty under any form whatsoever in the North African territories."

Thus the actual provisions of the Triple Alliance of 1891 were directly contrary to those of the Franco-Italian treaty ; and the treaty of 1891 was renewed, with this contradiction obtaining, both in 1902 and in 1912. Yet Prinetti assured Delcassé, in 1902, that in the renewal of the Triple Alliance " there is nothing directly or indirectly aggressive towards France, no engagement binding us in any eventuality to take part in an aggression against her ; finally, no stipulation which menaces the security or tranquillity of France." [1] What truth there was in this declaration the reader may judge from the facts just laid before him.

Finally, Prinetti assured Delcassé that : " No protocol or military provision in the nature of an international contract which would be in disagreement with the present declarations exists or will be concluded by her." In fact, a naval agreement had been drawn up in December 1900 [2] for the contingency of war against France and Russia ; and in November 1913, the Franco-Italian treaty being still in force and the above declaration on record, another naval agreement, equally directed against France, was entered into by Italy, as a member of the Triple Alliance.[3] We shall be told, perhaps, that the word " military " does not include " naval." But, in fact, there was also a military agreement drawn up in 1913.[4]

The facts thus established will enable the reader to form his own opinion on the " loyalty," " honour," or whatever the term employed may be, of the combination of the Triple Alliance with the Franco-Italian Treaty. Italians apparently regarded it as quite correct. Thus, in 1906, Tittoni said in the Italian Chamber : " This is not artifice, it is not Machiavellianism, it is not a double policy, as had been wrongly said ;

---

[1] Pribram, ii. p. 247.   [2] Ib., p. 87 note.   [3] Ib., i. p. 283.
[4] Ib., ii. p. 175. Salvemini says there was a military convention of March 1914 (see *Cronaca di Genova*, January 3rd, 1924). But this, perhaps, is a slip for 1913.

but it is simply the simple plain road to follow which presents itself inevitably to whoever really invites the preservation of peace. . . . If this is Machiavellianism, one must say that there is a Machiavelli in the direction of foreign affairs in each of the principal States of Europe." [1] That perhaps is a sound conclusion. Even Signor Salvemini, who is opposed to the methods of diplomacy, defends the Italian Government in this matter. The combination of the Franco-Italian Treaty with the Triple Alliance, he says, was " complicated but not really obscure, subtle but not disloyal." [2] We have given the reader the main facts ; he will judge for himself.

It should be added that if Italy, while bound by treaty to France, was making arrangements with the Central Powers for a naval war against her, it is also true that France, while bound by treaty to Italy, was determined to maintain her naval predominance in the Mediterranean. For in June 1912 Isvolski reports the following views of M. Poincaré, which are worth reproducing :

" As to the question of the formal withdrawal of Italy from the Triple Alliance, Poincaré agrees with you (Sazonoff) that there is no reason to aim at such a result, since it could only produce dangerous complications. It would be best to maintain the existing situation, for Italy is a brake on the Triple Alliance. Nevertheless, France must not forget that Italy belongs to the political group of her adversaries. That is why the French Government must see that Italy does not secure predominance in the Mediterranean. In the actual condition of naval armaments a simple mobilisation of the French fleet would be sufficient to make impossible any hostile enterprise on the part of Italy. ' You may be certain,' he said, laying special stress on these words, ' that France is firmly decided to maintain in the future, as now, the preponderance over Italy in the Mediterranean.' " [3]

Under the circumstances, it was natural that the renewal of the Triple Alliance did not imply any renewal of confidence between the signatories. Italy was alarmed at an apparent rapprochement of Russia and Austria. The King endeavoured to negotiate with the Tsar an equal part with those two

---

[1] Tittoni, *Italy's Foreign and Colonial Policy*, p. 63.
[2] See article in *Il Lavoro*, November 22nd, 1923.
[3] *Livre Noir*, i. p. 266.

Powers in the determination of Balkan issues, but received only polite assurances that Italy should know what had been concluded after the event.   Austria was even more intransigeant.   Thereupon the Italian Government deliberately unloosed the Irredentist propaganda which, for some time past, had been slumbering.   In 1903–4 war between the two States seemed to hang in the balance.   But neither, at that time, dared to take the risk, because the attitude of the other Powers was doubtful.[1]

The Germans also showed their usual mistrust of their ally.   If the war with France should come, said Kiderlen-Waechter, Italy would wait to see how the first battles went before coming to her decision.[2]   The French took precisely the same view of their new friend.   " In a general way," Isvolski wrote from Paris, " they think here that neither the Triple Entente nor the Triple Alliance can count on the loyalty of Italy ; that the Italian Government will employ all its efforts to keep the peace ; and that in case of a war it will begin by adopting a waiting attitude, and then join on the side towards which victory is inclining." [3]   Let the reader compare with this forecast the actual course of Italian policy in 1914–15.

Under these circumstances there was the usual hesitation about renewing the Triple Alliance.   What brought the matter to a head was the Italian war on Tripoli, which, after its long incubation in the womb of diplomacy, was finally delivered in 1911.   The result was a change in the " balance of power " in the Mediterranean, together with an increase in Italian self-confidence ; and the Germans were afraid that, unless Italy were held to the Alliance, she might proceed to war with Austria.   Italy, too, being alienated from France by the Tripolitan war (in spite of the fact that France had given her a free hand there), and being afraid of Slav aggression in the Balkans, was herself inclined to a renewal ; and this was agreed to by the parties in December 1912.   The text was not changed, so that Article 9 still read that Germany and Italy " engage to exert themselves " for the " maintenance of the territorial status quo " in Cyrenaica, Tripolitania and, Tunisia.   But since, as a matter of fact, that status had

---

[1] Salvemini, *Cronaca di Genova*, November 27th, 1923.
[2] Pribram, ii. pp. 165–6.   [3] *Livre Noir*, i. p. 365.

been changed by the Italian annexation of Tripoli, a new protocol was introduced stating that the territorial status quo in those regions " implies the sovereignty of Italy over Tripolitania and Cyrenaica." This is a good example of what States really mean when they guarantee a status quo. This little act of robbery Italy had managed to achieve with the consent of all the Great Powers ; and still, as before, by virtue of her treaty, on the one hand with Austria and Germany, on the other with France, it was open to her, when the Great War should come, to take sides according as her interests might seem to dictate.

V. The Mediterranean Agreements

Such then, in brief, is the history of the Triple Alliance. There is, however, one point of special interest to Englishmen on which it will be as well to say a few words. Up to the year 1900, or thereabout, British influence was thrown, on the whole, upon the side of the Central Powers and against France and Russia. What our Government then feared was French preponderance in the Mediterranean and the opening of the Straits to Russia. With a view to preventing these possibilities, and to consolidating their position in Egypt, the British Government entered, in 1887, into two agreements with Austria and Italy. These were known to and furthered by Bismarck, and may be taken as part of the system of the Triple Alliance.[1] The first agreement is dated February 12th, 1887. It provides for the status quo in the Mediterranean, the Adriatic, the Ægean and the Black Sea, with the usual addition that if the maintenance of the status quo becomes impossible, no modification shall occur except after a previous agreement between the parties. The third article runs : " Italy is entirely ready to support the work of Great Britain in Egypt. Great Britain, in her turn, is disposed, in case of encroachments on the part of a third Power, to support the action of Italy at every other point whatsoever of the North African coast district, and especially in Tripolitania and Cyrenaica." Put into plain language, this seems to mean that England gives Italy full leave to annex Tripoli when she likes in return for Italian support of the

[1] See Pribram for the texts, and also the German Documents, vol. iv.

seizure by England of Egypt. Whether the treaty implies armed support by Great Britain is left rather vague. The character of the co-operation, the British Government says, must be decided by them " when the occasion for it arises, according to the circumstances of the case."

The agreement of February was supplemented by another, in December of the same year. This starts in the usual way by stating that the object of the Powers is " the maintenance of peace to the exclusion of all policy of aggression." Its main object is the independence of Turkey, with special reference to the Straits. The Power that threatened that independence was, of course, Russia, though Russia is not mentioned. The agreement proceeds to affirm the independence of Bulgaria, except for the suzerain rights of Turkey, and " the desire of the three Powers to be associated with Turkey in the common defence of these principles." If Turkey should resist " illegal enterprises " in contravention of these principles, the three Powers will immediately come to an agreement as to " the measures to be taken for causing to be respected the independence of the Ottoman Empire and the integrity of its territory as secured by previous treaties." If, however, the Porte should " assume the character of complicity with or connivance at any such illegal enterprise," then the Powers will proceed to the " provisional occupation " of " such points of Ottoman territory as they may agree to consider it necessary to occupy in order to secure the objects determined by previous treaties." [1]

By these two agreements England had endeavoured to secure both her own position in Egypt and the status quo in the Mediterranean and the Balkans. She was not, in so many words, committed to war for these objects, but under certain circumstances, such as a Russian aggression on the Straits or on Bulgaria, or a French aggression on Morocco, she would, it seems, be morally bound to go to war. The treaties were secret, which meant, in this case, that though known to and favoured by Germany, they were not to be known either to Russia or to France, or to the Parliament or people of England. In this latter connexion attention must be drawn to the form

---

[1] Hoyos says that " the military arrangements between Rome and London were so far advanced that part of the Italian fleet, namely, the ships of the better class, were manned by English sailors, because it was thought that in that way they could be better employed " (p. 53).

of the agreement. This is peculiar, consisting of separate notes by the several parties, instead of the usual single document signed by all. The reason for this is given in a dispatch by the German Ambassador in London.[1] In Lord Salisbury's view, he writes, it was necessary to clothe the agreement in such a form as would allow the Government, in case of a question in the House, to deny the existence of an " alliance." Such denial was, in fact, more than once made in Parliament. Thus, when Sir Charles Dilke, in 1902, referred to the arrangement as a " virtual alliance," he was corrected by Lord Cranbourne, who even went so far as to say that " there was never a treaty or agreement with Italy." [2] Lord Lansdowne, a few days later, referred to it as an " exchange of views." [3] More important, however, than the name of the thing were its actual commitments. In 1888 Sir John Ferguson said, in answer to a question, that England " was not under any obligation to use military or naval action." [4] As England was bound, in certain contingencies, to proceed to the " provisional occupation " of points in Ottoman territory, this seems to be rather a questionable statement. Perhaps one may fairly assume that the British Government felt obliged to give some satisfaction to Italy, while at the same time they were unwilling to admit to the House of Commons that they were bound, in certain contingencies, to go to war. Probably they reckoned that, in the then position of the European constellation, the country would support war against France in the interest of Italy, should the occasion or the necessity arise. Moreover, pressure was put upon them by Germany; for Bismarck made it clear that, if England were determined to maintain her isolation from European entanglements, Germany might be compelled to take a different line in regard to French and Russian ambitions in the Mediterranean and the Straits. As he said, Germany herself has no interest in thwarting either; and he was only prepared to do so if England, on her part, were willing to contribute to his system of alliances for preserving the peace of the world.[5]

One other point may be noticed in this connexion. The

---

[1] Ger. Docs., iv. p. 304.   [2] Hansard, July 3rd, 1902, cx. p. 733.
[3] Ib., cxi. p. 660.   [4] Ib., February 22nd, 1888, cccxxii. p. 1184.
[5] Ger. Docs., iv. p. 300.

second article of the treaty of December 1887 refers to " the maintenance of the status quo in the Orient based on the treaties, to the exclusion of all policy of compensation." On the other hand, Article 1 of that treaty of 1887 between Austria and Italy which formed part of the Triple Alliance, said that, if those two Powers should find it necessary to modify the status quo " in the regions of the Balkans or of the Ottoman coasts and islands in the Adriatic and in the Ægean Sea by a temporary or permanent occupation on their part, this occupation shall take place only after a previous agreement between the two Powers aforesaid based on the principle of compensation." How this clause is reconcilable with the clause cited above from the agreement of the three Powers in December of the same year I must leave to those who are more skilled in the ways of diplomacy than I can pretend to be.

The agreement of 1887 has no period set to it, but it seems to have lapsed by 1894. It appears, however, that there was a new treaty entered into in that year, of which the text has not yet been published, but by which the British acquiescence in the Italian seizure of Tripoli was made even more definite than in 1887. " Thus supported," adds Signor Salvemini, " by friendship with France and England, Prinetti could proceed with complete security towards the renewal of the Triple Alliance;"[1] which Alliance, as we have seen, contemplated war against France.

To complete this part of our history we will refer to the Mediterranean agreement of May 1887 between Italy and Spain. In this Spain agrees " not to lend herself as regards France, in so far as the North African territories among others are concerned, to any treaty or political arrangement whatsoever which would be aimed directly or indirectly against Italy, Germany, and Austria, or against any one of these Powers." The second article repudiates " unprovoked attack " and also " provocation." The distinction is interesting, and marks perhaps some new shade of finesse in the minds of the diplomats ; but it does not appear what that shade may be. The agreement is in the form of two separate notes by the two Governments immediately concerned, and another by Austria-Hungary acceding to it. It was prolonged in

[1] *Il Lavoro*, November 5th, 1923.

1891, the year in which the first agreements of the Franco-Russian alliance were signed, and there is a new note on the part of Spain safeguarding the frontier line of the Spanish possessions in Morocco. The prolongation was for four years, and after that the treaty seems to have lapsed. At any rate, no further renewal appears in the texts that have been published. This treaty, it will be observed, completed the guarantee of the status quo in the Mediterranean, that guarantee, however, being well understood to be valid only until it should become desirable to alter it.

The Anglo-Italian treaty was directed, in veiled language but none the less clearly, against a possible French aggression in Morocco, and contemplated in such a " calamitous event " the appropriation of Tripoli by Italy.[1] But the Franco-Italian treaty of 1902 altered the whole situation. The French consented to trade Tripoli against Morocco, and perhaps an Anglo-Italian treaty of the same year endorsed that arrangement. The stage was thus set for great events. At the cost of two crises which shook all Europe the French secured Morocco ; at the cost of a first-class war the Italians took Tripoli ; that war unchained the Balkan wars ; and these in turn led to the Great War of 1914. Such were the actual results of this series of agreements to keep the peace. We will now turn to examine the other set of treaties constituting the Triple Entente.

[1] Pribram, i. p. 97.

CHAPTER IV

THE TRIPLE ENTENTE [1]

I. The Franco-Russian Treaty

THE Triple Entente was based upon three separate treaties : one between France and Russia, one between France and England, and one between England and Russia.

Of these the first only was an " alliance " proper, if by alliance be meant an engagement under stated conditions to go to war. This treaty dates from 1891 to 1893. It coincided, as we have seen, with Bismarck's dismissal from office and the lapse of the Reinsurance Treaty ; and it realised that union of the two Powers which had so often seemed to be imminent, and which it had been the main object of his policy to prevent. England, however, for another ten years remained attached, by sympathy or policy, to the Central Powers, and, in fact, it was fear of her adherence to the purposes of the Triple Alliance that helped to bring about the agreement between Russia and France.[2]

The ostensible object of the alliance was, as it always is, the preservation of peace. The mere news of the understanding between France and Russia, we are informed, had produced in Europe a " sense of security," of " pacification," to which she had long been a stranger.[3] Even the Germans, we are told, recognised the fact. " Germany knows well that she will not be able to separate us. She is but the more

[1] The history of the Triple Alliance is much better known to us than that of the Triple Entente ; for there, besides the texts of the treaties, we have also an historical account by Professor Pribram based on the Austrian archives, and a complete set of the German dispatches. But the States of the Triple Entente have not published their documents, so that we have only the texts and such subsidiary matter as can be gathered from Russian publications. For the text of the Franco-Russian Treaty, see the French Yellow Book, L'Alliance Franco-Russe, and Pribram, ii. App. B ; for the Anglo-French Treaty, de Martens, *Nouveau Recueil*, 2ᵉ Série, t. 32, and Morel, *Morocco and Diplomacy* ; for the Anglo-Russian Treaty, the *Nouveau Recueil*, 3ᵐᵉ Série, t. 1.

[2] See Yellow Book, No. 5, annex to No. 17 and note.

[3] Yellow Book, No. 24.

pacific for that. We also desire peace." [1] So the French Minister, and so also the Russian. He " does not believe that the Triple Alliance wants to risk war. The Emperor of Germany, the Emperor of Austria, and the King of Italy repudiate the idea, and they are sincere." [2] Why, then, one is inclined to wonder, since everybody wants peace, does not everybody disarm ? An answer to this question is given by the Russian Minister : " Although the Triple Alliance appears to be defensive, M. de Giers is convinced that war might break out by surprise, and it would never do to allow ourselves to be taken unprepared." [3] No better illustration could be given of the general truth that the existence of armaments is enough to provoke war. But there is another point. The French, as we have seen, [4] had never reconciled themselves to the loss of Alsace-Lorraine. As recently as 1887 there had seemed to be danger of war between her and Germany. The Tsar, therefore, is anxious that " Germany shall not be able to think herself directly menaced," and that " the party of immediate revanche shall not be in a position to drag us into an adventure." [5] Rather more bluntly the Russian General who is drafting the military convention says to his French colleague : " There is one thing which disturbs me : directly you have got the convention signed, will you not want to precipitate events and make war ? " [6] This is a little crude. The Tsar seems to frame the situation more exactly when he says : " You would not be good patriots, you would not be Frenchmen, if you did not cling to the thought that the day will come when you will be able to enter into possession of your lost provinces ; but between this very natural sentiment and the idea of a provocation to realize it—in a word, of revanche—there is a long step ; and you have proved many times—you have just proved it again— that you desire peace before everything, and that you will know how to wait with dignity." [7] There could hardly be a clearer indication of the state of mind of France. " We will never forget ; we will never resign ourselves ; only—it shall not be we who provoke the war ! "

But if Russia was anxious that war should not be pre-

---

[1] Yellow Book, No. 79.   [2] Ib., No. 21.   [3] Ib., No. 21.
[4] See above, pp. 48 seq.   [5] Yellow Book, No. 16.
[6] Ib., No. 53 note   [7] Ib., No. 90.

cipitated over Alsace-Lorraine, that is only because her interest did not lie there. It lay in Constantinople and the Balkans, and her natural enemy there was Austria. This is illustrated rather neatly by a little controversy that took place in the course of the negotiations. The French desired that the casus fœderis should arise whenever Germany were involved, even though it were Germany alone. The Russians, on the contrary, desired that it should arise only if Germany were supported by Austria or vice versa.[1] On this point the French view in the end prevailed. The reason why Russia was so much interested in the possibility of war with Austria was her ambition with regard to the Straits and Constantinople. It must be noted, however, that at this time she professed, on these points, a conservative attitude. " People suppose," said the Russian Minister, " that we covet Constantinople. We think, on the contrary, that nothing would be more unfortunate for Russia than to displace her centre of gravity. What would happen to our northern provinces and to St. Petersburg ? We desire that the Turks should remain guardians of the Straits."[2] Insinuations made to the Sultan about Russian aggression were " perfidious," for, in fact, the one object of Russia was to guarantee the status quo against the machinations of another Power.[3]

That other Power was England, who, after Germany and Austria, was the one at this time most suspected by her two traditional enemies. The grievance of France was Egypt, which we had occupied in 1882. The grievance of Russia was Constantinople, which we seemed always to be threatening to occupy. This joint mistrust of England is clearly expressed in the following dispatch of the Russian Minister : " The presence of British troops in the valley of the Nile is evidently an abnormal fact which disturbs the balance of power in the Mediterranean, creating, to the profit of England, a preponderance by which her friends and protégés, especially Italy, endeavour to profit. France has a great interest in bringing about the end of this occupation, and we have the same interest in seeing the Sultan enter once more into possession of one of the most important dependencies of his Empire."[4]

But the interest of Russia in Egypt was not so great as her interest in Constantinople and the Straits. In 1885,

[1] Yellow Book, No. 56.   [2] Ib., No. 21.   [3] Ib., No. 24.   [4] Ib.

as we have seen,[1] war had almost arisen on this question
between England and Russia, and both States posed as
champions of the independence of the unfortunate Porte,
while regarding the other as the disturber of the peace.
" You have yourself," the Russian Minister wrote to his
Ambassador at Constantinople, " signalised again and again
the attempts made by certain Powers of the Triple Alliance,
supported by England, to intimidate the sovereign of Turkey,
and, profiting by the accesses of fear and feebleness to which
he is unfortunately subject, to lead him to acts of a kind
which would cause Turkey to depart from the path of strict ·
neutrality." [2]   Thus, if there was to be war between England
and Russia, it would be about Constantinople and the Straits,
while, if there was to be war between England and France, it
would be about Egypt ; and neither Russia nor France were
prepared to support one another in arms on these issues.
About Egypt, indeed, even the French Minister enjoined
caution : " Finally, in the question of Egypt, you will not fail to
take account of the state of mind of the Russian Government,
to measure the action we can take without engaging ourselves
beyond what is prudent and necessary : not to discourage
the Sultan ; on the contrary, to support him in the idea that
he must not omit any occasion to affirm his suzerainty and to
recall England to her engagements, to make him understand
that, in this affair, as in all others, he has only France and
Russia to rely upon, to inspire him with confidence, and to
oblige him to give proof of a little more courage ; but not to
permit us to uncover ourselves too much nor to be brought
into a situation which would compel us to an effort in which
we should perhaps be isolated." [3]

On the basis of the considerations thus elaborated, a text
of the treaty was arrived at in two articles.   The first ran
as follows :

" In order to define and consecrate the cordial understanding
which unites them, and desirous of contributing, in common
agreement, to the maintenance of the peace which forms the
object of their dearest aspirations, the two Governments
declare that they will take counsel together upon every
question of a nature to jeopardise the general peace." [4]

[1] See above, p. 27.   [2] Yellow Book, No. 24.
[3] Ib., No. 22.   [4] Ib., No. 17 annex.

The Tsar seems to have been peculiarly anxious about the peaceable character of the arrangement. Indeed, at one point in the negotiations, he desired the insertion of a special article saying that if the French provoked war the treaty should be null and void. He was met, however, by the reply that only a " defensive " war was contemplated, and he renounced his idea.[1]

In this clause, it will be noticed, only the " preservation of peace " is referred to, not the " balance of power." But that was corrected a few years later. M. Delcassé was pre-occupied by the thought of what might happen if Austria-Hungary should break up, say at the death of the old Emperor. Some people—" on "—he thought, " perhaps wish this, some perhaps might favour it, or in any case might profit by it." Who is intended by " on " ? Presumably Germany. It would be a great mistake, Delcassé thought, if the effective alliance were to cease just at that crucial moment. But, in fact, the military convention which accompanied and defined the treaty would cease then, for its time limit was the duration of the Triple Alliance, and that must end automatically when Austria-Hungary ended. To meet this difficulty Delcassé visited Petersburg in 1899, and secured an addition to the objects of the treaty. It was now to envisage not only the " preser-vation of peace," but the " maintenance of the equilibrium between the forces of Europe." Since the " maintenance of equilibrium " (our old friend the " balance of power ") requires to be mentioned specially, it must be presumed not to be included in the maintenance of peace. It might even be incompatible with that. And in fact M. Delcassé remarked with some satisfaction that by the new clause " the scope (portée) of the alliance is singularly extended." At the same time, as logic required, the time of the military convention was prolonged. It was now to last as long as the treaty itself.[2]

The second article of the treaty runs as follows :

" In case peace should be actually in danger, and especially if one of the two Parties should be threatened with an aggres-sion, the two Parties undertake to reach an understanding on the measures whose immediate and simultaneous adoption would be imposed upon the two Governments by the realisation

----

[1] Yellow Book, No. 71.   [2] Ib., No. 95.

of this eventuality." [1] The only comment necessary here is the one we have so often had to make as to the absence of definition for the word " aggression." From 1899 onwards it would appear to include anything which might affect the " balance of power."

It will be observed that the provisions cited above are very vague in their phraseology. The reason is that the more definite agreement was to be embodied in the military convention. This was drawn up in 1892, and accepted in January 1894.[2] Its first article reads :

" If France is attacked by Germany, or by Italy supported by Germany, Russia shall employ all her available forces to attack (attaquer) Germany. If Russia is attacked by Germany, or by Austria supported by Germany, France shall employ all her available forces to fight (combattre) Germany." Whether any subtle distinction is intended between " attack " and " fight " I dare not pronounce. Perhaps the French held that the word " attack " could never apply to themselves.

If this article be compared with Article 2 of the Triple Alliance, it will be perceived, first, that, according to the treaties (supposing them to be observed), on the one hand, if France " attacks " either Italy or Germany the other Power will come in to fight her ; on the other hand, if Germany " attacks " either France or Russia the other Power will come in to fight her. At this date (1892) the " attack " would certainly have been held, by either side, to proceed from the other. The treaties thus between them secured that a war between France and Germany would immediately involve both Russia and Italy. Further, by the Austro-German alliance, " attack " on Germany by Russia would bring in Austria. England was still uncommitted ; and Italy was not yet engaged in that agreement with France which, as we have seen, gave her the excuse to fail her ally when the long-anticipated war at length occurred.

The military convention, being drawn up by soldiers, shows no illusions as to the " maintenance of peace." Thus the French General writes : " The General Staff of the French Army is penetrated by the principle that in such a struggle as this the essential thing is to pursue the

[1] Yellow Book, No. 17 annex.　　　[2] Ib.; No. 71.

destruction of the principal enemy. The ruin of the others would follow inevitably. In a word, Germany once con-quered, the Franco-Russian armies will impose their wills on Austria and on Italy. In this order of ideas France has sacrificed everything to the struggle against Germany." With this preface he proceeds to develop the military arrangements.[1] These are devised in view of the German plan, which has become known to the French.[2] It is calcu-lated that the Triple Alliance (including Roumania) will put 2,450,000 troops into the field against the 3,150,000 of the Franco-Russian combination.[3] This predominance in numbers seems to have been maintained by the latter down to the outbreak of the war.[4] But of course there was a continual attempt, on each side, to distance the other. Already indeed, as early as the August of this year (1893), we find the French arranging to meet a German increase : "France, in prevision of the new German law, has considerably reinforced her 'cadres.' Every effort will be made by the Government of this country to reinforce her peace-time effectives. Russia, on her side, we are sure, will take the measures that her loyalty and her accustomed penetration will dictate to her, whether to increase her forces or to improve their method of action." [5]

Hardly less important than the number of troops was the question of their mobilisation. Article 2 of the military convention runs as follows : [6]

"In case the forces of the Triple Alliance, or of one of the Powers composing it, should mobilise, France and Russia, at the first news of the event, and without the necessity of any previous concert, shall mobilise immediately and simul-taneously the whole of their forces, and shall move them as close as possible to their frontiers."

According to this clause, both Russia and France were bound to mobilise as soon as Austria should do so, although the treaty did not bind France to go to war if Austria alone should attack Russia. There had been a long dispute over this point. The French desired not to be under obligation to mobilise unless Germany did so ; for, if she did, " Germany would not hesitate to represent her action to the other Powers

[1] Yellow Book, No. 28.　　　　　[2] Ib., No. 54.
[3] Ib., No. 29 annex iii.　　　　[4] See below, pp. 368 seq.
[5] Yellow Book, No. 87 note.　　[6] Ib., No. 71.

as an aggression." [1] But the Russians, who expected the
war to break out (as it did) in connexion with Austria, were
determined that in that case, too, both parties should mobilise.
"There is no Germany," said the Russian General, "and no
'principal enemy.' There are the forces of the Triple Alliance.
If the bulk of the forces which threaten us is Austrian, we
must march against them and fight. Austria for us is the
principal enemy." "Quite wrong," the Frenchman replied,
"the principal enemy is ipso facto Germany." The reader
will observe how clearly the principle of the "preservation of
peace" was kept in view by these soldiers. But the French
fought in vain. On this point they had to give way, and the
clause was drafted in the manner cited above.[2] But from
this there resulted a curious situation. For the Generals
were agreed that mobilisation meant war. Mobilisation, said
General Boisdeffre, who was negotiating the convention, "is
the declaration of war; mobilisation compels one's neighbour
to do the same; mobilisation involves the execution of
strategic transport and of concentration." Whereto the
Tsar replied, "It is thus that I understand it." [3] This conversation has become famous, owing to the importance of the
question of mobilisation in 1914; but that discussion may
be reserved to a later place.

These then were the principal provisions of the Franco-
Russian alliance. In conclusion, a few words may be said
on the question of secrecy. On this the Tsar was insistent,
probably because he was anxious not to provoke Germany.
"What he would like would be to find a man with whom he
could treat 'seul a seul' without anyone knowing it." [4] This
would be possible in Russia. But the French were embarrassed by their Constitution and their public opinion. True,
the Constitution said that the President "negotiates and
ratifies treaties"; but also, he "informs the Chambers as
soon as the interest and security of the State permits." [5]
That, it is true, might be never; but Ministers, in any case,
must know about the treaty. On the other hand, it was recognised that the military convention should be kept secret;
and after all, it was the military convention in which the

---

[1] Yellow Book, No. 47.   [2] Ib., No. 53.
[3] Ib., No. 71.   [4] Ib., No. 76 annex.
[5] Loi sur les rapports des pouvoirs publics clause 7.

principal political clause was being embedded. This consideration perhaps decided the matter. At any rate, in the final text we read : " All the clauses enumerated above shall be kept rigorously secret." [1] In fact, the convention was not published until after the war.

II. The Anglo-French Treaties

We pass on to the Anglo-French and Anglo-Russian treaties. These are, formally, of a different kind to the one we have just been examining. They deal with particular causes of dispute between the States concerned, and they contain no provision about making war. It is for this reason, presumably, that the triple arrangement which resulted, between England, France, and Russia, was called an " entente," not an " alliance," and that, during the last days before the Great War, it was still uncertain whether or no England would come in. These treaties are also distinguished by the fact that they were published at the time when they were entered upon.[2]

Since they are concerned with lengthy and complicated solutions of a number of different issues, we need not, for our purpose, deal with them at length ; but certain general observations must be made. The first, and perhaps the most important, is this. The friction between Great Britain and Russia or France had several times, in the course of the last thirty years, brought us to the verge of war. Now it suddenly appeared that all these differences could be peaceably adjusted. Why now, and why not before ? Only one answer is possible. They were adjusted now because the parties wished to secure themselves against a fourth Power. This is only one illustration, but a powerful and convincing one, of the general fact that, in the international anarchy, no friendship can be formed or maintained unless it be countered by an enmity. Quarrels issuing in war are the permanent assumption of the situation ; and never, in the whole course of history, so far as we know

---

[1] Article 7 in Yellow Book, No. 57. The inclusion of political clauses in a military convention, and the claim that the latter may be kept secret, even when " treaties " must be published, is playing, we may be sure, a considerable part in present-day arrangements, and may easily defeat the purpose of the Covenant that all treaties shall be registered and published.

[2] There was, however, also a secret treaty with France, not published till later. See below, p. 113.

it, has there been a genuine arrangement on the part of all States to maintain the peace, as the first and most necessary of all policies. The League of Nations is the first serious attempt in that direction.

We must not, however, travesty the intentions of the Powers of the Entente. Lord Oxford and Asquith asserts that, since our hands were free, there was nothing provocative in our attitude to the Triple Alliance ; [1] and Sir Edward Grey plainly intended and desired to keep the peace. But in the European anarchy pious intentions, even when genuine, count for very little ; and the fact remains that, from the date of the formation of the Entente, crisis after crisis supervened, that Europe was again and again on the verge of war, that armaments increased and military and naval conventions multiplied, until at last it is hardly paradoxical to say that the European War came of itself, although nobody at that moment wanted it. The proof of this statement will be found in the following chapters. But in England there was, from the beginning, one observer at least who saw whither we were drifting. " This agreement," Mr. Churchill writes, " was acclaimed by the Conservative forces in England, among whom the idea of the German menace had already taken root. It was also hailed, somewhat short-sightedly, by Liberal statesmen as a step to secure general peace by clearing away misunderstandings and differences with our traditional enemy.[2] It was, therefore, almost universally welcomed. Only one profound observer raised his voice against it. " My mournful and supreme conviction," said Lord Rosebery, " is that this agreement is much more likely to lead to complications than to peace." [3]

We will now proceed to speak briefly of the contents of the treaties, beginning with those made with France. These adjusted a number of old disputes in various parts of the world. But for our present purpose those only are important which dealt with Egypt and Morocco. They were two, one public and one secret. The public treaty contained a recognition by France of the position of England in Egypt. This closed a long and acrimonious controversy, and established

---

[1] *Genesis of the War*, p. 64.
[2] France, of course, not Germany. Younger readers may require to adjust their ideas.
[3] Churchill, *World Crisis*, i. p. 22.

in permanence that British occupation which had been undertaken as a temporary measure, and which we had again and
again promised to abandon.[1]   What was the quid pro quo for
France ?   It concerned Morocco, and the method of granting
it is characteristic.   Article II of the treaty begins : " The
Government of the French Republic declare that they have
no intention of altering the political status of Morocco."
Those acquainted with the methods of States in picking up
territory must have suspected, on reading this, that it meant
the opposite of what it said.   And, in fact, the second clause
of the article proceeds to state that it " appertains to France "
to " preserve order in that country and to provide assistance
for the purpose of all administrative, financial, and military
reforms which it may require."   The further intentions of
the Governments were consigned to the secret treaty, first
published by a French newspaper in November 1911.   Even
this is evasively framed.   Article I begins :   " In the event
of either Government finding itself constrained by the force
of circumstances to modify its policy in respect to Egypt or
Morocco."   The meaning of this is further but discreetly
explained in Article III, which lays down that the part of
Morocco which faces Gibraltar should fall to Spain " whenever the Sultan ceases to exercise authority over it."   The
full intention is, however, only explained in the treaty of
France with Spain, signed in the same year, 1904.   Here, too,
there is first a public declaration, stating that the two
countries " remain firmly attached to the integrity of the
Moorish Empire under the sovereignty of the Sultan " ; then a
secret treaty, providing for the partition of that empire
between France and Spain " in case the continuance of the
political status of Morocco and of the Shereefian Government
should become impossible, or if, owing to the weakness of
that Government and to its continued inability to uphold
law and order, or to any other cause, the existence of which
is acknowledged by both parties, the status quo can be no
longer maintained."

What really happened then, in these treaties, was that the
world was publicly assured that the independence of Morocco
under the Sultan was to be maintained, while privately the

---

[1] According to an article in *Foreign Affairs*, May 1924, we had given
sixty-six pledges in this sense !   I have not verified this arithmetic.

parties agreed that the country should be occupied and partitioned. That was the price the British paid for the recognition of their position in Egypt and for the consolidation of that new understanding with France which was to issue in the war against Germany.

III. The Anglo-Russian Treaty and the Treaty of Björkoe

The Anglo-Russian treaty was similar to the Anglo-French; that is, it settled a number of questions which had previously been irritating and even dangerous. These concerned Tibet, Afghanistan, and Persia. It is the latter country which interests us, since it became, at a later date, one of the principal fields of the friction between England, Russia, and Germany. To this we shall recur in another chapter. But before concluding this one, we will refer to a treaty made by Germany in 1904 and 1905 with Russia, which, if it had become operative, would have forestalled the entente of that country with England. In 1904 the Russo-Japanese War broke out. Germany was favourable to the Russians and England to the Japanese, with whom she had formed an alliance in 1901. There followed the usual recriminations about unneutral acts. Finally the Kaiser, who was corresponding with the Tsar in a very intimate way, proposed, towards the end of 1904, a Russo-German treaty, to which, after its signature, French assent was to be secured. As proposed at first, it would seem that the treaty was intended to " localise " the Russo-Japanese War : that is, to prevent England from coming in by the threat that, in that case, Germany would come in on the other side. But later the reference to the immediate war was dropped, and the treaty was to become operative only at the conclusion of the peace.[1]

The first article runs : " In case one of the two Empires should be attacked by a European Power, its ally will aid it in Europe with all its forces by land and sea." From the German point of view, this can only have referred either to England or to France. In fact, at this time, the Kaiser was

---

[1] See the text in Ger. Docs., v. xix. p. 457, and Isvolski, *Memoirs*, p. 58, The date is July 1905.

feeling hostile to England, and we find him writing to the Tsar in the November of 1904 : " An excellent expedient to cool British insolence and overbearing would be to make some military demonstration on the Persio-Afghan frontier, where the British think you powerless to appear during this war." [1]

So far then as Germany was concerned the matter was simple enough. But the position of Russia was more complicated. Was she to be involved in war against her own ally France ? Or against the Power with which that ally had just made an entente ? The Kaiser's view was that, since the treaty was defensive, it could never come into operation against France unless France made an " aggressive " war. And if she did that, the Franco-Russian treaty, being also one of defence, could not come into operation either. Since there is no test of aggression, this contention was not very convincing. But, further, it was the idea of the treaty that France should herself become a party to it ; and the fourth article ran : " His Majesty the Emperor of all the Russias, after the entry into force of this treaty, will take all the measures necessary to initiate France into the agreement and to engage her to associate herself with it as an ally." The Kaiser's view was that France would feel compelled to join, once the treaty was in operation, and would then " press upon England to remain quiet and keep the peace, for fear of France's position being jeopardised." [2] It was important, however, that France should not know about the treaty until it had been signed, because she might inform England, and England might then join Japan and attack Germany, which would destroy the " balance of power."

The German Chancellor was from the beginning a party to the Kaiser's action. So also, apparently, were Count Lamsdorff and Count Witte. But here there is some confusion and probably some duplicity ; for it appears also that both these statesmen worked to defeat the treaty.[3] It was indeed obviously incompatible with Russian obligations to France, and against these it finally came to grief. For when Nelidoff, the Russian Minister at Paris, was consulted, he

---

[1] *Kaiser to Tsar*, November 17th, 1904.   [2] Isvolski, p. 53.
[3] An interesting correspondence between Lamsdorff, the Tsar, Nelidoff, and others, on the treaty, will be found in *Die Kriegsschuldfrage*, November 1924.

replied, without even referring the question to the French Government, that the French would never enter into such a treaty. No doubt that was the case, for, as we have seen, even before the Entente with England, they had always refused any reconciliation with Germany which would involve the abandonment of Alsace-Lorraine. The following little piece of correspondence is illuminating in this connexion. Witte said to one of the French Ministers in 1905, first " that the Emperor William has nothing but friendly feelings for France, and that his most cherished desire is to form with her relations not merely amicable but intimate "; secondly, " that far from desiring to destroy the Franco-Russian Alliance, he attaches the greatest importance to it, and that he would draw it together with his own hands, if there were need and if he had the power." Whereupon the French Minister ironically replied : " Would not the love of the Kaiser for the Franco-Russian Alliance go so far that he would be willing to join it ? " [1]

The final result was a declaration by the Russian Government that, since there was no prospect of the French adhering to the alliance, it must be understood that the first article of the treaty could not apply to a war between Germany and France, and that the bonds uniting Russia to France must be maintained as they were " until the establishment of a triple agreement." [2] This reserve on the part of Russia in effect cancelled the treaty, though the Kaiser held it to be valid as late as 1907.[3]

For the moment we may arrest our story here. We have traced in sufficient detail the series of treaties which laid the basis for the Great War. They were all made, ostensibly, for the sake of preserving peace; and some, or even all, statesmen may have desired that the peace should be kept. But among armed Powers, pursuing objects that can only be gained by war and united in treaties directed against one another, there can be no peace. The history of Europe during the years we are considering is one long demonstration of this general truth. We shall now proceed to examine more in detail the series of crises which arose from the situation described and preluded the final catastrophe.

---

[1] Bourgeois et Pagès, p. 318.   [2] Ib., p. 319.
[3] For all this, see Ger. Docs., xix. B, chap. cxxxviii.

CHAPTER V

MOROCCO AND THE CONFERENCE OF ALGECIRAS

I. The Previous History

THE complexity of inter-State relations is very embarrassing to a historian who desires, above all things, to be clear and succinct. If he follows strictly the chronological order of events he can hardly disentangle each single thread in the mesh. If he disentangles the separate threads, he is apt to obscure their interconnexion. On the whole, however, it seems best to pursue the second plan, indicating only in passing the bearing of remoter events upon the chain of causation that is being specially attended to.

The first crisis which was to follow the new orientation of European policy was provoked by events in Morocco. This north-western corner of Africa was of interest to the Powers for various reasons of the ordinary kind. First, it lies opposite to Gibraltar and, in occupation of a strong Power, might interfere with British control of the entrance to the Mediterranean. Secondly, it has a coast-line on the Atlantic, and, under similar conditions, might become a danger to British shipping travelling to the Cape. Thirdly, it adjoins Algeria, which had been French since 1837, and where, since its conditions were " unsettled," incidents on the frontier could always happen, or be produced. Fourthly, it had natives that might be conscripted for wars to maintain Right. Fifthly, there was no knowing how valuable its trade might become, and therefore it might always be useful either to monopolise that trade for oneself or to prevent someone else from monopolising it. Last, but not least, it·had important deposits of iron, and was therefore a natural object for the cupidity of any Western State. These are all reasons why Morocco should become a storm-centre of European politics.

Previously, however, to the year 1904 the storm, though always brewing, had not in fact broken. There were the usual disputes between the natives of the country and the Europeans settled there for purposes of trade ; the usual frontier episodes ; the usual intrigues and counter-intrigues. But the Powers, for many years, were rather prowling about the prey than venturing to take their spring ; and that for the usual reason, that they were afraid of one another. Morocco, in this respect, was like the Turkish Empire.   Everybody was looking forward to its seizure or partition, but no one quite liked to bring it about.

This attitude is frankly expressed, so far as France is concerned, by a French writer : " Rather than arrive at a ' lame ' (boiteuse) solution, France prefers to temporise, so long as she can preserve the independence of Morocco and the sovereignty of the Sultan. Her diplomacy is that of a watch-dog." [1] The watch-dog, it must be added, was waiting till it could safely turn into the wolf. Bismarck, who, like most European statesmen, was fond of giving away what did not belong to him, promised, as early as 1883, to support France " morally and diplomatically " whenever she might think the moment had come for declaring a Protectorate.[2] But there were other Powers besides Germany to be reckoned with. We hear, from French sources, of British projects against Morocco as early as the nineties of the last century. Since our position was still not assured in Egypt, we might, it was thought, have to fall back on the Cape route for our connexions with India. For this purpose a port on the Moroccan coast would be very convenient in our hands and very inconvenient in those of an enemy Power. There was also talk of handing over the protectorate of Morocco to Italy, who was not yet reconciled to France by the treaty of 1902, and was still bound to England, Spain, and Austria by the Mediterranean agreements.[3] But this idea, if it were ever seriously entertained, was ruined by the Italian disaster at Adua and the fall of the pro-English, anti-French Crispi. A

---

[1] Pinon, p. 130.   [2] Eckardstein, *Isolierung Deutschlands*, p. 90.
[3] Bérard, *L'Affaire Marocaine*, p. 61. Cf. Ger. Docs., x. p. 17, where Lord Salisbury, contemplating a partition of Turkey, throws out the idea that Italy might have Morocco (August 1895).

year or two later the British, as we have seen, were angling
for a German alliance ; [1] and it is interesting to note that
they suggested a partition of Morocco between the two States.
England was to take Tangiers ; for, at that time, it was the
possible seizure of that port by France that she feared. So
much so that the Governor of Gibraltar (unless we are mis-
informed) had orders, in 1900, to seize it at any moment on
the receipt of telegraphic instructions.[2] The quid pro quo
for Germany was to be certain ports upon the Atlantic, in
particular Casablanca, Mogador, and Rabat. We miss here
a definite mention of Agadir, the inclusion of which would
have made the dramatic irony complete. These places, it was
admitted, lay outside the British " sphere of interest." They
appear to have come within it a year or so later, when we
had decided that the enemy was Germany, not France.[3]

The Anglo-German negotiations came to nothing ; partly,
it would seem, because Lord Salisbury, who, at first, was
favourable to the project, reverted to his traditional preference
for France, partly because the Germans did not care to take
the risk of trouble with France about Morocco unless the
gain to themselves should be more substantial. What they
wanted was that England should join the Triple Alliance ;
and they thought that by degrees she might be drawn in to do
so.[4] Germany, indeed, seems to have shown, at this time, considerable caution on the whole question of Morocco ; for she
was approached, we are told, not only by England but by
France. She might take, so the French Government discreetly
hinted, Tangiers and Madagascar if, in return, she would
allow France to absorb the rest of Morocco and Siam.[5] The
gestures of the Powers, in these moments of balance between
alternative policies, are more instructive perhaps than anything
else as to the nature of diplomacy.

It was not till after the turn of the century that England
definitely passed from the German to the French camp.
Previously France was the potential enemy, and of that our
occupation of Egypt was a principal cause ; for the French

---

[1] See above, p. 60.   [2] Ger. Docs., xvii. p. 325.
[3] Eckardstein, ii. p. 359. But Eckardstein must always be read with
caution. We have, at present, no British information about this episode ;
but presumably some light will be thrown upon it in the later volumes of
the *Life of Lord Salisbury.*
[4] Ger. Docs., v. xvii. chap. cxiii. Cf. ib., chap. cix. pp. 15, 41.
[5] Ib., v. xvii. p. 107. Cf. Hammann, *Vorgeschichte*, p. 119.

thought that they had a vested interest in the reversion of that country, and that it was robbery for any other Power than themselves to steal it. It may be worth while for an Englishman to have his attention called to the light in which his policy was viewed, at this time, by his future ally. The following passage is cited from M. Pinon : [1] " It was the time when England was content with her splendid isolation. She feels bad-tempered when other nations claim to share in the partition of the world. She acts often enough with unjustifiable arrogance and intolerance. She occupies Egypt, contrary to all right, and in spite of reiterated promises refuses to evacuate it. She creates everywhere obstacles to our explorers and our traders. In Uganda she provokes the massacre of the black Catholics who were under French protection. She labours to establish her Protectorate in Morocco.[2] In Touat she stirs up the Moroccans and the Touareg against Algeria. She encourages, in defiance of our rights solemnly guaranteed by her, the intrigues of the Methodist ministers in Madagascar. She has an agreement with Italy against us in the Mediterranean. She furnishes arms to all our enemies—Samory, Béhanzin, Rabah. She incites the Siamese to resistance, and the Annamites to revolt. In all the Colonial wars, in all the insurrections against France, we find the hand of England, her agents, her money. And everywhere it is she who complains of the audacities of our explorers and the usurpations of our officers." Does the reader rub his eyes ? Let him but wait patiently, and all will be well again. He has but to turn over two pages, and he will find the author, when he comes to describe the Franco-British Entente, writing in a more conciliatory strain : " There was not—properly speaking, there never has been—in France (though it has sometimes been said that there was) any anti-English opinion

[1] Pinon, p 79.

[2] A little additional information, about that in particular, is not without interest. As early as 1891 we find Lord Salisbury suggesting a joint warning to France by England, Italy, and Spain. At this date, it will be remembered, the Mediterranean agreements *re* the status quo were in force (see above, p. 99). Germany, however, though sympathetic, refused overt action, and the matter was dropped. The French, nevertheless, checked their action, and do not seem to have renewed it, in a way to alarm the other Powers, until England was involved in the South African War. They then made another advance on the Moroccan frontier, to the great alarm of Italy, and our Ambassador in Madrid is reported to have said that England would tolerate no more aggression there. The boundary must be fixed by an international commission. (Ger. Docs., xvii. chap. cxiii, especially pp. 299, 331.)

or anti-English policy." The reader has, in these short extracts, a good picture of the scientific precision, the absence of prejudice, and the clear unbiased judgments of those who instruct us in history and politics.

II. The Anglo-French Rapprochement

In the year 1898 Delcassé became Foreign Minister, and held that post for seven successive years. His first act was to prepare for the seizure of Morocco. With that in view, he turned to Spain and proposed to her a treaty of the kind usual in these cases. The two States, said the draft, had a special interest in the " maintenance of the territorial, political, economic, administrative, military, and financial independence of Morocco," and they will not enter with any other Power " into any engagement which may tend to establish in that country any foreign influence." On the other hand, if anything should occur to make the maintenance of the status quo impossible, then—why then the two States will partition Morocco ; and they proceed to do it, on paper. The Convention, they continue, is " absolutely pacific " ; but in case it should be necessary to have recourse to arms, the countries will inform one another what they propose to do. It need not be added that the agreement is to be kept secret.[1]

So far, so good. But there was a fly in that otherwise pure amber. Spain did not dare to offend England ; and M. Delcassé found that, if he wanted to do a deal about Morocco, he must do it with the first Sea-Power. The Franco-Spanish treaty thus came to nothing ; whereupon M. Pinon heaves a sigh of relief. For the proposed arrangement, being favourable to Spain, must have been, for that very reason, unfavourable to France. " It was a piece of good fortune that there should have been found in Spain a Ministry to refuse a Convention which would have been disastrous for us, and one asks oneself how any French Government could ever have accepted it."

England and France meantime, as we have seen, had made up their minds to fall into one another's arms, on the understanding that France should drop her opposition to the British theft of Egypt, while England should permit France to steal

[1] Text in Pinon, p. 313. The date is 1902.

Morocco. The decencies, of course, were to be preserved. The public treaties therefore announced the determination of the two States to preserve the independence of Morocco, while the partition was arranged for in secret documents.[1] The French got to work quickly, though not quickly enough to satisfy some of their critics. In December they sent up an agent to Fez to press upon the Sultan the necessity of reforms. Very likely these were desirable; for " in 1900 Abdul Aziz, who had succeeded his father, Muley Hassan, in 1894, at the age of thirteen, took over the reins of government; but though the young ruler was intelligent and attractive, his passions for bicycles and motor-cars, fireworks and photography, and countless other temptations of European civilisation, emptied the treasury and disgusted his conservative subjects. The uncertain Algerian frontier and the savagery of the tribes led to continual friction, and the French authorities, military and civil, uttered loud complaints." [2] The situation was typical. It was the story of Tunis, of Egypt, and, later, of Tripoli. The Great Powers proceed, in such cases, by measures that are well understood. They complain of disorder, and introduce military control; they lend money to a frivolous ruler, foreclose upon his finances, and thus assume, by steps more or less gradual, according to circumstances, the control of the Government and of the economic resources of the country. So in this case. " After receiving the blessing of Great Britain on her work in Morocco, France turned to the task of reform with new zeal." Her Minister was instructed to explain to the Sultan that she only wanted to help him—poor man !—in maintaining order. " I am certain," he said, " that you recognise the pressing necessity of reforms which will increase the authority of the Government and in which France will help you." That is stage one. It is immediately followed by stage two. " To assist these reforms France advanced in June twenty-two million francs, guaranteed on the customs, and the news was at once telegraphed to all the Powers." Next, a French mission was sent up to Fez to explain to the Sultan that " the first need was the restoration of order, and French officers would therefore aid in the training of the police.

---

[1] See above, Chap. IV, p. 112.
[2] Gooch, *History of Modern Europe*, 1878-91, p. 340.

Roads and telegraphs were also required, and a State Bank would be useful." The Sultan replied that "while most of the suggested reforms were practicable, some were very difficult to accept."[1] All seemed to be going according to programme, when suddenly there came a disconcerting intervention.

III. The German Intervention

A year had passed since the making of the Moroccan treaties. The public treaty between France and England had been duly and officially communicated to the German Government by the British. It had not been so communicated by France. Delcassé, however, had privately informed the German Ambassador of its existence, though apparently he had not communicated the text.[2] But, in any case, the text was published at once, and the German Chancellor had expressed himself as satisfied with it.[3] During the months that followed something must have happened. Possibly the Germans had heard rumours of the secret treaties, though it does not appear that they had actually seen the texts.[4] Dr. Dillon says[5] that : " A friend of mine and of his (the Kaiser's) said to him : ' There is nothing in it (the secret treaty) except what everybody knows ; and that is harmless enough.' But the Kaiser replied : ' If that be so, why was it hidden from me ? The concealment makes me suspect something that has not emerged into the light. And whether or no it is there, I am warranted in suspecting it.' " The reader has profited little by this book if he does not agree with the Kaiser. We know now what the secret treaties did

---

[1] Gooch, *History of Modern Europe*, 1878–91, p. 348.
[2] Reventlow, ed. 1916, p. 260 ; Bérard, *L'Affaire Marocaine*, p. 370.
[3] Tardieu, *La Conférence d'Algéciras*, p. 4.
[4] See Valentin, p. 54 ; Hammann, *Vorgeschichte*, •p. 130. But cf. the Kaiser's note to a dispatch of February 1905 : " And the fellows (the Spanish) won't even confess what the devil the pact is that they have entered into " (Ger. Docs., xxi. p. 191, note 14). That the additional secret treaty entered into by France and Spain in September 1905 was known to the Germans is stated by Tardieu (*Algéciras*, p. 156). Witte reports the Kaiser as saying, of the public treaty of 1904, that it had " forced us to show that no treaties in which German interests are involved can be made without her consent, let alone without her knowledge " (p. 420). But it seems more likely, from the passage quoted in the text, that the Kaiser was speaking of the secret treaty.
[5] *Eclipse of Russia*, p. 331.

contain, and the reader may judge for himself whether really their contents were "harmless enough." No doubt they seemed so to British and French statesmen.

It has been suggested, further, that the German intervention was due to the Russian defeat by the Japanese and the consequent certainty that Russia could not intervene in a European war, if one should occur. But this view seems to be excluded by the German documents recently published. The Battle of Mukden did not take place until March 1905, whereas the intervention was decided upon at the end of 1904. The German account of their delay in action is that they wanted first to settle with the English in Egypt, as they did by a treaty of June 1904 ; and also, that they wanted to see how Franco-Spanish policy would develop.[1] For the intervention itself their reasons were prestige, and the fear that the French would monopolise the trade of Morocco—a fear not removed by the formal recognition, in the public treaty, of free trade. How much they were also influenced by a desire to weaken the Entente it is not easy to decide. Hammann, of the German Foreign Office, clearly had that point in mind.[2] It was denied by Count Metternich to Lord Lansdowne,[3] and the denial was emphasised with every appearance of sincerity by the Chancellor.[4] The Kaiser has the rather ambiguous note : " That is not what we want, or, anyhow, we don't avow such a purpose. We only want to maintain our rights in Morocco." [5] In a later note he says that his instructions had always been that the " Algeciras conference is to be the stepping-stone of the agreement between France and Germany." [6] Since his idea, at this time, was first to unite Russia and Germany, and then to induce France to join them,[7] it seems fair to conclude that his policy in Morocco was to be contributory to the same end. But there is no reason to suppose that that was the exclusive motive. There were also the others, to which we have referred, and in view of the secret treaties they seem to be amply justified.

Whatever may have been the motive of the intervention, it was made with the violence and clumsiness characteristic of the Germans. On March 21st, 1905, the Kaiser landed

---

[1] Ger. Docs., xx. p. 160.   [2] Ib., p. 312.   [3] Ib., p. 633.
[4] Ib., p. 642.   [5] Ib., p. 313.
[6] Ib., xxi. p. 567 note.   [7] See Treaty of Björkoe above, p. 115.

at Tangiers and formally took the Sultan of Morocco under his protection. He insisted on the latter's independence, and expressed both his determination to do all in his power to safeguard German interests in Morocco and his hope that, under the Sultan's sovereignty, " a free Morocco will remain open to the peaceful competition of all nations, without monopoly or annexation, on a policy of absolute equality." This important demonstration was made contrary to the Kaiser's own judgment and under pressure from his Chancellor, Prince Bülow.[1] This is shown by a letter he addressed to the latter, which is worth citing. " Read my telegrams," he writes, " before the visit to Tangiers. You confessed to me yourself that you had been so anxious that, when you received the news that I had got away, you had an attack of hysteria. I landed to oblige you, because my country demanded it, mounted a strange horse, although my left arm was crippled and hindered my riding, and risked the loss of my life. I rode among the Spanish anarchists because you wanted it, and because your policy was to benefit by it ! "[2]

But if the Kaiser was opposed to that particular venture, he was none the less convinced of the necessity of intervention. Just before the landing he had applied to President Roosevelt asking him to join with him " in informing the Sultan of Morocco that he ought to reform his government, and that if he would do so we would stand behind him for the open door, and would support him in any opposition he might make to any particular nation which sought to obtain exclusive control of Morocco."[3] France and Spain, he said, were a " political unity, who wished to divide up Morocco between themselves and debar her markets to the rest of the world." He added, in words which suggest the deeper underlying motive : " Since thirty-five years Germany has been obliged to keep an armed defensive against France. As soon as France discovers that Germany meekly submits to her bullying, we feel sure that she will become more aggressive in other quarters, and we do not consider a demand for a revision of the Treaty of Frankfort to be far off."

[1] Eckardstein, *Isolierung Deutschlands,* p. 100 ; Brandenburg, p. 189; Ger. Docs., xx. p. 263 note.
[2] Ger. Docs., xix. p. 497.   [3] Roosevelt, i. p. 468.

It should be added, further, that Germany had a Colonial party which, like all such bodies, was always crying out to her to take everything before other people took it. Already, in the spring of 1904, this party was busy. They demanded, for instance, that " if the status quo should be modified in favour of France, the German Empire should receive compensations at least equal to the increase of French power, compensations corresponding both to the importance of its economic interests in the country, to the need of its fleet for naval stations, and the need of its population for expansion." One must add, then, to the grounds of the German action the fact that they objected to being ostentatiously left out while the world was being partitioned. There is a play in which one of the characters has but one remark to make. He rushes on to the stage at a critical moment, shouting, " And me ! " So, no doubt, the Germans. And to anyone who objected they were quite entitled, according to the tradition of European morals and policy, to reply : " Well, why not ? I've as good, or as bad, a right as you ! "

IV. Delcassé's Resignation

The French did object strongly, and so did their allies. Germany's intervention, they thought, was both an impertinence and a menace. Germany was not a Mediterranean Power. Why should she interfere ? But then, by what right was Britain a Mediterranean Power ? By the right of conquest. By what right was Britain or France a Far-Eastern Power ? Once more, by the right of conquest. And by what right could Powers, accepting for themselves all the consequences of that right, pretend to debar another Power from asserting similar claims ? " Germany was a parvenu. She had arrived too late on the scene. She should be contented with what the older Powers might allow her." But why ? Had England done so, since the seventeenth century ? Had France ? Had any Great Power ? While Might was the recognised and only principle of international policy, no such claim could be plausibly or reasonably advanced. Germany had the same Right as any other Power. And that Right was Might.

But, further, Germany had a juridical ground to advance.

In 1880 a public treaty, to which thirteen other States were parties, had been signed with Morocco. It dealt with a practice that had grown up whereby the European residents of foreign Powers took under their " protection " natives of the country and so exempted them from native law. The practice had led to abuses whereby criminals were enabled to evade justice ; and the treaty of 1880 limited and defined the practice in question. But its seventeenth article ran as follows : " The right of most-favoured-nation treatment is recognised by Morocco for all the Powers represented at the Conference." What did this mean ? French publicists, when the question arose in 1905, argued that the article was governed by the whole tenor of the treaty, and referred only to the particular issue of " protecting " natives. Some Germans also, it appears, took the same view.[1] The treaty, no doubt, was ambiguous, as most international treaties are, either intentionally or unintentionally, and I do not propose to argue the matter ; the less so as, in fact, the French contention was not seriously sustained, either by the French or by the other Governments. The Germans claimed that, by virtue of the treaty of 1880, the status of Morocco could not properly be altered except by the common act of all the States that had signed that treaty. They therefore demanded a conference of those States to deal with the whole question. The issue was thus propounded. What would the Powers do ?

The answer to this question depended, in the first place, upon France. Could she, under existing conditions, afford to risk war with Germany ? Delcassé, the author of the rapprochement between France, Spain, and England, said emphatically, " Yes." He went further, and declared that he had from England a promise of armed support— that she would mobilise her fleet and land one hundred thousand men in Schleswig-Holstein. That such an offer was ever made by, or on behalf of, the British Government was denied at the time by the Foreign Office, and has been denied since by Lord Oxford and Asquith.[2] But Delcassé must have had some assurances, on which he relied, from somebody. Count

---

[1] See Tardieu, pp. 39 *seq.* Lord Lansdowne also suggested this view, but does not seem to have pressed it. Ger. Docs., **xx.** p. 416.

[2] Ger. Docs., **xx.** p. 663 ; Asquith, p. 90.

Reventlow attributes them to King Edward.[1] In any case the British Government were, in fact, ready to go to war, if France did so. But M. Rouvier, the new French Minister, was too prudent for that. He knew that France was inadequately prepared, and he had always favoured reconciliation with Germany. He therefore rejected Delcassé's policy, took over himself the direction of the Foreign Office, and in June accepted the resignation of the bellicose Minister.

This was what is called a " diplomatic victory " for Germany, and probably for the moment it averted war. How it was received by the Germans may be inferred from a story told by Isvolski. He narrates that he met the Kaiser in the summer of 1905 at Copenhagen. They spoke of the Treaty of Björkoe, then just signed.[2] Isvolski said that France would never become a party to it, because of Alsace-Lorraine. The Kaiser thereupon replied : " I threw down the glove to France à propos of the Moroccan affair, and she dared not pick it up. Having then declined to fight Germany, France has lost for good and all any claim she might have had in respect of her lost provinces." [3] That some such conversation did occur seems probable enough, and it illustrates the real menace that the Kaiser was to peace ; not because he wanted war, but because he so constantly thought and spoke in terms of it. At any rate, as the future was to show, the German " diplomatic victory " was as dearly bought as such victories usually are.

Meantime Delcassé's resignation eased the tension. There were indeed at this crisis two men who were particularly dangerous to the cause of peace, and either of whom, it seemed, might have unbalanced the precarious equilibrium of Europe. One was Delcassé, the other the all-powerful Holstein of the German Foreign Office. In this connexion it seems worth while to cite the following remarks, credited by Eckardstein to the French Socialist Jaurès : " In all the serious crises, of international as of domestic politics, it is a matter of the first importance whether capable and honourable men are at the head of affairs or whether the fate of the nation

---

[1] Ed. 1916, p. 291. Cf. an article by Mendelssohn-Bartholdy in *Wissen und Leben*, February 1st, 1925, based on vol. xx. of *Die Grosse Politik*. He thinks Lord Bertie may have been responsible. On this, as on so many other points, we must wait for the publication of British documents.
[2] See above, p. 115.   [3] *Memoirs*, p. 7.

is in clumsy or, it may be, criminal hands. In the former case the crisis is overcome ; in the latter it leads usually to a catastrophe which has to be liquidated by the unhappy, unsuspecting peoples. Woe to Europe if the Chauvinism which has declined so remarkably among us in France should lift its head again under the leadership of men like Delcassé. Personally, I do not question your Kaiser's love of peace, nor that of the great mass of the German people. But I fear that a small number of criminals and ambitious men may not only poison your people in Germany but among us too may bring into power a new and dangerous Chauvinism." [1] Holstein was to continue to influence German policy. But Delcassé was removed, and the situation thereby rendered, for the moment, less tense.

Meantime Rouvier, the French Premier, who was still opposed to the summoning of an international conference, endeavoured to negotiate further with Germany. What he desired was a general agreement between the two States, arrived at by them independently.[2] His views were thus represented to Eckardstein by his friend Armand Lévy : " As to an alliance, however desirable it may be for both parties, one cannot of course go so fast ; but that is no reason why one should immediately impose the other alternative and utter this terrible word " war." The idea of a friendly rapprochement of the two nations, which perhaps might gradually lead up to an alliance, has been mooted also between Prince Radolin (the German Ambassador in Paris) and myself." [3] Rouvier, indeed, went further ; for he offered the Germans a port on the Atlantic coast of Morocco.[4] A similar offer, it is true, had been made a few years before by England, but then Germany was the friend and France the enemy. Rouvier's proposal can hardly have been acceptable to the

[1] Eckardstein, *Isolierung Deutschlands*, p. 143.
[2] Ger. Docs., xx. pp. 356, 361, etc.
[3] Eckardstein, *Isolierung Deutschlands*, p. 104.
[4] Ib., p. 107. Cf. Bishop's *Roosevelt*, i. p. 476 ; Caillaux, *Agadir*, p. 25. It is interesting to note that in 1911 M. Georges Louis, French Ambassador at St. Petersburg, was explaining to the Tsar that France could not allow Germany to occupy a Moroccan port because " a German settlement in Morocco would be a menace to our Algeria. It is our vital interests that we are defending." Was it, then, "our vital interests" that M. Rouvier was proposing to sacrifice in 1904 ? The "vital" and the "non-vital" change places with extraordinary rapidity in the diplomatic game. And perhaps the only real meaning of "vital" is, what we are prepared, under present conditions, to go to war about (see Judet, *Georges Louis*, pp. 156–7).

British Government, if they knew of it ; [1] but it might, one would think, have been acceptable to the Germans. In fact, however, they rejected it. The reason given by the Kaiser to Roosevelt was that they were pledged in honour to stand by the Sultan, and could not therefore proceed to partition his territory. " Here," he said, " is a curious case. We may be forced into war, not because we have been *grabbing* after other people's land, but because we *refuse to take it.*" [2] Whether this was really the motive determining German policy I dare not affirm. If it were, that policy would stand out in a favourable light in comparison with that of France and England, who, while asserting to the world their determination to maintain the independence of Morocco and the sovereignty of its ruler, had arranged secretly for its partition between France and Spain. At any rate the attempts at a separate deal between France and Germany broke down. Germany continued to press for an international conference, and the tension once more became acute.

V. British Policy

Meantime what was British policy ? From English sources we have, as yet, almost no evidence, and we must piece together what we can from elsewhere. One thing is clear. British mistrust of Germany, by this time, was very strong. On this subject it will be useful to cite the words of an impartial outsider, friendly to both States. " Each nation," President Roosevelt wrote,[3] " is working itself up to a condition of desperate hatred of the other ; each from sheer fear of the other. The Kaiser is dead-sure that England intends to attack him. The English Government, and a large share of the English people, are equally sure that Germany intends to attack England." But he proceeds, " in my view this action of Germany in embroiling herself with France over Morocco is proof positive that she has not the slightest intention of attacking England. I am very clear that England utterly overestimates, as well as mis-estimates, Germany's singleness of purpose, by attributing to the German Foreign

[1] Lord Tweedmouth, however, told the German Ambassador that the British Government would not object. Ger. Docs. xxi. p. 187. Grey shared this view in 1906, but in 1911 took the opposite one ; see i, pp. 117, 220.
[2] Roosevelt, ib., p. 476.   [3] Ib., p. 472.

Office the kind of continuity of aim which it had from '64 to '71." The truth of these last words is borne out by all we learn of German diplomacy during the ten years preceding the war, and nowhere more than in the Moroccan episode. German policy is confused and hesitating. It does not work consistently for anything, and, least of all, for war.

The British, then, were ready to back France, if it should come to war. Some Frenchmen accused us further of egging her on ; [1] but that does not seem likely. It is more probable that the British Government were anxious to stand firmly by France on this the first occasion when the Entente was tested ; and the more so, because they knew of the German attempt to make a Continental bloc of Germany, Russia, and France. The Treaty of Björkoe, which was intended to lead to that result, was signed in July 1905.[2] The British Government were exercised, at that time, by the position in the Far East, and they feared a renewal of the combination formed there in 1895.[3]

That the Far East was the danger-point was clear also to the Kaiser. For we find him writing, in June 1905 : " My people are sure that England would now back France by force of arms in a war against Germany, not on account of Morocco, but on account of Germany's policy in the Far East. The combined naval forces of England and France would undoubtedly smash the German Navy, and give England, France, Japan, and Russia a more free hand in the Far East." [4] He also reports that " England has made a formal offer to France to enter into an offensive and defensive alliance which would be directed against Germany." [5]

As to this alleged offer we are still in obscurity. M. Poincaré also says that M. Delcassé " laid before his colleagues the written proposition for an agreement which had been transmitted to him a few days before by M. Paul Cambon on behalf of Lord Lansdowne." [6] It looks therefore as though some such proposal had been made by the Conservative Government. But that Government went out of office at

---

[1] See, e.g., Ger. Docs., xx. pp. 479, 482. Mr. Balfour, on the other hand, announced to the German Ambassador that British support of a war against Germany was only conceivable in the case of German aggression (ib., xxi. p. 475).

[2] See above, p. 115, and Ger. Docs., xx. pp. 173, 177, 627.
[3] See below, p. 284. [4] Roosevelt, p. 476. [5] Ib.
[6] *Origins*, p. 82.

the end of 1905, and we have clear evidence that Sir Edward Grey, who succeeded Lord Lansdowne at the Foreign Office, declined to give an engagement to the French that England would assist her in arms in case she were attacked by Germany. He refused even a verbal assurance to that effect; and he did not see how it could be put into writing without converting the Entente into an alliance. Such a change might be brought about by circumstances; but the pressure of circumstances was not as yet such as to require it. If the change were made, it must be communicated to Parliament. " No British Government could commit the country to such a serious thing and keep the engagement secret." [1]

The proposal then, if proposal there was, to convert the Entente into an alliance did not materialise. But that both Sir Edward Grey and his predecessors were prepared to go to war in support of France seems clear.[2] Mr. Roosevelt tells us that, in the middle of 1905, the British Ambassador at Washington, Sir Mortimer Durand, " was bitter about Germany, and, so far as he represented the British Government, it would appear that they were anxious to see Germany humiliated by France's refusal to enter a conference, and that they were quite willing to face the possibility of war under such circumstances." Roosevelt comments : " I did not think this showed much valour on their part, although, from their point of view, it was sagacious, as, of course, in such a war, where the British and French fleets would be united, the German fleet could have done absolutely nothing, while on land, where Germany was so powerful, it would be France alone that would stand, and would have to stand, the brunt of the battle." [3] Later the President says that : " It seemed to me that it would be useless to speak to England, for I felt that, if a war were to break out, whatever might happen to France, England would profit immensely, while Germany would lose her colonies and perhaps her fleet." [4] These were the President's impressions, and they are not without interest. They show, at any rate, that, in his opinion, the British Government would not have been averse to war. M. Tardieu seems to have had the same impression, for he says that war was regarded by many Englishmen as

[1] *Life of Campbell-Bannerman*, ii. pp. 253 seq.
[2] Cf. Ger. Docs., xxi. pp. 45 seq.   [3] Roosevelt, p. 475.   [4] Ib., p. 483.

" desirable and probable." [1] These, no doubt, are guesses, though made by intelligent men, in positions which gave them opportunities for sound judgments. More important and more authentic is the account given by Sir Edward Grey himself, in his famous speech of August 3rd, 1914. He tells us that, at the turn of the year 1905-6, he was asked by the French Ambassador whether, in case of war, we would give armed support to France. Sir Edward, in reply, said : " I could promise nothing to any foreign Power unless it was subsequently to receive the whole-hearted support of public opinion here if the occasion arose. I said, in my opinion, if war was forced upon France then, on the question of Morocco—a question which had just been the subject of agreement between this country and France, an agreement exceedingly popular on both sides—that if, out of that agreement, war was forced on France at that time, in my view public opinion would have rallied to the material support of France. I gave no promise, but I expressed that opinion during the crisis, as far as I remember, almost in the same words to the French Ambassador and the German Ambassador. At the same time I made no promise and I expressed no threats, but I expressed that opinion." Lord Loreburn, who cites this passage, expresses the opinion that public opinion at that time would have been vehemently opposed to war. [2] It is a matter of conjecture ; but evidently much would depend on how the war came upon the scene. In such matters the Foreign Secretary, the Cabinet and the Press have the power to determine opinion. It would have been easy to represent the French as a peaceable, innocent people and the Germans as hectoring bullies, for no one then knew anything about the secret treaties. Moreover, the fate of Gibraltar and of the entrance to the Mediterranean were likely to appeal much more to the British than the quarrel between Serbia and Austria did in 1914. So that it is at least questionable whether the then House of Commons would have overthrown the Government rather than sanction war.

War, at any rate, was considered so possible that military and naval authorities were agitated ; and the French Ambassador suggested that, under the circumstances, it would be desirable that British and French naval and military experts should consult together. Sir Edward Grey consented, without

---

[1] *Conférence d'Algeçiras*, p. 78.   [2] *How the War Came*, p. 77.

informing the Cabinet. His explanation, later, was that he was busy electioneering and that there was no opportunity to summon a Cabinet meeting. To that Lord Loreburn retorts that the Cabinet met in January 1906, and after that regularly, and that the conversations must have continued for some time.[1] Sir Edward, however, he suggests, might reply that by the end of January the crisis had passed and there was no reason to inform the Cabinet. Into that controversy we need not here enter.[2]

VI. The Conference

We will now return from the danger of war—which accompanies the whole crisis—to the German proposal for a conference. The French, as we have seen, were very unwilling to assent to this, even after the resignation of Delcassé, and the British supported the French view. One interesting argument adduced by M. Rouvier may be cited, for it shows the unwillingness of Great Powers to submit their disputes to the arbitration of lesser ones. " It would not," said the French Minister, " be consistent with the dignity of a Great Power to submit itself to what might be the decisive voice of some secondary signatory State such as Sweden or Denmark." So long as Great Powers take that view there can be no reality in the League of Nations and no arrest of war.

There was every appearance, then, that the breach might come over this question ; and it was, apparently, only the friendly intervention of President Roosevelt that led France to waive her objection.[3] It was necessary, however, that she and Germany should agree about the programme of the Conference. Here there were difficulties ; and it would seem that they were surmounted by the intervention with the Kaiser, first of President Roosevelt in June,[4] secondly of Count Witte in September.[5]

---

[1] Loreburn, pp. 80-1.
[2] For the military commitments started at this time, see below, p. 375.
[3] Roosevelt, p. 478.
[4] Ib., p. 485.   " Every means was used by Germany to make France understand that if she refused the Conference there would be war ; and to make assurance doubly sure, a special envoy was sent from Berlin to Paris for that express purpose. This was Prince Henckel v. Donnersmarck " (Churchill, *World Crisis*, 1. p. 31).
[5] Tardieu, pp. 12, 77.   Count Witte (*Memoirs*, p. 421) says that it was consent to the holding of the Conference which he elicited from the Kaiser ; but this must be a lapse of memory. Cf. Ger. Docs., xx. pp. 579 note and 590.

Thus at last, after all these dangers and delays, the Conference met at Algeciras on January 16th, 1906 ; and we are fortunate enough to have a full account of it from a competent French politician, M. Tardieu. His book contains details and documents of great interest ; but even more interesting than these, to a student of diplomacy, is the attitude of the author. If we are to believe him, France throughout was innocent, honourable, pacific, sinning, if at all, only by pardonable errors of judgment ; Germany was all wrong from beginning to end, sinister, violent, irrational ; while the other Powers are to be judged by the degree and constancy of the support they gave to France. And yet throughout, so cunning is the air of fairness and impartiality, that a careless or prejudiced reader might easily suppose he was reading history. What, in fact, he is reading is a pro-French pamphlet. But once he has grasped that fact, he will find the pamphlet to be useful, even for the immediate matter with which it deals, and still more so as an illustration of the way in which recent history is often written.

The programme of the Conference had been agreed to between the French and Germans in the course of the year 1905. In a document of July 8th [1] it was laid down that the German Government was not pursuing " any purpose which may compromise the legitimate interests of France in Morocco, or which may be contrary to the rights of France resulting from treaties or arrangements, and in harmony with the following principles :

" 1. The sovereignty and independence of the Sultan.
" 2. The integrity of his Empire.
" 3. Economic liberty without any inequality.
" 4. The utility of reforms in the police and the finances, the introduction of which would be regulated for a short time by international agreement.
" 5. The recognition of the situation made for France in Morocco by the contiguity, along an immense frontier, of Algeria and the Shereefian Empire, and by the special relations resulting therefrom between the two adjacent countries, as well as by the special interest which results for France in the prevalence of order in the Shereefian Empire."

[1] See Tardieu, Appendix iv.

The reader who is acquainted with the secret treaties knows what to think of such " principles " as the " sovereignty and independence of the Sultan " and the " integrity of his Empire." On this subject M. Tardieu has a very illuminating remark. The French, he says, had as their one great object " to prevent the Germans from setting foot in Morocco " For that reason they insisted, " by a manœuvre conducted in a superior way," on the assertion of Moroccan independence.[1] A few lines further on our author says : " Morocco was, and was bound to be, the great objective of French policy." It would be impossible to state more frankly the duplicity of the French. All who knew of the secret treaties must have known that they were countenancing a fraud. The British and Spanish of course knew, since they were parties to the treaties. The Germans at least suspected. The Americans, presumably, and the smaller States were kept in the dark. It was with these treaties in the background that the Conference assembled.

Its full membership was one hundred and fifty persons. The States represented were Germany, Austria, Belgium, Spain, the United States, France, Great Britain, Italy, the Netherlands, Portugal, Russia, Sweden, and of course Morocco. Of these States, France, Russia, and Great Britain [2] acted throughout in close co-operation. Austria, on the whole, supported Germany, yet not completely nor passively. The position of Italy, on the other hand, was peculiarly awkward, since in the year 1900 she had made the agreement with France which contemplated the appropriation of Morocco by that country, while Italy, in compensation, was to take Tripoli.[3] Giolitti and Tittoni, it is true, assured the Germans that " there does not exist between Italy and France any agreement, political or military, which is in contradiction with the Triple Alliance or can diminish the value of our obligations

---

[1] *Le Mystère d'Agadir*, p. 408.

[2] See Tardieu, pp. 60 seq., 87, 158. Sir Edward Grey said to M. Cambon, on January 31st, 1906, that " at present French policy in Morocco, within the four corners of the Declaration exchanged between us, was absolutely free, that we did not question it, that we suggested no concessions and no alterations in it, that we left France a free hand and gave unreservedly our diplomatic support, on which she could count " (*Life of Campbell-Bannerman*, ii. p. 254). Cf. Churchill, *World Crisis*, i. p. 32 : " Sir Henry Campbell-Bannerman authorised Sir Edward Grey to support France strongly at Algeciras."

[3] See above, p. 94.

with the allied Powers." ¹ But Rudini held that the agreement of 1900 was opposed at any rate to the spirit of the
Triple Alliance, and that, if he were Minister, he would prefer
to denounce it.² And San Giuliano said that "as a loyal
man he would not conceal the fact that he would not have
made the agreement with France, although he denied that it
was 'directly' contrary to the Triple Alliance." ³ We will
not dwell upon these subtleties. The fact remains that Italy
could not support Germany at Algeciras and was bound to
support France. This fact was emphasised by the appointment of Visconti Venosta—" the sly old fox," as San Giuliano
endearingly called him ⁴—to represent Italy at the Conference ;
for it was he who had concluded with France the agreement
of 1900. Italy, then, was working throughout on the side
of France. Spain, bound both to England and France by
secret treaties, in spite of some hesitations and fears supported them throughout. The small States of Europe took
no line of their own, preferring to avoid trouble. But—and
this was a determining factor—the United States went whole-
heartedly with the Triple Entente. It is indeed clear, from
President Roosevelt's account, that, on the information
available to him, he thought France was right. But that
information was incomplete if, as seems to be the case, he did
not know of the secret treaties. His attitude is sufficiently
indicated in a phrase he used to the French Ambassador,
Jusserand : " The important point was for them (the French)
to get the kernel of the nut, and they did not have to consider
the shell." ⁵ From M. Tardieu's account it is clear that
Mr. White, the representative of the United States, worked
in close co-operation with France and England. Only once
did he suggest an arrangement to which the French objected,
and, on their objection being taken, promptly abandoned it.
Under these circumstances Germany was faced from the
beginning with defeat. She had pressed for the Conference,
and the French had resisted it ; but it was the French, with
their treaties, their allies, and their clever diplomacy, who
were to come out with flying colours, and it was the Germans
who were to fail at every point. It should be added that the
work actually done at Algeciras, even when private conver-

¹ Ger. Docs., xx. p. 96.　　² Ib., xxi. p. 231.　³ Ib., p. 35.
⁴ Ib., p. 335.　　⁵ Roosevelt, p. 488.

sations are taken into account, was but part of the whole
proceedings ; for the Ambassadors were busy also at every
capital, and their action had much to do with the results
finally reached.   The formal sittings of the Conference
were for the most part merely records of decisions made
elsewhere.

What the French were bent upon throughout was to prevent
the " internationalisation " of Morocco.   To that idea, which
is the inspiration of the League of Nations, which underlies
the " mandatory " system, and which alone can bring any
peace to the world, they were radically opposed.   Morocco
was to be theirs, as the secret treaties with England and
Spain had provided.   Their allies, of course, supported them
in this view; and thus, ironically enough, the only representative of the international solution was Germany.   I do
not wish, however, to attach any undue importance to this
fact ; for Germany might just as well have taken the other
line had there been then a chance that Morocco might have
fallen to her instead of to France.

VII.   The Police

There were three points in particular which raised this
issue of international control.   One was the question of equal
opportunities for commerce.   But, in fact, this point was
granted by the French from the beginning.   It was embodied
in the secret as well as the public treaty, and it was too
important for England to be openly jettisoned by France.
The German anxiety on this matter was probably genuine,
and certainly natural, considering the record of France in
Madagascar and elsewhere.   But it was unnecessary.   That
door was open, at any rate for the time being.

The other questions were those of the police and the bank ;
and in both of these the French fought hard and, on the whole,
successfully, for French control.   The police, as the Germans
saw, and as everyone must have admitted, was the crucial
point.   For the right and duty of police meant, in fact, the
military, and so the political, control of Morocco.   Accordingly
a great part of the discussions, negotiations, and conflicts of
the Conference turned upon this point.   The behaviour of the
French in this matter seems to have been peculiarly dishonest.

The Germans had pressed them hard to abandon formally, before the Conference, any claim to the police of the western coast. Rouvier had refused. Public opinion, he said, would not allow such an abdication. On the other hand, he was willing to give a verbal promise that the mandate should not be claimed at the Conference. To this compromise the Germans assented, by the mediation of Count Witte. But at the very time that Rouvier gave this promise he had entered into a secret treaty with Spain, dividing the police of the ports between the two countries. Even this treaty, it appears, was somewhat ambiguous, for it left three ports unaccounted for. The French thought it clear that these would go to France, but the Spanish may have thought otherwise. The important point, however, for the moment was that the question of the police in the ports, regarded by the Germans as reserved for international control, had been quietly settled by the French and Spanish in a secret treaty.[1] This treaty, moreover, the Germans came to know during the Conference.[2] Is it very surprising if they were suspicious and intransigeant ?

This being the situation, an obstinate duel followed between the Germans and the French. The former made proposition after proposition intended to save the ports from French control. They proposed, first, that the police should go entirely to Spain, an idea which seems, for a moment, to have appealed to the Spanish, in spite of the secret treaty, but which they finally rejected, owing, no doubt, in part, as M. Tardieu suggests, to close and vigilant Anglo-French pressure. " The manœuvre," he says, " thus failed. But it was not of a nature to inspire confidence."[3]   The Germans next proposed that foreign officers to control the police should be appointed by the Sultan ; that an officer of some small Power should inspect and report to the diplomatic body at Tangiers ; and that that body should have a general control.[4] The French were shocked. " We could not admit the annulling of the special interest of France, respect for which we had been promised, nor the creation at our doors of an international organisation in which the liberty of the Sultan would serve

---

[1] Sept, 1, 1905. See Tardieu, pp. 58, 156, 377. For Rouvier's verbal promise see Ger. Docs. v. xx. chap. cl., esp. p. 582. Tardieu's constant implication that there was no such promise is plainly contrary to facts.
[2] Tardieu, p. 156.   [3] Ib., p. 145.   [4] Ib., p. 175.

as an instrument of European intrigues, as menacing to our peace in Algeria as to our Continental security." But the matter was delicate. It would never do to involve France in the reputation of intransigeance, nor to give the Germans an excuse for breaking off the Conference. The French therefore decided to offer what would look like a compromise. The police instructors should be French and Spanish, but there should be some kind of nominal international control, consisting of a report made to the Powers by the French and Spanish officers and presented by Italy.[1] " The practical result would be the same," M. Tardieu comments (meaning that Franco-Spanish control would be in fact established), but it would look like a concession. " It is interesting to note," he remarks, " that M. Rouvier and M. Révoil each hit upon this idea independently and almost simultaneously." [2] It was arranged that the plan should be presented by Mr. White as though it were an American proposal, and should be pressed upon the Germans by President Roosevelt ; and Mr. White promised not to " uncover the French " in his conversations with the German representatives. " Under these conditions the combination lost its inconveniences, to retain only its advantages." True, Italy was given a certain privilege in the matter of the report to the Powers, and Italy was a Mediterranean Power. " But our engagements with her, and the policy of disinterestedness which she had promised to pursue in Morocco, preserved us from all uneasiness so far as she was concerned." [3] It was explained to the Germans that the question of control could not be discussed until the Franco-Spanish nationality of the officers had been accepted ; and the French representative " did not fail to indicate to his German colleague how our reply, so prompt and so moderate, proved our desire to arrive at agreement." But alas ! Those unconscionable Germans remained obstinate. The French plan, they said, did not appear to be compatible with the international character of the police ; and they suggested that the French should make some other proposal. " With much reason, M. Révoil replied that there was little chance of agreement between two negotiators of whom one would not make any concession at all." [4] We have

---

[1] Tardieu, p. 180.   [2] P. 179 and note.
[3] Ib., p. 181.   [4] Ib., p. 187.

seen that, in Tardieu's own view, it was precisely the French who were making no real concession.

There followed, however, an awkward episode. The Spanish representative came to the French and announced that Spain, in her desire for an understanding, renounced the Franco-Spanish combination. She would consent that, for the next three years, the police should be organised by the Sultan, with Moroccan instructors under the control of the diplomatic body, and she invited France to accept this solution. Against this plan M. Révoil " was in duty bound to offer an energetic protest." The Germans evidently had been putting pressure on the Spanish. The new proposal would be " not a concession, but an abdication." He invoked the secret treaty, he invoked British support, he insisted on the need of drawing closer the bonds of union in order to resist the German pressure. " There was no German pressure," the Spaniard replied. But, says M. Tardieu, in fact it was being exercised with " unheard-of violence " in all the capitals, and above all in Madrid. This German pressure, no doubt, was somehow a thing different in kind to the French pressure, which, on M. Tardieu's own showing, was equally active everywhere. The result was that " the Spanish project was thrown back into the limbo from which it should never have issued." [1] The deadlock therefore continued, to the accompaniment of recriminations in the Press of both parties. The base Germans continued their diplomatic pressure at the various courts. So did the noble French. In Italy, especially, the Germans were embarrassing. They explained that Germany was defending the " general interests of Europe " and counted upon " the fidelity of her ally." " The situation of Italy," M. Tardieu justly remarks, " was difficult." For, as we know, by her secret treaty with France she had promised Morocco to the latter in return for Tripoli ; while, on the other hand, she was a member of the Triple Alliance and had secured thereby the promise of Germany to support her in a war against France, precisely in the case that France should encroach upon Morocco. These are the embarrassments of secret and contradictory treaties. But a brilliant idea occurred to the Italian Minister. The Italian delegate to Algeciras, he said, had only consented to go there on the condition that he was

[1] Tardieu, p. 189.

left unhampered by instructions ! [1] It would be better, therefore, if the German Chancellor should address himself directly to him. " Then," says M. Tardieu, " by a ' combinazione ' thoroughly Italian, and for that matter perfectly honourable, they advised us discreetly of this procedure, in order to give M. Révoil the opportunity to take his measures." [2] Still this, after all, was but " a precarious expedient." The trouble was that, whereas the French expected from Italy a positive support of all their proposals, the Italians seemed inclined to think that their obligations were only negative, not to oppose them.[3] " Evidently," exclaims M. Tardieu, " a Judaic gloss on a treaty conceived in another spirit ! " Accordingly a strong offensive was opened by the French and British Ambassadors at Rome, and also at Madrid. " If Spain, yielding to German pressure, should forget her engagements, she would but displace the obstacles she was endeavouring to escape. For Anglo-French resistance would take the place of German resistance." [4] " In the treaties," M. Jules Cambon argued, " resided in fact, for Spain as for us, the only guarantee for to-morrow. What to-morrow would be, no one knew. It might, given the general state of Europe, be more difficult for Germany than for us. And who knows if it would not offer us, sooner than we thought, the opportunity to execute in Morocco the engagements of 1904 and 1905 ? " [5] In other words, who knew how soon France and Spain might be in a position to carry out that partition of Morocco on which they had agreed with Great Britain, and which they were still determined to pursue, although the sovereignty and independence of Morocco was the basis on which the Conference at Algeciras was professedly proceeding. The Spanish Minister was impressed. The firm ground of procedure, he admitted, was the treaties. Thus, M. Tardieu comments, " at Madrid, as at Rome, we checkmated the German effort." [6]

Meantime, in Paris, the German Ambassador was endeavouring to enter into separate discussions with M. Rouvier. But the French Premier " stopped him at the first word. It was Germany who wanted the Conference. We were there.

---

[1] This does not seem to have been strictly true. Visconti-Venosta received instructions, but he seems to have been reluctant to communicate with his Government. See Ger. Docs., xxi. pp. 335, 343.
[2] Tardieu, p. 199.   [3] Ib., p. 206.   [4] Ib., p. 207.
[5] Ib.   [6] P. 208.

There we must stay." M. Révoil at Algeciras had full powers ;
it was with him that negotiations must be pursued. " C'était
la sagesse même," says M. Tardieu, and no doubt, under the
circumstances, it was.[1] Nevertheless, direct conversations did
take place between French and Germans, not, however, at
Paris, but at Berlin. A French ex-Ambassador, M. de Courcel,
met the German Chancellor, Prince Bülow. The latter,
" with the seductive graciousness and the frank optimism
which he knows how to display to those whom he desires to
convince, repeated to Baron de Courcel the vague and amiable
things that many of our compatriots had already heard.
' What was all this obstruction and delay at the Conference ?
It was time to end it. Germany wanted nothing but to save
her face. Why not arrive at a compromise ? Let France
take one port and police it with Frenchmen. Let the other
ports be assigned to international control, the police to be
recruited from all the countries concerned, including France
and Germany. France will then be the only country to have
a port under her own control. Germany would only ask for
one if some other Power should claim one. Come, let's be
sensible and agree. This is my last word.' " [2]

Horror of the French and of M. Tardieu ! " This last
word was the most impossible of all ! Germany must either
have failed to understand our policy or she must have believed
us resigned to every abdication." For Spain, no doubt, would
ask for a port too ; and then Germany would ask for one,
" which was as good as saying that we should partition
Morocco by installing Germany there. And, apart from
everything else, what would England say ? " [3] One wonders
indeed what England would say ; just as one wonders what
she would have said when, a few months earlier, the French
Government had offered to Germany in sovereignty that
port—nay, ports—into which it would now have been an
incredible " abdication " to permit her to step. As to partition, that, we know, had already been arranged ; but it was
to be partition between France and Spain. How monstrous,
then, that there should be even an oft-chance of Germany
getting a bit ! The effusive suggestion of Bülow was accordingly turned down by the French.

The next manœuvre was an approach by the Russian

[1] P. 201.   [2] P. 243.   [3] P. 244.

statesman, Count Witte, to the Kaiser himself. Why not make concessions ? They would be so much easier for Germany than for France. France, after all, had " rights." And then, how difficult was the position of Russia between France and Germany ! " Give to France, who is nervous about your intentions, a pledge of your spirit of conciliation by accepting, of course with appropriate guarantees, the solution she proposes." [1] Alas ! the Kaiser was adamant. He not only refused, he developed counter-grievances of his own. " We have given the French the police of the frontier. What more do they want ? And look at their Press ! If Russia desires to avoid a rupture she had better address herself to France. Still, if the French choose to accept . . ." To accept what ? The very proposal of von Bülow, the " most impossible of all ! " The Tsar, " disturbed, saddened, above all, astonished," said he could not understand. He promised to assist France with all the means in his power. But at this point President Roosevelt intervened. He was convinced, he tells us, that Germany was aiming, in effect, at the partition of Morocco, which was the very reverse of what she was claiming to desire. The President does not say why he had arrived at this conclusion, which seems to be contrary to all the evidence at our disposal. However, he wrote to the Kaiser, repeating substantially the French proposal, namely, the control of the police by French and Spanish officers, who should report both to Morocco, and to Italy as representing the Powers.[2] The Kaiser replied that such an arrangement " would be tantamount to a Franco-Spanish double mandate, and mean a monopoly of these two countries which would heavily curtail the political and the economic positions of the other nations." [3]

The French, meantime, had decided that it would now be safe to bring the question before a full meeting of the Conference. They calculated that they would have on their side England, Russia, Spain, and Portugal. The United States would not vote, the question being European, but were known to be favourable to the French. Their vote was therefore " morally " one for France. Germany, Austria, and Morocco would be on the other side. Belgium, Sweden, and Holland would abstain, or vote with the majority. The only trouble was that Italy was still hesitating ; she would

[1] P. 247.　　[2] Roosevelt, pp. 489 seq.　　[3] Ib., pp. 492 seq.

not vote against the French ; but, why should she vote at all ?
" Baron Sonnino applied to this case of international conscience the resources of a mind which combines with the
tenacity of the Semite all the suppleness of the Italian."
" We sympathise with you," he said, " but why press us to
vote ? Why put us in a difficult position ? France will
triumph morally. Count upon Time, that great physician,
who works for Russia, for France, for everybody except for
Germany." [1] Thus argued the Minister of the Power bound
to Germany by the Triple Alliance. But the French were
not thus to be repulsed. " Did Baron Sonnino hope that
this harmonious music would lay our vigilance to sleep ?
Probably not ! At any rate, we could not leave him in that
illusion." No ! The treaty of 1902 was clear. France was
to favour " the development of Italian influence " in Tripoli ;
Italy must do the same for France in Morocco. " We could
not admit any other interpretation of the contract which
bound us to her." To French pressure was added British.
" M. Egerton continued his demonstrations. Or he put
insidious questions. Was it true that the Marquis Visconti-
Venosta intended to abstain from voting ? That would
produce, in London and elsewhere, an unfortunate effect. If
Italy did not vote, England would be displeased and would
not be the only Power to be displeased." The reader will
remember that, on a previous occasion, when pressed by the
Germans, the Italian Government had escaped by saying
that their delegate had only accepted his position on condition
that he was left free to vote as he chose ; and that this
manœuvre was enthusiastically approved by M. Tardieu.
But now, when France was applying the pressure, it was a
different matter : " Affirm as they might that the Marquis
was free to take what action he chose, no one neglected to
put pressure on the Italian Government, of which, after all,
M. Visconti-Venosta was but the representative and the
mandatory." [2] Wonderful, is it not, how circumstances
change opinions ! But all this pressure failed to elicit a
firm assurance from the Italian Government ; and the French
were driven to conclude that their best chance was direct
pressure at Algeciras. They were justified ; for the first
test vote taken at the Conference, on March 3rd, gave a

[1] Tardieu, p. 253.   [2] Ib., p. 254.

majority of 10 to 3 for the French, and in that majority Italy was included. Only Morocco voted with Germany and Austria.[1]

The ground seemed now to be clear ; and on March 8th the French drew up a proposal, on which they had previously agreed with the British and the Spanish, and which, of course, was in accordance with the arrangements of the secret treaties. It gave the officers of the police to France and Spain.[2] But the very day before this proposal was to be laid before the Conference the Rouvier Ministry in France was defeated and resigned. " It was to be feared," cries Tardieu, still palpitating with the sensation, " that this mad action, committed without regard to external difficulties by an agonising chamber, might provoke in Germany illusions which might translate themselves into new demands at Algeciras." [3]   At first this anxiety appeared to be misplaced, for all continued to go well.   The German representative seemed to admit that the police might be Franco-Spanish ; and the Austrian delegate intervened to suggest an appropriate bridge between the disputing parties.[4] This proposal, when it appeared, was naturally a compromise. But it was one horrifying to the French.   For it suggested that the police in four of the ports should be French, and in three Spanish ; but that in one port, Casablanca, the Sultan should choose, as controlling officer, either a Swiss or a Dutchman, and that this officer should be inspector-general of all the police throughout the country. This would never do ! The French immediately got to work to propose a further compromise. They would admit a kind of international inspection (to which hitherto they had avoided committing themselves) if the Germans and Austrians would abandon the exceptional régime for Casablanca. But—O those Germans ! When Sir Arthur Nicolson proposed this arrangement to their delegate, he was met by a direct No !   " My Government has said its last word.   That last word is the Austrian proposal. Take it or leave it ! " [5]   The Italians and French came, in their turn, to plead, but received the same reply.   The Germans became " aggressive and menacing " ; the German Press re-echoed this tone ; and the German Ambassadors received orders to explain to the Governments to which they were accredited that France refused all concessions, and that everyone at Algeciras was against her. "Never had our position been more grave. Never had the results achieved been more compromised."[1] But this view, as it proved, was too pessimistic. Sir Edward Grey telegraphed to Sir Arthur Nicolson : "To avoid all misunderstanding I repeat once more that I shall support France to the end, and that she will not yield on Casablanca."[2] The Russian Minister made his position equally clear in the same sense.[3] Even President Roosevelt was no less opposed to the Austrian project. It seemed to him "to provide for a potential partition of the territory, in violation of the principle upon which we have agreed with Germany." For it constituted three spheres of interest, and the nations to whom those spheres were granted "may be expected in the ordinary course of events to enter into complete control."[4] He did not want this. But then, neither did he want Morocco to be divided between France and Spain. He therefore proposed that, in all the ports, the police officers should be both French and Spanish, so as to avoid separate spheres of interest altogether. Dismay of the French ! "It was the worst of all the mishaps we had to fear. On this American plan, there remained nothing of the spirit which had presided at the elaboration of the Franco-Spanish agreements, nothing of the very terms of the agreements."[5] The President did well to prevent a partition in which Germany might have a part ; but he did very evil (no doubt in ignorance !) to prevent a Franco-Spanish partition, in which the lion's share would go to France. The worst of it was that "to reject this combination was a difficult business. We ran the risk of annoying President Roosevelt, whose active assistance had been so useful to us." And, on the other hand, of course, those wretched Germans would take advantage of his proposal to "annihilate the Franco-Spanish agreements."[6] "We were caught in a trap without being able to incriminate anybody." Cruel situation ! But "our diplomacy had the honour, on this occasion, to despair neither of itself nor of others." The friends of France rallied round her. The French themselves, without directly rejecting

[1] P. 320. [2] P. 347. Cf. Grey, i. pp. 104 seq. [3] P. 331.
[4] Bishop, p. 498. [5] Tardieu, p. 386. [6] Ib., p. 386.

the American proposition, were able to indicate its inconveniences. In fine, the Americans abandoned their plan, and
the French breathed again. Only one difficulty remained.
The Conference evinced a desire to decide for itself how the
ports should be partitioned between France and Spain. This
was distressing to the French ; the more so as the Spanish
developed an obstinate wish to have the police of Tangiers,
although, by the secret treaty, it was to be, for fifteen years,
Franco-Spanish. They proposed to exchange Casablanca for
Tangiers ; and that, M. Tardieu admits, would be " logical "
since Tangiers lay opposite to Spain. But then, the Germans
would object to sole French control at Casablanca ; and it
would be awkward " to unveil under the fire of Germany the
arrangements of 1904." [1] There followed a fierce little dispute
between the two States, which was only adjusted the day
before the question was brought up at the Conference.
Tangiers, it was finally decided, was to have a mixed police,
with a French chief ; Casablanca a mixed police with a
Spanish chief ; two of the other ports were to go to Spain,
four to France ; and with a sigh of relief M. Tardieu was
able to conclude " the essential was thus acquired." It
was. The French, supported by Spain, Russia, and England,
had put through all their claims as provided in the secret
treaties. The ground had been laid, by an international
conference, for the partition of Morocco. The Germans,
who had demanded that Conference, were defeated ; the
French, who had opposed it, were victorious ; and one of
those diplomatic triumphs had been achieved which were
the prelude to the Great War.

VIII. The Bank

The right to police Morocco was the essential one on which
the control of the country would depend. Compared with
that, the question of the Bank was subordinate. But it
provided some points of interest. As we have already noticed,
one of the earliest steps taken in the absorption of a country
by a European Power, is a loan or loans to the ruler. He
wastes this money, fails to pay the interest, and thus invites
financial control by the " peacefully penetrating " Power ;

[1] Tardieu, p. 393.

and this, in turn, requires and leads up to military control
The classic case, in recent British history, is Egypt. In
accordance with this well-recognised principle of European
States, the French had lent, in 1904, to the Sultan of
Morocco, sixty-two and a half million francs at 5 per cent.[1]
What Morocco actually obtained was 48 millions, the banks
making a profit of 12,500,000 francs, and the Moroccan paying
interest on the full amount.[2] So far, so good. But in
this matter, as in that of the police, those miserable Germans
made trouble at Algeciras. The Conference proposed a
State bank for Morocco ; and the question then arose who
should control it. The Germans said " equal control by all
the Powers," thus reducing France, as M. Tardieu indig-
nantly notes, to " the same rank as Sweden or the Netherlands."[3] Such a bank, he says, would be " not a financial
establishment, but a political instrument of war against the
influence and rights of France."[4] In opposition to this
monstrous idea, France, from the beginning, insisted that
she must command a majority on the board of control.[5] On
this question, as on other points, the Germans opposed the
French.[6] And it is interesting to note that the French
pursued the same policy as in the case of the police—that of
inventing what would look like concessions, but were not
really such, in order to retain in the end all the essentials of
their claim. Thus, at one point, they thought of adjourning
the whole question, so that the Conference should not deal
with it at all. This would look like a concession, for, after
all, the original idea of a State bank was French. " On the
other hand, while we should make the most of our merits in
renouncing the project, we were pretty sure not to lose anything by the renunciation." For a private bank, created by
the French, would serve the same purpose, and was not
likely to meet with serious competition. " It was an elegant
expedient which lessened the tension without compromising
our interests, and might, if it succeeded, avoid friction without
inflicting upon us any injury."[7] There were reasons, however, why this proposal was not, in fact, brought forward,
and it is here cited only to illustrate the mentality of the

[1] Tardieu, p. 31. [2] Morel, *Morocco*, p. 41. [3] Ib., p. 142.
[4] Ib., p. 186. [5] P. 235, etc. [6] P. 233, etc.
[7] Ib., p. 338-9.

French. The projects and counter-projects actually advanced
need not detain us. In general, in this matter as in that of
the police, France was sure of the support of the majority
of the Conference. Yet her position, M. Tardieu tells us, was
not quite so strong, and she had to make some concessions
to internationalism. That is comprehensible. For it was one
thing to hand over Morocco to France, another to make
commercial or financial sacrifices. The French were thus
driven, in the end, to admit international control of the bank.
But after all, as M. Tardieu remarks, the important point
was that France should have a majority in the Council of
administration. And this she secured. The Council was to
have fourteen members. France had one, as one of the Powers
concerned, and two as the "consortium" responsible for
the loan of 1904 ; she had also an assurance that the British,
Spanish, Portuguese, Russian, and Italian members would
vote with her. "If one notes further that the bank was
governed by French law, that the seat of the Council of
administration was at Paris, and that the rights of the French
shareholders over the whole of the receipts from the customs
were expressly reserved, one will conclude that, in this
matter as in that of the police, we had preserved the essential
interests which it was our business to defend, and that, of
the principles which directed our policy, we had abandoned
only so much as was needed by the new form given to the
discussion by the meeting of the Conference." [1] Parfait !
Further comment would be superfluous.

The conclusions of the Conference were embodied in what
is known as the General Act of the Conference of Algeciras,
dated April 7th, 1906.[2] We need not follow the matter
much farther. But one or two points may be noticed. The
Act opens as follows : " In the name of God Almighty ! (The
Signatories) inspired by the interest which attaches to the
reign of order, peace, and prosperity in Morocco, and having
recognised that this desirable end could only be attained by
means of the introduction of reforms based upon the three-
fold principle of the sovereignty and independence of His
Majesty the Sultan, the integrity of his Dominions, and
economic liberty without any inequality, have resolved,

[1] Ib., p. 454.
[2] The French text in Tardieu, App. 12 ; English in Morel, App. 12.

etc." The sovereignty and independence of His Majesty and the integrity of his Dominions ! Let the reader recall the terms of the secret treaties between France and England, and France and Spain, partitioning that same territory ; let him remember the previous suggestions for a partition between England and Germany ; let him recall the struggle at the Conference over the police, and the motives underlying that ; and let him then estimate the exact significance of that opening phrase : " In the name of God Almighty ! "

One other point is to be noticed in the Act. Its last article runs as follows : " All existing Treaties, Conventions, and Arrangements between the Signatory Powers and Morocco remain in force. It is, however, agreed that, in case their provisions be found to conflict with those of the present General Act, the stipulations of the latter shall prevail." Nominally, then, the secret treaties were set aside by the Act. Did the French, did the Spanish, admit that consequence ? The course of events will show.[1]

IX. The Menace of War

In spite, however, of all this, it may be urged that the Conference did, at least for the time being, avoid war. That is true. And war was very near.[2] It was a great thing to avoid it, even though it were only for the moment. The danger was fomented, as usual, by the Press of all the countries concerned. In England, *The Times* took the lead in this campaign. Lord Haldane described it as " past curing " (Unverbesserlich). He also described Mr. Maxse, of the *National Review*, as a " madman."[3] King Edward expressed regret for the incitements of the Press, which seemed to be bent on sowing mistrust between England, France, and Germany. He referred particularly to a recent article in the *Observer*.[4] The British public, as Count Bernstorff explained, were astoundingly ignorant of foreign affairs, and therefore entirely under the influence of the Press ; and having once formed their opinion in this way they " believe,

[1] See below, p. 186. Perhaps, however, treaties between the Powers *about* Morocco are not included ?

[2] See, e.g., Tardieu, pp. 214, 344, etc.

[3] Ger. Docs., xxi. p. 429 ; cf. xx. p. 614, where *The Times* is accused of spreading false news.

[4] Ib., xxi. p. 477.

with a kind of stupid obstinacy, what they are determined
to believe."[1] This is true, but perhaps not truer of the
English than of other peoples. The German Press was not
behind the British, and its effect was the more serious because
it was believed to be inspired by the Government. The
French, especially the *Temps*, and its brilliant correspondent,
M. Tardieu, were no less active;[2] M. Clemenceau admitted
the fact, but urged that in France the Press was free.[3]
Other Frenchmen informed the Germans that the French newspapers were bought by British gold, and Mr. Beit endorsed
the statement, adding that the same was true of Russia.[4]
In any case, the Russian Press was not behind that of other
countries. For years, Baron Greindl writes,[5] "there has been
a Press campaign with the object of throwing suspicion on
Germany and attributing to her all kinds of ambitious projects and occult interventions which are purely imaginary."
In the April of 1905 a German observer notes that the Press
campaign was lamentable and reminds him of that which
preceded the Franco-German War.[6] Four months later the
German Chancellor, referring to the extravagances of the
French Press, says that, if the Germans begin to reply in
the same style, a breach is probable.[7]

The Press of all countries thus kept simmering a risk of
war which was anyhow serious enough. In June 1905, Delcassé
is urging the French Government to send cruisers to Tangier
to counter the German move; Rouvier replies that that
would mean war; but Delcassé retorts: "Oh no, that is
all bluff."[8] In December 1905, Mr. Beit informed Rouvier
that, in Paris no less than in London, they were afraid of a near
outbreak of war.[9] The English, as we know, were prepared
to back France in a "defensive" war. But, as Count
Metternich pointed out, there was no definition of defence;
and "if the French should cross the German frontier to-morrow,
the next day everyone in England would say that they had
been compelled to do so by the challenge of Germany."[10]
Mr. Beit reported to the Kaiser that Sir John Fisher was eager

---

[1] Ger. Docs., xx. p. 610.   [2] Ib., xxi. p. 557.
[3] Ib., xx. p. 692; xxi. p. 584. For the freedom of the French Press,
see above, pp. 42 seq.   [4] Ib., xx. p. 692; xxi. p. 584.
[5] Belgian Despatches, ii. p. 127.   [6] Ger. Docs., xx. p. 330.
[7] Ib., p. 573.   [8] Ib., p. 407.
[9] Ib., p. 692.   [10] Ib., p. 674.

for a " preventive " war ; [1] and from all we know of him that is likely enough. Everything, it seems, was prepared for the catastrophe, which might have come then as easily as in 1914. The Conference did at least stave it off. But as it did nothing to remove the chronic causes, the result was mere postponement. The further history of the Moroccan question we will leave to a later chapter.

[1] Ger. Docs., xx. p. 694. Cf. below, p. 404.

CHAPTER VI

THE ANNEXATION OF BOSNIA

I. Previous History

WE pass now to the Balkan Peninsula. The importance in world-history of that tiny area is out of all proportion to its intrinsic interest. The perpetual quarrels of these barbarous little States, at feud with a barbarous Empire, are not an edifying subject of contemplation. But it so happens that this ulcer on the inflamed surface of Europe was the point to which the peccant humours of several Great Powers converged. These petty States were thus able to determine a great catastrophe; for, as a Russian statesman put it in 1913 : " Under present circumstances, by virtue of the network of alliances and ententes which exists, every separate manifestation of any Power in the field of Balkan affairs may bring about very rapidly a great European war." [1]

The inhabitants of the Balkan Peninsula were deposited there, in various strata, by the tribes that invaded Europe on the break-up of the Roman Empire. In Roumania only, as the name suggests, was there an earlier layer of people civilised by that Empire and afterwards overlaid by the newcomers ; a fact reflected in their Latin language and Latin sympathies. The earlier struggles, conquests, and defeats of these various populations need not detain us. We may observe, however, in passing, that there was a Bulgar " Empire," so-called, in the tenth and eleventh centuries, a Bulgar-Vlach Empire in the twelfth and thirteenth, and a Serb Empire in the fifteenth. For the memory of such facts, exploited by literature, helps to determine the policies of States, which are always ready to impart into the conditions of the present the achievements of an imperialism long past, and better to have been long forgotten.

Upon these populations impinged the Turks, and reduced

[1] Isvolski, January 1913, *Livre Noir*, ii. p. 20.

them all, except the Montenegrins, to subjection. In this condition they vegetated in a long obscurity. But the nineteenth century brought with it nationalism, and wars for " liberation "; and by the period with which we are concerned, Greece, Serbia, Bulgaria, and Roumania had obtained their freedom. But the little States thus established did not comprise within their boundaries all the populations which they claimed as belonging to their nationality. Macedonia remained Turkish ; and the bulk of the people of that province were said by Serbs to be Serbian, by Bulgarians to be Bulgarian, and by Greeks to be Greek. Further, and yet more important, there were populations of Serbs, Croats, Slovaks, Slovenes, and Roumanians included in the Austrian Empire. The virus of nationality had thus not completed its work, at the period with which we have to deal, and it seemed that it could not do so without at least three wars ; one, of the Balkan States against Turkey, another, of the same States against Austria, and a third, between those States themselves to determine the fate of Macedonia. All these wars were in due time produced. They were even, perhaps, what is called " inevitable," seeing that Empire had not, and has not, learnt to consider the welfare and wishes of populations, nor one population to respect the liberties and rights of another. What was not " inevitable " was the enlargement of an Austro-Serb war into one between the Great Powers. That was due to the general anarchy which we are analysing. Three of these Powers had, or thought they had, an interest in the Balkans : Russia, partly because she was a Slav nation, but more because she wanted the political control of the peninsula ; Austria-Hungary, because her population comprised Serbs, Croats, and Roumanians who could only be united with the free States of the same stock by breaking up her Empire, and also, because she desired the hegemony of at any rate the western portion of the Peninsula ; [1] and Italy, which, after becoming a " Great Power," desired to control the eastern coast of the Adriatic. The interest

---

[1] In 1900 the Austrian Minister, Count Goluchowski, summed up the Austrian position in the Near East as follows :

(1) She cannot allow any other Power to occupy Albania and close the Adriatic.

(2) She cannot allow the union of Serbia and Montenegro.

(3) She cannot allow the Russians to occupy Constantinople. (Ger. Docs., xviii. chap. cxvii. p. 99.)

of Great Britain was more indirect, being concerned, previously to the Anglo-Russian entente, with keeping Russia
out of the Mediterranean, and therefore out of the Balkans.
France was also interested in the Mediterranean, and therefore opposed, for the same reason, to Russia. The " balance
of power " motives of these latter Powers were, it will be
observed, of a different and less urgent kind than the Austrian
concern for the preservation of an Empire. Lastly, the
interest of Germany in the Balkans was determined, until
1890 or thereabouts, solely by her relation to Austria. Up
to that date she did not care who had Constantinople nor
who occupied the Peninsula. Bismarck's policy was one of
partition of the territory into spheres of influence, the eastern
for Russia, and the western for Austria. But to this he could
never get a firm assent from the two Powers concerned.

The first Balkan crisis which falls into our period was
that of 1908, caused by the Austrian annexation of Bosnia
and Herzegovina. But to explain that we must recur to
the Russo-Turkish War of 1877 and the Treaty of Berlin.
When Russia was drifting into war, under the double pressure
of the Pan-Slavist agitation and the Bulgarian atrocities, she
made a treaty with Austria to keep her quiet. This, the
Treaty of Reichstadt, signed in January 1877, gave Austria
permission to annex the Turkish provinces of Bosnia and
Herzegovina. Later, by a treaty with the Turks, of July
1878, she accepted " occupation " instead of " annexation,"
and this was the arrangement sanctioned by the Treaty of
Berlin, which said that the provinces should be " occupied
and administered " by Austria. No one doubted that this
was equivalent, for practical purposes, to annexation. The
Austrians certainly took that view. Still it did not follow that
it was " honesty " to have it " thus set down " ; and set
down it actually was in the League of the three Emperors
(of Russia, Austria, and Germany), 1881-7. " Austria-
Hungary," says a protocol of that Act, "reserves the right to
annex these provinces at whatever moment she shall deem
opportune." The reader is asked to observe once more
this interesting word " right." [1]

[1] Nekludoff (p. 20) adds, that the annexation was further sanctioned by
Russia (1) in 1879, at a select and secret session of the Congress of Berlin,
(2) in 1897, on the occasion of the Emperor Francis Joseph's visit to St. Petersburg, (3) at Mürzsteg. I have not been able to verify these statements one
way or the other.

Not all the Powers, however, were satisfied with this occupation. Crispi, in particular, objected, in the interest of the Italians. Bismarck thereupon obligingly said, " take Albania." [1] Lord Derby made the same suggestion. [2] " I expressed," says Crispi, " the opinion of the Italian Government to Derby and Bismarck, who both replied, " prenez l'Albanie," with a simultaneousness which struck me as astonishing. I naturally demanded : " Qu'est que nous devons en faire ? " Whereupon Derby said : " C'est toujours un gage," and Bismarck added : " Si l'Albanie ne vous plait pas prenez une autre terre turque sur l'Adriatique." [3] It was thus that the Great Powers interpreted their solemn and repeated pledges to maintain the territorial integrity of the Turkish Empire. But Crispi, unfortunately, did not want Albania, and continued to object to Austria having Bosnia.

The Serbs, naturally, were equally opposed to this particular piece of theft, because the population concerned was largely Croat ; and the Serbian statesman Mijatovich tells us that " Johann Ristich, the only representative of Serbia at the Berlin Congress, told me on his return that when, heart-broken, he went to Count Schuvaloff and asked him how he could sacrifice Bosnia and Herzegovina to Austrian occupation, the Count answered : ' Don't be alarmed. Have patience. In ten years' time we will have a great war, and all this will be changed.' " [4] The " great war " took more than ten years to come, but otherwise the prophecy was sound.

Meantime, the Austrians found themselves involved in a rather considerable war before they could subdue and pacify their prize. But they finally succeeded and produced, it would appear, that kind of improvement in general conditions which the British produced in Egypt. What they did not, apparently, achieve, any more than we in the other case, was the good will of the population. That is the drawback of all imperialism, even the most successful and benevolent. Meantime, events moved on. In 1885 the then Bulgaria united to itself Eastern Rumelia. This was contrary to the

---

[1] Crispi, ii. pp. 31.   [2] Ib., p. 73.
[3] Ib., iii. p. 279. According to Professor Salvemini, Lord Salisbury again, in 1895, offered to Italy Tripoli and Albania, to soothe her, because the British would not let her land troops at Zeilah in the Abyssinian War (*Cronaca di Genova*, November 8th, 1920).
[4] Mijatovich, p. 228.

Treaty of Berlin. It was, however, provided for by the League of the Three Emperors, formed after the date of that treaty. "The three Powers," says Article 4, "will not oppose the eventual reunion of Bulgaria and Eastern Rumelia within the territorial limits assigned to them by the Treaty of Berlin, if this question should come up by force of circumstances." In spite, however, of this clause, it was two Powers of that same League, Austria and Russia, who did in fact object, while England and France acquiesced without protest ; [1] a further proof that it depends upon the particular situation of Europe, and of this or that State or States, whether a breach of treaty will be objected to, and by whom. The objection of Austria turned, presumably, on the fear that a big Bulgaria would be under Russian influence. She therefore supported Serbia in her attack on the new State, and saved her from the consequences of defeat. But Russia also objected to the big Bulgaria, because it had been achieved without her help, and because it showed no intention of being subservient. This question, in itself so insignificant, kept Europe for some years in a state of crisis. Bismarck had to work hard to keep Austria from war with Russia ; and the usual Anglo-Russian hostility was further increased by friction in the east. Still, the crisis passed by without actual war.

In 1893 there was a Bulgarian insurrection in Macedonia, accompanied by the usual massacres. Bulgarian policy seems to have been to promote such occurrences in order to keep the Macedonian question before Europe. In this they were successful ; for at last, in 1903, by what is known as the agreement of Mürzsteg, the policing of the provinces was handed over to the joint control of Austria and Russia,

---

[1] The Serbs at first took their ground on the breach of treaty. Then Mijatovich, recognising that public opinion in England approved of the Bulgarian annexation of Rumelia, and finding that the signatory Powers would not defend the sanctity of treaties, shifted his position to the " balance of power " and claimed " territorial compensation " for Serbia. At one time, the Serbs thought of taking this compensation not out of Bulgaria, but out of Turkey, by invading the vilayet of Kossovo. Later, King Milan told Mijatovich that the real object of the war was neither the balance of power nor compensation (still less, of course, the breach of treaty), but " to provoke war between Russia and Austria. My uncle George here present can confirm what I say to you now, and what I confided to him on the eve of the war." Uncle George did confirm it. " He enlarged upon the fact, thought that the King's idea was one of political genius, and that it was a misfortune, not only for the Balkan nations, but for the whole of Europe, that it had not succeeded." A typical piece of diplomatic history ! See Mijatovich, p. 47.

the maintenance of the status quo in the Balkans being, at this time, the policy of both those States. Thus events went rumbling on, largely underground, until a dramatic stroke startled the world. The Serbian king, Alexander, was murdered, in a singularly brutal manner. The murder in itself, being but one example of the most common feature of Balkan politics, need not have been significant. But in fact it was. For the murdered king had belonged to the Obrenovich family, and that family, for many years, had been under the influence and protection of Austria. His successor, Peter, who profited by the murder and was perhaps privy to it, was a Karageorgevich. His accession accelerated a drift, which had already begun, away from Austria and towards Russia ; [1] and it is possible that Russian diplomacy was accessory to the murder.[2] Acts so crude are reprobated by Foreign Offices and Courts ; but those institutions have agents in remoter places who are less respectable than their employers. A Serbian writer, in a position to be well informed, reports further that the assassination was supported by an Austrian agent ; for that, already, the Austrian Government was at feud with King Alexander and expected subservience from King Peter.[3] If that be the case, disillusionment followed. For the new monarch turned to Russia, and from his accession may be definitely dated [4] that anti-Austrian policy of Serbia which was the immediate cause of the Great War.

The friction between the two States was increased, in 1906, by the war of tariffs known as the " pig war." [5] The Anglo-

---

[1] Russian regard for Serbia was of much later date than is often supposed. E.g. in 1887 we find a Russian Minister speaking of " cette petite sale cochonne de Serbie " (Ger. Docs., v. p. 213).

[2] Eckardstein, i. p. 257. [3] Bogitshevich, pp. 12 seq.

[4] Cf. Mijatovich, p. 232.

[5] This is a good example of the way in which a trade war may constitute one cause of a military war. The effects on the trade relations of the two States is indicated by the following figures :

Austrian imports to Serbia, in percentage of total Serbian imports :

1905	..	..	..	..	..	..	60 %
1906	..	..	..	..	..	..	50 %
1907	..	..	..	..	..	..	36 %

Serbian exports to Austria, in percentage of total Serbian exports :

1905	..	..	..	..	..	..	90 %
1906	..	..	..	..	..	..	42 %
1907	..	..	..	..	..	..	16 %

See an article by Baernreither, " Unsere Handelsbeziehungen zu Serbia," in the *Oesterreichische Rundschau*, October 1911, xxix. p. 9.

Russian entente still further encouraged Serbia in her new course ; and her hostility to Austria was raised to fury by the latter's annexation of Bosnia in 1908.

II. The Balkan Treaties

Before dealing with the effects of this dynastic change on the policy and relations of the greater European Powers, it will be convenient to pause and consider the treaties which regulated, at this time, the relations of some of these Powers with the Balkan States.

In the year 1881, Austria-Hungary and Serbia had entered into a treaty embodying the following points : [1]

First, Serbia recognised the inclusion in the Austrian monarchy of Bosnia, Herzegovina and Novibazar, and promised not to tolerate religious or other intrigues directed against that monarchy. Austria assumed the same obligation towards Serbia.

Secondly, Austria promised to maintain and strengthen the Obrenovich dynasty with all her influence, and to recognise for it the title of king, if the head of the Serbian State should choose to assume it.

Thirdly, Austria-Hungary promised to use her influence with the other European cabinets to second the interests of Serbia ; while Serbia agreed that " without a previous understanding with Austria-Hungary " she " will neither negotiate nor conclude any political treaty with another Government and will not admit to her territory a foreign armed force, regular or irregular, even as volunteers." [2]

Lastly, Austria promised not to oppose territorial acquisitions by Serbia in the south (with the exception of the Sanjak of Novibazar), and to use her influence with the other Powers to win them over to an attitude favourable to such acquisitions.

It is clear that, by this treaty, the relations of the two States became as close as they could well be made, however surprising that fact may be to those who remember only the events immediately preceding the Great War. The treaty

[1] See Pribram, i. p. 51; also Mijatovich, ch. 3.
[2] For explanation, or rather modification, of this article, see Pribram, i. p. 61.

was concluded originally for ten years. But it was prolonged, in 1889, till 1895, with certain modifications. Of these the most interesting are the following : [1]

First, Austria-Hungary declares that she "will take all measures to prevent by every means and even by armed force every hostile excursion which might be directed from Montenegro against Serbia and her royal dynasty through the territory placed under the administration of the Imperial and Royal authorities," that is, through the Sanjak of Novibazar. Austria will also exercise her good offices with the Porte, to induce that Government to adopt a similar attitude.

Secondly, Austria-Hungary will recognise and support with other Powers the territorial extension contemplated in the original treaty ; "which extension may be carried in the direction of the valley of the Vardar as far as the circumstances will permit."

It is evident, from these two treaties, that so far from Austria being the enemy of Serbia during these years, she was her protector and friend, and even a champion of her territorial extension. So rapid are the changes which the relations of States undergo, and so rotten the foundations on which their friendships or enmities rest. A change of dynasty, a tariff war, were enough, as we have seen, to destroy the whole of this edifice and to convert Serbia into the bitterest foe of the Dual Monarchy.

So much for Austria and Serbia. We come now to Austria and Roumania. By a treaty concluded in 1883 [2] these two States agreed as follows :

"If Roumania, without any provocation on her part, should be attacked, Austria-Hungary is bound to bring her, in ample time, help and assistance against the aggressor. If Austria-Hungary be attacked, under the same circumstances, in a portion of her States bordering on Roumania, the casus fœderis will immediately arise for the latter."

This treaty was directed against Russia, which was definitely mentioned in the first draft. The mention was omitted in deference to a criticism of Bismarck, who wrote: "It would be better if Russia were not specially named, for fear an indiscretion on the part of Roumania (which Count Kálnoky too holds to be possible) should give new material

[1] Pribram, i. p. 135. [2] Ib., p. 78.

to the jingoes in Russia." [1] It may be noticed, in passing, that Bismarck also objected to the inclusion of the word " security " as one of the objects of the treaty, on the ground that " security is a very elastic idea which, under given circumstances, might justify an aggressive war." [2] The same criticism, it may be added, applies to the word " attack," which occurs in the clause cited.

By this treaty, then, each party agrees to defend the other against Russia. And, no doubt, Roumania's readiness to enter into it was due to the treatment she had received in the Treaty of Berlin, which had rewarded her for procuring victory for Russia in the Turkish War, by appropriating to that empire part of the Roumanian province of Bessarabia.[3] The treaty was negotiated under the auspices of Bismarck ; Germany acceded to it in 1883, and Italy in 1888.[4] Thus, although by the Triple Alliance Italy was not pledged to assist Austria against attack by Russia alone, by this treaty she was so pledged, if the attack should take place " in a portion of (Austria's) States bordering on Roumania." In entering into this obligation she must have been influenced by her fear of Russian aggression in the Balkans, and of its possible consequences in the Adriatic.

This Roumanian treaty, of course, was secret, like all the others; and it is interesting to note that, in March 1914, Count Czernin, then the Austrian representative in Budapest, being anxious about the relations between that Empire and Roumania, suggested that the publication of the treaty might clear matters up. The treaty, he said, was known to no one in that country, except the King, Bratianu and Maiorescu ; and the Roumanian representatives abroad were pursuing in Macedonia a policy favourable to the Entente. He suggests that by a " fortunate accident " the existence of the treaty should be made public ; and that the denial by Roumania (which must, of course, follow) should be so conceived as to be, in effect, an admission not a denial. The result would be, he thought, to clear up the relations between the two countries; for either the King would override the opposition of public opinion or he would definitely succumb to it. In either case the Austrian Government would

---

[1] Ger. Docs., iii. p. 273.
[2] Ib.
[3] See above, p. 10.
[4] Pribram, i. pp. 83, 85.

know where it stood. The little episode seems worth citing as a further illustration of the ways of diplomacy.[1] It may be added that, according to the Bulgarian statesman Guéchoff, a further treaty was entered into between Austria and Roumania in 1900, whereby Austria recognised the claims of Roumania on Silistria and a part of Bessarabia.[2] The original treaty was renewed in 1892, 1896, 1902, and 1913. It was thus in force when the Great War broke out. But Roumania repudiated it, and joined the party against whom she had made the treaty. This, no doubt, may and will be defended, on the ground that it was not Russia that "attacked" Austria, but Austria that "attacked" Russia. For since the term "attack" has no clear meaning, all treaties involving that word are ambiguous, and any interpretation defensible.

The two treaties just referred to contemplated war between Russia and Austria. Nevertheless, in 1897, these two States entered into an agreement "based on a principle of reciprocal confidence and loyalty" providing for the maintenance of the status quo in the Balkans and discarding all idea of conquest there. Austria-Hungary proposed further, in case the status quo should become impossible, that Albania should be independent, and the rest of the territory to be disposed of (i.e. Macedonia) divided between the existing Balkan States. To these latter arrangements, however, Russia declined to assent, inasmuch as they "touch upon questions of the future" which it would be very difficult to decide at present."[3] This agreement, taken in connexion with the others, gives a position with which we are now sufficiently familiar in other examples; namely, the status quo, so long as it is convenient to maintain it; and, when it ceases to be convenient, such and such changes. The situation contemplated did in fact occur in the Balkan War of 1912–13; and the two Powers concerned did, at that time, abstain from appropriating Balkan territory and consented to the division of the spoils among the Balkan States; though not until friction between them had nearly produced the European War. Of these events we shall have to speak later. Meantime, a later treaty of 1904 confirmed that of 1897:

---

[1] Conrad, iii. ; Anlage, x. p. 788. [2] Guéchoff, p. 61 See below, p. 309.
[3] Pribram, i. p. 185.

" Austria-Hungary and Russia, united by identical views as to the conservative policy to be followed in the Balkan countries, and much satisfied with the results obtained so far by their close collaboration, are firmly decided to persevere in this course." [1]

This treaty, it will be observed, dates from the year after that Mürzsteg agreement [2] by which the policing of Macedonia was handed over to the two States in question. No particular good seems to have happened to Macedonia in consequence ; but the co-operation of Russia and Austria was, for the time being, assured.

These agreements with Austria are to be accounted for mainly by the fact that Russia was withdrawing from active politics in the Balkans because she was occupied with her adventure in the Far East. This phase ended with her defeat by Japan in 1905, and thereafter she turned back to the south-west. The saying attributed to a Russian states-man is thus a fair rendering of the truth : " So long as Russia was occupied in the Far East, the Balkans were put under a glass bell, so that no changes should be accomplished there before Russia could return to an active policy in the Orient." [3]

Meantime, in 1902, a military convention had been entered into between Russia and Bulgaria.[4] This convention, apparently, remained in force until the Great War. At any rate the Russian Minister, Sazonoff, writes of it as still in force in 1913, and says that it has " so far benefited us exclusively, as Bulgaria was bound by its stipulations. We are asked to do nothing more than for political and economic reasons we should have been unable to refuse, even if no such treaty had existed." [5]

By this convention [6] the obligations of Bulgaria to Russia are, that she must give military aid " in case of a simulta-neous armed conflict with Germany, Austria-Hungary, and Roumania, or with Austria-Hungary and Roumania ; and

---

[1] Pribram, i. p. 237. [2] See above, p. 159.
[3] Cited by Reventlow, p. 347, ed. 1918.
[4] This is the date given by Guéchoff, p. 61, by Siebert, p. 315, by Nekludoff, p. 75, and by Georges Louis, in Judet, p. 209. Bogitshevich, on the other hand, who gives the text, dates it 1909. Conrad also gives 1909 (i. p. 205). Possibly there were two conventions ?
[5] Siebert, p. 315. But cf. Georges Louis in Judet, p. 209.
[6] Text in Bogitshevich, p. 89, and, in part, in Conrad, i. 205. Bogit-shevich omits the concluding sentence of Article I, as given by Conrad.

likewise in case of an armed conflict of Russia with Turkey, regardless of who has taken the initiative in the conflict." This clause is unusually frank. It makes no pretence that the casus fœderis arises only in case of " aggression " or " attack " or whatever the phrase may be, by the enemy. On the contrary, it clearly contemplates that the initiative may be taken by Russia, and binds Bulgaria, even in such a case, to assist her. On the other hand, Bulgaria is not required to take action in case of war between Russia and Roumania alone. But, as we have seen, by the treaty of the Powers of the Triple Alliance with Roumania, that contingency could not in fact occur, unless, by any chance, those Powers should decide that Roumania had been the aggressor.

What the position amounts to then is, that war between Roumania and Russia would immediately bring in, on the one side, the other Powers of the Triple Alliance, on the other side, Bulgaria. But also, by the Franco-Russian alliance, it would bring in France, unless France chose to say that it was Russia who had been responsible for the " attack." Nothing could illustrate more clearly the weight thrown on the undefined and indefinable word " attack," or the precarious uncertainties on which the peace of Europe was thus made to hang.

When we turn from the obligations laid on Bulgaria in this convention to those assumed by Russia, we find brutal frankness replaced by the usual ambiguities. Thus : " If Austria-Hungary, in combination with any other Power, should attack Bulgaria without provocation on the part of the latter, Russia agrees to provide Bulgaria with active armed support." And again, if Turkey should attack Bulgaria " without provocation by the latter," Russia will take such and such military measures. Here are all the familiar phrases, on which we need not comment further, though it would be rather interesting to know why Bulgaria consented to be tied, in words, more tightly than Russia.

We come next to another interesting clause :

" In case of a favourable outcome of the armed conflict with Austria-Hungary and with Roumania, or with Germany, Austria-Hungary, and Roumania, Russia promises to support Bulgaria in expanding her territory in the district peopled with Bulgarians between the Black Sea and the right bank of the Lower Danube, and in her other frontiers," that is, presumably, in the Dobrudja and in Macedonia.[1]

But the most revealing article is the fifth, which says :

" In view of the fact that the realisation of the high ideals of the Slavic peoples upon the Balkan Peninsula, so near to Russia's heart, is possible only after a favourable outcome of Russia's struggle with Germany and Austria-Hungary, Bulgaria accepts the holy obligation, both in the event mentioned and also in the event of the accession of Roumania or of Turkey to the coalition of the above-named Powers, to make the utmost exertions to avert provocation to the further expansion of the conflict." We have here a quite definite statement by Russia that she regards war with Austria and Germany as certain, and as a necessary condition of the fulfilment of the ambitions of the Balkan Slavs. It is a clear indication, in a formal treaty, of the expected and intended imminence of the Great War ; and it is from Russia, not from Germany, that the indication comes.

Finally, it appears that in 1908 Austria-Hungary approached Bulgaria, promising her Macedonia and holding out the hope of a partition of Serbia. But this offer Bulgaria rejected.[2]

Taking these treaties as a whole, we get the following results :

1. The status quo in the Balkans is to be preserved so long as it is convenient to the various parties to preserve it.

2. Everybody is expecting and desiring its alteration, when the time shall be ripe.

3. For this purpose the spoils have already been divided. Austria first promised them to Serbia, and later offered them to Bulgaria, with a piece for Roumania. Russia assigned them to Bulgaria.

4. The other Great Powers concerned are taking their positions, with a view to the expected war.

5. Austria and Russia are bound, at the same time, *both*

---

[1] In 1912 we find the Bulgarian Minister, Daneff, endeavouring to persuade Russia to include Adrianople in the Bulgarian sphere (Siebert, p. 344).

[2] Siebert, p. 345. This statement is given on the authority of the Bulgarian Minister, Daneff. Mijatovich, too, expresses a strong suspicion that a treaty was actually concluded (Mijatovich, pp. 240–4; cf. Friedjung, ii. p. 241). That Bulgaria was in fact, during the crises of 1908, working with Austria rather than with Russia, seems clear from the dispatches in *Is Germany Guilty ?*, ii. pp. 30, 34, 36, 39.

by treaties of peace and common action, *and* by treaties contemplating war between them.

6. Russia has frankly stated that only by war with the Central Powers can she and her Balkan friends obtain their objects.

We may add that in the January of 1907, Aehrenthal reported to the German Ambassador in Vienna [1] that he has reason to suppose that England, France, and Italy are working against Germany and Austria ; and that, in that view, they are endeavouring to bring about a rapprochement between Serbia and Bulgaria,[2] and to arouse feeling against Austria in Albania. The aim, of course, would be to weaken Germany.

Such is the actual picture, about the year 1908, of that peaceful Europe, in which, according to the war-time myth, the one disturbing factor was Germany.

III.   The Annexation

We will now turn to the crisis of 1908. In the year 1906, Count Aehrenthal became Foreign Minister of Austria-Hungary. He appears to have been a man of confident temperament, who believed not only in the continued existence of the monarchy, but in the possibility of " breathing new life " into it. He was an adherent of an understanding with Bulgaria, as an offset against Serbia, now, as we have seen, hostile to Austria ; and his views on the whole subject of the Balkans are worth quoting in his own words : " The antagonism between Bulgaria and Serbia is already a factor with which we can reckon. In Bulgaria, the conviction prevails that the road to Macedonia must pass over the body of the Serbian State, and it is certain that a violent struggle for the possession of Uskub must break out between Serbia and Bulgaria. If, in this conflict, we support the Bulgarian cause and favour the creation of a great Bulgaria at the cost of Serbia, the necessary preparation will have been made for laying our hand upon the rest of Serbia at a favourable moment of the European constellation. We should then have the secure frontiers of which I have spoken : an

---

[1] Ger. Docs., xxi. p. 388.
[2] Cf. *Is Germany Guilty ?*, ii. p. 34, Annex 6, App. 5, where Milovanovich reports Isvolski as saying : " Russia and England are endeavouring to alienate Bulgaria from Austria-Hungary."

Albania become independent under our protection, a Montenegro with whom we should be in friendly relations, and a
great Bulgaria bound to us by gratitude." [1] It is curious
to find an Austrian statesman relying on the great Bulgaria,
just as Russia had relied upon it thirty years earlier, and
imagining that gratitude is a quality to build upon when the
relations of States are involved.

It will be observed that, in this memorandum, Aehrenthal
contemplates the division of Serbia between Austria-Hungary
and Bulgaria. That this was his ultimate aim seems clear.[2]
As to the status quo, he remarks : " We respect it only so
far and so long as it suits us " ; [3] thus stating frankly what
was the real attitude of all the statesmen and all the countries
concerned. He found, however, on reflexion, that the present
moment would not be a good one to carry out the Serbian
partition ; a decision which much distressed Conrad, the more
thoroughgoing Chief of the General Staff.

On the other hand, the annexation of Bosnia was decided
upon, in principle, even before the Turkish revolution. The
reason was, apparently, the agitation carried on there against
the monarchy, and supported by the Serbs of the independent
kingdom.[4] But the Turkish revolution brought things to a
crisis ; [5] for the Young Turks seemed likely to reassert
Turkish authority in the provinces, a possibility which was
made acute by the proposal that Bosnia should send delegates
to the new Turkish Parliament. Aehrenthal, accordingly,
determined to act quickly,[6] and in October he announced the
annexation. But before doing this he had endeavoured to
prepare the way with the Powers most immediately interested.
Of these, the most important was Russia. Since 1897, as we
have seen, the Tsardom had been bound by treaty with Austria
to maintain the status quo in the Balkans. In the negotiation of that agreement Austria had proposed that her
" right " to the annexation should be recognised ; but Russia

---

[1] Cited Friedjung, ii. p. 241, Mem. of August 9th, 1908. Cf. Conrad, i.
p. 107.
[2] Cf. Conrad, i. p. 528, and also Brandenburg, p. 283.
[3] Ib., p. 574.
[4] Conrad, i. pp. 91, 511; cf. Brandenburg, p. 263.
[5] Conrad, i. p. 628.
[6] There is evidence that he was also influenced by the internal condition
of Austria-Hungary, and the desire to do something which would strengthen
his position (Brandenburg, p. 287).

had prudently replied that " the annexation of these two provinces would raise a more extensive question, which would require proper scrutiny at the proper time and place." [1] The proper time and place had now arrived, or so the Austrian Minister thought. On the other hand, Isvolski, now Foreign Minister of Russia, thought that the time had come to realise the " historic mission " of his country in the Near East and, in the first place, to achieve the opening of the Straits, the closure of which had been affirmed in the Austro-Russian Agreement of 1897.[2] Why not do a deal and get Austria to concede the opening, in return for Russian recognition of the annexation of Bosnia ? Isvolski made a proposition in this sense, in a memorandum of July 2nd, 1908.[3] Finally an agreement was reached between the two statesmen, at Buchlau, on September 16th, 1908. No text of the agreement has been published, and perhaps it was only verbal. At any rate, it gave rise, later, to violent controversy. It seems that Aehrenthal announced his intention to annex Bosnia, and his willingness that Isvolski should proceed to the opening of the Straits,[4] one ship only to pass at a time, and Constantinople not to be seized. After the event, in Aehrenthal's view, an international conference was to be summoned to give effect to both these actions.[5] Isvolski, on the other hand, according to his own account, had always said that both changes were contrary to public law, and had understood that the consent of the Powers was to be obtained beforehand, not afterwards. He also said that the date of the annexation was not fixed at Buchlau. He admits, indeed, that Aehrenthal had informed him of the date, by a letter which he received on October 2nd, in Paris ; but he

[1] Pribram, i. p. 293.

[2] See Pribram, i. p. 185 ; and *Drei Conferenzen*, Anlage, i.

[3] In this Memorandum, according to Friedjung (ii. p. 220), Isvolski accepted both the annexation of the provinces and that of the northern part of the Sanjak. But Conrad (ib., p. 107) seems to say that only the Sanjak was conceded, and in exchange for that concession Constantinople and the Straits were to be conceded by Austria.

[4] On this v. Schoen says : " I know from having been his colleague at Constantinople what M. Isvolski thought as to this. His idea was that the Straits should be open to Russian warships, but not to the ships of other nations. Thus the fortified Straits were to be a sally-point for Russia and barricaded to the others. The Turkish fortresses were to be of service to Russia, and if possible with the help of German material and German backing " (p. 82). Cf. Grey, i. p. 180.

[5] Friedjung, ii. p. 228.

complains that, by that time, the project had been already made known to the French Government, which had also been informed that Russia gave her consent.

That Isvolski was dissatisfied with the Austrian attitude, shortly after the Buchlau interview, is clear from v. Schoen's account of an interview with him : " M. Isvolski," he says, " seemed far from satisfied with the convention of Buchlau. He spoke in a tone of irritation of Aerenthal's adventurous scheme, which he put down to personal ambition. He pointed to the necessity for solving the question they raised at a conference, if not a congress, and hinted that, if we stood by our ally, he would be obliged to lean more on the Western Powers than he wished." [1]

On the other hand, it is affirmed that the annexation had been agreed to again and again by Russia. We have seen that this was, in fact, the case in the League of the three Emperors (1881--7), and the permission is said to have been repeated as late as July 2, 1908.[2]

The controversy between these two statesmen is not of great interest, except for the further light it throws upon the character of diplomats. Aehrenthal may have lied. Isvolski certainly did. For we find him saying, on October 5th, to a Serbian Minister, that he had made Russia's acceptance of the annexation of Bosnia conditional upon the evacuation of the Sanjak ; and on October 13th, stating to another Serbian that he had never consented to the annexation at all.[3] This duplicity is so common that we need only observe it in passing. It is more useful to excerpt two passages which occur in the course of the recriminations. The first deals with the Press, and runs as follows :

" The French Press, which received 1,400,000 francs for its friendly attitude towards each of the last two Russian loans, had had neither a refresher nor a retaining fee in this case of Austria versus Russia ; consequently it went over to the enemy, on the principle " whose bread I eat his song

---

[1] Schoen, p. 81.
[2] Friedjung, ii. p. 220. The controversy between the two statesmen is summed up in two articles which appeared in the *Fortnightly Review* of September and November 1909. These are signed respectively : " Vox et præterea nihil," and " Audi alteram partem," and are attributed respectively to Isvolski and Dillon.
[3] Bogitshevich, pp. 113, 117.

I sing." [1] The other deals with the consequences of the embroilment : " Every trumpery little question may now be magnified into an international issue, because the two Empires, whose unanimity and desire of peace formerly reduced the number of dangerous disputes, are now themselves, at loggerheads with each other." [2]

The announcement of the annexation produced an enormous reverberation in Europe. The Serbs were furious ; for it seemed to deprive them definitely of their hope of one day uniting with themselves the Croat population of Bosnia, and of that access to the Adriatic which they had long, and not unreasonably, desired. Protests and demonstrations were organised. " Down with Austria " and " Long live Serbian Bosnia " resounded through the land. The windows of the Austrian Embassy were smashed and an Austrian flag burnt. A " holy war " was preached, and in the Assembly a minority of 66 to 93 actually went as far as to vote for war.[3] The arguments (if such they are to be called) were of the usual kind. It was a matter of " life and death." " The existence of the Serbian State was endangered." [4] For by now the Serbia which had lived in close alliance with Austria from 1881 to 1893 could not live at all unless it broke up the Austrian Empire. How violent the feeling was may be illustrated by an article which appeared in a Serbian newspaper, announcing the imminent annexation, and calling for " immediate mobilisation and war to life and death against the monarchy," with the interesting addition that " only in that case will other Powers support Serbia." [5] Even as early as March, another newspaper had written, à propos of the proposed Austrian railway through the Sanjak : " War to annihilation must be declared against Austria-Hungary. Either we must make of Serbia a huge cemetery, or we must create greater Serbia." [6] The Serbian statesman Milovanovich reports Protich as saying : " Between us and Austria-Hungary there can only be peace and good neighbourhood if Austria renounces her position as a Great Power, if she makes up her mind to assume the rôle of an

---

[1] *Fortnightly Review*, September 1909, p. 401.
[2] Ib.   [3] Friedjung, ii. pp. 181-2.
[4] *Is Germany Guilty ?*, ii. p. 32.   [5] Conrad, i. p. 113.
[6] Ib., p. 134. I have not thought it necessary to discuss this project of the railway, which came to nothing. See Brandenburg, p. 264.

eastern Switzerland." The issue could not be better put. And British imperialism, at any rate, should be able to understand what really lay between Austria-Hungary and Serbia.

In Austria-Hungary, on the other hand, both Croats and Slovenes welcomed the annexation, for it seemed to bring them nearer to a union of the Slavs of the monarchy in an autonomous State. Even the Czech leader Kramarz supported it. Had not Austria, he said, for thirty years fulfilled a " civilising mission " in Bosnia ? But Kramarz had been warned by Russia not to oppose the annexation, because she was not in a position at present to take up the cause of the Slavs ; [1] and he changed his tone when Russia changed hers.

While thus the Slavs of Austria approved the annexation, other parties went still further and shouted for war with Serbia. The usual fever which, in a crisis long prepared behind the scenes, sweeps away into primitive passion the ignorant and deceived masses, was raging now throughout the monarchy. At the top, influential people, like Conrad, who was always urging war against somebody or other, were pressing for a military decision. To this, however, the Archduke Francis Ferdinand seems to have been opposed. At any rate, he told the Bulgarian Minister, Daneff, that, " when the Bosnian crisis was at its acutest and everything was ready for war against Serbia, I was almost the only man who vetoed military action." [2] Both States made military preparations, and these, as always, increased the danger of the situation. Thus the Russian Minister in Belgrade writes to Isvolski on March 17th : " The situation is becoming acuter. The news which reaches here of increased military preparations by Austria may compel Serbia to similar measures. These would be regarded by Austria as provocation." We get in this passage one meaning, at any rate, of that word " provocation," which appears so frequently in the treaties.[3]

Turkey, naturally enough, was also indignant ; for, after all, it was her province (nominally) that had been annexed. She did not, however, threaten war, but adopted that weapon of the commercial boycott which seems to be peculiarly

[1] Friedjung, ii. pp. 235–6.
[2] Ib., p. 269 note. Friedjung explains that the Archduke thought Italy, not Russia, the real enemy.
[3] Siebert, p. 256. For the military tension, see aso Conrad, i. pp. 116, 125, etc.

suited to Orientals. Austrian trade suffered severely, and Austria in the end had to settle the matter by paying a money compensation.

IV. The Policies of the Powers

Our main interest, however, is not in the actions and reactions of the States immediately concerned, but in the effects produced on the policies of the Great Powers. We have already seen how Austria and Russia were entangled with the Balkan States, and how, through the system of alliances, the other Powers were liable to be drawn in. We will now proceed to indicate the policy of these States during the crisis. And, first, we will consider Germany.

Her position was now very different from what it had been in the time of Bismarck. For the Bagdad railway was in course of construction, and she had become the most influential power in Constantinople. She was, therefore, no longer indifferent, so far as her own interests were concerned, to the fate of the Balkans and of Turkey. On the contrary, it was essential to her to keep open the overland route to the East and to prevent the extension in the Balkans of Russian influence. She had therefore an interest of her own in the crisis provoked by Austria-Hungary, as well as the interest of supporting her ally. But the attitude of German statesmen seems to have been far from unanimous. Von Schoen, who was told by Aehrenthal of his intentions a month before the event, expressed some anxiety and doubt about the probable result.[1] It would seem almost certain that he must have communicated the news to his superiors. But we are assured that the Kaiser, at any rate, heard of the annexation for the first time on the day on which it was made public (October 5th).[2] He was much disturbed, described it as a piece of brigandage, and said that it might be the signal for the break-up of Turkey, and the loss of all the influence built up there by Germany in the last twenty years. Marschall v. Biberstein supported him in this view. But v. Bülow, the Chancellor, did not. It seems incredible that he should not have known what had been communicated a month before to v. Schoen. But he speaks as though he

[1] Schoen, p. 77. [2] Brandenburg, p. 274.

had only just received the news. Anyhow, Austria, he thought, must be supported now that she had acted, otherwise Germany would lose her only ally. The Kaiser assented, though very reluctantly. England, he said, would inscribe on her banners the defence of treaties, and Edward VII secure a great triumph. But these considerations did not alter the mind of the Chancellor. He believed, and rightly, as it turned out, that the crisis would end without war ; and he determined to support Austria without any reserve. In the words of v. Schoen, he " was not averse to letting things take their course to a climax and to a trial of strength between the Central Powers bloc and the Triple Entente, which was not yet firmly established, as he was convinced that none of the Powers would draw the sword, and that, when it came to a question of bending or breaking, Russia would climb down from her high horse and would also call her vassal Serbia to order." [1] That, in fact, is what happened on this occasion. It is also what did not happen in 1914. Now, as then, the Germans were playing with fire.

We will turn now to England. Her policy is regarded, as usual, by Continental writers, with much suspicion, but in fact it seems to have been simple enough. In the first place, the one-sided repudiation of a European treaty has usually seemed to the British not to be the way to play the game. A well-known example is our protest against the Russian repudiation of the Treaty of Paris, in 1870. True, we take this action only when it otherwise suits our policy. We did not, for instance, object to the repudiation of the Treaty of Berlin by Bulgaria, when she united with Eastern Rumelia in 1885. Still, it is true that the British have cared more about the formal sanctity of treaties than some other Powers. But further, in this case, we objected to the blow struck at Turkey ; for that State had just accomplished a revolution which was popular in England, and which, for the moment, strengthened British influence with the Porte. Moreover, we were (probably) annoyed with Austria, who had refused certain propositions laid before the old Emperor at Ischl in August 1908. What precisely these were we do not know. An Austrian historian speaks of a memorandum drawn up by Lord Curzon proposing the division of the Near

[1] Schoen, p. 83. Cf. also Grey, i. p. 191.

East between the Powers of the Triple Alliance, with a bit
for Italy and Austria, but nothing for Germany.[1] Whether
or no this is true I dare not affirm. In any case it seems
probable that the object of the visit was to bring Austria
over to the orbit of the Entente. But the old Emperor
proved intransigeant, and " this time," he said, " the King
of England was not pleasant with me." [2]

So much seems to be true about British policy. Much
more is alleged by German and Austrian critics. We are
regarded as the Power which was anxious to push the crisis
to the point of war. King Edward is reported to have made
the remark : " We have fine allies ; France won't and Russia
can't fight." Mr. Winston Churchill's speech of September 11th, 1914, is cited, in which he said that there would
have been war in 1909 had not Russia given way. But that
is a statement of fact, and does not imply regret. Hellferich,
too, asserts that the British endeavoured to " sharpen the
conflict " ; [3] and the German and Austrian Ambassadors in St.
Petersburg accused the British Ambassador (Sir A. Nicolson)
of widening the breach between Russia and Austria.[4]

But the dispatches published by Siebert and in the
German White Book, " Is Germany Guilty ? " do not bear
out these accusations. The British, like the French, appear,
in this crisis, to have worked for peace. They endeavoured to moderate Serbia's demands as well as to
discover a method of satisfying Austria. Thus the Russian
Chargé d'Affaires in London writes on February 27th to
Isvolski : " Great disquietude prevails here, because the negotiations between the Powers for the prevention of an Austro-
Serbian conflict make no progress. In England, at present,
special importance is attached to the question of territorial
concessions in favour of Serbia, in the firm conviction that
an adherence to such demands must inevitably lead to war.
Here they would feel disposed, in general,[5] to support every
proposal which might facilitate a final understanding between
Austria and Serbia, but with the provision that the Powers
that would act in common must be perfectly clear concerning

---

[1] See Sosnosky, ii. p. 158, note 2. [2] Friedjung, ii. p. 225.
[3] P. 70. Cf. Conrad, iii. p. 66, and Brandenburg, p. 284.
[4] Friedjung, ii. p. 277.
[5] I have altered the English translation here. The German is " würde
man überhaupt geneigt sein."

the fact that Austria cannot be expected to make territorial concessions." [1] England, in fact, though she asked for a conference, did not press the demand. She was ready to accept anything Russia would accept ; as was natural, since the question was one that did not very closely concern her. More important than the attitude of England, was that of France. For without France, Russia could not, in any case, risk war with Austria, which would mean, also, war with Germany. But France did not want war at this time. After her diplomatic victory at Algeciras she was endeavouring to come to an understanding with Germany ; and in February 1909 that treaty about Morocco had been made which was to bear such meagre and unsatisfactory fruits.[2] Moreover, France disapproved of Russia's coming to an arrangement with Austria without her knowledge ; and Isvolski, in his tour of the European chancelleries, found a very cool reception at Paris. On the other hand the French appear to have regarded England as the danger to peace. Thus Isvolski reported that Clemenceau "judges the relation between Germany and England with great pessimism, and is convinced that it will lead to war. He is afraid that, in the moment of a conflict with England, Germany will find some excuse to fall upon France. The French statesman therefore was in terror (perhorreszierte) of any closer alliance with England, whereby France might be drawn into the German-English conflict." [3] France, it is true, was ready to fulfil her treaty obligations to Russia, should the occasion arise ; that is, should Germany " attack " France. " Pichon," says Isvolski, " has not ceased to let the Berlin Cabinet thoroughly understand that France follows the policy of the Russian Government in this crisis at all points, and that it will uphold in the most loyal manner the treaty of alliance which binds her to Russia. . . ." But, he adds, the French Minister went on to say that : " As this creates an extraordinarily serious situation for the two countries, neither of which wishes war, I have considered it my duty to seek for means by which this danger may be forestalled and not to have recourse to extreme decisions." [4]

[1] Siebert, p. 233. Cf. Grey, i. 190. [2] See below, p. 188.
[3] Friedjung, ii. p. 226. Cf. Reventlow, p. 364, who states that the *Temps* was warning England against putting pressure on France.
[4] Siebert, pp. 238-9, March 3rd, 1909.

The attitude of the French Government, we are told, was further influenced by the fact that a conflict would have found " no echo in the French population." [1] The " French population " presumably, means business men, politicians, and journalists. But, a fortiori, there is no reason to suppose that the bulk of the people desired war. In any case the important fact is that, for the reasons given, the French Government was opposed to war in this crisis, that it made this clear, and that this attitude reacted on Russian opinion. If France had adopted the same attitude in 1914, what might not the effect have been upon the course of events ?

As to Italy, she too had been informed, as early as September, of the intended Austrian move, though not of its exact date ; and apparently she had approved it. On September 28th, Tittoni said to the Austrian Ambassador : " Don't betray me, but at bottom I am almost contented with your annexation." [2] He wanted, however, first, assurance about the Straits, the Sanjak, and Article 29 [3] of the Berlin Treaty. If he was satisfied on these points, then that entente between Austria, Russia, and Italy would become possible "which you wish and which I, for my part, regard as not only desirable but necessary." The assurances were given, and Aehrenthal was able to say that he regarded the agreement between Italy, Russia, and Austria as concluded in principle.[4] It looks at this point as though a rapprochement between the Triple Alliance and Russia might have been possible, had the arrangement between Aehrenthal and Isvolski worked out as the latter desired.[5] But later, Italy took up a hostile attitude, and the king complained of

---

[1] Siebert, p. 266. Later, in the same dispatch, the Russian Ambassador at Paris remarks that public opinion, in France, as well as in England, demands more and more a closer rapprochement between Russia, France, and England. What does " public opinion " mean here ? The translator of the dispatches remarks that " M. Nelidoff must have mistaken his own for public opinion," and the suggestion does not seem improbable, except that the word " mistaken " is perhaps itself mistaken.

[2] Friedjung, ii. p. 231.

[3] This is the article which gives to Austria-Hungary the " maritime and sanitary police " of the coast of Montenegro, etc.

[4] Friedjung, ii. pp. 230-1.

[5] In the book by Judet on *Georges Louis* there are a number of references to common action by Isvolsky and Tittoni, and to the idea of an Austro-Italo-Russian entente; see, e.g., pp. 175 and 203. It is stated also that when Muravieff died in 1908 there was found in his pocket a draft of such an agreement. Cf. the agreement of Racconigi, below, p. 221.

the annexation as a " dagger stroke at the Berlin Act." [1]
Whether there was a misunderstanding here too and Italy
expected the question first to be referred to a conference
of the Powers, or whether she changed her attitude to
bring it into accord with that of England, is not clear. In
any case she ended by ranging herself with the other Great
Powers.

It will be clear, from this summary, that Isvolski, whatever
he may have intended, found no support among the Powers
for a solution by war. Russia, just emerged from her defeat
by Japan, was not capable of facing alone a conflict with
Austria and Germany. There remained, however, the danger
that Serbia might provoke Austria to war, or Austria embrace
the opportunity of crushing Serbia ; and, in that event, no
one could say what the consequences might be. The Powers
therefore determined to acquiesce in the annexation, and to
put pressure on Serbia to abstain from the demands for
territorial compensation which she was putting forward ;
for these Austria had made it clear that she would never
concede. On the other hand, Serbia might expect, and
Austria was ready to concede, economic compensation, and
some kind of access to the Adriatic. But Serbia was very
reluctant to assent to this compromise. Military preparations on either side increased the tension. But the action
of Germany saved the situation. She made a proposal that
Russia should put pressure on Serbia to keep her quiet, while
Austria, on her side, should abstain from attack ; but that
the annexation of Bosnia should be recognised by the Powers,
not by a conference, but by a communication of notes.
These were, no doubt, hard conditions for Isvolski, who, only
a fortnight earlier, had assured the Serbian Government that
" the act of annexation will, in the last resort, not receive our
signature." [2] But he ended by accepting the note, apparently.
before it had even been seen by his allies.

The German note has often been represented as a peculiarly bad case of bullying. It certainly contained one strong
phrase : " If the Russian Government thinks it cannot support our well-meant proposal we must let things run their

---

[1] Friedjung, ii. p. 255. See also Tittoni's speech of December 3rd and 4th,
in *Italien der Driebund und die Balkan-verträge*, Berlin, 1913.
[2] Siebert, p. 247.

course." [1] But it does not seem to have been conceived as an "ultimatum" and it was sent only after friendly consultation of the Chancellor with the Russian Ambassador. [2] The Tsar telegraphed to the Kaiser to thank him for finding the way out; [3] and when Prince Bülow retired from the German Chancellorship, Isvolski specially thanked him for his services. [4] This latter point, however, should not be stressed, for. Isvolski was an accomplished liar; and there seems to be no doubt of the bitter feelings towards Germany which he carried away from the crisis. In this connexion it may be worth while to transcribe a note written by the French diplomat, Georges Louis, in October 1914. "Isvolski has not forgiven me for frustrating his action in the Balkan business. He is in part the cause of the Tripoli business and of the Balkan business; he has not ceased to pursue an adventurous policy, dangerous to peace, and consequently contrary to our interests. All his policy is dominated by his rancour against Austria from 1910 on; again in 1911, in the Morocco business, and in 1912 and 1913. He wanted war to break out over Serbia, because it was in connexion with her that he had to yield to Austria in 1909. He is right, therefore, in speaking of 'my war' when he speaks of the war which is covering France with blood and ruins." [5] British statesmen, too, are said to have been angry, especially the Ambassador to Russia, Sir Arthur Nicolson. But there is no sign of irritation in the dispatches by Sir E. Grey published in the Siebert collection; and in a note of March 19th the Russian Chargé d'Affaires in London writes to Isvolski that "England's chief reason for expressing herself in favour of a conference is due to Russian wishes; if the Russian Government now considers it possible to give up this idea the British Government is also prepared to be satisfied with an exchange of notes." [6]

The real difficulty was Serbia, who was asked to abandon claims which, as we have seen, she, or certain elements of her public opinion, regarded as essential to her "existence." But for some time before the German note the other Powers had been endeavouring to modify the intransigeance of Serbia,

[1] Schoen, *Erlebtes*, p. 79; Eng. trans., p. 85; Brandenburg, pp. 281–2.
[2] Friedjung, p. 271. Brandenburg, p. 283.
[3] Brandenburg, p. 284.   [4] Friedjung, p. 283.
[5] Judet, *Georges Louis*, p. 149.   [6] Siebert, p. 258.

and none more actively than Russia.[1] Naturally, after accepting the German note, they refused to support her opposition ; and on the last day of the month she accepted the solution. The note in which the acceptance was given ran as follows :

" Serbia recognises that her rights were not affected by the action taken in Bosnia and that accordingly she will acquiesce in the decisions which the Powers will adopt in reference to Article 25 of the Treaty of Berlin.[2] Besides accepting the decisions of the Powers, Serbia promises to abandon the protest and opposition which she has made, since last October, in respect of the annexation, and promises further to change the direction of her policy towards Austria-Hungary and in future to live with the latter on a footing of friendly relations."[3] This was a sufficiently complete repudiation, in words, of Serbia's previous attitude.

V. Conclusion

In looking back over this crisis the reader is invited to pay special attention to the following points :—

1. So far as Austria and Serbia are concerned the situation was much as it was in 1914. Serbia had ambitions which were incompatible with the continued existence of the Austrian Empire. That was the reason of her passionate reaction against the formal annexation of two Turkish provinces, which were as much, or as little, part of the Austrian Empire as Egypt was of the British.

2. The reason that, on this occasion, events did not lead to a world-war, was the unpreparedness of Russia and the unwillingness of France and England. Otherwise, all the elements of the conflict were already present.

3. The desire of Russia, supported by England, to have the matter discussed at a European conference, was legitimate. It was a recognition that international treaties ought not to be set aside by the one-sided action of a single Power. True, the change proposed in this case was only the formal recognition of what was already a fact. But

[1] Siebert, pp. 243 seq., 257. Cf., for Grey, ib., p. 252.
[2] The article assigning to Austria-Hungary the occupation of Bosnia.
[3] Cited in Conrad, iv. p. 95.

forms are not unimportant, even in a world so unscrupulous
about realities as that of Europe was.

4. The Austrian action, technically wrong, was supported
and carried to victory by Germany.

5. The effects of the solution thus arrived at, in a world
of States whose relations were of the kind we have described,
was merely to postpone the final conflict. It is this last point
that is of the greatest importance for our present purpose, and
some citations in illustration of it may fitly conclude our
survey. That Austrian militarists, headed by Conrad v.
Hoetzendorf, were angry and disappointed goes without
saying. It must, however, be added that, given the whole
state of Europe, and especially the relations between Serbia,
Austria, and Russia, their position is intelligible. They
believed, and perhaps rightly, that they could have had
their war with Serbia at that moment, without necessarily
involving other Powers, because of the unpreparedness of
Russia and the unwillingness of France ; and they saw that
the present settlement settled nothing, for it left the whole
tangle of antagonisms and ambitions very much as it was.
" Anyone," wrote an Austrian General, " who has the opportunity and the intelligence to judge of the structure and
feelings of the popular elements in Serbia, elements which
here and in the neighbouring territories are filled with
unquenchable hatred for us, and consider the day of revenge
merely postponed—anyone who is clear that this people,
from lack of a sufficiently developed intelligence, is kept
continually in excitement by irresponsible agitators, is accustomed only to force, but yields to that and ends by complete
submission—anyone who so considers must regard with the
deepest regret the turn that has suddenly been given to
events. The more so as it is precisely the present moment
that would have been suitable for taking the final step
recognised as necessary by all good patriots, and for making
up, by an imposing development of our forces, for our
omissions in the past.

" The peace imposed (in Bosnia) only by military force
and, even so, not completely, upon the forces of the opposition, which wait only for the withdrawal of our troops and
the opening of the so-called Landtag—this peace will no
doubt, given the peculiar character of our administrative

apparatus, and the merely temporary strengthening of our military forces, come to an end when this latter ends ; then the agitation will set in again, in its usual audacious form, and will be supported by the Serbian and Montenegrin neighbour-States, which meantime will have regained consciousness." [1]

This is a true forecast of what was to happen. On the other hand, would war itself really solve the question ? Aehrenthal hesitated to answer in the affirmative. He did indeed look forward to an absorption of Serbia in the Monarchy, but saw no possibility of that solution at the moment. The best that could happen would be an "indemnity" of 500 millions, and the occupation of Belgrade as a pledge. In that way Serbia might be held, as long as possible, under Austrian pressure. But that result did not seem sufficient to justify a war. In the end this view prevailed over that of the soldiers. Yet even as late as March 29th the military solution seemed to have gained the day.[2]

But the result was that the situation for Austria was really worse than before ; for Serbian irredentism had been provoked, and the formula she was constrained to sign was nothing but words. That by itself need not have mattered very much to Europe. But, as we know, the Serbian question threatened at every moment to involve Russia and so Germany, France, and England. Here, too, in that larger world, the effects of the crisis were all to increase the menace. A few passages may be cited in illustration of this fact.

Bogitshevich says : [3]

" From this time forward all the political activities of Russia were directed, in the most intense manner, towards the creation of as large a combination of Powers as possible against Austria-Hungary and Germany, with the very clearly recognisable purpose to compel a decision by force of arms at a chosen moment favourable to Russia."

Milovanovich, the Serbian Minister, reports (October 1908) that Isvolski " condemned most severely Austria-Hungary, which had lost the confidence of Russia and the Western Powers ; he expressed the conviction and the hope

[1] Conrad, i. p. 164.   [2] Brandenburg, pp. 283, 285.
[3] *Causes of the War*, p. 22.

that this proceeding would soon be avenged in bloody fashion against Austria-Hungary," although " for the present any collision must be avoided, as the ground was neither militarily nor diplomatically prepared." [1]

The Serbian Minister at St. Petersburg wrote, March 6th, 1909, that Chonjakov (President of the Duma), reporting an audience with the Tsar, had said : " The Tsar has the feeling that a future collision with the Germanic people was unavoidable and that one had to prepare oneself for it." Asked the question what Rumania would do if Austria attacked Serbia, Chonjakov replied : " We have done what no other State has done up to now, in that we have declared before the whole world that we are not now in a position to wage war. Nevertheless, we shall regard any oppression of Serbia as the beginning of a European conflagration in which we are not able now to take part. This would blaze up in the future, however, when we are in the position to raise our voice." [2]

The Serbian Minister at Petersburg said to his Government :

" The change in Russian policy has called forth dismay and exasperation in Parliamentary circles. The wrath against France becomes increasingly greater. Germany's statement produced a terrific effect. Unprepared for war and with only a minimum portion of its forces at its disposal, Russia fears that Germany, which stands at the zenith of its readiness and power, will take advantage of this chance at any cost to attack and annihilate Russia. It therefore advises us to wait patiently as far as possible. Gutshow said to me : ' In this case we should only enter the war if the existence of Russia were involved, otherwise not at all, as we would be defeated ; when our equipment is complete we shall discuss matters with Austria-Hungary. Do not now begin a war, for that would be suicide ; conceal your intentions and prepare yourselves ; your days of joy will come.' " [3]

The consequence of this attitude of the Powers was, as it always is, the increase of armaments. On this point we will conclude with the words of Mr. Churchill :

" The Teutonic triumph was complete. But it was a

[1] *Is Germany Guilty ?*, ii. p. 33.
[2] Ib., App. 10, p. 38, March 19th, 1909.
[3] Ib., App. 8, p. 36, March 3rd, 1909.

victory gained at a perilous cost.   France, after her treatment in 1905, had begun a thorough military reorganisation. Now Russia, in 1910, made an enormous increase in her already vast army ; and both Russia and France, smarting under similar experiences, closed their ranks, cemented their alliance, and set to work to construct, with Russian labour and French money, the new strategic railway systems of which Russia's western frontier stood in need." [1]

[1] Churchill, *World Crisis*, i. p. 36.

CHAPTER VII

AGADIR

I. The Franco-German Agreement of 1909

IF the Balkan crisis of 1908–9 passed without war, that was partly because the French were endeavouring to come to an agreement with Germany about Morocco. To that question we must now return. It will be remembered that we saw, in a previous chapter, that the French, with the help of their allies and friends, had succeeded, by the Act of Algeciras, in retaining that joint Franco-Spanish control of the police which had been arranged for in the secret treaty of 1905, and which left the two States free, as and when opportunity should arise, to pursue the policy of partition agreed upon in the secret treaties of 1904. These treaties were still regarded as binding, in spite of the fact that the Act of Algeciras formally declared that any agreement in contravention of the Act was void. Thus Sir Edward Grey said to the German Ambassador in November 1911 : " We must take into consideration our treaty obligations to France " ; [1] and Isvolski reports that, even as late as March 1912, " the Spanish Government adheres obstinately to the exact text of the secret treaty of 1904." [2] Nevertheless, the German intervention had not been without effect. In the first place, a considerable body of French opinion, unacquainted with the secret treaties, was anxious to carry out loyally the provisions of the Act ; that is, to maintain the sovereignty and independence of the Sultan. Thus, " from the close of 1906 down to the very eve of the Fez expedition, the French Chamber passed resolution after resolution, by large majorities, expressive of its determination to observe the Algeciras Act, and disclaiming intervention in the

[1] Cited *Camb. Hist. Foreign Policy*, iii. p. 441.
[2] *Livre Noir*, i. p. 207.

internal affairs of Morocco." [1]   And M. Caillaux tells us that
French public opinion, and in particular that of M. Jaurès,
and his friends, appeared to favour the policy of " avoiding all
initiatives, outside the range of the Act of Algeciras, of letting
our rights and our special interests sleep, of consolidating and
fortifying the power of the Maghzen, of calling upon
the Powers, and especially Germany, to collaborate with us
in this work." [2]   " A contemptible policy," M. Caillaux comments ; and goes on to urge his objections to the Act of
Algeciras. The objections are not without force. But what
is interesting to us is the fact that, in the mind even of a
statesman so prudent and pacific as M. Caillaux, a public act,
solemnly signed after months of deliberation by fourteen States,
is treated as a " piece of waste paper, " to be circumvented or
broken as soon as possible.   " Our problem was nothing less
than to regain all the ground lost since 1905, and to repair
the consequences of the serious diplomatic check which we
had suffered." [3]

In the second place, the Germans had shown that it would
be difficult to swallow up Morocco without first conciliating
them, and it was therefore to conciliation that the French
Government turned.   Germany's intervention in Morocco had
been based, formally, upon her commercial interests there ;
and it was in this matter that the French sought an understanding.   By an interesting section of the Act of Algeciras
the following agreement had been made between the Powers :

1. " That in no case shall the rights of the State over the
public services of the Shereefian Empire be alienated for the
benefit of private interests."

2. " Should the Shereefian Government consider it necessary to have recourse to foreign capital or to foreign industries
for the working of public services, or for the execution of public
works, roads, railways, posts, telegraphs, or other, the Signatory
Powers reserve to themselves the right to see that the control
of the State over such large undertakings of public interest
remains intact."

3. Such concessions shall " be subject to the principle of
public awards on tenders, without respect to nationality, as
regards all matters which, by the rules observed under the

---

[1] Morel, p. 112.   [2] *Agadir*, p. 27.   [3] Ib., p. 29.

laws of foreign countries, admit of the application of that principle."

4. The call for tenders for such works shall be submitted to the "diplomatic body," i.e. the representatives of the Powers in Morocco.

5. The contract shall be awarded to the person (whatever his nationality) submitting the most generally advantageous offer.[1]

This is an interesting attempt to secure equal and free competition. But it was precisely these clauses, upon the violation of which the attempt at Franco-German co-operation was to be based. The opportunity was offered by the crisis of 1908. That, as we have seen, had been terminated by the intervention of Germany, indicating that, in case of war, she would stand by Austria. But this intervention had also embittered the relations of the Powers. Germany therefore was anxious " to calm Russia and France ; she wishes even to satisfy the latter, in order to draw her into her game."[2] France embraced the opportunity, and the result was an agreement between France and Germany, signed in February 1909.[3] It runs as follows :

" The Government of the French Republic and the Imperial German Government, being equally anxious to facilitate the execution of the Algeciras Act, have agreed to define the meaning which they attach to the articles of that Act with a view to avoid in the future all sources of misunderstanding between them.

" Therefore,

" The Government of the French Republic, firmly attached to the maintenance of the independence and integrity of the Shereefian Empire, being resolved to safeguard the principle of economic equality, and, consequently, not to obstruct German commercial and industrial interests in that country ;

" And the Imperial German Government, pursuing only economic interests in Morocco, recognising on the other hand that the special political interests of France in that country are closely bound up with the consolidation of order and internal peace, and being resolved not to impede those interests ;

---

[1] See Articles 105 seq. of the Act. [2] Caillaux, p. 32.
[3] For text, see Caillaux, p. 31, and Morel, p. 303.

" Declare that they do not pursue nor encourage any measure of a nature to create, in their favour or in that of any Power, an economic privilege, and that they will endeavour to associate their nationals in affairs for which the latter may obtain a concession."

The agreement was supplemented by the following letter from the German Minister of Foreign Affairs to the French Ambassador in Berlin : " I am entirely in agreement with you that the political renunciation (désinteressement) of Germany does not affect the situations already acquired by German nationals ; but it does imply that her citizens will not be candidates for the functions of directors or counsellors for those public services of Morocco which have, or may assume, a political character, nor for the functions of instructors in those services. On the other hand, it is understood that, in those affairs which permit of an association of German and French interests, account will be taken, so far as possible, of the fact that French interests are more important than German interests." [1]

What was the effect of this agreement ? French writers take it to be a recognition by Germany of the political predominance of France. " To France," says M. Pinon, " the difficult task of establishing in Morocco order and internal peace, without which no commerce is possible ; but to France also the benefits of this task, that is to say, under a form more or less attenuated, and at a date more or less remote, the essentials of the attribute of sovereignty." And in support of this view the German Chancellor is cited as having said " in substance," to the French Ambassador : " Now Morocco is a fruit which is ripening for you and which you are sure to pluck ; we ask of you only one thing, to be patient, and to consider public opinion in Germany." [2] In yet stronger words the *Journal des Débats* wrote : " We can now cash the Act of Algeciras." [3] M. Tardieu takes the same view. The treaty, he writes, was " a blow at the principles of Algeciras and the Act henceforth was relegated to a back place." [4] The reader will observe that this view regards it as a matter of course that a treaty between two States can cancel an Act signed

[1] Caillaux, p. 32.   [2] Pinon, *France et l'Allemagne*, p. 186.
[3] Gooch, *History of Modern Europe*, p. 462.   [4] *Agadir*, p. 10.

by fourteen States. So sensitive is the opinion of Governments and journalists to international obligation !

It seems clear, then, that the treaty was regarded, at the time, by some interpreters, as superseding the Act. But for this very reason it seemed to other critics to be dangerous. M. Caillaux, for example, calls it an " untenable compromise." For though " it disengaged us in some measure from the régime of internationalism," it was nevertheless " insufficient, incomplete from the political point of view, impossible, or at least very dangerous to put into action, from the economic point of view." [1] M. Caillaux goes further. He says that by this agreement, France had " deceived her allies," and that " without obtaining from Germany anything but the appearance of liberty of action in Morocco." [2]

In this severe judgment M. Caillaux appears to be thinking rather of the economic than of the political implications of the treaty. It had been agreed that, in a number of important enterprises, such as strategic railways and harbours, the Germans would not compete for concessions against the French ; but that, in the case of enterprises which neither have nor are likely to assume a political character, the two States will act together and share the concessions they may obtain. Was it, then, intended to set aside that principle of equal and fair competition by all States which was laid down in the Act of Algeciras ? The point is not clear. The Germans seem to have taken the view that they, at any rate, must have their half share, and that, if the French chose to consider the rights of other States, they could meet such claims out of their own quota.[3] But what the other States had a right to was fair and equal competition for the contracts, and on one occasion at least the British seem to have insisted on their right. It was presumably in this connexion that King Edward said (if he did say it) that the treaty was " made against us." [4]

In spite of this, however, the British Government seems to have welcomed the treaty. For when, in February 1909, King Edward visited Berlin, accompanied by Sir Charles Hardinge, the latter, as we are informed by the Russian Ambassador in Berlin, " congratulated the Chancellor upon the conclusion of the Morocco agreement between Germany

and France. The London Cabinet sees in this a valuable
pledge of peace and is prepared to support all further efforts
of this kind." [1] Sir E. Grey also is reported as saying to the
French Ambassador in London " that the new agreement
represented a new guarantee for peace and that it was certainly desirable." He added, however, that " he did not
believe that the Franco-German understanding was a very
profound one, and for this reason it would probably remain
a façade agreement." [2]

II. The Agreement Breaks Down

In this matter Sir Edward was a true prophet. For whatever may have been the intentions of the parties, the course
of events showed that it was impossible to work the treaty.
There were three important departments to which it might
apply : (1) mines, (2) railways, (3) other public works ; and
in all of these the arrangements projected broke down. Let
us take first the mines.

Here the position appeared to be not unfavourable, for
already, as early as 1907, an international society, the Union
of Mines, had been formed, in which France had 50 per cent.
and Germany 20 per cent. of the capital, the remaining Powers
being thus in a very small minority. So far, well and good.
But unfortunately a different and wholly German group,
Messrs. Mannesmann, were also in the field ; they had advanced
money to the Sultan, Mulai Hafid, at a time when he was only
a pretender, and had received in exchange extensive concessions from which " they hope to draw, if not much minerals,
at any rate much profit." [3] The Union, therefore, found it
advisable to negotiate with this other interest. But the
negotiations were difficult and protracted, and the German
Government was hampered in its dealings with the matter by
the fact that, as time went on, the German nationalists took the
Mannesmann brothers under their patronage ; and of this fact
the firm made every possible use. [4] The negotiations dragged
on and nothing had been concluded when the march to Fez
and the mission of the *Panther* altered the whole situation.

With regard to public works, difficulties no less serious

---

[1] Siebert, p. 491.   [2] Ib., p. 488.
[3] Tardieu, p. 45.   [4] See v. Schoen, pp. 117 seq.

arose. A company was formed, in February 1910, entitled the " Société maroccaine de travaux publics," in which France had 50 per cent. of the shares, Germany 26 per cent., and seven other Powers less amounts, including 6¼ per cent. for England.[1] This company was to take over both the construction and the operation of enterprises, creating subordinate companies for each. The work of construction was to be assigned, in the case of important works, to that nation which could offer the most favourable conditions. But the operation, so at least the French intended, was to be in the hands of the French, and so was the personnel. The company got to work quickly and put forward a number of schemes ; but none of them had been adopted by the end of June 1911. There had always been some objection ; precisely what, it is not easy now to discover, nor is it important for our present purpose. Most difficult of all was agreement about the railways, because here the political and military interests of the French demanded complete control, at any rate of " strategic " lines. A remark of M. Tardieu on this subject illuminates clearly the French point of view. Speaking of " strategic " lines, he says : " As the Sultan would not intervene, as France would put up the money, as the military engineers would be the only agency to be considered, we should not fall under the Act of Algeciras, and should escape adjudication."[2] But then, there was always the question, which railways, precisely, should be called " strategic " ? Worse, M. Pichon, pressed by the Germans, consented that two strategic lines, to be paid for by French money, should be constructed by the Société maroccaine.[3] The Germans then proposed that neither Government should allow any of its nationals to compete with the Société. The French objected, partly because they anticipated British objections. And they were right. For the British Government informed the French that they appeared to be creating an economic " condominium " with Germany, and that this was inadmissible. Further difficulties arose about the personnel. The Germans claimed a share of this proportionate to their share of the capital in the Société. The French objected. And agreement had not been reached when the episode of the *Panther* occurred.

[1] Tardieu, p. 61.   [2] Ib., p. 75.   [3] Ib., p. 76.

Meantime, there had been proceeding another negotiation, not directly connected with the treaty of 1909. The French had established, in their Congo Colony, the system which had made a hell of the Belgian Congo. They had given up all the property in the soil and its products to companies, and thus made the natives, to all intents and purposes, serfs for collecting rubber and ivory. The terrible consequences were exposed by the persistent efforts of Mr. E. D. Morel in England, assisted by all that was generous and humane in France. It is characteristic of M. Tardieu that, in dealing with this matter, he gives the reader no idea of what really lay behind the scenes, and treats the whole agitation as a piece of British hypocrisy, prompted only by the interests of British traders. On all that side of the question, however, we must not here digress. Our present concern is the trouble that arose between France and Germany. One of the companies which had obtained enormous concessions in the French Congo was the N' Ghoko Sangha. But the company had not been successful in exploiting its territory, and a good deal of the trade therein continued to be done directly between the natives and the Germans of the Cameroons. According to French law, this was illegal. After much controversy, in the course of which the Company extorted from the French taxpayers an enormous indemnity, a " consortium " was formed between Germans and French to work the territory. This arrangement was violently attacked in France, partly by those who were opposed to the whole method of exploitation, partly by those who thought the French were giving away much in return for little. In the end the opposition became so strong that the Government withdrew the concession and cancelled the indemnity. The German colonial party were furious, and the German Government embarrassed and annoyed. " You have cancelled your engagement," they said, " you have set our colonials on our back. What are you going to do by way of compensation ? " At every point, in every region, negotiations had broken down. The Germans were angry and mistrustful, and not without reason. For, as a Frenchman writes : " In four months neither the good will of Germany, evident in this matter, nor the urgency of our Ambassador (in Berlin), nor the pressure of circumstances recommending us to conciliate suspicious critics at a time

14

when we needed their approval, none of these things had induced us to conclude an arrangement based on the Act of Algeciras, signed by us, and by which there would have been achieved a first realisation of the agreement of 1909. . . . The Frenchman, in the first moment, lets himself go, then pulls himself up, hesitates, temporises. The more the German urges, the more he withdraws. . . . At the first difficulty, the German raises his demands. In vain. For the Frenchman shams dead. Then events develop. Discussion ceases. Silence and forgetfulness. The Frenchman, like a man who has escaped from an adventure, congratulates himself on his astuteness. But the patient German remembers. He seeks revenge, finds it, prepares it. It will be Agadir." [1]

While thus the agreement of 1909 failed to reconcile the economic interests of France and Germany, political crises continued to occur. One of the most serious was that of the deserters of Casablanca. The French possess a " foreign legion " recruited for colonial service. In September 1908 the German Consul at Casablanca assisted some of these legionaries in an attempt at escape. The French rearrested them, and there was an armed struggle between French and Germans. The episode was not, in itself, of any importance, but it is the kind of thing, in the international anarchy, that precipitates war ; and it had nearly done so in this case, before the common-sense solution of a reference to the Hague Tribunal was adopted. How nearly war broke out is indicated by a statement of M. Tardieu that " King Edward let the French Government know that he would place at its disposal on the Continent, if peace were broken, five divisions of infantry and one division of cavalry to hold the left wing in the second line." [2] This seems likely enough to be true. For the organisation of the overseas force had been entered upon as early as 1906 ; and the determination of the British Government to support France in a war for Morocco, should the occasion arise, was never in doubt. The world-war was nearly let loose by the trifling dispute of Casablanca.

[1] Bourbon, L'Énigme Allemande, p. 30. Cf. Caillaux, pp. 90-1.
[2] Cited by Gooch, p. 460.

III. The March to Fez

That dispute was one between French and Germans.
But also, between French and Moroccans, there was a continual
smouldering war. The Conference of Algeciras, it will be
remembered, had assigned the police of the ports to France and
Spain, and had left a general presumption that " order " was
to be maintained by France. But what appears to Europeans
as " order " is apt to appear to natives as subjugation.
" Servitudinem faciunt, pacem appellant," we may say,
parodying the Roman historian. The Moroccans showed no
enthusiasm for " order," and the French were not well equipped
for enforcing it. There had recently been a revolution which
had ended in the deposition of Abdul Asiz, and the substitution
of his brother, Mulai Hafid. The latter had been recognised
by the French, but only after a series of episodes, thus summarised by M. Tardieu : " Our intimacy with Mulai Hafid was
of recent date, and grave memories separated us from him.
He had founded his kingdom on hatred of the French ; and
though, once recognised, he was necessarily under obligation
to forget the passions of a pretender, yet it might be feared
that, either in his own mind or among his adherents, there
might linger the misgivings of a past epoch." [1] Besides this
" lingering of misgivings " there were current questions in
dispute. The French had occupied, and still held, a province
of Morocco on their frontier ; further, they were claiming
" indemnities " for the war they had waged against the Sultan.
In March 1909 an agreement was reached which, M. Tardieu
complains, was entirely in favour of the Sultan. This seems
an odd view, for the Sultan recognised his debt, and agreed
to employ for his army French instructors and French
only.[2] There followed, however, not peace, but " a further
period of anarchy." " We had suppressed fear without
awakening self-interest. We were to be treated as a quantité
négligeable. From June 1909 to February 1910 the correspondence of our consulates is nothing but one long complaint
against the vexatious proceedings inflicted by the orders of
the Sultan on French nationals and protégés." For example,
the French residents were positively taxed. Frontier troubles
also continued, and the Sultan's agents assumed an attitude

[1] Tardieu, p. 90.   [2] Ib., p. 95.

" more and more intransigeant, more and more hostile to the French. Our compatriots are dispossessed and ruined. All their contracts with the natives remain a dead letter." Alas ! The native, like some other animals, is very vicious. He defends himself when he is attacked.

These disputes, nevertheless, were arranged, or pretended to be arranged, by another treaty of March 1910.[1] But there remained the question of loans. The Sultan had admitted that he must pay for the war ; and that can only be done, in these cases, by borrowing from the creditor. But also he required money to pay both for his pleasures and his soldiers ; since, as M. Tardieu points out with irrefutable logic : " Without money no soldiers, for in the absence of pay they desert. Without soldiers no money, for taxes do not come in unless they are collected. It was a vicious circle." It was. And one repeated often enough, with much profit to Europeans.

In May 1910 a first loan was agreed to between the Sultan and the Bank of Morocco, the Germans and British combining with the French to insist upon its " urgent necessity." The object of this loan was, first, to pay the Sultan's private debts, contracted with European firms ; secondly, to pay the French war indemnity, by annual instalments. But these latter payments did not materialise, since the Sultan contracted new debts as fast as he paid the old ones. No sooner, indeed, had he signed the first loan, than he set out for Paris to contract another.[2] The destination of this was, partly to pay yet more debts, partly to pay soldiers, partly to pay for public works. But, once more, as M. Tardieu laments, there is a fatal defect. The new loan was not guaranteed by the French Government. It was therefore a mere " scrap of paper."

Meantime, the Moroccan Army was not improving. The French, as we have seen, had the exclusive right to provide it with instructors. But these were few, and there were difficulties about increasing their number. French public opinion was displeased by the Sultan's methods of reducing recalcitrant tribes, which, no doubt, were not exactly humane, though he had not yet been instructed by Europeans in the arts of poison-gas and bombs. There were disputes, not only as to the number of the instructors, but as to the use to be made, or not to be made, of them. There were disputes also

---

[1] Tardieu, p. 100.　　　　[2] Ib., p. 123.

between the French Foreign Office and War Office. Meantime, anarchy in Morocco continued. And the French commander was left to do what he could with a doctor, an interpreter, and some ten officers.[1] Such was the situation when the Europeans of Fez were pronounced to be in danger.

What that means, any European knows. Natives may kill one another as much as they like. Europeans may kill natives as much as they like. But let natives, driven to desperation, threaten to kill Europeans, and especially European women and children, and then—then, by God ! We have seen it in India ; we have seen it in China ; we have seen it in Africa. But were the Europeans really in danger ? On that point there is the usual conflict of evidence [2] and the truth is probably lost to history. What is certain is that, on the one hand, the French agent on the spot sent home alarming reports ; [3] and that, on the other, when the French expedition reached Fez, the European colony was safe.[4]

Whatever may have been the truth on this point, whether the French expedition was sent in response to a real danger, or in order to alter the status of Morocco, the result was an international crisis. Was the expedition, or was it not, in accordance with the Treaty of Algeciras ? Nothing very definite on this point was to be extracted from the Act itself, which had merely recognised, in a general way, the special political interests of France, and entrusted to her and to Spain the policing of the ports. The French instructions to their commanding officer were all in good order. He was to do nothing that might injure the independence of the Sultan or diminish the prestige of his sovereignty. " No occupation of new territories was in view. The operation of the force was to be as rapid as possible and terminated as quickly as possible." [5] But, on the other hand, we are informed by M. Tardieu that, in the opinion of M. Jules Cambon, French Ambassador in Berlin, " Morocco was and ought to be the great object of French policy." [6] We find the French Commander-in-Chief writing : " If France does not take in hand the effective control of Morocco, anarchy is irremediable." The French Cardinal, Lavigerie, wrote : " Algeria and Tunis

---

[1] Tardieu, p. 153.   [2] Cf. Caillaux, pp. 91–2.
[3] Tardieu, pp. 365 seq.
[4] Siebert, p. 587 ; Yellow Book, " Affaires du Maroc," vi. 1912, No. 307.
[5] Tardieu, p. 374. Cf. Siebert, pp. 587–8.   [6] Tardieu, p. 408.

will be incomplete and menaced so long as Morocco is not under the domination of France." And M. Tardieu adds the convincing comment : " Nothing was more evident. The protectorate of Morocco is a necessary consequence of the domination of France in Algeria, and the completion of the work accomplished during eighty years in North Africa." ¹ Whatever may have been the intentions, or the refusal to have intentions, on the part of the French Government, everyone knowing anything of history must have realised that the expedition to Fez would be the end of the ambiguous situation which had been maintained since the Act of Algeciras. What was doubtful was, whether the crisis would end in a French protectorate, or a European war.

Such, from the first, was the view of experienced statesmen. Thus Sir A. Nicolson, as reported by the Russian Ambassador in London, " did not conceal from me the fact that the Morocco question is disquieting the London Cabinet. He believes that France will be compelled to occupy Fez ; that the situation in the city appears to be threatening ; that a mere expedition for the protection of Europeans would not be a particularly alarming undertaking, but that the experience of all European States, beginning with England, shows that it is easier to occupy a city than to withdraw again." ² Similarly, Isvolski, at Paris, commenting on the official account of the French intentions, says : " I have no reason to doubt Cruppi's sincerity, but I am not yet convinced that his optimism is justified. To my question as to whether he could tell me, even approximately, how long the French would occupy Fez, he answered evasively, and I believe he does not take into account how difficult it will be to carry out the contemplated regimé." ³ Finally, when M. Caillaux came into power in June, he immediately decided that there were only two alternatives : either to evacuate Fez, or to give compensation to Germany. But the former course, he says, it was " impossible to think of ! It would be a humiliating rout." ⁴ The evidence is thus complete. Whatever may have been in the mind of M. Cruppi when the expedition was started, once Fez was reached there was to be no return to the pre-existing situation.

¹ Tardieu, pp. 408 seq.   ² Siebert, p. 581, May 1911.
³ Ib., p. 588.   Cf. *Livre Noir*, i. p. 107.
⁴ P. 115.   "Either Morocco for France," he said, " or war."

IV. Agadir

Everything, thus, was proceeding in the ordinary way towards the French annexation of Morocco, when suddenly the Germans struck a dramatic and challenging blow. On July 1st, 1911, they sent a gunboat to the Moroccan port of Agadir. The vessel had a crew of only 125 men, later increased to 274, and none of these were ever landed. But the stroke fell like a bomb into the chancelleries of Europe. What did it mean ? Was it a prelude to war ? Did it imply, as the British feared, a German naval station on the Atlantic ? Some years earlier, the reader will remember, they had offered this accommodation to the Germans.[1] But now France was the friend and Germany the enemy, and what would once have secured their Empire had become a menace to be conjured, if necessary, by war.

Sir Edward Grey took action at once. He " informed the German Ambassador that he had seen the Prime Minister, and that we considered the situation created by the dispatch of the *Panther* to Agadir as so important that it must be discussed in a meeting of the Cabinet. The next day I asked the German Ambassador to come and see me again, and said that I must tell him that our attitude could not be a disinterested one with regard to Morocco. We must take into consideration our treaty obligations to France and our own interests in Morocco." [2] This was a line consistent with that adopted in 1904-6 and demanded by the secret treaties. The days went on, the French discussions with the Germans seemed to be running into the sand,[3] and on July 21st, Sir Edward repeated his warning : " I pointed out that the Germans were in the closed port of Agadir ; that, according to native rumours,[4] they were landing and negotiating with the tribes, so that, for all we knew, they might be acquiring concessions there, and that it might be even that the German flag had been hoisted there at Agadir, which was the most suitable port on that coast for a naval base. The longer the Germans remained at Agadir, the greater the risk of their developing a state of affairs which would make it more difficult

---

[1] See above, p. 120.
[2] Hansard, November 27, 1911, v. xxxii. p. 46, and Grey, i. p. 222.
[3] See Siebert, p. 580.   [4] Apparently quite unfounded.

for them to withdraw, and more necessary for us to take some steps to protect British interests." [1]

Sir Edward's fear of a German naval station on the east coast of Africa was probably genuine. [2] It was shared by Sir Francis Bertie, at Paris, who, as Isvolski reports, "personally believes that Germany is only waiting a favourable opportunity to declare the Act of Algeciras as no longer existent, in order to occupy one or two ports, among them Mogador." This idea of the Germans declaring the Act of Algeciras non-existent may strike the reader as humorous, in view of what the French were actually doing. But the fear was no doubt genuine that "a heavy blow would thus be struck to British interests and the channels of communication with South Africa would be threatened." [3] It was also true that, in 1904, the idea of a Moroccan port had been pushed by certain Germans, and had been considered by the Chancellor; [4] but he had abandoned it as unwise, and we have no evidence that it had been taken up again. The German Ambassador accordingly, on being addressed by Sir Edward in the words quoted above, replied at once that his Government had no intention to seize a port. [5] But this declaration did not satisfy Sir Edward. "The German Ambassador," he tells us, "was not in a position to make any communication to me from the German Government." The Ambassador, thereupon, telegraphed to the German Foreign Office, and a reply was dispatched confirming what he had said, that there was no intention to take a port.

But before this message reached London a further step had been taken in England. On the morning of this same day, July 21st, Mr. Churchill visited Mr. Lloyd George, and found that that energetic statesman had made up his mind. We were drifting into war, the Minister thought, and Germany was acting as though Britain did not count. We must speak out and speak at once. That evening he was to address the bankers at their annual dinner and he "intended to make it clear that if Germany meant war she would find Britain against her." He intended to show what he had prepared to say, not to the Cabinet, which met that day, but afterwards, to the Prime Minister and Sir Edward Grey. What would they say, he asked. "I said," Mr. Churchill replied, "that

---

[1] Hansard, v.s., p. 48.   [2] Grey, i. p. 220.   [3] Siebert, p. 582, May 11th.
[4] Ger. Docs., xx. pp. 170, 202, 228.   [5] Reventlow, p. 406.

of course they would be very much relieved ; and so they were, and so was I." [1]

Mr. Lloyd George accordingly, after agreement with Sir Edward and with Mr. Asquith, made his famous speech at the Mansion House. The passage about Morocco has been cited in an earlier chapter.[2] It is an admirable specimen of the way in which the devotion of blind and ignorant masses is exploited for dubious policies. What was really at stake was the simple point, who is to steal Morocco ? The rest was the rivalry of States, due to their ambitions and their armaments. But few of those who read Mr. Lloyd George's speech could be aware of this. He asked, in effect, for men to come and die ; and that they are always ready to do, if they are told the cause is their country's. It is enough that certain phrases should be used, certain passions stimulated ; and the more noble and heroic such passions may be judged to be, the more tragic is the irony of their abuse.

The speech had, of course, enormous reverberations. But if it aroused patriotism and jingoism in England, it had the same effect in Germany. " The masterful (herrische) words of Lloyd George," writes the then German Chancellor, " were bound to create great excitement in Germany. The World-Empire which, later, we were accused hypocritically of seeking, England claimed for herself in these words, which declared that every war was just which Great Britain might wage to secure respect for her hegemony." [3]   Count Metternich immediately made a stiff protest; and Sir Edward replied that the Ambassador's words were such " that the feeling of national dignity rendered it impossible for him to answer or make any statement." [4]   When statesmen begin to talk about honour and dignity we are very near indeed to war.

On the afternoon of this day Mr. Churchill was walking with Mr. Lloyd George by the fountains of Buckingham Palace, when a messenger from Sir Edward Grey caught them up, requesting the Chancellor to come at once to the Foreign Secretary. " My speech ! " cried the Chancellor. His head, perhaps, would be asked for, like Delcassé's ! When they reached Sir Edward's room, the latter said : " ' I have just

---

[1] *World Crisis*, i. p. 46.   [2] See above, p. 33.
[3] Bethmann-Hollweg, *Betrachtungen zum Weltkrieg*, p. 31.
[4] See Benckendorf's account in Siebert, p. 594.

received a communication from the German Ambassador so stiff, that the fleet might be attacked at any moment.' The First Lord (Mr. McKenna) arrived while we were talking and a few minutes later hurried off to send the warning orders.'' Mr. Churchill proceeds . '' They sound so very cautious and correct, these deadly words. Soft, quiet voices, purring, courteous, grave, exactly measured words, in large peaceful rooms. But, with less warning, cannons had opened fire and nations had been struck down by this same Germany. So now the Admiralty wireless whispers through the ether to the tall masts of ships, and captains pace their decks absorbed in thought. It is nothing. It is less than nothing. It is too foolish, too fantastic to be thought of in the twentieth century. Or is it fire and murder leaping out of the darkness at our throats, torpedoes ripping the bellies of half-awakened ships, a sunrise on a vanished naval supremacy, and an island well guarded hitherto at last defenceless ? No, it is nothing. No one would do such things. Civilisation has climbed above such perils. The interdependence of nations in trade and traffic, the sense of public law, the Hague Convention, Liberal principles, the Labour Party, high finance, Christian charity, common sense, have rendered such nightmares impossible. Are you quite sure ? It would be a pity to be wrong. Such a mistake could only be made once—once for all.'' [1] Mr. Churchill, at least, had the imagination to realise what was at stake.

V. The Meaning of the German Coup

It would seem, from the facts thus detailed, that, in the view of the British Government or of those members of it who were controlling foreign policy, the Germans, when they went to Agadir, intended to annex that port ; that the British regarded such an intention as a casus belli ; that they indicated that fact through Mr. Lloyd George's speech ; and that the Germans, confronted by that threat, abandoned their purpose. Is that view of German policy correct ? We are now in a position to say that it was not. The last occasion on which a partition of Morocco had been proposed was, as we have seen,[2] during the discussions of an Anglo-German alliance in 1901 ; at which time it was the two

[1] *World Crisis*, p 48.   [2] See above, p. 120.

States negotiating who were to be the beneficiaries. Later,
in 1903, we have indications of a discussion between Spain
and Germany. This was in connexion with the French
plan of a Franco-Spanish partition, leaving England out in
the cold ; and the Germans seem to have put in a claim to
be considered.[1] But nothing came of this, since the English
intervened energetically with Spain. Instead there came
the Anglo-French entente. From that time on, not only
have we no evidence of German manœuvres to take Moroccan
territory, we have evidence to the contrary. In December
1909 the Sultan of Morocco offered Germany a port on the
Atlantic. The Germans took the view that to accept this
would be to violate (1) the integrity of Morocco as guaranteed
at Algeciras, (2) an agreement of 1907 between England,
France, and Spain, for the preservation of the status quo in
the Mediterranean, and in the parts of Europe and Africa
washed by the Atlantic, (3) the agreement made with France
in this same year 1909. " The seizure of a coaling station,"
said the Secretary of State, " would be regarded in France as a
disloyal action and a breach of our agreement." Further, the
object of the Sultan, he thought, was to make bad blood between
Germany and France. To prevent this the Germans themselves informed the French of the offers made.[2] On this
occasion, then, they showed the most scrupulous regard for
their international engagements. Was their conduct different
in 1911 ? The papers of Kiderlen-Waechter, who handled
the question in that year, show beyond dispute that it was
not. Already in 1910 we find him saying that the Germans
can do nothing in Morocco without the consent of the English ;
and that, since England has a debt of honour to support
France, Germany must abandon Morocco and seek compensation elsewhere.[3] This idea, indeed, is of earlier date, for
already in 1905 M. Tardieu reports v. Kühlmann as saying
that Germany would disinterest herself in Morocco in exchange
for concessions in the Congo.[4] The French expedition to
Fez caused a revival of this policy ; and as early as July 7th
the German Ambassador in Paris said to the French Foreign
Minister that " Germany has no territorial ambitions in

[1] Ger. Docs., xvii. p. 355.
[2] Ib., v. xxiv chap. 182, p. 472, etc.
[3] Kiderlen-Waechter, ii. p. 233.
[4] Mystère d'Agadir, p. 438; cf. Siebert, p. 601, 1911.

Morocco. It is in the Congo that she perceives a possible field for negotiations." [1]

This was, from the first, the attitude of the German Government. No doubt there were elements of German opinion which had a different view. The Pan-Germans were breathing fire and slaughter, as such people do in all countries. They were a nuisance to Kiderlen-Waechter. " These people," he says, " want us to annex not only Morocco, but the department of the Rhone. We shall do neither ! What lunacy ! " And again : " A leader of the National Liberals has been to me to congratulate us on having secured the annexation of Morocco, as the result of our action at Agadir. I tried to make clear to him that really we did not intend to set foot in Morocco. But the ox simply did not believe me." [2]

On the other hand, the Secretary well understood the bearing and consequences of the French expedition to Fez. The French, he said, had been spreading over the country like a drop of oil. Yet it had never been possible to say, " now the moment has come, at which you have broken the Act of Algeciras." [3] The undermining process had proceeded slowly but surely, until at last, with the expedition to Fez, the situation had become clear. Yet even then the Minister held his hand ; for if he were to come out at once for " compensation " the French would draw back and deny that they were violating the Act. He therefore temporised until the moment seemed ripe for the stroke of Agadir. Then, and before the Mansion House speech, he took the matter up with the French, with a view not to taking any part of Morocco, but to finding compensation elsewhere. The compensation he wanted was the French Congo, and he asked for it all. The French Ambassador, confronted with this demand, " almost fell down backwards." " Why," he cried, " even a bit of it would be hard to defend before Parliament ! " But Kiderlen was unmoved. " It is the last opportunity we have of seizing, without war, something useful in Africa. Bits of the Congo, however fine, with rubber and ivory, are of no use to us. We must reach the Belgian Congo, so as to be parties in any division of that territory that may follow, and while it remains undivided, to make connexion across it

---

[1] *Mystère d'Agadir*, p. 435. [2] Kiderlen-Waechter, ii. pp. 122-3.
[3] Ib., p. 132.

with our African colony." [1] For the Germans, like the British
and the French, wanted an African empire. Had they not
as good, or as bad, a right ?

To achieve this purpose, Kiderlen-Waechter was prepared
to go very far. If the French are obstinate, he said, we must
take our stand on the Act of Algeciras, and demand that
they observe it too. " I don't think that they will take up
the glove, but they must be made to feel that we are determined to go to the bitter end." [2] He found it, however,
very hard to get the consent of his master ; for the Kaiser was
determined not to run the risk of war, and twice the Secretary
threatened resignation. [3]

VI. The Anglo-German Tension

Such was the position of affairs when Mr. Lloyd George
delivered his Mansion House speech. It was based, as we now
know, upon a quite erroneous idea as to what the Germans
were intending, and was received with the usual torrent of
excited comment in the British and French Press. It is worth
while to observe the view taken of these demonstrations by
the German Government. We were engaged, said the Minister,
" in amicable discussion with France on a subject which did
not touch in any way upon British interests, directly or indirectly. If England had any representations to make, we
might expect that she would make them through the usual
diplomatic channels. The English Government cannot be
in doubt that the method they have adopted will not advance
that friendly understanding between ourselves and France
which they profess to desire. If they had intended to confuse
and complicate the political situation, and to precipitate a
solution by force, they could have chosen no better method
than the Chancellor's speech." [4] These views the German
Ambassador was instructed to bring before Sir Edward Grey.
He did so, and, as we have seen, the result was that the latter
professed that the honour of England had been impugned
and regarded war as imminent. Thus a sheer misunderstanding nearly precipitated the catastrophe. We thought
that the Germans intended to seize an Atlantic port. In

---

[1] Kiderlen-Waechter, ii. p. 129.   [2] Ib.
[3] Ib., pp. 129, 134.   [4] Ib., pp. 135-6.

fact, they were only intending " compensation " in the Congo, a matter in which we had no direct interest. And over this confusion war might have broken out. Is it necessary to point the moral ?

The port of Agadir, however, was only one episode in this crisis. Quite apart from that, the British, now as in 1905-6, were bound by treaty to support the French in Morocco. On this point Sir Edward's position was rather difficult. For even while he was threatening the Germans with war if they took Agadir, he was prepared to hand over the whole territory to France. The Germans did not fail to rub this point in. Thus, in one of the interviews between Sir Edward and the German Ambassador, we find the latter remarking that if Sir Edward " attached so much importance to the inviolability of Moroccan territory, he should apply first and foremost to France for explanations " ; an observation to which Sir Edward does not seem to have replied, presumably because no reply was possible.[1]

But if Sir Edward could not defend his policy, at least he made perfectly clear what it was. As early as the end of May, in an interview with Count Metternich, he had said " that the agreements between England and France imposed on England the obligation to support France ; that the British Government was of opinion that France was not only justified, but obliged to protect the interest of the French, English, and other foreigners in the capital of Morocco ; that the situation in Fez was growing worse daily, and that, consequently, intervention on the part of France would be of advantage to the entire world." The German Ambassador thereupon referred to the contingency that the French occupation of Fez might be of considerable duration. Sir Edward replied that, even in this case, the English standpoint would remain unchanged, and that he did not believe that German interests would be in any way violated ; for, according to the agreement concluded between France and Germany, Germany had renounced all political influence, on condition that her economic interests should be protected against all political entanglements. " England in any case and under

---

[1] July 21st. See the account of the interview as given by the German Foreign Secretary to the Reichstag on November 27th, cited Morel, p. 338. Sir Edward's version to the House of Commons does not include this passage.

all circumstances would fulfil her obligations to France."
This account of what passed between Sir Edward and Count
Metternich was confirmed by the former, who added that
" Count Metternich had asked what the consequences would
be if the Morocco Government came under French influence
and the Algeciras Act were violated. Sir Edward replied that,
in the event of entanglements, all English obligations would
become operative. "[1] This last phrase looks as though it
could have only one meaning ; namely, that England would
support her ally, if necessary by arms, supposing that that
ally should tear up an international agreement, signed by
fourteen States.

M. Caillaux, nevertheless, still had his doubts. " I know,"
he wrote, " like all who have studied closely the history of
the British people, the considerable influence exercised on the
Government of this great country by the higher administrative
officials ; but I know also that the men who at this moment
represent the majority in power in the House of Commons,
entertain very different sentiments. Sir Francis Bertie (British
Ambassador at Paris) does not conceal this fact, and what he
has said to me on the subject is not reassuring. There is, so
it seems to me, an uncertainty in the mentality of the rulers
of Great Britain."[2] Accordingly, at the end of July, he instructs
his Foreign Minister to ask a definite question ; and M. de
Selves telegraphs to England an inquiry whether, if Germany
should install herself at Agadir or elsewhere in the Empire of
Morocco, England would accept the accomplished fact. The
French Ambassador replies, on July 28th, that, if the Germans
should take possession of Agadir, Sir Edward Grey will consult
his colleagues in the Cabinet. " Evasive reply ! " comments
Caillaux, " and somewhat disquieting."[3] Twice, he adds,
in the course of the negotiations, he asked a similar question,
on August 23rd and September 5th. He received the reply
that the concession of a protectorate to France would justify
territorial concessions in the Congo, and that, if the negotiations
broke down, the only way out would be to propose the summoning of a conference. Sir Edward thus refrained, on being
asked the definite question, from giving carte blanche to France.
One may perhaps suppose that he purposely spoke more
strongly to the Germans than to the French ; and that his

[1] Siebert, pp. 583-4.   [2] *Agadir*, p. 139.   [3] Ib., p. 140.

position really was, " If the worst comes to the worst, we shall support France in arms, but we shall try everything else first."

The result of Sir Edward Grey's attitude was that M. Caillaux determined to try a deal with the Germans ; and he found them, as we know they always had been, ready to negotiate, on the basis that in exchange for a free hand in Morocco, France should give Germany what she was asking for—" compensation " in the Congo.

On this basis, then, at last, the French and Germans began to negotiate seriously ; and in the end they reached an agreement which gave to the Germans a portion of the French Congo in exchange for what was, in effect, a French protectorate in Morocco. The negotiations were conducted at Berlin between the French Ambassador and the German Foreign Secretary. They were difficult and hazardous, and more than once the danger point was reached. The Germans at first asked for the whole of the French Congo, but offered in exchange their own colony of Togoland. " Plutôt le conflit," the French Minister exclaimed ; [1] and by the middle of August " the situation was more grave than on the morrow of Agadir." [2] Seven different proposals were put forward to secure agreement ; [3] and all this time it was hanging in the balance whether millions of Europeans should perish because the Governments of two States could not agree as to how they would divide between them a piece of equatorial Africa to which neither had any right except that of theft by arms. The Governments, it is true, on both sides were egged on by " public " opinion, which meant, in this case, as it usually does, " jingo " opinion ; and it is some satisfaction to know that in both countries there was disappointment at the result finally reached. Once more Europe had escaped, by the skin of the teeth, from the Great War.

The treaty finally arrived at [4] gave to France the substance of a protectorate in Morocco though without actually using the word. This was the main result. But there are one or two points, relevant to the purpose of this book, to which it will be worth while to call attention. The first is concerned with Article 4 of the treaty. This article declares that free trade shall be maintained in Morocco not (as in the Act of

[1] Caillaux, p. 138. [2] Tardieu, p. 479.
[3] Ib., p. 487. [4] English text in Morel, App. xv.

Algeciras) for thirty years, but for an indefinite period. On this the Germans had insisted. But the provision was very distasteful to French patriots, who, like most patriots, were protectionists. The Moroccan arrangement would constitute an exception in French policy, which had long aimed, throughout the French Empire, at the exclusion of foreign goods wherever they might compete effectually with French. French critics, accordingly, complained bitterly. " I do not believe," said one, " that there is in the world a country whose sovereignty is thus limited for eternity, whose economic development is hampered for eternity." [1] Considering that Great Britain had taken a similar engagement in Egypt, the truth of this remark seems questionable. But now, note! M. Cambon, the French Ambassador in Berlin, who had conducted the difficult negotiations, thus expressed himself in a private letter to M. Caillaux : " In diplomatic law (Droit) perpetual conventions are the only ones which can be denounced at an opportune moment." M. Caillaux proceeds : " Was it really a *sacrifice* to which we consented when we renounced an arrangement (the thirty-year limit) which had a value in form and appearance only, not in substance and reality ? " [2] We have here a quite definite statement that the free trade clause, just because it was nominally " for ever," was one the French might hope, at a convenient moment, to denounce, and was therefore more convenient than if it had contained a time limit.

Secondly, M. Caillaux's principal satisfaction with the result reached was the fact that he could now draw conscripts from Morocco. In his preface he says, speaking with approval of the colonial policy of Jules Ferry, that that statesman and those who followed him had taken up the policy of ancient Rome, " poor in Roman citizens, rich in the number of her subjects, supplying the absence of Latin soldiers by Gaulish legions. Colonial expansion became the complement, or rather the buttress, of their general policy ; it gave to France the material power, the weight, necessary for her affirmations of Right in Europe." [3] The result, he concludes, is that " France could prepare for eventualities which she did not seek." " Did not seek ! " No doubt. Who did ? Did not seek, but intended to be prepared for !

[1] Cited Tardieu, p. 565.   [2] Caillaux, p. 205.   [3] Ib., p. 6.

It may be added that the recognition of the French protectorate was rather the beginning than the end of trouble. The Moroccans, naturally, had not been considered in the dealings of the Powers with their country, because all the Powers cared about was, who should get the loot and on what terms. In the following year, accordingly, we find the French engaged in continual war, just as the Austrians had been in Bosnia. Thus : " Hardly had the French Government concluded a treaty with the Sultan of Morocco than disorders began, consequent on the new state of things in the Shereefian Empire. In the very heart of the country, in its capital, a revolt suddenly broke out, in the course of which a large number of French subjects perished. According to the latest information there are 70 dead, of whom 15 are instructing officers, 40 private soldiers, and 13 civilians ; among the wounded there are 4 officers and 66 private soldiers. In addition, it appears that massacres have taken place in the Jewish quarter in Fez, and that the houses and shops of the Jews have been pillaged. The number of Jews killed is more than a hundred, and among the survivors terror and destitution prevail. . . ." The causes of this insurrection, it is said, are firstly the negligence of the French military authorities ; but also " the new agreement with reference to the Protectorate, accepted unwillingly by the population, the prolongation of the Franco-Spanish negotiations, diminishing in the eyes of the Moroccans the prestige of the French, finally the Italo-Turkish war and the obstinate resistance of the Tripolitan Arabs. In general, the latest European conquests in Mussulman countries could not fail to have repercussions, above all, in Morocco, where sentiments of independence and ardent fanaticism so long protected this savage country against European invasion." [1] Such were the beneficent results of European civilisation in Morocco. The reference to Tripoli reminds us of a further illustration of a similar kind ; but to that we shall turn in the next chapter.

Meantime, we will pause a moment to consider what had been the attitude of Russia during the crisis we have been describing. It appears to have been of a moderating character.

[1] *Livre Noir*, i. p. 237. Dispatch from Isvolski, April 25th, 1912. Cf. ib., p. 321, events of August–September of the same year. As I write the Moroccans of the Riff are still struggling successfully against the Spanish and the French, fourteen years after the proclamation of the Protectorate.

For Russia did not wish to be drawn into war over Morocco
any more than France had wished to be drawn in over the
Balkans in 1908–9. Thus, for example, Isvolski, then Russian
Ambassador in Paris, expressed astonishment that France
should resist Germany's demand for territorial compensation
in the Congo : " The fact that Germany renounces Morocco
is a considerable victory for you. You will have henceforth
in North Africa the most admirable Empire imaginable. And
you grudge the *pourboire* which the German Empire claims !
Really, I don't understand you." The very fact, he urged,
that Germany demeaned herself to a policy of *pourboire* was
an appreciable success for France ; and he added that Russia
would not engage in war for the Congo. " Perhaps we might
support you—though it would be difficult—if it were a question
of Morocco." [1] More important, perhaps, than this unwillingness to be drawn into war over Morocco was the fact, which
Isvolski stresses, that Russia was not yet ready. " We
need two years at least to reorganise our forces before we
shall be in a position to face such a struggle." M. Louis,
then French Ambassador at St. Petersburg, interviewing the
Tsar, received the same impression. The Tsar said that, " if
occasion arose, he would honour his signature, but that Russia
was not ready, that we must be prudent and try to arrange
with Germany." [2]

VII. The Imminence of War

It seems clear, then, that though Russia would have gone
to war if the occasion contemplated in the treaty should occur
—that is, if France should find herself at war with Germany—
she did not want war, because she was not ready for it, and,
therefore, put pressure on France to prevent it. Sir Edward
Grey also did not want it, though he too would have made
it if war had broken out between France and Germany.
Did Germany want it ? Clearly the Kaiser did not ! " The
Emperor William," writes the Russian Ambassador at Berlin,
" at the first outbreak of the crisis resolved not to let it come
to war." [3] Nor did Kiderlen Waechter want it. But he was
reckless enough to play the threat of war in the course of his
dealings with France. France herself, by her advance on

[1] Caillaux, p. 142.   Ib., p. 144.   [3] Siebert, p. 609.

Fez, precipitated the crisis. We need not endeavour to apportion responsibilities. The point is that war, though it was avoided in the end, was very near. Thus, there was talk of replying to the *coup* of Agadir by sending a French and a British warship there. M. Caillaux reports that his Foreign Minister, without consulting him, made this proposal to the British on his own initiative. The British, however, wisely determined against it. Had they consented, what might not the result have been ! [1] M. Caillaux himself, it would seem, was prepared for war, if the Germans had asked for anything in Morocco.[2] Again, M. Caillaux tells us that he had received a report from his Under-Secretary of State, a document of " indisputable authenticity," saying that, in conversation with the Ambassadors of certain Powers, the German Foreign Secretary had remarked that " the attitude of France made war almost inevitable, that in any case the situation cannot long remain stationary, that it must develop quickly into peace or war ; but that he had not much confidence in the first solution." [3] In August Sir Edward Grey asked the Russian Ambassador in London what Russia would do in case of complications. Benckendorff replied that he " had not the slightest doubt but that the terms of the treaty would be strictly carried out." Whereupon Sir Edward said : [4] " I will tell you why I believe we must know this. In the event of war between Germany and France, England would have to participate. If this war should involve Russia, Austria would be dragged in too, for although she has not the slightest desire to interfere in this matter, she will be compelled by force of circumstances to do so. There is no doubt that, in such an event, the situation in Albania will become aggravated. Consequently it would no longer be a duel between France and Germany—it would be general war." Sir Edward's position is perfectly clear in this passage. He would go to war, if war should arise, even between France and Germany only. But he foresees that such a war would mean a world war.[5] In complete accordance with this Isvolski tells us that, in the summer of 1911, England had been prepared to move against Germany not only her fleet but her expeditionary force.[6]

---

[1] Caillaux, pp. 108, 110, 111. [2] Cf. above, p. 198.
[3] Caillaux, p. 174. [4] Siebert, p. 598.
[5] See Brandenburg, *passim*, and Grey, in Siebert, p. 599. [6] Siebert, p. 611.

This is confirmed by the conversation held by Colonel Bridges with the Belgian Officer Jungbluth, in April 1912.[1] So that we may probably trust the following note in Wilfrid Blunt's *Diaries*: " I asked George (Wyndham) whether, in the late crisis about Agadir, troops would have been landed in France, and he said that orders had been given for an expedition, though it was no longer possible to send more than 80,000 instead of 160,000."[2] The next sentence in the *Diaries* runs : " We three shot Buzland's and Sheppard's beat, and got 19 wild pheasants with 166 rabbits. George and all of us shot extremely well, notwithstanding our overnight's discussion." Lastly, it is interesting to note that, in the protocol of the Franco-Russian military conference, dated August 1911, the chiefs of staff of the two countries were agreed that the words " defensive war," in the Franco-Russian treaty, " cannot be interpreted in the sense of a war to be conducted defensively. On the contrary they affirm that it is an absolute necessity for the French and Russian armies to take a vigorous and, so far as possible, simultaneous offensive."[3]

It should, perhaps, be added that there is some evidence that the German attitude was affected by the financial crisis which arose out of the fear of war. Mr. Norman Angell emphasises this fact in his *Great Illusion*. M. Caillaux makes the same suggestion. It is reported, he says, that in the last days of August, some of the great German financiers were asked if they could find funds to finance a short war of two months. The financiers said " No." " Perhaps," he comments, " this account is not quite exact, perhaps the facts have been exaggerated." M. Cambon also reports that the financial crisis counted for much in the more conciliatory attitude of the German Government.[4] This, for what it may be worth. At any rate, war was very near, though we have not found evidence that it was the German Government, any more than the French or the British, which was responsible. It was near because of that whole state of Europe, which at last produced it in 1914. And the fact that it was then produced shows that we must not flatter ourselves that it can be prevented by a mere financial crisis. For war is a kind of suicide, and when suicide is in the air, finance will not stop it ;

[1] See below, p. 379.   [2] *Diaries*, October 13th, 1911, p. 381.
[3] *Livre Noir*, ii. p. 419.   [4] See Caillaux, pp. 194 seq.

any more than it will prevent it, after it has begun, from being pursued to the bitter end.

It is more likely that the real reasons why war did not actually break out are those given in a dispatch of the Russian Ambassador in Berlin : " First, Emperor William at the first outbreak of the crisis resolved not to let it come to war ; and secondly, the Ambassador of the French Republic, M. Cambon, has displayed unusual cleverness and tact. He had to fight simultaneously with an extremely strong opponent at Berlin, the German Secretary of Foreign Affairs, and a very strong opponent at Paris—the influence of those political circles whose object was to prevent an understanding with Germany." [1]

But although war was staved off, it continued to impend ; for the relations of States continued to be as they were before. Thus the Serbian Minister in London reports as early as September 1911 a conversation held with M. Cambon, which he sums up as follows : " France is conscious that in any case the war will be forced upon her. But France together with her allies is of the opinion that the war must be post-poned to a more distant period, i.e. 1914–15, even at the cost of greater sacrifice. The necessity of this postponement is not dictated so much by the material military preparation of France, which is excellent, as by the reorganisation of the supreme command, which is not yet carried out. This delay is also necessary for Russia. England alone will have no advantage from it, as each year brings a decrease of the supremacy of its fleet over the German ; but nevertheless England, in view of the preparations of its allies, advises France to come to an agreement with Germany for the present." [2] In December 1911 Isvolski, after ascribing the preservation of peace to the " resolute attitude of the three Entente Powers," goes on to write as follows : " I do not indulge in optimism as to the future. After the crisis just experienced the political situation in Europe is less secure than ever. Beyond all doubt any local collision between the Powers is bound to lead to a general European conflict, in which Russia, like every other European State, will have to participate. With God's help, the conflict may be postponed for a while, but that it may come at any moment we must bear in mind, hour by hour, and we must arm against it hour by hour." [3]

[1] Siebert, p. 609, October 13th.
[2] *Is Germany Guilty ?*, ii. p. 43. Cited also Bogitshevich, p. 109.
[3] Siebert, p. 612.

It will be observed that, in his view, God cannot do more than postpone the struggle. His impotence may be reasonably ascribed precisely to M. Isvolski's counsel of arming against the conflict " hour by hour." For " Gegen die Dummheit," says the German poet, " kämpfen die Götter vergebens."

Lastly, let us listen to M. Tardieu, who was actively concerned in the two crises of Morocco, and has written the most elaborate history of them. What does he think the result has been on the future peace of the world ? It is thus that he concludes his book on the *Mystery of Agadir*.[1] " The country deserves, by the wakening of its moral forces, to be better protected against bad shepherds. It has too long admitted as a valid excuse the idealism which the Socialists invoke. It discerns to-day the utilitarianism that lurks beneath these, and resists the dissociation of its living forces. It understands what it owes to its Army. It escapes from the pacifist dream. It regains the sense of realities. In 1911 it affirmed its resolution. It would be found ready in the same circumstances to affirm it again. The Governments of yesterday could believe that regard for life counselled weakness. This same regard will counsel energy to the Governments of to-morrow." Let the reader observe. " Idealism," " Utilitarianism "—these are the enemy ; the Army is the friend. Regard for " life " means war, means what we saw for four years from 1914 to 1918. There was no peace in prospect, there could be no peace, while the armed anarchy continued ; and not one among the statesmen or nations of Europe dreamed of putting an end to it. The crisis of 1911 merely prepared the way for those of 1912, 1913, 1914. And the peace of 1919 ? Has it prepared the way for anything better ? If it has, it will not be because of its own provisions, nor because of the intentions or beliefs of statesmen and soldiers and sailors. It will be because of the determination of that plain man, whom I would like to imagine as reading these words, that States shall cease to make it their principal object to steal territory and markets, shall begin to think of real people and their welfare, and consequently shall take seriously and develop into reality that League of Nations whose feeble and precarious existence is the only barrier against a renewal, on an incalculably more terrible and destructive scale, of the Great War of 1914.

[1] Tardieu, pp. 604–5.

CHAPTER VIII

TRIPOLI

I. Previous History

IN previous chapters we have had occasion to notice that Italy, since her unification, completed in 1870, had been preoccupied with her position in the Mediterranean, and consequently afraid of the expansion of France, Austria, and Russia. Of England one might say that the new kingdom was only not afraid because she was too much afraid to do anything but remain on friendly terms ; for she could never face the British Navy. Hence her insistence that the Triple Alliance must never have a point against England.[1] In the years previous to the turn of the century her principal antagonism had been to France ; an antagonism that was reciprocated, for France could not forgive her for joining Germany and Austria in the Triple Alliance. The Mediterranean agreements of 1887[2] with England and Austria were intended to safeguard her position in the Mediterranean ; and it is clear that, in these earlier years, Salisbury thought war against Russia in defence of Austria a very possible contingency for England. Both in these agreements, and in the Triple Alliance, the status quo in the Mediterranean was the object guaranteed ; and in the latter, as renewed in 1887, it was made clear that, in case of French aggression in Morocco or in Tripoli, the casus belli would arise on Italy's demand.[3] For during these years the principal fear of Italy was that France might seize Tripoli. True, the integrity of the Turkish Empire had been guaranteed by the Powers both in the Treaty of Paris (1856) and in that of Berlin (1878). But, as we have abundantly seen, this obligation was held very lightly by the statesmen of Europe. France had

[1] See above, p. 85.   [2] Above, p. 99.   [3] Above, p. 88.

occupied Tunis, England, Egypt ; and it was plain that only considerations of force, not those of right, would prevent a further dismemberment of Turkey. If, however, Tripoli was to be taken, Italy meant to take it. Hence the trouble.

At Berlin, while the Powers were drafting the clause about the integrity of Turkey, they had been very free in their discussion of eventual partition. " By a secret stipulation with England," said the French Minister, Waddington, in 1893,[1] " I obtained carte blanche for France in Tunis, which, later on, permitted us to establish there our protectorate without the occurrence of any European incident." This is substantially confirmed by a dispatch of Lord Salisbury to Lord Lyons (1878), in which he says : " If France occupied Tunis to-morrow we should not even remonstrate. But to promise that publicly would be a little difficult, because we must avoid giving away other people's property without their consent, and also because it is no business of ours to pronounce beforehand on the considerations which Italy would probably advance upon that subject." [2] The permission thus given to France was, of course, secret. But the Italians were already alarmed and had to be placated. Thus in August 1879 that same Waddington who had received the promise from England declared to the Italian Ambassador, on his " word of honour," that " as long as I am a member of the French Government nothing of the sort will be attempted ; no occupation of Tunis or any other place will take place without your co-operation, without a previous recognition of Italy's right to occupy another point of relative and justly proportioned importance." [3] This, of course, on that principle of " compensation " with which we are sufficiently familiar ; the compensation, in this case, to be given out of the territory of the same Power whose integrity both States had joined in guaranteeing the previous year. Again, in July 1880, Freycinet said that " for the present France had no intention of occupying Tunis, but that the future was in God's hands " ; [4] a remark hardly calculated to soothe Italian apprehensions, since the " act of God " is as incalculable in diplomacy as in the humbler sphere of the common law. As things turned out, that act did occur as early as the following

---

[1] Crispi, ii. p. 99. Cf. Woolf, p. 95. [2] *Life*, ii. p. 333.
[3] Crispi, ii. p. 105. [4] Ib., p. 107.

year, when, presumably under divine compulsion, the French sent an expedition to occupy Tunis. Nothing more was heard for the moment of "compensation" to the Italians. Indeed, in a conversation of the previous year, the Italian Ambassador had taken a high line on that subject. "Why will you persist in thinking of Tunis?" Freycinet had asked. "Why not turn your attention to Tripoli, where you will have neither ourselves nor anyone else to contend with?" Whereto the Ambassador replied that the suggestion of compensation "reminded me of the advice Bismarck gave to Napoleon III, to take Belgium and leave the Rhine provinces alone. I said that we sought possession neither of Tripoli nor of Tunis; that we desired only that the Regency there be maintained in status quo. I added that Tripoli must not even be mentioned as a compensation should France one day occupy Tunis, unless Tripoli should meantime have ceased to belong to the Ottoman Empire." In reply to this Freycinet reiterated that the matter was in God's hands, but that if He should compel France to occupy Tunis, Italy should be informed as long beforehand as possible.[1] God, however, as we have seen, acted with somewhat unprecedented celerity, and there does not seem to have been time to warn Italy of His intentions. In the course of 1881 France had established her military footing in Tunis, and the proclamation of a Protectorate was only a question of time and opportunity. Italian indignation was, perhaps, tinged with regret. For her Foreign Minister stated, in 1894, that at the Conference of Berlin it had been suggested that Italy herself might take Tunis, without any objection being raised by the Powers.[2] If that were so, Italy had missed an opportunity. Whether or no the Powers, or some of them, or one of them, had really offered Tunis both to Italy and to France we must leave undecided; merely observing that it is not, in itself, an improbable contingency.

From that time on, until the agreement of 1902, there was continual friction between Italy and France. The occupation of Tunis was one of the reasons, perhaps the principal one, for Italy's joining the Triple Alliance,[3] and for her insisting, at its renewal in 1887, upon the introduction of the clause which enabled her to call upon Germany for

armed support if France "should extend her occupation or
her protectorate or her sovereignty, under any form whatsoever, in the North African territories, whether of the vilayet
of Tripoli or of the Moroccan Empire." [1] In the same year,
1887, she secured that treaty, or agreement, with England,
which seemed to suggest that England might support her by
war in such a contingency. [2] In 1890, Crispi, the protagonist
of Italian claims in Africa, being then in office, a somewhat
acute crisis arose. The French were extending the "hinterland" of Tunis in such a way that it would include territory
which Italians held to belong to the hinterland of Tripoli.
The point in question was the control of the caravan route
from Tripoli down to Central Africa. Italians felt that the
future of the territory which they intended some day to
seize was being compromised. Their trade with Central
Africa would be interfered with ; the "balance of power"
in the Mediterranean would be upset. True, the trade in
question was negligible, or even non-existent. And as to
the balance of power—"the more one learns of it the more
extraordinary a phenomenon it seems to be. To the horror
of Wellington and other statesmen who were not Frenchmen,
it was upset and destroyed by the French in 1830. Nothing
happened, and despite its destruction in 1830, it still existed,
to be destroyed and upset again by the French in 1881. And
yet, less than ten years later, it is still found to be existing
in the nightmare of an Italian General, who is horrified by
the consequences which will follow if the French—who
destroyed the balance of power in the Mediterranean in 1830
by seizing Algeria and in 1881 by seizing Tunis—are allowed
once more to destroy the indestructible by seizing Tripoli in
1890." [3] The situation was intensified by rumours that the
Bey of Tunis had promised France the protectorate of that
territory after his death. Italy approached Germany. But
the Germans held that the Triple Alliance had nothing to do
with Tunis. [4] They did, however, approach Lord Salisbury
on the subject. But he was unsympathetic. France, he
said, had raised at the Congress of Berlin the question of
compensating Italy with Tripoli, but he had opposed the
idea. Now he was afraid that if Italy pressed her objec-

[1] See above, p. 88, and Pribram, ii. p. 79.   [2] See above, p. 99.
[3] Woolf, p. 128.   [4] Ger. Docs., viii. pp. 240 seq.

tions to French expansion in Tunis, France might renew
that proposal, and thus precipitate the break-up of the
Turkish Empire. Count Hatzfeld, on the other hand, was
afraid that if Italy's interests were too much neglected she
might be tempted to pass into the other camp. To which
Lord Salisbury replied that English democrats would never
stand for war with France over Tripoli. There was some
reason for Count Hatzfeld's fear that Italy might join France.
For, in fact, the Italian Ambassador in Paris had a discussion
with M. Ribot in which the question of Italian " compensation "
was definitely approached. " I reminded Ribot," he reports,
" of the offers of co-operation which M. Jules Ferry had made
in former days, first to me, and then to the Ambassador, offers
which Mancini had repulsed ; and I added that, should an
offer of co-operation in some similar undertaking be made
to-day, there was now a Minister at Rome (Crispi) who
would certainly be willing to consider it, because, despite all
reports to the contrary, I was well aware how anxious he
was to bring about a reconciliation between our country
and France, if this could be done with advantage to Italy."
M. Ribot seems to have replied with great frankness. The
difficulty was, he said, that any deal about Tripoli would be
met " with a decided *non possumus* " by the Sultan. But,
further and more important : " Public opinion in France
would condemn the Government should it lend its support
to Italy in such an undertaking, unless Italy would, in return,
consent to withdraw from the Triple Alliance. Until the
Triple Alliance, which constitutes an even greater offence to
the Tsar than to the French Republic, has been denounced,
no intimacy will ever be possible between Russia and Germany,
any more than between the Italians and ourselves. We
may not be openly hostile, but we can never be true friends." [1]
This is an interesting illustration of the general condition, on
which we have already dwelt, that France was determined not
to have friendly relations with Italy so long as the latter was
a member of the Triple Alliance. Crispi, however, had no
intention of sacrificing what had been his own creation, and
in November 1890 he raised the question of the renewal of
the alliance. In the same year, however, he fell from office,
and his successor, Rudini, either was or was believed by

[1] Crispi, ii. p. 469.

the Austrians and the Germans to be negotiating on friendly terms with France. The Germans became the more urgent for the renewal of the Triple Alliance. The Italians were in a strong position, and they managed, in the new agreement arrived at in 1891, to secure the inclusion of Tunis among those territories of North Africa where the status quo was to be guaranteed. Presumably their hope was that, in this way, they could call upon their allies for support in case of further extensions of French power in the hinterland.[1]

The next important stage in this history was the agreement between France and Italy, reached in December 1900. Under this it was provided that " if a modification of the political or territorial status of Morocco should result from French action in " safeguarding the rights " which are " the result for her of the proximity of her territory with that Empire, then Italy would reserve to herself, as a measure of reciprocity, the right eventually to develop her influence with regard to Tripolitania-Cyrenaica."[2] In plainer language, Italy agreed to let France steal Morocco, on condition that she in return might steal Tripoli. France was thus squared ; and, as we have seen, she began her action in Morocco a few years later, after squaring England. Italy, however, still held her hand. Perhaps she was waiting till she had also squared Russia. This was done by the agreement of Racconigi in 1909, the fifth article of which runs : " Italy and Russia engage themselves to regard with benevolence, the one Russia's interests in the question of the Straits, the other Italian interests in Tripoli and Cyrenaica."[3] This Racconigi agreement was received with some enthusiasm by the other Powers of the Entente. But the enthusiasm was not unmixed with perplexities. Thus we are told by the Russian Ambassador in London that : " Hardinge has stated to me that he shares the opinion of a part of the European Press concerning the strange position which Italy has assumed in respect to the grouping of the Powers. Chiefly, in the event of complications in the Near East, Italy would either have to be untrue to her ally, or act counter to her own national interests."[4] The dilemma, as we shall see, did in

---

[1] Pribram, ii. p. 99, and text of Treaty of 1891, Article 9.
[2] Ib., p. 244.
[3] Text in *Livre Noir*, i. p. 357. Cf. Judet's *Georges Louis*, p. 173.
[4] Siebert, p. 149.

fact present itself, precisely in this way, in 1912-13, after the outbreak of the Balkan wars. It then appeared that, for that occasion only, Italy preferred her old ally Austria to her new one France. She made up for that, however, by inclining to the new ally, and deserting the old one, in 1915. So there is " compensation " everywhere.

By the conclusion of the Racconigi agreement Italy had secured for her annexation of Tripoli the consent of Russia, in addition to that of France and of her partners in the Triple Alliance ; she had, it would seem, also secured the consent of England. At any rate, Signor Giolitti speaks of the " agreement with France and England which recognised our primary interest in Libya as a compensation for our dis-interestedness in Morocco and in Egypt." [1] Everything was thus prepared, so far as the Great Powers were concerned ; and Signor Giolitti, on assuming office in 1911, decided to take the long-anticipated step. " Many," he says, " wondered why the Government had come to this decision," and he is careful to explain what had really determined him. The reasons he gives are, first, the fact that while now " Western Africa, from Tunis to Morocco, was under the protection of European administration, Libya was very much behind the times. Slave markets were still held in Bengasi, and men and women taken by violence in Central Africa were sold in those markets : infamies which it was impossible to tolerate at the very gates of Europe." Signor Giolitti, perhaps, will hardly expect us to infer that it was the observation of these infamies which had determined Italian policy from 1871 onwards. There were, at any rate, other considerations to be taken into account. Prestige, for instance, and " national dignity." Then, the Young

---

[1] *Memoirs*, p. 250. Cf. a dispatch of the Russian Foreign Minister, August 1911 (cited Siebert, p. 158) : " In the course of the conversation (with the Italian Ambassador at St. Petersburg) I learned that France and England, as well as Germany and Austria-Hungary, are not only informed of Italy's intentions, but that they are not raising any objections to them."

See also Blunt's *Diaries*, July 24th, 1912 : " The truth is, that Italy was allowed to invade Tripoli without our disapproval at the Foreign Office, as part of Grey's policy of detaching Italy from the German alliance in favour of the Entente, which was gradually becoming a coalition. In this he succeeded four years later."

No doubt Sir Edward desired to detach Italy. On the other hand the British, like the French, were perplexed, because they were great Moham-medan Powers, and the reverberations of the Italian episode throughout the Mohammedan world were disquieting.

Turks had come to power and excited the political and fanatical feelings of the Mussulmans against Italy. The Banco di Roma too had "established considerable interests in Cyrenaica and Tripoli which it was the duty of the Italian Government to safeguard." The Banco di Roma had, in fact, for some years past been pursuing that policy of " peaceful penetration " by which territories are prepared for annexation, much as the boa-constrictor softens and moulds his prey before swallowing it. But in this case the penetration appears, from the financial point of view, to have been a failure. Indeed, things had arrived at such a pitch that the bank, " seeing itself in serious danger, had opened negotiations to cede all its interests to a group of Austro-German bankers." [1] Lastly, but not least, Italian nationalists were thirsting for the fray. They were, in Mr. McCullagh's words, " jingoes of an extreme and candid type. They believe in war for war's sake. They believe that the shedding of blood makes a nation virile, unifies it, intensifies the patriotism of the individual. Their motto is : ' If you feel decadent, go out and murder somebody.' " [2] The expression of this mood is unusually frank in modern Italy ; but the mood itself is one of the components of all jingoism, and even the blood-bath from which Europe has just emerged does not seem to have made it ashamed.

II. The Launching of the Enterprise

Such, then, were the reasons which determined Signor Giolitti to launch the long-delayed enterprise, in the autumn of the year 1911. The way, as we have seen, was well prepared with the States of the Entente. They had agreed to support Italy in her seizure of this piece of loot in return for her consent to their arrangements about Egypt, Morocco, and the Straits. They were bound in "honour" to support her, and on the whole they lived up to their duty. Thus, as early as the end of July, Sir Edward Grey promised that England would give " her sympathetic support " ; which, however, would only be " of a moral nature." He

---

[1] Giolitti, pp. 253, seq. Cf. McCullagh, pp. 14 seq.
[2] McCullagh, p. 4.

added " in a friendly and personal manner, that it was indispensable that any eventual action on our part should be justified by a flagrant violation of our rights, or by the evident demonstration of Turkey's intention to put us in an inferior position in Tripoli with respect to other nations." In particular he desired that we should " avoid any appearance that our action was determined by any desire on our part to obtain an economic position based on particular interests granted us by Turkey," as that would make it difficult for him to maintain in Parliament the " sympathy and moral support " he intended to display. More simply, he wanted to secure that Italy should maintain the open door after she had taken Tripoli.[1] Sir Edward thus laid down from the beginning the two conditions which would make it easy for him to support Italy before British opinion ; first, the show of a good moral cause, secondly, consideration for British trading interests. Unfortunately, when the time came, some part of the British Press was hostile. But Signor Giolitti knew why. He " knew they were newspapers that were under German influence because they upheld the scheme, then supported by some English political groups, of an understanding with Germany."[2] The reader will observe that it is inconceivable to this statesman that anyone could really have any moral objections to the course he was adopting. " Pro-Germanism " is the only way in which he can account for this perverse attitude. The French Government, as was to be expected, after the agreements of 1900–2,[3] was equally favourable to the Italian design. " Delcassé told Tittoni that all wishes and sympathies were for Italy. This friendly attitude of the French Government was also mirrored by the Press, which, apart from the incident of the *Manouba* and of the *Carthage*, followed our movement with much interest and sympathy."[4] Russia was equally friendly, though preoccupied with the possible reactions of the war on the Balkan situation.[5]

The Entente Powers, on the whole, came up well to their promises to sanction this piece of international brigandage. But with her nominal allies Italy seems to have had more difficulty. Signor Giolitti tells us that he did not inform

---

[1] Giolitti, p. 263.   [2] Ib., p. 264.   [3] See above, p. 94.
[4] Giolitti, p. 265.   [5] Ib.

them of his intentions before the end of September, being anxious "at one and the same time to spare them serious embarrassment and to assure ourselves against interference which, however well intentioned and friendly, would have complicated our situation." He adds that when Aehrenthal was at last informed he expressed his anxiety about the probable repercussions in the Balkans, and begged Italy to "consider the grave responsibility it might incur." But, says Signor Giolitti triumphantly : "It was too late ; Austria was faced by a fait accompli."[1] It appears, however, that, in fact, Aehrenthal was not sorry to have Italy's attention distracted from the Balkans. Conrad, on the other hand, wanted war with Italy and had to resign in December.[2]

Germany was really anxious. She was in friendly relations with Turkey, and her Ambassador there maintained "that the occupation of Tripoli would have as a result the immediate breaking out of a revolution in Turkey which would cause the fall of the Young Turks and consequent disorders directed against the European colonies. We were assuming," he insisted, "a very grave responsibility." The Kaiser advocated joint action with France to preserve peace in the Balkans and revived his old idea of a Continental combination against England.[3] On the very day before hostilities broke out the German Foreign Minister endeavoured to prevent the war. But, says the Italian Minister, "all these attempts to arrest our action at the last moment confirmed me in my intention to allow no time to elapse between our final determination to act and such action itself."[4]

For these motives, then, and with this preparation, the Italian Government determined to venture. The closest secrecy was maintained up to the moment of sending the ultimatum : "I came to an arrangement with San Giuliano that he was to remain at Fiuggi or Vallombrosa, on the pretext of taking his vacation, while I stayed at Cavour or Bardonnechia, so as to give the idea that nothing unusual was to be looked for. I remember that those newspapers most in favour of the Libyan enterprise reproved me caustically, for absenting myself from the capital and not keeping in close contact with the Foreign Minister and other members

[1] Giolitti, p. 266.   [2] Brandenburg, p. 333
[3] Ib., p. 334.   [4] Giolitti, pp. 268-9.

of the Cabinet. These remarks pleased me very much, since they showed that my stratagem was working well, and would have the effect of dissipating the Turkish Government's suspicions. The latter was, in fact, taken quite by surprise by our ultimatum."[1] That ultimatum was dispatched on September 26th, 1911, and, as Signor Giolitti explains, was " couched in such a way as not to leave any possibility of evasion open, and so to avoid lengthy discussions which were to be avoided at any cost. This idea governed the composition of every word of the document."[2] It governed also that of a later and more famous ultimatum.

In this document[3] the Italian Government set forth how they had long been representing to the Porte that " the state of disorder and neglect in which Tripoli and Cyrenaica are left by Turkey should come to an end." This was " required by the general exigencies of civilisation." The situation had become, of late, extremely dangerous " on account of the agitation prevailing against Italian subjects which is very obviously fomented by officers and other organs of the authorities." The Turks had even sent military reinforcements. The Italian Government therefore, " finding itself forced to consider the guardianship of its dignity and its interests, has decided to proceed to the military occupation of Tripoli and Cyrenaica." In a later manifesto, published in *The Times*,[4] it was explained that " Italian nationals have been surrounded by a hostile atmosphere not in keeping with the good official relations existing between the two States." A young girl had been abducted and married to a Mussulman. The Italian flag had been insulted more than once. The " genuine and beneficent work of economic progress and of civilisation " introduced by the Banco di Roma had been resisted. Italian subjects had been hindered from acquiring land. There had been assassinations. In fact the cup was full. The Turks replied[5] that the efforts of the Italians had been plainly directed to political, not merely economic influence, and that what they were aiming at was not an equal but a privileged, indeed a monopolistic, position. All this face-making need not detain us, for we know that, for years past, Italy had been preparing the ground for the

---

[1] Giolitti, p. 269.   [2] Ib., p. 276.
[3] Text in Barclay, p. 109.   [4] Ib., p. 114.   [5] Ib., p. 119.

seizure of Tripoli, quite apart from grievances of any kind; and we know also that, in doing so, she was only following the example of her stronger and more experienced rivals.

The course of the war we need not describe. It was waged with the usual ruthlessness—a ruthlessness, of course, denied by the country engaged and emphasised by citizens and correspondents of countries not involved. Nothing is more difficult to check than accounts of atrocities and nothing more certain than that they always occur.[1] More convincing, perhaps, than any alleged details is the following letter by Lord Roberts, who knew what war was, and who disclosed more than he intended : " That the means employed to re-establish what I have called the equilibrium of battle were severe is doubtless true, but in war it is usually the severest measures that are in the long run the most humane. No soldier will put credence in the reports that women and children were deliberately killed by the Italians, but doubtless, in the act of clearing the hostile villages behind the Italian lines, many innocent people suffered with the guilty. Such things are unfortunately inevitable in war." [2]

III. The Policies of the Powers

Our present interest, however, is not in the conduct of the war, but in its diplomatic accompaniments. We have seen that both Austria and Germany regarded with apprehension the Italian enterprise, and indeed that the Germans did their best to stop it. As events proceeded the friction with Austria became acute. For Italy, unable to win a quick victory in Africa, in what soon became a guerilla war, was led to attempt pressure on the Turks by attacking them elsewhere. She had promised not to carry her operations into the Adriatic nor into Albania, " knowing that the militarist element in Vienna would try to profit thereby." Nevertheless, an episode occurred in that region which " drew an energetic protest from Austria," who complained of " a flagrant breach of our promise to localise the war in the Mediterranean " and " threatened serious consequences if such occurrences did not cease." [3]   Later, a cruiser squadron

---

[1] See McCullagh, and also a letter published by Wilfrid Blunt, *Diaries*, App. to vol. ii. p. 452, in the edition of Martin Secker.

[2] Cited Barclay, p. 17 note.   [3] Giolitti, pp. 282-3.

appeared at Beirut, and two Turkish warships were sunk ; whereupon Austria sent a protest " accusing us of having bombarded an open city." [1] A little later, the Italian Government informed Berchtold (who had just succeeded Aehrenthal) that she intended to occupy some of the Greek islands. Berchtold replied that this was contrary to Article 7 of the Treaty of the Triple Alliance, and a reference to the text seems to show that he was right.[2] But, needless to say, his interpretation was denied by the Italians. Finally a compromise was reached, whereby Austria agreed to the occupation of the Dodecanese. The occupation was said to be temporary—a provision which, according to Signor Giolitti, " made it impossible for Austria to claim compensation." It did not, however, make it impossible for Italy, during the peace negotiations, to claim sovereign rights to the islands. Whereupon the Turkish envoy remarked : " If you really want to keep those islands, do so ; but do not ask for our consent, which we will never give. . . . The question of the islands does not exist for me." [3] It existed, however, very much for the Italians, who were still in possession when the Great War broke out. Such are the amenities, and such the results, of diplomacy and war.[4]

These disputes with Austria might easily have been serious. Germany preserved a more friendly attitude, but thought the war should be ended on some terms short of the definite annexation of Tripoli and Cyrenaica. To this, however, the Italians, who, in order to avoid such embarrassments, had announced the annexation at an early stage, opposed an obstinate refusal.

The Powers of the Entente would have liked an earlier ending of the war. They had, indeed, given their assent to the annexation ; but still, awkward consequences were ensuing. For both England and France were great Mohammedan Powers, and their subjects were becoming restive. Thus we find M. Barrère, the French Ambassador at Rome, pointing out to his Russian colleague " that his Government

---

[1] Giolitti, p. 296.   [2] See above, p. 87.   [3] Giolitti, p. 324.
[4] Giolitti, p. 369, has an interesting passage on the islands. He says, among other things, that England " made it clearly understood that, even at the cost of war, she would not permit any of the Ægean islands to remain in the possession of a Great Power. In this England had the support of France."

was very much worried over the spirit prevailing among the
Mohammedan subjects of France, and wanted the war to
end as soon as possible." [1]   Incidents of the war increased
the friction. The Italians stopped French ships.[2]   The
French, so the Italians complained, took no adequate steps
to prevent the transport of contraband of war through Tunis
to Tripoli.[3]   Worse, when the Italians occupied the islands,
it was feared, not without reason, that this would result in
annexation—a circumstance which "would run directly
counter to the interests of France in the Mediterranean." [4]
Financial considerations also caused friction. "Italian public
opinion accuses a French financial group of wishing to grant a
considerable loan to Turkey to be guaranteed by the harbour
tolls of Smyrna and Beirut. If this rumour should prove
true it would be regarded as a violation of neutrality." [5]
In short, "the present war has greatly increased the
feeling of national consciousness among the Italians,
and, as they say, they do not intend to allow any foreign
tutelage." [6]

The reference just made to financial interests tempts us
to cite also the following interesting little fact. In March
1912 the Russian Ambassador at Rome writes to his Government as follows : "As the French Ambassador here (in Rome)
told me, the (French) Press is under the control of the French
insurance companies, who have invested nearly 300 millions
in life insurance here and fear the loss they would suffer if a
State monopoly for life insurance should be introduced into
Italy. . . . The German Ambassador very skilfully takes
advantage of the mistakes made by the rivals of his country
and has commissioned the German journalist Mühling to
influence the German Press in favour of Italy." [7]   This
kind of complication, no doubt, created, in French public
opinion, a certain measure of distrust or hostility. But it
should be consoling to those who fought the war for democracy
to know how firmly M. Poincaré dealt with such manifestations : "Neither Government," he informed the Russian
Ambassador, "had allowed itself to be influenced by public
opinion." [8]   The position, nevertheless, was rather difficult,

[1] Siebert, p. 171.   [2] Giolitti, p. 291.   [3] Siebert, p. 172.
[4] Ib., and also p. 184.   [5] Ib., p. 173.   [6] Ib., p. 166.
[7] Ib. Cf. Giolitti, p. 233.   [8] Siebert, p. 181.

and the French Government was anxious for an early conclusion of the war.

So was the British; for in the British Empire, too, the Mohammedans were becoming restive. Further, British opinion was disturbed by the horrors of the war.[1] And apart from this, the general political situation was causing anxiety; for the growing friction between Italy and France might have the effect of driving Italy back towards the Triple Alliance. "In England," writes the Russian Foreign Minister, "they are beginning to be uneasy, as they fear there that in the event of disagreement between Italy and France, Italy will again become more closely associated with the Triple Alliance. In this case, Tripoli might, in Italian hands, become a convenient naval base of operations for the Triple Alliance in the Mediterranean."[2] The same anxiety was shown by Russia[3] and by France.[4]

As early as October the Russians had proposed to Turkey an agreement whereby the latter should permit the passage of the Straits by Russian warships in return for a guarantee of Constantinople and the Balkans. But to this plan the French were cold and the British hostile. The Germans, who were also consulted, had divided counsels, and Austria was naturally reluctant. This project therefore came to nothing.[5] But in the spring the Turks closed the Straits, in consequence of Italian attacks, and trade began to suffer. The question was then raised, had the Turks the right to exclude merchant ships? Signor Giolitti answers this question categorically in the negative.[6] But the point does not seem to have been so clear to other statesmen. M. Poincaré, for instance, hints doubts.[7] In any case, the Russians were not in a mood to rest their case on international law alone. "Public opinion," their Ambassador said to Sir Edward Grey, "would not concern itself with the responsibility of Turkey or Italy, nor with any treaty rights, but would simply and unanimously demand that the Straits be reopened to Russian trade, and the Government would certainly have to yield. I further said that, at the present moment, it was not so much the question of Right or Wrong, but we had to deal with facts, and that

---

[1] Siebert, p. 164.   [2] Ib., p. 179.   [3] Ib., p. 180.
[4] Ib., p. 186.   [5] Brandenburg, p. 335.   [6] *Memoirs*, p. 300.
[7] Siebert, p. 170.

TRIPOLI

a further development of the disputed points might assume
unexpected proportions." [1] From this it would appear that
the Russian Government was indifferent to the question of
legal right and proposed to act as her own interests might
dictate. M. Poincaré, however, hinted that the position they
were adopting might logically lead to the neutralisation of
the Straits. "We should not," writes the Russian Ambassador, "in his opinion, lose sight of this fact, so as not to
get into a conflict ourselves with our own political interests
and aspirations." [2] Whether that point would have finally
determined the attitude of Russia does not appear, for the
difficulty was settled by Turkey yielding to her demands.

It may be added that, although, from the point of view
of the Straits, Russia may have desired a quick ending of
the war, there was another consideration which worked in
the opposite direction. She was engaged, at the time, in
discussions with Turkey about her position in Persia, and she
preferred that the war should continue until that question
was adjusted; since in time of war Turkey would be compelled
to be more accommodating than she might be in time of
peace.[3] In short, to use the words of Signor Giolitti:
"When we thought it convenient to move the field of war
from Libya to the Ægean, everywhere we turned we found
British, German, Russian, French and even American, but
never Turkish interests." [4]

All this is a natural result of the European anarchy, and
it led to attempts on the part of the Powers to bring the
war to a conclusion. It was proposed that the States of the
Entente should first agree upon what looked like reasonable
terms, and then communicate these to the Central Powers.
It was, however, difficult to draft the formula. Both the
Russians and the British objected to the phrase proposed
by the French, that "the Powers must, above all . . . confirm in writing their disinterestedness"; for they were
unwilling to exclude from the discussions the question of the
Straits. And we find Sir Edward Grey referring to the
promise he gave Russia in 1908,[5] and saying that, while at
that time the promise referred to the future, now "circumstances had changed, and that if the Russians wished to

[1] Siebert, p. 168.   [2] Ib., p. 171.   [3] Ib., p. 331.
[4] Memoirs, p. 350.   [5] See above, pp. 65, 66.

bring up the question he did not desire to rule it out." [1]
Similarly, Poincaré and M. Paul Cambon were now in favour
of opening the Straits to the Russians, in order to re-establish
in the Mediterranean the " balance of power " disturbed by
the Italian successes. [2] Ultimately a formula of intervention
was agreed upon between the three Powers. But then the
belligerents objected : " Turkey because she is afraid she will
be ousted from the Balkans altogether ; Italy, because she
evidently wishes alone to decide the fate of the islands occupied
by her—an occupation which, by the way, is considered inadmissible in London." [3] Thus the attempt to end the war,
in this way, failed ; and hostilities might have continued
indefinitely, were it not that it became evident that the Turks
would have to face a new war in the Balkans. That was
precisely the contingency which the Austrians and the
Germans had been fearing all along, but which, it would seem,
the Italians contemplated with a certain satisfaction. [4] The
Turks were driven to make peace in order to meet the
new enemy, and they accepted the Italian sovereignty over
Tripoli and Cyrenaica. The partition of the Turkish Empire,
so far as North Africa was concerned, was now complete ;
England, France, and Italy, all signatories of the treaties
guaranteeing that Empire, being the beneficiaries. And
Europe turned to deal with the last crisis before the one
which ended in the Great War.

Signor Giolitti discusses and rejects the view that the
war for Tripoli [5] necessarily precipitated that catastrophe ;
and, no doubt, it is always conceivable in history that something might have happened otherwise than it did. But
taking a common-sense view of causation, it was the war for
Tripoli that encouraged the Balkan States to rise and throw
off Turkish rule, and it was the Balkan wars that led directly
to the Great War. That will emerge clearly from our later
chapters. Meantime, since our interest is in the European
anarchy, we may briefly sum up this example of it. The
five Great Powers of Europe, having all of them solemnly
affirmed, in public treaties, the integrity and independence
of the Turkish Empire, agree with Italy, in a series of secret
agreements, that as far as they are concerned she may take

---

[1] Siebert, pp. 186, 190.   [2] Ib., p. 184.   [3] Ib., p. 191.
[4] Giolitti, p. 341.   [5] Ib., p. 351.

Tripoli. In the course of the war the Russian Government, annoyed by the closure of the Straits, announces that, treaties or no treaties, it will insist on their being opened ; and the fact that the opening was in fact arranged without an act of war does not do away with the significance of this action. The Governments which have given Italy carte blanche fulfil their promise by standing aloof while she carries out her piece of brigandage. But they are embarrassed by the repercussion of events in the Mohammedan world, and, at any rate in the case of England, by a public opinion which, in its simple way, is indignant at an outrage which it does not know to have been sanctioned by its own Government, and at atrocities which it does not choose to attribute to the very nature of war. Meantime, in France, another section of " public opinion " is working, for reasons of profit, against the policy of the French Government. And the war drags on, while the Governments debate, till it ends in the annexation to Italy of a tract of barren desert, of questionable value either for colonisation, for trade, or for defence. It is thus that the business of nations is conducted, and thus that it will continue to be conducted, unless and until public opinion becomes better informed and more intelligent through the supersession of animal passion by reason, knowledge, and humanity.

CHAPTER IX

THE BAGDAD RAILWAY

I. The Earlier History of the Enterprise

As we have frequently had occasion to observe in the course of this book, one of the principal objects of cupidity, and therefore of strife, to the Great Powers of Europe, was the vast primitive and unorganised Empire of Turkey. The French had cultural and military associations there dating from the Crusades, and their right, by tradition and treaty, to the protectorate of the Christians, gave them an excuse to intervene, whenever their interests or their pride might require it; the Russians were always looking to Constantinople and the Balkans; while the British and the Austrians were united in the determination to keep them out of both. These Powers were the original protagonists in that perpetual wrestling-match known to history as the Eastern Question; and the following passage gives a good summary of the situation as it existed for many years previous to 1870:
" Astride across Europe and Asia the Ottoman Empire represented, for all the nations of the Old Continent, the cosmopolitan centre where each had erected, by dint of patience and ingenuity, a fortress of interests, influences, and special rights. Each fortress watched jealously to maintain its particular advantages in face of the enemy rival. If one of them obtained a concession or a new favour, immediately the commanders of the others were seen issuing from their walls, to claim from the Grand Turk concessions or favours which should maintain the existing balance of power or prestige.
. . . France acted as protector of the Christians; England, the vigilant guardian of the routes to India, maintained a political and economic position; Austria-Hungary mounted guard over the route to Salonica; Russia, protecting the

Armenians and Slavs of the South of Europe, watched over the fate of the Orthodox. There was a general understanding among them all, tacit or express, that none should better its situation at the expense of the others." [1] With the unification of Italy and of Germany new forces began to operate in the complex " balance." Italy, almost from the beginning, became both the accomplice and the rival of Austria in maintaining the status quo in the Balkans. Germany, under Bismarck's prudent and pacific control, claimed nothing in the peninsula for herself, but recommended its division into distinct spheres of influence for Russia and Austria. But, in little more than a decade after his retirement, Germany had produced, in the Middle East, yet another whirlpool, in the rapids which were sweeping Europe into war.

The cause of this disturbance was a great economic enterprise which, in a world of reasonable humane and progressive men, would have met, on all sides, with enthusiastic co-operation ; being nothing less than the project of a railway across the Turkish Empire, linking the capitals of Europe with the Persian Gulf, unlocking, to the common benefit, the mineral and agricultural resources of that vast territory, substituting productive labour for stagnation and brigandage, and benefiting everybody alike by the energy, brains, and skill of the youngest competitor in the industry of the world. This is how such an enterprise must have been viewed by States unarmed, and therefore unsuspicious, uncovetous, and therefore unaggressive, instructed, and therefore not the easy prey of military, diplomatic, and financial adventurers. But the States of Europe were not, and are not, of this kind ; and the germ of the Bagdad Railway, flung into the cauldron of the armed anarchy, evoked the only spectre that can emerge from that witches' kettle, the fiery countenance of the spirit of war.

It is interesting to note that the plan of a railway across Turkey to the Persian Gulf was, in the first place, British. It was conceived by a young officer as early as 1831, and twenty-five years later enthusiastically supported by Lord Palmerston and Lord Stratford de Redcliffe.[2] A concession was actually granted by the Sultan ; but funds were not forthcoming and the scheme was abandoned. The con-

[1] Pierre Albin, *D'Agadir à Serajevo*, p. 81.   [2] Earle, p. 176.

struction of the Suez Canal by a French engineer revived the plan, for it was felt that the new route to the East must be countered by another, under British control. But Beaconsfield's purchase of the control of the Canal, in 1875, allayed the anxiety and quashed the enterprise. In 1878, however, the idea came up again, in connexion with Lord Salisbury's scheme of a " pacific penetration " of Turkey by England.[1] But financial support was not forthcoming, and the advent of a Liberal Government dismissed the project once more into limbo. Ten years later the Sultan proposed the extension of a British railway (Haidar Pasha-Ismid) to Angora and ultimately to Bagdad ; and at the same time the British chairman of the Ottoman Debt Administration endeavoured in vain to form an Anglo-American syndicate to construct a railway from Constantinople to Bagdad.[2] But these ideas also failed to materialise. The British had had their chance, and the scheme was to pass to other hands. In the same year, 1888, the German enterprise was floated. A German syndicate received a concession for a railway to Angora, and in 1903 the concession was extended to the Gulf. From that moment the scheme was involved in that whole network of intrigue, bluff, fears, and threats which is called international politics.

An enterprise such as this has two aspects, distinguishable, though intimately connected. It is first economic ; and there seems to be no reasonable doubt that this motive was the one which prompted the actual promoters in Germany. But, even from this point of view the scheme was bound to create opposition ; for in proportion as it should succeed it must interfere, at one point or another, with existing interests and privileges. There were other railways in Turkey that might be affected ; for instance, a British company running from Smyrna inland, which feared the effect on its profits of the development of other ports and objected to the grant of a kilometric guarantee, which it did not itself possess, to the new company by the Turkish Government.[3] There was a British navigation company on the Tigris, which had long had a practical monopoly of the river-transport and which would be seriously affected by railway competi-

---

[1] See above, p. 66, and *Life*, ii. p. 306.   [2] Earle, p. 31.
[3] Ib., p. 189, and Hansard, cxx. pp. 1358 seq.

tion. The directors, " in defence of their interests, wrapped
themselves in the Union Jack, and called upon their Home
Government for protection ; they were patriotic to the last
degree, and were determined that the custody of a privilege
highly important to British commerce should never pass to
Germany except over the dead bodies of the principal
partners." [1] Then there were British shipping companies
afraid of a diminution in their freights to India if the new
land route should be established. These pointed out, in
accordance with the usual economic fallacy, that if the Turkish
customs were raised to meet the subvention to the railway,
the subsidy would in fact be paid by British importers.

Not less agitated were the existing interests of Russia,
and perhaps even more fantastic in their contentions. The
new route, it was urged, would compete with the trans-
Siberian ; why, when the one went south to the Gulf and the
other north to Vladivostok, it is not easy to perceive. But,
worse, if Mesopotamia should become once more the granary
of the world, what would become of the landlords of Russia
and their exports of corn ? If the oil of Mesopotamia were
developed, what would happen to the oil of Russia ? If
Germany should penetrate Persia, what about Russian trade
there ? Similar considerations agitated the French. The
railway would interfere with the sea route to India via
Marseilles ; it might interfere with the export of silk to Lyons.
How could one tell ?

Such conflicts of vested against prospective interests are
the very substance of economic life, as it is conducted in
the modern world. But then, in such conflicts, there are
always progressive as well as obstructive forces, and the
former, in the long run, are apt to win. What made the
Bagdad enterprise a factor in the friction that leads to war
were not economic but political considerations. What, said
the Governments of the Entente, are the Germans really
after ? Economic development ? *Credat Judæus!* Of
course they want to steal something ! Of course they want
to attack somebody ! For Governments judge the motives
of other Governments by their own, and they are not likely
to believe in a disinterestedness which they are aware that
they do not possess themselves.

[1] Cited, Earle, p. 191.

What then *were* the Germans after? Unfortunately, no one could be sure. So far as the initiators of the project are concerned there is no evidence to make us doubt that their motives were economic gain and prestige. Germany had a population of sixty millions, a rapidly growing foreign trade, and therefore a continually increasing need of raw materials and new markets. Their colonial empire was small and still undeveloped, and their Navy, when the project was launched in 1888, non-existent. Their future, therefore, was precarious, so far as it depended on transport by sea. On the other hand, they were the greatest military power on the Continent. They would be safer, therefore, in expanding upon land. If they could make and keep Turkey strong against Russian, or British or French aggression, and strong under their own influence and patronage, they might develop, in security, enormous resources and markets, profiting themselves without interfering with the profit of others. There was nothing aggressive in such a scheme. But it was launched in a world that could not think or act except in terms of offence and defence, so that the effect of the enterprise on the balance of power was certain to become the predominant consideration.

Now, beyond doubt, in this respect its potentialities were considerable. The railway would bring Germany to the frontiers of Persia, and thence, by " economic penetration," to the frontiers of India. It would bring her to the Persian Gulf, so that she could threaten India by sea. It would bring her closer, if not actually close, to the Russian frontier in Armenia. Nor was that all. It would immensely increase the military strength of Turkey, for it would enable her, for the first time, to concentrate quickly at a given point the troops dispersed over her vast empire, to enforce the military service that was now so largely evaded, and to become, in alliance with Germany, a very important force in the event of that world-war which all States were always expecting and always preparing for. Although, therefore, it does not seem to have been true that the railway was planned with a view to political and military expansion, it clearly could be employed in that way ; and German jingoes were not slow to emphasise this point. They showed how the line, via Damascus, south to Palestine, might be used to threaten

Egypt ; as, in fact, it was, in the Great War. They spoke
of Turkey becoming, in the case of war with England, a
centre of Mohammedan propaganda against British rule in
India. These possibilities, of course, were referred to as
means of defence when England should attack Germany ;
for no State admits that it might itself be the aggressor.
But they were none the less alarming to the English.[1] Such
utterances of irresponsible people throw, of course, no light
upon the intention of the Bagdad Railway ; but they indicate
its possible uses ; and in a world always preparing for war
these possible uses become, much more than actual intentions, the determinants of policy. When England had joined
the group hostile to Germany, she began to regard her as
the potential enemy. That is why the Bagdad Railway
became an additional source of international friction, instead
of the beneficent enterprise, appealing equally to all States,
which it would have been in a sane and peaceable world.

II. The Attitude of England

Such was the general position. We will now proceed to
examine more closely the particular policies of the various
Powers ; and first we will consider our own country. For it
was British opposition to the scheme that was most pertina-
cious and most effective. Not, indeed, at first ; for, as we
have seen [2] about the turn of the century, England was
proposing an alliance with Germany. If that had been
successful, we should, no doubt, have supported the railway
with enthusiasm ; and, in fact, during the earlier years,
both our Governments and what passes for our public opinion
were favourable. The German enterprise, we then thought,
would block the Russian approach to the Gulf and to India.
Thus, for example, Lord Salisbury is reported as saying in
1900 : " We are not at all unfavourably impressed by the
grant of the concessions in question to Germany. On the
contrary, we welcome them, for in this way Germany comes
into line with our own interests in the Persian Gulf." [3] The
Germans, too, though with more hesitation, were willing, at

[1] See Rohrbach, *Bagdad-Bahn*, pp. 18 seq., ed. 1911. Lord Ronaldshay
cited him in the House of Commons (Hansard, 1911, xxiii. p. 628).
[2] See above, p. 61.
[3] Ger. Docs., xvii. p. 373. Cf. Earle, p. 178.

that time, to co-operate with the British. Eckardstein, for example, describes a discussion in the German Foreign Office, where it was agreed that the scheme must be carried through in conjunction with England.[1]

But this favourable attitude of the British was reversed by their entente with France, followed by that with Russia. The change began to be evident in the course of the year 1903, when the Germans obtained their concession for the continuation of the railway from Konia to Bagdad. The British Government seems at first to have been favourable to the scheme, and to the investment in it of British capital, subject to the condition that the control should be international. This meant equal shares for Germans, British, and French. In the words of Lord Cranborne, then Under-Secretary of State for Foreign Affairs, the object of the Government was " not to support a German railway but to turn a German railway into an international railway." [2] But immediately a violent opposition was organised in the Press. It was maintained that, although the holdings of Germany, Great Britain, and France were to be equal (25 per cent. each), yet the remaining 25 per cent. (10 per cent. Swiss, 10 per cent. Anatolian railway and 5 per cent. Austrian) would, in fact, be controlled by Germany, who would thus have in all a half share of the whole enterprise.[3] The outcry in the Press is somewhat mysterious, and it is possible that it was engineered, in part, by Russia, who was doing the same thing in France.[4] But interests and strategic fears also played their part. Thus, the British Smyrna-Aidin Company, as we have already noticed, feared the effects of the new enterprise upon their profits. They were represented in the Commons by Mr. Gibson Bowles, who informed the House that he " did not object to the railway, because all railways were good feeders of ships. But this was not a railway ; it was a financial fraud and a political conspiracy—a fraud whereby English trade would suffer, and a conspiracy whereby the political interests of England would be threatened. It amounted to a military and

[1] Eckardstein, ii. p. 177.   [2] Hansard, 1903, cxxvi. p. 120.
[3] *Fortnightly Review*, 1903, v. lxxiii. p. 819.
[4] This suggestion is made by Sir Clinton Dawkins, as cited by von Gwinner in the *Nineteenth Century*, June 1909, v. lxv. p. 1091.

commercial occupation by Germany of the whole of Asia Minor." [1]

The frankly interested patriotism of Mr. Gibson Bowles was supported by the fears of more important persons. British imperialists had decided that our control of the Persian Gulf must not be threatened by any foreign Power. Thus Lord Lansdowne said, in 1903, that " we should regard the establishment of a naval base or of a fortified port in the Persian Gulf by any other Power as a very grave menace to British interests, and we should certainly resist it with all the means at our disposal." He added, however : " I say that in no minatory spirit, because, so far as I am aware, no proposals are on foot for the establishment of a foreign naval base in the Persian Gulf." [2]   At a later date Lord Curzon, even more emphatically, said that " he would not hesitate to indict as a traitor to his country any British Minister who should consent to a foreign Power establishing a station on the Persian Gulf." But before 1903 Lord Curzon had already taken steps to provide against that contingency and had established a " protectorate " over the Sheik of Koweit, which made it impossible for him to consent to the establishment of a foreign Power at the mouth of the Gulf without British approval ; [3] and it was Koweit which, according to the scheme then under consideration, was to be the terminal port of the railway. British interests, therefore, appeared to be duly safeguarded. Nevertheless, for reasons which have not been fully elucidated, Mr. Balfour suddenly changed his policy. On April 7th he had spoken in favour of British participation ; on April 23rd he withdrew his support.[4] From some remarks of Lord Cranborne it would appear that it was the public agitation that had prevented the British Government from obtaining the terms they thought necessary. " We were not able," he said, " to get the terms ; and I go further and say that the outcry which was made in this matter—I think it a very ill-informed outcry—made it exceedingly difficult for us to get the terms we require." [5] The truth is probably contained in the following letter by Sir Clinton Dawkins, a British

[1] Hansard, 1903, v. cxxvi. p. 109.   [2] Ib., cxxxi. p. 1348.
[3] Earle, p. 198.   For the question of Koweit from 1899 to 1903, see Ger. Docs., v. xvii. pp. 465 seq.
[4] Earle, p. 185.   [5] Hansard, 1903, v. cxxvi. p. 121.

financier interested in the project, who wrote, in 1903 : " The
fact is, that this business has become involved more or less
in politics here and has been sacrificed to the very violent
and bitter feeling against Germany exhibited by the majority
of newspapers and which is shared by a large number of
people." He adds : " This is a feeling which is not shared by
the Government or reflected in official circles." [1]

Whatever may have been the cause of the Government's
withdrawal, their action, even from the point of view of
British interests, was very questionable. The best-informed
historian of these events describes it as a " colossal diplomatic blunder"; for, as he points out, the Entente between
England and France which was concluded the following year
would have given the control of the railway to those Powers
acting jointly. They would have commanded a majority in
the Directorate,[2] and so have been able to checkmate any
attempts by Germany, had such been made, to convert the
enterprise to her own purposes. " Sir Henry Babington
Smith," says Professor Earle, " assures the author that there
was nothing in the arrangement suggested by the Deutsche
Bank which would have prevented eventual Franco-British
domination of the line." [3] It seems difficult to resist the
conclusion that, even on the narrowest view of British interests,
a bad mistake was made. Still more was this the case if we
take the standpoint of world peace and progress. For ten
years more the Bagdad Railway was to add its quota of poison
to the diplomatic cup, only to be settled, in the end, on terms
less favourable to Great Britain than those rejected in 1903.
But the Government, on this occasion, seems to have been less
to blame than what is called public opinion ; that is, the
combination of obstructive interests and ignorant jingoism
which commonly passes for such in international affairs.

From 1903 then, until the settlement of 1914, the railway
was a continuing cause of international friction. The three
Powers of the Entente steadily opposed it, at any rate till
1910, and even after that date, though, from then onwards,
the opposition was crumbling. Their principal weapon was

---

[1] Cited in *Nineteenth Century*, June 1909, p. 1090.
[2] The Germans would have possessed, with their Turkish collaborators,
only fourteen out of the thirty votes in the Board of Directors. Earle, p. 188.
[3] Earle, p. 188. For the newspaper agitation in England, cf. Ger. Docs.,
xvii. p. 436.

the control by the European Powers of the Turkish customs. This control was originally set up, as in China, to secure revenue in payment of the foreign debt. But it was used as a bargaining instrument between the Powers in pursuit of their own interests, without much reference to those of Turkey. From the Turkish point of view there was no doubt about the benefits of the railway. But the condition of its construction was a " kilometric guarantee," that is, the payment by Turkey of a fixed sum per kilometre constructed. This money could most conveniently be found by raising the customs ; and they could not be raised above the 8 per cent. fixed by the treaties without the consent of the Powers. The Turkish Government, in 1903, requested permission to raise them by 3 per cent. This was agreed to, but not until 1906 and " after prolonged and irritating negotiations " ; and " even then the higher duties were assented to under a number of restrictions which rendered difficult the diversion of the increased revenue to the payment of railway guarantees ; elaborate regulations were incorporated in the treaties prescribing expensive reforms of the Government of Macedonia and costly readjustments in the Customs administration." [1] After the Turkish revolution of 1908 there was a further request for permission to raise the duties ; but this was still resisted by Great Britain. By the end of 1909, indeed, Sir Edward was inclined to give his assent ; but he required not only political conditions, especially the control of the Gulf sector, but also that the " surplus shall not benefit the German enterprise," i.e. shall not be used to finance the kilometric guarantee.[2] He also said that the British Government could not give its consent " without corresponding advantages to British merchants." [3] The two other Powers of the Entente seem to have been less tenacious than England. At any rate, we find the British Ambassador in Constantinople complaining that " all the Powers with the exception of England were apparently willing to consent to the increase without setting up any condition regarding the Bagdad Railway." [4] But this was too pessimistic a view.

[1] Earle, p. 96.   v. Tschirschky writes (February 1907) that the British attitude on this question is "one of the most striking examples of the hostility of English policy" (Ger. Docs. v. xxi. p. 481).
[2] Siebert, pp. 502, 514.   [3] Ib., p. 522, 1910.
[4] Ib., p. 504, November 1909.

The three Powers, in fact, continued to act together on this issue. And even after the Potsdam agreement of 1910, whereby Russia formally withdrew her opposition to the railway, she held herself free to support Britain in the matter of the Customs.[1] British opposition was only withdrawn when she had made sure that the railway, in its last section to the Gulf, would not be under German control; and that was not until 1914.

III. The Gulf Section

The control of this section then was the keynote of British policy. Yet as early as 1906 the Germans had shown themselves conciliatory on the point. Our authority here is Lord Haldane.[2] At the end of 1907, he tells us, the Kaiser was at Windsor. He there met Lord Haldane and had a conversation with him on the subject of the railway. He was sorry, he said, that there was so much friction, but he did not know what we wanted as a basis of co-operation. Lord Haldane said that he could not answer for the Foreign Office, but that, speaking for the War Office, the one thing we wanted was " a gate to protect India from troops coming down the new railway "; and by " gate," he explained, he meant " the control of that section which would come near the Persian Gulf." " I will give you the gate," the Kaiser replied. He proposed that that section of the line should be Anglo-German, and the terminal harbour British, subject to the condition that it should always be open to peaceful transit.[3] Lord Haldane warmly recommended this plan to Sir Edward Grey. The latter was favourably disposed, but he had agreed with the French and Russians that he would make no arrangement with the Germans without their participation.[4] To that the Germans would not assent; and their reasons are interesting. " We should have found ourselves," they said, " round the table alone, in face of three Powers not friendly to us, and bound together among themselves." [5] Was the German attitude unreasonable? Not more so, I venture to think, than that of any other Power would have been, under similar circumstances. Germany had just emerged defeated

[1] Siebert, pp. 544, 561. Cf. below, p. 250.   [2] *Before the War*, p. 48.
[3] Cf. v Schoen, p. 62.   [4] Siebert, p. 536.   [5] v. Schoen, p. 62.

from the Conference of Algeciras, and was naturally reluctant to repeat the experience. On the other hand, Sir Edward's unwillingness to deal with her apart from the other Powers of the Entente, was strictly honourable, for he had pledged himself to that course. Another proof, if any were needed, that under the system of alliances and counter-alliances no harmony or peace was possible for Europe.

The next step we hear of is an idea, supported by Mr. Churchill, of a separate concession, to be granted by the Turks to England, for a railway from Bagdad to Koweit.[1] But the Turkish Government replied that the concession had already been given to the German company. They were, however, prepared to give, to England and to France, equal control with Germany over that section. But this does not seem to have satisfied the British, and we find their Ambassador in Constantinople writing : " We have always demanded the control and construction of the line south of Bagdad and cannot content ourselves with less." [2] Yet, at the same time, we find anxiety on the part of the Russians and French, lest the British be doing a separate deal with Germany.[3] These fears were groundless, for in April 1910 we learn that : " The opposition of the London Cabinet and the renewal of its claims upon the Bagdad–Basra section has again brought the entire matter to a standstill, to the marked displeasure of Germany and Turkey." [4] Nevertheless, a certain change seems to have taken place in the British attitude ; for in this same month of April we are informed that " the British Government no longer deems it possible to bring the entire Bagdad–Basra line into its own possession, and is ready to share it with Germany ; demanding, however, predominance for itself both in the question of construction and exploitation." [5] What led, perhaps, to this more conciliatory attitude was the suspicion that the Germans might raise the money, without recourse to the Customs, out of other Turkish revenues.[6]

Nevertheless, in July 1910 we find the British Government once more making to the Turks the proposal for a railway from Bagdad to Basra under exclusive British control,

---

[1] Siebert, p. 501.
[2] Ib., p. 505, November 1909.
[3] Ib., pp. 503, 510.
[4] Ib., p. 518.
[5] Ib. Cf. p. 519.
[6] Ib., pp. 518, 519, but cf. p. 522.

and stating that, unless this should be favourably considered, Britain would not agree to the customs increase.[1] The Turks, no doubt for the reasons given above, declined. Whereupon Sir Edward Grey proposed a British share in the proposed section of at least 55 per cent. In July the Turkish Minister submitted two counter-propositions : either the internationalisation of the section, or its construction by the Ottoman Government. Nothing seems to have come of these proposals ; and in 1911 the Turks produced a scheme whereby the Turkish Government should have a 40 per cent. share, and the German, French, and British 20 per cent. each. But this was refused by Sir Edward Grey, presumably because the Turkish 40 per cent. would really be controlled by the Germans.[2] It was not till 1914 that an agreement was reached between all the parties, whereby the terminus of the railway was to be Basra, unless and until the British should consent to its prolongation to Koweit. This arrangement gave the British a veto on the prolongation of the railway to the Gulf. At the same time it assured to the British company the monopoly of navigation on the Shat-el-Arab, Tigris, and Euphrates. It should be added that two British representatives were added to the directorate of the railway to see that the principle of equal rates for all countries was fairly carried out. The agreement was initialled, but not signed, when the war broke out.[3] Thus, at length, was British opposition overcome in this long tug-of-war ; of war literally, as well as metaphorically, for war was in the offing all the time.

IV. Russian Policy

What, meantime, had been the attitude of the other Powers of the Entente ?

Russia, as we have already noted, was opposed from the outset to the scheme. There were, first, the economic objections to which we have referred. On that subject a remark of the Kaiser's seems to be pertinent. It is, he said, " the old Russian system, to oppose and if possible stop

---

[1] Earle, pp. 226 seq.   [2] Ib., p. 226. Cf. Siebert, pp. 558, 576.
[3] Cf. Hansard, liii. p. 391 (1913) ; Valentin, pp. 142-3 ; Lichnowski, pp. 395-6. The agreement is printed by Professor Earle in the *Political Science Quarterly*, March 1923, p. 29.

every economic development which she cannot fully and exclusively control. Given the economic backwardness and inertia of the Russians, that leads, in all the neighbouring countries, to conscious stagnation. It is the same on the Lower Danube. The policy of the Russians is intelligible from their point of view, and with their inner structure; whereas that of England towards the Bagdad Railway is foolish even from the English point of view." [1] But in the case of Russia, as in that of England, it was political considerations that were predominant. They wanted to exclude all foreign Powers. They suggested, therefore, that Turkey should build, if at all, solely out of her own funds, and promised, in that case, to ask for no concessions themselves. The Porte replied that the concession to the Germans was granted and could not be withdrawn; whereupon Russia remarked that the existing tranquillity in the Balkans was due to her efforts, and that, if she were to disinterest herself in the matter, Turkey would experience the consequences. On this the German Ambassador observes, not without reasons, that it meant condemning Turkey to economic collapse, a result desired by Russia in pursuit of her own purpose of swallowing up, one day, the Turkish Empire.[2] That was in 1900. Next year the Russians protested against the proposed direction of the railway across Northern Armenia to Mosul. Such a line, they said, would be a strategic menace to the Caucasus; and they threatened to collect from Turkey the arrears of an indemnity due under the treaty of Berlin unless that route were abandoned.[3] The Turks submitted to this pressure, and it was arranged that the line should be carried across Central Anatolia to Konia, and the Cilician gates. But still the Russians were uneasy; and in December 1901 Count Witte stated categorically that he considered the construction of the railway by any other Power than Russia as a menace to the imperial interests of the Tsar.[4] Later, in 1903, we find Russia applying for a counter-concession to the Gulf by Lake Van and the Tigris.[5] This, too, the Turks refused.

These Russian fears were treated, at first, with scant respect by the British. We had not yet made the Entente,

[1] Ger. Docs., xvii. p. 448 note. [2] Ib., p. 380.
[3] Earle, p. 149. [4] Ib. [5] Ger. Docs., xvii. p. 450.

and the traditional suspicion of Russia was still in the ascendant. But that was altered in a year of two. The British became the leading opponents of the scheme, and were supported by Russia as well as by France. Yet already, as early as 1907, when the Entente with England was well under weigh, Russia was weakening about the railway. We have, in evidence of this, an interesting account of a meeting of the Russian Ministerial Council in February 1907.[1] The Ministers expressed themselves as opposed to the enterprise, on strategic as well as economic grounds; but also they saw no chance of being able, for any length of time, to stop it. They therefore inclined to the policy of seeking " compensations " from Germany. Unfortunately, "the Bagdad Railway is so injurious to Russian interests that we can scarcely hope to receive compensations of real importance to us. Hence we must content ourselves with paralysing, as far as possible, its harm." The Russian demands should be :

(1) Germany to guarantee "that no branch lines be built in the direction of the Persian frontier, as, for instance, Khanekin "; the fear being that German and British trade might compete with Russian in North Persia.

(2) That Turkey should build no railways in the north (i.e. towards the Caucasus frontier) without Russian consent.

(3) The treaty of 1900 with Turkey, giving Russia a monopoly of railway development in Northern Anatolia and Armenia, must be extended in the Russian interest.[2]

This reluctant determination of the Russian Government to come to terms with Germany was, very likely, due to her knowledge of the German willingness to come to terms with England. But the proposed Anglo-German agreement, as we saw, fell through, because Sir Edward Grey insisted on associating France and Russia with the negotiations. This result was very welcome to the Russians ; and determined them not to proceed with their own idea of making a separate arrangement with Germany. But a similar situation arises again in 1909. Once more the Germans are suggesting British control of the Gulf section. Once more Sir Edward Grey has said that France and Russia must participate in the discussions. " The necessity," he says, " of inviting Russia and France to participate renders it difficult for the British

Government to take part in the building of the railway." [1]
The Russians, none the less, were still afraid that he might
go back upon them. "It is not clearly discernible," writes
Isvolski, "whether England is not attempting to evade her
former promise that all four Powers must negotiate together." [2]
But this doubt, he seems to admit, was unfounded. Still, as
the Russian Ambassador at Constantinople writes, "in any
case we must reckon with the possibility of England and
Germany effecting an understanding on this question with
comparative ease." [3] In the end, Russia approached Germany and made the separate arrangement known as the
Potsdam Agreement (November 1910). Whether or no this
was a breach of the understanding that none of the three
Powers should do a deal with Germany without consulting the
others, may be left undecided. Apparently both Sir Edward
Grey and M. Pichon knew that negotiations were going on ; [4]
but apparently also neither was made aware of their scope
until they were concluded ; and the Potsdam Agreement
created dismay in the other Powers of the Entente.

V. The Potsdam Agreement

So far as the Bagdad Railway was concerned, the provisions of the Agreement were as follows :

(1) Germany recognised the Russian sphere of interest in
Northern Persia, and undertook not to seek concessions for
railways, roads, telegraphs, or other means of communication
in that region.

(2) Germany agreed that Russia should obtain from
Persia the concession for a railway from Teheran to Khanekin
on the Persian frontier, which place was to be linked up
to the Bagdad Railway at Sadijeh.

(3) In return Russia promised to abandon her opposition
to the Bagdad Railway. [5]

It will be observed that, so far as the branch to Khanekin
is concerned, this agreement represents a complete change of
view from that adopted in 1907. [6] Then the object was to

---

[1] Siebert, p. 502. [2] Ib., p. 504. [3] Ib., p. 507.
[4] Earle p. 243 ; Hansard, 1911, xxi. pp. 82 and 243.
[5] A German draft is given in *Die Kriegsschuldfrage*, March 1924, p. 62.
The final treaty, of August 1911, is given, ib., p. 63. Cf. Brandenburg,
p. 314 ; Schuster, p. 226 ; Earle, p. 239 ; *Livre Noir*, ii. p. 334.
[6] See above, p. 248.

prevent the construction of the line from Teheran to Khanekin, and thence to the Bagdad Railway ; now that line is to be constructed by Russia. The reason is that Russia has now made up her mind that she could not exclude Germany from Persia, and had better, therefore, admit her on Russia's own terms.

As we have said, the agreement, when it became known, or known in part, created something like consternation in England, and, to a less extent, in France. What distressed Sir Edward Grey, as might be inferred from his whole policy, was the possible strategic menace to India. In the first place, had the Russians, he asked, given their consent to the extension of the railway right down to the Gulf ? If so, England's bargaining position about that section would be much weakened. In the second place, the Bagdad Railway was now to be connected with North Persia. Under whose control ? " He deems it extremely important that, should we connect Khanekin with a point in Northern Persia, whatever Germany's participation may be, the control and management of this branch-line in our Persian sphere of interest should remain solely in Russian hands, to the exclusion of every kind of German interference." Sir Edward gave a reason for this. He said, we must not forget the Pan-Islamic movement. Persia is Mohammedan, as is Afghanistan ; and since both Russia and England possess numerous Mohammedan subjects, a Turkish army commanded by German officers, controlling a railway which is under German influence, would be a permanent danger, the importance of which must not be underrated." [1] Finally Sir Edward hopes that Russia has preserved her freedom not to consent to the increase of the Turkish customs. Otherwise, this weapon, so important for England, might be blunted.

These two points then, the extension of the railway to the Gulf, and the branch-line between Khanekin and Teheran, were the ones on which British anxiety turned. With regard to the first, the Russians replied that the term " Bagdad Railway " in their agreement meant only the railway as far as Bagdad. Also, that they still retained the right to resist the increase of the customs. On that head, therefore, they were in a position to reassure the British.[2] But the difficulty

[1] Siebert, p. 538, January 1911. [2] Ib., p. 537.

of the Khanekin–Teheran branch remained. By the Potsdam agreement the concession for this line was reserved for Russia, but would be transferred to Germany if the line were not built within a certain time.[1] The question was, Could Russia raise the capital? She sounded the British Government, but was informed that it could not itself guarantee a loan, and that a guarantee would be necessary from Russia;[2] and this the Russians could not give. In an interesting dispatch of June 1911 the Russian Ambassador in London tells us that " the Anglo-Russian convention does not afford any basis upon which an English protest against German control of the said line might be raised." Nevertheless he strongly urges his Government not to permit such control : " Should the German control come into effect, our convention with England would be shaken and its political effect would be called into question. A railway line under German control would give this Power first-rate political influence in Persia ; therefore England would also have to reckon with Germany at Teheran, and this would involve negotiations which it is believed here would be most welcome to Germany. It is evident that the whole situation would be changed, to the detriment of our interests and of our position in Persia. This refers to the exercise of the financial control on the part of Germany. The consequences just explained would all the more be bound to set in, if we gave up the construction of the railway. Such a renunciation would—this must not be doubted—give the coup de grâce to the Anglo-Russian policy in Persia, and an Anglo-German combination would supplant the Anglo-Russian convention of 1907."[3] This passage is interesting in illustration of the kind of confidence the Powers really have in one another under the conditions of the international anarchy. We have already seen the British fearing a Russo-German approximation. We now see the Russians fearing an Anglo-German one. So true is it that there is not and cannot be any real mutual confidence in these combinations of robber Powers. Sir Edward Grey, indeed, seems to have been so much disturbed by the Potsdam agreement and its results that he was thinking of resigning. On February 9th the Russian

[1] See Brandenburg, p. 314, and the text in *Die Kriegsschuldfrage.*
[2] Ib., p. 555.   [3] Siebert, p. 574.

Ambassador in London writes that "great efforts were necessary to dissuade him from his original intention of tendering his resignation and withdrawing from public life. Our attitude in the railway question has shaken his inner conviction that Russia still possesses full liberty of action in her sphere of interest, and he believes that England should first have been asked in so important a matter. As he possesses no documents on which he could have supported himself officially, he regarded his resignation as the only way out." [1]

This passage seems to support the view that, while Sir Edward may have known, and probably did know, of the fact that the Russians were negotiating with Germany, he did not know at the time what was being negotiated. It is not easy, from the documents at our disposal, to follow precisely the further negotiations with regard to this Khanekin branch. But it would seem, from a dispatch of September 1911, that the Russian Minister obtained assurances from the Germans that they would not "construct any branch-lines of the Bagdad Railway in the territory included between it and the Russian and Persian boundary north of Khanekin, nor lend any support to any enterprise of that sort." [2] This perhaps settled the question more or less to the satisfaction of England. At any rate, in published dispatches, we hear no more of the point, nor of any further opposition by Russia to the Bagdad Railway. The final settlement of the question, as we have seen, came in 1913-14; but it does not appear that any new concessions were then made to Russia. So far as she was concerned the Potsdam agreement was final.

VI. French Policy

We will turn now to the French. They, as we have briefly noted, had an interest of a sentimental kind in Turkey, and especially in Palestine and in Syria, dating back to the Crusades. This fact cannot be ignored, because it is the kind of fact that influences some sections of public opinion. We will summarise the position in the words of Professor Earle : [3] "French nationals recalled with pride the rôle of France in the Crusades;

[1] Siebert, p. 550, February 1911. [2] Ib., p. 576. [3] P. 153.

they remembered that Palestine itself was once a Latin kingdom ; they believed that Christians in the Levant looked to France as their protector, and that this protection had received formal recognition under the capitulations, negotiated by Francis I and extended by his successors from Henry IV to Louis XV. They knew that the French language was the language not only of the educated classes in Turkey, but also, in Syria, of the traders, so that it could be said that a traveller in Syria might almost consider himself in a French dependency. They were proud of the fact that the term Frank was the symbol of Western civilisation in the Near East. They were aware of the far-reaching educational work of French missionaries. France, to their mind, had done a great work of Christian enlightenment in the Moslem stronghold, Turkey. Was the Government of the Republic to be backward in asserting the interests of France when Bourbons and Bonapartes had so ably paved the way for the extension of French civilisation in the Holy Land ? "

More important, however, than these considerations was the actual situation of the Great Powers. France was hypnotised by her fear of Germany and her alliance with Russia ; and her position, she felt, would be seriously weakened if German influence should be extended throughout Turkey, and Russian influence extruded. " Before long," said a speaker in the Chamber, " the railway will make of Asia Minor a veritable German colony. It will tend to annihilate for ever French influence. It is also an anti-Russian work par excellence." [1] Again, even more sweepingly : " The power which the Bagdad Railway will give to all the Germans of the Ottoman Empire will necessarily do harm to all the French of this same Ottoman Empire." [2] There, in a phrase, is the passion which creates and maintains armaments and wars. How, it may be asked, does the harm that might be done by Germans to French in Turkey compare with the harm actually done by them in France, as a result of the war created by precisely such sentiments as those quoted ? These patriots were also exercised by fear that the French protectorate over the Christians might be weakened and were candid enough to avow

[1] *Journal Officiel*, March 20th, 1902, p. 146, cited by Chéradame, p. 281
[2] Chéradame, p. 298.

openly that, in this connexion, it was less the Christians they
cared about than the political prestige of France. " Her moral
protectorate," we are told, " is the basis of her material
influence." [1] The railway " implies a complete economic
control over the Turkish dominions which must sooner or
later lead to a political protectorate." It will be a " constant
menace to other Powers." It will imply " a complete rupture
in favour of Germany of the balance of World-Power."
" For the last thirty years Germany has sought an outlet
for her teeming populations and her expanding industries."
Terrible crime, indeed! Only, it must be added, that by
1903 German emigration had ceased, so that there was no
idea of exporting " teeming populations." But the " expanding industries " ? Well, so long and so far as nations believe
that the trade of one is ruinous to the trade of another, so
long will they continue to ruin both trade and civilisation,
by making wars to prevent one another from trading.

This kind of opposition, sentimental and economic, to
the new scheme, it was necessary to mention, because it is
part of the causation of events. But there were other interests working in the opposite direction. French finance was
anxious, from the first, to participate in what was likely to
be a great source of revenue. There were, first, those who
had investments in Turkey, and who foresaw that the value
of their property was likely to be enormously enhanced by
the railway : " It was estimated in 1903 that French investors
controlled three-fifths, amounting to a billion and a half of
francs, of the public obligations of the Imperial Ottoman
Treasury. French promoters owned about 366 million francs
in the securities of Turkish railroads, and over 162 million
in various industrial and commercial enterprises in Asia
Minor. French banks had approximately 176 million francs
invested in their branches in the Near East. The total of
all French investments in Turkey was more than two and a
half billion francs. The French-controlled Imperial Ottoman
Bank, the French-owned Smyrna–Cassaba Railway, and the
French-administered Ottoman Debt Council all favoured the
promotion of the Bagdad Railway idea." [2] Another group of

[1] Chéradame, p. 303.
[2] Earle, p. 154. The Smyrna–Cassaba Railway here referred to connected,
at Afiun-Karahissar, with the line from Constantinople to Konia, which was
to be continued to Bagdad.

French railways, in Syria, would connect with the line to Aleppo.[1] These railways therefore were bound to profit by the German scheme. The Ottoman Bank agreed, in 1899, to participate in the financing of the railway,[2] and one of its officers became a Vice-President in 1903. The bank held its shares until the settlement of 1913, when they were repurchased by the Germans.[3] These facts are worth attending to, because it is sometimes assumed that " capitalistic " interests always make for war. They make, in fact, for war or peace, according to circumstances. In the present case, they were making for co-operation with Germany, and, so far, for peace.

If French finance were thus favourable to the Bagdad Railway, the French Government was not, at first, opposed. M. Delcassé, later the creator of the Anglo-French Entente, supported it from 1899 to 1902 ; so did M. Rouvier ;[4] and the Chamber upheld them. But in October 1903 the Government changed its attitude and ordered the Bourse to exclude the shares of the railway from its quotations. The motives of this change of policy are not altogether clear. Professor Earle tells us that it was " a consequence of a persistent clamour on the part of the French Press that the construction of the Bagdad Railway, which was popularly considered a menace to French interests, should be obstructed by every effective method at the disposal of the Government." [5] The popular clamour, no doubt, was instrumental   But two other facts must be remembered ; first, the hostility of Russia,[6] and the well-authenticated fact that the Russian Embassy was in the habit of bribing the French Press ; secondly, the attitude adopted, in the spring of 1903, by Great Britain,[7] and the fact that the negotiations for the Entente were already proceeding.[8] It seems likely that, at this time, the two Powers agreed to pursue in common a policy of opposition to the railway.

At any rate, from 1903 onwards until 1910, the three States of the Entente stood together against the railway. Then came the Potsdam agreement, as to which, at first, the French, like the British, seem to have been much disturbed.

[1] Earle, p. 165.   [2] Ger. Docs., xvii. p. 394.
[3] Earle, p. 248.   [4] Ib., pp. 155–6.
[5] Ib., p. 157.   [6] Cf. Ger. Docs., xvii. pp. 446–7.
[7] See above, p. 240.   [8] Ger. Docs., xvii. p. 452.

The French Ambassador in London, we learn, was afraid, like Sir Edward Grey, that Russian consent might have been given to the building of the last section of the line to the Gulf, and he observed that " France and England would be quite isolated in future." [1] He felt easier on being informed that he was under a misapprehension. But again : " Pichon," we read, " is convinced that the admission of Germany into our (the Russian) sphere of influence (in Persia)—while France, for our sake, has retired from all activity in that country in the question of the foreign advisers—would call forth very vigorous attacks on his policy in France, and might be interpreted as separation, on our part, from the Triple Entente." [2] We may, perhaps, conclude that M. Pichon, like Sir Edward Grey, though he may have known of the fact of the Russo-German negotiations,[3] was not informed of the actual direction they were taking. French opposition, however, was not as strong as British, and probably was mainly due to the latter. For the Russian Ambassador in London writes to Sazonoff in February 1911, that : " France's opposition was from the very beginning not very categorical. Sir Edward Grey therefore finds that England is now far more isolated in this question than before." [4] The truth is that France was looking for compensations. Even before the Potsdam agreement, the Young Turks were endeavouring to propitiate her by concessions in Turkey. They favoured the extension of the Smyrna–Cassaba railway from Soma in Western Anatolia to Panderma on the Sea of Marmara, giving " the highest kilometre guarantee ever granted a railway in the Ottoman Empire." They opened negotiations with the Ottoman Bank for the award to a French-owned company of a concession " for a comprehensive system of railways in Northern Anatolia, " and for " extensive concessions to the French-Syrian railways." [5] Finally, on the conclusion of the Anglo-German Agreement as to the section from Bagdad to the Gulf there was concluded also, early in 1914, a secret Franco-German agreement which is made public for the first time, in summary, by Professor Earle.[6] The details of this arrangement need not here concern us. The main points are that, for purposes of railway development, the French secured a sphere of influence for themselves

[1] Siebert, p. 535.   [2] Ib., p. 548.   [3] Earle, p. 243.
[4] Ib., p. 557.   [5] Ib., pp. 245–6.   [6] Ib., p. 248.

in Northern Anatolia, and Syria, in return for a recognition of the German sphere in the regions traversed by the Bagdad Railway. They agreed also that "appropriate diplomatic and financial measures should be taken to bring about an increase in the revenues of the Ottoman Empire"; which means, presumably, that raising of the Custom duties which the Entente had been opposing since 1907. In return, the Deutsche Bank agreed to purchase from the Ottoman Bank all the latter's shares and debentures of the Bagdad Railway.

VII. Conclusion

These three agreements—the Potsdam, Anglo-German, and Franco-German—concluded this long and tangled business. Looking back upon it, the following reflections suggest themselves. First, the opposition of the British and of the Russians was mainly, if not exclusively, "strategic" in character. German penetration into Turkey was feared by the British on account of the security of India; by the Russians on account not so much of the security of Russia—they can have felt no fears as to that—as of the effect upon their prospects of absorbing Turkey themselves. The British had had to choose whether Russia or Germany was the enemy most to be feared, and had decided, in 1907, that it was Germany. Whether their foresight was justified, for a near future, may be matter for discussion. For a far future, it certainly was not; because, as events have shown, the whole situation was to be quickly transformed; and now, it would seem, we are back again on the old basis, with Russia as the potential foe. As to the French, they had less strategic concern in Turkey, but they fulfilled what they regarded as their obligations to their allies and what they thought likely to injure and thwart their principal enemy, Germany.

On the other hand, the great economic interests of the future, as distinguished from the lesser vested ones of the past, were all in favour of the enterprise. This was most clearly the case in France; but, in the end, the same view prevailed also in Russia, when, by the Potsdam agreement, they admitted the trade of Germany into their sphere of interest in Persia. Only in Great Britain do the economic as well as the political interests seem to have maintained

18

their opposition, and they achieved a short-sighted and
transient victory by securing the perpetuation of their
monopoly of the traffic on the Shat-el-Arab.

On the whole, then, we may conclude that the opposition
to the Bagdad Railway was mainly political ; and it has been
interesting to note the mistrust, constantly arising, between
the Powers of the Entente, as to their mutual fidelity to
this policy. But that was not all. There are clear indications
that any attempt by one Power to come to terms with Germany was resented by the others, just because it might have
led, if successful, to a new grouping. Thus, in 1909, when
discussions of an informal kind were proceeding, between
German and British representatives, as to the Gulf section
of the Railway, and when Sir Edward Grey loyally told
the other Governments what was going on, there was a
flourish of alarm. "The English communications," writes the
Russian Ambassador at Constantinople, "have made a
painful impression on the Paris Cabinet." "The French
Ambassador (at Constantinople) is of the opinion that
England is more and more, concentrating all her energies on
the domination of the roads leading to India—the Persian
Gulf and the Indian plains—and England appears to be less
and less interested in Constantinople and the Turkish problem
proper. The London Cabinet has safeguarded itself by its
conventions with Russia against an extension of Russian
influence in the Persian Gulf. The projected treaty with
Germany completes England's sovereignty in the Persian
Gulf. England will then attempt to free herself in Egypt
from the obligations to obtain Turkey's sanction in certain
political and financial matters, and once this is attained
England will no longer take an active part in the other
questions. But this cannot be desirable for France." For,
if England should come to an agreement with Germany,
" the result would be two opposing groups : France and
Russia would stand alone, which has to be prevented from a
political point of view." [1]   At the same time Pichon, we are
told, then French Foreign Minister, " is alarmed by the inner
political struggle in England, which distracts the attention
of the British Government from questions of foreign policy.
In view of the present situation in France, however, it is of

[1] Siebert, pp. 510 seq., December 8th, 1909.

the utmost importance that England continue to play her former leading part in European matters and act as a check on Germany. Should England recede to the background, bellicose intentions might once more arise in Germany, which would be dangerous to France." [1] We find here, quite definitely stated, the desire of France to keep England unreconciled with Germany in Turkey, in order to have her on the French side in the Franco-German conflict in Europe. The latter throws its shadow over the whole East, and makes of what should have been a purely economic enterprise a first-class political, and therefore military, issue.

The Russians were no less mistrustful of an Anglo-German rapprochement, and for the same reason. Thus the Russian Ambassador at Constantinople writes that "the possibility of an Anglo-German rapprochement is disadvantageous and harmful to France and Russia;" [2] and adds : "I myself go further, and reckon with the possibility of a Franco-German understanding respecting the Bagdad Railway, which, so far as French capital is concerned, already exists. . . . In that case we are threatened by disadvantageous isolation should we not by then have arrived at an understanding with Germany and Turkey." [3] It was this fear, as we have seen, that led to the Potsdam agreement, which in turn seemed, for a time, as though it might break up the Anglo-Russian Entente.

It may, no doubt, be urged that the German menace was so great that these alarums and excursions were justified. But so far as the Railway and the Persian Gulf is concerned, I find no evidence that either the interests involved, or the German Government, regarded it as anything but an economic venture from which, of course, they hoped that Germany would profit, but from which also all other States would profit too. The strategic advantages that might accrue to Germany are of course obvious. But that is no proof that she intended to provoke a war in order to exploit them. Germany seems to have been as innocent as any Great Power can be in the European anarchy. But, in fact, none of them can be innocent ; for they all live in a perpetual state of mutual fear and antagonism, expecting war, and therefore bound always to prepare for war. The moral of the whole episode is that economic enterprises of the

[1] Siebert, p. 512.　　[2] Ib., p. 515, December, 1909.　　[3] Ib., p. 515.

greatest value to civilisation may be arrested on account of political and strategic considerations arising from the anarchy of armed States.

The issue, as we have seen, found a settlement by 1914, but after so much friction that von Jagow was still waiting, when the war broke out, for an " appropriate moment " to publish the Anglo-German agreement, " when the danger of adverse criticism was no longer so acute." [1] The settlement was a belated triumph of common sense over fear, ambition, and greed. But one such triumph was not enough to reverse the effect of years of friction and conflict. It is thus that its effect is summarised by M. Cambon, the French Ambassador in Berlin : " I do not think that the agreement will affect the great body of public opinion on both sides of the Vosges. It will not, unfortunately, change the tone of the French Press towards the Germans. . . . There is no doubt whatever that the majority, both of Germans and French, desire to live at peace ; but there is a powerful minority in each country that dreams of nothing but battles and wars, either of conquest or revenge. That is the peril that is always with us ; it is like living alongside a barrel of gunpowder which may explode on the slightest provocation." [2]

[1] v. Jagow. Cited Earle, p. 268.   [2] Cited Earle, p. 268.

CHAPTER X

PERSIA

I. Peaceful Penetration

THE story of the Western Powers in Persia, during the years preceding the Great War, is but one variety of a common situation ; a weak, incompetent State standing in the way of the development of one or more aggressive and predatory neighbours, and presenting thus at once an object of their rivalry, a temptation for their financiers, an opportunity for their diplomats and soldiers, and one contributory cause of the friction that was to eventuate in the World-War. Persia lay in the line of expansion both of the British and the Russian Empires, and, in the normal course of events, it would be between these that it would become a bone of contention. So, in fact, it was beginning to be, about the time when our present inquiry begins. But that revolution in British policy which took form, first, in the Entente with France and then in that with Russia, though it did not terminate Anglo-Russian friction, subordinated it in a common antagonism to the new interloper, Germany. Germany entered upon the scene by the route of the Bagdad Railway which, as we have already seen, from 1903 onwards, became a new and acute centre of inflammation in the chronic fever of the world. It alarmed both the British and the Russians about their position in the East. True, if the British had succeeded in arranging that treaty of alliance with Germany which they were pressing for in the years 1898–1901, they would have welcomed German extension in the East as a counterweight to Russia. We have indeed already noticed that as early as the year 1885 Lord Randolph Churchill suggested a partition of Persia into British and German spheres of influence ; [1] proposing thus

---

[1] Above, page 37.

to adopt the same policy with Germany against Russia that was afterwards adopted with Russia against Germany. For there are "laws" determining the policy of States, though they are based only on calculations, or miscalculations, of national interest, as conceived, or misconceived.

The Anglo-Russian agreement was made in 1907. But, before that, financial interests had been at work, and we hear, for example, of a concession given to an Englishman for the production, sale, and export of all the tobacco of Persia. The concession, of course, was given by the Shah, and, equally of course, the profit was to go to him, not to his subjects. It appears that the capital of the proposed British corporation was £650,000, and that it expected to net an annual profit of £371,000. Not a bad percentage on the capital! But then, there were the risks, and in this case they proved to be considerable. For the concessionaires had reckoned without the religion of the Persians, which forbade them to touch tobacco soiled by the hands of infidels. The tobacco accordingly was boycotted, and the concession withdrawn. But in "compensation" for its withdrawal the Persian people were mulcted of half a million. This they borrowed from a British bank—"The Imperial Bank of Persia"—at 6 per cent. So that British interests, on the whole, were pretty well paid for doing nothing, and paid, of course, by the Persian peasants.[1]

There were also, as usual in these cases, loans to the Persian State, to be expended on the personal amusements of the Shah ; and security for these was given in the form of control over Persian revenues. Thus Russia lent 22½ million roubles in 1900, and 10 million in 1902 ; and we read that, "having got his money, the Shah set off again on his travels this summer for another tour in Europe," where he expended 6,000 francs a day in hotel bills.[2] Already, by 1900, a French resident is writing that "from concession to concession Persia will soon be entirely in the hands of foreigners."

This kind of story is so familiar, all over the world, wherever the capital of industrial States sees an opportunity to make money out of the vices of native rulers and the taxation of oppressed populations, that it is hardly worth while to dwell upon it at length. But perhaps the reader may be interested

[1] Browne, *Persian Revolution*, pp. 31 seq.   [2] Ib., p. 104.

to know how it appeared to a Persian patriot. Here, therefore, is a passage from the writings of Sayyid Jamal ud Din, translated by Professor Browne : [1]

" Verily the King's purpose wavereth, his character is vitiated, his perceptions are failing and his heart is corrupt. . . . He hath sold to the foes of our faith the greater part of the Persian lands and the profits accruing therefrom, to wit, the mines, the ways leading thereunto, the roads connecting them with the frontier of the country, the inns about to be built by the side of these extensive arteries of communication, which will ramify through all parts of the kingdom, and the gardens and fields surrounding them. Also the tobacco with the chief centres of its cultivation, the lands on which it is grown, and the dwellings of the custodians, carriers, and sellers wherever these are to be found. He has similarly disposed of the grapes used for making wine, and the shops, factories, and wine-presses appertaining to this trade throughout the whole of Persia ; and so likewise soap, candles, and sugar, and the factories connected therewith. Lastly there is the bank. And what shall cause thee to understand what is the bank ? It means the complete handing over of the reins of government to the enemy of Islam, the enslaving of the people to that enemy, the surrendering of them and of all dominions and authority into the hands of the foreign foe. In short, this criminal has offered the provinces of the Persian land to auction amongst the Powers, and is selling the realms of Islam and the abodes of Muhammad and his household (to whom be greeting and salutation) to foreigners. But by reason of the vileness of his nature and meanness of his understanding he sells them for a paltry sum, and at a wretched price. (Yea, thus it is when meanness and avarice are mingled with treason and folly !) " [2]

II. The Division of Persia into Spheres of Interest

The quaintness of an Oriental idiom may perhaps bring home to the reader, with a certain vividness, the real nature of the transactions by which the West has accomplished, all over the world, its policy of " peaceful penetration " as a

[1] *Persian Revolution*, p. 17.
[2] Cf. other articles from the Persian Press, ib., pp. 173 seq.

prelude to political absorption. But our present subject is not that, though that is germane to it. We will pass on, therefore, to the act which was to determine the fate of the Middle East during the critical years which preceded the Great War. In 1907 Sir Edward Grey made the Anglo-Russian rapprochement. This agreement, as we know, constituted not a formal alliance, but the settlement of a number of outstanding questions. In other words, it decided that Britain and Russia, instead of quarrelling about their differences, would arrange them in a friendly way ; a most sensible plan, were it not that it developed into a joint hostility to German purposes and policy. So far as Persia was concerned, the agreement begins plausibly enough : " The Governments of Great Britain and Russia, having mutually pledged themselves to respect the integrity and independence of Persia, and sincerely desiring the preservation of order throughout that country and its peaceful development, as well as the permanent establishment of equal advantages for the trade and industry of all nations." What could be more satisfactory ? Only, oddly enough, the method adopted to secure these admirable purposes was the division of Persia into three spheres of influence, one British, one Russian, and one intermediary and neutral.[1] It would seem to us odd if that method had been adopted by France and Germany to secure the integrity and independence of Belgium. What, one wonders, would Belgium have said ? And what England ? The meaning of this division into spheres is explained in later clauses of the agreement. Great Britain and Russia respectively pledge themselves that neither will seek for itself, nor support in favour of its subjects, or of the subjects of third Powers, any concessions of a political or commercial nature—railways, banks, telegraphs, roads, transport, insurance, etc.—in the sphere of the other country : nor will oppose the grant of such concessions to that other. The effect of this is plain. Developments of transport vital for Persia are barred, unless either England chooses to introduce them in the south-east or Russia in the north. Why is this ? The diplomatic correspondence now at our disposal gives the answer. What the two States are thinking of, primarily, is military transport. They are both afraid of some Power, and we know of which. The agreement is

[1] A map showing the spheres will be found in Shuster and in Browne.

directed against German expansion eastwards and northwards. Sir Edward Grey is thinking of the Indian frontier, and Russia of the Caucasus.

The agreement thus subordinated the economic development of Persia to the military policies of her two powerful neighbours ; and probably that is all that Sir Edward Grey intended it to do. For in the same year, 1907, the British Minister in Teheran issued to the Persian Government an explanatory commentary. The British and Russian Governments, he said, are in perfect accord on two fundamental points:

(1) That neither of them will interfere in the affairs of Persia, unless injury is inflicted on the persons or property of their subjects ;

(2) That negotiations arising out of the Anglo-Persian agreement must not violate the integrity and independence of Persia. " Neither of the two Powers," says the memorandum, " seeks anything from Persia, so that Persia can concentrate all her energies on the settlement of her internal affairs." The object of the two Powers is not in any way to attack, but rather to ensure for ever, the independence of Persia. Especially they intend " not to allow one another to intervene, on the pretext of safeguarding their interests." This important document, curiously enough, was unknown to the British Foreign Office up to the year 1912. Still it exists, and it imposed a formal obligation on the Governments concerned.[1]

There is no reason to doubt that this document represents the real intentions of Sir Edward Grey. He did not want to partition Persia, nor even to influence her domestic policy. His object was to keep out Germany. This was the impression of the Russian Ambassador in London, who wrote, in August 1910 : " England desires no more annexations ; she knows from experience how a Government may be forced to resort to such a measure. She does not wish to occupy Persia, because she is convinced that this cannot be done without a war. England is less interested in what happens in Persia than in preventing any other Power, except England and Russia, from playing any rôle there. This applies particularly to Germany and Turkey—of course for political reasons." [2]

---

[1] See text in Shuster, p. 28, and Browne, p. 190.
[2] Siebert, p. 92. I have corrected the English translation, which is rather obscure as printed.

These words, no doubt, express accurately Sir Edward's wishes. But wishes, in these cases, do not count for much. Russia, as well as England, had a finger in the pie, and her finger was nearer and more active. The Russian Government may have intended to keep to the terms of the agreement. But, as we know in the case of the Balkans, and as we shall see in this case, Russian agents on the spot had the habit of acting independently of the wishes or orders of their Foreign Office. Moreover, such arrangements naturally lead to further encroachments ; for the native Government is weak and recalcitrant, civil tumults ensue, "order" is endangered, incidents, in a word, are always occurring to disturb the status quo, even though the intention of all parties may be to maintain it. The common sense of the situation was well expressed in a cartoon of *Punch*, where the British lion and the Russian bear are represented as mauling between them an unhappy Persian cat. The lion is saying, " You can play with his head and I can play with his tail, and we can both stroke the small of his back " ; while the cat moans, " I don't remember having been consulted about this." [1]

III. The Powers, Germany and Persia

The essential truth of this cartoon is shown by the whole subsequent history, which we will now proceed to summarise. In the year 1906 the Persian Shah had been shot, a new Shah set up, and a representative body called the Medjlis created. But the new Shah proved to be a debauchee and a tool of the Russians. A conflict broke out between him and the Medjlis, in which he seems to have been supported not only by the Russians but by the British. In June 1908 the Medjlis was forcibly dissolved. The nationalists assembled at Tabriz and the Shah proceeded to besiege them. Thereupon the Russians sent troops to Tabriz to " restore order." Nevertheless, and in spite of this intervention, the counter-revolution was defeated, the Shah was deposed, his son, a boy of twelve, appointed in his place, and a new Medjlis assembled. The Shah fled to Russia. That might have seemed to be the end of the business, and would have been so, presumably, had such events taken place in Europe. It was thus that Louis Philippe, and later

the Empress Eugénie, took refuge in England ; and England
did not endeavour to exact from France money for their
support.   In this case, however, Russia and England intervened to secure an agreement whereby the Persian Government should pay a pension to the ex-Shah, so long as he
remained abroad and made no attempt to regain the throne.
For the next two years the Persian Government was in
the hands of the nationalists, entrenched in the Medjlis ;
and the history of these years may be fairly described as a
continuous conflict between them and the two Powers who had
them in their grip.[1]   For the " independence and integrity "
guaranteed in the Anglo-Russian agreement turned out to have
a singularly narrow application.   There was almost nothing
commonly done by sovereign States which the Persians found
themselves permitted to do.   Do they want to raise a loan ?
The tutelary Powers at once object to its being raised from
anyone but themselves, and, above all, from Germany.   They
consult together as to their line of action.   The British
propose that " a statement be drawn up of outstanding debts,
and a declaration made to Persia that we intend to insist not
only on the settlement of these claims, but also on that of all
other advances made, should Persia persist in her intention
to mortgage the revenues of the country as security for a loan
to be granted by a third Power.".   This seems to the Russian
Foreign Minister a little too obvious.   " We must try to avoid,"
he says, " making any such declaration, as we might be accused
of wishing to prevent Persia from obtaining credit in any other
countries."   He proposes, therefore, conditions which will
have the same effect without so obviously revealing the
intention.[2]   But in April 1910 one Cohen arrives in Paris,
having secured from one of the Persian Ministers the option
for the conclusion of a loan of 200 million francs, with the
Customs and Telegraph revenues as security.   The object of
the loan was to pay off the debts due to the British and Russian
Government, thus restoring the financial position of Persia.
The French Minister at Teheran asked his Russian colleague
what he thought of the plan.   " I answered that the payment
of the sums due to us was by no means compatible with our
interests, since this would open the door for the political influence of foreigners in this country."   " Foreigners," the context

---

[1] See British Blue Book, 1911, v. 103.   [2] Siebert, pp. 78-9.

suggests, means citizens of other States than those essentially
" native " ones, Russia and England. The French, being
allies of Russia, were accommodating. They quashed the
scheme, informing the enterprising Jew that " only such
financial operations would be allowed to be carried through
here which had been first submitted to the consideration of
Great Britain and Russia. . . . The Foreign Minister gave me
the assurance that, in all Persian affairs, France would permit
of nothing being undertaken which could be disagreeable to
Russia and England. The financial circles have been duly
informed of this." [1]

So much for loans. There were similar difficulties about
concessions. As we have seen, the Anglo-Russian agreement
bound the two States each to abstain from asking concessions
for railways or other means of communication in the sphere
of the other. The reasons for this were, primarily, strategic,
and directed against the Germans. The dispatches show a
continuous anxiety of Sir Edward Grey on this subject.[2]
But, naturally, differences of opinion arose between the
Persians and the two Powers ; and we find the Russian
Foreign Minister writing to his representative at Teheran that
the Persian regent " might be told, that any grant of concessions to foreigners, without Russia and Great Britain having
been previously consulted, will be regarded by us as an act
of hostility and will have the most serious consequences for
Persia." [3]

The attitude of Germany, in the face of this situation,
must appear, to an impartial observer, singularly moderate
and conciliatory. Alone, in the face of unceasing opposition
by the Powers of the Entente, she was carrying through the
great and beneficent scheme of the Bagdad Railway. It
was a natural and reasonable consequence that she should
be able to tap the trade of Persia. The Anglo-Russian agreement had been made without any consultation with her, and
she might fairly have said she was not bound by it. But
she adopted no such attitude. She admitted the special
interests of the two Powers in Persia ; she admitted their
monopoly of " strategic " concessions, such as railroads ;
but she claimed to be left in at least as good a position as

---

[1] Siebert, pp. 85-6.   [2] E.g. Siebert, pp. 68, 70, 73, 75.
[3] Ib., p. 80. Cf. p. 85.

other Powers, and to exercise all rights which the agreement
had not reserved to Great Britain and Russia. Yet even
over this limited claim disputes arose in which all the technical right appears to have been on the side of Germany.
For instance, in connexion with a certain loan, it was proposed that seven French financial officials should be appointed
by the Persian Government.[1] The Germans protested against
the admission of French officials, if German officials were to
be excluded; the more so as " the Persian Government, for
its part, would certainly be willing to appoint various German
officials." This episode led to some slight difference of opinion
between Sir Edward Grey and the Russians, the latter being
inclined, on this occasion, to be more intransigeant than the
former. Sir Edward, indeed, clearly thought the protest well
founded. The Germans, he said, acknowledge the privileged
position held by the Russians and the British, but claim that,
where other nationals are admitted at all, all nations must
be treated equally. This principle, he observes, is easy to
defend and difficult to assail; although in this case " we are
unable to uphold it."[2] He proposes, therefore, that the
appointment of Frenchmen be dropped, and that the officials
be chosen among nationals of countries which are not Great
Powers.[3]

Similar difficulties arose about concessions. In connexion
with this same loan the Germans urged that its terms " were
of a nature to exclude foreign trade and to render Persia's
independence illusory." Grey disputed this view and apparently, for the moment, satisfied the Germans.[4] But there
remained the question of the neutral zone. That, at least,
was open to commercial penetration by any Power? Certainly it was, so far as the Anglo-Russian agreement was
concerned. But the two Powers were agitated at the idea
that Germany might get concessions there.[5] And by 1912 we
find that the Russians have proposed, and Grey is prepared to
accept, the annulling of the neutral zone, and its inclusion in
the sphere of influence of one or both of the Powers.[6]

Enough has been said to indicate the kind of friction

---

[1] This was an Anglo-Russian loan of £400,000, 1910. See Cd. 5656, 1911,
ciii, pp. 539, 550, etc.; see also Siebert, p. 72.
[2] Siebert, pp. 65–6. [3] Ib., p. 67. [4] Ib., p. 77. [5] Ib., p. 80.
[6] See *Livre Noir*, ii. p. 351. By the treaty of 1915 between England and
Russia it was assigned to the former.

that was arising between the two Powers and Germany. The former justified their conduct by their fears of strategic penetration by the Germans. There appears, however, to be no evidence of such intentions. On the other hand, the great enterprise of the Bagdad Railway gave the Germans a legitimate interest in the trade of Persia, as well as of Turkey. Conciliatory though they seem to have been, it was unreasonable to suppose that they would, or should, acquiesce in a permanent exclusion from Persian concessions. They took, however, no violent step, but endeavoured to reach an agreed settlement. In April 1910 we find the German Chancellor proposing to the British that the whole Persian question shall form part of a general political convention, to be concluded between the three Powers. Germany might waive all claims to concessions for railways, telegraphs, and the like within the British sphere ; while England should grant Germany a proportionate share in the supply of materials. In the case of loans and of official appointments, Germany should receive the same share as other third Powers. In the Russian sphere Germany might similarly renounce all claims to concessions, while Russia should grant Germany equal rights in all commercial questions and should undertake to connect her railways in Northern Persia with the Bagdad Railway, not to interfere with international traffic on that line, and to facilitate the connexion of the German line with Teheran.[1] Nothing appears to have happened with regard to the British part of this proposal. But the Russian part is plainly the preliminary to the Potsdam agreement, concluded at the end of the year. As we have seen,[2] the difficulty, or one difficulty, about that agreement, from the point of view of Sir Edward Grey, was that it left open the possibility that railways in Persia might be constructed and controlled by Germany. For that and other reasons Sir Edward was so much disturbed that he contemplated resignation. But the difficult moment passed, and right up to 1912 we find the two Powers still engaged in excluding Germany from all concessions in Persia, and thus intensifying the friction which led, in the end, to the Great War. That aspect of the matter we will now leave, and return to the tragic events which were occurring in that unhappy country. For the play of the Russian bear by now was becoming serious to the cat.

¹ Siebert, p. 18.   ² See above, p. 250.

IV. The Bear Squeezes the Cat

As might have been, and perhaps was, foreseen, when the Anglo-Russian agreement was made, it was very difficult for England to exercise any real control over Russian policy in Central Asia. Russia was there on the spot; she could pour troops at any moment across the Caucasus; her agents were numerous, unscrupulous, and out of hand. Sir Edward Grey, no doubt, genuinely desired that the division of Persia into spheres of influence should not lead to its partition. It is not impossible that the Russian Government had the same intention. But that Government was a long way off, and the men on the spot, we may pretty certainly affirm, had different intentions. There had been always a strong current of opinion in Russia against the division of Persia into spheres of interest, for the reason, frankly expressed in 1901 by Count Witte, that : " Persia, together with the waters which bathe its shores, must remain the object of Russian material and moral protection." [1] The Entente is hardly likely to have obliterated this point of view. At any rate, it soon became evident that Russia, in every crisis, would be anxious to take more drastic measures than Sir Edward Grey could approve, though he was willing to go further in the direction of coercion than liberal British opinion. This was shown as early as the attempt at counter-revolution by the Shah in 1908. At that time, as we saw, the Russians advanced troops to Tabriz, on the usual plea of the security of the lives of foreigners. These troops were not withdrawn, but remained encamped outside the city, till the moment came for them to play a terrible and tragic part. It may be added that Colonel Liakhoff, the Commander of the Cossacks in the employ of the Shah, was a Russian citizen, and took an active part in the attempted counter-revolution. Further, when the Nationalist leader was marching on Tabriz, the Russian Legation called upon him to halt. Clearly, then, whatever may have been the intentions of the Russian Government, the Russians on the spot were against the Persian Nationalists and in favour of the reactionary Shah. The latter, however, was defeated and, as we have seen, withdrew to Russia, under a firm obligation never to return to Persia. The Persian Government then

Browne, p. 102.

proceeded to look for a capable and disinterested foreigner who would help them to reform their finances. They applied, without success, for a Frenchman and for an Italian,[1] and ultimately secured an American, Mr. Shuster. The European Powers were much disturbed by this appointment. Russia and England had made an agreement that they would not permit the Persian Government to nominate to office subjects of any Great Power, lest Germany should insist on the appointment of Germans; and Sasonoff called the attention of Sir Edward Grey to this point. Sir Edward, however, pointed out that the agreement concerned only subjects of European Powers. " He fears that it will be difficult to protest against Americans ";[2] and he " does not believe that the Persians will appoint any other foreigners except Americans, if Russia and England should declare that in such a case they will have to insist on the appointment of Russians and Englishmen."[3] The truth was, no doubt, that Sir Edward could not take the risk of offending America, and Mr. Shuster's appointment went through. He arrived to take up his duties in May 1911.

Mr. Shuster was a plain, honest American, determined to do his duty to Persia, without regarding European intrigues. His single-mindedness radiates from every page of his fascinating book. But such a man is, of all men, the most distasteful to professional diplomats, engaged, as they so commonly are, in discreditable operations which cannot be defended in the light of day. Mr. Shuster was neither unreasonable, nor impolite, nor unperceptive. But he was determined, if he could, to restore the finances of Persia. Equally the Russians were determined that he should do nothing of the kind; for they relied on the chaos of the financial situation for tightening their grasp on the country. " Mr. Shuster's mission," an Englishman in Persia wrote, " was doomed at its inception, seeing that a prosperous Persia would have brought about weakened Russian control."[4]

Mr. Shuster, as we have said, arrived in May 1911, and by June he had produced a law for the reorganisation of the finances. It was an essential part of the new project that the Customs revenue, mortgaged for the European loans, should be under the control of the new Treasurer-General. Against

---

[1] Shuster, App. E, p. 404.
[2] Grey says (i. 169) that he himself suggested an American.
[3] Siebert, p. 104.   [4] Shuster, App. E, p. 405.

this arrangement " the Russian, French, German, Italian, and Austro-Hungarian Legations rained protests upon the Persian Foreign Office ; and Mornard (the Belgian head of the Customs service) said he would not obey the law nor recognise the Treasurer-General." But the Treasurer stood firm, and the Belgian, in the end, consented to serve under him. So far, so good. But for the execution of the new law it was further necessary to create a special gendarmerie to collect the taxes ; since, as Mr. Shuster puts it : " The Persian peasants, labouring classes, and small property-owners are not intractable in the matter of paying their dues to the Government, but the peculiar conditions in that country demanded that the Government should be able to show the necessary force with which to exact the taxes before it could hope to receive them on the mere demand of civilian officials." [1] For the command of this force a competent European was required, and Mr. Shuster selected an officer of the British Indian Army, Major Stokes, who was well acquainted with the Persian language, and was at the time military attaché to the British Legation in Teheran. Immediately the Russian Government protested. " The appointment of Stokes would have an unfavourable effect on public opinion in Russia, . . . and the Russian Government might be under the obligation of demanding compensations, such, for example, as the reorganisation of the Persian forces by Russian officers." [2]

Technically, the Russian objection was that it was proposed to employ Major Stokes, for a time, in the Russian sphere of influence. The real objection, no doubt, was, that he might contribute to the restoration of Persian finances. Sir Edward felt compelled to support this objection. He therefore signified that Stokes must resign his position in the Indian Army, if he accepted a post under the Persian Government. The Major, accordingly, applied for his discharge. It was refused.[3] Further, in August, Sir Edward communicated a note to the Persian Government warning it that, if it persisted in the appointment, " the British Government will recognise Russia's right to take such steps as she thinks are necessary in order that her interests in Northern Persia may be respected." Mr. Shuster wrote a strong protest to the British Ambassador on this interference with Persian sovereignty. He

---

[1] Shuster, p. 70. [2] Siebert, p. 105. [3] Shuster, pp. 106, 112.

did not either deny or ignore the provisions of the Anglo-Russian Convention. He merely pointed out that " Stokes was not a bank, a railroad, or a political or commercial concession of any kind."[1] Sir Edward does not seem to have contended that the appointment of Stokes was contrary to the letter of the Convention ; but he thought it contrary to the " spirit," which no doubt it was, if the spirit implied the complete domination of the Persian State by the two Powers.

Things had reached this point when suddenly, on July 18th, news arrived that the ex-Shah, Mohammed Ali, had landed in Persia at a point on the Caspian. According to the agreement signed by Great Britain and Russia at the time of his defeat and flight in 1909, both Governments were pledged to do all they could to prevent his return. Whether the Russian Government endeavoured to fulfil this obligation we are not likely ever to know beyond dispute. Certain facts, however, are suggestive. Thus, ten days before the Shah landed, the Russian Minister at Teheran announced, at a large dinner party, that within a few weeks the Persian constitutional Government would have ceased to exist.[2] Further, the ex-Shah had had an interview at Vienna with that notorious Russian diplomat, Hartwig, who was so largely influential in stirring up the Balkan trouble in 1913.[3] Finally, he passed the Russian Customs disguised as a merchant, with a false passport, and carrying in packing-cases three Austrian cannon, labelled " Mineral water."[4]

It may be noticed, further, that the Russian Minister asked Mr. Shuster whether he would remain Treasurer-General under the returned Shah, promising him, in that case, the full support of the Russian Government. This little episode by itself is enough to characterise the real attitude of the Russian authorities in Persia, whatever may have been that of the Government at St. Petersburg.[5]

On hearing of the arrival of the Shah the British and Russian Governments declared that they would be neutral in the complications likely to follow. Grey further remarked that, according to the terms laid down by the two Governments, the Shah's pension should now be stopped. But the Russians replied that they could take no action, now the Shah was in

[1] Shuster, p. 77.   [2] Ib., p. 117.   [3] Ib., p. 107.
[4] Ib., p. 128.   [5] Ib., p. 118.

Persia ; that Russian public opinion was against any intervention on their part ; and that the Persian reactionaries
welcomed the return of their ruler—which no doubt was the
case.[1]

There followed civil war in Persia, in which once more
the nationalist forces triumphed and the ex-Shah was defeated.
The Persian Government thereupon pronounced the confisca-
tion of the estates of the rebel leaders, and especially of two
brothers of the ex-Shah. Mr. Shuster, as Treasurer, was
responsible for the execution of this order, and he dispatched
gendarmes to execute it. Cossacks, under Russian officers,
resisted them. Next day Mr. Shuster sent another party,
and found a force of Cossacks established in the garden of the
house he was commissioned to seize. His officer requested
the Russian consul to withdraw this force, and the consul
refused. The gendarmes then proceeded to disarm the
Cossacks, which was done without resistance, and the Government took peaceable possession of the property. But presently two Russian officers arrived with a party of Cossacks,
arrested the gendarmes and their officers, and conveyed them
as prisoners to the Russian Consulate. The Government in
Russia upheld this action of their agents on the spot. They
were thus openly protecting Persian rebels against the legitimate action of the Government that had defeated them. At
the same time they took the opportunity of exacting further
concessions. They insisted on the replacement of the Persian
military police at the estate in question by Cossacks, and
also on an apology. "Contrary to all expectation," the
Persians refused. The Russians repeated their demands in
writing, and threatened, in the event of a refusal, to break
off relations with the Persian Government. They received
no reply, broke off relations, and ordered a Russian division
to advance upon Kaswin, leaving it to the discretion of the
Minister whether it should proceed further to Teheran in order
to expel the Persian gendarmerie by force.[2]

This was embarrassing to Sir Edward Grey. He did,
indeed, consider the Russian demands as not unnatural ;
though he would himself have adopted somewhat milder

---

[1] Blue Book, v. 122, 1912–13, pp. 175 seq. The British Ambassador at
St. Petersburg acquits the Russian Government of conniving at the return,
" whatever negligence may have been shown by the local authorities at Baku."
[2] Siebert, pp. 116–17.

measures, such as the occupation of the Persian custom houses ; " but he looks upon the sending of troops as a perilous measure, both as regards Persian affairs per se, as also with respect to its reaction on the Anglo-Russian agreement." [1] What this meant was that British public opinion was becoming agitated, and Sir Edward was perplexed how to deal with it. Once more the Entente seemed to be threatened. " Should the unity of our action in Persia come to an end, this would necessarily mean the disruption of the entente. It would result—in a far shorter period than is generally believed—in a new orientation of English politics." [2] " It was regrettable," said Sir Edward, " that the Russian ultimatum based itself on the question of the property of the Shoa Es Sultanah. This entire question was somewhat trivial and from the Russian standpoint not wholly justifiable." [3]

Nevertheless, the Persian Government, under pressure from Sir Edward, did in the end accept the original demands of the Russians. But immediately the latter presented another ultimatum. They now demanded :

1. The dismissal of Mr. Shuster ;
2. The assurance of the Persian Government that they would not appoint foreigners without having previously obtained the approval of the Russian and English Legations at Teheran ;
3. The payment of the costs of the Russian expedition by the Persian Government.[4]

This, the reader will observe, is all according to the best precedents, in the dealings of the Christian Powers with weak and disorganised Orientals. But since, on this occasion, it was Russia, not Britain, who was playing the bully, there was, as we have noted, a considerable disturbance of British public opinion. Sir Edward was once more perplexed. He did not venture to object to the two first demands ; for, as he remarked, " Shuster did not follow the advice we gave him ; he has brought us into a very difficult position, and we shall have to come to some agreement with the Persian Government on the question of foreign advisers, in order to obviate again being placed in such a position." [5] But he regrets the demand

[1] Siebert, p. 117.   [2] Ib., p. 128.   [3] Ib., p. 129.
[4] Ib., p. 127.   [5] Ib., p. 129.

for an indemnity, on the ground that Persian funds were required to keep order in Persia, and especially on the southern trade route, where British interests were suffering. He also urged that Russian troops should occupy Teheran only in case of extreme necessity. "I fear that the St. Petersburg Cabinet does not sufficiently take into account how unexpectedly the Persian question, if it be not properly handled, may bring about a discussion of foreign policy as a whole. If demands be made which we cannot declare to be covered by the Anglo-Russian Convention, then the Persian question would be lost sight of, and the question of foreign policy in general, Russia's as well as England's, would take its place. This would be regrettable, and I am in the greatest anxiety." [1] Sir Edward goes on to suggest that, if he can overcome, with Russian connivance, the present difficulties, "we could perhaps form a Persian Government which would recognise the necessity of taking Russia's interests into account, instead of continually setting up opposition." The "independence" of Persia, the reader will observe, is becoming "small by degrees and beautifully less," as the effects of the Anglo-Russian agreement develop. But, alas! the Russian Government, in spite of appeals from their Ambassador in London, showed no inclination to meet Sir Edward's modest demands. "For your personal information," writes the Russian Minister to his agent at Teheran, "we have by no means the intention of rendering the demands we shall lay before the Persians dependent on the approval of the British Minister." [2]

The Persian Ministry was inclined to accept the new Russian ultimatum. But the Medjlis refused. "It may be the will of Allah," said a member, "that our liberty and our sovereignty should be taken from us by force, but let us not sign them away with our own hands." [3] The result was that the Medjlis was forcibly dissolved by the ex-Cabinet,[4] and, at the end of the year, Mr. Shuster resigned. The Russians had thus succeeded completely in their determination to prevent the reorganisation of the Persian finances. But that was not enough; the Persians must be properly punished. As we have seen, Russian troops had entered Kaswin, and

[1] Siebert, p. 130.   [2] Ib., p. 126.
[3] Shuster, p. 182.   [4] Ib., p. 199.

towards the end of December we learn that the Persian Chargé d'Affaires at St. Petersburg was complaining that "encounters with our troops had taken place at Resht and Tabriz, the blame resting with the Russians." The Russians, of course, replied that "according to our information, the Persians had attacked." [1] About the same time, a Russian Viceroy in the Caucasus is issuing orders to the Russian troops to advance upon Teheran without halting ; to "take energetic measures against refusal to work, boycott, and robbery " ; to take the Persian volunteers prisoners, and, "should they resist," destroy them.[2] A day later, "the attacks on our troops and the mutilation of our wounded rendered energetic reprisals necessary, and I considered it desirable to instruct general Woropanoff to blow up the Tabriz citadel and to establish military tribunals to mete out justice. . . . The verdicts must be carried out at once. Furthermore, a considerable compensation is to be demanded from the population of Tabriz for the families of the killed and wounded. Similar measures to be taken in Enzeli and Pesht, and in other Persian towns in which encounters have taken place." Further, "all culprits should be dealt with by courts-martial, on the spot in Persia, and not sent to Russia to the Caucasian prisons, as these are overcrowded, the trials would be long drawn out, and the punishment would not be severe enough in proportion to the transgressions." [3] These instructions were duly carried out ; that is, there was a general massacre by the Russians in Tabriz, and, among other episodes, the chief priest and two others were hanged, with several other high officials, on the sacred day of the 10th Muharram. " The effect of this outrage on the Persians," wrote a British journalist,[4] " was that which would be produced on the English people by the hanging of the Archbishop of Canterbury on Good Friday." But, as the Russian *Novoe Vremya* explained, " in this case true humanity requires cruelty. The whole population of Tabriz must be held responsible and punished. . . . There is a limit even to Russian indulgence." [5]

So ends, for the moment, this little episode of European imperialism. Let us recapitulate. Persia is a weak and

---

[1] Siebert, p. 136.   [2] Ib.
[3] Ib., p. 137.   [4] Shuster, p. 202.
[5] Ib. For further details of these Russian atrocities, see Professor Browne's *Reign of Terror*.

incompetent Oriental State, with a preference for religious
and poetical discussion over administration, economic development, and war. Near her are two great Empires : one the
Russian, which has already crossed the Caucasus ; the other
the British, impinging on her across the dependent State of
Baluchistan. For many years these two Empires have
been on the verge of war, for no other reason than the fact
that they were coming into contact, and therefore, according to the recognised tradition, must fight. But suddenly a
curious transformation scene occurs. Another Empire, the
German, begins penetration on the west of Persia, and seems
to threaten the Persian Gulf, which has been equally a subject
of cupidity to both Empires. By a surprising volte face they
suddenly discover that, after all, they have no ground for
quarrelling, and unite to keep out the new intruder. Persia
is solemnly declared, without her own approval or choice, to
lie within their " sphere of influence." She is to be independent ; the integrity of her territory is to be guaranteed ; only,
in compensation, she must do, in all respects, exactly as her
neighbours may require. Persia, under these happy conditions,
shows a certain unintelligible recalcitrance : ungrateful country !
Germany also makes impertinent demands. Finally, one
of the two Empires does a deal, behind the back of her
partner, with the country they both mistrust, admits German
trade into the northern sphere of Persia, and so far under-
mines the agreement that Sir Edward Grey trembles on the
verge of resignation. But this little betrayal of the main
purpose of the conspiracy only tightens the grip of the bear
upon the cat. An attempt on the part of the unhappy and
struggling victim to reform her finances, by the help of an
honest and independent American, is the signal for more
and more violent squeezes. The lion, whose tail is exposed
to twisting in many parts of the world, and even—oh, shame !—
by his own Englishmen, grows uncomfortable. Could not the
bear be a little more considerate—just for friendship's
sake ? The bear is polite, but unfortunately unable to alter
his course of behaviour. With a final squeeze he extrudes
from the cat's belly that alien morsel, Mr. Shuster, and
destroys a number of tiresome parasites, among others the
Oriental equivalent of the Archbishop of Canterbury. Thus,
while affirming the integrity and independence of Persia,

Russia had put a stop, once for all, to her attempts at reforming her Government and her finances. She had now only to sit down and wait till events should sound the hour for the final deglutition of the victim. Only—events happened otherwise!

And England? We have seen the part that England played. It was neither honourable nor humane. But what could she do? Protests were unavailing. Does anyone recommend war? We might, no doubt, have broken off the entente with Russia; or we might never have formed it. True! We should then have avoided complicity with the Russian enterprise in Persia. But Persia would be likely to have suffered rather more than less. In any case, the reader can hardly have followed the story, as it has been developed in the preceding chapters, without seeing that, under any and every combination, the World-War was on its way. For States whose policy is conducted according to the traditions and principles we are examining can produce nothing but war. The episode of Persia is, indeed, one of the most discreditable on record. But it is one episode only in that long tale of futile slaughter which constitutes the history of international relations.

CHAPTER XI

THE FAR EAST

I. Japan Adopts Western Civilisation

EVENTS in the Far East were not connected directly with the outbreak of the Great War. But they had some indirect effect on the causation, the course, and the result of it, and we will therefore deal briefly with them, so far as they are relevant to our subject.

The recent history of the relations of the European Powers with China dates from what is called the Opium War between that country and England. This war was caused, specifically, by Chinese obstruction to the importation of opium from India, and, more generally, by the obstacles put in the way of British trade. It was concluded by the Treaty of Nanking, 1842, which sanctioned British trade at certain ports, and gave to foreign traders rights of residence in the Empire. These provisions were immediately extended to other Powers, and from that time on the history of European relations to China is one of continual aggression, military and financial, by the former, and continual defeat by the latter. For China had committed the unpardonable offence of having a weak army, and of despising the soldier as compared with the official and the merchant. Accordingly, during the last half of the nineteenth century, she lost to Russia a large tract in the north, to France Annam and Indo-China, to Britain Burma, and to Japan Formosa and Korea.

These latter losses were due to the Sino-Japanese War of 1895. Japan, by that date, was a Power organised on the western model. After over two centuries of exclusion from intercourse with other States, during which she had enjoyed a civilisation unique in beauty, in harmony, and in peace, she had succumbed to the restless determination of the Western Powers that there should be no part of the world exempt from their curiosity and their greed. The expedition of the American, Commodore Perry, in 1858, had opened her doors to the world. But Japan was unlike other Eastern societies. Organised, for centuries past, on a feudal system curiously resembling that of the Middle Ages in Europe, she had retained, even in time of peace, the military virtues without the military savagery. Further, she had, as her earlier relations with China had shown, an extraordinary capacity for assimilation. When, therefore, she admitted European influences, it was not to succumb to but to master them. With incredible rapidity she became an industrial and military State on the most modern plan ; and her diplomacy followed her material development. By 1895 she was ready to put into practice her newly acquired talents. She picked a quarrel with China about the peninsula of Korea, won a crushing victory over that ramshackle Empire, and seized the peninsula of Liaotung and Port Arthur. Her success had been complete. But it brought her up at once against the Western world, which she could not imitate without challenging. Russia had her eye on Port Arthur ; France was the ally of Russia ; Germany was preparing to assert her commercial and political influence in the Far East, and had reasons for fostering friendly relations with her restless neighbours in Europe. The three Powers accordingly intervened to deprive Japan of Port Arthur. This disappointment was accepted by the victor with the stern philosophy inherited from her feudal past. In illustration we may cite the words of Count Hayashi, published at the time :

" It must never be forgotten that discontent is the prime factor which incites men to greater activity and diligence. We should therefore retain our discontent to spur us on to greater diligence, with a view to one day dispersing the gloom around us. We must persistently suffer the insufferable and support the insupportable for the sake of what the future will have in store for us. In this way we shall truly promote the strength and prosperity of our nation.

" We should exert ourselves to develop our commerce and our industries, for these are the principal factors of national expansion. Commerce and industry produce wealth. We must also devote more attention than ever to building up, on scientific principles, our Army and Navy.

" We must continue to study according to Western methods,

for the application of science is the most important item of warlike preparations that civilised nations regard. If new ships of war are considered necessary, we must build them at any cost. If the organisation of our Army is found to be wrong, it must at once be renovated. If advisable, our whole military system must be entirely changed. We must build docks to be able to repair our ships. We must establish a steel factory to supply guns and ammunition. Our railways must be extended so that we can mobilise our troops rapidly. Our overseas shipping must be developed so that we can provide transports to carry our armies abroad.

" This is the programme that we have to keep always in view. We have suffered hard things, and we must suffer yet harder things before we arrive at our destiny. Whilst our preparations are in the making, things will not be easy. Our taxes will increase, our people will suffer distress, our Government officials must work for small salaries, and amidst a discontented populace. Political parties will use the distress to raise political disputes, and our whole Empire may feel unhappy. But if we always keep in view the great ends which I have indicated, then we shall endure all these things gladly.

" Peace has been restored, but it cannot be a lasting peace. We must sacrifice ourselves, we must work for those who come after us, we must face difficulties, even as ' combing our hair in the rain and bathing in the wind.' Many will be disappointed and discontented, but they must endure all their disappointment and discontent in silence and with a brave heart.

" If they were private merchants they would endure and continue struggling. As a nation we must do the same. The actions of the Great Powers are like those of individual merchants. Each one seeks his own gain, and if he cannot at once win continues with increased energy until he does so at last." [1]

It will be admitted that the political philosophy of the West had been well conned by its disciples in Japan. It was to bring forth in due time characteristic fruits. For the moment, however, as we have seen, Japan was checkmated by a combination of Western Powers, and it is relevant to our purpose to explain how that combination came about.

[1] Hayashi, p. 104.

II. Japan is Deprived of the Fruits of Victory

Russia was the Power most obviously interested. Her interest was partly what may be called the normal desire of European Powers to seize territory for the sake of seizing it. " Emperor Nicolas," Count Witte writes, " was anxious to spread Russian influence in the Far East. Not that he had a definite programme of conquest. He was merely possessed by an unreasoned desire to seize Far Eastern lands." [1] But the Count himself had motives more intelligent and intelligible. He was engaged on the great enterprise of the Siberian Railway, which he desired to carry across Manchuria to Vladivostok. Further : " I clearly saw that it was to Russia's best interests to have as its neighbour a strong but passive China, and that therein lay the assurance of Russia's safety in the East." The stress, in Count Witte's mind, was perhaps rather on the word " passive " than on the word " strong," in that interesting conjunction of terms. But, whatever the reason, it was the interest of Russia that China should remain, for the time being, unpartitioned. Hence : " it appeared to me obvious that it was imperative not to allow Japan to penetrate into the very heart of China and secure a footing in the Liaotung Peninsula, which, to a certain extent, occupied a dominating position." Count Witte therefore proposed a kind of self-denying ordinance : That China remain unchanged, and that no Power be allowed to increase its territorial possessions at China's expense." [2] For these reasons Russia took the lead in opposing the terms which Japan was to exact from China. France was bound to Russia by the alliance recently concluded, and was willing therefore to give diplomatic support. Great Britain, on the other hand, decided to stand aloof. She was asking, at the time, for no further territorial concessions for herself ; although, when the German Ambassador, Count Hatzfeld, remarked that, nevertheless, if other Powers were to take anything England would not be left behind, Lord Kimberley smiled, and pointing to the map of China, said that thereon was marked the not very important point which, in such a

[1] Witte, p. 83.
[2] Ib., p. 83. Cf. Dillon, *Eclipse of Russia*, p. 246, and Ger. Docs., ix. pp. 265, 270.

case, England would seize. Count Hatzfeld thought that
Tschusan was intended, and probably he was correct.[1] A
day or two later the British Minister said definitely that
England would not intervene ; upon which the Kaiser, with
a clear appreciation of the principles of diplomacy, commented : " Then the British have secured themselves by
secret agreements with Japan." But I know of no evidence
that this, at that time, was true.[2]

England thus stood out, but Germany was coming in.
Her motives were various and complicated. First the Kaiser
had his eye upon a port in China. He had already mentioned
this matter to the Tsar.[3] Amoy had been thought of, so
had Tschusan, but the most persistent idea was Kiaochow.[4]
The Chinese, the Kaiser clearly saw, would not be willing to
give him what he wanted. They did not understand the
motives of Christendom. " The conception of moral conquests
is altogether foreign to them. Force is the only language
they understand," [5] writes a German diplomat. And again :
" A delicacy in making demands which might be suitable
in Europe would be out of place in China and would not be
understood." After all, as the Russian Ambassador in Peking
had cheerfully remarked, " in China there is room for us all—
for us, for France, and for Germany." [6]

In spite, however, of his low opinion of the mentality of
the Chinese, the Kaiser seems to have hoped that an intervention against Japan would give him a claim upon their
gratitude. That was one reason why he joined the Franco-
Russian movement. But there were others. He hoped that,
by taking action in this matter, Russian policy might be
" nailed " to the East, and that her attention might continue
to be distracted from the Balkans and the German frontier.[7]
At the moment, indeed, the usual friction between France
and Germany was making itself felt. The Kaiser had been
disturbed, he tells the Tsar, " in the midst of these peaceful
occupations and the quiet hunting," by news of threatening
military measures by the French. Russian officers are
fraternising with them, and though " I perfectly know that

[1] Ger. Docs., ix. p. 264. Cf. ib., xiv. p. 93.   [2] Ib., ix. p. 268.
[3] Dillon, *Eclipse of Russia*, p. 248; *Kaiser to Tsar*, p. 11, April 26, 1895;
Memoirs, p. 61 ; Ger. Docs., xiv. p. 12 note.
[4] Ger. Docs., xiv. pp. 47 note and 128.   [5] Ib., p. 40.
[6] Ib., p. 49.   [7] Ib., ix. p. 358.

you personally do not dream of attacking us, still you cannot be astonished that the European Powers get alarmed at seeing how the presence of your officers and high officials in official way in France fans the inflammable Frenchman into a white passion and strengthens the cause of Chauvinism and Revanche." [1]

His preoccupation, then, with the possibility of a Franco-Russian attack was one reason why the Kaiser desired to " nail " Russia to the East. But further, he was influenced by one of his grandiose dreams—the future conflict between East and West.

" The development of the Far East, especially its danger to Europe and our Christian Faith, is a matter which has been greatly on my mind ever since we made our first move together in spring. At last my thoughts developed into a certain form and this I sketched on paper. I worked it out with an artist [2] —a first-class draughtsman—and after it was finished had it engraved for public use.

" It shows the powers of Europe represented by their respective genii called together by the Archangel Michael—sent from Heaven—to *unite* in resisting the inroad of Buddhism, heathenism, and barbarism for the defence of the Cross. Stress

---

[1] *Kaiser to Tsar*, September 26th, 1895, p. 19.

[2] " The Yellow Peril cartoon stated by the *North German Gazette* to have been specially designed by the Kaiser for presentation to the Tsar. The same paper describes the engraving which was carried out by Professor Knackfuss, of Cassel, as follows : ' On a plateau of rock bathed in light radiating from the Cross . . . stand allegorical figures of the civilised nations. In the foreground is France shading her eyes with her left hand. She cannot altogether believe in the proximity of danger, but Germany, armed with shield and sword, follows with attentive eye the approach of calamity. Russia, a beautiful woman with a wealth of hair, leans her arm as if in close friendship on the shoulder of her martial companion. Beside this group Austria stands in resolute pose. She extends her right hand in an attitude of invitation as if to win the co-operation of still somewhat reluctant England in the common task. . . . In front of this martial group of many figures stands unmailed the winged Archangel Michael, holding in his right hand a flaming sword. . . . At the foot of the rocky plateau stands the vast plain of civilised Europe. . . . In the foreground is the castle of Hohenzollern, but over these peaceful landscapes clouds of calamity are rolling up. . . . The path trodden by Asiatic hordes in their onward career is marked by a sea of flame proceeding from a burning city. Dense clouds of smoke twisting into the form of hellish distorted faces ascend from the conflagration. The threatening danger in the form of Buddha is enthroned in this sombre framework. A Chinese dragon, which at the same time represents the demon of destruction, carries this heathen idol. In an awful onset the Powers of Darkness draw nearer to the banks of the protecting stream. Only a little while and that stream is no longer a barrier ' (Berlin Correspondent, *Morning Post*, November 11th, 1895)." Note by the Editor of the letters.

is especially laid on the *united* resistance of *all* European
Powers, which is just as necessary also against our common
internal foes, anarchism, republicanism, nihilism. I venture
to send you an engraving begging you to accept it as a token
of my warm and sincere friendship to you and Russia." [1]

III. Europe takes " Compensation "

For these various reasons the German Government, on
the initiative, as it would seem, of the Kaiser, ranged itself,
in the Far East, on the side of that alliance which had just
been formed against it in the West. Under pressure of the
three Powers, Japan abandoned Port Arthur. The Chinese
ought, no doubt, to have been grateful. But no! They
still refused to offer Germany a port. There was nothing left
except " to wait till the Chinese give us an excuse for reprisals "; [2] and it was not necessary to wait long. Towards
the end of 1897 a band of Chinese robbers murdered two
German missionaries. The opportunity had come. " I am
firmly determined," the Kaiser cried, " to abandon our over-
scrupulous policy, which is condemned throughout East Asia,
and at last to convince the Chinese with all my force, and if
necessary with the most brutal ruthlessness, that the German
Kaiser does not allow himself to be played the fool with,
and that it is a bad business to have him for a foe." [3] In
pursuance of this heroic resolution the Germans seized Kiaochow
and exacted the exclusive right to construct railways and to
open mines in the whole province of Shantung, a country
larger, in area and population, than England. They also,
of course, in accordance with European precedent, took an
indemnity for their military expenses.

But the matter did not end thus. There were the other
Powers to be considered. For, as we have had occasion more
than once to observe, it is a principle of European diplomacy
that if one Power makes an advance anywhere others must
do so too, by way of " compensation." The compensation
for Russia, it would seem, had been already discussed. For
before the fortunate opportunity of seizing Kiaochow arose,
the Kaiser, on a visit to Petersburg, had not only gained the
Tsar's previous assent to that step, but had suggested that

[1] *Kaiser to Tsar*, pp. 18, 19.   [2] Ger. Docs., xiv. p. 45.   [3] Ib., p. 67.

Russia, when the contingency should occur, should take Port Arthur by way of making things even.[1] The contingency had now occurred, and the question was discussed at the Imperial Council. Count Witte opposed the step, and carried the Council with him. But afterwards Count Muravieff persuaded the Tsar that Britain was intending to seize the port in question, and that it would be well to anticipate her. The Tsar, accordingly, gave his order, and a Russian squadron entered the harbour and ran up the Russian flag. The action of Russia had thus come full circle. In 1895 she had saved Port Arthur for China from the Japanese. In 1897 she took it for herself. It was a neat and characteristic example of diplomacy and war. The Kaiser was delighted. In an excess of enthusiasm he telegraphed to the Tsar : " Please accept my congratulations at the arrival of your squadron at Port Arthur. Russia and Germany at the entrance of the Yellow Sea may be taken as represented by St. George and St. Michael shielding the Holy Cross in the Far East and guarding the gates to the continent of Asia." [2]

There remained England, who, while she had approved of the German appropriation of Shantung, was alarmed by Russia's appropriation of Port Arthur. She accordingly appeased her public opinion by taking Wei-hai-wei.[3] The whole series of events, it will be agreed, made a fairly complete compensation for the murder of two German missionaries by irresponsible robbers; and the Chinese must have been more than ever impressed by the morals and the power of Christianity.

But, alas! these heathen were unteachable; for in less than three years the Boxer movement broke out. Moreover, on this occasion, it was not merely missionaries who were attacked : the foreign embassies in Pekin were surrounded and besieged, and the German Ambassador murdered. The Kaiser rose to heights of prophetic inspiration : " Pekin," he cried, " must be attacked and razed to the ground. This is the fight of Asia against all Europe " ; and he summoned Europe to revenge, in the name of its prophet Jesus.[4] Europeans in China, naturally enough, were filled with terror. They appealed to their Governments to threaten the destruc-

---

[1] Isvolski, *Memoirs*, p. 124 ; Dillon, *Eclipse of Russia*, p. 248.
[2] Ger. Docs., xiv. p. 129.   [3] Ib., p. 161.   [4] Ib., xvi. p. 14.

tion of the imperial tombs if a hair of the heads of the ambassadorial staff, or of those they were sheltering, should be injured. This heroic measure was too much, even for the Kaiser.[1] But it was decided to send a military expedition up to the capital, and, after much negotiation, the command was given to a German, Count Waldersee. The Count arrived somewhat late upon the scene, when Pekin had already been taken. But his record of what he found is worth transcribing, as a record of the righteous vengeance of the West :

" Throughout the whole stretch of country from Taku to Tien-tsin I found—as also in no inconsiderable sections of Tien-tsin itself—a state of terrible devastation. So far as the eye could reach, on the country-side in question, one could see nothing but ruins in which not a single Chinaman could still live, and the whole stretch from here to Pekin, in so far as I have been within the reach of the advancing armies, is, I am told by my Chief of Staff, Major-General von Schwarzhoff, in the same condition ; while in Pekin terrible destruction has been done by fires and looting. According to a conservative estimate, 300,000 inhabitants (but probably many more) have become homeless along the line of march and are now living in the open, and this will remain possible only for a little time longer owing to the good weather prevalent at this period of the year. There can be no doubt, however, but that presently there will be famine and epidemics. I believe that great numbers of the homeless and the foodless will begin to plunder the rest of the population and will join the Boxers ; I am convinced that this kind of fighting has created more Boxers than were killed in battle." [2]

The honour of Jesus Christ had thus been satisfactorily vindicated. But such services deserve and require terrestrial reward. Accordingly, the allied troops, the Embassy staffs, and the Europeans generally took their compensation in the form of loot. " Immense damage," says Count Waldersee, " must have been done during the three days of authorised looting (followed by much private looting), but nothing approaching an estimate of the losses entailed on the inhabitants has as yet been made out. Every nationality accords the palm to some other in respect to the act of plundering, but it remains the fact that each and all of them went in hot and strong for

---

[1] Ger. Docs., xvi. p. 26.   [2] Waldersee, p. 216.

plunder." Admirers of Mr. Bernard Shaw will be interested to note that, on this occasion, the English lived up to his conception of their character. They saved their conscience while they secured the loot. " In the case of England," writes the Count, " this phase of war-making is covered over with certain formalities. The booty had to be handed over and placed in the spacious apartments of the Legation for public auction a good many days later. The money forthcoming from this, like the prize-money, was distributed in accordance with a certain scale among the officers and non-commissioned officers. Hence it is intelligible that no Englishman sees anything to be shocked at in looting." [1] " The amount of damage," the Count goes on, " done to the country down to date by ravage and plunder will never be calculable, but it must be immense." And he concludes : " Unfortunately the looting has not failed to be attended by other excesses : outrages on women, barbarities of all descriptions, wanton acts of incendiarism, etc."

It was thus that, by murder and robbery, the Christian Powers taught the Chinese not to attempt to resist murder and robbery. But though they were agreed upon their vengeance, they were agreed upon little else. The Russians were inclined to recover the friendship of the Chinese by leaving them secure at Pekin, while they established themselves in what they really wanted, Manchuria. The British were alarmed at precisely that possibility. The Germans endeavoured to keep on terms with both, and even went a long way towards supporting the British. We must not here pause to disentangle all these complications. Nor will we dwell at length on the long and sordid disputes about the amount of the indemnity. Everyone, of course, was putting in the most extravagant claims, and everyone was accusing other people of doing the same. The Americans endeavoured, without much success, to impose some degree of moderation. But at last the amount to be exacted was fixed ; and the salt tax was impounded and put under foreign control to secure the necessary revenues. In addition, the foreigners appropriated a large tract of ground in Pekin ; and an arch, one knows not whether to call it triumphant or mortuary, was erected by the Chinese, at their own expense, to commemorate the murder of v. Ketteler.

[1] Waldersee, p. 219.

Justice had been vindicated, profit made, and the chains of European finance riveted more firmly than ever on the decaying body of the Chinese Empire.[1]

IV. The Anglo-Japanese Alliance

The next event of importance was the conclusion of the Anglo-Japanese alliance. This, on the face of it, was a startling innovation ; for it admitted a yellow race, on terms of equality, into the cockpit of the whites. But, as we have seen, Japan had qualified for this position by adopting, with singular thoroughness and in an extraordinarily short time, both the militarism and the diplomacy of Europe. And there were the usual reasons for the alliance. Both Powers feared a third Power, Russia ; and when that is the case, there are two recognised methods of dealing with the situation. Either you make an alliance, in the form of " defence," with another Power or Powers having the same fear. That, as we have seen, was the origin of the Austro-German and the Franco-Russian alliances. Or you turn to the Power you are afraid of and make up your differences there, at the price of common action against some other Power which you are both beginning to fear more than you fear one another. That is what the British did, a year or two later, with that same Russia, against which they had made the alliance with Japan ; and that is what Japan was considering, even at the very time when her negotiations with England were proceeding. It might even be thought, by a purist, that Japan went a little beyond the usual line ; for at the moment when, through one of her statesmen, she was negotiating with England an alliance directed against Russia, through another she was negotiating with Russia an alliance directed against England. It was, however, in the end, the former that triumphed ; England thus securing a good champion against Russia during the few years that intervened before she herself became an ally of that country.

There were, however, difficulties in this negotiation. The British Government saw, and dreaded, the possibility that, if they joined Japan, the world-war might break out in the Far East.[2] They would have liked a guarantee that the free hand

For all this see Ger. Docs., v. xvi. chap. civ   [2] Hayashi, p. 166.

which Japan was to secure in Korea should not be used for
" aggression " against Russia.[1] But as it was impossible to
say beforehand what aggression was, that could not well be
arranged for. Further, and, no doubt, more important, the
British thought that the treaty, as proposed by Japan, would
be one-sided. They were to recognise Japan's interests in
Korea. But what British interests was Japan to recognise ?
The British suggested India. But Japan politely said no.
In the end, however, the treaty was signed, on January 30th,
1902. It begins, in the kind of language to which we are
accustomed in these documents, by the statement that the
parties, " having recognised the independence of China and
Korea, declare themselves to be entirely uninfluenced by
any aggressive tendencies in either country " ; and it goes on
to state that, while both countries have " special interests "
in China, Japan, in addition, " is interested in a peculiar degree,
politically as well as commercially and industrially, in Korea."
It then lays it down that, if either of the parties, in the defence
of their respective interests, as above described, should become
involved in war with another Power, the other party will
maintain a strict neutrality ; but that, if any other Power
or Powers should join the hostilities against the ally, the other
party will come to its assistance by war. This means, in
plainer language, that if Japan should become involved in
war with Russia, England would remain neutral ; but that if
Russia's ally, France, should join in, England would go to war
in defence of Japan. Or, on the other hand, that if Great
Britain should become involved with Russia, Japan would remain neutral ; but if France should come in also, Japan would
go to war in defence of England. Russia was the expected
enemy. With Germany, both England and Japan were still
anxious to retain friendly relations, and, originally, there was
talk of including her in the alliance. Thus, in October 1901,
Count Hayashi said to Lord Lansdowne : " What are your
plans with regard to including Germany in the agreement ? "
and Lord Lansdowne replied : " We think that it will be best
to negotiate with you first, and later we can invite Germany
to join in the negotiations and come into the alliance."[2]
The Japanese Government, it appears, desired, up to the end,
the inclusion of Germany. But the period of the negotia-

[1] Hayashi, p. 168.   [2] Ib., p. 131.

tion of the treaty was also that of the last flicker of the long
and slow-burning taper of Anglo-German friendship. Public
opinion on both sides had been worked up to fever-heat by
the Boer War. In the October of 1901 Mr. Chamberlain made
his famous anti-German speech, and Lord Lansdowne, presumably, did not feel that he could take the risk of actually
embarking on a treaty of alliance with the object of so much
popular animadversion.[1]

The treaty, then, was directed against a possible Russian
aggression. But, as we have observed, at the very time of
its negotiation, the Japanese were also considering the alternative possibility of a treaty with Russia, which presumably
would have been directed against the British. We learn
from Count Hayashi that the view was held, by some persons
in Japan, that this latter would be the preferable arrangement.[2]
And it is interesting to note that one of the Count's reasons
for urging an alliance with England was the possibility, which
he already foresaw, that otherwise England herself might join
Russia.[3] Further, we find Count Hayashi suggesting to his
Government that it might be well to encourage the idea
of a Japanese alliance with Russia, as that might stimulate
the English to checkmate such a move by favouring the
Anglo-Japanese combination.[4] In fact, the Japanese were
working at both schemes at once. For while Count Hayashi
was pressing the one idea in London, Prince Ito was discussing the other in St. Petersburg, on the basis that Russia
should have a free hand in Manchuria, and Japan a free hand
in Korea.[5] This situation, not unnaturally, roused the suspicions of Lord Lansdowne. He said that " if it were the
intention of the Japanese Government to negotiate a convention or agreement with Russia, whilst the negotiations with
Great Britain were in progress, the British Government would
be very angry." [6] The Marquis Ito, on the other hand, held
that " all negotiations for an Anglo-Japanese alliance ought
to be suspended until we are quite sure that it is hopeless to
attempt to conclude a convention with Russia." [7] The Marquis
appears to have pressed his view with great insistence. But

---

[1] For the treaty, see besides Hayashi's *Memoirs*, Eckardstein's *Lebenser-
rinnerungen*, and also the Ger. Docs., xvii. chap. cx, and the notes there,
which show that Eckardstein, as usual, must be read with caution.
[2] Hayashi, p. 81.   [3] Ib., p. 84.   [4] Ib., p. 123.
[5] Ib., p. 138.   [6] Ib., p. 145.   [7] Ib., p. 155.

on December 7th, 1901, the Japanese Cabinet definitely rejected his plan, and decided upon the English alliance.[1] Whether, if Marquis Ito's scheme had gone through, the Russo-Japanese War would have been avoided, must remain a matter of speculation. But very likely, in that case, there would have been, instead, a war of Russia and Japan versus England ; the one certain thing, in all these arrangements, being that the war will break out somewhere, between some Powers or other.

Under the circumstances it is not unnatural that the publication of the Anglo-Japanese treaty, upon which the Japanese insisted, and which took place in February 1902, should have caused a sensation in Russia. Count Lamsdorff, the Russian Foreign Minister, we learn, " is completely astounded by the Japanese communication, and very serious about the unmistakable direction of the point of the agreement against Russia." It was monstrous, he thought, thus to anticipate warlike developments " at a moment when nobody is thinking of war." [2] This Russian reaction was particularly agreeable to the Kaiser. The treaty, he thought, was a not undeserved punishment upon the Russians " for their flirtation with England, their passivity during the South African War, their coyness towards us, and their insusceptibility to the well-meant winks (Winke) of his majesty." [3] The Kaiser also thought it would be advisable to warn China that if any Power were injured in its rights or interests, the required measures would be taken—naturally, against China.[4] Count Lamsdorff's reaction, under these circumstances, was to recur to the idea of a combination of all the Continental Powers of Europe. Austria and Italy, he thought, would be available, and France would join.[5] But Germany was cold to this invitation. She explained that, in case of hostilities in the Far East, she had not the means of bringing her army to bear. She observed, further, that French plans of revenge were fostered by the Russian alliance. What guarantee had she that Russia would not be swept away into common action with France against Germany ? The Russians, in reply, explained that their influence with France was all-powerful, that no French Minister could remain in office if he were

[1] Hayashi, *Memoirs*, p. 100 note.   [2] Ger. Docs., xvii. p. 155.
[3] Ib., p. 156.   [4] Ib., p. 157.   [5] Ib., p. 157.

distasteful to Russia, and that Russia would never allow France to attack Germany.[1] But Germany remained obdurate to the siren's voice ; and all that Russia could do was to enter into an agreement with France, which takes note of the Anglo-Japanese agreement, expresses concurrence in its principle of maintaining the status quo, and adds that, since the Powers were obliged to " envisage the case in which either the aggression of third Powers or new troubles in China, putting in question the integrity and the free development of that Power, should become a menace to their own interests," they " reserve the right to take counsel together on the means of safeguarding those interests." [2] This formally pacific engagement alarmed the British. They had hoped, by the publication of the agreement with Japan, to have warned France off from taking part in a Russian war against that Power. But now ? " The Russo-French note has dissipated this illusion, and opened the way to a certain feeling of insecurity." [3] The world of armed States is indeed precarious and dangerous !

On this occasion, however, British anxiety was misplaced. Two years later, when the Russo-Japanese War duly arrived, France did not intervene on the side of Russia. She hardly could, for the entente with England was now achieved, and it would have been rather a strong step to begin the new arrangement by a war. Had England been drawn into the war it would, more likely, by that time, have been against Germany, who favoured Russia just as we favoured Japan, and who was beginning to assume that honourable place of enemy-in-chief so long occupied by France or by Russia. It so happened that the Anglo-Japanese treaty was renewed while the Russo-Japanese War was still in progress. Not only so, but it now assumed a closer form. Not only was India included in the scope of it, but " unprovoked attack or aggressive action " on the part of a single Power in respect to China, East Asia, or India would give rise to the casus fœderis. This, however, did not affect the war then in progress, in reference to which there was a special article, running as follows :

" As regards the present war between Japan and Russia, Great Britain will continue to maintain strict neutrality, unless some other Power or Powers shall join in hostilities against Japan, in which case Great Britain will come to the

[1] Ger. Docs., xvii. p. 161.   [2] Ib., p. 180.   [3] Ib.; p. 181.

assistance of Japan, and will conduct the war in common and make peace in mutual agreement with Japan." [1] France being ruled out, it seems that only Germany was left as the Power whose intervention might possibly have given rise, in this way, to the casus fœderis. But things did not go as far as that, and the two combatants were left to deal with one another alone. The result was a crushing victory for Japan, and, as future historians may have to record, a turning-point in the history of the world. For the first time, for centuries, an Oriental Power had played the Western game and won it ; and who can say whether the next few centuries will not be marked by a counter-offensive of the East against the West ?

V. Japan and Russia Join Hands

The victory of Japan was followed by a peace of almost unexampled moderation, conducted under the friendly auspices of President Roosevelt. Japan took Port Arthur and the peninsula of Liaotung. She also became suzerain in Korea, and proceeded thereafter, by the usual steps, to the position of sovereign, inflicting, in the course of her advance, cruelties and injustices upon the helpless population even more ruthless than might be justified by European example.[2] But she abandoned the claim for an indemnity from Russia, and left behind her, in that country, so little bad feeling that, almost before the blood was dry on the bayonets, or the corpses rotted in the ground, the two enemies had joined hands to exploit Manchuria in common. By a treaty of 1907 they agreed to respect the independence and territorial integrity of China ; and we know what that kind of treaty usually portends. There followed a clause which had presumably more genuine significance—namely, that they will respect the rights accruing to them from the treaties, conventions, and contracts in force between them and China.[3] This clause was in the public treaty. But there was also a secret agreement, of which the text does not appear to have been published, which divided Manchuria into a Japanese and Russian sphere of interest.[4]

[1] See text in MacMurray, i. p. 516.
[2] See *The Tragedy of Korea*, by F. A. Mackenzie.
[3] See Willoughby, p. 315, and MacMurray, i. p. 657.
[4] Siebert, p. 17.

This latter was not the only treaty which was to complicate the affairs of the Far East. In 1909 the United States put forward a programme not only affirming the independence and territorial integrity of China, but suggesting that the railways of Manchuria, by whomsoever constructed, should remain Chinese property. There appeared, at once, a curious difficulty in getting this principle accepted. Germany and England did, indeed, express their " agreement in principle." [1] But by now England was tied to Russia, in the Far East as in Persia, and Russia objected to the American proposition. In particular she objected to the idea of the construction of a railway from Chinchow to Aigun. " Its accomplishment," she said, " will open up a new route, giving access from the south not only to the Chinese Eastern Railroad but, directly, to Russian possessions at Aigun. This shows adequately the strategic and political importance of the enterprise." [2] Japan, taking a different line, remarked that the railways of Manchuria were " dedicated exclusively to commercial and industrial uses," and that the American project was therefore superfluous.[3] Further, in the course of the discussion, Russia observed that she had a treaty with China of the year 1899, whereby the latter had promised that she would build no railways north of Pekin except either with Chinese or with Russian capital, and that, " in no case, would any other Government be allowed to participate." [4] Whether the existence of this agreement was consistent with the declaration given by Russia, in the Treaty of Portsmouth, that she had not in Manchuria " any territorial advantages or exclusive concessions in impairment of Chinese sovereignty, or inconsistent with the principle of equal opportunity," I will leave to the casuists of international relations. Sir E. Grey thought that the Chinchow–Aigun scheme was not really incompatible with the treaty of 1899, though no doubt Russia was " formally in the right." [5] However, the American scheme failed of acceptance, and Russia and Japan proceeded, in the year 1910, to celebrate their victory by a new treaty, or rather two—one public and one secret. By the public treaty, the two parties agreed to " lend each other their friendly co-operation with regard to their respective railway lines in Manchuria, and to respect the status quo in that

---

[1] Siebert, p. 10.   [2] Willoughby, p. 321.   [3] Ib., p. 325.
[4] Ib., p. 322.   [5] Siebert, p. 15.

province as determined by the various treaties and agreements exchanged between them and China." In case any event arises of a nature to menace the status quo above mentioned, the parties will " enter into communication with each other to arrive at an understanding as to the measures they may judge it necessary to take for the maintenance of the said status quo." [1] By the secret treaty the parties recognise once more their spheres of interest, as already defined by the secret treaty of 1907, agree to abstain each from any interference in the sphere of the other, and, in case the interests of either should be threatened, pledge themselves to agree on the necessary measures to support one another.[2] We have already come across this type of treaty in Persia and in Morocco, and we know what it signifies. It is interesting to note that both treaties, the public and the secret, were shown to Sir Edward Grey by the Russians, and that, according to a dispatch of Count Benckendorf, he " is very much satisfied with the steps taken by the Russian Government and requests me to forward you his best thanks. He has watched with satisfaction the development of good relations between Russia and Japan within the last three years, and is extremely satisfied by the confirmation of his observations as furnished by me." [3]

VI. Russia and China

The " good relations " between Russia and Japan were, of course, based upon the exploitation of China ; and China, as too often, was showing herself recalcitrant.   In July 1910, the Russian Chargé d'Affaires at Pekin writes that " the only peaceable means of exercising pressure on China at present is to lay down a double track on our Siberian railway. This measure alone is feared by the Chinese." [4]   In December of the same year we have the protocol of a ministerial council held at St. Petersburg.[5]   In the discussion, a difference of view appeared between the Foreign Minister and the Minister for War.   The latter " recommends as necessary, on strategic grounds, the annexation of North Manchuria to Russia."   His reasons were that " Japan is taking open measures for the

[1] Willoughby, p. 329 ; MacMurray, i. p. 803.   [2] Siebert, p. 17.
[3] Ib., p. 19.   [4] Ib., p. 19.   [5] Ib., p. 24.

annexation of Southern Manchuria," while China is reorganising her military forces, and colonising Manchuria with a view to war. The Minister for Foreign Affairs, M. Sazonoff, differed. He declared, indeed, that " he was perfectly convinced that the annexation of Northern Manchuria was, for us, an imperative necessity." But he regarded the present moment as unfavourable, as "America, England, perhaps even Japan, would oppose our plans and we could expect no support from any quarter whatever." The Minister of Commerce then observed that "the annexation of Northern Manchuria is connected with the risk of a great war." But the Minister of Finance remarked that "three years ago the Governor of the Amur territory pronounced war with Japan to be unavoidable "; ¹ yet "our relations with this State are at present perfectly normal." "The conclusion of the treaty of June 21st testifies to our confidence in Japanese policy, and we need not reckon with a war with this country in the immediate future." The Prime Minister then stated his position. He agreed with the Foreign Minister that " the violent separation of a province from China cannot be justified by legal considerations. We know how expensive such annexations prove to be in the long run, and to what international complications they lead. The purpose of such annexations would not be understood in Russia." This last sentence seems rather surprising. But it must not be thought that the Minister was against annexation. "Naturally," he proceeded, " it would be impossible to declare that Northern Manchuria will never be annexed by Russia ; political events in future might make it necessary for us to do so, should the political situation be favourable at the time. By safeguarding at present all our privileges in Manchuria we can best prepare for the possibility just referred to. We must not withdraw from Manchuria, but attempt to strengthen our position in this country, in order to fulfil our mission there in the proper manner at the proper time." The decision reached was that the Council " regards an annexation as dangerous at the present moment, but is of opinion that the trend of events may force Russia to this step. All Ministers must therefore be guided by the consideration that our stipu-

¹ That is to say, in 1907, the very year when the Russians and Japanese made their first treaty towards the partition of Manchuria.

lated privileges in Northern Manchuria must be maintained in full, to permit, eventually, an annexation at some future date." In conclusion, "the Ministerial Council sanctions the measures proposed by the Minister of Foreign Affairs to exert pressure upon China. In case of necessity, however, there must be no shrinking from forceful measures."

The "measures proposed" seem to have led to the emission of an ultimatum in the next month or so.[1] The ultimatum elicited a reply which "is of an accommodating nature and can be regarded as satisfactory on the whole,"[2] and thus matters rested for the moment.

But in 1912 the Chinese revolution broke out, and presently Yuan Shih Kai was established in power. Whereupon "Russia and Japan," writes M. Sazonoff, "must use the present favourable moment to fortify their position in China." A new agreement with Japan is contemplated, and also one with China, involving among other things "an acknowledgment on the part of the Chinese Government that the Chinese Eastern Railway[3] possesses not only freedom of action in purely technical railway questions, but can also assume the entire administration of the expropriated zone."[4] "Our political interests," the Foreign Minister goes on to observe, "are directly opposed to the maintenance of China's territorial integrity"—an interesting commentary on the public treaties making that territorial integrity the object of the policy of Russia and Japan. Lastly, by May of 1912 we find that not only Manchuria but Mongolia is in question, and that the Russian Minister has now been able to assure himself that "we need at present fear no opposition on the part of foreign Powers, should we deem it necessary to take the above-mentioned military measures in Northern Manchuria, Mongolia, and West China." The American Ambassador had received instructions to make no objection, and Sir John Jordan said that "no other Power would attempt to oppose our measures." "You can now undoubtedly proceed without anxiety in West China and outer Mongolia, my English colleague told me, and will only have to take Japanese interests and desires into account in Manchuria."[5] This attitude of the British, presumably, is to be explained, in part, by the fact that they wanted a revision

[1] Siebert, p. 29.   [2] Ib., p. 30.   [3] Under Russian control.
[4] Siebert, pp. 34-5.   [5] Ib., p. 38.

of their treaty with Russia about Thibet, so as to give them
" freedom of action " in that country.[1]

But we must not pursue further the operations in the
Far East of those who were later to do battle for Liberty
and Right. Enough has been said to show that all was prepared, in that quarter, for the outbreak of the Great War
which everyone anticipated and everyone professed not to
want. England, Russia, and Japan were firmly united at
the cost of China. Germany was isolated. It only remained
for Japan, who coveted the inheritance of China, to turn her
out of Shantung and enter herself. This she duly did, when
the war broke out, rejecting the assistance of China, and keeping
her out of action until she had made secret treaties with her
allies for taking all she wanted. China was then invited to
join in the war, in order that she might expel German traders
and missionaries. She did so, and it was not until the Peace
Conference opened that it was revealed to her that her allies
had previously and secretly bargained away her own territories
and rights.

[1] Siebert, p. 41.

CHAPTER XII

THE BALKAN WARS

I. Russia and the Central Powers after 1909

WE will return now to take up the story of the Balkans, which we left at the settlement of the Bosnian crisis in 1909. That crisis was followed by a certain rapprochement between Russia and Austria. In October 1910 Sazonoff explained to Kiderlen-Waechter that the Governments of those countries had " found a common point of view, which it was necessary to adopt to maintain peace in the Balkan Peninsula." This was, apparently, a return to the principles of 1897, whereby both States guaranteed the status quo. "And if," said Sazonoff, " more confidential relations between Russia and Austria became necessary, in the interests of peace, and if owing to recent events such relations should not be possible, the Russian Government would not refuse to treat with Vienna by the intermediary of German statesmen, who in that case would serve as the connecting link between us." [1] Next day the German Chancellor, Bethmann-Hollweg, said to Sazonoff, " on his own initiative," that " if Austria-Hungary should not remain faithful to the principles enunciated by Count Aehrenthal, and should manifest aggressive dispositions in the Balkans, she would not find, on the side of her ally, a support which is not stipulated for in any treaty, and which is not in conformity with German interests." [2]

Thus, ostensibly, an understanding had once more been reached between the Central Powers and Russia about the Balkans. But that this was merely temporary, and intended, at any rate by Russia, as a stop-gap, until events and circum-

[1] *Livre Noir*, ii. p. 333.
[2] Ib. Cf. Brandenburg, p. 363, and Kiderlen-Waechter, ii. p. 187, where Germany is shown taking that line in September 1912.

stances should change, is strongly suggested by a comment of the Russian Ambassador in Paris, who writes to Isvolski, in February 1910 :

" An agreement of this sort, concluded for a certain number of years, would leave the Balkan States at perfect liberty, in regard to their internal development as well as to their mutual relations, which they might develop in every possible way. At the same time Russia would be placed in a position which would enable her to develop her military forces in all security and to prepare herself for those events which cannot be avoided. In the meantime the further evolution of the Ottoman Empire would be clearer—the problems would mature, and we should be able to meet the events that are to be foreseen much better equipped than otherwise." [1]

Are we to infer that at this date Russia had definitely determined on war ? No! There is seldom anything as clear-cut as that in diplomacy. There was to be war some time ; only not quite yet. Thus we are told by M. Nekludoff that, in 1911, when he was received by the Tsar before taking up his post at Sophia, the autocrat said to him, " after an intentional pause, stepping backwards and fixing me with a penetrating stare : ' Listen to me, Nekludoff ; do not for one instant lose sight of the fact that we cannot go to war. I do not wish for war ; as a rule I shall do all in my power to preserve for my people the benefits of peace. But at this moment, of all moments, everything which might lead to war must be avoided. It would be out of the question for us to face a war for five or six years—in fact till 1917. . . . Though, if the most vital interests and the honour of Russia were at stake, we might, if it were absolutely necessary, accept a challenge in 1915 ; but not a moment sooner—in any circumstances or under any pretext whatsoever." [2] Had this remark

---

[1] Siebert, p. 283, February 3rd, 1910. In view of these remarks, it may be noted further that December 1909 is the date given by Bogitshevich for the military convention between Russia and Bulgaria referred to on page 165. If this be correct we should have here an excellent example of the methods of diplomacy. For in that case, at the very time at which Russia was ostensibly renewing friendly relations with Germany and Austria, she had also entered into a convention in which it is stated that " the realisation of the high ideals of the Slavic peoples upon the Balkan Peninsula, so near to Russia's heart, is possible only after the favourable outcome of Russia's struggle with Germany and Austria-Hungary."

[2] *Diplomatic Reminiscences*, p. 5.

been the Kaiser's instead of the Tsar's, all our war-historians would have been citing it as a definite proof of the guilt, and the sole guilt, of Germany. I do not cite it as a proof of the guilt, still less the sole guilt, of Russia. I cite it as one more illustration of the state of mind of all ministers and all princes— "The war will come. We don't want it ; but we must be ready. And when it comes . . . ! "

Next year, in the summer of 1912, the Emperors of Russia and Germany met at Baltischport. On this occasion the German Chancellor expressed himself satisfied with the existing relations of the Powers, and insisted on Germany's need of peace to consolidate her industry. Sazonoff thereupon asked the Chancellor " whether the Berlin Cabinet would, if necessary, use its influence at Vienna in order to prevent Austria from penetrating farther into the Balkans. Bethmann-Hollweg promised this without hesitation, and pointed out that he could unconditionally renew the assurances he had already given me at Potsdam." [1] In that year, therefore, as in 1909, all was friendly upon the surface. Yet it was in this very year, 1912, and before the meeting at Baltischport, that the Serbo-Bulgarian treaty, contemplating war with Austria, was drawn up, with the full knowledge and approval of Russia, and that a Naval Convention was entered into between Russia and France.[2] So much for these diplomatic amenities.

II. The Racconigi Agreement

Let us turn now from Russia to Italy. Italy, as we saw, was prepared, in 1908–9, to fight on the side of Austria, if war had then come about. She still adhered to the status quo in the Balkans. But if it should be modified she still insisted on getting " compensation." And since Austria had now handed the Sanjak of Novibazar back to Turkey, she entered, in December 1909, into an agreement supplementary to Article 7 of the Triple Alliance, extending the principle of compensation to that territory.[3] But at the same time she entered into what is known as the Racconigi Agreement with Russia. By this arrangement, as we have seen,[4] she recognised

[1] Siebert, p. 647.   Page 399 below.
[3] Text in Pribram, i. p. 241.
[4] See above, p. 221.   Cf. Brandenburg, p. 306 ; Livre Noir, i. p. 357.

Russia's claim to the Straits, while Russia recognised hers to Tripoli. But, in addition, the following clauses were adopted concerning the Balkans :

"1. Russia and Italy should devote themselves, in the first place, to the maintenance of the status quo in the Balkan Peninsula.

"2. In any eventuality which may occur in the Balkans they should apply the principle of nationality, by developing the Balkan States, to the exclusion of any foreign domination."

If we compare this agreement with those by which Italy was bound to Austria,[1] we shall find that her position was something like this :

1. The status quo is to be maintained in the Balkans for the present.
2. If it be disturbed, and if Austria takes anything, Italy shall get " compensation."
3. Austria in fact shall *not* take anything. Italy and Russia will see to that.

The fact, if not the terms, of the Racconigi Agreement seems to have become known to Turkey, and to have aroused some intelligible anxiety. For we find the Grand Vizier, on the one hand, congratulating Russia on " a significant victory won by Russia's diplomacy over Austria-Hungary " (with whom, as we have seen, Russia had just renewed the bonds of amity), but, on the other hand, hinting politely that " the Turkish Government has learned that, at Racconigi, the eventuality that it might not be possible to maintain the status quo in the Balkans was also discussed, and that in this case Russia and Italy had promised each other compensations at the expense of Turkey." The Russian Ambassador at Constantinople thereupon suggests that " we should give the Grand Vizier some information concerning the negotiations at Racconigi and try to persuade him that the word ' compensation ' was not mentioned." In fact, it was not. What was mentioned was Tripoli and the Straits, and what was contemplated as possible was the expulsion of Turkey from the Balkans. When, therefore, the Ambassador

---

[1] See Triple Alliance, art. 7.

suggests that "some" information should be given to Turkey, he cannot mean " all " or even " much." [1]

Turkey, however, was not the only Power disturbed by rumours of the Racconigi Agreement. For we find the Russian Chargé d'Affaires at Berlin writing to Isvolski of " the feeling of suspicion which Germany of late has been harbouring concerning our foreign policy ; for the Germans seem ever and again to fear the efforts of the enemies of Germany to isolate her. The ratification of a long series of international conventions to which Germany was not a party, as well as the fear of a conflict with England, which has increased since the Russian rapprochement with England, have called for this distrust on the part of Germany." [2] It is the fashion among advocates of the Entente to say that this German fear of isolation or " hemming in " was illusory. Whether it really was, or no, readers will judge from the whole story we are telling. But even if it had been, that would have made no difference to the situation. It was inevitable, in the conditions of the European anarchy, that Germany should take that view, as soon as England, France, and Russia had begun to work together. The best intentions on the part of the enemy Powers, even if we supposed them to exist, could not alter this fact. For the fact results from secret alliances and engagements in a world of armed States ; and it would result none the less, under those conditions, even if all the States really were, as they all pretend to be, innocent of harmful intent. But if they really were all innocent, they would all disarm and conduct their diplomacy in the light of day.

III. The Balkan States Combine

Enough has been said to show that the crisis of 1908–9 had settled nothing. The Great Powers were still watching one another and endeavouring, while they kept the peace, to improve their positions in view of the anticipated war. The next shocks that were felt on the surface, as a result of this underground travail, were, as we have seen, not directly connected with the Balkans. They were the Moroccan crisis

[1] Siebert, p. 155. The translation of " einige " by " certain " is ambiguous, and I have substituted " some," which is a correct translation of the German. I do not know what the Russian original may be.

[2] Ib., p. 500, March 18th, 1910.

of 1911 and the Italian war for Tripoli. But meantime the situation in the Balkans was also developing towards war. For our present purpose the rights and wrongs of this war, as between Turkey and the Balkan States, may be left undiscussed. There was here, as we know, a case of misgovernment for centuries, producing, as it usually does, in the oppressed, the same vices that distinguish the oppressor. At first there were hopes that the Turkish revolution might bring relief. But the Young Turks soon showed that they were more, not less, nationalistic than their predecessors. The usual rebellions and massacres recommenced, and the Balkan Christians [1] may well have felt that they had no hope but in war. But then, why not have their war and settle it, if they could, without involving the rest of Europe? That, as we have seen, was precisely the difficulty. For Austria, Russia, and Italy all regarded themselves as concerned in the disposition of the Balkans; and none of them had any interest, either in Balkan liberties or in the cessation of massacre and torture, at all comparable to their interest in their own policies of power.

It followed from this situation that, whenever the Balkan States should make a bid to escape from their oppressors, they must enlist the support of some one or other of the Great Powers; and the Power that lay nearest to hand was Russia. Russia, in fact, was already engaged in efforts to bring about an alliance between the Balkan States. As to the nature and purpose of that alliance, there were at first two policies.[2] One was that advocated by Tcharykoff, the Russian Ambassador at Constantinople. His plan was to maintain a weak Turkish Empire as a vassal state to Russia, and to make it a member of the proposed alliance. What, in that case, the alliance would be for, does not very clearly appear. It could hardly be to deliver the Balkan States from Turkey; for which reason it could not be expected to commend itself to them. Presumably the intention was to direct it against Austria.[3] In any case the proposal was broken against the resistance of the Turks.[4] The other alternative was pursued, ultimately to success, by Hartwig and Nekludoff, the Russian Ministers at Belgrade and Sophia. It was an alliance definitely directed

[1] " Who, after all, aren't real Christians at all," as Queen Victoria once remarked. No doubt they were not. But who are?
[2] See Friedjung, iii. p. 170.   [3] Cf. Valentin, p. 111.
[4] Tcharykoff retired March 1912 (Friedjung, iii. p. 172).

against Turkey, though, as we shall see, it had also a point
against Austria. Negotiations in this sense began as early
as 1909.[1] At first the approaches from Serbia were coldly
received by King Ferdinand of Bulgaria. But by the end
of 1911 he is wavering ; for the interesting reason that he
" has more and more convinced himself, in the course of the
last few weeks, that constant and close relations for their
mutual support were being kept up between Russia, France
and England, and he is convinced that the forces of these
three Powers are superior to those of Germany and Austria." [2]
A better example could not be adduced of the way in which
Balkan policies were determined by those of the Great Powers,
and of the tacit assumption, so terribly justified by events,
that the Balkan problem would involve a European war. In
the same conviction we find the Bulgarian Minister, Guéchoff,
anxious as to the effects of a Balkan alliance upon Austrian
policy, and asking what guarantees Russia could give to
Bulgaria.[3] Finally, however, the difficulties were overcome,
at any rate on paper, and the treaties of alliance completed
in the course of 1912.[4]

IV. The Treaty between Serbia and Bulgaria

The first of these treaties was concluded between Serbia
and Bulgaria ; and it is important to note that the Russian
Ministers at Sophia and Belgrade were actively engaged in
furthering it. " The negotiations," says M. Nekludoff, " were
to be conducted with the utmost secrecy, and only the respective Russian Ministers were to be allowed to know what was
going on. In point of fact M. Hartwig and I were the constant
arbiters, continually consulted and referred to in each difficulty,

---

[1] Siebert, p. 276.   [2] Ib., p. 317.   [3] Ib., p. 316.
[4] The texts of these treaties will be found in *Nationalism and War in the
Near East*, and also in Guéchoff, *L'Alliance Balkanique*. There is an English
translation of the treaties between Serbia and Bulgaria in Bogitshevich,
App. viii. The treaties were published by the *Matin* in November 1913.
According to Valentin (p. 112), King Ferdinand of Bulgaria turned the
point of the Serbo-Bulgarian treaty away from Austria and against Turkey.
This means, I suppose, that he arranged that the war should be against
Turkey, not against Austria ; the treaty, as is shown in the text, contemplating
both. On the previous page, Valentin says : " His idea was, if possible,
to liquidate European Turkey peaceably, and he therefore arranged a military
combination with Serbia against both Austria and Turkey." This seems
a curious idea of a peaceable liquidation, and I cannot pretend to understand it.

however small, by the parties." [1] Further, these Russians constantly consulted their Minister, either M. Sazonoff or his substitute, M. Neratoff.[2] So that this treaty must be taken to be as much an indication of Russian as of Balkan policy.

The treaty is dated March 1912. It is accompanied by a "secret annex" of the same date (the treaty itself, of course, being also secret) and followed by a military convention of June 12th, which, as is usually the case, contains also important political clauses. In these documents the following points are laid down :

1. By the first article of the treaty the two States guarantee reciprocally, by force, their political independence and their territory.

2. The second article runs as follows :

"Both contracting parties agree to support one another, with all their forces, in case any one of the Great Powers should make the attempt to annex or to occupy or seize with its troops, even provisionally, any territory situate in the Balkans and at present under Turkish rule, in case either of the two States considers that such act is injurious to its vital interests and constitutes a casus belli."

Here the phrase "any one of the Great Powers" is ambiguous. But the Power thought of cannot be Turkey, which could not "forcibly acquire" its own territory ; it cannot be Russia, since the treaty was being shaped under Russian patronage. It must therefore be Austria or Italy, or both. But the Agreement of Racconigi seems to rule out Italy, who is now acting with Russia. There remains Austria, and Austria is, in fact, specially named in the military convention that completes the treaty.

But Roumania, it would seem, is also contemplated. M. Guéchoff says [3] that the reason for this is a treaty which he alleges to have been entered into by that country with Austria in 1900, whereby Austria recognised that the desire of Roumania to annex a part of Bessarabia, Silistria, and if possible Rustchuk, Shumen, and Varna, was "very legitimate." If such a convention existed,[4] it must have

---

[1] Nekludoff, p. 52. M. Poincaré's version of these facts is that the treaty, though communicated to Russia, was "undoubtedly" not inspired by her. The reader will form his own opinion of the correctness of this statement (*Origins of the War*, p. 111).

[2] Ib., p. 55.   [3] *Memoirs*, p. 61.   [4] Pribram does not give it.

presupposed a European war, as otherwise Bessarabia could not come into question. In any case, however, Roumania was formally tied to the Triple Alliance.

The Austrian, or Austro-Roumanian, war seems then to be the only one contemplated in the treaty proper. For some reason—presumably that of an even greater secrecy—the articles dealing with Turkey were put into a secret annex, of the same date as the treaty. The first article, defining the casus belli, is so complicated that it will be better to cite it textually. It runs :

" In case internal troubles should arise in Turkey of a nature to endanger the national or public (d'État) interests of the Contracting Parties, or of one of them, or in case internal or external difficulties in which Turkey should be involved should imperil the maintenance of the status quo in the Balkan Peninsula, that one of the two Parties which should first arrive at the conviction that military action should be taken shall address itself in a reasoned proposal to the other Party, which will be bound immediately to enter into an exchange of views and, if it does not agree with its ally, to give a reasoned reply." There follows a reference to Russian arbitration, to which we shall return immediately.

It will be observed that, in this article, first, the grounds of a possible war upon Turkey are very elaborately stated. That, however, is immaterial, as the Parties intended to make war whenever it should seem convenient to them ; and the moment came, in fact, a few months after the treaty was signed. Moreover, it seems worth while to note that in a first draft, made by the Bulgarian, Rizoff, among the " casus fœderis " is one comprehensive one—" if the interests of Bulgaria and Serbia require the liquidation of the question " ; [1] and also that, in a draft made by the Serbians, the text runs : " In case one of the Contracting Parties, estimating that the situation in Turkey requires it, and that the general conditions in Europe are favourable, should address to the other a proposition to take action to free the Bulgarians and the Serbs from the Turkish yoke." [2] Clearly it was " aggressive " war against Turkey that was intended.

The real difficulties were not concerned with the casus belli. They were concerned with the much more material

[1] Guéchoff, *L'Alliance Balkanique*, p. 22.   [2] Cf. p. 31.

point of the division of the spoils. Macedonia was claimed alike by Bulgars and Serbs, and the conclusion of the treaty was preceded by a long wrangle as to how that province should be distributed among the victors. In the negotiations the Bulgars wanted it to be made " autonomous," [1] hoping for a later opportunity of annexing it. But to this the Serbs would not agree. In the end the territory was divided into three zones, one of which was reckoned as Bulgarian, another as Serbian, while the third was divided between them, but pro- visionally only, in case autonomy should be found imprac- ticable, and subject to the arbitral decision of the Tsar. It is important to note that the division assigned to Serbia Northern Albania, and that her disappointment at being deprived of this by the Powers was one of the causes of the second Balkan War.

The reference to arbitration by the Tsar brings us to the point that the treaty was not only negotiated, as we have seen, under the stimulus and with the assistance of the Russian Representatives in the Balkans, but also contained clauses definitely inviting Russian mediation and approval. Thus, in the first article of the secret annex, it is provided that, if the two Parties agree to take action against Turkey, they shall communicate their decision to Russia, and the action shall be taken only if she does not disapprove. If the two Parties do not agree, the matter shall be referred to Russia for her decision, which shall be final. Only if Russia refuses to pronounce can independent action be taken. Thus, according to the treaty, war could not be declared until Russia had been consulted. There seems, however, to be no evidence that she was in fact consulted, before the war broke out. At any rate, she appears to have disapproved of it. So that this clause of the treaty must have been violated.

The defenders of Russia, one would suppose, must be hard put to it to justify her action in this matter. She had agree- ments with Austria and with Italy to maintain the Balkan status quo. She had a promise from Germany, made in 1910, that the latter would not support Austria in aggressive action there. And of this promise she secured the renewal, in the summer of 1912,[2] when she actually had in her pocket the treaty between the Balkan allies which contemplated the

---

[1] Guéchoff, p. 26.   [2] See above, p. 304.

destruction of that status quo by war against Turkey or Austria, or both. What would have been said by Englishmen or Frenchmen about such manœuvring, had it been brought home to Germans, we may easily conjecture. But the human mind is a curious thing; and it seems possible that, in spite of the actual terms of the treaty, M. Sazonoff may have regarded it as " defensive " and hoped to be able to prevent war from materialising in action until Austria or Turkey or both had begun an " attack." This view is, in fact, suggested by his conduct when the Balkan States took the bit into their teeth in the October of 1912, and also by some of his recorded remarks. Thus, on hearing of the first overtures, he exclaimed to Nekludoff : " Well, but this is perfect ! If only it could come off ! Bulgaria closely allied to Serbia in the political and economic sphere ; five hundred thousand bayonets to guard the Balkans—but this would bar the way for ever to German penetration, Austrian invasion." [1] And when he communicated the news of the treaty to Isvolski in Paris, he describes it as being " for the common defence and protection of the interests of both sides, in case of a change in the status quo on the Balkan Peninsula, or in case a third Power makes a sudden attack upon one of the contracting parties." [2] Again, as Nekludoff tells us, Kokovtzoff and Sazonoff " had given Paneff (the Bulgarian Minister) to understand, in a very amiable but firm manner, that we should not under any circumstances allow ourselves to be drawn into an active policy in the Balkans " ; [3] and Nekludoff continually endeavours to persuade his readers, if not himself, that the treaty, in the construction of which he had played so great a part, somehow was not intended to lead to war. One must suppose, therefore, on the part of the Russians, either simplicity or duplicity of a very high order. For our purpose it does not much matter which view is taken.

Sazonoff communicated the fact of the negotiation of the treaty to his Ambassadors in Paris and London at the end of March.[4] Its existence was thus made known to Poincaré and to Grey.[5] But there is no evidence that they were shown the text. The French Minister, de Selves, knew, even before this, that a treaty was under negotiation, as we are informed

[1] Nekludoff, p. 45. Cf. p. 55.   [2] *Is Germany Guilty ?*, ii. p. 62.
[3] Nekludoff, p. 83.   [4] Siebert, p. 339.   [5] Ib.

by Guéchoff in an interesting little anecdote. The Bulgarian and Serbian negotiators, he tells us, Stancioff and Milovanovich, who were then visiting Paris, were discussing the matter in the Opera House, when M. de Selves passed by and said to them, with a smile on his lips : " I pass by you in order not to divide you." Whereupon Stancioff " completed the thought " of M. de Selves by adding, " But to unite and bless us " ; to which M. de Selves, " Yes, yes, to bless you. You are doing good work."[1] The French Minister, therefore, it would seem, approved of the negotiation of the treaty ; but we do not know that he was aware of its actual text. This does not seem to have been shown to M. Poincaré until he visited St. Petersburg in August. On seeing it, he immediately protested : " It is really a convention for war. Not only does it reserve arrières pensées for the Serbs and Bulgarians, but it may be feared that their hopes may seem to be encouraged by Russia, and that the eventual partition may be a bait for their cupidities." This common-sense view of the situation may have startled Sazonoff. He admitted, indeed, that his own Minister at Sophia (that very Nekludoff who had helped to negotiate the treaty) had described it as a " treaty of war " ; but he still urged that Russia's right of veto would suffice to maintain peace.[2] The best commentary on this odd idea is the actual course of events.

V. The Treaty between Bulgaria and Greece

So much for the Serbo-Bulgarian treaty. We will pass now to the treaty between Bulgaria and Greece, which seems to have been negotiated independently and to have been signed before any communication about it was made to Serbia.[3] Unlike the other, it was directed exclusively against Turkey. After starting, in the usual way, by affirming the desire of the two countries for peace and the purely defensive character of their agreement, it pledges the parties to assist one another by arms if either should be attacked by Turkey, " either in its territory or by a systematic violation of the

[1] Guéchoff, p. 42.
[2] Bourgeois et Pagès, pp. 352–3 ; *Livre Noir*, i. p. 324, ii. p. 342.
[3] Siebert, p. 345.

rights derived from treaties and the fundamental provisions of the Law of Nations." This unexceptionable definition of the casus belli probably did not give rise to much dispute, since both parties intended to take an early and favourable opportunity of making an aggressive war. On the other hand, there was as much wrangling about the division of the spoils in this treaty as in the other. Guéchoff wanted an autonomous Macedonia, which might lead up later to its incorporation in Bulgaria. But this idea, naturally, did not commend itself to Greece. In the end, no division of the territory was made, nor yet any reference to Russian arbitration. Both parties, no doubt, hoped that events would favour their claims when the time for action came.

The treaty was followed by a military convention, drawn up at the beginning of October, by which time the Serbo-Bulgarian treaty had been made known to Greece. This convention, as is usual in such documents, contained further political articles. For the most part these only make more explicit the commitments of the treaty; but there is one new clause which runs as follows: " In case one of the contracting Governments should declare war upon a State other than Turkey, without a previous understanding and without the consent of the other Government, the latter is released from the obligations of Article 1, but is nevertheless bound to observe, throughout the duration of the war, a friendly neutrality towards its ally." [1] This is the only reference, in the treaty or the convention, to the possibility of war with any other State than Turkey; and there can be little doubt that it had reference to that war with Austria-Hungary which is contemplated in the Serbo-Bulgarian treaty. In such a war, then, Greece would be bound, at the least, to be benevolently neutral.[2]

The treaties we have examined are like two sides of a triangle, and one would have expected a third between Serbia and Greece. But there is, at present, no evidence that such a treaty existed. Nor does there appear to have been one between Montenegro and any of the other Balkan States. Sazonoff, indeed, definitely discouraged the idea that Monte-

[1] Article 4.
[2] I have found no evidence as to whether, or when, this treaty was communicated to any of the Great Powers. But I should think it most probable, under all the circumstances, that it was communicated to Russia.

negro should join the Serbo-Bulgarian alliance : " I emphasised that I should consider such an action a mistake, because there is open enmity between Montenegro and Serbia, and any political treaty would be insincere, quite apart from the fact that such an alliance would immediately become known to Austria." [1] There seems, however, to have been an interview between Bulgarian and Montenegrin Ministers, whence resulted " the impression that Montenegro was ready to march with us." [2] The impression was justified, as events showed. We are also told of a military convention between the four States,[3] but this does not seem to have been published.

The diplomatic arrangements thus completed were accompanied by military preparations which seem to have included large deliveries of money, guns, uniforms, and other war materials both by France and by Russia.[4] Russia also engaged in a trial mobilisation of her Western Army and raised her peace establishment by a million men ; and on September 30th an order was sent out by the Tsar to the effect that mobilisation would mean war against Germany.[5] We hear also of a proposed new military convention between Russia and Bulgaria in 1912 ; but it is not clear whether this was ever concluded.[6]

VI. The War Breaks Out

Thus, by the end of September 1912, Serbia, Bulgaria, and Greece were ready for war with Turkey, and also, if events should so turn out, for war with Austria. They were naturally anxious to attack Turkey while she was still engaged with Italy. But Russia, although she, too, contemplated war as a necessity of the future, yet was not anxious to have it precipitated at that time. As we have seen, she was not herself ready ; [7] and all our evidence shows that she endeavoured to prevent the outbreak. Thus, as early as May 30th, 1912,

[1] Siebert, p. 345.   [2] Guéchoff, p. 71.   [3] Valentin, p. 112.
[4] Friedjung, iii. pp. 179, 188. Cf. Guéchoff, p. 75.
[5] See Friedjung, ib., p. 188, who says that the order was discovered by the Germans during the war. Dobrorolski says that it was issued " under the influence of the difficulties with Austria," but was revoked in November 1912 (Die Kriegsschuldfrage, April 1924, p. 80).
[6] Nekludoff, Diplomatic Reminiscences, p. 75. Cf. Siebert, p. 344.
[7] See above, p. 303. Cf. Georges Louis, pp. 157, 167, and, for the year 1912, p. 185 : " She (Russia) avoids compromising herself in the wake of Italy, but never abandons the idea that great events are perhaps at hand."

we have the report of an interview between Sazonoff and the Bulgarian Minister Daneff. Daneff " began the conversation with rather uncompromising statements. He pointed out how difficult the financial burden made it for Bulgaria to be in constant readiness for war without being able to exploit, in a diplomatic way, the present difficulties of Turkey. An immediate settlement of the Macedonian question becomes, therefore, all the more imperative for Bulgaria. In consequence of the Turkish administration of this territory the Bulgarian element is losing ground. This situation leads many circles in Bulgaria to believe that those parts of Turkish territory which are gravitating towards Bulgaria should be acquired by force of arms." Whereupon Sazonoff " found no difficulty in proving to Daneff how little an active step on the part of Bulgaria, and the complications arising therefrom in the Balkans, would please Russian opinion and our Government, and how improbable it was that events would take a turn favourable to Bulgaria in case of a general collision. At subsequent conversations I found Daneff more reasonable on that question." [1]

But whatever Russia may have intended or desired, the Balkan States were on tiptoe for war. Thus, in August, the Bulgarian Minister in Rome declared that " if Turkey refuses immediately to introduce reforms in Macedonia and to appoint a Christian Governor, his Government will be forced to declare war on Turkey, as otherwise a revolution would break out in Bulgaria." [2] In the same month the Russian Ambassador at Constantinople writes : " Encouraged by the conclusion of secret alliances, and convinced of their superiority, the Balkan States have only one idea—not to allow the favourable moment to pass and to throw themselves into the fight as soon as possible. The existence of such plans has been confirmed under my very eyes, almost hourly, by the ever-increasing nervousness of my Balkan colleagues here. All of them, and chief among them the Bulgarian Minister, continually address the following question to me : ' When will Russia at last begin to act ? ' It is possible that the general tension will become so great that the Balkan States will no longer ask themselves whether Russia, too, will move, and that they will take up arms against her will." In such a case, he adds,

---

[1] Siebert, p. 313.   [2] Ib., p. 357.

probably Bulgaria will invest Constantinople. This will be
" a menace to our (Russia's) historic ideals," and he concludes,
in the usual way, that " we must be armed." [1]

On September 30th the Balkan States simultaneously
mobilised ; [2] and it is curious to find Nekludoff, one of the
negotiators of the Serbo-Bulgarian treaty, telling us that
" when the mobilisation was announced we (Russia), like all
the other European Cabinets, were aghast." [3] The Powers
endeavoured, at the last moment, to stop the now obviously
imminent war. On October 8th they sent a joint note to
the Balkan States declaring, first, that they reprobate energetically any measure which might lead to a rupture of the
peace ; secondly, that they will themselves take in hand the
reform of Turkish administration ; thirdly, that if war does
break out, they will not allow any modification of territorial
arrangements in European Turkey—in other words, that the
States may fight, but that if they do they shall take no spoils. [4]
Whether the Powers really thought that this step would
prevent war we are not in a position to affirm or deny. Their
Ministers in Bulgaria clearly did not ; for it is thus that
Nekludoff describes the scene at Sophia, when the note of the
Powers was presented to the Bulgarian Government :

" Having assembled at the house of our senior, we decided
to make the prescribed declaration the very next day to
M. Guéchoff, one after the other and in a verbal form, but
strictly identical. To effect this we drew our communication
up together, and each of us was to read the text to M. Guéchoff.
It is not difficult to guess that not one of us expected any
result from this proceeding. The evening before my French
colleague and I had confessed as much to one another. The
next day, when I was on my way to the Foreign Office at the
appointed hour, I met Count Tarnowski, the Austro-Hungarian
Minister, coming out of his legation.

" ' Well, so we are going to take our famous step, are we ? '
he asked, with a sarcastic smile.

---

[1] Siebert, p. 357. [2] Friedjung, ii. p. 187.
[3] Nekludoff, p. 106. His explanation is that " our diplomatic chiefs
in St. Petersburg simply were filled with what M. Isvolski, in a speech made
at the Duma some time before, had called, ' healthy optimism ' ; " an optimism which, he adds, " had led Russia to the brink of war." I cannot pretend
to solve these enigmas.
[4] The Kaiser did not approve of this policy. He thought that the Balkan
States should have their chance of making good. Brandenburg, p. 364.

" ' Certainly,' I replied.

" ' And you think that something will come of it ? '

" ' I doubt it.'

" ' And I am quite sure that nothing will,' replied my colleague sharply. ' Europe is simply placing herself in a ridiculous position.'

" I did not answer, but in my heart of hearts I could not but agree that Tarnowski was perfectly right." [1]

It seems likely that, in making this declaration, some of the Powers, at any rate, did so in the persuasion that the Balkan States would be defeated by Turkey, and desired to save them from themselves. This was probably the position of Sazonoff, and possibly it was also that of Sir E. Grey. For Benckendorff writes that : " Grey had already excluded territorial gains in Turkey's favour ; in a reversed sense he seemed to be less positive. That is all I can say." [2] At any rate, so soon as it became apparent that the Balkan States would be victorious, we hear no more of the status quo.

At the same time that they made this declaration to the Balkan States, the Powers addressed a note to Turkey, saying that they themselves intended to take up the question of reforms. Both communications had the kind of reception that might have been anticipated. The Turks replied that they proposed to introduce reforms themselves, independently of any foreign pressure. The Balkan States replied that reforms were indeed most desirable, but that they thought it more hopeful to achieve them by their own direct action. On October 12th [3] accordingly they addressed an ultimatum to Turkey and, receiving no reply, declared war on October 18th. [4]

The war that followed had two phases. The first, after a series of victories by the Balkan States, culminated in the capture of Adrianople, and was concluded by a truce on December 12th. Peace negotiations were begun in London. But while they were drawing themselves out the Young Turks seized power in Turkey and denounced the truce. War

[1] *Diplomatic Reminiscences*, p. 109.
[2] October 22nd, 1912 ; Siebert, p. 373.
[3] Montenegro took action a few days earlier, on October 8th, " in order," says Bogitshevich, "that her ruler might successfully conduct his operations on the Stock Exchange at Vienna " (p. 37).
[4] All these documents in Guéchoff, pp. 87 seq.

was thus resumed at the beginning of February 1913. After another four months of fighting and further victories by the Balkan States, the plenipotentiaries once more assembled in London, and the Treaty of London was drawn up and signed on May 30th.   But before it was ratified there broke out, at the end of June, the war for the spoils between the Balkan States.   This was concluded within the month, and the whole crisis ended with the Treaty of Bucharest, signed on August 10th.   With the military events of these months we need not concern ourselves.   It is, however, relevant to the purpose of this book to remind the reader of the action of Roumania.   That little State had long had her eye on a piece of territory in the Dobrudja, which she could only get by making war on Bulgaria.   She was, however, astute enough to hold her hand during the first Balkan war.   When the second broke out her forces were intact, and she took what she wanted practically without fighting for it.   This neat little action is hailed by M. Poincaré in the following enthusiastic passage :

" Far from joining with Bulgaria, Roumania shook off Austrian tutelage. . . . Roumania found by instinct her natural road, and King Carol compelled himself to bow to the wishes of his people, who refused to be involved in a plot against Serbia." [1]

It is curious how war is always a plot when made by one's enemies, and a heroism when made by one's friends.

VII. The Policies of the Powers

Our concern, however, is not primarily with the duplicities of the Balkan States, but with the policies of the Great Powers.   None of these Powers, not even Russia, seems, at this moment, to have wanted to let loose the European war. They therefore, as we have seen, endeavoured to deter the Balkan States by declaring that, whether they fought or no, they should not alter that Balkan " status quo," the maintenance of which was the avowed object of so many treaties. After the successes of the Balkan States the Powers made no further attempt to give effect to their solemn declaration. But they did attempt, and ultimately with success, to avoid

[1] Poincaré, p. 150.

a European war. For this purpose, on the proposal of Poincaré,[1] their representatives met in London, after the truce of December, under the presidency of Sir Edward Grey, to agree upon a common policy. This Conference, assembled, not, after a war, to arrange terms of peace, but in a difficult crisis to agree upon common action, was something new in diplomatic history. It substituted personal talk round a table for dispatches and telegrams, and was thus a first rudimentary approach to the machinery of a League of Nations. An interesting testimony to its usefulness is given by Sazonoff in a dispatch of February 1914, where he says :

" Of late we have frequently been able to convince ourselves that we lack an organ which would unite the views and the common action of the Powers, an organ such as the Ambassadorial Conference in London last year. The correspondence resulting from this lack leads to delays which have an injurious effect on the progress of affairs." [2] True, while the Powers were divided as we have seen they were, and pursuing such objects as they were pursuing, no great confidence could be had in the power of a piece of machinery to avert catastrophe. But on this occasion, at any rate, the Conference succeeded. This seems to have been due, in great part, to the patience and skill of Sir Edward Grey, to whom the German Ambassador to England, Prince Lichnowski, gave the following honourable testimonial : " Sir Edward Grey conducted the negotiation with prudence, calmness, and tact. As often as a question threatened to become complicated he suggested a formula of agreement that met the case and was invariably accepted. His personality won him equal confidence among all who took part in the conferences." [3] Lichnowski says further that : " On every issue we (the Germans) took the view-point of Austria and Italy, while Sir Edward Grey almost never supported that of France or of Russia. On the contrary, in most instances he lent his support to our group in order to give no pretext for war such as was subsequently furnished by a dead Archduke." But this statement is disputed, not only by the German Foreign Secretary, v. Jagow,[4] but also by Benckendorff, the Russian

[1] Siebert, pp. 382–3, etc.   [2] Ib., p. 712.   [3] Lichnowski, p. 49.
[4] *Remarks*, p. 133. Jagow, however, is not a very trustworthy witness.

Ambassador in London, who writes that, while Germany and England have met on the basis of compromise, English diplomacy " has gone to the last limit of firmness to make the compromise turn in favour of Russia and the Balkan States, while the German attitude, though in favour of Austria, has been much less decisive." [1] The matter, however, is not of much importance. It is enough to notice that, on this occasion, Germany, no less than England, was working for peace. [2]

The Conference met in December, suspended its formal sittings when the second war broke out, at the beginning of February, but reassembled when that war was finished and peace discussions were renewed in London. It then sanctioned an arrangement which divided Macedonia between Serbia, Greece, and Bulgaria, and left Turkey with only a small province in Europe east of the Maritza. But it reserved, for its own disposal, the question of Albania ; for that might have occasioned, and nearly did occasion, the European war.

We must dwell, therefore, on that question a little more in detail. A study of the Serbo-Bulgarian treaty, and of the negotiations that led up to it, seems to show that what Serbia really wanted, and intended to take, was a port on the Adriatic, if not the whole of Albania. It was in the hope and expectation of obtaining that that she made such large concessions to Bulgaria in Macedonia ; and it was when that was refused her that she went back upon her agreement, proposed to keep for herself what had been assigned to Bulgaria, and so led up to that war between the victorious States which ended in Bulgaria's defeat and her complete exclusion from Macedonia. The action of the Great Powers in the Albanian question thus involved war between the Balkan allies. But, on the other hand, it was the only way of avoiding war between the Powers themselves. For Austria was determined that no territory on the Adriatic should go to the Serbs, or to their allies the Montenegrins ; and in this matter she was supported by Italy. The reason is clear. Austria, already an Adriatic Power, did not want, established on the sea, a Power which she knew to be her bitter and irreconcilable enemy ; while Italy wanted no change, unless it were an autonomous

---

[1] *Livre Noir*, ii. p. 304, February 25th, 1913.   [2] Cf. Grey, i. p. 275.

Albania ; for, if Austria were expelled, she preferred to be there herself. Thus, during this episode, we find Austria and Italy working together and making the question of the Adriatic the one on which war or peace hung. The solution finally agreed to by all the Powers was that the territory, formerly Turkish, that bordered the Adriatic between the coasts of Montenegro and Greece should be formed into an independent Albanian State.[1]

Two questions remained, however, which proved very difficult to adjust. In the first place, the solution adopted by the Powers was unacceptable to the Balkan States. For the northern part of the new Albania contemplated by the Powers had been assigned to Serbia in the Serbo-Bulgarian treaty ; and, during the second war against Turkey, Serbia had occupied San Giovanni di Medua and Durazzo, Greece had occupied Janina, and Montenegro was besieging Skutari. What the Balkan States wanted was to partition all Albania among themselves.

In the second place, the Great Powers were in dispute as to the boundaries of Albania. Austria desired the widest possible extension, so as to include in the new State Janina, Ochrida, Prizren, and Skutari ; while Russia, more favourable to the claims of the Balkan States, proposed a narrower limit, excluding those towns. And between these conflicting views the Powers had somehow to decide.[2] The danger-point turned out to be Skutari. The Powers decided that it should be included in Albania. But the Montenegrins were besieging it, and showed no intention of letting go ; and this caused a very dangerous situation. For it was possible that Austria might intervene by force to drive away the Montenegrins, that Russia might take their side, and that the European war might be thus precipitated. This is only one example of the constant fact that a very small question may determine very great issues, when behind it there lies a whole series of ambitions, suspended precariously in a " balance of power," and easily to be dislodged, at a touch, into universal ruin. On this occasion the crisis was finally surmounted by the withdrawal of Montenegro in May.

[1] An interesting account of the physical features and the population of Albania will be found in Conrad, ii. p. 157.
[2] A map of the district with the various suggested boundaries marked, will be found in Sosnosky, ii. p. 374.

The above is a brief summary of events from October 1912 to May 1913. We will now examine, more in detail, the policies of the Powers. And, first, we will take the States most immediately involved, beginning with Austria-Hungary.

VIII. Austrian Policy

The interest of Austria in the Balkans, as we have already explained, was direct, whereas that of all other States was indirect ; for the satisfaction of the ambitions of the Balkan States, especially of Serbia, meant the disruption of the Austrian Empire. It was impossible, therefore, that Austria should look with indifference on the situation created by the victories of the Balkan allies. But what was to be done ? Conrad, now once more Chief of the General Staff, was bent, as always, upon war. His memoirs read like the story of the Sibylline books : Do it now, or you will have to pay more for doing it later. Chance after chance, he urged, had been missed. Now was perhaps the last chance. Austria must fight Serbia, and, if necessary, Russia too. Italy meantime, with good luck, could be fobbed off to a future occasion. But these views of the General Staff do not seem to have had any influence on Austrian policy. Berchtold hesitated and veered, but never came out on the side of war. The old emperor, it would seem, exercised a restraining influence. For Bogitshevich tells us " from an authentic source " that when the Berlin authorities reproached Berchtold with the indecisive and wavering policy of Austria, he replied that : " The conduct of Austrian policy had been made very difficult for him for the reason that, at the beginning of the Balkan conflict, his hands had been tied by his instructions, received from highest authority, to the effect that he might conduct matters as he pleased, save that under no circumstances was he to permit it to come to a conflict with Russia."[1] The Archduke Francis was also against war, at any rate up to May 1913.[2] Austria thus moved from concession to concession. She consented

[1] Bogitshevich, p. 49.
[2] See Conrad, *Aus meiner Dienstzeit*, iii. *passim*. I notice, however, that Pribram, a very trustworthy historian, says that already, in November 1913, the Archduke was trying to convince the German Kaiser of "The necessity of energetic action against the unreasonable demands of the Serbs " (*Austria's Foreign Policy*, p. 41).

to the division of the Sanjak of Novibazar between Serbia and Montenegro, she accepted the invitation to a Conference of the Powers, and she agreed to its recommendations.

On the other hand, this policy of peace she made conditional upon the exclusion of Serbia from territorial acquisitions on the Adriatic. Upon that understanding only did she agree to enter the Conference ; and the other Powers accepted the condition. The solution they adopted, as we have seen, was an independent Albanian State. Serbia's access to the Adriatic was to be provided for by giving her railway communication and the use, though not the proprietorship, of a port. To this compromise Austria assented. The final tension was due, as we have seen, to the difficulty of getting the Powers to agree among themselves as to the boundaries of Albania, and of inducing the Balkan States to accept their decision. Serbia, in particular, wanted the Adriatic coast, even more than she wanted Macedonia. It was, however, over the obstinacy of Montenegro that the most dangerous friction arose. For that little State, as we have seen, was engaged in besieging Skutari, which she was determined to incorporate in her own territory ; and she showed no willingness to relax her grip at the dictation of the Great Powers, who had decided that the town should belong to Albania. In this situation Austria became more and more impatient ; she threatened, if the Powers could not jointly compel Montenegro to withdraw, that she would act by herself. The consequence might easily have been a European war, because, in that case, Russia might intervene on behalf of Montenegro. Finally, however, the Montenegrins were induced, after taking the town, to withdraw ; so that, this time, the Powers were not precipitated into the gulf. The just comment is made by a diplomat who was, indeed, a Serb, but one with some sense of the relative proportion of things : " Owing to their mutual feelings of mistrust the Great Powers had come to such a miserable and shameful pass that their very existence or non-existence, the weal or woe of England, France, Germany, might depend upon the favour and ambition of a few politicians and fanatics, the representatives of small States which are less advanced in civilisation." [1]

---

[1] Bogitshevich, p. 53.

IX. Russian Policy

The second Power concerned in Balkan questions, though less directly than Austria, was Russia. Her interest was partly nationalistic, for the Balkan States were the " little brothers," and the "inevitable" war of Slavism versus Teutonism was an idea that had got firm hold of hot and idle heads. But this sentimentality would not have been likely to determine Russian policy, had it not been connected with other and more realistic motives. Constantinople and the Straits were a genuine Russian interest, for she was excluded from the Mediterranean permanently, so far as ships of war were concerned, and temporarily, even for her commerce, when the Porte was at war, as it had been recently during the war between Turkey and Italy. But the route to Constantinople led through the Balkan States ; and if the German Powers should permanently and finally control that route the fulfilment of Russian ambitions would become more difficult, if not impossible. Hence that constant friction between Austria-Hungary and Russia which was finally to produce the Great War.

It was this issue, as we have seen, that had made it so impossible, even for the genius of Bismarck, to keep on good terms both with Austria and with Russia. His retirement had been the signal for the final drift of Russia away from Germany and across to France ; and the statesmen and public opinion of Russia, by the date we have now reached, seem to have settled down to the conclusion that the coming of the Great War was merely a question of time. Still, as we have seen, the Russian Government, no more than the Austrian, wanted the war just then, although they thought it might in fact " come." Moreover, they were somewhat alarmed and dismayed at the very completeness of the victory of the Balkan States. For it seemed as though Bulgaria might advance even to Constantinople ; and then what would become of Russian ambitions there ? Thus, the first thing Russia did, at the very beginning of the crisis, was to make it clear to Bulgaria that she must limit her aims. On October 31st Sazonoff writes to his Ambassador in London saying that the Balkan States " have been assured of the full support of our diplomacy on the condition, well known to

Bulgaria, that all compensations, in the shape of reforms or territorial acquisitions, will be limited by a line which runs from the mouth of the Maritza by way of Adrianople to the Black Sea." [1] A little later he writes that : " A prolonged occupation of Constantinople by the Allies might force us likewise to send our fleet, which would remain there precisely as long as the Allies." [2] Grey accepted the Russian view, and the final peace treaty left Turkey with a strip of territory in Europe barring Bulgaria from the capital.

While thus, on the one hand, Russia was holding in check the ambitions of Bulgaria, on the other she was endeavouring to moderate those of Serbia. She accepted, though with reluctance, the Austrian contention that there must be no Serbian port or territory on the Adriatic, and she put strong pressure on Serbia to cause her to acquiesce.[3] She accepted also the creation of an independent Albania, pressing only, in the interest of Serbia, for a narrow limitation of the boundary eastwards. But while making these concessions she had always in view the possibility of war with Austria. Thus, on November 14th, Sazonoff writes : " All information at our disposal points to the fact that, at least for the present, Austria is not striving for any territorial acquisitions in the Balkans. Nevertheless Austria might—entirely according to the way things will develop and in consideration of the conflict with Serbia over the access to the Adriatic—resolve upon the annexation of Turkish or even of Serbian territory. In both cases it would be most important for us to be sure that, in case of an intervention on our part, France will not remain indifferent." [4] And again, November 20th : " It will be difficult for public opinion in England to understand that . . . a Serbian harbour on the Adriatic or the size of Albanian territory . . . might step by step lead up to the war." [5] It will be difficult for anyone to understand who is not steeped in the traditions and aims of statecraft.

X. Italian Policy

The position of Italy during this crisis was, as usual, more complicated than that of any other Power. For, as we have

[1] Siebert, p. 381, October 31st, cf. Brandenburg, p. 359.
[2] Ib., p. 387, November 6th.   [3] Ib., pp. 395–6.
[4] Ib., p. 401.   [5] Ib., pp. 405–6.

seen, she was tied up by opposite and incompatible treaties. By a treaty of 1901 she had agreed with Austria that, if any change should be made in the disposition of the Turkish province of Albania, it should be in the direction of autonomy.[1] Thus Italy was bound to support Austria in excluding Serbia and Montenegro from Albania. And this was also in accordance with her own interests, as she conceived them. For though she did not want Austria to strengthen her position on the Adriatic, she did not, any the more, want Serbia established there. These considerations, had the European war then broken out, would have led her to range herself beside Austria, to whom, of course, she was also bound by the Triple Alliance. On the other hand, she had her treaty with France, and the French were disposed to interpret this as meaning that Italy must remain neutral in any war waged by Germany against France, even if France should take the initiative in declaring war.[2] We have here a particularly interesting example of the general truth that, when it comes to the point, the interpretation of treaties of alliance depends on whether the States concerned want to go to war at all, and with, or against, whom. It is perhaps the desire to maintain this freedom that causes treaties to be drawn up in such ambiguous terms.

Of the disagreement, in this case, between Italy and France, we have an account in the dispatches of Isvolski.[3] He tells us that, in November, Tittoni, then Italian Ambassador at Paris, had an interview with Poincaré, in which he expressed anxiety at an alleged change of view of the Russian Government in favour of giving to Serbia a port on the Adriatic. The matter, he said, preoccupied him greatly ; for the Italian Government was engaged to defend the principle of the integrity of Albania, " and in case of war on that question Italy would be obliged to give Austria armed support." Poincaré replied that that was not a position compatible with the Treaty of Racconigi (as far as he knew it),[4] and was altogether contrary to the Franco-Italian convention of 1902,

---

[1] Pribram, i. p. 197. Friedjung, iii, p. 219, says there was a second treaty in this sense in 1909.
[2] See the article quoted above, p. 94.
[3] See *Livre Noir*, i. pp. 347 seq.
[4] It does not seem to be incompatible with the text of that Treaty as given, ib., i. p. 357 (see above, p. 305).

by virtue of which France has the right to count on the neutrality of Italy in case of war between France and Germany. Tittoni replied that the agreement with Austria about Albania had been prior to that with France [1] and also to that of Racconigi, and that it was undoubtedly obligatory on the Italian Government. This seems to be a frank admission that the Italian Government had involved itself in incompatible agreements. It was not unnatural that M. Poincaré should have been " astonished " ; for when the treaty with France was negotiated, it had been understood between the parties that it was " in harmony with the present international engagements of Italy." And now suddenly an engagement was sprung upon him of which he had never heard, and which was said to make it necessary, in certain contingencies, for Italy to go to war against France. Italy, no doubt, might reply that, in the particular war which was now being contemplated, it would not be the case that France, " as the result of a direct provocation," would be " the object of a direct or indirect aggression on the part of one or more Powers," or would " find herself compelled, as the result of a direct provocation, in defence of her honour or security to take the initiative of a declaration of war." It must always be a matter of opinion whether such conditions have, in fact, occurred ; and Italy, no doubt, had the occasion then arisen, would have defended her action by saying that France was the aggressor, which would have been as true, or untrue, as the opposite view. This indeed, appears to have been Poincaré's own opinion ; for when asked by Isvolski what value he attached " to the expressions, a little equivocal in my opinion," of the Franco-Italian treaty, he replied that, in his view, " the importance of the treaty lay in the fact that Italy had abandoned defensive and offensive preparations on the French frontier and concentrated her preparations on the frontier of Austria." But, he adds, " there is no doubt that, in the decisive moment, Italy will always find it possible to give to the agreement the interpretation she wants." [2] Such conduct, however, always causes the State that is disappointed to attribute treachery to the other. And in fact Isvolski

---

[1] In fact, the first agreement with France was made December 16th, 1900. The Austro-Italian treaty was concluded February, 1901.

[2] *Livre Noir*, i. p. 361.

tells us that the view was held in Paris " that neither the Triple Entente not the Triple Alliance can count on the loyalty of Italy, that the Italian Government will employ all its efforts to preserve the peace, and that, in case of war, it will begin by adopting a waiting attitude and then join the camp to which victory is inclining." [1] The reader is invited to compare this forecast with the actual conduct of Italy in the years 1914–15.

While, however, Italy was thus prepared to support Austria in case a general European war should arise over the question of Albania, she was also determined that Austria should not get any advantage of position from such a contingency. She was doing all she could to prevent that Power from taking independent military action against Montenegro. But should Austria nevertheless do so, Italy intended to occupy Valona, the natural object of her ambitions, as its possession would enable her to close the Adriatic. It was rumoured even that an agreement in this sense had been entered into between Italy and Austria.[2] But the withdrawal of Montenegro from Skutari precluded these developments.

Such were the policies of the Powers most immediately concerned with Balkan issues. What about the remainder ? What about France, Germany, and England ?

XI. French Policy

France, it must be remembered, was represented, now and till the outbreak of the Great War, by M. Poincaré, who succeeded M. Caillaux as Premier after the Moroccan crisis of 1911, became President in the beginning of 1913, and continued, in that position, to determine the foreign policy of his country. Whatever else may be thought about him, it will be agreed that he was nothing if not obstinate. The policy on which he might decide he would carry through whatever might be the cost ; and, in that sense, he was what is often called a " strong " man. His election as President was taken by the Russians to be a sign of renewed and vigorous support for the Alliance. " To-morrow," Isvolski writes on January 16th, " are the Presidential elections. God grant that Poincaré may not be beaten. It will be a catastrophe

---

[1] *Livre Noir*, i. p. 365.   [2] Ib., ii. p. 89.

for us, for it will be the début of an era of Combisme." [1]
A few days later he has an interview with the new President
and reports that " in his quality of President of the Republic
he would have full powers to exercise a direct influence on
the foreign policy of France." [2] And again : " The energy,
the decision, the whole character of M. Poincaré give us a
guarantee that in his quality of President of the Republic he
will not content himself, like M. Fallières, with a purely
passive and, so to speak, decorative rôle, but that he will
bring his influence to bear, by all means, at every moment,
on the course of French policy, principally in the domain of
foreign affairs. . . . That is why, during the next seven years,
we are completely assured against the apparition at the head
of the French Government and their diplomacy of such people
as MM. Caillaux, Cruppi, Monis, etc. . . . M. Poincaré
continues to come every day to the Foreign Office, and
M. Gonnart gives no reply, expresses no opinion, without his
knowledge and approval. M. Poincaré has expressed the
desire to see me often, even after his installation at the Elysée,
and has begged me to address myself directly to him whenever
I think it desirable. Such a departure from what is customary
here may be very profitable and convenient to us in the present
difficult circumstances." [3] It is clear from these passages
that M. Poincaré was determined himself to control French
foreign policy, and to control it in close co-operation with
the Russian Government. Further evidence of this intention is shown in the recall of M. Louis, the French Ambassador at St. Petersburg, and the substitution of M. Delcassé.[4]
M. Delcassé, it will be remembered, was the man who had
stood out for war with Germany in 1905, and had resigned
when his policy was rejected. His appointment made a
very bad impression in Germany ; for he " has acquired the
reputation of a convinced enemy of Germany, and it is to him
that they attribute the initiative of the ' Einkreisungs Politik.' " [5] That policy, it is true, was more commonly attributed,
in Germany, to King Edward. But it seems certain that
M. Delcassé was a principal exponent of anti-Germanism in
France. His appointment, therefore, was as welcome to the

[1] *Livre Noir*, ii. p. 9.   [2] Ib., p. 41.   [3] Ib., p. 19.
[4] See Judet, *Georges Louis*. Isvolski pressed constantly for his removal,
and Poincaré finally yielded.
[5] *Livre Noir*, ii. p. 36.

Russians as it was distasteful to the Germans. Isvolski
writes : " If—which may God forbid—the crisis comes, the
decision will be taken by the three strong personalities which
are at the head of the Cabinet—Poincaré, Millerand, and
Delcassé. It is a piece of luck for us that we shall have to
do with precisely these personalities, and not with the various
politicians of the moment who during recent years have
succeeded to the Government of France." [1]

It is clear, then, that Poincaré's accession to power
implied a determined and personal conduct of foreign affairs
and a closer intimacy with Russia ; and this fact had a considerable effect upon the development of the international
situation. In particular, it had one immediate and important
result. In the Balkan crisis with which we are dealing Poincaré
made it clear at once that, if the European war should break
out, France would be at the side of Russia. More precisely,
this meant that, if a war should arise between Austria and
Russia, and if Germany then should take the side of Austria,
France would consider that Russia had been " attacked " by
Austria and Germany, and that therefore the " casus fœderis "
had arisen. Poincaré gave this assurance to Isvolski as early as
September 1912 : " If the conflict with Austria brought about
an armed intervention of Germany, the French Government
recognises beforehand that this would be a casus fœderis, and
it would not hesitate a minute to fulfil the charges incumbent
on it vis-à-vis with Russia." [2] And more than once, in the
course of succeeding months, he reiterated the pledge.[3] Now
it will be remembered that the Franco-Russian Treaty defined
the " casus fœderis " as an " attack " by Germany, or by
Austria supported by Germany, upon Russia or upon France.
If, now, such a situation should arise as nearly did in 1912–13,
and as actually did in 1914—if Austria should go to war
with Serbia, if Russia should thereupon go to war with
Austria, and if Germany should come in to assist her ally—it
might have been equally open to France to decide either that
Russia or that Germany was the attacking party. The
importance of M. Poincaré's decision was that he determined
this moot point in the sense that France would fight. Pos-

---

[1] *Livre Noir*, i. p. 364.   [2] Ib., i. p. 326.
[3] See, e.g., Siebert, p. 403; *Livre Noir*, i. p. 362, ii. p. 20. And, quite explicitly, in November 1912 : "Si la Russie fait la guerre, la France la fera
aussi " (ib., p. 346).

sibly M. Caillaux or M. Combes or M. Monis might have decided otherwise, and, so deciding, might have prevented the Great War ; for Russia would hardly have fought if she had not been assured of French support. That is the exact importance of M. Poincaré's decision.

Why did he adopt it ? There is one little hint which it seems worth while to consider. The Franco-Russian Treaty, it will be remembered, was modified in 1899 by M. Delcassé, who was preoccupied in that year by the possibility of the disruption of Austria-Hungary. This, he considered, would disturb " the equilibrium between the forces of Europe," that is, more simply, the " balance of power." He therefore induced the Tsar to consent to the inclusion, among the objects of the treaty, of the " maintenance of equilibrium," in addition to the " maintenance of peace." This addition, as he said, singularly extended the scope of the treaty.[1] Henceforth the parties are ready to go to war not merely to preserve the peace—the usual claim—but (which may be incompatible therewith) to preserve the " balance." Now, in a letter of Isvolski, dated November 7th, 1912, occurs an interesting passage. A certain communication of Poincaré's, he says, which had been discussed in the Cabinet, expressed " a perfectly new standpoint of France in the matter of the territorial aggrandisement of Austria in the Balkans. Whereas France, up to the present, had declared that local, so to speak, Balkan events could not induce her to take any active measures, the French Government now appears to admit that an acquisition of territory on the part of Austria in the Balkans would affect the general European equilibrium and consequently also the special interest of France."[2] Here the " balance of power " is thought to be affected by an access of territory to Austria, whereas, in 1899, it was to be affected by the disruption of that Empire. Either event, of course, might be held to affect it. That is the nature of the balance of power. And we may perhaps conjecture that Poincaré and his Government had agreed to interpret their treaty in a sense which would involve a European war, not because Russia would have been " attacked " by Austria and Germany, but because the balance of power in the Balkans might suffer. This is the case against Poincaré. But we need not make too much of

[1] See above, p. 108.　　　[2] Siebert, p. 393.

it. For we know that the European anarchy made war inevitable, sooner or later, and that the part played by this or that statesman in postponing or accelerating it is a matter of secondary importance.

In accordance with this interest in the balance of power in the Balkans, we find M. Poincaré " full of the warmest sympathies for Russia and the Balkan States and resolved to continue to give us his most energetic assistance." [1] The Russian Ambassador in London, a rather good observer, goes so far as to say that, in recalling his conversations with M. Cambon (French Ambassador) and the attitude of M. Poincaré, " the thought comes to me as a conviction that, of all the Powers, France is the only one which, I will not say wishes war, but which would look upon it without great regret. In any case, nothing has shown me yet that France has taken an active part in working towards compromise. Now a compromise is peace, beyond compromise lies war." [2] We may add that, apparently, in the autumn of 1912, the French military authorities took the view that the French chances in case of a general war were good. For Isvolski tells us, on the authority of M. Poincaré, that " well-informed and responsible persons envisage with much optimism the chances of Russia and France in case of a general conflagration. This optimistic point of view is based on the consideration (among others) of the diversion that will be produced by the united forces of the Balkan States (except Roumania), who will draw against them a part of the Austro-Hungarian forces. A favourable element for Russia and France will be the immobilisation of Italy, who will be tied as much by the African war as by her special agreements with France." [3] The date of this dispatch is September 12th, 1912, so that already, before the Balkan war had broken out, " well-informed and responsible " persons in France were contemplating, in high spirits, the prospect of European war. Later, however, things changed. Turkey made peace with Italy, and, as we have seen, that country did not in fact consider herself " immobilised " by the treaty with France ; so that the situation was not as good as had been anticipated. This

[1] *Livre Noir*, ii. p. 15.
[2] Ib., p. 303. English translation in *Is Germany Guilty ?*, ii. p. 75, February 25th, 1913.
[3] *Livre Noir*, i. p. 326.

may have affected the attitude of France. At any rate, throughout the crisis she appears to have joined with the other Powers in working for peace. Thus it was M. Poincaré who first suggested the summoning of the Conference,[1] and endeavoured, together with Sazonoff, to induce the Balkan States to abstain from war ;[2] and though, as we have seen, he had promised to support Russia, if the European war should break out over the Balkans, yet he also said that, " Only an attack by Germany against Russia could give rise to the treaty obligation."[3] On the whole, we may conclude that M. Poincaré's position was like that of the other statesmen of Europe. The war, he thought, must " come " ; he was ready to take his part in it when it did ; but meantime he would rather it did not come—or not just yet ! For one reason, French public opinion was insufficiently prepared to comprehend the necessity for a war about the Balkans ;[4] and, further, financial interests were opposed to it.[5]

XII. German Policy

We will turn now to Germany. And, first, we have to observe that now, as in 1908 and 1914, Germany made it clear that, if the European war broke out, she should support Austria-Hungary.[6] Her attitude on this point is precisely analogous to M. Poincaré's about Russia, and as much, or as little, blame is to be attached to the one as to the other. Or, if we do choose to consider the relative blameworthiness of the two States, we may remember that the interest of Germany to prevent the Balkans from falling under Russian hegemony was, owing to the enterprise of the Persian railway, direct, while that of France was very indirect, being concerned only with the " balance of power." The view, so commonly taken in England, that it was natural and right for France to support Russia, but monstrous for Germany to support Austria, is a mere product of war-psychology.

But this determination on the part of Germany to support her ally, should the worst come to the worst, is no proof that she was working for war. All the evidence we have

[1] Siebert, pp. 382, 408, 422.   [2] *Livre Noir*, ii. p. 355.
[3] Ib., p. 356.   [4] Ib., ii. pp. 20, 342.   [5] Ib., p. 356.
[6] Siebert, p. 398 ; Bogitshevich, p. 45.   Cf. Kiderlen-Waechter, i. p. 197, speech in the Reichstag, November 25th, 1912.

points to the opposite conclusion. No doubt there were men in Germany who felt sure that the Great War would come, just as there were such men in France, and, no doubt, in all countries. But these men did not control policy ; and even they, or some of them, took the view, common to men of all nations, that when it did come it must be provoked by the other side. This is illustrated by an interesting correspondence between Conrad and Moltke. Conrad, as always, was for immediate war. Moltke replied : " I think that a European war must come sooner or later, in which the real issue will be the conflict between Germanism and Slavism. To prepare for this war is the duty of all States which uphold the banner of German culture. But the attack must come from the Slavs." [1] In precisely the same way, as we shall see, Benckendorff was urging that the attack must come from the Germans. If this attitude on the part of German soldiers is a proof of German responsibility for the Great War, then, by the same kind of evidence, all States are equally responsible. But whatever German soldiers may have thought or said during this crisis, the German Government was working consistently with the British to stave off the danger. In January 1913 the German Kaiser visited the Austro-Hungarian Embassy, and stated that if Austria-Hungary were involved in war Germany would support her ; but that his Ministry was working for peace, and that it would not be easy to convince the German people of the necessity of a war about Durazzo. This is an attitude precisely analogous to that of Poincaré, who promised to support Russia if it came to war, but felt that it would be difficult for French public opinion to understand the need of a war about the Balkans.[2] Again, in February, the Kaiser writes to the Archduke Ferdinand that everything must be avoided which might lead to war with Russia ; [3] and in March Conrad protests to Berchtold that he should not allow himself to be so much influenced by the German Emperor. " They held us back," he says, " in 1908, and now once more they want to bind our arms." [4]

It would not be necessary to dwell at length on the Kaiser's personal views were it not that the need to personify wicked-

[1] Conrad, iii. p. 146.   [2] Cf. Bethmann-Hollweg, p. 82.
[3] Conrad, iii. p. 155.   [4] Ib., iii. p. 169. Cf. also Sosnosky, ii. p. 380.

ness in some one person made him the centre of British hate during the war, and makes us still attribute to him an influence over foreign policy which in fact he did not possess. German policy was conducted by his Ministers, and in this crisis it was thrown, with the full approval of the Kaiser, on the side of peace. No better testimony is required than that of Sazonoff himself, communicated to the *Nazionale Zeitung* of Berlin in October 1913 : " German diplomacy," he wrote, " and particularly the German Secretary of State, have, from the beginning, seconded my efforts to bring about solidarity of action on the part of the great European Powers in the most loyal and forceful manner. M. von Kiderlen has personally laboured most zealously to promote an understanding between London, Paris, Vienna, and Petersburg, which has now happily been attained." [1] Evidence indeed abounds. Thus, in January 1913, the Russian Ambassador in Berlin writes : " The more I look about me, the more I listen, the more I come to the conclusion that in Berlin they wish at all costs to avoid war, and that they have in all probability made this clear to Vienna." [2] Again, Benckendorff, as we have seen, testifies to the accommodating spirit of Germany at the London Conference ; [3] and Bogitshevich tells us that " it is, in Vienna, ascribed to Germany's restraining influence that Austria gave up her demands to have the towns Djakowa and Dibra placed under Albanian sovereignty." [4]

Germany then, throughout this crisis, was working for peace, and with that in view was constantly putting pressure on Austria-Hungary. Indeed, as we have seen, it was precisely for that reason that Austrian militarists complained of her.

XIII. British Policy

Finally we come to England. Here, too, Sir Edward Grey was working throughout for peace. The suggestion for a Conference came, it is true, from M. Poincaré, not from him ; [5] and it would, presumably, have been held in Paris, not in London, but for the objection taken by Austria. On this point there is a remark of Isvolski which shows how carefully diplomats attend to what might seem, to the mere public, to be details. " For my part," he writes, " I must

---

[1] Bogitshevich, p. 38 note. [2] *Livre Noir*, ii. p. 24, January 30th, 1913.
[3] Ib., p. 304. [4] P. 47. [5] See above, p. 334.

confess that the deep distrust and lack of good will displayed towards me by Berlin and Vienna would, in case I should participate in the Conference, prove to be an unpropitious factor. In London the colourless Mensdorff and Lichnowski, who has not yet had time to create a position for himself, will not, of course, be able to cope with the influence of Benckendorff and Cambon. It seems to me that it would not therefore be particularly advantageous for us to insist upon the choice of Paris." [1] London, then, was chosen, and consequently Sir Edward Grey presided, with the admitted competence and success to which we have already adverted. He appears to have worked throughout in close co-operation both with Russia and with Germany. Only on the question of Turkey did some difficulty arise. For Grey was bound to take into account the feelings of the Mohammedans of the Empire, and therefore not to press too hardly on the Turks, who then, as always, had many friends in England. So, in the autumn of 1912, we find Sazonoff reporting to the Tsar: "All the actions of England are at present dominated by one paramount anxiety, viz. not to draw upon herself the anger of the Mussulman world, so that she might rely upon the Mohammedan part of the Indian population for the necessary security of British rule. Hence the seeming indifference to the fate of the Christians living under the sway of Turkey, which is contrary to England's former attitude ; hence the irresolute policy in Persia and Central Asia." [2] It is not necessary to comment upon this. Every Englishman knows how British statesmen and public opinion have oscillated between regard for the Turk and regard for the Balkan or Armenian Christians. But it is worth while to quote the passage that follows : " Apart from this, England is guided by the desire not to weaken the present Ottoman Government, in which the Anglophil Kiamil Pasha is playing an important rôle, as well as to prevent the Young Turks and Ferid Pasha from coming into power—the latter being a friend of Germany." The Young Turks, it will be remembered, did come into power early in 1913, and that perhaps helped to change Sir Edward's attitude to Turkey. But even before that Benckendorff is writing to Sazonoff : [3]

[1] Siebert, p. 428.   [2] Ib., p. 368, October 1912.
[3] Ib., p. 373, October 21st.

" The entire conversation with Grey proves that he has completely veered round in his opinions, in the interests of the maintenance of the Entente, and that he is resolved, for the sake of the Entente, to grant far greater concessions at the cost of Turkey than he was prepared to grant hitherto." Thus, in the end, there was no difference of policy, on the Turkish question, between England and Russia, and the frontier ultimately drawn was drawn with the approval of both States. It may be added that Grey was as anxious as Russia that no Balkan State should take Constantinople, and agreed that, when the question of the Straits was raised, it should be solved in favour of Russia.[1]

It is interesting to note, further, that, in regard to the possibility of a European war, Grey was as unwilling to commit himself as he was in 1914. Thus Benckendorff writes in November 1912 : " When I drew Grey's attention to the solidarity of the Triple Alliance, and asked him if he could tell me anything about England's attitude, in case our efforts to prevent an Austrian action were not successful, he replied, after some moments' reflection, that it was impossible for him to give a direct answer to a question referring to a possibility which, since his interview with Mensdorff, no longer appeared probable ; and also because the attitude of England depended, above all, on the attitude of the remaining Powers. The attitude of solidarity gave us valuable indications in that respect but no positive facts." [2]

On the other hand, just as in 1914, Grey made it clear to Germany that if the war *should* break out she must not count on English neutrality. Such, at any rate, appears to be the meaning of the very guarded statement he made to Lichnowski : " If all the Powers were at present making serious efforts to preserve the peace, England and Germany were those countries which are least interested in Balkan questions, and therefore most interested in the preservation of peace. If war should break out, the real cause would lie far deeper than the secondary causes which may provoke the war, so that he could see no serious guarantee that England and Germany would not both be drawn into the war." [3]

This statement, Benckendorff says, was made upon his

---

[1] Siebert, p. 387.   [2] Ib., p. 309, November 14th, 1912.
[3] Ib., p. 423, November 28th, 1912.

suggestion.[1] But he adds : " Grey's words did not convey to me the sense of a definite obligation towards ourselves." Sir A. Nicolson apparently was less cautious, for he " told Cambon, with every reservation, that if the Triple Alliance were fighting against the Entente, England would, he thought, take part in the war." But, Benckendorff adds, " Nicolson's views do not always reflect Grey's views." [2]

Grey, then, was endeavouring sincerely, and on this occasion successfully, to keep the peace. But his attitude is not exhaustively defined by this fact ; and we may suppose, with some confidence, that Benckendorff is judging correctly when he writes : " Monsieur Cambon seems to be persuaded, and I believe in this respect he is right, that England would certainly rather let war break out than let the power of France be endangered. This is one reason which would force arms into her hands. The second would be an ultimatum or a brutal attack on the part of Germany, whether against France or against Russia. Here the honour and national dignity of England would be touched, as the King has said. It is a mistake to believe that this point of view does not exist in England." [3] This last touch only was needed to complete the picture. 1912–13, like 1908–9, was a full-dress rehearsal of 1914. All the forces were drawn up, all the explosives assembled. Only, as it so happened, no one in those years fired the fuse. Europe had one last chance, the breathing space of a year.

So far as the Great Powers were concerned, they had come to their agreement by the end of May 1913. By the Treaty of London,[4] Turkey, on the one hand, and the Balkan allies on the other, agreed, first, that Turkey should hand over to the latter all her European territory west of the Enos–Midia line except Albania ; secondly, that the questions of Albania and of the islands be left to the Great Powers. There followed, however, at the end of June, the war for the spoils between the Balkan States. We need not concern ourselves here with this sordid and miserable business, which showed that these savage little States had well conned the principles of diplomacy and war long practised by their betters. But its results had

[1] Siebert, p. 425.   [2] Ib., p. 400.
[3] Is Germany Guilty ?, ii. p. 77.
[4] May 30th, 1913. Printed in Nationalism and War, p. 400.

a certain bearing upon the future history of Europe. Bulgaria had to cede Macedonia to Serbia and to Greece, and Silistria and part of the Dobrudja to Roumania. Serbia was thus enormously strengthened, in territory as well as in conceit, and, at the same time, left with a grievance, for she had been excluded from anything but railway access to the Adriatic. Thus aggrandised, she was an even greater danger to Austria-Hungary than she had been before ; and the perception that that must be so had induced the Dual Monarchy, even before the war was over, to face at the last moment that risk of war which hitherto she had declined. She approached her allies of the Triple Alliance with the question whether, if she went to war with Serbia, they would consider that the obligations of the Alliance arose. The episode was thus described, at a later date, by Giolitti : " On the 9th of August,[1] about a year before the war broke out, I, being then absent from Rome, received from my colleague, San Giuliano, the following telegram : ' Austria has communicated to us and to Germany her intention to act against Serbia, and defines such action as defensive, hoping to apply the casus fœderis of the Triple Alliance, which I consider inapplicable. I intend to join forces with Germany to prevent any such action by Austria, but it will be necessary to say clearly that we do not consider such eventual action as defensive, and therefore do not believe that the casus fœderis exists. Please telegraph if you approve.' I replied that : ' If Austria intervenes against Serbia, it is evident that the casus fœderis does not arise. It is an action that she undertakes on her own account, since there is no question of defence, as no one thinks of attacking her. It is necessary to make a declaration in this sense to Austria in the most formal way, and it is to be expected [2] that German action will dissuade Austria from her most perilous adventure.' "

This statement was made by Giolitti in December 1914, and it is characteristic of the way history is written at such

---

[1] This date is given also in his *Memoirs* (p. 372). But it can hardly be correct. The Peace of Bucharest was signed August 13th, and it seems probable the Austrians would have entered earlier. Giolitti accuses Austria of trying to drag Italy into war earlier in the crisis. But his account is not very convincing (see p. 360). It seems likely that the date was really July. Cf. Montgelas, p. 84.

[2] È d'uopo. I believe—subject to correction—that " expected " is a closer translation than " hoped."

times that M. Yves Guyot, reporting it, omits the references
to Germany, and concludes that, somehow or other, here
is a further proof of Germany's determination to have war
in 1914.[1] In fact, the episode rather suggests the contrary,
In any case, there is no shadow of evidence, so far as I am
aware, that Germany supported Austria's demand. M. Nekludoff,[2] indeed, who is certainly not a pro-German, says that
"Austria did in fact wish to intervene and to attack Serbia,
but she was stopped first by Italy's flat refusal to be associated
in such a policy, and secondly, and more especially, by the
veto of Germany." He goes on, indeed, to say that Germany
was only postponing for the moment a war which she already
intended to wage. But he gives no evidence of this, and his
statement adds nothing to what is known about the origins
of the Great War.

The war between Bulgaria and the other Balkan States thus
proceeded to its conclusion, without involving the Great
Powers. But even after the Peace of Bucharest was signed
Serbia refused to withdraw her troops from Albania, until at
last Austria was driven to send her an ultimatum. The other
Great Powers put pressure on her to yield, and so at last the
tempest of that year rumbled away into silence.

XIV. The Imminence of War

We have seen, nevertheless, how nearly the war broke
out in 1913. We will now pause and observe how, as always
in these crises, the danger was increased by arming and
counter-arming, the existence of the armaments being always
a condition and a cause of the imminence of war. In this
case Austria and Russia were the Powers primarily concerned,
and each was making preparations to counteract alleged
preparations by the other. Thus, in October 1912, Neratoff,
Acting Foreign Minister in St. Petersburg, writes that if the
Balkan States should win the war " diplomatic as well as
military proceedings on the part of Austria and Roumania
are not out of the question. The war preparations of both
States point to this possibility, preparations which are being
silently and carefully made, and to which the reports of our

[1] Yves Guyot, *Les Causes et les Conséquences de la Guerre*, p. 100.
[2] *Diplomatic Reminiscences*, p. 197. Cf. Brandenburg, pp. 381-2;
Montgelas, p. 83.

military agents at Vienna and Bucharest testify. Looked at from the political point of view, it would appear to be useful to oppose to these like measures on our part, these to be taken with the utmost caution, as silently as possible." [1] Again, in December, Sazonoff writes to his Ambassadors in Paris and London : " You can at the same time inform the Governments to which you are accredited that the Imperial Government has decided to maintain under arms the reserves in all Russia and the Caucasus. This measure can be realised without the necessity of publishing a special ukase." [2] In November 1912 Isvolski writes : " Austria is mobilising three army corps in Galicia, and has completed her military preparations against Serbia." [3] On the 18th he writes : " According to all the information received here, Austria is actually preparing the complete mobilisation of ten corps, of which a part is ostensibly disposed against Russia." [4] The French, he writes in the same dispatch, "regard with astonishment and with apprehensions which they do not conceal our indifference to the Austrian mobilisation." And referring to the possibility of the European war, he adds : " The French Government envisages this possibility with conscience and calmness, firmly deciding to fulfil its obligations to its ally. It has taken all the necessary measures ; mobilisation on the eastern frontier has been ' verified,' [5] the material is ready, etc." Lastly, Paul Cambon, French Ambassador in London, reported to Benckendorff that the English Fleet " is fully ready and fully mobilised, without attracting much outward attention, but yet in a way that caused the Admiralty great expenditure." [6] Everything, in a word, as in 1914. Yet can the reader honestly say which of the Powers is " guilty " of the situation ? Is it not rather the total result of the European anarchy, always ready, like the Trojan horse, to deliver, from its belly, war ?

War, nevertheless, was postponed that year ; but it was only postponed. For the main fact—the tension over the Balkans—was now more acute than ever. Serbian ambitions were whetted, not blunted, by her success ; Austria's danger was, therefore, increased ; and Russia was always in the back-

[1] Siebert, p. 361. [2] *Livre Noir*, ii. p. 1.
[3] Ib., i. p. 352. [4] Ib., p. 369.
[5] I do not know the exact meaning of this term. I suppose it means that the plans were gone through and found to be all in order.
[6] *Is Germany Guilty ?*, ii. p. 76, February 1913.

ground, to defend her protégé. To show how great the menace
had been, and still was, let us cite some characteristic utterances
of the men behind the scenes.

In 1913, after the conclusion of the war between the
Balkan States, Pashitch, the Serbian Minister, said to
Bogitshevich : " For the sake of acquiring Bosnia and Herzegovina likewise, I might have caused a general European war
to break loose, already at the time of the first Balkan war ;
but as I feared that in that case we should find ourselves
compelled to make greater concessions to Bulgaria in Macedonia, I desired, above all, to secure possession of Macedonia
for Serbia, in order that, when that was secure, we might then
move forward to the acquisition of Bosnia and Herzegovina." [1]
Bogitshevich states further that Pashitch said to the Greek
Minister, M. Politis, at the Bucharest Peace Conference :
" The first game is won ; now we must prepare for the
second, against Austria." [2] So also Hartwig, Russian Minister
at Belgrade, is reported to have said : " Turkey's business
is finished ; now it is Austria's turn." [3]

Whether or no these things were said (and I see no reason
to doubt that they were) they reveal the tendency and meaning
of Serbian policy, which is sufficiently shown by the whole
history we have recounted and by the actual terms of the
Serbo-Bulgarian treaty. The policy could not be carried to
completion without a European war ; and for a European
war M. Pashitch was perfectly prepared. The lives and
fortunes of millions of Russians, Englishmen, Frenchmen,
Italians, Germans, all completely ignorant of all the facts
and causes, were being cynically staked by this old fox in his
little corner of Europe. And he won the game.

Let us now further observe how the engine thus constructed
was actually working. On November 13th, 1912, the Serbian
Minister in Bucharest writes to his Foreign Secretary in
Belgrade : " The Ministers of Russia and France advise, as
friends of Serbia, that we should declare ourselves satisfied
with a guarantee of an unconditional free use of an Adriatic
port ; and the time will come when we shall be able to retain
some such port as our own. It would be better that Serbia,
which would be at least twice as large as formerly, should
strengthen herself and gather herself together, in order to

---

[1] Bogitshevich, p. 53.   [2] Ib., note 1.   [3] Judet, *Georges Louis*, p. 200.

await with as great a degree of preparedness as possible the important events which must make their appearance among the Great Powers. Otherwise, if a European war started, Europe will make Serbia responsible for the catastrophe." [1] Observe : " the important events which must make their appearance among the Great Powers." Russia and France knew the war was coming. I will not say that they " intended " to make it. The minds of diplomats endeavour not to " intend " anything so definite. The war, after all, was a tremendous risk. No one could say with certainty how it might develop. Still, said everyone, " it must come. We must be ready."

But they said also : " It must come in such a way that the enemy shall appear to have provoked it." This latter point is a constant refrain of Benckendorff, the Russian Ambassador in London, during the crisis we have been describing. To take only one passage. In December 1912 he writes to Sazonoff : " In this connexion I beg you to observe how extremely important it is that the blame for obduracy in the most difficult question at the Conference should fall upon Austria alone. It will not be easy to accomplish this, and yet everything may depend upon it. At the critical moment Grey will have public opinion on his side only if Russia has done all within her power to maintain peace, in so far as her position permits." [2] Isvolski takes the same line. He writes in December 1912 : " If, in spite of the moderation of our demands with regard to the solution of current questions, Austria nevertheless decides for some active step, the whole world will have seen that the war is due not to Russia or to any unreasonable demands by Serbia, but to the attempt of Austria and Germany to establish their hegemony in the Balkans. The French Government ought to be grateful to us for this way of putting the question, which is the more necessary in that it is only in these conditions that we can count upon England." [3] Thus did the children, creeping about in the dark in the powder magazine, chatter about the importance of not being the first to drop the match. It never occurred to any of them then, any more than now, to put out the matches and go out into the light.

[1] Bogitshevich, p. 98.   [2] Siebert, p. 426.   [3] *Livre Noir*, i. p. 370.

That the match would be dropped, that the explosion must come, no one seems to have doubted, unless it were Sir Edward Grey. " In a few years," writes Isvolski in November 1913, " perhaps sooner than we expect, a new crisis will arise in the Near East which will bring about the final collapse of the Ottoman Empire and the partition of Turkey." [1] In April of the same year Hartwig writes : " Serbia has only passed the first stage of her historical journey, and for the gaining of her aims she must still undergo a fearful struggle in which her whole existence may be at stake. Serbia's promised land lies in the territory of the present Austria, and not where her aims are now directed.[2] Under these conditions it is of vital interest to Serbia to place herself, by hard and patient work, in the necessary readiness for the inevitable fight in the future." [3] But perhaps the most notable passage at our disposal is one cited on a later page.[4] The reader is invited to turn and peruse it.

[1] *Livre Noir*, ii. p. 170.
[2] I.e. Macedonia.
[3] *Is Germany Guilty ?*, ii. p. 24.
[4] P. 350.

CHAPTER XIII

THE LAST YEAR

I. The Anglo-German Rapprochement

THE immediate sequel to the Balkan wars, as had been the case after previous crises, was an attempt at a rapprochement of the Powers. On the present occasion the Powers concerned were England and Germany. Negotiations had never altogether ceased, in spite of the failure of the efforts made to arrest the naval rivalry. And during the last year before the outbreak of the war an agreement was actually reached. The Germans, as we know, had long been complaining that they were denied their " place in the sun " ; and in fact, wherever they had tried to expand, whether in Africa or in Asia, they had been met by the tenacious opposition of one or other of the Powers of the Entente. In Africa, however, that tension, which more than once had threatened war, had been in the end relaxed by concessions ; and Germany had managed to secure territory in the East and in the West, including in the latter the piece of the French Congo acquired after the crisis of Agadir. The expansion of Germany had, indeed, been very small compared to that of either France or England, although her population was greater than that of either country ; and she had secured what she had only by the most obstinate tenacity, in the course of which her rivals, while taking the biggest slices themselves, had been inclined to treat her moderate claims as the sole source of friction. Still she had obtained something in West and in East Africa. And now, in the years 1913–14, negotiations proceeded between her and England dealing, in the first place, with the Portuguese colonies in Africa, and in the second, with the Bagdad Railway. The first question was an old one, going back to 1898. In

that year, as we have seen,[1] an agreement had been made
between the two countries looking to the partition of those
colonies between them. The agreement, at that time, came
to nothing. But now, after fifteen years, negotiations were
resumed. The boundaries of the respective " spheres of
interest " were revised, and the difficulty of the guarantee of
Portuguese colonial territory, renewed by the British in 1899,
was met by an agreement that the guarantee should not be
operative if the colonies should separate from the Mother
Country. To this was added an understanding that, if
Portuguese misgovernment should lead to the intervention
of another Power, England would not interfere. It seems
difficult to interpret these provisions otherwise than as a
veiled understanding that one or both Powers should intervene in the name of " Right," encourage the separation of
the colonies from Portugal, and then proceed to partition
them.[2] But however discreditable the Portuguese agreement
may have been to the States that entered into it, it had at
least the advantage of diminishing the chances of war between
them. The European anarchy does not permit of any but
bad solutions ; and while it lasts, the best that statesmen
can hope to do is to choose the lesser of two evils. The
agreement was initialled in October 1913. It was not signed,
because Sir Edward Grey, with an honesty for which he
deserves credit, was determined not to add to the number
of our secret treaties, and insisted on the publication not
only of this new agreement, but of those of 1898 and 1899.
The Germans did not want to publish, but finally agreed
that they would do so in the autumn of 1914. Before then,
Armageddon had begun.

The other much more important matter on which the
British and Germans reached an agreement was that of the
Bagdad Railway. We have already described the long and
complicated history of this enterprise, and we need not here
recapitulate. The agreement,[3] reached in May 1914, was
initialled, like the other, and waiting signature when the war
broke out. The German Chancellor was ready to sign by
the end of July. But by then the die was cast. Over this

[1] See above, p. 58.
[2] The treaty has not been published. But an account of it is given from
the German Documents, by Brandenburg, p. 399.
[3] See above, p. 246.

last-hour reconciliation fate had written the words "Too late." [1]

II. The Liman-Sanders Episode

It was not, then, between England and Germany that the occasion arose which launched the World-War. It arose, as had long been foreseen by shrewd observers, in the Near East. Long ago Bismarck had said : "I shall not live to see the Great War. But you will see it, and it will originate in the East." [2] To the Near East then let us turn. And, first, let us say a few words about an episode, small in itself, but dangerous enough, under the circumstances, to threaten the outbreak of war. In the latter part of the year 1913 the Turks had appointed a German general, Liman von Sanders, to reform their military organisation and to command the first army corps in Constantinople. The Russians were disturbed, for they feared that this arrangement might be fatal to their long-standing plan of seizing the Straits. Communications accordingly were entered into between the Powers of the Entente. France made it clear that she would support Russia, if necessary, to the point of war ; [3] England hesitated, proposed and withdrew, annoying and exasperating Russia ; but on the whole, and in the end, her influence appears to have been on the side of peace. On the other hand, the Germans seem to have shown an unusual measure of conciliation, in a matter where "honour" might have been held to be peculiarly involved. They conceded the point in question, asking only that nothing like an ultimatum should be presented to them, since that might precipitate the crisis. The most important evidence we have on this matter is contained in the minutes of a Council held at St. Petersburg just about the turn of the year 1913-14 ; and to these we will devote a few lines. [4] The view taken at the Council was that pressure should be put upon Turkey, according to that recognised principle of European statecraft, "when

---

[1] It may be worth while to add that, according to Mr. Churchill, the Admiralty had changed the view which they apparently held in 1911 about the danger of German naval stations. For, as he tells us, they thought colonial expansion would help to distract the menace from our coasts. "We were no enemies to German colonial expansion, and we would even have taken active steps to further her wishes in this respect" (*First World War*, i. p. 94).

[2] Cited, e.g., in Huldermann, *Albert Ballin*, p. 202.

[3] See Siebert, p. 704.　　　　　[4] See *Drei Konferenzen*, pp. 32 seq.

in doubt, bully the weak." The means of pressure discussed were a financial boycott and the occupation of some point on the Black Sea, such as Trapezunt. Since, however, Turkey might resist, and Germany might support her, the possibility of a European war immediately arose. In this connexion Sazonoff remarked that " so far as France is concerned the Russian Government can reckon on active support up to the fullest measure " (" tatkräftige Unterstützung bis aufs Äusserste "). For Delcassé had given the assurance that " France would go as far as Russia wanted." On the other hand, it was doubtful how far England would go : " England so far had lent no serious support to the efforts of the St. Petersburg Cabinet, and had indeed facilitated Germany's resistance to Russia's objections, by the fact of the presence of Admiral Limpus in Constantinople." Admiral Limpus was instructing the Turkish Navy, and that fact made it rather awkward for the British to object to a German general holding a similar position in the Turkish Army.

Russia and France alone, Sazonoff remarked, were hardly in a position to deal Germany a fatal blow. " On the other hand, if England took part, then, as Germany was well aware, she might be faced in six weeks with a social catastrophe." The Russian Government therefore, before taking decisive steps, must make sure that England would come in, supposing the military operations should take a turn unfavourable to Russia and France. Such intervention appeared, to the Foreign Minister, to be certain (unzweifelhaft). The President of the Council, Kokovtseff, then raised the question : " Is war with Germany desirable and can Russia wage it ? " He himself was of the contrary opinion, and the majority of the Council agreed with him. It was finally decided that, unless the active support both of England and France could be obtained, it was impossible to adopt a form of pressure which might lead to war with Germany. Meantime negotiations must be continued with that Power ; and these, as we have mentioned, were met in the end in so conciliatory a way that the crisis passed away without an explosion. Whoever may be to blame in this matter, it seems to be clear that Germany behaved with unexampled moderation.

III. The Balkans

But this episode, dangerous though it was, neither created nor eased the general situation in the Near East. It remains now for us to describe the position there, in the form it assumed after the Treaty of Bucharest. The Balkan wars, as we have seen, left everything in that region more precarious and unsettled than ever ; and, immediately, the diplomats were at work to make capital of the new situation. The original Balkan block had been broken up by the war. Bulgaria had gone out ; but then, Roumania had come in. To bind Serbia, Greece, and Roumania into a new alliance, favourable to the Slavs and hostile to Austria, became now the policy of Russia, in preparation for that " inevitable " war which was to destroy the Austrian Empire and realise the ambitions of the Slavs. This plan is developed in an interesting conversation held in February 1914 between the Serbian Minister Pashitch and the Tsar.[1] Some extracts from this deserve quotation. First, Serbia, Pashitch said, " desires the maintenance of peace in the Balkans, and that complications be avoided, for Serbia needs peace." Yes ! but why ? " In order to recuperate, and in order that she may arm herself afresh for the defence of Serbian national interests." What those interests are we have abundantly seen. Serbia wants time to prepare for the Austrian war. And meantime—peace ! How is this " peace " to be maintained ? First, Montenegro is to be united with Serbia, but in such a way that " the existence of the Montenegrin monarchy shall be assured." Next, Bulgaria. She has indeed behaved very badly, but has been " punished by God." And now " a state of harmony between Bulgaria and Serbia might be useful to both." This harmony might be produced by concessions made to Bulgaria (of course, in Macedonia) " in case she was willing to be of assistance in the solution of the Serbo-Croatian question "— that is, in the break up of the Austrian Empire. The Tsar, thereupon, inquires " how many Serbo-Croatians lived in Austria-Hungary, and what they were now believing and desiring ? " Pashitch told him that there were six millions, and informed him (what apparently he did not know) where

[1] Bogitshevich, p. 126.

they lived. There were also, he said, the Slovenes, who were " gravitating to the Serbo-Croatians." " Then I told him that just at this time there was a Slovene stopping at Petersburg who was working for the establishment of a Southern Slav bank, and was trying to win over the Russians to the project. This was very agreeable to the Tsar, and he said that it was very necessary that the Russian banks should take a greater interest in the Slavic countries. I then told the Tsar how great a reverse in sentiment had taken place among the Slavs of Austria-Hungary, how many Starcevic followers there were who formerly expected salvation from Austria, but now comprehended that this salvation could come to them only from Russia or Serbia, and that they could scarcely await the opportunity to see their desires fulfilled ; and then I told him that for every rifle we received we should have a soldier from these countries to carry it." How many soldiers, the Tsar asked, could Serbia put into the field ? Answer : Half a million, well clothed and armed. Whereupon the Tsar : " That is sufficient, it is no trifle, one can go great ways with that."

Passing on to the other Balkan States, it was agreed that Serbia must foster the alliance with Greece. The Tsar said that Roumania " had three and a half million co-nationals in Austria-Hungary and that these desired union with Roumania. Thereupon I said to him, the Transylvanian Roumanians were better nationalists than the Roumanians in Roumania, and King Carol had said to me that public opinion in Roumania had changed in favour of rapprochement with the Balkan States, and that he had to reckon with this fact, and had ordered mobilisation and action of the Roumanian Army to maintain the balance of power in the Balkans and better frontiers in the Dobrudja."

A project is then discussed for the marriage of the Crown Prince of Serbia to one of the Tsar's daughters ; and the Tsar concludes the interview with the words : " For Serbia we shall do everything. Greet the King for me and tell him in Russian : ' For Serbia we shall do all.' "

We see from this interview what kind of a " peace " Serbia was aiming at. So far as Roumania was concerned, the prospects for the new combination seemed favourable. For the Russian Minister at Bucharest writes, in January

1914, that " an important, or perhaps even a decisive, change
in public opinion has been brought about here in favour of
Russia. Besides, one must bear in mind that the events of
last year, which have inspired the Roumanians, and above all
their military leaders, with confidence in their own strength,
have at the same time also encouraged the efforts of the
irredentists. These are not so much directed against Russia
(i.e. in Bessarabia) as against Transylvania with its three
million Roumanians." [1] Roumania, it is true, had renewed
her alliance with the Central Powers in February 1913. But
what are treaties ? And especially what are treaties made
by a ruler and kept secret from the people ? 1916 was to
answer the question.

Montenegro, Roumania, Greece, all that looked favourable
enough. The trouble was Bulgaria, and here Russia had to
play a very careful hand. In an interesting letter of
March 2nd, 1914, Sazonoff writes to his Minister at Sophia : [2]
" The Russian representative can essentially adopt only a
waiting attitude. . . . The present Cabinet does not enjoy
our confidence. . . . It is difficult to effect a rapprochement
between Russia and Bulgaria and between Bulgaria and
Serbia, through the good offices of Russia, unless a complete
change in public opinion and a change of the Government
takes place. If the present Cabinet should be replaced by
a Coalition Ministry, with Malinoff at its head, we should
welcome such an event, in the consciousness of being able
to save Bulgaria from ruin. A ministerial change of this
kind would lead to active support on our part." The active
support suggested is the favouring of a Bulgarian loan in
Paris, which was intended, as we learn elsewhere, to counter
the efforts that were being made to raise a loan in Berlin.

In face of this Serbo-Russian policy, directed against the
very existence of the Austro-Hungarian Empire, what could
the latter do ? The most important evidence of Austrian policy
is contained in a memorandum addressed to the German
Kaiser, and completed just before the murder of Serajevo.[3]
This document points out that the result of the Balkan wars
is " anything but favourable " either to Austria or to the

---

[1] Siebert, p. 436.   [2] Ib., pp. 441 seq.
[3] *Austrian Documents.* i. pp. 1 seq. English translation in *Is Germany
Guilty ?*, ii. p. 6.

Triple Alliance. "The thought of liberating the Christian peoples of the Balkans from Turkish rule, in order to use them as weapons against Central Europe, has ever been the real political background of the traditional interest of Russia for these peoples." Hence the formation of the Balkan Alliance. In the war that followed, the first phase of the plan had been accomplished and the Turks driven out of the Peninsula. The result, however, had been, not a union of all the Balkan States, but a division into two groups "almost equally strong"—Bulgaria and Turkey on the one hand, Serbia, Montenegro, Roumania, and Greece on the other. "To eliminate this division, and to unite all the Balkan States, or at least a decisive majority, in order to modify the European balance of power, was the next task which Russia and France undertook after the crisis was ended." Their difficulty was to adjust the differences between Serbia and Bulgaria. This could only be done " if Serbia consented to give up to Bulgaria the part of Macedonia which she had taken in the Peace of Bucharest." Serbia would probably consent to this. There might be difficulties with Bulgaria. But Russian agents are at work there, paving the way for an overthrow of the present régime, while, at the same time, France and Russia are working to " bring about a complete isolation of Bulgaria, in order to make her more susceptible to the Russian plans." They are trying also to draw Turkey over to themselves, and to counteract her tendency to join, together with Bulgaria, the Triple Alliance. These efforts seem to be meeting with some success. As to Roumania, public opinion has undergone a decided change, and " to-day one cannot doubt that a large part of the Army, of the ' Intellectuals ' and of the people, are won over to the idea of joining a movement, the aim of which would be to 'free the brothers beyond the Carpathians'"— that is, those included in the Austro-Hungarian Empire. King Charles, indeed, was personally faithful to the Triple Alliance, but " he was unable to enforce his political ideas against the public opinion of the day, and it would be impossible, even though the treaty called for Roumania's assistance in case Russia should become aggressive,[1] for Roumania to fight on the side of Austria-Hungary." Indeed, the

[1] See above, p. 162.

Roumanian Minister of Foreign Affairs had admitted " that a rapprochement of Roumania towards Russia had taken place, and that a community of interests existed between the two States."

This picture, it will be observed, is substantially the same as that drawn from Russian and Serbian sources. We may take it for certain, therefore, that this was, in fact, the situation in the Balkans. What, under such conditions, was Austria to do ? The proposal of the memorandum is that the monarchy should accede to the propositions of Bulgaria, made a year ago and since frequently repeated, and should enter into a formal alliance with her. It should also favour an alliance between Bulgaria and Turkey. The negotiations of the treaty with Bulgaria should not be kept secret from Roumania, for it is hoped to impress Roumania with the dangers she will run if she joins the other party. This scheme is presented to Germany for her approval ; and at the close a special appeal is made to her, on the ground of the danger to herself involved in the expansionist policy of Russia. " One can hardly impute to Russia plans of annexing German territory ; but still, the extraordinary and warlike preparations, the construction of strategic railways near her western frontier, etc., are surely directed more against Germany than against Austria-Hungary. Russia has realised that the materialisation of her plans in Europe and Asia, born out of an absolute inner necessity, is sure to infringe upon important German interests, and will inevitably meet with powerful German resistance."

Such is the Balkan position, and such the intrigues of the Great Powers concerned, immediately before the last and fatal crisis. By a coincidence which suggests that the Power behind events is a dramatist, at the very moment when the document we have cited was completed, there occurred the murder of Serajevo. A postscript thereupon concluded thus : " The above memorial had just been finished, when the awful deed of Serajevo occurred. The entire possible consequences of this foul murder cannot at present be estimated. It serves, however, to prove the impossibility of bridging over the opposition between the Monarchy and Serbia, as well as the danger and intensity of the greater Serbian movement, a movement that will stop at nothing. Austria-Hungary has never been lacking in good will and accommodating spirit in order to bring about endurable relations to Serbia. But it has been proved by recent events that all these efforts have been in vain, and that the Monarchy, in the future as in the past, will have to reckon with an obdurate, uncompromising, aggressive antagonism of Serbia. All the more is the Monarchy faced with the imperious necessity to break with a strong hand the threads that her foes are trying to weave into a net about her head."

Will any British imperialist deny, to an Empire so situated, comprehension, and even sympathy ?

In conclusion, we will cite two remarks attributed to M. Poincaré in the beginning of this year, 1914.

" In two years the war will take place. All my efforts will be devoted to preparing for it." [1]

" Whatever be the issue, small or great, which may arise in the future between Russia and Germany, it will not pass by like the last. It will be war." [2]

---

[1] Judet, p. 231, January 12th.   [2] Ib., p. 233, March 14th.

CHAPTER XIV

THE HAGUE CONFERENCES

I. The Conference of 1899. Disarmament

In our first chapter we pointed out that the arming and counter-arming of States is a potent, indeed a principal, cause of war; and from time to time, in the course of our study, we have had occasion to illustrate this point more particularly. It will be useful now to bring together the main facts bearing on this topic during the period with which we are concerned.

We will deal first with The Hague Conferences. The first of these met in 1899, at the invitation of the Tsar. What the Tsar's motives may have been in summoning it was at the time, and probably always will be, disputed. In the international anarchy no State trusts the purposes of any other, and, as we shall see more particularly, Russia was thought to be merely playing for a pause in the armament-competition, during a period when she found it difficult, herself, to continue the strain. But it seems more probable that the Tsar was moved by a genuine sense of the evils of the armed struggle, and by a desire to do something to alleviate it. This desire was also felt, no doubt, in a more or less Platonic way, by some of the other statesmen of Europe. But the evidence is abundant that few of them believed that anything could or would be done. And, in fact, nothing was done. The blame for this is commonly put upon Germany, and there is no doubt about her hostility to the project. This was felt and expressed, at the very outset, by the Kaiser. " The whole plan," he writes in one of his vigorous notes, " is due merely to the financial exhaustion of Russia. Army increases, strategic railways, the rapid expansion towards China, the Siberian railway, all this has drained her dry, and all the while typhus rages in the land, taxes can hardly be increased, and culture is at the lowest ebb. All this must be counted in, along with the humanitarian nonsense of the Tsar. There's a bit of devilry in it, too, because anyone who refuses the invitation will be said to want to break the peace, and that at a moment when Russia cannot go further, while we others —Germany too—can begin again and make up for lost time." [1] It is rather amusing to compare with this private outburst the reply which the Kaiser actually addressed to the Tsar. It runs as follows : [2] " Prince Radolin has communicated to me, by your commands, the Memoir about the proposal for an International Conference to bring about a general disarmament. This suggestion once more places in a vivid light the pure and lofty motives by which your counsels are ruled, and will earn you the applause of all peoples. The question itself—theoretically, as a principle, seemingly simple —is in practice, I am afraid, eminently difficult, considering the great delicacy of the relations and dispositions of the different nations to each other, as well as with respect to the most varied development of their respective histories. Could we, for instance, figure to ourselves a monarch holding personal command of his army, dissolving the regiments sacred with a hundred years of history, and relegating their glorious colours to the walls of the armouries and museums (and handing over his towns to anarchy and democracy). However, that is only en passant. The main point is the love of mankind which fills your warm heart and which prompts you to this proposal, the most interesting and surprising of this century ! Honour will henceforth be lavished upon you by the whole world ; even should the practical part fail through the difficulties of the detail. My Government shall give the matter its most serious attention."

This passage is written in the Kaiser's own peculiar English. But translated into a more genuine idiom, and substitution being made of the British Navy for the German Army, it would express pretty well the sentiments of the great mass of Englishmen. Here, at any rate, is an account by the German Ambassador in London of a conversation with Lord Salisbury. " Lord Salisbury," he says, " in a private interview expressed himself very sceptically with reference to Count Muravieff's programme for the peace

---

[1] Ger. Docs., xv. p. 149 note 4.   [2] Ib., p. 151.

conference, but begged me to make no official use of his communications. He described the whole programme as ' pas sérieux.' Especially, it would be impossible, even if agreement could be reached about military and naval reduction, to secure the honourable fulfilment, by the individual Powers, of the arrangements arrived at. . . . From the statements of Lord Salisbury I received the distinct impression that this country will take part in the conference, and will recognise to the full the peaceable intentions of the Russian Tsar, but in the discussions will assent to nothing which may limit the further development and the fighting efficiency of the English fleet, or compel England to submit important English interests to the decision of third parties." [1] I can almost hear the sigh of relief with which any ordinary Englishman will greet these words. But they are only the English variant of those of the Kaiser, cited above.

Now for the French. In private conversation with Count Münster, the German Ambassador in Paris, Delcassé said : " In this conference we have precisely the same interest as you. You will not limit your forces at this moment nor agree to proposals of disarmament. We are in the same position. On both sides we wish to spare the Tsar and to find a formula to get round this question ; but we will not let ourselves in for anything which may weaken our forces on either side. To avoid a complete fiasco perhaps we may make a concession about arbitration. But this must not limit the complete independence of the great States." [2]

If this was the attitude of leading statesmen in England and in France, it must not be supposed that the initiative of the Tsar was approved by his own Ministers. One of the ablest statesmen of Europe was Count Witte. He was very conscious of the evils involved in the burden of armaments ; [3] but this is how he writes of the Conference :

" I congratulated (the Tsar) upon having taken the initiative in the great and noble task of bringing about universal peace, but I pointed out that the Conference was not likely to have any practical results. The sacred truths of the Christian faith were announced by the Son of God some two thousand years ago, and yet most of the people are still

[1] Ger. Docs., p. 170.   [2] Ib., p. 186.   [3] See, e.g., Dillon, p. 275.

indifferent to these precepts. Likewise many centuries will pass before the idea of peaceful settlement of international conflict will be carried into practice. Five years later we ourselves showed that our talk about disarmament was but empty verbiage." [1] Count Witte's views were shared by v. Staal, the Russian delegate to the Conference. " He knew well," he said to v. Bülow, " that most of the expectations which were bound up with the Conference could not be realised. But as the Dean of Russian diplomacy (he was seventy-five years old !) he had to see that the Conference did not result in a fiasco for his sovereign and his sovereign's country and house. Il s'agit pour la Russie d'une question de prestige et d'honneur." [2] The phrase is characteristic. No mention of the Russian people. No mention anywhere of any people. They were left to express their views, as they could, in their own blind, foolish way. Thus, as we learn from Mr. White, the American delegate, " books, documents, letters wise and unwise, thoughtful and crankish, shrewd and childish, poured in upon me ; in all classes of society there seemed fermenting a mixture of hope and doubt." [3] But let not the reader suppose that even the American Government was seriously bent upon the purpose of the Conference. No ! " The non-augmentation of land and sea forces," Mr. White was instructed, " is so inapplicable to the United States at present that it is deemed advisable to leave the initiative, upon this subject, to the representatives of those Powers to which it may properly apply " ; and as to the attempt to restrict the use of new weapons of war, " the expediency of restraining the inventive genius of our people in the direction of devising means of defence is by no means clear, and considering the temptations to which men and nations may be exposed in a time of conflict it is doubtful if an international agreement of this nature would prove effective." [4] The truth of that last sentence has been so amply verified by recent events that it may stand as a good example of American horse-sense. The method attempted at the Conference was, in fact, a mistaken one. But our present point is that nobody really meant to do anything by any method. That is made sufficiently clear, if it be not

[1] *Memoirs*, p. 97.
[3] White, ii. p. 252.
[2] Ger. Docs., xv. p. 193.
[4] Ib., p. 253.

clear already, by the following passage from the official French report on the Conference :—

" From the first meeting it was easy to see that the delegates of every Power, while appearing animated by the desire to respond to the humanitarian intentions of their own Governments, derived either from their own convictions or from the instructions of their Governments " (the same Governments that had the " humanitarian intentions "), " a resolve not to accept any measure which might result in really diminishing the defensive or offensive forces of their country, or even in limiting those forces." [1]

II. The Conference of 1899. Arbitration

Enough, perhaps, has been said to show that the attitude of the Kaiser and of his advisers was noticeable rather from the vigour of its expression than from any essential difference of opinion between him and the Ministers of other States. The idea of disarmament ran quickly into the sand. In place of it was taken up the question of arbitration.

On this matter, too, the Germans had very definite views. They are ably expressed in the following remarks of that sinister and mysterious Holstein, who was so potent a force behind the scenes in the German Foreign Office. He gives us a little essay, which might be called classical, in that current philosophy of the State, held openly by the Germans and less openly by most of the statesmen, journalists, soldiers, and sailors of every State during the years preceding the Great War :

" Subjects of international law are States, not individuals. It will therefore be formally difficult, and practically impossible, to isolate the individual Judge from the passions and interests of the Whole, in the way in which that happens, or is supposed to happen, in private law. Of all conceivable judges Great Powers are the least disinterested, for in every question of any importance that may come up all Great Powers are interested à un degré quelconque. An impartial decision is, therefore, excluded by the nature of things. But arbitration without guarantee of disinterestedness is nothing but ordinary intervention. The constitution of the so-called

[1] Cited Ger. Docs., xv. p. 203 note.

Court of Arbitration has therefore no purpose, save by clearing up the interests involved, to prepare the grouping for war, and thus war itself, or to facilitate the violation of the weaker party. Small disinterested States as subjects, small questions as objects of arbitral decision, are conceivable, great States and great questions are not. For the State— the more so the bigger it is—regards itself as an end, not as a means towards the attainment of higher aims lying outside it. There is no higher aim for the State than the protection of its own interests. But the latter, in the case of Great Powers, are not necessarily identical with the maintenance of peace, but rather with the subjugation (Vergewaltigung) of an enemy and rival by a well-constructed stronger group." So much for the general position. Now for the application : " The suspicion, therefore, lies near at hand that, in the thoughts of Russian diplomacy, if these rest at all upon the ground of reality, the Areopagus of the Great Powers is regarded rather as a means of force than of peace. To begin with, Russia would wish, perhaps, to make the Areopagus effective as a continental group against England ; later perhaps against other Powers, whether in the French or the Russian interest." [1] Shocking? Yes, when a German says it. But how is it when an Englishman or a Frenchman or an Italian (say a Fascist) thinks it ? There is, indeed, a good answer to it ; the answer that the State is not an end in itself, but a means to the happiness and well-being of its citizens ; that any war injures these more than anything else can injure them ; and that, therefore, any decision given anyhow, good, bad or indifferent, is better than recourse to war. But how many people are prepared to stand for this answer ? How many are not still in the toils, whether they know it or not, of what is called the " German " philosophy of the State ?

At any rate, whatever may be thought of this philosophy, it led the Germans to oppose arbitration for international disputes. But what about the other States ? " Not a single Power," writes Mr. White, " was willing to bind itself by a hard and fast rule to submit all questions to arbitration, and least of all the United States. A few nations were willing to accept it in regard to minor matters—as, for example,

[1] Ger. Docs., xv. pp. 188–9 ; cf. ib., pp. 281–2.

postal or monetary difficulties and the like." The reasons
for this caution it is hardly necessary to draw out. The
States knew that, on every important point, they would
prefer to fight. A characteristic passage in this sense may
be cited from a dispatch addressed to the German Foreign
Office by the Roumanian delegate. His Government, he said,
were opposed to any kind of compulsory arbitration and to
a permanent International Court. "The grounds for our
standpoint in this matter are too obvious for it to be
necessary for me to expound them further. Consider only
to what we might be led, under the still uncertain political
circumstances which surround us in the East, if arbitration
were made compulsory, with regard to the innumerable
difficulties of the most various kinds which we have with
our neighbours (especially Bulgaria)."[1] What this really
meant the reader will realise who has read our chapters on
the Balkans. Some of the delegates, no doubt, were more
serious than these in their desire to introduce arbitration
for a few minor causes of disputes. Mr. White even says
that all the German delegates, except Count Münster, were
" favourable to a good arbitration plan."[2] So, no doubt, was
the French delegate, the well-known pacifist, M. Bourgeois;
though Mr. White tells us that " everybody knows that France
has never wished for arbitration."[3] Lord Pauncefote, the
British delegate, was one of its keenest advocates. He led
the proposal for a permanent court, and was supported by the
United States and by most of the other delegations. The
Germans led the opposition; and they were only induced, in
the end, to accept that panel of arbitrators called The Hague
Court by the fear that otherwise they would be exposed to
the condemnation of public opinion and might irretrievably
ruin their relation to Russia.[4]

The Kaiser's notes appended to the dispatch in which his
Chancellor advised him to make this surrender are characteristic. He expatiates on the terrible results produced by
that " dreaming boy " the Tsar. He prays that Heaven
may forgive those " hypocritical Pharisees " the Americans.
Finally, he announces his consent in the following terms:
" To prevent the disgrace of the Tsar in the face of Europe

[1] Ger. Docs., xv. p. 262.   [2] White, ii. p. 298.
[3] Ib., p. 304.   [4] Ger. Docs., xv. p. 303.

I vote for this nonsense. But in my actions, now and here-after, I shall trust and invoke only God and my sharp sword." [1] Perhaps, if we had the private remarks of other rulers of Europe, we should find their sentiments much the same, whatever their language might be. We have, at any rate, some indication of the military and the naval point of view. " Germany is prepared for war as no other country is or can be ; she can mobilise her Army in ten days ; and neither France nor Russia nor any other Power can do this. Arbitration would simply give rival Powers time to put themselves in readiness, and would therefore be a great disadvantage for Germany." [2] Thus the representative of the greatest military Power. Whereto the representative of the greatest naval Power : " The Navy of Great Britain is and will remain in a state of complete preparation for war. A vast deal depends on prompt action by the Navy ; and the truce afforded by arbitration proceedings would give to other Powers time which they would not otherwise have to put themselves into complete readiness." [3] In conclusion we will add the following little anecdote :

Scene : A dinner in Amsterdam during the Conference.

Characters : SIR JOHN FISHER and COUNT MÜNSTER.

SIR JOHN : Why did not you answer the Queen's Speech and propose the toast ? You are the senior ambassador.
COUNT MÜNSTER : Staal, as President of the Conference, is the only man who has the right to do that.
SIR JOHN : President of that nonsense ! Does that count ? [4]

But more informing than these remarks of the statesmen, soldiers, and sailors, are the recorded actions of the Powers during the years that follow. In the autumn of the same year, 1899, in which the Conference was held, the relations, long tense, between England and the Transvaal reached the breaking-point. The Boers proposed arbitration. The British, who had championed arbitration at The Hague, refused. There followed the Boer War. During its course

---

[1] Ger. Docs., **xv.** p. 305–6.   [2] White, p. 265.
[3] Ib., p. 268.   [4] Ger. Docs., **xv.** p. 357.

occurred the troubles in China, the massacres, and the sack of Pekin. 1904 was the date of the Russo-Japanese War. Does anyone think that, whatever the Germans had done or not done at The Hague, any of these wars would have been prevented ?

III. The Conference of 1907

The defeat of the Russians was followed, in 1907, by the second Hague Conference. The initiative for this came from the United States, though the invitations were sent out by Russia. But the Russian attitude was different now from what it had been in 1899. Disarmament was then the main object of the Tsar, though not, as we have seen, of his Ministers. But now, after her defeat, Russia desired to build up her armaments again. Disarmament, therefore, was not included in the programme. It was the British Government who desired that it should be introduced, because they wished to limit expenditure on the Navy, in order to have money for the social reforms to which they were pledged. The Germans, however, announced that they would not take part in such a discussion. This is often brought up against them. But really, it was their frankness rather than their policy that distinguished them from the other Great Powers. It is incompatible with the " dignity " of a Great Power, a German diplomat said, to allow any other State to interfere in so vital a matter.[1] " It is an encroachment on the rights of the sovereign," said the Tsar.[2] Muravieff dismissed it as a " Utopia,"[3] and Isvolski as " a dream of Jews, Socialists, and hysterical women."[4] The Austrian Minister, Aehrenthal, agreed with Germany.[5] So did France, who did not expect any practical result, though she was prepared, for the sake of appearances, to take part in an academic discussion.[6] In England, King Edward regarded it as a piece of humbug.[7] Sir Edward Grey was sceptical.[8] So was Sir Charles Hardinge.[9] Lord Haldane agreed with the Kaiser and with King Edward,[10] and the Admiralty of course was opposed to the whole idea, as

[1] Ger. Docs., xxiii. p. 135. [2] Ib., p. 157.
[3] Ib., p. 105. [4] Ib., p. 163. [5] Ib., pp. 108, 158.
[6] Ib., pp. 125, 138, 153, 210, 211, 229. [7] Ib., pp. 84, 210.
[8] Ib., pp. 154, 215. [9] Ib., p. 207. [10] Ib., p. 86.

Admiralties and War Offices always are and always will be [1]
Even in America, President Roosevelt had " very little trust in
the coming Hague Conference," said that he regarded practical
results as unattainable, and added that in no case would he
permit anything to be proposed which might be unpleasant
to Germany.[2] The President, indeed, in the April of this
same year, expressed, in a public speech, the view that a
righteous war is better than an unrighteous peace.[3]   While
such views are held, there can be no chance of disarmament ;
for in order to enforce righteousness, one must be stronger
than the unrighteous.   It does not seem likely, in the face of
this evidence, that any result would have been reached at the
Conference, even if Germany had consented to the discussion.
Indeed, the view was pretty generally expressed that the best
thing to do was to humour the English by permitting them to
have their say, and then to give the whole project an imposing
and respectable funeral. This, as the German delegate
ironically reports, was, in fact, the effect of the brief one-day
discussion initiated by the British delegate.[4]

More serious than the discussion of disarmament was
that of the right of capture at sea.   This was a matter of
primary interest to England, as the greatest naval Power,
and one very awkward for her to handle, if she was also to
maintain her attitude as a lover of peace.   She was determined not to abandon the right ; and it is interesting to
find Sir Edward Grey arguing that, if there is to be war, the
more terrible it is, the more " humane " ; while the Germans,
on the other hand, discourse on the " inhumanity " of the
destruction of merchant ships.[5] Submarines had not yet
shown what they could do ; otherwise perhaps the English
and the Germans might each have adopted the point of view
of the other, without either of them abandoning the claim of
safeguarding humanity.   Even as it was, the German Admiral,
von Tirpitz, objected to the policy of his Government.   He saw,
or thought he saw, that the effect of the British proposals
might be to secure England's food supplies in war, without
giving security to those of Germany.   It is hardly worth
while to dwell upon these discussions ; for although they
led, in the end, to the Declaration of London, that was thrown

---

[1] Ger. Docs., xxiii. pp. 147, 158.   [2] Ib., pp. 95, 146.
[3] Ib., p. 231.   [4] Ib., p. 313.   [5] Ib., pp. 380, 349.

out by the House of Lords, and England entered the Great War free to starve out Germany, if she could. It was, indeed, as some students of the war seem to hold, the success with which this was achieved that finally determined the victory. Whether that be true we need not here discuss ; any more than we need debate the question whether the starvation of women and children is more or less humane than the drowning of sailors.[1]

The other subject of importance discussed at The Hague was that of Arbitration. Here, too, the Germans have been condemned for their opposition to the principle of compulsion, even for a small and limited class of cases ; and here, too, the evidence is that the other Powers, if more discreet, were hardly more favourable to the idea. The Austrian Minister formally declared that he could not accept compulsory arbitration, so long as the Balkan question remained unsolved.[2] Roumania had said the same thing in 1899,[3] and it would hardly be possible to declare more plainly that that question was to be settled by force. France, said the French Minister at Rome, would never consent to compulsory arbitration.[4] England was at first opposed, but afterwards changed her mind, apparently owing to influence brought to bear on King Edward by the Marquis de Soveral.[5] Germans, however, it is interesting to note, complain that, in spite of this, and in spite of the fact that there was a special arbitration treaty between Germany and England, the latter steadily refused to submit to arbitration the German claim to compensation for ships stopped in the South African War. The British said that they declined arbitration because the claim in question was unfounded ;[6] a position which clearly would defeat any treaty of arbitration. This does not look as though they could have been very enthusiastic advocates even of the limited measure of compulsion proposed at the Conference. Although, therefore, the opposition of Germany was more open and more avowed than that of other States, no State seems to have been enthusiastic for the proposal. Some of the delegates, indeed, notably M. Bourgeois, Mr. Choate, and Herr Lammasch, were honest and convinced

---

[1] For the discussion of capture at sea, see Ger. Docs., xxiii. chap. clxxii.
[2] Ger. Docs., xxiii. p. 134.   [3] Above, p. 362.   [4] Ger. Docs., xxiii. p. 138.
[5] Ib., p. 287.   [6] Ib., p. 343 note.

in their support of it.   But it was not possible, under the circumstances, to do more than pass a pious resolution recognising the " principle " of compulsory arbitration, declaring that certain topics are suitable for settlement in that way, and announcing that there had " disengaged itself from the discussion a highly elevated sentiment of the common good of mankind." This " highly elevated sentiment " presently translated itself into the Tripoli war, the Balkan wars, and the Great War.   And at the date of this writing, seven years after that war was concluded, the British, Japanese, and Italian Governments still refuse to adopt the clause in the Covenant which prescribes arbitration for certain categories of disputes.   It does not look as though the " Jews, Socialists, and hysterical women " have made much progress, as a result of the war to end war.

From this survey we may conclude that, however the blame may be distributed, there was not any chance that The Hague Conferences, under any circumstances, would have done anything to prevent the approaching catastrophe. Public opinion was either indifferent or unorganised throughout the world, and the diplomats and Governments had the game in their own hands.   The object, as they saw it, was to fend off a tiresome, incipient, but fortunately dispersed and feeble agitation.   They did this by fine words and phrases, while taking care that nothing more substantial should be adopted.   They thus kept what rhetoricians call their " swords " bright, and were able, when the time came, to enter into the war for Right, unhampered by rules which it might otherwise have been necessary to break.   The statesmen, the soldiers, and the sailors had then, as they still have, the world in their hands, to roll it about, as the apes did the ball in *Faust*.   " 'Tis clay, my kits, 'twill break in bits."   No matter !   The children must have their game.

CHAPTER XV

ARMAMENTS

I. Continental Armies

WE will proceed now to examine the competition in armaments, taking, first, the forces on land. We may usefully begin with a quotation from Mr. Churchill : " One must think," he says, " of the intercourse of the nations, in those days, not as if they were chessmen on the board, or puppets dressed up in finery and frillings, grimacing at each other in a quadrille, but as prodigious organisations of forces, active or latent, which, like planetary bodies, could not approach each other without giving rise to profound magnetic reactions. If they got too near, the lightnings would begin to flash, and beyond a certain point they might be attracted altogether from the orbits in which they were restrained, and draw each other into dire collision. The task of diplomacy was to prevent such disasters ; and as long as there was no conscious or subconscious purpose of war in the mind of any Power or race, diplomacy would probably succeed. But in such grave and delicate conjunctures one violent move by any party would rupture and derange the restraints upon all, and plunge cosmos into chaos." [1] This position of armed States is the one I have endeavoured, throughout this book, to keep before the reader's mind. I have also shown him, I think conclusively, that all the Great Powers had "subconscious" if not "conscious" purposes making for war. The plunging of cosmos into chaos was thus a practical certainty. In this chapter all we have to do is to bring together the more important facts about that competition in armaments which was at once the cause and the effect of the political tension.

The view is, or was, current in this country, and no doubt in other allied countries, that the Germans had, before the

[1] Churchill, i. p. 45.

war, an enormous preponderance of military force over any possible or likely opponents. This view is contradicted by the facts. If, to begin with, we take the numbers of men in the peace establishments of France and Russia, on the one hand, and of Germany and Austria, on the other, we find : [1]

Year.	France and Russia.	Central Powers	Franco-Russian Excess.
1899	1,470,000	950,000	520,000
1907	1,813,000	1,011,000	802,000
1914	2,239,000	1,239,000	1,000,000

These figures do not include those of Italy, still nominally the ally of the Central Powers, though it was pretty certain, since the agreement of 1902, that she would not take part in war against France. In fact, as we know, she took part with her. Her figures are :

1899	..	..	..	..	.. 258,000
1907	..	..	..	..	.. 284,000
1914	..	..	..	..	.. 273,000

So that even if these figures be added in, they still leave the Triple Alliance in a position of great numerical inferiority as compared with France and Russia. But perhaps they should be added in, as a matter of form, because, in March 1914, Italy entered into a new military convention with the Allies against whom she was to fight in 1916. [2]

The figures cited give the peace strength of the States concerned. War strength, of course, would be different, and here the greater population of Germany would tell against France. But so would the greater population of Russia tell against Germany. By 1914 the war strengths of the two combinations were estimated at :

France and Russia	..	..	5,070,000
Less 500,000 for the troops outside Europe, who would be late in arriving	.. .. ..	..	4,570,000
Germany and Austria	..	..	3,358,000
Franco-Russian excess	..	..	1,212,000 [3]

[1] Montgelas, p. 106.
[2] Eckardstein, *Isolierung Deutschlands*, p. 185 note.
[3] These are the figures given by Montgelas, and, so far as I know, they are not disputed. But I make no pretensions to technical knowledge on the

This superiority in numbers of the Franco-Russian combination is reflected in military expenditure. Here are the figures : [1]

1905–9

Austria-Hungary	..	..	£105,962,783
Germany	..	..	£195,647,224
Total	..	..	£301,610,007
France	..	..	£150,530,462
Russia	..	..	£215,485,152
Total	..	..	£366,015,614

1910–14

Austria-Hungary	..	..	£128,705,624
Germany	..	..	£252,378,319
Total	..	..	£381,083,943
France	..	..	£196,817,797
Russia	..	..	£279,659,470
Total	..	..	£476,477,267

In the year 1913 both the Germans and the French increased their military strength ; and the extreme effort then put forth suggested that, on both sides, the final struggle was believed to be close at hand. The German increase was financed by a capital levy of 50 millions, an operation which, it is urged, could hardly have been repeated. The projection of this scheme dates from a memorandum by Ludendorff drawn up in December 1912. He contemplates a war in which England will side with France and Russia, while Italy would, at most, immobilise a French army on the Alps. The violation of Belgium is anticipated, and also the operation of the English Expeditionary Force.[2] The Bill required for the increase was published on March 28th, 1913, and was motived by the weakening of the German position, owing to the first Balkan war, and also by the constant increase in French armaments.

---

subject. General Seely, in the House of Commons, estimated the Franco-Russian excess at the end of 1913 at some 700,000 (Hansard, June 1913, liii. p. 900). In any case, there seems to be no doubt as to the fact of excess.

[1] Morel, *Truth and the War*, pp. 93, 94.　　　[2] Ludendorff, i. p. 57.

The French have cited, in this connexion,[1] what is alleged to be a secret German report, dated March 19th, on the strengthening of the Army. After referring to the arrangements made for the British Expeditionary Force, to a possible attack by the British Fleet, to the improvements made in the French Army, and to the weakening of Austria's position by the Balkan wars, this document says : " It is our sacred duty to sharpen the sword that has been put into our hands, and to hold it ready for defence as well as for offence. We must allow the idea to sink into the minds of our people that our armaments are an answer to the armaments and policy of the French. We must accustom them to think that an offensive war on our part is a necessity, in order to combat the provocations of our adversaries." The memorandum proceeds to emphasise the desirability of opening out relations with influential people in Egypt, Tunis, Algeria, and Morocco, as well as Russia, in order to " prepare the measures which would be necessary in the case of a European war," and it adds that : " In the next European war it will also be necessary that the small States of Europe should be conquered or neutralised." This document has since been attributed by the *Temps* to Ludendorff. Ludendorff denies the authorship and doubts the authenticity of the report.[2] Even, however, if it were genuine, it would be as absurd to infer from it the policy of the German Government as it would be to infer that of the British Government from the extravagances of Lord Fisher. The other and very different document which really was written by Ludendorff,[3] in December 1912, states that, whereas the Triple Alliance is defensive in purpose and has all the weakness of such alliances, the Triple Entente has " marked offensive tendencies,"—Russia in the Balkans and France in Alsace-Lorraine—while the British are anxious to destroy the German Fleet. We have dwelt so long and so often on the vanity of the distinction between " aggressive " and " defensive " war, that it would be superfluous to say more.

Meantime, on March 10th, eighteen days before the publication of the German Bill, the French Government distributed to the Chamber a Bill to restore the three years' service.

[1] F.Y.B., No. 2 in C.D.D., p. 130.
[2] Ludendorff, *Franzözische Fälschung meiner Denkscrift von* 1912, Berlin, 1919.
[3] *The General Staff*, i. p. 57.

Their project must therefore have been prepared before the details of the German scheme became public.[1] It has been suggested that, in fact, the measure had been decided upon during M. Poincaré's visit to St. Petersburg in August 1912. But this is conjecture.[2] The French law was so unpopular that it is thought it could not have been long maintained. In any case, it is clear that both sides were straining their resources to the utmost; and the best comment on the situation is the following, made by the Russian Ambassador in Berlin :

" France certainly does not fall behind Germany in matters of national defence. But a further increase of the French Army, apart from the difficulties attending the introduction of a three years' military service, is rendered impossible by lack of men. It is beyond doubt that Germany's extraordinary military measures will also awaken a serious echo in Russia, all the more since we cannot be deterred by any such argument as the lack of men. Now the question arises, what will be the position of Europe, armed from head to foot in an armour of steel, and groaning under the insupportable burden of military taxes ? The tension, it would appear, will become such that at length war will become inevitable. But," he adds, " no matter how terrible may be the consequences of a general conflict, the advantages in my opinion would be all on our side." [3]

The Russian increases here predicted did, in fact, occur. In 1913, the effectives were increased by 135,000, and the period of service by half a year.[4] At the same time, a loan was raised in Paris for improvements in strategic railways and roads.[5] These efforts produced the inevitable result. Thus, in March 1914 the Russian Ambassador in Berlin reports :

" The growing military strength of Russia is causing ever more serious anxiety in Berlin. In the opinion of German Government circles the new heavy siege artillery in Russia will be finished by 1916, and from that moment Russia will step into the lists as a most formidable foe, with whom Germany will have to cross arms. No wonder that, in view

[1] Montgelas, note 13, p. 235.   [2] Cf. Poincaré, p. 137.
[3] Siebert, p. 672, March 14th, 1913.   [4] Montgelas, p. 105.
[5] *Livre Noir*, ii. p. 439. Another loan was raised in January 1914, to be applied to strategic railways (Jagow, i. p. 75).

of such considerations, the Germans are straining every nerve to be ready for war with us, and no wonder that they try to intimidate us so as to avert the suspicion that Germany is afraid of Russia. Nevertheless, it is my conviction that, between all the lines printed about Russo-German relations in the German newspapers of late, one may always read fear of Russia." And then, the characteristic conclusion : " Let me express the hope that they are not in error about this at Berlin, and that we are actually taking all measures for strengthening our military power, which must compel Germany to shrink from nothing in order to bring her preparedness for war to the highest pitch." [1] The German fear of Russia seems to have affected the soldiers as well as the general public ; for, as we are informed by Eckardstein, v. Moltke said to him, in June 1914 : " Russia at the moment gives me the greatest anxiety. We must take every precaution that no sudden surprises are presented to us from that quarter." [2]

The military preparations thus publicly made by the opposing Powers were, of course, accompanied by secret arrangements of the military and naval authorities. It so happens that the text of the meetings of the French and Russian military staffs, for the years 1911–13, have been published, and the reader who is curious may refer to them to see what were the expectations and hopes of these soldiers.[3] They certainly did not anticipate defeat, nor fear the conflict. It is hardly worth our while to follow out this matter in detail, and indeed no civilian can be competent to do so intelligently. But we may note that, in 1911, the French and Russian military chiefs declare that the word " defensive " war must not be interpreted in the sense of a " war to be conducted defensively " ; that the mobilisation of the German Army will oblige Russia and France to mobilise immediately and simultaneously, without waiting for previous agreement, although this result need not be produced by a mobilisation confined to Austria or Italy ; that the first great battles will be " in Lorraine, Luxemburg, and Belgium," and (interesting to Englishmen) that " in twelve days the French Army will be ready to take the offensive against Germany with the

---

[1] Siebert, p. 711.   [2] *Isolierung Deutschlands*, p. 186.
[3] *Livre Noir*, ii. pp. 419 seq.

aid of the English Army on its left wing." [1] There occurs
also, in this protocol, the statement that Russia will not be
able to wage war against Germany "with the certainty of
success" before two years, i.e. before 1913. So much for
the sudden unexpected and unprovoked attack of Germany
upon France and Russia.

These plans of the soldiers are a necessary result of the
armed anarchy. They are always being shaped and re-shaped
behind the scenes, now, when the war to end war has been
fought, just as much as before. They are not known to the
public at home, though they are discovered by the Secret
Services of Foreign States. They are the motions of the vast
engine of destruction always silently at work beneath the
cheerful rumours of the streets. Only now and again does
some sound, more pronounced and more ominous than usual,
penetrate to the ear of the Press, and, reverberating
thence, fill the peoples with a moment's alarm. One such
occurrence, which happened just before the final crisis, it
may be well to recall to the reader. In June 1914 there
appeared, in a Russian newspaper,[2] an article with the head-
ing : "Russia is Prepared. France Must Prepare Also."
"Russia," it runs, "does not permit herself to intervene
in the internal affairs of a foreign nation, but cannot remain
merely an unconcerned onlooker during a crisis in a friendly
and allied country. If the French Parliament feels itself at
liberty to comment on such internal affairs of Russia as army
contracts, which are connected with certain economic
advantages to the contractors, Russia can certainly not
remain indifferent in the face of a purely political question,
such as the three-year term of service, which constitutes a
cause of dissension between the parties of the French Parliament. In Russia there is no divided opinion with regard to
this matter. Russia has done everything to which her
alliance with France obliges her, and she now expects that
her ally will perform her obligations as well. It is known
all over the world what colossal sacrifices have been made
by Russia to perfect the Franco-Russian alliance. The
reforms made in the Russian military departments during
the training of Russia's armed forces exceed anything that
has ever been done before in this line. The contingent of

---

[1] *Livre Noir*, pp. 420 seq.   [2] *Birshewija Wjedomosti*.

recruits for this year has, by the latest ukase of His Majesty, been *raised* from 450,000 *to* 580,000 *men, and the period of service has been lengthened by six months.* Thanks to these measures, there are in service every winter in Russia *four* contingents of recruits under arms, making an army of 2,300,000 *men.* Only the great and mighty Russia can permit herself such a luxury. Germany has at her command over 880,000, Austria somewhere over 500,000, and Italy rather more than 400,000 men. It is thus *quite natural* that Russia *should expect from France* 770,000 *men,* which is only *possible* under the *three-year term of service.* It must be remarked that these army increases in time of peace are exclusively for the purpose of effecting *rapid mobilisation.* Russia is at the same time moving on toward new reforms, to the construction of a *whole network of strategic* railways, *for the most rapid concentration of the Army in case of war. Russia wants the same thing from France,* which she can only do by realising the three-year term of service. *Russia and France want no war,* but Russia is ready and France must be ready also." [1]

II. The British Expeditionary Force

Enough has been said to illustrate the effect of armaments upon the nerves of the Continental Powers. It remains to discuss the British contribution to this general unrest and fear. That contribution was, of course, mainly naval; but it so happens that even our small professional Army played a part of some importance. We will therefore add a brief statement about the origin of the expeditionary force.

In the year 1905-6, as we saw,[2] there was risk of war between France and Germany over Morocco. In that case the British Government might also be involved. "Accordingly, as early as April 25th, 1905, Sir F. Bertie informed M. Delcassé, on Lord Lansdowne's instructions, that in the event of the German Government seeking for a port on the coast of Morocco, the British Government would be willing to join the French in strong opposition to such a proposal; and they hoped that, if the question were raised,

[1] Kautsky, p. 53. Italics as printed. I have ventured to improve the English a little.　　[2] See above, Chap. V.

they would be given full opportunity to concert with the French Government the measures which might be taken to meet it." Lord Lansdowne also suggested that " the two Governments should treat one another with the utmost confidence and discuss all likely contingencies." [1] The position became acute at the end of the year 1905, and the soldiers got to work in a manner described, in some interesting detail, by Colonel Repington.[2] He tells us that, on December 28th, 1905, the French Military Attaché, Major Huguet, dined with him. The Major was anxious about the situation, particularly in view of the change of Government in England, and the fact that Sir Edward Grey had given no assurances that he would continue the policy of Lord Lansdowne. He thought that " the Germans might attack suddenly, and probably through Belgium." Next day Colonel Repington communicated the substance of this conversation to Sir Edward Grey. He also lunched with Lord Esher and saw Sir John Fisher at the Admiralty. " The Admiral thought that the Germans would beat the French. The latter had discussed co-operation with him, but all that he wanted from them was submarines at Dunkirk. He assured me that Admiral Wilson's Channel Fleet was alone strong enough to smash the whole German Fleet, and said that he, Fisher, was prepared, on his own responsibility, to order our fleets to go wherever they might be required." On January 1st Sir Edward Grey replied to Colonel Repington, saying : " I have not receded from anything which Lord Lansdowne said to the French, and have no hesitation in affirming it." This removed the fear of a change in British policy. The soldiers went on to discuss the possibilities of a war, and the best way of meeting them. For this purpose they dined, as seems appropriate, at " The Rag." Finally, it was decided that Colonel Repington, who was a " free lance," should draw up certain questions to be submitted by Major Huguet to the French military authorities. This was accordingly done in the first week of January, the questions being shown to the French Prime Minister and to the Minister of War. The details do not concern us here ; but one seems worth

---

[1] Spender, *Life of Sir Henry Campbell-Bannerman*, ii. p. 248.
[2] Repington, *First World War*, i. pp. 1 seq. Perhaps the most pregnant thing about this book is its title, upon which I would ask the reader to reflect. It may well be prophetic.

reproducing : " Major Huguet's account of the profound astonishment of the French General Staff when he announced to them the mission on which he had come was most amusing. He found them deeply engaged upon the elaboration of an academic plan for the invasion of England, and when he told them of the friendly British invasion which some of us contemplated, their jaws dropped, their pens fell from their hands, and they were positively transfixed with surprise." All, the Colonel proceeds, went well, and the questions, with the French replies, were taken to the Defence Committee. Later, conversations took place between the chief of the Belgian General Staff and Colonel Bernardiston, with regard to the landing of a British force " on the French coast in the neighbourhood of Dunkirk and Calais, and information was given as to the strength of the force and the time it would take to transport it. But it was perfectly understood that these conversations did not bind either Government, also that the entry of the English into Belgium would only take place after the violation of [Belgian] neutrality by Germany." [1]

Nevertheless, Sir Henry Campbell-Bannerman put it on record that " I do not like the stress laid upon joint preparations. It comes very close to an honourable undertaking, and it will be known on both sides of the Rhine. But let us hope for the best." [2] Campbell-Bannerman proposed to hold a Cabinet on the French question ; but in fact it was not held. For "when Sir Edward Grey returned, ten days later, the crisis had passed, and the question of military preparations had ceased to be urgent." [3]

Now let us listen to. Mr. Churchill's comments : " This was a step of profound significance and of far-reaching reactions. Henceforward the relations of the two staffs became increasingly intimate and confidential. The minds of our military men were definitely turned into a particular channel. Mutual trust grew continually in one set of military relationships, mutual precautions in the other. However explicitly the two Governments might agree and affirm to each other that no national or political engagement was involved in these technical discussions, the fact remained that they constituted an exceed-

---

[1] See the documents printed as an appendix to the Belgian Grey Book, C.D.D. p. 354.   [2] *Life*, ii. p. 257.   [3] Ib., p. 258.

ingly potent tie."[1] And again: "Her (Germany's) open attempt to terrorise France had produced a deep impression upon French public opinion. An immediate and thorough reform of the French Army was carried out, and the entente with England was strengthened and confirmed. Algeciras was a milestone on the road to Armageddon."[2] The phrase, "Germany's open attempt to terrorise France," is tendentious and must be considered in the light of the facts we have narrated in a preceding chapter. But otherwise the passage is most significantly true.

The crisis of 1906 passed; but from it dates the British preparation for military action on the Continent. Lord Haldane was instructed, in January 1906, to take the matter in hand. He found, on going into it, that there were " great deficiencies in the British military organisation of these days," and that " it would not be possible to put in the field more than about 80,000 men, and even these only after an interval of over two months." " There was nothing for it, therefore, but to attempt a complete revolution in the organisation of the British Army at home. . . . The outcome was a complete recasting which, after three years' work, made it practicable quickly to mobilise not only 100,000 but 160,000 men; to transport them, with the aid of the Navy, to a place of concentration which had been settled between the Staffs of France and Britain; and to have them at their appointed place within twelve days, an interval based on what the German Army required, on its side, for a corresponding concentration."[3] This work was accomplished by the end of 1910. That it was proceeding had, apparently, not been communicated to the Cabinet. Yet it was clearly a very important fact, for it was a recognition, in the strongest possible form, that the British were contemplating very seriously war with Germany, while they were making no preparation of this kind for war with any other State. The fact that, from the time of the Anglo-French Entente, Germany became the potential enemy, could not be more definitely expressed.

The next crisis involving imminent risk of war between France and Germany was that of Agadir in 1911; and, as

[1] Churchill, i. p. 32. [2] Ib., p. 33.
[3] Haldane, *Before the War*, p. 32.

we have seen, on this occasion British intervention was formally threatened by Mr. Lloyd George. Following this crisis, we have a document [1] reporting a conversation with the British military attaché in Belgium, in which the latter said that " the British Government, at the time of the recent events, would have immediately landed troops on our territory, even if we had not asked for help." The Belgian General protested that his Government's consent would be necessary for this. The military attaché observed that he knew that, but that, "as we were not in a position to prevent the Germans passing through our territory, Great Britain would have landed her troops in any event." This document proves nothing, except the rashness of military men ; but such rashness, continued behind the scenes over long periods of years, may easily end in morally committing one Government, or in raising unfounded expectations in another.

In this same year, 1912, the naval arrangement was made, whereby the French Navy was concentrated in the Mediterranean and the British in the North Sea. At the same time a letter was addressed by Sir Edward Grey to the French Ambassador. It ran as follows :

" From time to time in recent years the French and British naval and military experts have consulted together. It has always been understood that such consultation does not restrict the freedom of either Government to decide at any future time whether or not to assist the other by armed force. We have agreed that consultation between experts is not, and ought not to be, regarded as an engagement that commits either Government to action in a contingency that has not arisen and may never arise. The disposition, for instance, of the French and British fleets respectively at the present moment is not based upon an engagement to co-operate, in war.

" You have, however, pointed out that, if either Government had grave reason to expect an unprovoked attack by a third Power, it might become essential to know whether it could in that event depend upon the armed assistance of the other.

" I agree that, if either Government had grave reason to expect an unprovoked attack by a third Power, or something

[1] April 1912, C.D.D. p. 360, B.G.B. App. 4 (2).

that threatened the general peace, it should immediately discuss with the other whether both Governments should act together to prevent aggression and to preserve peace, and, if so, what measures they would be prepared to take in common. If these measures involved action, the plans of the General Staffs would at once be taken into consideration, and the Governments would then decide what effect should be given to them."

This letter, it appears, was written to reassure the French. M. Poincaré tells us that " we were unable to modify the distribution of our naval forces and abandon the protection of the Channel and Atlantic coasts, unless we could be assured that, in case of peril, there would be conversations on the attitude and, if need be, on the measures to be taken." [1] Sir Edward Grey, however, maintained at the same time, no doubt with strict truth, that " no alliance was concluded between the two Powers. They fulfilled the purpose rather of putting the substance of the military agreements in the proper light, agreements which had been entered into, between the Army and Navy authorities, for the eventuality that it should become necessary for the British and French naval and land forces to co-operate actively."[2] Lord Oxford and Asquith, not content with denying that there was an alliance, goes so far as to say that " there were neither military nor naval compacts."[3] I am not skilled in these verbal subtleties; but I venture to doubt whether, if an arrangement of this kind had been secretly concluded between the military authorities of the Central Powers, either Mr. Asquith or Sir Edward Grey or the British public would have accepted so complacently their obvious innocuousness. I doubt also whether either the French or the Russians took Sir Edward's statements quite at their face value. At any rate, we have this interesting remark by Isvolski: " The Anglo-French military convention has a character as complete and finished as the Franco-Russian convention."[4] But the Franco-Russian convention was the product of an alliance, and implied close co-operation in any war in which Germany should become engaged with either party.

---

[1] Poincaré, p. 72.   Cf. Loreburn, p. 98.   [2] Siebert, p. 721.
[3] *Genesis of the War*, p. 83.   For Grey's statement to Lichnowski in July 1914, see below, p. 407.
[4] *Livre Noir*, i. p. 367, December 1912.

Whatever the facts may have been, the British public was not to know them. And when, on March 10th, 1913, Lord Hugh Cecil asked whether this country was under any obligation to send a very large armed force to co-operate in Europe, he received from Mr. Asquith the reply, short and simple : " I ought to say that it is not true." [1] " I ought to say." Perhaps he " ought " ; and literally, no doubt, what he said was true. But how different would have been the effect of the whole truth, as outlined in the preceding pages. But that truth cannot be told, and never is told, in the international anarchy ; and men who, in other relations of life, are upright and honest beyond a question, are compelled to flounder obscurely in the mephitic atmosphere of secrecy. " Splendide mendaces," does someone say ? Perhaps ! But from such splendours sprang the greatest catastrophe in history.

III. The Anglo-German Naval Competition

The military arrangements between England and France did not, it may fairly be urged, have a very important effect on the outbreak of the Great War. But it was otherwise with the naval rivalry. The building of the German fleet, which began, on a large scale, with the programme of 1900, was not the only factor in the conversion of British policy from friendship with Germany to entente with France; but very quickly the growth of the German Navy became the principal source of antagonism between the two States. " When, early in the present century," Mr. Churchill writes, " our potential enemy, for the first time, became, not France, but Germany, our naval strategic front shifted from the South to the East Coast, and from the Channel to the North Sea." [2] British opinion, reflecting on this, is apt to comment : " Well, it was all the fault of the Germans. Why did they want a navy ? " But there seems not to be very much sense in this view, unless the objector is prepared to go further and ask : " Why does any State want armaments ? " The Germans wanted a navy for the usual reasons that determine all States to arm. They had, in the first place, a large and increasing merchant marine. What was to protect it in

[1] Hansard, v. i. p. 43.   [2] The World Crisis, i. p. 144.

case of war ? Were they to remain at the mercy, so far as
their seaborne trade was concerned, of any stronger naval
Power with whom they might be engaged ? They were no
longer economically self-dependent ; and the war, when it
came, showed that a blockade could defeat them, in spite of
all military victories. That was one important reason why
Germany should build a fleet. But there were others. Being
a State with a rapidly growing population, trading all over
the world, bursting with the pride and ambition which
dominates all Great Powers, Germany wanted to have a
colonial empire. The British, one would think, should be
the last people to be surprised or shocked at that. But if a
nation intends to build up a colonial empire, it will want a
navy both to gain it and to hold it. Moreover, Germany's
policy in all overseas issues was rendered impotent by her
weakness at sea ; a fact which we find continually emphasised in the Kaiser's notes to the German dispatches.[1]
Her military force could only help her on the continent of
Europe ; and, as we have just seen, even there it was out-
numbered by the combined forces of her possible enemies. It
could not help her at all in the Pacific, or in Africa, or in China,
unless she had also a navy at least strong enough to make
other States hesitate to attack her. The British did not
require a large army because they were, or thought themselves, secured by the sea. It does not follow that Germany
did not want a navy. Her position was less fortunate than ours,
and, if she was to be a World-Power, she must pay the price.

That price would be, of course, not only the cost of the
Navy, but also the dangers and complications in which it
would involve her with foreign Powers, and especially with
England. From this point of view, no doubt, it may be
urged that it was not worth while for Germany to take the
risk ; and, in view of what has happened, many Germans
now adopt that view. But, at that time, consider the pride
of all nations ; the blind passion for size and power ; the love
of bullying and the determination not to be bullied ; the
whole complex of superficial but uncontrollable emotions
which lies, like an ocean, waiting to be stirred by every wind
let loose, by the Press, by public meetings, by societies and

[1] An interesting illustration of this fact will be found in Ger. Docs., xiv,
pp. 592, 612, etc., dealing with the Samoan dispute of 1899.

associations, by the whole apparatus erected, in every country, in proportion to its size and its power, to drive men to their own destruction and to the destruction of mankind. Let our jingoes apply to the Germans the same standards they apply at home ; and let those who are not jingoes remember their impotence among their own countrymen. They will then, I think, admit that Germany was driven to build a navy by precisely the same forces that have built up navies and armies in all countries ; that her reasons were as good, or as bad as those of others ; and that if she had to pay the price, so do all States, sooner or later, though none will learn from the experience of others.

True, the Germans could not hope to build a navy equal to that of the British. But that was not the idea. The idea was that they could build one strong enough to make it advisable for the British to transact with them rather than to fight them. The memorandum attached to their Navy Bill of 1900 defined its object as follows : " To protect the Empire's sea trade and colonies, in view of present circumstances, only one method can avail—Germany must have a battle fleet so strong that even the adversary possessed of the greatest Sea-Power will attack it only with grave risk to herself. For our purpose it is not necessary that the German battle fleet should be as strong as that of the greatest naval Power ; for as a rule a great naval Power will not be able to direct his whole striking force upon us. But even if it should succeed in meeting us with considerable superiority of strength, the defeat of a strong German fleet would so substantially weaken the enemy that in spite of a victory he might have obtained his own position in the world would no longer be secured by an adequate fleet." [1]

In the course of the debate in the Reichstag this general position was illustrated, more particularly, with reference to England. " Then the Germans intended war with England ? " Intended it ? No, they intended only to be " prepared " for it ; and, like everyone else, were ready to assume that preparation for war would prevent war. The German Fleet, so Tirpitz maintained, would even make possible a real and peaceable understanding with England.[2] This was nonsense,

[1] Cited Asquith, *Genesis of the War*, p. 71.
[2] Haller, *Aera Bülow*, p. 74. Cf. Tirpitz, *Politische Dokumente*, passim.

of course, but not more so than the talk current in all countries before the war, and since, on the theme *si vis pacem para bellum*. In fact, of course, the effect and the only possible effect of the building of the German Fleet was to intensify Anglo-German enmity, and to prepare the Great War. As to the intended weakening of the British position, by making it too dangerous for her to attack Germany, the English were the last people to permit such a contingency as that to occur. " The school of v. Tirpitz," writes Lord Haldane, " would not be content unless they could control England's sea-power. They would have accepted a two to three standard because it would have been enough to enable them to secure allies and to break up the entente. Now it was vital to us that Germany should not succeed in attaining this end." [1]

The precise date at which this English reaction began to be felt it is not possible to determine. By 1905 Lord Roberts was conducting his missionary campaign in favour of conscription, and presumably this was in view of the possibility of a German invasion. In the autumn of that year Lord Haldane visited Berlin and discussed the subject with the Kaiser. The Kaiser said : " It was natural that, with the increase of German commerce, Germany should wish to increase her fleet—from a sea-police point of view—but that they had neither the wish nor, having regard to the strain their great army put on their resources, the power to build against Great Britain." Lord Haldane replied that " the best opinion in England fully understood this attitude, and that we did not in the least misinterpret their recent progress." But, he added politely, we propose " to maintain, for purely defensive purposes, our Navy at a two-power standard." [2]

In the same year, 1906, the " Dreadnought " was invented in England, with the result, of course, that it was imitated by other Powers, and that both the danger and the cost of naval competition was enhanced, without any alteration in its intensity. " In this same sense," v. Tirpitz tells us, " I could not help asking the Reichstag for the increased financial means necessitated by the transition to the Dreadnought type, which we were compelled to build, like all other navies of the world, by the British." [3] But the British at this moment had a newly elected Liberal Government, and a need for economy ;

---

[1] Haldane, p. 139. [2] Ib., pp. 42–3. [3] *Memoirs*, i. p. 202.

the Government took its risks, and the Naval Estimates of 1906–1908 showed a slight decrease instead of the usual increase.[1] This action, however, it would seem, was taken with much misgiving. " It was impossible," says Mr. Churchill, " to resist the conclusion, gradually forced on nearly everyone, that, if the British Navy lagged behind, the gap (between it and the Germans) would be very speedily filled." [2]

Diplomacy too was anxious and at work. In 1908 King Edward visited the Austrian Emperor at Ischl, and endeavoured, if we are rightly informed, to persuade him to influence Germany in the matter of naval estimates. The Emperor, however, seems to have declined.[3] The same year he met the Tsar at Reval, and we find Sir Charles Hardinge saying to Isvolski that Sir Edward Grey desired and intended the best of relations with Germany ; but that " in spite of that, one can't shut one's eyes to the fact that, if Germany continues her naval armaments in the same quickened ratio, in seven or eight years a very disquieting and strained situation may arise. Russia will then undoubtedly be the arbiter of the situation. For this reason we desire that, in the interests of peace and of the maintenance of the balance of power, Russia shall be as strong as possible by land and by sea." [4] The reader will observe the operation of that law that has no exceptions : " Increase of armaments produces increase of armaments." In August of the same year King Edward visited the Kaiser at Cronberg, and Lord Hardinge had a conversation with the latter, of which he has published an account.[5] He tells us that he represented strongly the apprehension caused in English public opinion by the German naval programme. The Kaiser pooh-poohed this anxiety, and said that he himself controlled German policy, and that his friendship for England was well known ; instancing his action during the Boer War when, as he affirmed, he had refused to assent to a Franco-Russian proposal for a coalition against England.[6] The German Navy represented no danger to England, and

---

[1] See Hirst, p. 63, and Churchill, i. p. 39.   [2] Ib.
[3] Hoyos, *Der Deutsch Englische Gegensatz*, p. 29.
[4] Siebert, p. 479, June 18, 1908.
[5] *The Times*, November 10th, 1924. A much fuller and more amusing account is given by the Kaiser (Tirpitz, *Politische Dokumente*, p. 69). The Kaiser may have embellished, but so may the Englishman have toned down.
[6] See above, p. 51.

the programme must be carried through. It was a matter of national honour. " No discussion with a foreign Government could be tolerated ; such a proposal would be contrary to the national dignity, and would give rise to internal troubles, if the Government were to accept it. He would rather go to war than submit to such dictation." At this point the reader is invited to turn his mind back to the year 1908, when British opinion was so bitterly disturbed because the Kaiser had sent a letter to Lord Tweedmouth in which, as was believed, he had endeavoured to check the growth of the British Navy.

The Kaiser also spoke of the British invention of the Dreadnought : " It was in England that the first Dreadnought had been built, in the greatest secrecy, and on its completion Admiral Fisher and the Press had at once announced that she was capable of sinking the whole of the German Navy. These statements had forced the German Government to begin building ships of a similar type, to satisfy public opinion in Germany." Lord Hardinge concluded that the object of the Kaiser's discourse was to urge " the greater advantage to England of friendship with Germany over the understandings with France and Russia." Very possibly he was right. The Kaiser was constantly anxious for such a rapprochement and not necessarily for sinister reasons. But he was singularly unfortunate in the tactics he adopted to promote his purpose.

Turning now to Germany, we find that, in July 1908, v. Bülow, then Chancellor, circulated a dispatch in which he said : " The tension between England and Germany is more serious. England desires to limit Germany's naval armaments in order to maintain her supremacy. Germany will therefore agree to no proposals which aim at a reduction of armaments by land or sea. If England's efforts take concrete form, Germany would take up arms. Meantime the German Fleet must be further developed." [1] That was uncompromising enough. But in the same year v. Bülow resigned, and it was his successor who conducted the next negotiations with England. In October the *Daily Telegraph* published that once famous interview with the Kaiser, by which he intended to show his good will for England, but which had, like

[1] Conrad, i. p. 95.

so many of his utterances, an effect contrary to what he desired.[1]

In the year 1909 we find v. Schoen, of the German Foreign Office, saying to Isvolski that : " The only clouds on the horizon were the relations with England : in this direction the atmosphere was charged with electricity. Of course, Germany could not admit that a foreign Power should dictate the extent of her naval armaments ; but the present situation would become dangerous, if protracted, for which reason an amicable solution must be found."[2] But the amicable solution was not found, and the situation became more and more dangerous. British public opinion was stampeded into one of its periodic panics,[3] both Government and Opposition joining in alarmist language. It was stated, by those responsible, that Germany would have 9 Dreadnoughts in March 1911, and either 17, or at least 13, in March 1912. Mr. Churchill and the Chancellor of the Exchequer disputed these estimates ; and, in fact, when the time came, the German figures proved to be 5 for 1911 and 9 for 1912. Mr. Churchill comments : " The gloomy Admiralty anticipations were in no respect fulfilled in the year 1912. The British margin was found to be ample in that year. There were no secret German Dreadnoughts, nor had Admiral v. Tirpitz made any untrue statement in respect of major construction."[4] The episode is characteristic. The Admiralty makes a campaign ; the Government and the House yield ; it turns out later that all the statements made were false ; but the ships are there, the money is spent, and the pretences under which it was obtained are forgotten. All this follows naturally from the fact of the naval competition ; and no doubt the Admiralty were conscious only of having performed their duty.

IV. The Anglo-German Naval Discussions

While thus the British Government yielded to an agitation based on false data, they were anxious also to come, if they

[1] For the details of this indiscretion, which seems to have occurred through a muddle in the German Foreign Office, see Schoen, pp. 102 seq.
[2] Siebert, p. 497.
[3] See Hirst, p. 65 seq.   [4] Churchill, p. 37.

could, to some agreement with Germany. The origin of this movement seems to date from a conversation held, in June 1908, between Albert Ballin, the German shipping magnate, a personal friend of the Kaiser's, and Sir Ernest Cassel, the financier, a personal friend of King Edward.[1] Sir Ernest stated that " fear of the German danger was the driving force of the whole policy of the Entente, and the latter was in fact a means for allaying the former." The agitation of the year 1908–9 seems, for the time being, to have prevented further developments. But a year later, in June 1909, there was a second meeting between the two friends.[2] On this occasion Sir Ernest said that England must maintain her naval supremacy " at all hazards and subject to no engagements of any kind," and that she could not enter into a naval arrangement with Germany alone, since she must also consider Austrian naval increases, and " the two dark horses " Italy and Russia. After discussion, however, it was agreed that it would be useful that a few sensible men should get together and consider the whole question. By sensible men it would seem that naval experts were meant. But, as matters developed, the Chancellor was brought in as well as v. Tirpitz, and finally the discussion took place between him and Sir Edward Goschen, the British Ambassador in Berlin. The Chancellor, however, was in constant correspondence with Kiderlen-Waechter, then German Ambassador at Bucharest, and seems to have taken from him the main direction of his ideas. The discussions took much the same course as the later ones of 1912. The Germans said that the first thing to be done was to make a political agreement, if only because it would thus be easier to overcome the professional opposition of the experts. The British replied that there was little hope in a political agreement unless the tension were first relaxed by a substantial naval reduction. But this the Germans were not prepared to accept. The most they suggested was a slackening in the pace of their programme, without a reduction in its scale. They produced a draft political agreement, which would bind the parties on either side to neutrality, not only if one of them were attacked by one or more Powers, but also if one of them " in virtue of existing agreements should come into the position of declaring war on a third

[1] See Huldermann, pp. 138 seq.   [2] Ib., pp. 145 seq.

party." [1]   The Germans illustrated the contingency they had
in mind by the case of an attack by Russia either on Austria
or on Japan.   In the first case Germany, in the second England, was pledged to defend her ally.   But what, of course,
was really in the minds of both parties was the bearing of
a war between Russia and Germany upon the position of
France.   As happened in 1914, and as was easily to be foreseen, under the system of alliances, if war arose between
Austria and Russia, and Germany came in to aid the former,
France would come in to aid the latter.   What would then
be the position of England ?   Neither now, nor in 1912, was
the Government ready to bind itself to neutrality.   They
suggested, as at the later date, an agreement that neither
party should make an " unprovoked attack " on the other.
But the Germans were not satisfied, and the negotiations
came to nothing, without, so far as the available evidence
goes, any bad faith on either side.

The naval competition accordingly continued.   In 1911
Mr. Churchill became First Lord of the Admiralty, "with
the express duty to put the Fleet in a state of instant and
constant readiness for war." [2]   In the same year came the
crisis of Agadir.   Von Tirpitz tells us that, in consequence
of the German diplomatic defeat, he went to the Chancellor
and told him that he must save the situation by a Supplementary Naval Bill.[3]   The Chancellor " denied the check,
and feared that a Bill would lead to war with England."   A
long tussle followed, in which Tirpitz, though making some
concessions, adhered to his Bill.   Its coming was announced
in the Reichstag on February 7th, 1912.   The next day
Lord Haldane arrived in Berlin.

We have, by now, several accounts of the negotiations
that followed,[4] and by piecing these together we can arrive
at something not very far from the truth.   The negotiations
were preluded by an approach from the British Government,
conducted by Sir Ernest Cassel,[5] who handed to the Kaiser

[1] For text see Kiderlen-Waechter, ii. p. 67.
[2] Speech at Dundee, June 5th, 1915.
[3] *Memoirs*, i. p. 211.
[4] By Asquith, Haldane, Bethmann-Hollweg, Tirpitz, Lichnowski, Churchill,
Ballin (in Huldermann).
[5] Mr. Harold Begbie, in the *Vindication of Great Britain*, p. 133, says :
" The invitation came from Germany."   This is not borne out either by
Bethmann-Hollweg or by Haldane.   But the point is not of much importance.

a memorandum expressing the views of Sir Edward Grey,
Mr. Churchill, and Mr. Lloyd George. The memorandum
proposed, on the one hand, that British superiority at sea
should be recognised, and the German programme not
increased, but, if possible, reduced ; in return, the British
would put no obstacles in the way of German colonial expansion, but would " discuss and further their colonial wishes
in this matter ; and both Powers should affirm that they
would take no part in aggressive plans or combinations
against one another." [1] Sir Ernest took back to London a
friendly reply, except for the statement that the Germans
would adhere to their present naval programme. This,
however, it was indicated, might be modified, if proof were
given of a friendly orientation of British policy ; and the
request was made that Lord Haldane, the War Minister,
should be sent privately to Berlin. This was done, as we
have seen, early in February 1912.[2]

But as in 1909, so now, there was a different emphasis in
the minds of the German negotiators from that in the minds
of the British. Lord Haldane laid the chief stress on a
naval rather than a political arrangement. "Any agreement," he said, " for settling our differences and introducing
a new spirit into the relations of the two nations, would be
bones without flesh, if Germany began by fresh shipbuilding,
and so forced us to do twice as much. Indeed, the world
would laugh at such an agreement, and our people would
think that we had been fooled." [3] The German Chancellor,
on the other hand, considered that a political agreement
was the necessary presupposition of a naval understanding.
Both points of view are, in fact, equally intelligible and
reasonable ; for the naval and the political friction were
part of the same complex. We did not worry ourselves
about French or Russian military or naval increases. On
the contrary, we approved of them ; and the reason was,
that those States were bound to us by political understandings.
There was not, however, much prospect of such a naval

[1] Bethmann-Hollweg, p. 49. Cf. Churchill, p. 95.
[2] Incidentally it is interesting to note, as bearing on political conditions in
Germany, that the Secretary for Foreign Affairs, Kiderlen-Waechter, who had
a special interest in these matters, was away on his holiday, and took no
part in what was done. See Kiderlen-Waechter, ii. p. 155.
[3] Haldane, p. 60.

reduction as would have eased British apprehensions. When Sir Ernest Cassel returned to England from his preliminary visit to Berlin he brought with him a " fairly full statement by von Bethmann-Hollweg of the new German Navy law." [1] Mr. Churchill and the Admiralty " devoured it all night long," and reported that the " naval increases are serious, and will require new and vigorous measures on our part." From the British point of view, therefore, the new German law would have to be considerably modified, if not withheld altogether, if there were to be a naval understanding. Lord Haldane, on his arrival, took a strong line on the subject, stating, from the outset, that for every keel laid down by the Germans we should lay down two. Tirpitz " thought the two-power standard a hard one for Germany, and indeed Germany could not make any admission about it." He gave his reasons : " I could only sacrifice military values on principle in return for actual and in a certain sense final guarantees, either naval (the proportion of 2 to 3) or political (an agreement regarding neutrality)." [2] The only concession that could be elicited from Tirpitz was the " sacrifice " of one of the ships contemplated in the new law of the year 1912. In return Mr. Churchill tells us that he himself " sacrificed two hypothetical ships." [3] But he adds, without appearing to reflect upon the natural reaction in Germany, that " the splendid gift of the *Malaya*, by the Federated Malay States, raised the figure of the first year from 4 to 5," so that, in fact, the British " sacrificed " only 1 ship, not 2.

This was nothing in the way of naval reduction. That method of approach had therefore to be abandoned ; and Lord Haldane consented to enter upon the discussion of a political agreement. The difficulties arising in this matter illustrate so fruitfully the main contention of this book that they are worth dwelling upon at some little length. The Germans first brought forward a proposal substantially the same as that which they had advanced in 1909 : [4]

" 1. The High Contracting Powers assure each other mutually of their desire for peace and friendship.

[1] Churchill, i. p. 95.
[2] *Memoirs*, p. 222. The proportion of 2 to 3, more accurately of 16 to 10 was, in fact, accepted by the British, but in 1913, not in 1912.
[3] P. 108.
[4] Haldane, p. 64. Only part of this is given in Bethmann-Hollweg, p. 52.

" 2. They will not, either of them, make any combination, or join in any combination, which is directed against the other. They expressly declare that they are not bound by any such combination.

" 3. If either of the High Contracting Parties become entangled in a war with one or more other Powers, the other of the High Contracting Parties will at least observe toward the Power so entangled a benevolent neutrality, and use its utmost endeavour for the localisation of the conflict.

" 4. The duty of neutrality which arises from the preceding article has no application in so far as it may not be reconcilable with existing agreements which the High Contracting Parties have already made. The making of new agreements, which make it impossible for either of the Contracting Parties to observe neutrality toward the other beyond what is provided by the preceding limitations, is excluded in conformity with the provisions contained in Article 2."

To this Lord Haldane objected. The reason he gives is that under Article 2 [1] " we shall find ourselves, were it accepted, precluded from coming to the assistance of France should Germany attack her and aim at getting possession of such ports as Dunkirk, Calais, and Boulogne, a friendly occupation of which was so important for our island security. Difficulties might also arise which would hamper us in the discharge of our existing treaty obligations to Belgium, Portugal, and Japan." Lord Haldane suggested a fundamental revision of the draft " by confining its terms to an undertaking by each Power not to make an unprovoked attack upon the other or join in any combination or design against the other for purposes of aggression or become party to any plan of naval or military combination alone or in conjunction with any other Power directed to such an end." [2] Bethmann-Hollweg tells us that, in the discussion of these two drafts, Lord Haldane admitted that the obligation upon England contained in his own was " too weak," but that, in his judgment, the German proposal went too far. Suppose, he said, we were to attack Denmark, either to seize a naval station, or for some other object disagreeable to Germany,

---

[1] *Sic.* But Article 3 seems to be intended.
[2] See also Bethmann-Hollweg, p. 52.

Germany must have a free hand. Similarly, if Germany were to let herself go (losstürzen) against France, England could hardly remain neutral. It would seem that the Chancellor endeavoured to meet this point by altering his draft, which appears in the version given by Mr. Asquith (presumably the final one), as follows : —

" 1. The High Contracting Parties assure each other mutually of their desire for peace and friendship.

" 2. They will not either of them make or prepare to make any (unprovoked) attack upon the other, or join in any combination or design against the other for purposes of aggression, or become party to any plan or naval or military enterprise alone or in combination with any other Power directed to such an end, and declare not to be bound by any such engagement.

" 3. If either of the High Contracting Parties becomes entangled in a war with one or more Powers in which it cannot be said to be the aggressor, the other party will at least observe towards the Power so entangled a benevolent neutrality, and will use its utmost endeavour for the localisation of the conflict. If either of the High Contracting Parties is forced to go to war by obvious provocation from a third party, they bind themselves to enter into an exchange of views concerning their attitude in such a conflict.

" 4. The duty of neutrality which arises out of the preceding article has no application in so far as it may not be reconcilable with existing agreements which the High Contracting Parties have already made.

" 5. The making of new agreements which render it impossible for either of the parties to observe neutrality towards the other beyond what is provided by the preceding limitation is excluded in conformity with the provisions in Article 2.

" 6. The High Contracting Parties declare that they will do all in their power to prevent differences and misunderstandings arising between either of them and other Powers."

On this draft Mr. Asquith cites the following comment by the Foreign Office :

" These conditions, although in appearance fair as between the parties, would have been grossly unfair and one-sided in their operation. Owing to the general position of the European Powers, and the treaty engagements by which they were bound, the result of Articles 4 and 5 would have been that, while Germany, in the case of a European conflict, would have remained free to support her friends, this country would have been forbidden to raise a finger in defence of hers."

Whether this comment is justified or no it is impossible to say, since everything depends on the interpretation of the term " aggression." Formally, if Germany should be the " aggressor," England would not be bound to neutrality, and would be able, therefore, to " raise a finger " in support of her " friends," that is of France. If, on the other hand, France should be the " aggressor," then England, according to her own declarations, would not wish to support her. But as there would certainly be differences of opinion as to who the " aggressor " was, there was no knowing how the treaty might work out.[1] The animus of the Foreign Office note seems to be unjustified ; but the substance of it was true. Germany might make an " offensive-defensive " attack on France. Equally, however, France might do the same to Germany. This formula thus broke down. But the discussions were continued in London. On March 4th, as we are informed by Lichnowski,[2] Sir Edward Grey suggested to the German Ambassador the following formula :—

" England will make no unprovoked attack upon Germany and pursue no aggressive policy towards her.

" Aggression upon Germany is not the subject and forms no part of any treaty, understanding or combination to which England is now a party, nor will she become a party to anything that has such an object."

Count Metternich " thought this formula inadequate," and one can see why. When is an attack unprovoked ? Who ever admitted to having made such an attack ? What additional security, therefore, does such a pledge give ? Count Metternich proposed to substitute : " England will observe at least a benevolent neutrality should war be forced upon Germany," or " England will therefore, as a matter of course, remain neutral, if a war is forced upon Germany."

A similar difficulty arises at once. When is a war " forced

[1] Cf. Grey, i. p. 253   [2] Lichnowski, p. 270.

upon " a country ? Who is to be the judge ? Sir Edward
" explained that if Germany desired to crush France, England
might be unable to sit still, though if France were aggressive,
or attacked Germany, no support would be given by His
Majesty's Government or approved by England." " Aggressive," " Attack "—the same ambiguity. Finally, says Lichnowski, Sir Edward proposed the following formula : " The
two Powers, being mutually desirous of securing peace and
friendship between them, England declares that she will
neither make nor join in any unprovoked attack upon Germany." The difficulty remains. When is an attack unprovoked ? In making this last proposition Sir Edward seems
to have said that, while he was convinced that there would
be no trouble so long as Bethmann-Hollweg was Chancellor,
it might be different when he was succeeded by someone
else. When these remarks were communicated to the Kaiser,
he burst forth in fury. " I have never in my life heard of
an agreement being concluded with reference to one definite
statesman, and independently of the reigning sovereign.
It is clear that Grey has no idea who is master here, namely
myself. He prescribes to me who my minister must be if
I am to conclude an agreement with England." [1] The Kaiser
thereupon wrote to Count Metternich, instructing him to
say that, the British Government having departed from the
basis which Lord Haldane had put forward, the negotiations
must be considered to have failed. The Ambassador was
now to suggest a new formula, an offensive and defensive
alliance, in which France should be included. His object, he
told the Chancellor, was to put England in the wrong if
she should decline. The Chancellor was compelled to let
the Kaiser's letter go, but, himself, told the Ambassador
to say that, unless a defensive alliance could be secured,
no change could be made in the German naval law.[2] But
Metternich expressed the opinion that nothing could be done
unless the law were dropped altogether ; and so the discussions ran into the sand. On April 25th the law was laid
before the Reichstag, and on May 14th it was adopted.
    From all this complicated history what are we to con-

---

[1] Brandenburg, p. 353. Cf. Tirpitz, p. 235.
[2] Brandenburg, pp. 353–4. A draft of a letter from the Kaiser to King
George, proposing the alliance, is printed by v. Tirpitz (*Politische Dokumente*, i.
p. 331). Whether this was ever actually delivered does not appear.

clude ? There seems to be no reason to doubt good faith
on either side ; but each suspected the other of trying to
get an advantage. The Germans wanted "neutrality."
"Ah," said the English, " and then you will attack France ! "
The English agreed not to make an "unprovoked" attack.
" Thank you for nothing," said the Germans. " We want a
little more than that ! " In the then situation of Europe
confidence was impossible between these two States, even
though both of them may, in fact, have had honest intentions.
The negotiations broke down, and the naval competition was
resumed.

There is, however, another piece of evidence which seems
to prove that the final breakdown was due to the veto of
France. For Isvolski writes to Sazonoff, in the December
of 1912, as follows : " From my conversations with Poincaré
and Paléologue I have been able to learn, very confidentially,
that à propos of the famous journey of Lord Haldane to
Berlin in February of this year, Germany had made to England
a quite concrete proposition, suggesting that the London
Cabinet should take a written engagement to maintain its
neutrality, in case Germany should be engaged in a war
not provoked by Germany. The London Cabinet informed
M. Poincaré, and apparently hesitated whether to accept or
reject his proposal. M. Poincaré pronounced himself in the
most emphatic way against such an engagement ; he informed
the English Government that since there did not exist,
between England and France, any written agreement of a
general political character, the signature of such an agreement with Germany would immediately end the existing
Franco-English relations. The objection had the effect
intended, and the London Cabinet rejected the German
proposal, thus provoking great discontent at Berlin." [1]
It might be inferred from this, by a historian as hostile to
France as most English historians have been to Germany,
that the French were determined to secure English assistance,
even in a war provoked by themselves against Germany.
But I do not suggest that conclusion. The French knew,
as well as anyone else, that these phrases, " provoked " and

---

[1] *Livre Noir*, i. p. 365. Cf. ib., p. 201, where it would appear that Poincaré was not at first opposed to the negotiations, but was induced to change
his attitude by the soldiers.

" unprovoked," had no clear meaning, and they did not want further to weaken an English obligation to themselves which they thought to be too weak already. Any arrangement with Germany, such as Sir Edward apparently desired to make, would have been suspect to them. In short, the alliances and ententes made it impossible to bridge the differences between the Powers.

The naval competition, accordingly, continued, although it was seen, clearly enough, to what catastrophe it was likely to lead—" to war within the next two years," Mr. Churchill said with prophetic vision.[1] Similarly, Count Metternich, the German Ambassador, prophesies war by 1915 at latest.[2] As we saw, the British Admiralty had been shown a summary of the new German Naval Law, before Lord Haldane went to Berlin. On his return he brought with him the complete text, handed to him confidentially by the Kaiser. The Admiralty found it even more formidable than they had supposed.[3] " Discussion about the terms of a formula," says Lord Haldane, " became rather futile, and we had only one course left open to us to respond by quietly increasing our Navy and concentrating its strength in northern seas. This was done with great energy by Mr. Churchill, the result being that, as the outcome of the successive administration of the Fleet, by Mr. McKenna and himself, the estimates were raised by over twenty millions sterling to fifty-one millions."[4] This " quiet " procedure was not likely to reassure the Germans. Tirpitz indeed professes to believe that their determination to continue building had made England more tractable. He must have known as little of England as the English knew of Germany. " Silence," says Mr. Churchill, " was restored, but it was not the silence of sleep. With every rivet that v. Tirpitz drove into his ships of war, he united British opinion throughout wide circles of the most powerful people in every walk of life and in every part of the Empire."[5]

One immediate result of the continued competition was the agreement with France by which the British Navy was concentrated in the North Sea and the French in the Mediterranean. Mr. Churchill, indeed, endeavoured to maintain, and very likely Mr. Asquith and Sir Edward Grey believed,

---

[1] Brandenburg, p. 352.   [2] Cf. Huldermann's *Ballin*, p. 188.
[3] Churchill, p. 102.   [4] Haldane, p. 72.   [5] Ib., p. 115.

that this arrangement did not bind us to take the side of France when or if the war broke out. But the real truth lay in what Mr. Churchill calls his " somewhat inconsequent " admission : " Consider how tremendous would be the weapon which France would possess to compel our intervention if she could say, ' On the advice of and by arrangement with your naval authorities we have left our northern coasts defence-less. We cannot possibly come back in time.' Indeed it would probably be decisive, whatever is written down now. Everybody must feel, who knows the facts, that we have the obligations of an alliance without its advantages, and above all without its precise definition." [1] The events of 1914 were to prove the truth of this contention.

We should not, however, be warranted, by this lamentable story, in the conclusion either that England " wanted " war with Germany or Germany with England. On the contrary, negotiations continued. In 1913 the English accepted the proportion of 10 to 16. In the same year they proposed a " naval holiday," which meant, in Tirpitz's view, " one more attempt to break the neck of the Navy Bill." [2] The Germans refused. Nothing more was done towards limiting the naval competition, and the British entered the World-War with their naval predominance unchallenged.

To conclude this discussion, it may be interesting to cite two utterances of Mr. Asquith, one of 1912 the other of 1914. In July 1912, during the progress of the Anglo-German negotiations, he said in the House : " Our relations with the great German Empire are, I am glad to say, at the moment, and I feel sure are likely to remain, relations of amity and good will. My noble friend, Lord Haldane, the present Chancellor, paid a visit to Berlin early in the year. He entered upon conversations and an interchange of views there which have been continued since, in a spirit of perfect frankness and friendship, both on the one side and on the other." [3] By that date Germany had already asked for an agreement which would pledge England to neutrality in case Germany " should become entangled in a war with one or more Powers in which it cannot be said to be an aggressor." [4] Thus, whatever iniquity or deceit there may have been in the German proposal was already

---

[1] Churchill, p. 113.
[3] Hansard, xli. p. 1393, July 25th, 1912.
[2] *Memoirs*, p. 233 note.
[4] See above, p. 393.

known to Mr. Asquith when he made this statement. In October 1914, after the outbreak of the war, he said, of the same German proposal : " They wanted us to pledge ourselves absolutely to neutrality in the event of Germany being engaged in war, and this, mind you, at a time when Germany was enormously increasing both her aggressive and defensive resources, and especially upon the sea. They asked us, to put it quite plainly, for a free hand so far as they were concerned, when they selected the opportunity to overbear, to dominate the European world." [1]

V. The Naval Agreements with Russia

We will now turn from the naval relations of England with Germany to those of France and of England with Russia. In July 1912, on the initiative of Russia, an agreement was entered into between that country and France, providing for the co-operation of their naval forces in all cases where common action is provided for in the treaty of alliance, and for a monthly exchange of information.[2] In August of the same year M. Paléologue, the French Ambassador in St. Petersburg, denied to the German and Austrian Chargés d'Affaires the existence of such a convention, while recognising, in general terms, that the chiefs of the general staffs of both nations had engaged in technical conversations of the nature of which he was not aware.[3] Whether this is merely the kind of statement which is understood, in diplomacy, to mean the opposite of what it says, or whether M. Paléologue was really, at that date, ignorant of the facts, we are not in a position to determine. We gather, however, that M. Poincaré's policy looked " to the complete development of the Triple Entente in military, diplomatic, and maritime matters in the interest of the European concert." [4]

The Franco-Russian naval convention was followed by one between France and England. The negotiations between this country and Germany were regarded, as we have seen, with alarm and repugnance by the other Powers of the Entente.[5] England herself, while endeavouring to come to

---

[1] Speech at Cardiff, October 2nd, 1914, printed in *The Justice of Our Case*, Liberal Publication Department, 1914.
[2] Yellow Book, chap. iv.   [3] *Livre Noir*, i. p. 308.
[4] Ib.   [5] Cf. Brandenburg, p. 401.

terms with Germany, was also anxious to be in a position to meet her victoriously if war should supervene. Thus it was that, no sooner had the naval conversations with Germany broken down, than a naval agreement was entered into with France. In September 1912 it was arranged that the third French naval squadron should be transferred from Brest to Toulon, to reinforce French preponderance in the Mediterranean. "This decision," said M. Poincaré to Isvolski, "has been taken in agreement with England, and as an ulterior development and complement of the agreements that have already been made between the general staffs of the French and British Navies. M. Poincaré assured me that while these agreements have not yet been clothed in diplomatic form they were none the less conventions of a clearly determined character between the general staffs." [1] In the same month M. Sazonoff was in England, and visited the King at Balmoral, where he had a conversation with Sir Edward Grey. In his report upon this to the Tsar he said that he had asked Sir Edward " what we might expect from England in the case of an armed conflict with Germany." He had pointed out that, in accordance with the naval agreement of Russia with France, the French Fleet would prevent the Austrians from breaking into the Black Sea ; and he asked whether the British Fleet could render a similar service by diverting the German squadron from the Baltic coast of Russia. Without hesitating, Grey stated that, should the conditions under discussion arise, England " would stake everything in order to inflict the most serious blow upon German power." He was not clear, however, that the British Fleet could safely enter the Baltic, in case of such a war, for fear of being bottled up by the Germans. He went on to " corroborate what I already knew from Poincaré," that England had engaged herself " in case of a war with Germany " [2] to come to the assistance of France both by sea and by land.

This is the account given of the conversation at the time by Sazonoff. We have also Sir Edward Grey's account, given from memory : " I remember," he says, " being asked the question whether, supposing Britain did go to war with Germany, we should restrict action to the use of our Fleet ; and being irritated not only by its hypothetical character but because it seemed unnecessary and unreasonable, I replied, with some impatience, that, of course, if Britain decided to enter into a war against Germany, she would have to use Fleet, Army, men, money, and every resource she had. That this would be so if we were in any great war should have been obvious to anyone. To construe such words as a declaration of an intention to go to war with Germany, and still more as an obligation to do so, would have been unpardonable." [1] Nevertheless, Sazonoff may have misconceived the situation. In his report he says nothing about the war being provoked by Germany, but twice over uses the phrase " in case of a war with Germany." He goes on, moreover, to say that King George " expressed himself still more decidedly than his minister. With visible emotion His Majesty mentioned Germany's aspirations towards naval equality with Great Britain, and exclaimed that, in case of a conflict, it would have disastrous consequences, not only for the German Fleet but also for German commerce, as the English would sink every German merchant ship they got hold of." These words, the Russian Minister adds, " seem to express not only the personal sentiments of His Majesty but the predominant opinion in England with regard to Germany." [2] It is difficult to resist the conclusion that the words of Sir Edward Grey, as is so often the case in conversations, made a different, and in this case a stronger, impression on M. Sazonoff than that intended by their author. And it was this impression that was the one communicated to the Tsar. No charge lies against Sir Edward ; but the charge which we are making throughout this book lies against the whole situation. For, taking the most genial view of the position of English Ministers, the facts are these : That while, on the one hand, they are assuring Parliament and the Germans themselves that their relations to the latter are friendly and correct, on the other hand they are assuring the Russians that if war with Germany should arise (by German provocation, it is assumed) then they will stake everything to inflict the most serious blow on German power.

The next phase in this discussion, of which we have definite information, dates from April 1914. In that month

---

[1] Grey, i. p. 298.
[2] *Livre Noir*, ii. p. 347; cited also in *Is Germany Guilty?*, ii. pp. 111 seq.

Paléologue, French Ambassador at St. Petersburg, telegraphs to Doumergue, the French Minister, reporting a
conference between the Tsar and Sazonoff. The Tsar had
referred to the possibility of the outbreak of hostilities
between Greece and Turkey. If that should happen, he
said, and if Turkey should close the Straits, he would open
them by force. Germany might then interfere on behalf of
Turkey and there would be " new complications threatening
the East." It was therefore urgent to arrange for a speedy
agreement with England. It would be very useful if the
President, M. Poincaré, would mention in his interview with
King George, who was about to visit Paris with Sir Edward
Grey, the arguments which, in his opinion, make urgent a
tightening up of Anglo-Russian relations.[1] This was done ;
there was a conversation between Doumergue, Paul Cambon,
and de Margerie, representing the French, and Sir Edward
Grey and Sir William Tyrell representing the English ;
also one between Poincaré, the King and Sir Edward. The
result was immediately communicated to Isvolski, the Russian Ambassador in Paris, who reports it to Sazonoff. In
this report [2] he notes, to begin with, the communiqué given
to the Press, to the effect that the three Powers had as their
aim " not only the maintenance of peace but also stability
and equilibrium." We have already noticed that this aim
of " equilibrium " had been added to the objects of the
Franco-Russian alliance in 1899, and that the fact of its
addition implies that the maintenance of equilibrium was
something different from the maintenance of peace, and
might therefore, presumably, be incompatible with that.[3]
To this view Sir Edward Grey now acceded. After this was
settled, Doumergue approached the question of the relations between France, Russia, and England. Sir Edward
said that " he would be ready to conclude with Russia an
agreement similar to those which exist between England and
France. He did not conceal, however, from Doumergue
that there were in England, not only among the members of
the Government's party, but also in the Cabinet itself,
elements prejudiced against Russia, and little disposed to
enter into closer relations with her. He expressed the hope,

[1] *Livre Noir*, ii. p. 258 ; *Is Germany Guilty ?*, ii. p. 113.
[2] *Livre Noir*, ii. p. 259.   [3] See above, p. 108.

however, that he would succeed in inclining Asquith and the other members of the Government to share his point of view." He went on to propose the communication to the Russian Government of the existing agreements between England and France, that is (1) the military and naval conventions between the general staffs, (2) the letters exchanged between Sir Edward and the French Ambassador in London in 1912 ; [1] and he suggested that the Russian Government should be asked what they thought of a similar arrangement. The convention with the Russians, however, could only be naval, since the British Army was already committed to the defence of France. He promised, on his return, to submit the question to his colleagues. "MM. Doumergue, Cambon, and de Margerie," the report continues, "all told me that they were astonished at the firmness and precision of the words of Sir Edward Grey, when he said that he was ready for a more intimate union with Russia ; they are persuaded that, if he spoke with reserve of the probable attitude of Mr. Asquith and of the other members of the Cabinet, with regard to this agreement, it was only as a matter of form, and that, if he had not been sure beforehand of their consent, he would have refrained from making such concrete proposals."

The next thing we hear is that the British Admiralty has been told to enter into relations with the naval authorities of France and Russia in order to draw up the technical conditions of naval co-operation between the three Powers. At the same time Sir Edward takes pains to communicate to the Russian Ambassador the text of his letter of 1912, in order to make it clear that "no alliance existed between France and England, and that therefore none would be implied by the new naval convention contemplated with Russia." [2] The Ambassador communicates this to Sazonoff, who replies that "the readiness of the British Government to begin without delay negotiations regarding the conclusion of an agreement between Russia and England which would concern joint operations of our naval forces in case of a common military action, has been received, on our part with a feeling of satisfaction. In the conclusion of such an agreement we see an important step towards bringing England

---

[1] See above, p. 379.   [2] Siebert, p. 721, May 23rd.

into closer union with the Franco-Russian alliance," and he adds : " I have called the attention of our naval authorities, in particular of our naval agent in London, to the great political significance of the impending negotiations which the latter will have to carry on with the staff of the English Admiralty." [1] The word " political " in this passage seems to be of considerable importance, as indicating the view taken by the Russians of the proposed convention.

In June we hear that the Russian captain, Wolkoff, has returned from St. Petersburg, with instructions for the negotiations with the British Admiralty. In these instructions there occurs the following interesting suggestion : " In the northern theatre of war our interests demand that England should fetter as great a portion of the German Fleet as possible in the North Sea. By this means the vast preponderance of the German Fleet over our own would be equalised and perhaps permit, in the most favourable circumstances, a landing in Pomerania to be made. Should it be possible to undertake this operation, its execution would be rendered extraordinarily difficult owing to the lack of transport vessels in the Baltic. The British Government might therefore assist us considerably by rendering it possible that a certain number of merchant vessels should be sent to our Baltic ports before the beginning of warlike operations, so that the lack of transport vessels might be made good in this way." [2] This landing scheme was not in fact attempted. But it is interesting to note, on the authority of Lord Fisher,[3] that Mr. Lloyd George and Mr. Churchill " magnificently responded " to the idea of constructing a great armada of 612 vessels, which were to land a million soldiers somewhere in the Baltic.

By this date, then—June 1914—the British, French, and Russian naval authorities appear to have got to work on plans for naval co-operation in case of war with Germany. But Sir Edward is taking the same line that he took about the military and naval agreements with France. There is no " alliance " ; politically he and Parliament remain free ; only, since there is danger of war, it is necessary to be prepared to act immediately, and for this preliminary plans are

---

[1] Siebert, p. 724.
[2] Ib., p. 726; *Is Germany Guilty ?*, ii. p. 116.   [3] Fisher, p. 55.

necessary.[1]   The consultations of the naval authorities appear
to have been arranged, like the military consultations with
France in 1906, without consulting the Cabinet.   In 1906 the
reason given was the General Election ;   in 1914 it was the
" difficulties in Ireland and the Budget." [2]   Sir Edward had,
however, reported to Mr. Asquith the results of his visit to
France, and the Prime Minister had " answered that he saw
no insurmountable difficulties against carrying out the plan
proposed in Paris."   " Since then Asquith has repeated this
to Cambon himself." [3]   " It is not to be assumed," the
Russian Ambassador continues, " that all members of the
Cabinet will give their sanction to this beforehand and without
opposition.   Nevertheless, the firm determination of the real
leaders of the Cabinet will carry the day, as I do not doubt in
the least, and then the real negotiations may begin." [4]   This
was written on May 18th.   What happened later, whether the
facts were or were not communicated to the Cabinet, and on
what date, we do not know.   Lord Oxford and Asquith, who
discusses at length the Haldane Mission of 1912, says nothing
in his book about these negotiations.

The formal reservation of our freedom of action was, no
doubt, quite sincere on Sir Edward Grey's part.   But it is
clear also that, by the pressure of the other Powers of the
Entente, and by his continually yielding to it, the net was
being drawn tighter around him.   Thus, for example, the
naval arrangements with France made it necessary for him
to give the assurance, in 1914, that the British Navy would
protect the north coast of France.   Whatever he may have
thought or intended, the Entente was being transformed into
something more and more like an alliance ;   and there is
evidence that this was, in fact, the view taken, at any rate
by the Russians.   For Benckendorff, writing to his Government in 1914, says : " After the results which have just been
described (the military and naval agreements) shall have
been achieved, we, as I believe, shall have attained the main
object in view, namely, to substitute for the hitherto far
too theoretical and pacific base idea of the Entente something more tangible."   He goes on to say that he is convinced
that a formal alliance is impossible ; but " I doubt whether

[1] See, e.g., Siebert, pp. 717, 721.
[2] Ib., p. 719.   [3] Ib.   [4] Ib.

a more powerful guarantee for common military operations could be found, in the event of war, than this spirit of the Entente, as it reveals itself at present, reinforced by the existent military conventions." [1]

The new commitments were, of course, to be kept secret. Questions were asked in the House; and, replying to one of these, Sir Edward repeated an answer, given earlier by Mr. Asquith, to the effect that : " If war arose between European Powers, there were no unpublished agreements which would restrict or hamper the freedom of the Government or of Parliament to decide whether or not Great Britain should participate in a war." " That," he said, " remains as true to-day as it was a year ago. No negotiations have since been concluded with any Power which would make the statement less true. No such negotiations are in progress, and none are likely to be entered upon so far as I can judge." [2] This statement was, to say the least, ambiguous. There were, it is true, no " political " agreements, in the precise sense of the term, committing us definitely to engage in war if Germany should become engaged with Russia or France. But there were military and naval agreements of which the House was ignorant, and of which Sir Edward was determined that they should remain ignorant. I do not propose to discuss the ethics of this. I adduce it as further evidence of the incompatibility of the armed anarchy with open and straightforward dealing.

More important, however, than the suspicions of the British were those of the Germans. Rumours were circulating in their Press, and the Government had become anxious. After Sir Edward's denial in the House, as cited above, the Chancellor wrote to his Ambassador in London that the British Minister's " denial of a naval convention " (observe the interpretation naturally given to Sir Edward's words) is " very gratifying." Had the rumours been true, the result must have been most disastrous upon Russian and French and therefore upon German chauvinism. " The result might have proved incalculable. In any case, the idea of the common mission of England and Germany for the guaranteeing of peace would have been fatally endangered at the very beginning by the complications that would probably have

[1] Siebert, p. 720.   [2] Hansard, lxiii. p. 458, June 11th, 1914.

arisen." [1] This was written on June 16th. On June 24th
Lichnowski, the German Ambassador, visited Sir Edward
and thanked him for " the frank and honest statement he
made in the Lower House disavowing the rumours of an
alleged Anglo-Russian naval convention," and emphasising
the importance of maintaining that intimate contact between
the two Governments which had existed during the crisis of
1912–13. " The Minister took cognisance of my remarks
with visible pleasure and stated that he too was endeavouring
to move forward with us hand in hand, and to remain in
close touch with us concerning all matters that came up.
There existed, so Sir Edward told me, no agreements between
Great Britain and her Entente companions that had not been
made public. . . . He wished, however, to be quite frank
with me, not desiring that I should be led in any way to
misunderstand him, so that he would take this occasion to
tell me that, in spite of the facts mentioned above, his relations
with the other two allies were to-day, as always, most intimate,
and that they had lost none of their earlier cohesion. He
stood in permanently close touch with the Governments
concerned on all important matters." [2] " No agreements that
had not been made public." Everything seems to turn upon
the meaning of the word " agreement." Apparently, in Sir
Edward's view, military and naval arrangements were not
" agreements "; but, unfortunately, they were such in the
minds of the Germans, and it was precisely about them that
they were anxious. Did Sir Edward think that the Germans
would understand him as he understood himself ? Possibly ;
and possibly they did so understand him. For, on July 15th,
Jagow, the German Foreign Secretary, writes to Ballin that,
after looking into the matter, he has come to the conclusion,
" to his most intense regret, that the report of the naval
agreement has, as a matter of fact, some foundation." Lichnowski, he says, has talked to Grey, and " Grey, after some
hesitation, failed to make a complete denial. Now there is
probably behind the affair, as a matter of fact, more than
Theodor Wolff (editor of the *Berliner Tagesblatt*) knows himself,
or the good Lichnowski is willing to believe. There is actually
in negotiation between London and Petersburg a naval convention by which . . . on the part of Russia very broad

[1] Kautsky, No. 3.   [2] Ib., No. 5.

military and naval co-operation is being sought." The convention is not yet concluded, and in fact Grey has " become a little dilatory." The Russians, on the other hand, are urgent. Grey will probably not oppose the conclusion of the compact in the end, if he does not meet with opposition from his own party or the Cabinet. " Like a Pilate, he may be able to persuade himself that the transactions are not really being conducted between the two Cabinets, but between the naval authorities. I will admit that it is an open question whether the English will not act with their unique casuistry and conclude the agreement with a mental reservation not to intervene at the critical moment if it should not suit them to do so, as a casus fœderis is intentionally not provided in the convention. But even if the convention should hang indecisively in the air, it would nevertheless have the result of materially encouraging Russia's aggressive tendencies." [1] Could not Ballin, the Secretary suggested, warn his English friends, e.g. Lord Haldane, of the consequences of such action ?

Ballin thereupon proceeded to London, and on July 24th dined with Lord Haldane and Sir Edward Grey. He asked the " indiscreet " question whether there was any truth in the rumours of an Anglo-Russian negotiation. Grey replied that " the friendly relations which were the result of the Haldane Mission " were stronger than ever, owing to the co-operation of the two States (England and Germany) in the Balkan crisis ; that England, however, had come to associate herself with a group of Powers, and naturally questions came up for discussion in that group. But " that no such naval convention existed, and that it was not England's intention to agree to any such convention." [2] The veracity or otherwise of this reply I will leave to the reader's judgment.

In any case, it is clear, from the evidence before us, that the Germans knew of the negotiations ; and we can infer how they knew. Siebert, an employé in the Russian Embassy in London, was sending copies of the dispatches that came to his office to Berlin. These have since been published, and they deal in some detail with the naval conversations. The Germans thus knew of what was going on at the very moment when Sir Edward Grey appeared to be denying it. It must be admitted that this transaction was not calculated to

[1] Kautsky, No. 56.   [2] Ib., No. 254.

reassure them as to the honesty and peaceable intentions of British policy.

In conclusion, it is interesting to note the following remark by Sir George Buchanan, our Ambassador at St. Petersburg :

" I did not announce the conclusion of an Anglo-Russian naval convention, because no such convention ever existed." This might be regarded as strictly true if the convention, though in preparation, was never actually concluded. And when the Ambassador adds that " I never even entered into negotiations with the Russian Government for the conclusion of a naval convention," we must infer that it was considered safer—or perhaps more in accordance with Sir Edward's personal view of what constituted an " agreement "—that the naval staffs alone should draft the convention, although Governments must start and Governments conclude it.[1]

[1] Buchanan, *My Mission to Russia*, i. p. 186.

CHAPTER XVI

THE LAST THREE WEEKS

I. The Murder of the Archduke

WITH the murder of Serajevo we come to those last weeks which have commonly been treated as though it were in them that the menace of war first arose, and as though the catastrophe were produced merely by a one-sided act of a single Power. The previous chapters have shown how trivial and false is this idea. For years the States of Europe have been drifting down the rapids of their own purposes and passions. They have now reached Niagara ; and at this point we might arrest our study without any loss to the truth we are driving home. But since to do that might seem paradoxical, we will follow the stream until it actually plunges over the brink. In doing so we are hampered still to some extent by imperfect information. But that affects, for the most part, small and subordinate points. The main facts, by now, are clear enough. We have only to put them together.

On June 28th, 1914, the Archduke Francis Ferdinand, heir to the throne of Austria-Hungary, was murdered, with his wife, at Serajevo in Bosnia, whither he had gone to a military review. The murderers were two young Bosniaks, Austrian subjects, but Serb by race. Of what lay behind the murder little was known at the time, though much was suspected, at any rate by the Austrians. Since that date a good deal of information has been dribbling out which tends to show that members of the Serbian Government were privy to the crime.[1] But at the time of the murder there was no proof of that available.[2]

[1] See, e.g., a number of papers in *Die Kriegsschuldfrage*. Also Stanojević; also an article in the *Contemporary Review*, January 1925, by Miss Durham.
[2] See Austrian Documents, i. No. 17.

The murder of Serajevo was not an isolated event. It was the climax of a long feud. The Austro-Serbian question, as we have seen, for many years past had been a principal menace to European peace. More than once it had almost led to a general war; and the conflict, so far from being settled in 1912–13, remained acuter than ever. We have called attention on the one hand to Serbian aspirations and their approval by the Tsar, on the other to the Austrian memorandum drawn up for submission to the German Government immediately before the date of the murder.[1] It was therefore, as we now know, a thing to be expected that Austria should take this occasion to settle with Serbia once for all.[2] And from the beginning Count Berchtold, the Austro-Hungarian Minister, took that view.[3] But there was one difficulty. In 1913 Germany had refused to support her ally. Would she take the same line now? Austrian policy would be influenced, if not altogether determined, by the answer to that question.

The murder, as we have seen, took place before the Austrian memorandum had been dispatched to Germany. The memorandum was now sent, with a personal letter from the Emperor to the Kaiser, and reached Berlin on July 5th.[4] What the Emperor felt on hearing the news of the Archduke's murder is indicated by the phrase cited by Conrad: " Everyone dies; I alone cannot die." [5] In his letter he said: " The outrage upon

[1] See above, pp. 350 seq.
[2] There were rumours that Austria and Germany had already determined to attack Serbia, at the interview between the Kaiser and the Archduke, held at Konopischt early in June. Mijatovitch says that, on that occasion, " warlike action was decided on," and that the assassination of the Archduke merely gave a plausible pretext for action " which was decided on some time beforehand " (*Memoirs of a Balkan Diplomatist*, p. 247). The Serbian historian Stanojević says (p. 54) that similar information was given to the Serbian conspirator, Dimitrievic, by the Russian General Staff. Poincaré also suggests that the manœuvres at Serajevo were intended as a jumping-off ground for this enterprise (*Origins of the War*, pp. 158–9). Jagow denies the statement (p. 101 note). But his assertion that the object of the interview was to show the Kaiser the Archduke's roses is not very convincing. Conrad tells us, on the authority of the old Emperor of Austria-Hungary, that the latter commissioned the Archduke to ask the Kaiser whether " we could count unconditionally on Germany in the future "; and that the Kaiser evaded the question (iv. p. 36). It seems pretty clear that if there were anything in the story, the murder would have led at once to immediate war without any ultimatum. If the Russian General Staff did really give Dimitrievic the information, it seems natural to suppose either that they were misled, or that they had their own objects. Cf. *Kriegsschuldfrage*, January 1925, p. 20; March 1925, p. 70; June 1925, p. 355.
[3] Aust. Docs., i. No. 3.
[4] Ib., i. No. 1.
[5] *Aus meiner Dienstzeit*, iv. p. 37.

my nephew is the direct consequence of the agitation carried on by the Russian and Serbian pan-Slavists, whose only aim is the weakening of the Triple Alliance and the breaking up of my Empire. According to all inquiries hitherto made, the Serajevo murder was not the bloody deed of a single individual, but a well-organised plot, the threads of which can be traced to Belgrade; and even if, as seems likely, it should be impossible to prove the complicity of the Serbian Government, there yet can be no doubt that its policy, aiming at a union of all the South Slavs under the Serbian flag, encourages such crimes as these, and that the continuation of this state of affairs forms a lasting danger to my dynasty and my countries." Apart from the assumption of the complicity of the Serbian Government, which at that time was not proved, this is a plain statement of a plain fact. Serbian aspirations were incompatible with the continuance of the Austro-Hungarian Empire; and the murder of the Archduke was connected with these aspirations, from whatever source it may have originated.

II. German Policy

The Emperor was preaching to the converted. For on the margin of a dispatch in which the German Ambassador at Vienna described his efforts to enjoin caution upon the Austrian Government the Kaiser had already written : " Let Tschirschky be good enough to drop this nonsense ! The Serbs must be disposed of, and that soon—right soon ! " [1] And though, at his first reception of the note, he maintained a cautious attitude, saying that, in view of possible European complications, he must consult his Chancellor, after lunch he authorised the Austrian Ambassador to say to his master that, should war result between Austria and Russia, Germany would stand at the side of her ally. Only, he added, let Austria act quickly, for this was the favourable moment.[2] On the afternoon of the same day he discussed the situation with the Chancellor, Béthmann-Hollweg, and with the Under-Secretary of State, Zimmermann. He repeated what he had said to the Ambassador, and found, as he had anticipated, that the Chancellor agreed with him. Francis Joseph must be assured of German support in case of war ; but it was not the business

[1] Kautsky, No. 7.   [2] Aust. Docs., i. No. 6.

of Germans to dictate to him what steps he should take. Their business was to prevent the conflict between Austria and Serbia from developing into a European war.[1]

The German position was thus taken definitely at the outset. Perhaps the best exposure of its motives is to be found in a dispatch sent a fortnight later by the Secretary of State to the Ambassador in England. This may be conveniently cited here :

" Austria, which has forfeited more and more prestige as the result of her lack of vigour, hardly counts any longer as a really Great Power. The Balkan crisis weakened her position still further. Our group of allies has also been weakened by this retrogression of Austria's position as a Power.

" Austria no longer intends to tolerate the sapping activities of the Serbians, and just as little does she intend to tolerate longer the continuously provocative attitude of her small neighbour at Belgrade—see the talk in the Serbian Press— and that of Mr. Pashitch. She fully realises that she has neglected many opportunities, and that she is still able to act, though in a few years she may no longer be able to do so. Austria is now going to come to a reckoning with Serbia, and has told us so. During the whole Balkan crisis we mediated successfully in the interest of peace, without forcing Austria to passivity at any of the critical moments. The fact that, notwithstanding that, we have often, with injustice, been accused of trimming and shuffling, makes no difference to me. Nor have we at the present time forced Austria to her decision. But we neither could nor should attempt to stay her hand. If we should do that, Austria would have the right to reproach us (and we ourselves) with having deprived her of her last chance of political rehabilitation. And then the process of her wasting away and of her internal decay would be still further accelerated. Her standing in the Balkans would be gone for ever. You will undoubtedly agree with me that the absolute establishment of the Russian hegemony in the Balkans is, indirectly, not permissible, even for us. The maintenance of Austria, and, in fact, of the most powerful Austria possible, is a necessity for us both for internal and external reasons. That she cannot be maintained for ever,

[1] Kautsky, No. 15; Aust. Docs., i. No. 11; Bethmann-Hollweg, *Betracht ungen*, i. p. 135.

I will willingly admit. But in the meantime we may perhaps be able to arrange other combinations.

" We must attempt to localise the conflict between Austria and Serbia. Whether we shall succeed in this will depend first on Russia, and secondly on the moderating influence of Russia's allies. The more determined Austria shows herself, the more energetically we support her, so much the more quiet will Russia remain. To be sure, there will be some agitation in Petersburg, but, on the whole, Russia is not ready to strike at present. Nor will France or England be anxious for war at the present time. According to all competent observation, Russia will be prepared to fight in a few years. Then she will crush us by the number of her soldiers ; then she will have built her Baltic Sea fleet and her strategic railroads. Our group, in the meantime, will have become weaker right along. In Russia this is well known, and they are therefore determined to have peace for a few years yet. I readily believe your cousin Benckendorff [1] when he says that Russia wants no war with us at present. Sazonoff assures us of the same thing, but the Government of Russia, which is still attached to peace and half-way friendly to Germany to-day, is constantly growing weaker, while the feeling of the Slavic element is becoming more and more hostile to Germany. Russia's fundamental treatment of us was clearly indicated last fall. During the Balkan crisis she could not thank us enough for our peaceful influence. But no sooner had the crisis passed than her unfriendly behaviour recommenced—on account of Liman, etc. If we cannot attain localisation (of the conflict) and Russia attacks Austria, a casus fœderis will then arise ; we could not throw Austria over then. We stand in the midst of an isolation that can scarcely be called ' proud.' I desire no preventive war, but if war should come we cannot hide behind the fence.

" I still hope and believe, even to-day, that the conflict can be localised. In this matter the attitude of England will prove of great significance. I am fully convinced that local opinion in that country will not be enthusiastic over Austria's procedure, and I admit that all your arguments in this line are correct. But we must do all that is possible to prevent her becoming too enthusiastic in the Serbian cause, for it is

[1] Russian Ambassador in London.

a long road from either sympathy or antipathy to the fanning of the flames of a world conflagration. Sir Grey [*sic*] is always talking of the balance of power represented by the two groups of Powers. It should, therefore, be perfectly obvious to him that this balance of power would be utterly destroyed if we should desert Austria and she should be demolished by Russia, and also that the balance of power would be made to totter considerably by a world conflagration. Therefore, if he is honourable and logical, he must stand by us in attempting to localise the conflict. But now, satis superque ; it is one o'clock in the morning. If these arguments in favour of our policy are, perhaps, not sufficient to convince you, I know, nevertheless, that you will stand behind them." [1]

From this important document certain things emerge clearly. First, though Germany will not dictate to Austria, she will leave her a free hand to deal with Serbia as she thinks right ; for her maintenance as a Great Power is necessary, at any rate for the present, in Germany's own interest. Next, Germany must try to " localise " the conflict, that is, to confine it to Austria and Serbia ; and this, it is believed, will be possible, for Russia is not yet ready to strike. Thirdly, if war should result between Austria and Russia, Germany must, in self-defence, support Austria. Lastly, " the attitude of England will prove of great significance." [2]

---

[1] Kautsky, No. 72, p. 135 ; Jagow, *Untersuchungs-ausschuss*, Beilage i. p. 27.

[2] What the Germans really thought about the chances of war with England is not very clear, probably because their guesses oscillated, as guesses will. There is a very strong passage in a dispatch from the Bavarian Ambassador in Berlin (Kautsky, App. 8, No. 2, p. 618), which says that in the opinion of the Under-Secretary of State, both England and France will exercise a pacifying influence on Russia, since neither wants a war " at the present moment." England, on the other hand, would " scarcely permit " the destruction of Serbia. " A war between the Dual Alliance and the Triple Alliance would be unwelcome in England at the present time, if only in consideration of the situation in Ireland. Should it, however, come to that, according to all opinion here, we should find our English cousins on the side of our enemies, inasmuch as England fears that France, in the event of a new defeat, would sink to the level of a Power of the second class, and that the ' balance of power,' the maintenance of which England considers to be necessary for her own interests, would be upset thereby." This view was very close to the facts, so far as England is concerned. On the other hand, the evidence seems to be that, in this initial stage, war with England was not regarded by the Germans as a very serious possibility, though a possibility it clearly was. Cf. Conrad (*Aus meiner Dienstzeit*, iv. p. 157), who says that it was hoped and expected that England would remain neutral. See also Aust. Docs., i. No. 15 (July 12th), where it is said that the German Government believes it has clear indications that England would not take part in a war arising out of a Balkan question, even if Russia and France should be involved.

The position is, not that Germany wants a European war, but that, on the contrary, she must endeavour to avoid it. She cannot, however, shrink from war with Russia, if Russia should insist on intervening. This attitude was maintained, as we shall see, up to July 28th.

Further, Germany attached great importance to secrecy and rapidity of action, so that the other Powers might be taken by surprise and brought face to face with an accomplished fact, before they had time to consult as to what they should do. In this way, it was hoped, the crisis might be over and its results accepted before it could develop European complications. For this reason the Kaiser was advised not to abandon the trip to the North Sea which had been already arranged. He left Berlin on July 6th ; but before his departure he interviewed several military and naval officers. These interviews, later, became involved in the propaganda of the Entente, whose Press maintained that a Council had been held at which war had been decided upon. There seems to be no ground for these assertions. What happened was that, on the afternoon of the 5th and the morning of the 6th, the Kaiser had a series of conversations with various highly placed officers, though not with either v. Moltke or v. Tirpitz, the heads of the Army and the Navy, both of whom were away on leave and neither of whom was recalled. He informed those whom he interviewed of the attitude adopted towards the Serbian crisis. He made it clear that he did not anticipate the intervention of Russia ; but since such intervention was possible, and since it might be supported by France, it was well that the minds of the soldiers and sailors should be prepared. No mobilisation, nor preliminaries thereto, followed these conversations. But the Navy accelerated the completion of some ships already in course of construction, replenished its stock of coal, and sent a ship of war down the Kiel Canal. The Admiralty also arranged with the Foreign Office that they might be warned in time to recall the Fleet to home waters if a conflict with England should loom in sight.[1] No special military preparations seem to have been made. " The regular mobilisation work had

---

[1] Cf. Kautsky, No. 125. The Fleet on July 25th was off Norway (see Tirpitz, *Memoirs*, i. p. 253).

been concluded on March 31st. The Army was always ready." [1]

We must now turn back from Germany to Austria. On July 7th there was held at Vienna a Crown Council of which we have the minutes.[2] Count Berchtold, opening the proceedings, reported that " the conversations at Berlin had led to a very satisfactory result, inasmuch as both the Kaiser Wilhelm and Herr Bethmann-Hollweg had assured us most emphatically of the unqualified support of Germany in case of military complications with Serbia." This meant, of course, support in case of war with Russia, which, as Count Berchtold plainly said, might be the consequence of trouble with Serbia. But since Russia was planning a coalition of the Balkan States against Austria, the " logical " course was to anticipate her by quick action against Serbia, and thus to arrest the whole design. We see from this how important to Austria was the promise of German support,[3] and how clearly the possibility of Russia's intervention was foreseen by her Government.

In the discussions that followed two questions were raised. First, whether war against Serbia should be definitely determined upon, or whether a diplomatic humiliation would suffice. The general opinion was in favour of the former course ; but Count Tisza, the Minister-President of Hungary, urged that demands should first be made upon Serbia which, though hard, should not be impossible for her to accept ; only if she refused to accept should military action follow.

[1] General Waldersee, Kautsky, *Preliminary Remarks*, p. 48. See the reports of the officers concerned, in the *Untersuchungs-ausschuss*, and also the documents cited in Kautsky, *Preliminary Remarks*, p. 46 and Supp. 8.

[2] Aust. Docs., i. No. 8.

[3] Cf. Conrad, *Aus meiner Dienstzeit*, iv. pp. 36 seq., and Hoyos, *Der Deutsch-Englische Gegensatz*, p. 78 : " Count Berchtold was not an unconditional supporter of immediate war against Serbia, any more than was the Emperor Francis Joseph. What he wanted to avoid was new tension in the international situation caused by a threat on our part, as had happened in 1908 and 1912, which, nevertheless, should not result in a final settlement of the Serbian question. We could not endure any longer the continual unrest caused by our Serbian neighbour. The repeated mobilisations of our reserves threatened to undermine discipline in the Army, trade and industry stood still, and it seemed to all parties, at that moment, that war was preferable to preparedness for another six years." I cite this because of the important last sentence, showing clearly, as everything shows, how preparation for war brings war about. There can be no doubt, so far as all the evidence goes, that once Austria had received carte blanche from Germany, she was determined to have her war with Serbia, and that, even after Germany had turned round and was trying desperately for peace.

Referring to the possibility of a European war, Tisza pointed out that it would be a " frightful calamity under present circumstances." Later the situation might be better. Russia, for instance, might be diverted to the Far East and Bulgaria be secured as an ally.

The other question discussed was the treatment of Serbia in case of war. Berchtold held that, having regard to the attitude of Russia, the kingdom might be " diminished " but not annihilated. Tisza agreed, but added that in no case could he consent to the annexation of territory by Austria, for he did not think it wise that yet more Serbians should be incorporated in the Dual Monarchy. The general opinion of the Council was that action against Serbia must be rapid ; that mobilisation should not precede, but follow, the presentation of the demands ; but that these demands should be such that Serbia could not accept them, so that an ultimatum and war must ensue.

The next day, Count Tisza had an interview with the Emperor, in which he urged once more the position he had taken up at the Council.[1] War against Serbia, he said, would involve Russia, and that would mean a world-war. The demands should not therefore be so conceived as to make war inevitable ; and if war should follow, it must be clear that it had not been provoked by Austria. The note to Serbia should therefore be couched " in a moderate, not a threatening, tone." Then, if she refused to accept the demands, the responsibility would rest on her. It is evident that Count Tisza had a clearer sense of the realities of the situation than his colleagues. But he was, apparently, in a minority of one, and he gave way to the majority. By July 14th complete agreement was reached as to the character of the demands to be presented to Serbia. A draft of the note was then made,[2] and the text was finally adopted at a Crown Council held on the 19th.

At this Council war against Serbia was taken for granted, and the discussion of her fate was resumed. Count Tisza insisted once more on his view that " no inch of Serbian territory must be annexed by Austria." Count Berchtold agreed that " as things now are " Austria should not annex. She should content herself with distributing Serbian territory

---

[1] Aust. Docs.. i. No. 12.　　　　[2] Ib., i. No. 19.

to Bulgaria, Greece, Albania, and perhaps also Roumania. In this way Serbia might be so diminished as to be no longer dangerous. But no one could tell how affairs in the Balkans might shape. The States referred to might become hostile, in which case it would be necessary, if Serbia were to be properly reduced, for Austria to annex the territory herself. Count Tisza, however, adhered to his view, and finally, on his proposition, it was decided to announce, when the war began, that " the monarchy is waging no war of conquest and does not intend to incorporate the (Serbian) kingdom." But it was made clear that " of course strategically necessary corrections of frontiers and the diminution of Serbia to the advantage of other States, as well as such temporary occupations of Serbian territory as may be necessary, are not excluded by this resolution." [1] There remained the question of the date when the demands upon Serbia should be presented. The day fixed was the 23rd,[2] and it was selected in order that the contents of the note might not become known before the French President, who was about to visit St. Petersburg, had started on his journey home. So punctilious, indeed, was the procedure on this point that the time of presentation was altered, later, from 5 to 6 p.m., for fear the news should reach the President before his departure.[3]

III. Germany and the Ultimatum

As we have seen, the German Government had taken the line that the note must be drafted independently by Austria. Nevertheless, the German Secretary of State was very anxious to see the text before anyone else. He was continually pressing this point upon the Austrian Ambassador in Berlin,[4] as well as upon the German Ambassador in Vienna,[5] who in turn presses it upon the Austrian Government.[6] As early as July 12th the Ambassador announces, on the authority of Berchtold, that the note will include a demand for a proclamation by the King forbidding the Greater Serbian propaganda and for the admission of an Austrian authority to

---

[1] Aust. Docs., i. No. 26.   [2] Ib., i. No. 26.
[3] Kautsky, Nos. 93, 96, 112, 127.
[4] Untersuchungs-ausschuss, p. 28.   [5] Kautsky, Nos. 77, 83.
[6] Aust. Docs., i. Nos. 39, 40.

supervise this condition.[1] On the 18th the Bavarian Chargé d'Affaires at Berlin reports to his Government, on the authority of v. Jagow, that the note will contain the following demands : [2]

1. The issuing of a proclamation by the King of Serbia which shall state that the Serbian Government has nothing to do with the Greater Serbian movement, and fully disapproves of it.

2. The initiation of an inquiry to discover those implicated in the murder of Serajevo, and the participation of Austrian officials in this inquiry.

3. Proceedings against all who have participated in the Greater Serbia movement.

A respite of forty-eight hours is to be granted for the acceptance of these demands. " It is perfectly plain," the report proceeds, " that Serbia cannot accept any such demands, which are incompatible with her dignity as a sovereign State. Thus the result would be war."

Whether this last sentence is quoted from v. Jagow, or whether it is a comment by the writer of the dispatch, is not clear. But in any case thus much was known in Berlin, on the 18th, about the contents of the note, although the text was not finally adopted in Vienna until the following day. In the same letter the Bavarian Chargé d'Affaires adds : " They are of opinion here that Austria is face to face with an hour of fate, and for this reason they declare here, without hesitation, in reply to an inquiry from Vienna, that we would agree to any method of procedure which they might determine on there, even at the risk of a war with Russia." [3] It is clear from all this that precisely those demands of the Austrian Note which were least acceptable to Serbia were, in fact, known to v. Jagow as early as the 12th, and that he made no protest. He hardly could, indeed, since Austria was taking precisely the action recommended to her by Germany. This, however, did not prevent him, on July 20th, from telling the Serbian Chargé d'Affaires that he " was not acquainted with the demands which Austria-Hungary intended to make." [4]

[1] See a letter from Tschirschky, cited *Untersuchungs-ausschuss*, p. 119.

[2] Kautsky, Supp. IV, No. 2, p. 616.

[3] Ib. For further extracts from Bavarian dispatches, cf. *Untersuchungs-ausschuss*, No. 36, p. 89.

[4] Kautsky, No. 91.

The final text of the note was delivered to Tschirschky, in Vienna, on the 21st, and forwarded by him, by post, to Berlin, which it reached on the 22nd.[1] Almost at the same time it was handed to the Foreign Office in Berlin by the Austrian Ambassador.[2] On the evening of the 22nd v. Jagow told the Austrian Ambassador that he thought the note "too strong in form and content." The Ambassador replied that it was too late to alter it, as it had already gone to Belgrade and would be presented there next morning. This, as v. Jagow remarks, was an " error " on the part of the Ambassador, since it was not to be presented till the evening of the 23rd at 6 p.m. Von Jagow goes on : " I expressed to the Ambassador my astonishment that the communication was too late for us to take action about it." [3] On the honesty of this the reader will form his own opinion. But there is no doubt that what followed was a case of the lie direct. On the 23rd v. Jagow telegraphed to the German Ambassador in London that " we are not acquainted with the Austrian demands." [4] On the 24th (or 25th) he " repeated very earnestly " to the British Chargé d'Affaires at Berlin that, " though he had been accused of knowing all about the contents of that note, he had in fact had no such knowledge." [5] On the 24th he informed the Italian Secretary for Foreign Affairs that " we are not informed in detail about the Austrian Note, nor do we wish to be," [6] and on the same day he directed the German Ambassadors in Paris, London and St. Petersburg to say that " we exercised no influence of any kind with regard to the contents of the note and had as little opportunity as any other Power to adopt an attitude in connexion with it before its publication." [7]

There is thus no doubt as to the attitude of the German Government. Whether or no their representatives abroad were fully informed, we do not know ; but on the 21st the Chancellor had sent a note to St. Petersburg, repeated on the 22nd to Paris and London, in which the Ambassadors were instructed to say that " neither the procedure nor the demands

---

[1] Kautsky, No. 106. The statement of Count Wedel, in Kaut., Supp. 9, p. 652, is therefore inaccurate.
[2] Zimmermann, in the *Untersuchungs-ausschuss*, p. 33, and Jagow, ib., p. 30.
[3] Ib., p. 30, of Bethmann-Hollweg, *Betrachtungen*, p. 139.
[4] Kautsky, No. 126. [5] B.B.B., No. 18.
[6] Kautsky, No. 145. [7] Ib., No. 153.

of the Austro-Hungarian Government can be regarded as otherwise than moderate and proper," and that, if they are not accepted, that Government " would have no alternative except to exert strong pressure, which may take the form of military measures." [1] Presumably these instructions were intended to be fulfilled after the delivery of the note, and they imply a knowledge of its contents. Yet, on the 26th, v. Schoen in Paris " affirmed that Germany had been ignorant of the text of the Austrian Note and had only approved it after its delivery " ; [2] and on the 25th, in St. Petersburg, Pourtalès, with his Austrian colleague, published a note in the Press, stating that the German Government had not influenced the Austrian Note nor known beforehand what its terms were.[3] The determination to keep the Powers of the Entente in the dark was certainly carried out with thoroughness.

IV. Serbian Policy

Meantime, during these days June 28th to July 23rd, what were the other Powers about ? We will speak first of Serbia, though here the records are very imperfect. The Government, of course, repudiated all responsibility for the murder ; and the documents published turn mainly upon the Serbian Press propaganda, which is explained as being evoked in response to that of Austria. The Press on both sides was doing its best to inflame passions, and we need not attempt the hopeless task of determining on which side the principal blame lay. That the Serbs were as much in the dark as other States as to the contents of the expected Austrian Note seems clear from a dispatch by the Serbian Minister at Vienna, in which he says : " It is very difficult, indeed almost impossible, to ascertain here anything positive as to the real intentions of Austria-Hungary. The word has been passed round to maintain absolute secrecy about everything that is being done." But the Minister fears the worst. " The general conviction prevails here that it would be nothing short of suicide for Austria-Hungary once more to fail to take advantage of the opportunity to act against Serbia. It is believed that the two opportunities previously missed—the annexation of Bosnia and the Balkan

[1] Kautsky, No. 100.   F.Y.B., No. 57.   [3] Pourtalès, p. 21.

War—have been extremely injurious to Austria-Hungary. In addition, the conviction is steadily growing that Serbia, after her two wars, is completely exhausted, and that a war against Serbia would, in fact, merely mean a military expedition to be concluded by a speedy occupation. It is also believed that such a war could be brought to an end before Europe could intervene." [1] In view of this situation the Serbian Government took the view that, while they would meet any reasonable demands of Austria-Hungary dealing with the question of the murder and with the punishment of any individuals on Serbian territory who might be proved to have been responsible, yet " if Austria transported the question on to the political ground and said that Serbian policy, being inconvenient to her, must undergo a radical change, and that Serbia must abandon certain political ideals, no independent State would or could submit to such dictation." [2] This sentence raises the whole issue. The " political ideals " cherished by Serbia involved the destruction of the Austro-Hungarian Empire; and it was precisely to put an end to that ambition that Austria was preparing her action. The " ideals " of the two States were incompatible, and while they adhered to them on both sides there was no possible solution except war.

V. Russian Policy

Next, let us consider Russia, on whose policy everything turned, since upon it depended the answer to the question whether or no an Austro-Serbian war should develop into a world-war.

Sazonoff, the Foreign Minister, was much disturbed from the beginning. As early as July 6th, the day before the Austrian Council was held, he " pointed out in a friendly way " to the Austrian Chargé d'Affaires " the disquieting irritation which the attacks of the Austrian Press against Serbia are in danger of producing in this country." " No country," he said, " has had more to suffer than Russia from crimes prepared on foreign territory. Have we ever claimed to employ, in any country whatsoever, the procedure with which your

[1] S.B.B., No. 31.
[2] B.B.B., No. 30. Cf. Kautsky, No. 86, and S.B.B., No. 30.

papers threaten Serbia ? Do not embark on such a course." [1]
On the 13th the German Ambassador at Petersburg reports
that " M. Sazonoff, when I spoke to him about the assassination
for the first time, dwelt only briefly upon a condemnation
of that crime, while he could not find enough words with
which to criticise the behaviour of the Austro-Hungarian
authorities for permitting the excesses against the Serbs." [2]
As to the assumption that the murder was the result of a
Greater Serbian plot, nothing, he said, had been proved, and
it was unjustifiable to hold the Serbian Government responsible. " Russia would many times have had the same right
to call the French Government to account for assassinations
that were planned on French soil and carried out in Russia."
Pourtalès thereupon remarked that the murder was a warning
to all monarchies to bear in mind their common interests
and the common dangers by which they were threatened."
But this suggestion appears to have left Sazonoff rather cold ;
" a restraint," says the Ambassador, " that can only be
explained by the unmitigable hatred of the Minister for
Austria-Hungary, a hatred which is absolutely clouding more
and more all clear and calm judgment here." [3]

On the 18th the Minister declared that he could not
tolerate an Austrian ultimatum to Serbia. [4] By the 21st
he had become " quite anxious." He vented his wrath, " as
usual," says the German Ambassador, on Austro-Hungarian
policy. He was ready to admit that the Emperor and Count
Berchtold were friends of peace ; but " there were powerful
and dangerous elements at work which were constantly gaining
ground in both halves of the Empire, and which did not
hesitate at the idea of plunging Austria into a war, even at
the risk of starting a general world conflagration." He mentioned, particularly, Count Forgach, an " intriguer of the
basest sort," and Count Tisza, " who is half a fool." It is
interesting to hear what diplomats say of one another when
they are talking frankly. There seems no reason to quarrel
with the description of Count Forgach. As to Count Tisza,
he may indeed have been " half a fool," but on this occasion,
as we have seen, he was the one man who tried, and tried
in vain, to temper Austrian policy. To Sazonoff's outburst

---

[1] F.Y.B., No. 10. [2] Exclamation point by the Kaiser in the margin.
[3] Kautsky, No. 53. [4] Oman, p. 18.

Count Pourtalès riposted with his view of the Serbs and their agitation, his remarks on that subject being commented later, in the margin, by approving exclamations from the Kaiser. Sazonoff continued excitedly, saying that, in any case, Austria-Hungary, if she was absolutely determined to disturb the peace, ought not to forget that in that event she would have to reckon with Europe. Russia could not look on indifferently at a move at Belgrade which aimed at the humiliation of Serbia. " La politique de la Russie," he concluded, " est pacifique mais pas passive." [1] Yet on this same day Count Benckendorff is saying in London that " nobody in Russia was thinking of war ; the armaments were purely the result of all the surplus and improved finances. Therefore it was much to be regretted that ill-feeling which was wholly unjustified and was based only on scandal and false reports could arise. Frank talk would probably lead quickest to the object desired. Belgrade was being pacified as much as possible." [2] That Belgrade was in fact being " pacified " seems to be true. But also it must have been dawning on the German Government, after receiving the reports of Pourtalès, that the prospect of localising the war was very dim.

VI. French Policy

We will turn next to France. M. Poincaré, as we have seen, had given his word to Russia, in 1912, that he would support her in a war arising out of German aggression in the Balkans.[3] It so happened that, just at this time, he had arranged to visit Russia ; and that, as we have seen, was the reason why the presentation of the Austrian Note was delayed. The President sailed from Dunkirk on the 16th, reached Cronstadt on the 20th, and left, on his return journey, on the afternoon of the 23rd. He was quite in the dark as to what was brewing in Austria-Hungary, but also, and therefore, anxious. M. Paléologue, the French Ambassador at St. Petersburg, has described, with the gusto of a melodramatic novelist, the tense and enthusiastic atmosphere of those days. On his way to Cronstadt to meet the President he lunched with the Tsar on his yacht, and had a conversation with him as follows :

[1] Kautsky, No. 120. [2] Ib., No. 85. [3] See above, p. 331.

" One question," the Tsar said, " occupies me above all others : our Entente with England. We must get her to enter into alliance with us. It would be a pledge of peace."

" Yes, sire ! The Triple Entente cannot be too strong if it is to preserve the peace."

" I am told that you are anxious about the intentions of Germany."

M. Paléologue replied that he was anxious.

The Tsar reflected a moment, then : " I cannot believe that the Kaiser Wilhelm wants war. . . . If you knew him as I do, if you knew all the charlatanism there is in his attitudes ! "

Whereto M. Paléologue : " Perhaps I do too much honour to the Kaiser when I consider him capable of willing or even of accepting the consequences of his gestures. But if war were threatened, could he or would he prevent it ? No, sire, in all sincerity I do not think so."

The Tsar remained silent, took a few puffs at his cigar, then said in a firm tone of voice :

" It is all the more important that we should be able to count upon the English in case a crisis arises. Unless she has completely lost her reason, Germany will never dare to attack Russia, France, and England together."

There follows a romantic account of the scene as the French warship, bearing the President, comes into view. " The spectacle is magnificent. In a vibrating silver light, on waves of turquoise and emerald, the *France*, leaving a long furrow behind her, advances slowly, then stops majestically. The formidable ironclad which carries the head of the French State justifies eloquently her name. It is indeed France that approaches Russia. I feel my heart beat." [1] From this magnificent equipage descended, surely with something of bathos, the square figure and obstinate countenance of M. Poincaré. For the next three days all was festivity and speeches. The President, as always, was faultless in his orations. The strains of the Marseillaise celebrated his comings and goings. And it is interesting to learn that at the same time workers in the suburbs of the capital were being cut down by Cossacks for singing the same tune.[2] It may be interesting, too, for the reader to hear how that

---

[1] Paléologue, pp. 2-3.   [2] Kautsky, No. 203.

complex history we have described, with the imminence of war, the waiting on tiptoe of all the Powers, and above all of France and Russia, for the moment when, through someone else's blunder or fault, they might take what they wanted by war—how that history represented itself on the lips of the first magistrate of France : " Nearly twenty-five years have elapsed since, with a clear vision of their destinies, our countries agreed upon a common diplomatic policy, and the happy results of this lasting association are seen every day in *the equilibrium of the world*. Based on community of interests, consecrated by *the pacific will of the two Governments*, supported by armies and fleets that know each other, esteem each other and are accustomed to fraternise together, tested by long experience and *completed by invaluable friendship*, the Alliance in which the illustrious Emperor Alexander II and the lamented President Carnot took the earliest initiatives has certainly given proof of its beneficent action and its unshakable solidity. Your Majesty may rest assured that, to-morrow as to-day, France will pursue, in close and daily co-operation with her ally, *the cause of peace and civilisation* for which the two Governments have never ceased to labour." [1]

Magnificent ! But behind this noble façade the rats were gnawing. What was it that was going on in this uncanny silence ? The President interviewed the Ambassadors of the Powers. Sir George Buchanan " did not attempt to hide from me the anxiety he felt in consequence of Austria, the silence and the mystery surrounding her future intentions." The Italian Ambassador " gave me friendly assurances that the movements of the troops in Italy were solely due to the railway strikes." Count Pourtalès, the German, " greeted me with irreproachable courtesy." But Count Szápáry, the Austrian, " while extremely polite, displayed great reserve." [2] The President discussed with the Tsar the obscure and disquieting situation. He expressed the view that " the only way to preserve the general peace is to open a broad debate between all the Great Powers, avoiding the opposition of one group to the other. That was the method which had served so well in 1913. Let us adopt it again." The Tsar agreed. Nothing could be more correct. On the 22nd a great banquet

---

[1] Poincaré, p. 187. Italics as printed in the text.   [2] Ib., pp. 188-9.

was held. " Three long tables were prepared under half-open tents, in the midst of a garden in full bloom. The flower-beds, newly watered, exhale a fresh vegetable odour, delightful to breathe after the torrid day. I am one of the first to arrive. The Grand Duchess Anastasie and her sister the Grand Duchess Militza welcome me with enthusiasm. The two Montenegrin Princesses exclaim, talking together : ' We are living in historic days, sacred days ! To-morrow, at the review, the bands will play nothing but the " Lorraine March " and the " Sambre and Meuse." I received to-day from my father [1] a telegram in cipher in which he says that before the end of the month we shall have war. What a hero, my father ! He is worthy of the Iliad ! See, this little bonbon-box which never leaves me. It contains the soil of Lorraine —yes, the soil of Lorraine ! I gathered it beyond the frontier when I was in France with my husband two years ago. And see—see there, on the table of honour ! It is covered with thistles. I did not choose that there should be any other flower. They are thistles from Lorraine. I picked some plants on the annexed territory, brought them here and had the seeds sown in my garden. . . . Militza, go on speaking to him, keep the Ambassador in talk, while I go to receive the Emperor.'

" At dinner I am placed on the left of the Grand Duchess Anastasia. And the dithyramb continues, interrupted by prophecies : ' The war is coming ! Nothing will be left of Austria ! You will get back Alsace-Lorraine. Our armies will join at Berlin. Germany will be destroyed ! ' Then abruptly : ' I must check myself. The Emperor is looking at me.' Under the severe glance of the Tsar the Montenegrin Sibyl suddenly calms herself." [2]

Thus, then as always, Romance, dreaming of the future ! Three short years, and where would Russia be, and where the Tsar ? But the Montenegrin Princesses were not dis-appointed. From the ruins of the Tsardom, from the frag-ments of the Austrian Empire, from Germany tortured, mutilated and starved, from France triumphant but prostrate, from England staggering and blind, rose, like a phœnix—Jugo-Slavia !

On the 23rd the *France* sailed away, majestic as she had

---

[1] The King of Montenegro.   [2] Paléologue, pp. 14-15.

arrived. It was 10 p.m., and four hours earlier the Austrian
Note had been delivered in Belgrade. Suddenly the gulf had
opened, and the President's journey home was made in a
murky gloom lit up by flashes of lightning. On the 26th
M. Poincaré learned that the Kaiser had curtailed his trip
and returned to Kiel ; then, that the German squadron had
left the North Sea. On the 27th : " A German cruiser met
us and saluted us very correctly in passing. A German
destroyer, on the contrary, made a right turn about on
sighting us and made off at full speed in the direction of the
Kiel Canal." A wireless message to Berlin followed, which
the *France* intercepted but could not interpret. It was not
till the 29th that the President reached Dunkirk and stood
once more on French soil. [1]

VII. British Policy

Meantime, what has England been doing ? Our first notice
is on July 6th,[2] when the German Ambassador called and
asked Sir Edward whether he could not persuade Russia to
induce a submissive attitude in Serbia. A general discussion
followed, in which Lichnowski spoke of Russian hostility to
Germany, while Sir Edward said he had no knowledge of any
such feeling. The conversation then passed to the rumours
of a naval agreement between England and Russia.[3] " The
Minister," the Ambassador reports, " was distinctly impressed
by my communications and thanked me for the frank discussion that had been carried on in our customary agreeable
and friendly fashion." On the 9th there was another interview, dealing with the military and naval conversations,
in the course of which Sir Edward said that " he had been
endeavouring to persuade the Russian Government to adopt a
more peaceful view and to assume a more conciliatory attitude
towards Austria. Very much would depend," he thought,
" on the kind of measures that were under consideration and
on whether they might not arouse Slavic sentiment in such a
fashion as to make it impossible for M. Sazonoff to remain
passive under them." " In general," the Ambassador reports,
" the Minister was in a thoroughly confident mood, and

---

[1] Poincaré, pp. 198 seq.   [2] Kautsky, No. 20.
[3] See above, pp. 399 seq.

declared, in cheerful tones, that he saw no reason for taking a pessimistic view of the situation." [1]

On July 15th the British Ambassador at Vienna telegraphed home a "forecast of what was about to happen" [2] received from a "private source." This forecast has not been published and we do not know whether it was correct. Meantime Prince Lichnowski is trying, without much success, to enlighten his Government as to the probable trend of English opinion. It is to be expected, he says, that "local sympathies here will turn instantly and impulsively to the Serbs just as soon as Austria takes to violence." [3] On this dispatch v. Jagow comments : "That is unfortunately all true." [4] But his only reply to the Ambassador is an instruction to remind the British Government of the assassination of King Alexander of Serbia and his Queen in 1903 and of the feeling then excited in England. "We are concerned at present with a pre-eminent political question, perhaps the last opportunity of giving the Greater Serbian menace its death-blow under comparatively favourable circumstances. If Austria neglects this opportunity, her prestige will have come to an end, and she will constitute a still weaker factor of our association." [5] But Lichnowski is unconvinced. He replies, reminding his Government of the attitude adopted by English opinion towards the struggle for Italian independence, "in spite of the bombs of the Mazzinists." [6] Later, on the 16th, he returns to this theme : "What I do believe myself able to state with certainty is that, in case of war, it would not be possible to influence public opinion in this country to the disfavour of Serbia, even by conjuring up the bloody shades of Draga and her paramour, whose removal has long been forgotten by the English public, and thus belongs among historic events, with which, as far as non-British countries are concerned, people here are in general less familiar than is perhaps one of our average third-form boys at home." [7]

Meantime Sir Edward is getting anxious. On the 15th the Russian Ambassador reports of him that although "he had received no disquieting news from Vienna during the

[1] Kautsky, No. 30.   [2] B.B.B., No. 161.
[3] Kautsky, No. 43, July 14th.   [4] Ib., No. 52, note 2, p. 115.
[5] Ib., No. 48.   [6] Ib., No. 52.   [7] Ib., No. 62.

last few days, nevertheless he did not seem to be very reassured. He considers this outbreak of national passions as very dangerous, the more so since there are very few elements which would be able to restrain them. He says that we can no longer count upon Germany being the peacemaker under all circumstances." "I have no doubt," Count Benckendorff adds, "that Grey has used very plain language in Berlin and Vienna." [1] Whether he had, we do not know. But he did, at any rate, use plain language to the Austrian Ambassador, who called on the 23rd to tell him privately the main points of the Austrian Note. As to these the Minister reserved judgment till he could see the text. But he went on to say that, up to now, he had avoided speaking on the subject, because Austria regarded it as a matter between herself and Serbia. He recognised the strength and the difficulty of the Austrian case; but he drew attention to the gravity of the situation. "If four great States, Austria-Hungary, Germany, Russia and France, should be involved in war, a condition would result which would be equivalent to the economic bankruptcy of Europe. No credit to be had, the industrial centres in an uproar, so that in most countries, no matter who were victorious, 'many an existing institution' would be swept away." "Sir Edward," says the Ambassador, "was cool and objective as always, friendly and not without sympathy for us. He is undoubtedly much disturbed and very anxious about the possible consequences." [2]

VIII. The Austrian Note is Delivered

It was on this same day that the Austrian Note was delivered. It begins by reciting the text of the Serbian promise, given in 1909, to live in the future on good neighbourly terms with Austria-Hungary. It then accuses Serbia of breaking this undertaking and encouraging criminal agitation against the Dual Monarchy. It affirms that the murder of the Archduke was planned in Belgrade, and that the duty is now imposed on the Austrian Government to put an end to these intrigues; and it proceeds to demand from the Serbian Government a formal condemnation of anti-Austrian machinations, and a promise to proceed against such with the

[1] Siebert, p. 734. [2] Aust. Docs., i. No. 59. Cf. B.B.B., No. 3.

utmost rigour. Finally, it presents the following points for acceptance :

1. Suppression of anti-Austrian publications.
2. Dissolution of the propaganda society called Narodna Odbrana.
3. Elimination from public instruction of anti-Austrian propaganda.
4. Removal from the Government service of all officers and functionaries guilty of such propaganda, the Austrian Government to supply the names.
5. " To accept the collaboration in Serbia of representatives of the Austro-Hungarian Government for the suppression of the subversive movement directed against the territorial integrity of the monarchy."
6. " To take judicial proceedings against accessories to the plot of the 28th June who are on Serbian territory ; delegates of the Austro-Hungarian Government will take part in the investigation relating thereto."
7. To proceed at once to the arrest of two men, Tankositch and Ciganovitch.
8. To prevent the illicit traffic in arms across the frontier.
9. To furnish explanations as to certain utterances of high Serbian officials who have expressed themselves in terms of hostility against the Austro-Hungarian Government.
10. To notify that Government, without delay, of the execution of the above measures.

The reply of the Serbian Government is expected by 6 p.m. on the 25th.[1]

These terms, as we know, were intended to be such as no self-respecting Government would accept. Sir Edward Grey said that he " had never before seen one State address to another independent State a document of so formidable a character." [2] But precedents are rapidly established in international affairs ; and after the Italian Note to Greece in 1923, and the British Note to Egypt in 1924, the procedure adopted by the Austrian Government seems to have become normal. In the year 1914, however, it surprised and shocked the

---

[1] See text in B.B.B., No. 4, and also in Kautsky, Supp. 1, p. 603.
[2] B.B.B., No. 5.

statesmen ; and it was, in the then circumstances of Europe, a plain menace to the peace of the world.

In a reasonable society the question of Serbian guilt would have been referred to an international court, to be tried by due process of law. The French did, in fact, make the suggestion that " the Triple Entente should ascertain the possibility of substituting for the Austro-Serbian investigation an international inquiry." [1] Similarly, Sazonoff, stating that Austria " could not be both accuser and judge in her own cause," proposed that " the documents in relation to the inquiry be laid before the Cabinets of the six Powers." [2] But the German Ambassador made the reply which Ministers of all States always make when their own conduct or that of their allies is at stake : " Austria would object to this suggestion, just as any Great Power would have to refuse to submit itself to a court of arbitration on a case in which vital interests were at stake."

The idea of an international inquiry was thus plainly chimerical and can hardly have been seriously entertained by any of the Governments. There was no method available except the broken reed of diplomacy ; and the Governments of the Entente set to work by that method to do what they could to postpone a war for which they were not yet ready. Serbia was urged to make her reply as conciliatory as possible, and Austria to extend the time limit.[3] At the same time Sazonoff made it plain that if Austria were to " devour " Serbia Russia would go to war with Austria.[4] Nevertheless the German Ambassador at St. Petersburg, reporting this, adds that, in his opinion, " despite the great excitement unquestionably predominating in Government circles here, precipitate steps in this direction are not to be looked for at present." The words " precipitate " and " at present " may mean next day, or next week, or next month. But, precipitate or not, there was no doubt about the Russian intention, and it is plain that that intention was based on the promise of French support. " Russia," said Sazonoff to the British Ambassador, " if she feels secure of the support of France, will face all

[1] Poincaré, *Origins*, p. 195.
[2] Kautsky, No. 160. Cf. ib., No. 204.
[3] Poincaré, p. 195 ; B.B.B., Nos. 12, 13 ; R.O.B., No. 16 ; F.Y.B., No. 38.
[4] Kautsky, No. 204, July 25th.

the risks of war." [1] But though Russia was determined to fight if there were war between Austria and Serbia, yet she did what she could to prevent war ; and the extraordinarily humble character of the Serbian reply was due, no doubt, to her advice. For Serbia, of course, herself would fear war if she were not sure of Russian support, and would therefore do what Russia advised.

We will now proceed to follow the efforts made by the Powers of the Entente to get the period set by the ultimatum extended. They had only two days wherein to operate, so that time was the essence of the situation. It was not until 10 a.m. on the 25th that Sir Edward Grey's proposal for an extension,[2] supported by France and by Russia, reached Berlin. The German Secretary of State informed the French Ambassador that he had telegraphed it " this very morning " to Vienna.[3] He wired also to Lichnowski at 1 p.m. : " Have communicated proposal of Sir Edward Grey to Vienna." [4] But the telegram actually sent was not dispatched till 4 p.m. It contained Sir Edward's proposal as transmitted by Lichnowski, and added : " Have replied to London that I would communicate Sir Edward Grey's proposals to Vienna." [5] The difference between " have communicated " and " will communicate " may be accidental. But there is no doubt about the times at which the telegrams were dispatched. To both was appended the statement that, since the ultimatum expired that day, and Count Berchtold was at Ischl, the Secretary did not believe that the extension demanded would be possible.

On the same day a request for an extension of time was received at Berlin from Russia. The Russian Chargé d'Affaires asked for an interview with the Secretary of State, but was told that he could not be received until 4.50 p.m. He therefore wrote a note conveying the message entrusted to him. The exact hour of this note is not given, but it must have been some time before 4.50.[6] The evidence, then, seems to be fairly complete. The Germans forwarded the proposal, by telegram, six hours after they received it. If forwarded at once, it would have been late enough. Sent when it was, it would certainly be too late ; for telegrams appear to have

[1] B.B.B., No. 17.   [2] Ib., No. 18.   [3] F.Y.B., No. 41.
[4] Kautsky, No. 104.   [5] Ib., No. 171   [6] Kautsky, No. 172.

taken from two to three hours to arrive, and the time limit expired at six.

Meantime, at Vienna, the Russian Chargé d'Affaires sent a telegram to Count Berchtold, who was away at Ischl. This was dispatched about eleven, and we hear no more of it. But the Chargé d'Affaires the same morning had an interview with v. Macchio, of the Austrian Foreign Office, in which he put forward the same request for an extension of time. Von Macchio telegraphed the request to Ischl, and was ordered, in reply, to give a direct refusal.[1] On the same day (hour not given) Count Berchtold sent a dispatch to his Ambassador at St. Petersburg. " We were aware," he says, " from the first of the possibility that our dispute with Serbia might involve us in war with Russia. Should events prove that Russia considers the moment for the great settlement with the Central European Powers to have already arrived, and should she be therefore determined on war from the beginning, the instructions that follow are superfluous." Should she, however, " think better of it," the Ambassador should point out that Austria-Hungary has " no selfish motives " ; that she desires no Serbian territory ; that she does not intend to interfere with Serbian sovereignty ; but that " any further tolerance of Serbian intrigues would undermine our existence as a State and our position as a Great Power, thus also threatening the balance of power in Europe. . . . Our action against Serbia, whatever form it takes, is conservative from first to last, and its object is the necessary preservation of our position in Europe." This is only a re-statement of the Austrian case as given to the public. But the following sentence deserves special notice : " I assume that your Excellency, in the existing circumstances, has established a close understanding with your German colleague, who will certainly have been enjoined by his Government to leave the Russian Government no room for doubt that Austria-Hungary, in the event of a conflict with Russia, would not stand alone." Attention must also be called to the following, which was toned down in the Red Book published in 1914 :—

" We shall go to the furthest point in the enforcement of our demands, and shall not shrink from the possibility of European complications." [2]

---

[1] Aust. Docs., ii. Nos. 27, 29.   [2] Ib., No. 42.   Cf. A.R.B., No. 26.

But if Austria, backed by Germany, was determined not to shrink from war with Russia, Russia was equally determined not to shrink from a war which would involve all Europe. On this same day—25th—at 5 p.m., a Ministerial Council was held at St. Petersburg. Sazonoff, we are informed, was very violent on the subject of the outrage (Vergewaltigung) which was being committed on " our Slav brethren." He appealed to the " soldierly instincts " of the members. Only a military demonstration, he said, would keep Austria in order ; and, accordingly, measures preliminary to mobilisation (Kriegsvorbereitung) were ordered to be taken the next day.[1] On this Dobrorolski, Chief Mobilisation Officer of the Russian Army, comments : " The war was already a thing settled, and all the flood of telegrams between the Governments of Russia and Germany served but to arrange the ' mise en scène ' of the historical drama." But this seems to be the observation of a man looking back, not forward. There was yet to be many a slip between the cup of blood and the lips of the millions who were to quaff it.

IX. Mediation Proposals

The efforts of the Powers of the Entente for an extension of the time limit were thus foredoomed to failure. At two minutes before 6 p.m. on July 25th the Serbian reply was handed in to the Austrian Ambassador at Belgrade.[2] It was unexpectedly conciliatory, accepting all the demands of the Austrians except 6 and in part 5.[3] " It was plain," said Sir Edward Grey, " that this acceptance of Serbia's was to be attributed solely to the pressure exerted from St. Petersburg." [4] But the Austrian Government, as we know, was predetermined not to be satisfied. As early as July 23rd, the day of the presentation of the note, Count Berchtold had instructed his Minister at Belgrade that any reply short of unconditional acceptance was to be treated as rejection, and to be followed by his immediate departure. The very time of his train was

[1] Sukhomlinoff, *Erinnerungen*, pp. 351 seq., who, however, is not, it must be admitted, the best of witnesses. Cf. Pourtalès, p. 18. Of the probable consequences of military measures Sazonoff had been strongly warned by Sir G. Buchanan (see B.B.B., No. 17).

[2] Aust. Docs., ii. No. 26.

[3] Text in B.B.B., No. 39 ; Aust. Docs., ii. No. 47.

[4] Kautsky, No. 277.

named, 6.30 p.m.[1] By that train the Minister, in fact, left,
and before 8 p.m. he had telegraphed from Semlin, in Austria,
to his Chief.[2] He can hardly have had time even to read
the Serbian reply, much less to consider it. On the same
day the Austrians released to the Powers the long indictment
they had prepared on the Serbian agitation.[3] But it was not
till the 28th that they circulated the reply to their note,
with their own comments.[4] We need not pursue this topic
further. The Austrians, according to plan, have precipitated
their war with Serbia. There remained the vital question :
Will the European war follow ?

On the 26th, the day following the presentation and
rejection of the Serbian Note, Sir Edward Grey proposed a
conference between the representatives of England, France,
Germany, and Russia " for the purpose of discovering an
issue which would prevent complications." [5] The idea was
conceived on the model of the London Conference of 1912-13,
and it implied mediation between Russia and Austria-Hungary
by the Powers less immediately concerned. Already, on the
previous day, Sir Edward had been informed that Russia
would accept such a proposal.[6] In transmitting it to Berlin,
Lichnowski said that, in the opinion of British diplomats, the
conference was " the only possibility of avoiding a general
war." But a condition of its success was the cessation of
military activities. " Once the Serbian border was crossed,
everything would be at an end, as no Russian Government
would be able to tolerate this, and would be forced to move
to the attack of Austria, unless she wanted to see her status
among the Balkan nations lost for ever." " The localisation
of the conflict, as hoped for in Berlin, was wholly impossible,
and must be dropped from the calculations of practical
politics." This latter point the Ambassador earnestly reiter-
ates on his own behalf, and ends by expressing " the humble
wish that our policy be guided, solely and alone, by the need
of sparing the German nation a struggle in which it has
nothing to gain and everything to lose." [7] This dispatch of
Lichnowski reached the German Foreign Office at midnight.
The Chancellor showed it to the Kaiser, and made thereafter

[1] Aust. Docs., ii. No. 1.   [2] Ib., No. 26.   [3] Ib., No. 48.
[4] Ib., No. 96.   [5] B.B.B., No. 36.   [6] Ib., No. 17.
[7] Kautsky, No. 236.   Cf. ib., No. 265.

the marginal note : " His Majesty disapproved of Lichnowski's point of view." [1] On the 27th, at 1 p.m., he replied to London : " We could not take part in such a conference, as we would not be able to summon Austria before a European court of justice in her case with Serbia." [2] Germany thus rejected the proposition which Russia had accepted. Her reasons are pretty clear. She knew that Italy disapproved of her action. To go to a conference, therefore, would mean that she would be outvoted by three to one. Apart from this, she was too deeply committed to Austria to be willing now to call her off. And further, underlying the whole situation, was that ancient fetish of the " balance of power " which dominates, at all times, the policy of all Powers. " The impression is constantly gaining ground here," Lichnowski writes from London, " that the whole Serbian question has devolved into a test of strength between the Triple Alliance and the Triple Entente." Whereon the German Under-Secretary of State comments : " Where will the balance of power be if Austria gives in ? " [3] Where indeed ? Echo could only answer, Where ? And the next thing she had to repeat was the crack of rifles and the boom of guns throughout the continents of Europe, Asia, and Africa. Verily the " balance of power " is a jealous god !

Germany, then, rejected Sir Edward's proposal and recurred, in spite of the warning she had received, to her original idea of " localisation." Meantime, on the morning of the 27th, Sir Edward had seen the text of the Serbian reply. He informed Lichnowski that, in his opinion, it amounted to an acceptance of all the points except that of the participation of Austrian officials in the inquiry. If Austria refused to be satisfied, it would be a proof that she was seeking an excuse to crush Serbia. Russia would regard this as a challenge, and the result would be " the most frightful war that Europe had ever seen, and no one could tell to what such a war might lead." He begged Germany, therefore, to put pressure on Austria. " He was convinced that it lay in our hands to bring the matter to a settlement by means of the proper representations, and he would regard it as a good augury for the future if we two should again succeed in assuring the peace of Europe by means of our mutual influence on our

[1] Kautsky, No. 265, note 2.   [2] Ib., No. 248.   [3] Ib., No. 265, note 4.

allies." [1]   This dispatch reached Berlin at 4.30 p.m. on the 27th, and at midnight the Chancellor forwarded it to Vienna with the following comment : " Since we have already refused one English proposal for a conference, it is impossible for us to waive à limine this English suggestion also. By refusing every proposition for mediation, we should be held responsible for the conflagration by the whole world and be set forth as the original instigators of the war. That would also make our position impossible in our own country, where we must appear as having been forced into the war." [2] This is not a very strong kind of pressure ! But there is worse behind. At 9.15 on the same evening the Austrian Ambassador in Berlin telegraphed to Count Berchtold to inform him that, in the immediate future, mediation proposals by England would be brought to the notice of the Austrian Government. He continued as follows : " The German Government assured me in the most binding way that it does not identify itself in any way with the proposals. On the contrary, it is directly opposed to them, and forwards them only in order to take account of the English request. The reason for doing so is that it is of the utmost importance at the present moment, to prevent England from making common cause with Russia and France, and that is what might happen if Germany refused to forward English proposals. The German Government, in the case of every such request by England, would explain to her, in the most explicit way, that it did not support in any way such requests for intervention, and only forwarded them in order to meet the wishes of England." So, on the present occasion, v. Jagow had promised to forward the British request, but had said that " he could not support it, since the Serbian conflict was a question of prestige for the Austro-Hungarian Monarchy, and Germany too was affected by it." The Secretary had given Sir Edward's note to Tschirschky (German Ambassador in Vienna) without ordering him to lay it before Count Berchtold. " He was thus enabled to inform the British Cabinet that he did not directly refuse the British requests, but had, in fact, forwarded it to Vienna." In conclusion, the Secretary had said, " though he had acted as intermediary, he was absolutely opposed to the acceptance of the English requests for intervention with

[1] Kautsky, No. 258.   Ib., No. 277.

Austria-Hungary," and only handed on the proposals "in order to meet England's wishes." [1]

Later, after the war was over, both the Chancellor and the Secretary of State affirmed that this report by Szögyény could not be a correct account of what the Secretary had said.[2] We need not press the point, nor is it very important. In any case, it is clear that, although Germany forwarded to Austria Sir Edward's request, she did not herself endorse it. At the most she left the matter in Austria's hands.

But Austria, as we know, was determined, at all risks, to have her war with Serbia. Already, at 3.30 p.m. on the 27th, the German Ambassador in Vienna had sent to his Government the following telegram :

" They have decided here to send out the declaration of war to-morrow, or the day after to-morrow at the latest, chiefly to frustrate any attempt at intervention." [3] In fact, the declaration was sent " to-morrow "—that is, the 28th—at 11 a.m. ; [4] and it was another step on the declivity that was now sloping sharper and sharper to the pit.

Meantime, on the 27th, Sazonoff was still talking in a concilatory way with Pourtalès. The moment had come, in his opinion, to " build a golden bridge " for Austria. Far from his mind was any idea of humiliating her. He begged Germany to co-operate with her in persuading her to modify her demands. " There must be a way of giving Serbia her deserved lesson, while sparing her sovereign rights." [5] But on the 28th he telegraphs to his Ambassador in Berlin : " In consequence of the declaration of war by Austria against Serbia the Imperial Government will announce to-morrow (29th) the mobilisation in the military conscriptions of Odessa, Kieff, Moscow, and Kazan." [6]

---

[1] Aust. Docs., ii. No. 68.
[2] *Is Germany Guilty ?*, p. 47 ; Jagow, p. 118.
[3] Kautsky, No. 257. Cf. Aust. Docs., ii. No. 78.
[4] Kautsky, No. 311. When the declaration was submitted to the Emperor for his signature it contained a statement that " Serbian troops have already attacked near Temes-Kubin." Later the Minister informed His Majesty that this information had not been confirmed, and he had therefore eliminated the statement from the note (Aust. Docs., ii. No. 97, iii. No. 26). It would be interesting to know whether the statement had ever been believed or was a sheer invention. But we do not know, and must leave this little episode with a note of interrogation.
[5] Kautsky, No. 282.
[6] Romberg, p. 35. Already on the 24th Russia had decided, " in principle," to mobilise these districts (*Tages-Aufzeichnungen*, p. 7).

This is an important decision, to which we shall return later. But it did not, in Sazonoff's view, put an end to the possibility of mediation. It only changed its character. For on the same day he telegraphs to London, saying that, although the declaration of war " clearly put an end to the idea of direct communication between Austria and Russia," yet " action by London Cabinet in order to set on foot mediation with a view to suspension of military operations of Austria against Serbia is now most urgent." [1] Meantime Serbia makes a strong appeal to her protector, expressing " the hope that this act, which disturbs the peace of Europe and revolts her conscience, will be condemned by the whole civilised world and severely punished by Russia." [2] The " conscience " of Europe is a rather nebulous affair. But the policies of Europe had brought about, as we know, a situation in which Serbia could count upon Russia, Russia upon France, and France upon England. Little Serbia thus stood on the verge of satisfying her national ambitions at the cost of the peoples and civilisations of three continents.

X. Germany Reverses Her Attitude

But at this very moment there had taken place, in the German attitude, a change which might, even yet, have saved the situation. This change, no doubt, was due, in great part, to an increasing anxiety about the prospects of the Central Powers in the event of a European war. Italy, it was becoming clear, would not come in on the side of her allies.[3] Roumania, in spite of the loyalty of the King, was very doubtful. England maintained her reserve, but in that reserve lay the possibility of her intervention. These facts, from this time onward, weighed more and more in the German calculations. But, also, the Serbian reply was unexpectedly submissive. Was there now any need of war ? The Kaiser definitely thought not. He had seen, on the 27th, a dispatch announcing the imminence of the Austrian declaration of war.[4] At 10 a.m. on the 28th, an hour before that declaration was presented, he wrote to the Secretary of State saying that he has read the Serbian reply that very

---

[1] For these two telegrams, see B.B.B., No. 70.   [2] S.B.B., No. 47.
[3] See Aust. Docs., iii. No. 32, and below, pp. 481 seq.   [4] Kautsky, No. 257.

morning, and that he was " convinced on the whole that the wishes of the Danubian monarchy have been acceded to. The few reservations that Serbia makes in regard to individual points could, according to my opinion, be settled by negotiation. But the note contains the announcement, orbi et urbi, of a capitulation of the most humiliating kind, and as a result every cause of war falls to the ground." He goes on, indeed, to say that the note is only a " scrap of paper " which must be translated into acts before it has value. The Serbs are " Orientals," and " therefore liars, tricksters, and masters of evasion." A " douce violence " must be exercised, and he suggests the occupation of Belgrade by Austria, to be held as a hostage until the demands made have actually been complied with. " On this basis I am ready to mediate for peace with Austria. Any proposals or protests to the contrary by other nations I should refuse regardless." He ends by ordering the Chancellor to submit to him a proposal in this sense, for communication to Austria.[1] At the same time he directs the Adjutant-General to inform the Chief of the General Staff that, since Serbia has accepted in essence all the demands, there is no occasion for war.[2] The Chancellor acted on these instructions, prepared a note, and submitted it to the Kaiser. The note was dispatched, by telegram at 10.15 p.m. and reached its destination at 4.30 a.m. on the 29th. It is sufficiently important to be cited verbatim :

" The Austro-Hungarian Government has distinctly informed Russia that it is not considering any territorial acquisitions in Serbia. This agrees with your Excellency's report to the effect that neither the Austrian nor the Hungarian statesmen consider the increase of the Slavic element in the Monarchy to be desirable. On the other hand, the Austro-Hungarian Government has left us in the dark concerning its intentions, despite repeated interrogations. The reply of the Serbian Government to the Austrian ultimatum, which has now been received, makes it clear that Serbia has agreed to the Austrian demands to so great an extent that, in case of a completely uncompromising attitude on the part of the Austro-Hungarian Government, it will become necessary to reckon upon the

[1] Kautsky, No. 293. [2] See Bülow, *Erste Stundenschläge*, p. 96.

gradual defection from its cause of public opinion throughout all Europe.

"According to the statements of the Austrian General Staff, an active military movement against Serbia will not be possible before the 12th of August. As a result, the Imperial Government is placed in the extraordinarily difficult position of being exposed in the meantime to the mediation and conference proposals of the other Cabinets, and if it continues to maintain its previous aloofness in the face of such proposals, it will incur the odium of having been responsible for a world-war, even, finally, among the German people themselves. A successful war on three fronts cannot be commenced and carried on on any such basis. It is imperative that the responsibility for the eventual extension of the war among those nations not originally immediately concerned should, under all circumstances, fall on Russia. At M. Sazonoff's last conversation with Count Pourtalès the Minister already conceded that Serbia would have to receive her deserved lesson. At any rate the Minister was no longer so unconditionally opposed to the Austrian point of view as he had been earlier. From this fact it is not difficult to draw the conclusion that the Russian Government might even realise that, once the mobilisation of the Austro-Hungarian Army had begun, the very honour of its arms demanded an invasion of Serbia. But it will be all the better able to compromise with this idea if the Vienna Cabinet repeats at Petersburg its distinct declaration that she is far from wishing to make any territorial acquisitions in Serbia, and that her military preparations are solely for the purpose of a temporary occupation of Belgrade and certain other localities on Serbian territory in order to force the Serbian Government to the complete fulfilment of her demands, and for the creation of guarantees of future good behaviour— to which Austria-Hungary has an unquestionable claim after the experiences she has had with Serbia. An occupation like the German occupation of French territory after the Peace of Frankfort, for the purpose of securing compliance with the demands for war indemnity, is suggested. As soon as the Austrian demands should be complied with, evacuation would follow. Should the Russian Government fail to recognise the justice of this point of view, it would have against it the public opinion of all Europe, which is now in the process of turning away from Austria. As a further result, the general diplomatic, and probably the military, situation would undergo material alteration in favour of Austria-Hungary and her allies.

"Your Excellency will kindly discuss the matter along these lines thoroughly and impressively with Count Berchtold, and instigate an appropriate move at St. Petersburg. You will have to avoid very carefully giving rise to the impression that we wish to hold Austria back. The case is solely one of finding a way to realise Austria's desired aim, that of cutting the vital cord of the Greater Serbia propaganda, without at the same time bringing on a world-war, and, if the latter cannot be avoided in the end, of improving the conditions under which we shall have to wage it, in so far as is possible.

"Wire report." [1]

This note is, from many points of view, open to criticism. The Germans' objection to a world-war seems to be only that the odium of it might fall upon Germany. They are also very much afraid of seeming to interfere with Austria's liberty of action. But the note does, nevertheless, definitely suggest that Austrian occupation of Serbian territory should be limited, and should be followed by withdrawal when the Austrian demands have been complied with. It further urges that "an appropriate move" should be made at St. Petersburg, which can only mean an arrangement between Austria and Russia along the lines indicated. And even if the reader be inclined, as he may be, to think, at this point, that the evidence of a change of mind in Germany is not very strong, he will be convinced, as the story proceeds, by the growing intensity of the Chancellor's appeal to his recalcitrant ally.[2]

The pressure thus put upon Vienna was reported, on the 29th, to the British Ambassador at Berlin,[3] and was welcomed warmly by Sir Edward Grey.[4] It looked like a possible way out. Why did it fail?

---

[1] Kautsky, No. 323.
[2] See, e.g., Kautsky, Nos. 385, 395, 396; and below, pp. 452 seq.
[3] B.B.B., No. 75.　　　　[4] Ib., No. 77. Cf. ib., No. 103.

XI. Armaments Begin to Function

There were two sets of facts working concurrently to defeat it. The first was the universal apprehension caused by the ever-increasing armaments of all the Powers. This factor, of course, was operative from the beginning, being, as we know, a principal cause of the chronic unrest of Europe.[1] But at the point we have now reached it begins to dominate the whole situation. On the 28th, as we have seen, Russia had announced, for the 29th, her partial mobilisation [2] against Austria. On the same day Count Berchtold telegraphed to Berlin pressing Germany to declare that partial mobilisation in Russia would be followed by total mobilisation in Germany. This was the usual diplomatic device of meeting threat by threat. What action would the German Government take at this critical moment ? The uncertainty and confusion involved in the diplomatic blind-man's buff is well shown by a statement made by the Bavarian Minister in Berlin. He reports to his Government : " Germany's procedure was rendered very difficult by the fact that no one knew whether the measures taken in Russia and France were meant as a bluff or were serious." [3] That was a question necessarily most disquieting to the General Staff. On the 29th, for the first time, so far as we know, they intervened with a memorandum on the whole situation. They pointed out, with great lucidity, the obvious facts : " Russia has announced that she will mobilise against Austria if Austria invades Serbia. Austria will therefore have to

---

[1] See, e.g., Kautsky, Nos. 216, 230, 264, 274, 275, 276, 281, 291, 295, 296, 327, 337.

[2] The views of a layman on what constitutes " mobilisation " are not of any interest. But a soldier has defined it as follows :

(1) In a narrower sense, the passing of the Army from peace strength to war strength—that is, the calling up of reserves. This happened in 1908-9, between Austria and Serbia, and also in 1912-13 between Austria and Russia.

(2) Not only this, but the concentration of troops at the frontier. Since the use of railways for this purpose this could be done very quickly. Consequently, it has always, once started, been carried to the end, and followed by war. This, presumably, is the meaning of the statement made by General Boisdeffre in 1892, and endorsed by the Tsar, that " mobilisation means war." This is repeated in the Russian mobilisation order of 1912 (cf. Bethmann-Hollweg, p. 150).

(3) There were also " preliminary measures "—the " last stage before mobilisation."

[3] Kautsky, Supp. IV, No. 18, p. 630.

mobilise against Russia. The collision between the two States will then have become inevitable. But that, for Germany, is the casus fœderis. She therefore must mobilise too. Russia will then mobilise the rest of her forces. She will say: 'I am being attacked by Germany.' Thus the Franco-Russian alliance, so often held up to praise as a purely defensive compact, created only to meet the aggressive plans of Germany, will become active, and the mutual butchery of the civilised nations of Europe will begin. . . . After this fashion things must and will develop, unless, one might say, a miracle happens to prevent at the last moment a war which will annihilate for decades the civilisation of almost all Europe." The memorandum ends : " The military situation is becoming from day to day more unfavourable for us, and can, if our prospective opponents prepare themselves further unmolested, lead to fateful consequences for us." [1] It will be agreed that a more serious document was never presented to any Government. There is no evidence here of a desire to precipitate war. On the contrary, the memorandum shows, on the face of it, a more realistic sense of what such a war would mean than is to be found in most of the dispatches of the diplomats. On the other hand, the General Staff, no doubt, like many people in Europe and most well-informed soldiers, expected war at some near date, and very likely believed that it would be better for Germany that it should come now rather than later. We are, in fact, told that " the Chief of the General Staff, Commander-in-Chief v. Moltke, knows with absolute certainty that a war of aggression against Germany was planned and prepared for between Russia, France, and England for the year 1917. Moltke considers Russia to be the head of the conspiracy." It was fortunate, he held, that the mine was exploded at Serajevo, before Russia was ready and while the French Army was in a state of transition.[2] If this were Moltke's belief it would, of course, influence him in the pressure he put on his Government during the critical days.

However that may have been, the German Government were faced with this report. What did they do ? In the first

[1] Kautsky, No. 349.
[2] Ib., App. IV, No. 35, report of the Bavarian Minister at Berlin, August 5th.

place, they sent orders to their Ambassador in St. Petersburg to warn the Russian Government of the dangers of mobilisation.[1] Next, they held, on the evening of the 29th, a Ministerial Council, under the Presidency of the Kaiser.[2] The minutes of this Council have not been published. It was suggested by the French Ambassador [3] that mobilisation was decided upon, but rescinded next day ; and this, if true, might explain the false report issued by the *Lokal Anzeiger*.[4] But in fact, the Germans did not mobilise on that day ; and this resistance to the pressure of the General Staff by the Government is further proof that, at that stage, Germany was sincere in her effort to avoid war. What defeated that effort was the course of events in Russia, to which we will now return.

At 11 o'clock on the morning of the 29th, Count Pourtalès had an interview with Sazonoff. He spoke to him of the pressure Germany was applying in Vienna. The Minister replied that he was glad to hear of it, but that, unfortunately, Vienna, as yet, had given no sign of entering upon conversations with St. Petersburg. He then informed the Ambassador that, in consequence of the Austrian mobilisation, he had decided himself to mobilise in the districts on the Austrian frontier. Pourtalès protested strongly. Sazonoff replied that no threat of war was intended, for " in Russia mobilisation was far from meaning war, as it did among the Western nations ; the Russian Army would doubtless be able to remain under arms for weeks to come without crossing the frontier." Pourtalès may have felt sceptical as to this. He would certainly have done so had he known, as we know now, that the French and Russian General Staffs were agreed that mobilisation meant war.[5] He replied that " the General Staffs of the possible opponents of Russia would not be willing to sacrifice the advantage of getting a start over Russia in the matter of mobilisation, and would press for counter measures. I earnestly begged him to consider this peril. M. Sazonoff assured me most solemnly once again that not the least thing was to happen to us. I replied with emphasis that, while the idea of a threat of war was far from

[1] Kautsky, No. 342.
[2] Ib., Supp. IV, No. 15, p. 629, and references below.
[3] F.Y.B., No. 105.   [4] See below, p. 458.   [5] See above, p. 111.

my mind, he was acquainted with the obligations of our alliance with Austria."[1] When the Ambassador had left, Sazonoff discussed the interview with some of his colleagues. Did Germany really intend to put pressure on Vienna ? Or was she only trying to postpone Russian mobilisation in order to gain time for her own preparations ? Thus, at this crucial moment, we come, in Russia as in Germany, upon the doubts and fears engendered by the darkness in which discussion was proceeding.[2] Between 6 and 7 p.m. Pourtalès appeared again to deliver a warning from his Government. He was to " call M. Sazonoff's serious attention to the fact that further continuance of Russian mobilisation would force us to mobilise, and in that case a European war could scarcely be prevented."[3] To his communication Sazonoff replied shortly : " Now I have no longer any doubt as to the real causes of Austrian intransigeance." Thereupon Pourtalès sprang from his seat and cried : " I protest with all my might, Mr. Minister, against this insulting assertion "; to which Sazonoff replied coolly that " Germany had still the chance to convince him by her actions of the erroneousness of his assumption." This is the Russian account.[4] Count Pourtalès himself says that Sazonoff received his message with obvious emotion, and replied merely that he would communicate it to his master.[5]

XII. The Partial Mobilisation of Russia

However that may have been, this interview finally decided Sazonoff to order partial mobilisation against Austria. He telegraphed to his Ambassador at Paris as follows : " The German Ambassador declared to me to-day the resolution of his Government to carry out its own mobilisation if Russia does not cease her present military preparations. These, however, are only a consequence of the mobilisation of the VIIIth Corps in Austria, which has already taken place,[6] and the obvious disinclination of Austria to agree to any form of peaceful settlement of its own conflict with Serbia.

---

[1] Kautsky, No. 343.   [2] Tages-Aufzeichnungen, p. 18, and note 24.
[3] Kautsky, No. 342. The Tages-Aufzeichnungen give a different version of Pourtalès's communication. See Die Kriegsschuldfrage, September 1924, p. 350.   [4] Tages-Aufzeichnungen, p. 18.   [5] Pourtalès, p. 46.
[6] On the evening of the 25th, according to Montgelas.

" Inasmuch as we cannot fulfil Germany's request, we have no option but to accelerate our armaments, and to reckon with the probable eventuality of war. Will you bring this to the knowledge of the French Government ? " [1]

Shortly after the departure of Count Pourtalès the telephone bell rang. The Tsar was calling up to say that he had just received a telegram from the Kaiser. Of this we have the text.[2] After referring to the murder of Sarajevo and emphasising the common interest of all sovereigns to secure its punishment, the Kaiser proceeds : " On the other hand, I fully understand how difficult it is for you and your Government to face the drift of your public opinion. Therefore, with regard to the hearty and tender friendship which binds us both from long ago with firm ties, I am exerting my utmost influence to induce the Austrians to deal straightly to arrive at a satisfactory understanding with you. I confidently hope you will help me in my efforts to smooth over difficulties that may still arise."

To this communication from the Tsar the only answer of Sazonoff was to report his recent interview with Pourtalès, and to point out how discrepant the Ambassador's tone was from that of the Kaiser. This must mean (apart from questions of manner) that, whereas Pourtalès had dealt with the dangers of the armament situation, the Kaiser dealt with the possibilities of avoiding war. Obviously there is no contradiction between the two positions.[3] However, the Tsar, after listening to his Minister, decided to reply to the Kaiser asking the reason of the discrepancy alleged.[4] It was in the same telegram that the Tsar proposed reference of the Austro-Serbian dispute to The Hague; a suggestion which the Kaiser punctuates by a note of exclamation in the margin.

This telegraphic conversation with the Tsar was followed by a discussion between Sazonoff and the soldiers. The latter pointed out that partial mobilisation would interfere seriously with a later general mobilisation which, it seemed likely, would have, after all, to be ordered. The decision

[1] See *Is Germany Guilty ?*, ii. p. 120. Cf. F.Y.B., No. 100 ; Romberg, p. 41, No. 304. This latter is one of the telegrams omitted in the publication of 1914.
[2] Kautsky, No. 335.   [3] Cf. Pourtalès, *Am Scheidewegen*, p. 49.
[4] See Kautsky, No. 366.

was therefore reached to proceed at once with general mobilisation—that is, against Germany as well as Austria-Hungary ; the Tsar's consent was obtained, and telegrams communicating the news sent to Paris and London.[1] At some time this same evening Sazonoff received the Austrian Ambassador. The question of the interruption of conversations between St. Petersburg and Vienna was discussed,[2] and a friendly tone appeared to have been established, when suddenly Sazonoff received a telephonic message announcing the bombardment of Belgrade. Thereupon, as the Austrian Ambassador reports, the Minister's manner was transformed. " You only want to gain time," he cried, " by diplomatic discussion while you go on and bombard an undefended town. What will you not take, once you have the capital in your hands ? "—" and other such childish expressions." [3] " What is the use of our conversing further, when you go like that ? " Sazonoff concluded, and the Ambassador left him " in a highly excited condition." We do not know the hour of this conversation. If it occurred before the decision to substitute general for partial mobilisation, it was, one may suppose, partly responsible therefor.

The issuing of the order for general mobilisation was the duty of General Dobrorolski, and he has told us how he went to the telegraph office to dispatch the message. It was then about 9 p.m. on the 29th. He handed the dispatch to the head of the office and the typewriters got to work to copy it. While this was proceeding—at 9.30—Dobrorolski received an order to suspend the operations. The Tsar had commanded the substitution of partial for general mobilisation. Dobrorolski withdrew all the copies of his telegram and left the office.[4] Later, about midnight, he returned to dispatch the order for partial mobilisation. The cause of this change in the Tsar's mind was a second telegram received from the Kaiser,[5] in which he said that he was mediating at Vienna, and added : " Of course, military measures on the part of Russia, which would be looked on by Austria as threatening,

---

[1] *Tages-Aufzeichnungen*, p. 19 ; Paléologue, p. 35. The telegram to Paris is, perhaps, that given R.O.B., No. 58, and Romberg, p. 340, No. 1551, though that does not explicitly say whether the mobilisation is partial or general. No such telegram is printed in the B.B.B.
[2] See below, p. 454.   [3] Aust. Docs., iii. No. 19.   [4] Dobrorolski, pp. 25–6.
[5] Kautsky, No. 359, sent out from Berlin at 6.30 p.m.

would precipitate a calamity which we both wish to avoid, and jeopardise my position as a mediator which I readily accepted on your appeal to my friendship and help."

The news of the substitution of partial for general mobilisation was conveyed to Sazonoff at 11 p.m. Two hours later another interview took place between him and the German Ambassador.[1] The usual positions were taken on both sides. The Minister said that only Germany could stop Austria. Pourtalès retorted with the thesis of "localisation," and the impossibility of German interference with Austrian sovereignty. Besides, Austria had promised not to take Serbian territory. That ought to satisfy Russia. "Not at all," Sazonoff retorted. "Russia could not allow Serbia to become a vassal State of Austria." Pourtalès then recurred to the Russian mobilisation against Austria, which, he said, now overshadowed the Serbian problem and menaced the peace of Europe. Sazonoff replied that there could be no question of countermanding this; but he said nothing about the order and counter-order of total mobilisation.[2]

Meantime the decision for general mobilisation had been communicated to Paléologue, the French Ambassador, at 11 p.m. The information, the Ambassador tells us, "made me jump." "Would it not be possible," he urged, "to be content for the moment with partial mobilisation?" Reasons, however, were given against that course which he was compelled to admit were strong.[3] After midnight, the Ambassador was informed of the substitution of partial mobilisation for general, and he telegraphed the news of this latter to Paris. On the 30th, Isvolski had an interview with the French War Minister. The Minister said that he did not wish to interfere with Russian preparations, but suggested that, in view of the efforts being made to preserve the peace, they should be as secret and as little provocative as possible. He also said to the Russian military attaché, that "we (the Russians)

---

[1] According to the Russian account, Pourtalès asked for the interview (*Tages-Aufzeichnungen*, p. 20). According to Pourtalès himself, Sazonoff sent for him (*Am Scheidewegen*, p. 46).

[2] According to the Russian account (cf. also F.Y.B., No. 103, and B.B.B., No. 97), it was in this interview that Sazonoff produced his last formula for reconciliation (see below, p. 457). But Pourtalès says it was certainly at the later interview, next day, that this occurred (see *Tages-Aufzeichnungen*, p. 20, note 30).

[3] Paléologue, pp. 35–6.

might declare that, in the higher interests of peace, we were ready for a time to slacken in our preparations ; which, however, would not hinder us from pursuing and even intensifying them, though we might, as far as possible, abstain from transport of troops." [1]

XIII. Austria Resists German Pressure

Meantime, what was Austria doing ? We have seen that, on the evening of this day, 29th, Sazonoff had had a conversation with the Austrian Ambassador, which had been interrupted by the news of the bombardment of Belgrade. In that interview he had complained that conversations between St. Petersburg and Vienna had been interrupted. The basis for this complaint seems to have been a conversation held on the 28th between Berchtold and the Russian Ambassador at Vienna. The Ambassador had suggested that " the Serbian reply might be taken as the starting-point for an understanding " ; but the Minister had refused, on the ground that such a discussion would be intolerable to public opinion, the more so as the declaration of war had already been made. [2] Reporting further, on the 29th, Berchtold adds that, though he had declined to discuss the Serbian Note, he had kept open the possibility of further conversations on the general subject of Russian and Austrian relations ; [3] and on that same day the Austrian Ambassador at St. Petersburg had repeated that suggestion. [4] Knowing, as we do, the Austrian determination to get on with the Serbian war, we may perhaps assume that Berchtold was endeavouring to fob off Russian intervention by inconclusive conversations without coming to a definite breach. At any rate, on the 29th, he interviewed the Russian Ambassador, but without saying or admitting anything which altered the situation. [5] On the

---

[1] Romberg, p. 49, No. 210. This telegram is omitted from the original Russian Orange Book. Romberg comments : " This telegram is an irrefutable proof that, both for Petersburg and for Paris, all further negotiations for the maintenance of peace, the proposals of Grey and the efforts of Germany in Vienna, served only as covers for the military preparations which were being secretly pursued in Russia and France." This extravagant conclusion is characteristic of a good deal of German propaganda.

[2] Aust. Docs., ii. No. 95, report sent to Petersburg at 11.40 p.m.

[3] Ib., iii. No. 23.　　　　　　　　　[4] Ib., iii. No. 19.

[5] Aust. Docs., iii. No. 45.

same day, at 2.30 p.m., he informed Berlin that instructions have gone to Count Szápáry to begin conversations with Sazonoff.[1] The Germans, meantime, were urgently requesting that " in order to prevent a general catastrophe, or at least to put Russia in the wrong, Vienna should inaugurate and continue the conferences proposed by Germany." [2] They were persistent in their efforts to persuade Austria to put into execution the plan proposed by her, and accepted by England ; and their urgency was increased by the warnings and appeals Lichnowski was sending from London. Twice on the 29th Sir Edward had seen him and had left upon his mind the impression that " unless Austria is willing to enter upon a discussion of the Serbian question, a world-war is inevitable." [3] " Mediation seemed to him now to be urgently necessary if a European catastrophe were not to result." While England could stand aside so long as the conflict was confined to Austria and Russia, yet, if Germany and France should be involved, " the British Government would, under the circumstances, find itself forced to make up its mind quickly." This he said because he wanted to " protect me from disappointments and himself from the reproach of bad faith." [4] In the language of diplomacy, this was equivalent to a declaration that, if France and Germany were involved, Britain would come in against Germany ; and, plainly, it was so understood by the Germans. They forwarded Lichnowski's dispatches to Vienna in the early hours of the 30th,[5] and to the second of them the Chancellor appended the following note : " We stand, in case Austria refuses all mediation, before a conflagration in which England will be against us ; Italy and Roumania, to all appearances, will not go with us, and we two shall be opposed to four great Powers. On Germany, thanks to England's opposition, the principal burden of the fight would fall. Austria's political prestige, the honour of her arms, as well as her just claims against Serbia, could all be satisfied by the occupation of Belgrade or of other places. She would be strengthening her status in the Balkans, as well as in relation to Russia,

[1] Kautsky, No. 433.
[2] Kautsky, No. 385, sent out from Berlin at 4.10 a.m. on the 30th, reached Vienna at 6 a.m.
[3] Ib., No. 357.   [4] Ib., No. 368.   [5] Ib., Nos. 384, 395.

by the humiliation of Serbia. Under these circumstances, we must urgently and impressively suggest to the consideration of the Vienna Cabinet the acceptance of mediation on the above-mentioned honourable conditions. The responsibility for the consequences that would otherwise follow would be an uncommonly heavy one, both for Austria and for us." [1] This latter communication reached Vienna at noon on the 30th. It was brought to the German Ambassador while he was at lunch with Berchtold, and read by him to the Minister immediately upon their rising from table. " The Minister," he reports, " listened pale and silent while it was read twice—Count Forgach taking notes—and said at the conclusion that he would make a report to the Emperor about it." [2]

What effect had these urgent communications upon Austrian policy? In the first place, Berchtold saw the Russian Ambassador; but though he spoke to him about the complaint of Sazonoff that conversations had been broken off, he said nothing about the points urged in the German Note.[3] Secondly, he conveyed to Germany, at 2.30 p.m., a communication which amounted to an acceptance of the German proposal. " Instructions have gone to Count Szápáry for him to begin conversations with Sazonoff. Count Szápáry is authorised to explain to the Russian Minister the note to Serbia, which of course has been superseded by war, and to receive every suggestion that may be made further on the part of Russia, as well as to discuss with Sazonoff all questions directly touching on Austro-Hungarian relations. . . . Furthermore, the Minister will tell the Russian Ambassador —and as a matter of fact the Minister made note of the following appropriate points in my presence—that the Monarchy has no idea of making any territorial acquisitions in Serbia, and that after the conclusion of the peace it intends to occupy Serbian territory purely temporarily, in order to compel the Serbian Government to the complete fulfilment of its demands, and for the creation of guarantees for future good behaviour. Just to the extent

---

[1] Cf. also Kautsky, No. 441, which, however, was not sent (ib., No. 450).
[2] Ib., No. 465.
[3] Aust. Docs., iii. No. 45 ; B.B.B., No. 96. It is possible that this interview was held before the arrival of the German Note ; but the account of it was not sent to Petersburg until 1.40 a.m., on the 31st.

that Serbia fulfils the conditions of peace the evacuation of
Serbian territory by the Monarchy will follow." [1]   On this
the Kaiser notes : " Thus practically my proposition accepted
and handled as I telegraphed it to the Tsar as my view."
This communication was forwarded by the Germans to their
Ambassador in England [2] as well as to Pourtalès at St.
Petersburg.[3] The Germans then clearly believed that they
had gained their point with Austria.   But, in fact, we do not
find any dispatch from Berchtold to St. Petersburg of the
kind which he promised that he would send.[4] There is no
evidence, then, that he ever sent it ; and there is striking
evidence to suggest the contrary.   For, on the 31st, the
German proposal was brought before a Ministerial Council
at Vienna, in order to discuss what formal reply should
be given.   Berchtold then reported that he had seen
the Emperor ; that the latter had said that a stoppage of
hostilities against Serbia was impossible ; and that the
British proposal could not, therefore, be accepted in
substance,[5] though the form of the reply should be conciliatory.[6]   He explained that, if Austria should secure
a victory only of prestige, she would have gained nothing.
It was useless merely to occupy Belgrade.   For the
Serbian Army would remain intact, and in a year or two
the Monarchy would have to face a new attack under
less favourable conditions.   Count Tisza agreed.   He proposed to reply that Austria was ready to consider the British
proposal, but only under condition that the military operations against Serbia were continued, and the Russian mobilisation stopped.   Herr von Bilinski said that he found this
proposal " extraordinarily clever " and that it would help
to gain time.   As to a conference, the remembrance of the
one held in London (1912–13) was so painful that public
opinion would rise against a repetition of such a farce.
The proposal of Tisza was then adopted unanimously.[7]

[1] Kautsky, No. 433.   [2] Ib., No. 444.
[3] Ib., note 3. For reception by Sir Edward, see ib., No. 489.
[4] The dispatch referred to above, Aust. Docs., iii. No. 45, deals only with the
question of the interruption of conversations, mobilisation, etc., and it
was, perhaps, an account of an interview held before the arrival of the last
German Note.
[5] In meritorischer Hinsicht.
[6] Dass wir in der Form unserer Antwort Entgegenkommen zeigen.
[7] Aust. Docs., iii. No. 79. Cf. B.B.B., 133, No. 135,

Whether the Austrians intended, or no, to deceive the Germans we need not pronounce. But it is clear that they had not really accepted the German proposal in the sense in which the Germans thought it had been accepted ; and still less in any sense which was likely to satisfy the Russians.

XIV. The Russian General Mobilisation

To Russia we must now return. We left events there at the point when, by the command of the Tsar, acting on his own responsibility, partial mobilisation had been substituted for general. The order had been sent out at midnight. But neither Sazonoff nor the military chiefs had changed their opinion. They still thought partial mobilisation a fatal mistake, and they returned to the charge on the 30th. Sukhomlinoff and Januschkevitsch telephoned to the Tsar at 11 a.m. to try to shake his resolution. But he was firm and threatened to cut short the conversation. Januschkevitsch had only just time to beg him to see Sazonoff. After a few moments' silence he consented, and an interview was arranged for 3 p.m. At that interview, "for nearly a whole hour" Sazonoff urged upon the Tsar that war had become inevitable. Germany had clearly determined upon it, for otherwise she could easily have brought her ally to reason. "It was better to proceed with our preparations without fearing that by doing so we might precipitate events, rather than, from fear of provoking war, to be surprised by it." It would be impossible to put more clearly the menace involved in armaments. Everyone must be prepared, yet everyone's preparations involve a threat to others, which will precipitate the very event that is dreaded. The Tsar felt the dilemma. He resisted long, and it is interesting to note that what finally decided him was an intervention by a General Tatischtscheff. During a moment of silence, the General observed : "Yes, it is hard to decide." The Tsar replied, in an irritated voice : "It is I who decide," and he decided in favour of general mobilisation. On such small things, in the last resort, may great events depend. Sazonoff hastened to the telephone in the palace and gave the news to Januschkevitsch, adding : "Now you can cut off the telephone." This last remark referred to a previous conversation, in which it had been arranged that the General, after receiving and giving the order, should disappear, so that there might be no chance of another counter-order from the Tsar.[1]

This decision was reached sixteen hours at latest after the issue of the order for partial mobilisation. In that short time, presumably, no steps had been taken which might make the change confusing and difficult. The necessary signatures for the new order were quickly obtained, and at 5 p.m. Dobrorolski was once more at the telegraph office. " At 6 o'clock all the apparatus was ready to receive the telegram. I entered the room. A solemn silence prevailed among the operators. Each sat before his instrument and waited for the copies of the telegram, that was to dispatch to all the ends of the Russian Empire the news of the summoning of the people to the great conflict. Suddenly, a few minutes after six, all the instruments began to tap. It was the opening moment of the great epoch. At 7 p.m. the answers began to pour in. The order for mobilisation had been received." [2]

Meantime at noon [3] on this day (30th) Pourtalès had had another conversation with Sazonoff.[4] He had been instructed to inform the Minister of the proposal Berlin was pressing on Vienna, and to warn him against the consequences of mobilisation.[5] Sazonoff repeated that he could not be satisfied by a declaration of territorial disinterestedness from Austria. To do so would be to risk the life of the Tsar. This observation, if serious, is an interesting proof of the strength of Russian public opinion. Pourtalès replied that, in that case, they were at a deadlock. " In strong words I represented to the Minister how fearful would be this war, the scope of which it was impossible to foresee. No means should be omitted to stop the rolling stone. A compromise must be reached if possible. One could surely be found if there were good will on both sides." Under this pressure Sazonoff wrote down the following formula : " If Austria declares that in recognition of the fact that its conflict with Serbia has assumed the character of a question of European interest,

[1] *Tages-Aufzeichnungen*, pp. 28-9. Cf. Paléologue, p. 38.
[2] Dobrorolski, pp. 28-9.   [3] Above, p. 451, note 2.
[4] *Am Scheidewegen*, p. 50 ; Kautsky, No. 421.   [5] Kautsky, No. 380.

it declares itself ready to eliminate from its ultimatum those points which infringe on Serbia's sovereign rights, then Russia agrees to suspend all military preparations." [1] There was not much chance that Austria would have accepted this formula, since she had always refused to reconsider the terms of her ultimatum ; and this Pourtalès pointed out. He was unable however to persuade the Minister to further concessions ; and he forwarded the proposal, as drafted, to his Government, which circulated it to the other Powers. Sir Edward Grey then secured the Russian assent to an amendment, so that, in the end, the formula ran as follows : " If Austria consents to stay the march of her troops on Serbian territory, and if, recognising that the Austro-Serbian conflict has assumed the character of a question of European interest, she admits that the Great Powers may examine the satisfaction which Serbia can afford to the Austro-Hungarian Government, without injury to her sovereign rights as a State, and to her independence, Russia undertakes to preserve her waiting attitude." [2] The formula, as thus amended, might be more acceptable to Austria since it does not touch on the terms of the ultimatum. In fact, however, it never came to acceptance or rejection, for the Russian mobilisation precipitated the war. It remains for us to describe that final episode.

XV. The Last Hours

At 1 p.m. on the 30th an announcement of German mobilisation appeared in the *Lokal Anzeiger* in Berlin. Various suggestions have been made as to the meaning of this ; as, that mobilisation had, in fact, been decided upon in the evening of the 29th ; or that it was desired, by this news, to precipitate a mobilisation in Russia. But these suppositions do not seem to be supported by any evidence. The announcement was immediately contradicted ; [3] and it had, in fact, no influence in precipitating Russian mobilisation ; for that, as we have seen, had been extorted from the Tsar between 3 and 4 p.m., nothing, at that time, being known in

[1] Kautsky, No. 421.
[2] B.B.B., No. 132 ; R.O.B., No. 67 ; F.Y.B., No. 113.
[3] F.Y.B., No. 105 ; R.O.B., No. 62.

St. Petersburg, and therefore nothing said, about the rumour. On the evening of this day v. Moltke urged upon the Austrians a general mobilisation.[1] Conrad tells us that, when he read this message to Berchtold, the Minister exclaimed : " Success ! (das ist gelungen). Who rules ? Moltke or Bethmann ? "[2] On this same evening the Kaiser telegraphed to the Austrian Emperor urging once more the plan of " halt in Belgrade."[3] To this the Emperor replied that immediately after receiving the Chancellor's dispatch he had heard of the mobilisation of Russia against Austria[4] and had in consequence mobilised his whole army.[5] The terms of this note, which presumably were supplied by Berchtold, are further evidence of the intransigeance of Austria-Hungary : " In the consciousness of my grave obligations toward the future of my Empire, I have ordered the mobilisation of my entire armed forces. The movements of my army against Serbia, now in progress, can suffer no disturbance through the threatening and challenging attitude of Russia. A rescue of Serbia by means of Russian intervention, at the present time, would bring about the most serious consequences for my territories, and therefore it is impossible for me to permit such an intervention. I am aware of the full meaning and extent of my decision, at which I arrived with confidence in the justice of God, combined with the certainty that the strength of your defence will, with unflinching fidelity, furnish security for my Empire and for the Triple Alliance." Before the Kaiser replied to this, the final catastrophe had been precipitated by the news of the total mobilisation of Russia. This reached Berlin at about 11.30 a.m. on the morning of the 31st.[6] The Germans, as we saw, had abstained from mobilising on the night of the 29th. They dared not abstain now. At 1.45 p.m. they declared " Kriegs-

---

[1] Aust. Docs., iii. No. 34, sent out from Berlin at 7.40 p.m.

[2] *Aus meiner Dienstzeit,* iv. p. 153.

[3] Kautsky, No. 395, urging the acceptance of mediation. This reached Vienna at noon on the 30th.

[4] News received about 7 p.m. on the 30th (Kautsky, Nos. 385, 386).

[5] Aust. Docs., iii. No. 49 ; Kautsky, No. 482. This telegram was sent at 1 p.m. on the 31st. The mobilisation against Russia was ordered at 11.30 a.m. on the same day (Bülow, *Erste Stundenschläge,* p. 144 ; Montgelas, p. 139).

[6] Kautsky, No. 473 ; Bülow, *Erste Stundenschläge,* p. 146. This was the very hour of the mobilisation of Austria against Russia.

gefahr." [1] At 1.45 p.m. they telegraphed this news to Austria,[2] saying that mobilisation would follow, that war would then be inevitable, and that " we expect from Austria active participation in the war with Russia." [3] The ultimatum to Russia followed at 3.30.[4] At about the same hour the Tsar sent a telegram to the Kaiser, saying that Russian mobilisation had been provoked by Austria, that for technical reasons it could not be stopped, but that " we are far from wishing war. So long as the negotiations with Austria on Serbia's account are taking place my troops shall not take any provocative action. I give you my solemn word for this. I put all my trust in God's mercy and hope in your successful mediation in Vienna, for the welfare of our countries and for the peace of Europe." [5]

When Pourtalès presented the German ultimatum, at midnight, Sazonoff still harped upon the comparative innocuousness of Russian mobilisation and the desire of the Tsar for peace. But the Ambassador replied that the Tsar's promise to refrain from war depended upon his reaching an agreement with Austria. Could the Minister promise that, even if such agreement were not reached, Russia would keep the peace ? Of course, the Minister could not. " In that case," I replied, " nobody can blame us for our unwillingness to allow Russia a longer start in mobilisation." [6] The assumption of the Ambassador plainly was that agreement with Austria was impossible ; and all we know of Austrian policy confirms that view. But on this point a last ambiguity was to drag its way, for another forty-eight hours, through the Chancelleries of Europe. On the 31st, after the general mobilisation of Russia had been made known, the Austrian Ambassador interviewed Sazonoff, to convey to him the instructions sent him on the 30th.[7] He had decided, he reports, to ignore the Russian mobilisation, partly because he did not wish to disavow the statement, telegraphed by

---

[1] See Kautsky, No. 341, where it is said that Kriegsgefahr, " although it would not yet mean mobilisation, or the calling in of any reserves to the colours, would nevertheless increase the tension."

[2] It seems from Aust. Docs., iii. No. 72, that the news of the Russian mobilisation, sent off by the Ambassador at 11.25 a.m. on the 31st, did not reach Vienna from Petersburg until 9 a.m. on the 1st August.

[3] Kautsky, No. 479.   [4] Ib., No. 490.

[5] Ib., No. 487. Cf., for a later telegram, ib., No. 546.

[6] Ib., No. 536.

[7] Aust. Docs., iii. No. 45. See above, p. 454. For Szápáry's interviews with Sazonoff, ib., Nos. 75, 97.

the Kaiser to the Tsar, that Austria was ready to continue conversations, partly because " it seemed to me opportune, in order to establish our technical position, that we should have given an extreme proof of good will, in order, so far as possible, to put Russia in the wrong." His Government, he told the Minister, was ready to discuss the ultimatum to Serbia " so far as concerned its interpretation." He was aware that Russia took the view that the form of the note should be softened, while the Austrian position was merely that its meaning might be explained. This was, of course, a discrepancy; but " it seemed to me to come to essentially the same thing." Sazonoff welcomed this statement with a satisfaction that is rather surprising. It was good news, he said ; the question could now be treated in the way he had always desired. The Ambassador appears to have been rather disturbed by this warm reception of his words, and dwelt once more upon the discrepancy between the Russian and the Austrian points of view. He concludes his report with the words : " In view of my reserve on the subject of the Russian mobilisation, your Excellency will be perfectly at liberty to say that my observations have no longer any significance (meine Eröffnungen als gegenstandlos zu erklären). On the other hand, I thought it important to have taken a step which can be said to go as far as possible in the way of conciliation. Should your Excellency consider diplomatic negotiations, even now, to be practicable or opportune, here is a foundation laid for them." It seems clear, from this account, that the Ambassador was concerned rather with putting Russia in the wrong than with offering any new concession from Austria. For such concession he had, in fact, no authority. But he seems to have spoken in such a way that Sazonoff thought a concession had been obtained. For he telegraphed to his Ambassador in France that Austria was willing to enter into a discussion of the " contents " of the ultimatum ; that he hoped the British Government would conduct the negotiations ; but that, for success, it was important that Austria should stop her military operations against Serbia.[1] This communication was, apparently, the basis of Sir Edward Grey's latest efforts to secure a com-

[1] Romberg, No. 1592, p. 51.   This dispatch does not appear in the Orange Book as published in 1914.

promise. He suggested [1] that Austrian military action against Serbia should proceed for the present, but that Russia should stop her mobilisation against Austria. It seems probable that Austria might have accepted such a proposal, since it would have allowed her to continue her military operations against Serbia, while Russia countermanded hers against Austria. But it is hardly possible that Sazonoff would have accepted it. As we have seen, what he wanted was a modification of the terms of the Austrian ultimatum ; Austria, meantime, to arrest her operations against Serbia. We have, however, no Russian source to inform us how he received Sir Edward's proposal. The German Ambassador in Paris says on the 1st : " It is officially reported here that Sir Edward Grey's proposal of a general suspension of military preparations has been accepted in principle," [2] and the French Prime Minister tells the Ambassador that " Russia has agreed to the suspension of military preparations on condition that the other Powers should act in the same way." [3] This was a different suggestion to the one put forward by Sir Edward ; but it is hardly credible that Russia was really prepared to accept even this, after the receipt of the German ultimatum. If she had been, she would surely have replied in that sense to Germany. Nor does it seem possible that Austria had consented, or would consent, to stop her military preparations against Serbia. We must conclude, unless and until further evidence is produced, that these last efforts of Sir Edward were based upon a misapprehension by Sazonoff of the real nature of the offer conveyed in his interview with Szápáry ; that they would, in any case, have broken down ; and that they were certainly made impracticable by the German ultimatum.[4]

XVI. How France Came In

We have thus traced the steps by which Russia came into war with Austria and Germany. Let us now turn to

[1] B.B.B., Nos. 133, 135. The proposals Nos. 110 and 111 seem to precede the communication from Russia.
[2] Kautsky, No. 571. [3] F.Y.B., No. 125.
[4] Unfortunately the dispatches published between London and St. Petersburg of August 1st and August 2nd are very scanty. We do not, therefore, know what was really passing. It may be added that Sazonoff's Apologia, R.O.B., No. 77, contains no reference to this last effort for peace.

France. To her, too, Germany sent an ultimatum, at the same time as to Russia, but with a time limit of eighteen instead of twelve hours.[1] There was, however, the Germans thought, just a possibility of French neutrality; and they directed their Ambassador that, in case France should choose that course, she should be required to hand over in pledge the fortresses of Toul and Verdun.[2] In fact, however, the French had never had any idea of remaining neutral. They had given their promise to Russia as early as 1912, had repeated it during the present crisis, and did so again, most emphatically, on August 1st.[3] But though the French had made up their minds, they were not anxious to say so. On receiving the German Note the Premier said " that he had no news of any general Russian mobilisation, only of precautionary measures. Therefore he was not willing quite yet to give up the hope of avoiding the extreme event. He promised to give an answer on the neutrality question by one o'clock to-morrow at the latest." [4] That the Minister had no news of the general Russian mobilisation was true, in the sense that the news, as transmitted by their Ambassador at St. Petersburg, did not arrive until after this interview.[5] But, as we have seen, the French Government was informed on the 30th of the partial mobilisation [6] and had advised the Russians to pursue their preparations, keeping them as secret as possible. So that this remark of the French Minister may be regarded as a terminological inexactitude. As to the postponement of a reply to the German inquiry until 1 p.m. next day, the object of that was frankly explained by the President. " It will be much better," he said, " that we should not, in adhering to the alliance, have to declare war. If Germany declares it against us, the people of France will rise with greater ardour to defend its soil and its liberty." [7] We have seen, again and again, that one of the objects of diplomacy is to make sure that, when the war which all are

---

[1] Kautsky, No. 491. [2] Ib., No. 491.

[3] Romberg, p. 58, No. 222; p. 60, No. 225. These dispatches are not included in the Orange Book as published in 1914.

[4] Kautsky, Nos. 528, 571.

[5] See Romberg, p. 53, No. 215. The interview was at 6.30 p.m. The news from the Ambassador at Petersburg arrived at some later hour. (But cf. Montgelas, pp. 162-3, and *Kriegsschuldfrage*, August 1923, May 1924.)

[6] Which can hardly be what is meant by the phrase " precautionary measures " (see above, p. 451).

[7] Poincaré, p. 249.

anticipating breaks out, it shall appear to have been provoked by the other side. M. Poincaré's remarks are therefore quite in accordance with diplomatic philosophy. But
there were other and additional reasons why it was preferable
that the Germans rather than the French should precipitate
hostilities. For a French declaration of war, a vote of the
Chambers was necessary ; and the President, though he had
no doubt that he could obtain such a vote, preferred to avoid
a public discussion upon the obligations of the Russian
alliance. Again, there was the effect upon English opinion
to be considered. For Sir Edward was still holding his hand,
and any suspicion that the French were the aggressors might
determine British opinion in the wrong direction. There
was also a military reason. French mobilisation had not
begun, and it was desirable that there should be as long a
time as possible to develop it before actual war broke out.[1]
For all these reasons France gave no definite reply to the
German ultimatum on the 31st ; but she proceeded to
mobilisation on the 1st.[2] Meantime the Germans extended
the time limit of their ultimatum by two hours.[3] This
brought it down to 3 p.m. on the 1st ; but even at 5.30 the
Ambassador was still conversing with the Premier, who maintained that there was yet a possibility of settlement on the
basis of Sir Edward's last proposal.[4] " He could not abandon,"
he said, " his hope for peace."

But by now the time limit appointed for Russia had
passed, and at 7.10 p.m. the declaration of war was handed
in at St. Petersburg. " I asked M. Sazonoff," says the
German Ambassador, " three successive times, whether he
could make me the declaration demanded concerning the
suspension of hostile measures against Austria and us. After
my question had been answered in the negative three times,
I handed over the note as instructed."[5] In Beethoven's
5th symphony three notes followed by one run all through
the first movement, and the master gives the indication " so

---

[1] Romberg, p. 61, No. 225. It appears from this that M. Poincaré was
contemplating a delay of ten days. But also, that he was afraid that
Germany would attack at once, in order to make the mobilisation more
difficult. Perhaps the brevity of the dispatch obscures the position really
taken.

[2] 3.40 p.m. See B.B.B., No. 136. The decision was taken at midday
(see Bülow, *Erste Stundenschläge*, p. 166, who cites the authorities).

[3] Kautsky, No. 543.   [4] Ib., No. 598.   [5] Ib., No. 588.

klopft das Schicksal an die Tür." Between these two commonplace men, each convinced he was right, those three questions and answers decreed the death of millions of men, the collapse of some States and the birth of others, the ruin of Europe, perhaps of our civilisation. Such instruments do the Powers use to bring into operation the decrees whereby, for purposes unknown to us, they govern the frail and impotent race of mankind.

Germany and Russia being thus at war, nothing remained for the French Government but to endorse, at the cost of the nation, the catastrophe thus brought about by years of secret diplomacy. The nation accepted the decree with dramatic propriety. Ministers, the President tells us, came away from the meeting of the Chambers " in a state of inexpressible emotion, and repeated to me as one man : " If only you could have been there with us. France has never been so fine ! "

XVII. How England Came In

By August 1st, then, there was war between the four Continental Powers. But the fate of England still hung in the balance. Sir Edward Grey, as we have seen, from the beginning of the crisis, had tried plan after plan to keep the peace of Europe. He had supported the extension of the time limit in the Austrian ultimatum.[1] He had proposed a Conference of the Powers, or failing that, mediation between Austria and Russia.[2] He had besought Germany to put pressure on Austria.[3] He had proposed the " Halt in Belgrade " followed by the mediation of the Powers.[4] He had supported the last Russian formula and secured its amendment, to make it more acceptable to Austria.[5] Whatever may be thought about the other Powers, the evidence is conclusive that the British Government strained every nerve to avoid the war. Moreover, Sir Edward saw clearly, from the beginning, where the danger lay. As early as July 15th he told the German Ambassador that " everything would depend on the kind of intervention (by Austria) that might ensue. In no

[1] Kautsky, No. 157 ; B.B.B., No. 26.
[2] B.B.B., Nos. 24, 25, 36, 67 ; Kautsky, No. 236.
[3] B.B.B., No. 36.   [4] B.B.B., 88, Kautsky, No. 368.
[5] B.B.B., Nos. 103, 104.

case ought a diminution of Serbian territory to be considered." [1]
On the 25th he said to the German Ambassador that " He
counts with certainty on the Austrian mobilisation being
followed by that of Russia," and that " Without (German)
co-operation, all attempt at mediation would be futile." [2]
At the same time he was careful not to give the impression
either that England would keep out of the war, under all
circumstances, or that she would, necessarily, come in.[3] His
position was that, if the war were confined to the east, England
would not be involved ; but that it would be different if
France should take part.[4] Nevertheless, he refused to give
France a definite assurance.[5] He has been blamed for
this. It has been said that, if he had put himself frankly
on the side of France and Russia, the war might have been
avoided. Possibly that is true. But Sir Edward has his
defence. " On my remarking," said the Austrian Ambassador
in London, " that I counted on him to keep them quiet in
St. Petersburg, he replied that two opposite views were urged
upon him : to put himself unconditionally upon the side of
Russia and France, which might prevent the war (I interjected
that it would have the opposite effect), or to make it clear
that England, under no circumstances, would side with
France and Russia. The latter course, he assured me, would
not prevent the war." [6] It may be inferred from this that
Sir Edward believed that any assurance he might give to
either party would but precipitate events.[7] He was determined to give no excuse for aggression on either side, and to
use his influence, to the last, in the endeavour to preserve
peace.

This attitude he maintained against very strong pressure
from France. For on the 31st the French President addressed
the following letter to the King :

" CHER ET GRAND AMI,
    " In the grave circumstances through which Europe
is passing, I believe it to be my duty to communicate directly
to your Majesty the information the Government of the
Republic has received from Germany.

[1] Kautsky, No. 52.   [2] Ib., No. 179.
[3] B.B.B., No. 47.   [4] Kautsky, No. 368.
[5] B.B.B., No. 119.   [6] Aust. Docs., iii. No. 42, July 30th.
[7] In his book Grey takes a different line (see ii. pp. 40 seq.).

" The military preparations that are being made by the Imperial Government, notably in the immediate neighbourhood of the French frontier, are every day assuming additional intensity and acceleration. France, determined to do until the last all that she can for the maintenance of peace, has so far confined herself strictly to indispensable measures of precaution. It does not appear that her prudence and her moderation will abate the determination of Germany—far from it. We are therefore, perhaps, in spite of the discretion of the Government of the Republic and the calmness of public opinion, on the eve of the most formidable events.

"From all the information that is reaching us, it is clear that if Germany were certain that the British Government would not intervene in a conflict in which France would be engaged, war would be inevitable ; and that, on the other hand, if Germany were certain that the Entente Cordiale would be operative, in such case, even to the battlefield, there would be the greatest chance that peace would not be broken.

" Undoubtedly our military and naval agreements leave your Majesty's Government entirely free, and in the letters exchanged in 1912 between Sir Edward Grey and M. Paul Cambon, Great Britain and France are merely pledged the one to the other, to conversations in the event of European tension, with a view to considering whether there is ground for common action.

" The intimate character, however, that public opinion in both countries has given to the *entente* between Great Britain and France, the mutual confidence in which our two Governments have unceasingly worked for the maintenance of peace, the sympathy your Majesty has always manifested for France, encourage me to make known to you quite frankly our feelings, which are those of the Government of the Republic and of the whole of France.

"I believe that henceforth the last possibilities of peace depend on the language and the conduct of the British Government.

" We have ourselves, since the beginning of the crisis, recommended to our allies a moderation to which they have adhered. In accord with the British Government and in conformity with the latest suggestions of Sir Edward Grey,

we shall continue so to act. But if all the efforts at conciliation come from the same side, and if Germany and Austria
are able to speculate on the abstention of Great Britain, the
demands of Austria will remain inflexible and an agreement
between Russia and her will become impossible.

"I have the profound conviction that at the present moment
the more Great Britain, France, and Russia present a strong
impression of unity in their diplomatic action, the more we
may still rely on the preservation of peace." [1]

But even this letter produced no definite assurance. The
King's reply was as follows :

"CHER ET GRAND AMI,

"I appreciate to the fullest extent the sentiments
that have led you to write to me in such a cordial and
friendly spirit, and I am glad that you have set forth your
views so fully and so frankly.

"You may be assured that the present situation in Europe
has been the cause of much anxiety and preoccupation to
me, and I am thankful to think that our two Governments
have worked so amicably together in order to try to find a
peaceful solution of the questions in dispute.

"It would be a source of deep satisfaction for us if our united
efforts should end as we wish, and I am not yet without hope
that the terrible events that appear to be so near may yet be
avoided.

"I admire the constraint that you and your Government
are exercising in abstaining from taking, on your frontiers,
the final military measures, and in adopting an attitude that
can in no sense and in no way be interpreted as a provocation.

"I am personally making the strongest efforts with the
Emperors of Russia and Germany for the purpose of finding
some means by which the present military efforts may be,
in any case, postponed, so that time may be gained for calm
discussion between the Powers.

"I intend to prosecute these efforts unceasingly, so long
as there remains any hope of an amicable settlement.

"As to the attitude of my country, events are happening
so rapidly that it is difficult to foresee future developments,

[1] Poincaré, pp. 238–9.

but you may be assured that my Government will continue to discuss freely and frankly with M. Cambon everything that may arise and that may present an interest for our two nations.

" Believe me, Monsieur le Président, your sincere friend,
" GEORGE R.I." [1]

The first overt act taken by Sir Edward was in connexion with Belgium. It was common knowledge among the soldiers of Europe that if there were war between France and Germany the German Army would invade by that route. On the 31st accordingly the British Minister addressed a note both to France and to Germany asking whether they would respect Belgian neutrality.[2] The French answered that they would.[3] The Germans said that they were not in a position to reply.[4] In fact, they had sent to their Ambassador in Belgium, as early as July 29th, a sealed note, to be delivered when orders to that effect should be given. In this note they said that France would attack Germany through Belgium, and that Germany must anticipate this attack by herself invading Belgium ; that they hoped Belgium would not regard this as a hostile act ; but that, if she did, and if she attempted resistance by force, the result would be war with Germany.[5] But even Germany's refusal to promise respect for Belgium's neutrality did not precipitate the British Government into war. Sir Edward merely observed to the German Ambassador that " if there were a violation of the neutrality of Belgium by one combatant, while the other respected it, it would be extremely difficult to restrain public feeling in this country." [6] Upon this, the Ambassador asked whether England would remain neutral if Germany agreed not to violate Belgium. But Sir Edward declined to give this assurance. The Ambassador then asked what the conditions of British neutrality were. Would a guarantee of the integrity of France and of her colonies suffice ? Whereupon Sir Edward said : " I felt obliged to refuse definitely any promise to remain neutral on similar terms, and I could only say that we must keep our hands free." [7] This was on

---

[1] Poincaré, pp. 249–50.   [2] B.B.B., No. 114.   [3] Ib., 125.
[4] Ib., No. 122.   [5] Kautsky, No. 375.
[6] B.B.B., No. 123.   [7] Ib., No. 123.

August 1st. In the same interview Sir Edward observed that " he had also been wondering whether it would not be possible for Germany and France to remain facing each other under arms without attacking each other, in the event of a Russian war." On which the Kaiser comments : " The rascal is crazy or an idiot." [1] Later, on the same day, Sir Edward telephoned to the German Ambassador, asking him if he could give the assurance that, in case France should remain neutral in a Russo-German war, the Germans would not attack the French. [2] The reply to this was that, " of course," they would refrain from attacking France, if French neutrality were guaranteed by the British Fleet and Army. [3] We know now what, apparently, Sir Edward did not know then, that France was pledged again and again to assist Russia in arms, in case of war between her and Germany. Presumably Sir Edward communicated with France and received that reply. At any rate, the Ambassador informed his Government that the "suggestions of Sir E. Grey, which were founded on the wish to secure France's permanent neutrality, if possible, were made without previous communication with France and without knowledge of the mobilisation, and have since been abandoned as entirely hopeless." [4]

On August 2nd, a Cabinet meeting was held, after which Sir Edward gave to the French Ambassador the following memorandum : " I am authorised to give an assurance that, if the German Fleet comes into the Channel or through the North Sea, to undertake hostile operations against the French coasts or shipping, the British Fleet will give all the protection in its power." [5] We know, from the naval arrangements between England and France, that this was the very least the British could do. The promise, indeed, was given explicitly because " it was essential to the French Government, whose Fleet had long been concentrated in the Mediterranean, to know how to make their dispositions, with the north coast entirely undefended." At this point, therefore, the naval agreements, which had been so carefully concealed from Parliament and the public, begin to bear their natural and inevitable fruit. It would have been dishonourable, no doubt, to do anything less than this. But the " honour " of

[1] Kautsky, No. 596. [2] Ib., No. 562. [3] Ib., No. 575.
[4] Ib., No. 631. [5] B.B.B., No. 148.

the nation had been committed behind its back. Yet even now the Government did not regard war as certain. It was the invasion of Belgium that gave them an unassailable case. On August 4th they sent their ultimatum to Germany, and by midnight that day the country was at war.

In all this history of the last fortnight before the outbreak of the war there seems to be only one point which might be charged against Sir Edward's policy, and it is, in fact, commonly charged against him by the Germans. They say that he did not put pressure upon Russia, or none that was adequate, in spite of requests from the German Government.[1] We are hardly in a position at present to discuss this matter, for the communications of the British Government with the Russian do not seem to have been completely published. The British Ambassador in St. Petersburg did undoubtedly, in the earlier days, point out to Russia the danger of mobilisation, and press her to abstain from it.[2] But otherwise there is no evidence that Sir Edward was urging moderation in St. Petersburg, and there is some evidence to the contrary. Thus, on July 25th, he is reported to have said, in answer to a request from the German Ambassador, that it was " quite impossible " for him to " bring conciliatory pressure to bear " at St. Petersburg.[3] And again : " In Paris, Baron v. Schoen vainly endeavoured to induce France to adopt joint action, with Germany, towards Russia for the preservation of peace. The same attempts were made in London. In both capitals the answer was given that any action taken should be at Vienna, as it was Austria's inordinate demands, her refusal to discuss Serbia's few reservations and her declaration of war that threatened to provoke a general war. France and England are unable to bring any moderating pressure to bear upon Russia, as, so far, that Power has shown the greatest moderation." [4] This was written at some time before the 29th. On that day the German Ambassador had an interview with Sir Edward in which he " entreated the Minister to warn St. Petersburg against any precipitate decision and especially to prevent a general mobilisation there that would affect our frontiers also. The

---

[1] Cf. Kautsky, No. 199 ; Tirpitz, *My Memories*, i. p. 253, etc., etc.
[2] B.B.B., No. 17. [3] R.O.B., No 20.
[4] Ib., No. 53. Cf. Romberg, p. 36, No. 198.

consequences would be beyond description." " The Minister," he tells us, " promised me again to use his influence in this direction and to strive to keep them as cool-headed as possible." [1] Whether Sir Edward fulfilled this promise we have no documentary evidence to show. The 29th was the critical day, so far as mobilisation was concerned, and English pressure in St. Petersburg might have strengthened the effect produced by the Kaiser's letters. Yet it is difficult to believe that such pressure would have made very much difference. What was important to Russia was French support, and of that she had full assurance. One may say, I think, without much fear of being refuted by later revelations, that Russia would have risked war even without any certainty of British support. For consistently from the beginning she had made it clear that she would not stand by to see Serbia crushed by Austria. It is possible that Sir Edward was afraid that to stop Russia's preparations might encourage Germany to precipitate the war. But we must leave the question until further publications throw a fuller light on British policy.

XVIII. The Real Moral

This may conclude our account of the slipping down of Europe into war. The process may be regarded as " inevitable " or as " accidental," according as we look at the deeper or the more superficial causes. We may even, and if we are Englishmen we probably do, seek the real cause in the villainy of some man or men. No doubt, if a poet of insight and dramatic gifts were to investigate the conduct of individual statesmen, he would find among them evidence in plenty of frivolity, shortsightedness, obstinacy, flurry, and confusion. But his last judgment, I believe, would be, not how wicked, but how small they were ; what little puppets, knocking away with lilliputian hammers the last stays that restrained the launch of that great death-ship, War. Let the reader listen for a moment to some few utterances, wrung, at the last, from the pale and stuttering lips of these homunculi, as there opens upon their vision the last end of their long, subterranean travail. We will take first this,

[1] Kautsky, No. 357.

from the German Kaiser, written in the urgency of the moment when it dawned upon him that England too would enter the war against him :

" Frivolity and weakness are to plunge the world into the most frightful war, which eventually aims at the destruction of Germany. For I have no doubt left about it.: England, Russia, and France have *agreed* among themselves— after laying the foundation of the casus fœderis for us through Austria—to take the Austro-Serbian conflict for an *excuse* for waging a *war of extermination* against us. Hence Grey's cynical observation to Lichnowski : ' As long as the war is *confined* to Russia and Austria, England would sit quiet, only when we and France *mixed into it* would he be compelled to make an active move against us,' i.e. either we are shamefully to betray our allies, *sacrifice* them to Russia, thereby breaking up the Triple Alliance, or we are to be attacked in common by the Triple Entente for our *fidelity to our allies* and punished, whereby they will satisfy their jealousy by joining in totally *ruining* us. That is the real naked situation *in nuce*, which, slowly and cleverly set going, certainly by Edward VII, has been carried on, and systematically built up by conversations afterwards denied between England and Paris and St. Petersburg ; finally brought to a conclusion by George V and set to work. And thereby the stupidity and ineptitude of our ally is turned into a snare for us. So the famous ' *encirclement* ' (Einkreisung) of Germany has finally become a complete fact, despite every effort of our politicians and diplomats to prevent it. The net has been suddenly thrown over our head, and England sneeringly reaps the most brilliant success of her persistently prosecuted, purely *anti-German world policy*, against which we have proved ourselves helpless, while she twists the noose of our political and economic destruction out of our fidelity to Austria, as we squirm *isolated* in the net. A great achievement, which arouses the admiration even of him who is to be destroyed as its result ! Edward VII is stronger after his death than am I who am still alive ! And there have been people who believed that England could be won over, or pacified, by this or that puny measure ! Unremittingly, relentlessly, she has pursued her object, with notes, holiday proposals, scares, Haldane, etc., until this point was reached. And we walked into the net and even went into the one-ship programme in construction with the ardent hope of thus pacifying England! All my warnings, all my pleas, were voiced for nothing. Now comes England's so-called gratitude for it! From the dilemma raised by our fidelity to the venerable old Emperor of Austria we are brought into a situation which offers England the desired pretext for annihilating us under the hypocritical cloak of justice, namely, of helping France on account of the reputed 'balance of power' in Europe, i.e. playing the card of all the European nations in England's favour against us! This whole business must now be ruthlessly uncovered and the mask of Christian peaceableness publicly and brusquely torn from its face in public, and the pharisaical hypocrisy exposed on the pillory! And our consuls in Turkey and India, agents, etc., must fire the whole Mohammedan world to fierce rebellion against this hated, lying, conscienceless nation of shopkeepers; for if we are to be bled to death, England shall at least lose India. W." [1]

He must be, I think, a dull and unimaginative man, who does not feel, behind the grotesqueness, the tragedy of this outburst. The conception of the real causes of events is imperfect enough; whose conception, indeed, at that time was or could be perfect? But this cry of rage and despair is genuine in every note; and it would be more profitable for the English to listen and consider, than to laugh or to sneer. For what matters, in all human affairs, is not merely what you do, or what you think, or what you suppose your-self to think, but how your acts appear to other people. In that appearance, you may be sure, there will be more truth than you are ready or able to perceive.

Or listen to this duet between two statesmen, Bethmann-Hollweg and Sir E. Goschen, both conscious of virtue, both at that moment sincere, both so pitifully helpless in the face of what both nevertheless had contributed, though it were unwittingly and unwillingly, to produce:

" . . . I found the Chancellor very agitated. His Excel-lency at once began a harangue, which lasted for about twenty minutes. He said that the step taken by His Majesty's

Government was terrible to a degree ; just for a word—
' neutrality,' a word which in war-time had so often been
disregarded—just for a scrap of paper, Great Britain was
going to make war on a kindred nation who desired nothing
better than to be friends with her. All his efforts in that
direction had been rendered useless by this last terrible step,
and the policy to which, as I knew, he had devoted himself
since his accession to office had tumbled down like a house
of cards. What we had done was unthinkable ; it was like.
striking a man from behind, while he was fighting for his
life against two assailants. He held Great Britain responsible
for all the terrible events that might happen. I protested
strongly against that statement, and said that, in the same
way as he and Herr von Jagow wished me to understand
that, for strategical reasons, it was a matter of life and death
to Germany to advance through Belgium and violate the
latter's neutrality, so I would wish him to understand that
it was, so to speak, a matter of ' life and death ' for the
honour of Great Britain that she should keep her solemn
engagement to do her utmost to defend Belgium's neutrality
if attacked. That solemn compact simply had to be kept,
or what confidence could anyone have in engagements given
by Great Britain in the future ? The Chancellor said :
' But at what price will that compact have been kept. Has
the British Government thought of that ? ' I hinted to His
Excellency as plainly as I could that fear of consequences
could hardly be regarded as an excuse for breaking solemn
engagements, but His Excellency was so excited, so evidently
overcome by the news of our action, and so little disposed to
hear reason that I refrained from adding fuel to the flame
by further argument. As I was leaving he said that the
blow of Great Britain joining Germany's enemies was all
the greater that, almost up to the last moment, he and his
Government had been working with us and supporting our
efforts to maintain peace between Austria and Russia. I
said that this was part of the tragedy which saw the two
nations fall apart just at the moment when the relations
between them had been more friendly and cordial than they
had been for years. Unfortunately, notwithstanding our
efforts to maintain peace between Russia and Austria, the war
had spread and had brought us face to face with a situation

which, if we held to our engagements, we could not possibly
avoid, and which unfortunately entailed our separation from
our late fellow-workers. He would readily understand that
no one regretted this more than I." [1] A " somewhat painful
interview," the Englishman comments.

Two days before this, on August 2nd, the English
Premier, who is not commonly accused of sentimentality,
had discussed the situation with the German Ambassador
in London. " Tears," we are told, " repeatedly stood in
the eyes of the old gentleman, and he said to me : ' A war
between our two countries is quite unthinkable.' " [2] In
forty-eight hours the " unthinkable " was a fact. It was
past the holding back by either of these well-meaning
statesmen. Listen again for a moment to Sir Edward Grey.
He has been interviewing the Austrian Ambassador, who reports
as follows : " Grey is in despair that his efforts to maintain
the peace have gone to ruin. Again and again he said of
the war, ' I hate it, I hate it ! ' He recalled all the efforts
we had made together, in the previous year during the Balkan
Conference. He had earnestly hoped that, once the present
danger were passed, it might be possible to preserve the peace
for years. ' I was quite ready, if ever Russia had been
aggressive—in the case of France it was not likely that she
should—to stand by Germany, and that we might come to
some sort of understanding between the Powers. Now all
that was shattered, and the universal war, with all its horrible
and revolting consequences, had broken out.' " [3]

An interview followed between the Ambassador and
Lord Rosebery, who, we are told, " judges rightly that in
this crisis it is above all Russia that is to blame. We fight
for a balance of power without seeming to see that we are
going to establish the supremacy of Russia all over the
world." [4] O prophecy ! There was perhaps more truth
in Sir Edward's forecast : " It is the greatest step towards
Socialism that could possibly have been made. . . . We shall
have Labour Governments in every country after this." [5] If
that were to come true, perhaps we might also, at last, have
peace. But the future is dark, and I do not choose to add
my prophecies to the rest.

[1] B.B.B., No. 160. [2] Kautsky, No. 676.
[3] Aust. Docs., iii. No. 159. [4] Ib. [5] Ib.

It is not to emphasise my own agreement or disagreement that I have cited these utterances, but rather to indicate the little tragedy, that lies in the foreground of the great one, like the figures of Siegmund and Hunding in the *Walküre*, backed by the lightning, and the storm, and Wotan's apparition. Does it not seem to the reader a little grotesque and unreal to pursue meticulously, across the enormous stage, the moral rights and wrongs of these puppets? But if we choose to do so, then it seems clear that, in that last month, a preponderance of blame lies upon the statesmen of Austria, Germany, and Russia. But how came it about that it was possible for these little men to let loose a world-catastrophe? They did not desire it; they did not will it; at most, they took the risk of it. But whence came the risk? The answer is the one we have been giving from the beginning of this book—the anarchy of armed States pursuing by war the maintenance, or the extension, of power. Let us then, in conclusion, summarise the course of events, as seen from that, the only realistic standpoint.

For years the little State of Serbia had been undermining the Austrian Empire. She had done so by the same impulse and the same right as that which had inspired and justified Italy during the Austrian occupation. What was the Empire to do in self-defence? One can conceive a world in which Austria would not have wished to hold down a nationality against its will. But that would not be the world of history, past or present. Never has an empire resigned before the disruptive forces of nationality. Always it has fought. And I do not believe there was a State in existence that would not, under similar circumstances, have determined, as Austria did, to finish the menace, once for all, by war. So long as power is the object of States, so long will such policies be pursued; and in the mouth of what State does it lie to blame another?

The pertinent question is, therefore, why was the war not localised, as Austria and Germany intended and desired? There is only one answer to this: because Russia did not choose to allow it. Why not? Because of her affection for her Slav brethren? Hardly, I think; though that sentiment played, no doubt, a part in her public opinion. Listen to this remark of Sazonoff made to the Austrian Ambassador: " Perhaps he ought not to say so, but he had no feeling at all for the Balkan Slavs. These were, in fact, a heavy burden to Russia, and we could hardly imagine what they had to suffer from them." [1] The real motive of Russian policy, we may be sure, was expressed by Sazonoff when he said, in conversation with the British Ambassador, that " during the Balkan crisis he made it clear to the Austrian Government that war with Russia must inevitably follow an Austrian attack on Serbia. It was clear that Austrian domination of Serbia was as intolerable for Russia as the dependence of the Netherlands on Germany would be to Great Britain. It was, in fact, for Russia a question of life and death." " Life and death ! " Once more that ambiguous phrase ! The " life " of a State, in this context, means its power ; and for that, the lives of its people may be sacrificed indefinitely. But why was the question of the Balkans one of " life and death " for Russia ? The answer is that she wanted Constantinople and the Straits ; that she wanted access to the Mediterranean ; that she wanted extension of territory and influence; that she had an "historic mission " ; that she must make herself secure ; in short, the whole farrago of superstitions that dominates all States under the conditions of the armed anarchy.

If then we really desire to put the " moral " question in a way in which it is worth the trouble of answering, we must inquire which has the greater justification—a State (Austria) which is defending itself against disruption, or one (Serbia) which is desirous to extend its power by the disruption of its neighbour. That, really, was the question between Austria and Russia. I should answer, myself, if I thought it worth while to answer, that the justification lies with Austria, and the aggression with Russia. The reader may not agree ; but at any rate that is the point at issue.

It may perhaps be replied that Russia would have accepted, and France and England favoured, a punishment of Serbia which should not interfere with her " sovereignty " or her " independence." But would that really have been a solution ? It would but have given Serbia time to wait until she was better prepared for the great venture. So, at least, the Austrian Government had come to think ; and will any candid Jugo-Slav care now to deny it ? With every year

[1] Aust. Docs., ii. No. 73.

that passed the Austrian position would get worse and the
Serbian better. So at least the Austrians thought, and not
without reason. They took their risk, according to the
usual canons in such matters. They may be accused of
miscalculation, but I do not see how they can be accused
of Wrong, by anyone who accepts now, or who accepted
then, the principles which have always dictated the policy of
States.

We come next to Germany. Against her has been
directed most of the moral indignation of the victorious
Powers. That this is not justified by the facts should be
clear, after our analysis. For, although Germany backed
Austria at the beginning, in the last day or two she was
endeavouring, vainly, to call her off. But, the reader may
ask, why did she back Austria at all? For the same kind
of reason that made France back Russia : because of the
" balance of power " ; because, if Austria were defeated, she
would be left isolated among her enemies ; because her
economic enterprises extended right across Asia, and she
could not afford to have them cut in two by Balkan States
under Russian control ; because she was pledged by her
alliance to defend Austria ; because, in a word, of all those
considerations that are always valid for all States. German
diplomacy was cumbrous, stupid, and dishonest. Granted,
it was ! But German policy was such as any State would
have adopted in her position. The Powers of the Entente
say that the offence was Germany's backing of Austria.
Germans say that the offence was Russia's backing of
Serbia. On that point, really, the whole controversy turns.
To my mind, the German position is the more reasonable.
But what, after all, is the use of such discussions? When
States are so aligned as were those of Europe before the
war, war is coming, let them do, or say, or think what
they may.

And France? France entered for the sake of the balance
of power and to recover Alsace-Lorraine ; and her technical
success in waiting till the declaration of war came from
Germany does not alter the position. It had been known,
for at least two years past, it was reaffirmed more than
once during the crisis, that if Germany came in against
Russia, France would come in against Germany. We

have seen how the preparations for that war were being conducted by the two allies. We have · heard their pledges of mutual faith. Nevertheless, they did not "want" war? No! Who did? But they thought it worth while to have it, rather than not to have it, under the conditions then given. But they would not have started it? Who can say? At any rate since 1912 they would always have entered when Russia did. And does anyone who has perused the previous chapters, and who realises the state of Europe, believe that Russia would not have started it a year or two later?

And England? More seriously and more hopefully than any other Power, England was working for peace. She was less entangled than the Continental Powers; and she had a Government and a Foreign Secretary more pacific, perhaps, than has ever before been vouchsafed to any State in history. But let us not exaggerate. England, after all, though not allied with France and Russia, nor tied to them by any firm agreement to go to war, yet, for the last ten years had been drawing closer and closer to their side. She had military and naval commitments to France which were like a suction pipe to draw her, whether she would or no, into the war. And that approximation to the other two Powers of the Entente was made for no other reason than the maintenance of the balance of power. We had become more afraid of Germany than of our traditional enemies, France and Russia. After all our commitments to France it would have been base to desert her. Agreed! But what were the objects for which those commitments were made? Our own power, our own empire, our own security. Is it a crime, then, the reader may ask, to think first of those things? I am not saying so. What I am saying is something more important : that for so long as the States of the world arm with a view to war, pursue policies which can only be fulfilled by war, make alliances in expectation of war, conduct their relations in secret because of war, for so long war will come, until war shall end mankind ; and for so long will every object which gives a reason why States should exist, the prosperity of the mass of the people, the pursuit of knowledge, the practice of art, the cult of human relations, be sacrificed to that Moloch, who offers in return nothing but the prospect of sacrificing again. Is it not time we stopped our disputes about who was the good or the bad boy, and began at last to take stock of the real situation? The time is short, and the danger imminent.

XIX. Italy Comes In

Before the war was over, it had swept into its orbit almost all the world, civilised and uncivilised. Pathans from India were meeting in the scrub natives of Central Africa. Yellow men from China were carrying munitions to black men from Senegal. The whole of North America was swept into the vortex. From the farthest ends of the vast and distracted globe men came pouring in their millions to die and to kill under the black cloud of lies raised by politicians and pressmen to cover up the naked facts it has been our business to unveil. Of this vast movement of human automata we cannot pause to speak. But there was one Power in Europe so intimately bound up with the story we have had to tell that we must not leave unnoticed its entry into the enormous carnage.

Italy was a member of the Triple Alliance. Why, then, did she not stand, from the beginning, beside her allies? "Because the cause was unjust," the reader may reply. There were, indeed, many men in Italy who thought so; and their opinion, no doubt, weighed with the Government. "Marquis di San Giuliano," wrote the German Ambassador as early as July 14th, "insisted that the Italian Government could never take up arms against the principle of nationality." [1] But also, from an early date, the rulers of Italy began to nibble at "compensation," relying upon Clause 7 of the Triple Alliance.[2] By that clause compensation was due to either Power if the other should occupy, either permanently or temporarily, territory "in the regions of the Balkans or of the Ottoman coasts and islands in the Adriatic or the Ægean Sea." Would this clause cover the occupation by Austria of Serbian territory? The Italians said "Yes"; the Austrians said "No";[3] on the usual principle, well understood

---

[1] Kautsky, No. 42.
[2] See text, as renewed in 1912, and cf. above, p. 86.
[3] E.g. Aust. Docs., iii. No. 79, pp. 78 seq.

in diplomacy, that the terms of a treaty are to be interpreted by the ambitions and conveniences of the States concerned, and that the question at issue must never be submitted to any impartial tribunal. A long wrangle thereupon began between the two Governments ; and it was probably for that reason that the Austrians did not show to Italy beforehand the text of their ultimatum, although she was an ally.[1] In her pursuit of " compensation," Italy was supported by Germany, who from the beginning took the Italian view of the meaning of the treaty. In doing so, she was influenced, no doubt, less by the terms of the document, than by a perception of the importance of Italy's assistance, in case the war became general, and by the fact that, so far as she herself was concerned, there was no objection to Austria making concessions. For every State is apt to think that it is only common sense and justice that other States should abandon territory, however inconceivable and monstrous it may seem that they should abandon any themselves. Germany, it seems, was kept well informed of Italy's claims by her Ambassador there ; and we find the Secretary of State writing, as early as July 15th, that " according to our information the cession of Valona, for instance, would not be regarded at Rome as acceptable compensation. In fact, Italy seems to have abandoned for the present her desire to fix herself firmly on the *altera sponda* of the Adriatic. As I may remark, in strict confidence, the acquisition of the Trentino is the only thing that would be regarded as ample compensation by Italy." [2] But what appeared reasonable to Germany, appeared to Austria as blackmail. " Whether the war be localised or general, Italy wants to discount the issue and be paid her price beforehand." [3]

Nevertheless, as events developed, as it became more and more clear that what was in prospect was a general war,

[1] Conrad tells us definitely that it had been agreed between Austria and Germany that the contents of the ultimatum should not be made known either to Roumania or to Italy (see *Aus meiner Dienstzeit*, iv. p. 80), and gives as the reason for the omission of Italy that " there was no reason to doubt of Italy's assistance, as pledged by treaty " (ib., p. 154). Italy's assistance is the last thing Conrad himself believed in, as his whole book shows. The Austrian Government may at first have believed in it. Germany was more sceptical. Yet in a dispatch of the Bavarian Minister in Berlin we are told that, as late as July 30th, the Chancellor was of the opinion that " Italy was standing by the Triple Alliance and had only announced certain modifications in her method of rendering assistance " (Kautsky, Supp. iv, No. 18).

[2] Kautsky, No. 46.　　　　　[3] Aust. Docs., iii. No. 88.

and as Germany became more and more urgent, Austria consented reluctantly to admit the possibility of compensation ; and as a result of the Council held on July 31st, Count Berchtold gave to the Italian Ambassador the following undertaking : " I consider that a divergence of view on the interpretation of Article 7 forms an element of uncertainty in our relations, present and future, which might be prejudicial to the intimacy of the two Powers.   I accept the interpretation given to the article by Italy and Germany, on condition that Italy observes a friendly attitude with regard to the operations of war already in process between Austria-Hungary and Serbia, and will fulfil her duties as an ally if that conflict should bring about a general conflagration." [1] But this concession was not sent to Italy until August 1st, and on that day she had already decided upon neutrality. The concession therefore lapsed.   But that did not end the matter.   For though Italy declared that she was not bound by the Triple Alliance to support Austria in war, since she regarded her as the aggressor, yet she " reserves her right to determine subsequently in what way she can assume an attitude favouring the allies while preserving her own interests." [2]   The Austrians accepted this declaration with the best grace they could.   They hoped that, if Roumania and Turkey should join the Central Powers, Italy might yet be induced to do the same.   Meantime, talk about compensation might be evaded by the reply that as yet no Balkan territory had been occupied.[3]   But the Germans knew Italy better than Austria did ; and they immediately protested against this treatment of the question of compensation.   " Italy," they said, " was on the point not merely of neutrality, but actually of joining the other side." [4]   The discussion of compensation did, accordingly, proceed.   On August 4th, the Italian Minister explained his views frankly. Nice, he said, was French, and had been given up by Italy. Tunis, no doubt, was a fine colony but Italy had enough of them.   As to Albania, that might suit a mixed State, like Austria, but would be a burden to a national State like Italy. It would be different with the Trentino.   That would be the

---

[1] Aust. Docs., iii. No. 87.
[2] Kautsky, No. 568.   Cf. ib., No. 700.
[3] Aust. Docs., iii. No. 117.   [4] Ib. No. 137.

only compensation thinkable. The Austrian Ambassador, at this point, broke off the conversation sharply. But he adds the comment : " That San Giuliano should begin already to speak of the Trentino is characteristic and a bad sign." [1]

It would be premature to suppose that already, at this point, Italy was preparing to enter the war against her allies. She did not know yet how the war would go. She was, however, arranging her position so that, whatever happened, she might get hold of something. But the Austrians were still intransigeant, since they did not know, any more than Italy, what the course of the war might be. The sordid contest between the Central Powers and those of the Entente for the fair hand of Italy was fought out by bribery on both sides.[2] But the Entente had the longest purse and was freer to promise, since it was not its own goods that it was giving away. Moreover, by the spring of 1915, the Entente looked more like winning. The result was the treaty of April 1915, whereby Italy agreed, in return for enormous territorial gains,[3] to enter the war against her allies, and on the side of liberty, democracy, and the ending of war. What else is to be said on this subject may be reserved for our final chapter.

[1] Aust. Docs., iii. No. 127.
[2] For the later stages, see the Austro-Hungarian Red Book : " Diplomatische Aktenstücke betreffend die Beziehungen Oesterreich-Ungarns zu Italien in der Zeit vom 20 Juli, 1914, bis 23 Mai, 1925."
[3] See below, p. 486.

CHAPTER XVII

CONCLUSION

I. The Secret Treaties

WE have thus brought Europe and the world to the beginning of the Great War. We have examined, fairly and squarely, the evidence at our disposal about the origins of the catastrophe; and, in all that evidence, nowhere at any point have we found a trace of any of the purposes which, during the struggle, both sides attributed to themselves. The war did not arise out of a desire for justice, liberty, democracy, or anything of the kind. It was a product of the international anarchy, as we have analysed it.

Its origins being such, it is natural that its results should be of the same kind. And so, in fact, they were. Hardly had the struggle begun before the Governments of the Entente, while their propaganda was making the world ring with catchwords, were drawing up that series of secret treaties which barred the way to any peace save one which should transfer territory and power from the vanquished to the victors. These treaties may be summarised as follows: [1]

By an agreement with Russia in March 1915,[2] the British and French approved the annexation by Russia of Constantinople, the west coast of the Bosphorus, the Sea of Marmara, and the Dardanelles, Southern Thrace up to the Enos-Midia line, the coasts of Asia Minor, between the Bosphorus the river Sakaria and a point to be determined later on the gulf of Ismid, the islands of the Sea of Marmara and Imbros and Tenedos. At the same time, Russia agreed to the incorporation of the " neutral zone " in Persia into the British sphere

[1] See texts in Cocks, and also De Martens, IIIe Série, v. 10.
[2] De Martens, ib., pp. 347 seq.

of influence. This agreement recognised at last the age-long ambition of Russia, so long thwarted by the war or diplomacy of England, France, and Italy.

By a second agreement between Great Britain, France, and Russia,[1] those States partitioned among them the greater part of the Turkish Empire. The division was as follows : Russia was to obtain the provinces of Erzerum, Trapezunt, Van, and Bitlis, together with parts of Southern Kurdistan ; France, the coastal strip of Syria, the vilayet of Adana, and the territory east and north of the Russian frontier ; England, the southern part of Mesopotamia, with Bagdad, and Palestine, with the ports Akka and Haifa. Thus at last had the Powers taken their spring. Turkey was partitioned, and the victorious States were to enter into their kingdom, swallowing up, among other things, the Persian railway. For the principal point of victory in war is, and always has been, the reaping by the victor where he has not sown.

Meantime, as we have seen, after much manœuvring, bribing, and counter-bribing, Italy had decided to enter the war. Her booty was assigned her by a treaty of April 26th, 1915.[2] She was to receive the Trentino, Cisalpine Tyrol to the Brenner frontier (including that purely German territory for which the inhabitants had fought in the past so long and so well, with so much praise from lovers of liberty in Europe), Trieste, Gorizia, and Gradisca, all Istria as far as the Quarnero, the Istrian Islands, Dalmatia with most of the adjacent islands, and Valona. Albania, solemnly created by the Powers as a free State two years earlier, was to be partitioned between Montenegro, Serbia, and Greece, except for a small piece in the centre, which was to be " autonomous and neutralised," Italy being charged with the representation of its relations with foreign Powers. Italy was also to keep the islands of the Dodecanese, which she was still occupying in defiance of her solemn promise to evacuate them. Further, since she was interested in the " balance of power in the Mediterranean," she was to be given her piece of the Turkish booty in the south of Anatolia. In Africa, the frontiers of her existing territory were to be adjusted in her favour. " The present arrangements," of course, " shall be held secret."

[1] March 6th, 1917, De Martens, ib., p. 353.   [2] Ib., p. 329.

Such were the terms upon which Italy consented to enter the war for Right. But her claims, though acceded to, do not appear to have been popular with her allies. "Italy's ambition," M. Paul Cambon is reported to have said, "inspires her to all kinds of mischief." "She had announced again and again that she had come into the war solely to conquer the territories she coveted." Further, "there can be no doubt that in forty-eight hours after the peace is signed Italy will be in the arms of Germany." So M. Jules Cambon. Whereto his brother: "Italy will do nothing for us. She has only one idea, to perfect her preparations for joining in the economic struggle after the war when all the other allies are exhausted." These remarks would, no doubt, be denied if it were thought worth while to deny them, and they may not be exact in phraseology; but I hardly think a judicious reader will doubt their substantial authenticity.[1]

We come next to Roumania. She, too, like Italy, had to be bought, and she exacted a good price;[2] not only Transylvania proper, but also Bukovina and all Hungary up to the river Theiss.

Next came a treaty signed separately by France and Russia,[3] without the knowledge of England, and dealing with the Franco-German frontier. Alsace-Lorraine was to be restored to France without any consultation of the inhabitants; the Saar, rich in coal but wholly German in population and sympathies, was also to go to France; and the whole German territory on the right hand of the Rhine was to be cut off from "political and economic" dependence upon Germany, and formed into an "autonomous and neutral" State, to be occupied by French troops until Germany should have fulfilled all the conditions to be laid down in the treaty of peace.

Such, in outline, were the treaties. In none of them was any mention made either of disarmament or of a League of Nations. What all the Governments were looking to, in Europe and in Asia, was simply the partition of their enemies' territory. The young men perished, or returned mutilated, impoverished, wrecked; and the Allied Powers, having won the victory, proceeded to implement the terms.

[1] See Sixte de Bourbon, *passim*, especially pp. 28, 99, 173–4.
[2] Treaty of August 17th, 1916, De Martens, ib., p. 342.   [3] Ib., p. 370.

II. Reasons for Modifications of the Treaties

But meantime certain things had happened. In Russia there had been a revolution, and consequently the secret treaties had ceased to be valid. The new Russian Government repudiated them, and the Allied States were glad enough to do the same. The abandonment of Constantinople and the Straits to Russia, we may be sure, had never been welcome, either to the English or to the French. In this connexion, a remark attributed to Jules Cambon is illuminating. " Certain people," he said, " make ideal allocations of territory to all the nations : Constantinople for Russia, for instance. That was a great mistake. . . . Then the entire Adriatic to Italy ! As for ourselves, we shall be left as cold as charity." But, the ambassador added, there was at least one consolation : " There are territories for us, too, in the Turkish Empire." [1] Constantinople and the Straits thus remained an open question. Poland, too, now freed from the Russian incubus, could be disposed of at her own will, and that of the Allies.

That, then, was one thing that had happened. The other was that America had come into the war ; and America, unlike the other victors, had no axe of her own to grind. Her people accepted at its face value the account of the origin and motives of the war dealt out by European propaganda. The President, no doubt, knew better. But he preferred the cause of the Entente, and his entry into the war had done much to assure victory, and a little to introduce a better tone. The consequence of all this was that, in certain respects, the treaties of peace were better than the secret agreements we have analysed. The principal achievement of President Wilson was the Covenant of the League of Nations. In the drafting of this the English took a considerable part : but it was the President's influence, from 1917 onwards, that had made its introduction possible. Further, the English and Americans, working together, prevented the realisation of the more extreme French claims, as embodied in the secret treaty with Russia. And, finally, General Smuts was able to introduce the mandatory theory for some of the territories transferred.

[1] Sixte de Bourbon, p. 28.

All this was to the good. Still, the general truth remains, that the treaties of peace were conceived on the traditional lines aiming at the weakening of the defeated enemy and the strengthening of the victors by transferences of territory and by indemnities which, in this case, were reckoned at a figure so absurd that the history of the succeeding years has consisted largely in a belated reduction of them to a sum which, even yet, is known by instructed people to be fantastic.[1] But that subject is too large and too technical for our present discussion. We will content ourselves, therefore, with indicating the main points of the territorial annexations.

III. The Treaties of Peace

First, in Europe, France secured not indeed all she desired, nor all she had provided for in her treaty with Russia, but still a great deal. She took Alsace-Lorraine; she separated from Germany the area of the Saar, with its important deposits of coal; and this area, though it is nominally under the control of the League, she has managed in fact to govern in what she conceives to be her own interest.[2] She occupies the left bank of the Rhine;[3] and she has invaded, contrary to the treaty (as the British, at any rate, maintain), the rich coal district of the Ruhr, whence she is only now withdrawing after the demonstrated failure of her enterprise. Thus, until quite recently, she has relied for her defence against

[1] The decision finally to abolish Reparations was taken by the Lausanne Conference in June, 1932. On the German side the preparatory diplomatic work had been Brüning's, but owing to the delay of the Conference in meeting its fruits were reaped by the Right-wing and aggressively nationalist Chancellor, Franz von Papen.—F.H.

[2] In accordance with the Treaty of Versailles a plébiscite was held in the Saar in January, 1935, at which there voted: For reunion with Germany, 90·35 per cent of the population; for the status quo, 8·83 per cent; for union with France, 0·4 per cent. The territory was, therefore, reunited with Germany in March of the same year.—F.H.

[3] By the terms of the Treaty of Versailles this area was divided into three zones, due to be evacuated five, ten, and fifteen years respectively from the enactment of the Treaty. The first or Cologne zone was evacuated in January 1926. By an agreement made at the Hague Conference in August, 1929, at which the British representative was the then Foreign Secretary, Mr. Arthur Henderson, the evacuation was finally completed on June 30, 1930. This was the last great diplomatic success of Stresemann, who died in October, 1929. But he lived to see the evacuation of the second zone. This had been occupied not only by French but also by Belgian and British troops. —F.H.

Germany on the old device of disarming and holding down the enemy; a device which, when that enemy is powerful, has never succeeded, and never can succeed, in achieving that object,[1] but which has always resulted, and always must result, in new wars.

Even more richly than France was Italy rewarded. She took the greater part of what had been promised in the treaty of 1915. Only in her claim to Fiume was she checked by the determination of President Wilson; and there too she has, in the end, after a filibustering semi-war, gained very much what she wanted. Since then she has made a bid to seize by force the island of Corfu; and she appears, under her Fascist Government, to be determined to defeat all efforts at permanent disarmament and peace.

Russia, having undergone a revolution, was left out in the division of the spoils, but that only gave to France and her Allies a freer hand in the East. The new Poland has taken the " corridor " which separates East Prussia from the rest of Germany; she has been assigned, by the League of Nations, acting under the restrictions of the treaty, the richest part of Silesia; and, by a deliberate and successful defiance of the League, she has appropriated to herself the city of Vilna, and a large adjoining territory.

There remains, in Europe, what used to be the Empire of Austria Hungary. Here the Allies had the best opportunity for carrying out their avowed principles; for here the new doctrine of nationality could be combined, roughly, with the old one of spoils. All the more interesting is it to note that it was precisely Austria-Hungary which, during the earlier part of the war, the Allied Governments were willing, not indeed to leave intact, but to compensate for necessary losses, if, by so doing, they could secure a separate peace. For the enemy, at any rate in the view of England and France, was not Austria-Hungary, but Germany. The negotiations of 1917, of which we have an account by Prince Sixte de Bourbon,

---

[1] The outstanding achievement of the Nazi régime, and the dominant fact in subsequent European history, has been the rearmament of Germany. This, being contrary to the Treaty of Versailles, at first proceeded more or less in secret, but in March, 1935, a German degree re-establishing universal compulsory military service was published, and in June, 1935, an Anglo-German naval agreement was signed. In March, 1936, Germany re-occupied the de-militarized zone of the Rhineland in breach of the Treaty of Locarno. —F.H.

are very illuminating from this point of view. The suggestion was made to square Austria by offering her territory in Germany, such as Silesia and Bavaria. But the Austrians replied that, at that time, the provinces in question were not in the possession of the Allies who were disposing of them. Africa was next considered. " The Prince suggested that one of the Italian colonies might meet his (the Emperor Karl's) requirements. Tripoli was barred as a too recent acquisition which would yield nothing, and was too close to Italy. There remained Erythræa and Somaliland. The latter in particular had a future before it, and was quite unknown to the great majority of the Italians; he could say confidently that they would not resent its cession; while, from the Austrian point of view, the novel experience of an African dominion could only be pleasant, especially when it was taken in exchange for a crowd of blustering and uncontrollable irredentists. A negro was, in short, better value than an irredentist." [1] These negotiations, in the end, broke down. The war proceeded to the bitter end; and, in accordance with the secret treaties, the Austro-Hungarian Empire was broken up. That operation may have been desirable for the health of Europe; but not in the way in which it was carried out. For the new States were permitted to destroy not only the political but the economic unity of the area, and have pursued, ever since, a policy of protective tariffs which has gone far to ruin it. In addition, since it is impossible, in that region, to draw such frontiers as will result in wholly national States, and since even what might have been possible in that way was ruled out by the secret treaties, the new States comprise minorities of alien and recalcitrant populations, and have been treating these with no less rigour, to say the least, than that exercised in the past by Hungary. The nationality problem in Europe is unsolved; and, it may be added, it is insoluble by any frontier-drawing so long as race-hatred and contempt dominate the nations. But those feelings are only intensified by war, which is thus the worst way of attempting a solution. There is no solution except justice, temperance, and benignity; and how should such qualities supervene upon years of savage warfare?

I have confined myself so far to Europe; but the results

[1] Sixte de Bourbon, p. 139.

of the war are not less unsatisfactory in the rest of the world, and perhaps even more ominous for the far future. The British, who have again and again declared themselves " satiated," have nevertheless overeaten themselves in Africa and Asia; a process that seems likely to result in a severe attack of indigestion. Everywhere in the world they are at loggerheads with their subjects. They have just challenged Japan to a naval competition; and they have alienated that immense reserve of force, the republic of China. Russia, for whom the agonies of the war were prolonged and intensified by the military and economic depredations of her former Allies, now threatens a junction with China, and possibly with Japan.[1]   In Morocco, the French and Spanish are involved in a serious war with the native ruler of the Riff; so recalcitrant to the blessings of civilisation are these obstinate tribes, fourteen years after their transference, against their will, to the French. While through the rest of French Africa the native populations watch, with eager eyes, the methods of modern warfare, accept conscription for reasons of their own, and wait gladly for events that may give them their chance in the future. What a world made safe for democracy! what a triumph for liberty, justice, and the rights of small nations!

IV. The Way to Salvation

Such, then, are the results of the war and the peace. Seldom has a lesson been taught with such uncompromising thoroughness. Whether it has been learnt is another matter. There is little evidence in the policies of States to show that it has. Europe is armed, suspicious, and covetous, even more than she was before the war. Yet there are currents below the surface which do not find expression in policy. The governing classes, perhaps, are enjoying their last term of

---

[1] It might indeed seem the case in China in 1926 that new Bolshevism was but old Tsarist imperialism writ large. From 1923 to July, 1929, the influence of a Russian mission led by Borodin was strong in the Left wing of the Kuomintang, the Chinese nationalist party. But at the latter date Borodin and his mission were expelled by the Hankow Government of Feng Yu-hsiang. Further, there has subsequently taken place a complete reversal of Russian foreign policy with the incidental consequence that it does not now appear to be the policy of the Russian Government to support Communist movements in China.   The present antagonism between Russia and Japan is too well-known to need comment.—F.H.

office, and a new world is fermenting underneath. But if that world does not achieve peace, it might as well be old as new; for, though the leaders may be changed, the direction will be the same—down into the pit.

That the way to salvation is the development of the League of Nations into a true international organ to control, in the interests of peace, the policies of all States will be generally admitted by those who have any constructive ideas; and the way in which this could be done has been often enough pointed out. All States must enter the League. The legal openings left for war must be closed, as was provided by the Protocol. There must be, by consequence, a complete apparatus for the peaceable settlement of all disputes. There must be a genuine application, by States with discontented minorities, of the rules laid down by the League. There must be arrangements for an equitable distribution of important raw materials, and the abandonment of protective policies. And, above all, there must be general, all-round disarmament.

Obviously, we are far enough from the adoption of this programme; and one reason is that political opinion, in all countries, has hardly begun to perceive the perils, and is therefore recalcitrant to the remedies. That is why this book was written. There must be knowledge as well as good will, and that knowledge must be widely disseminated. A book of this kind, it is true, cannot hope to be read by very many. It is of necessity complicated, like the facts, and it can hardly help being tedious to any but trained minds. But the facts it deals with may nevertheless be mastered by young students, and through them filter down to larger audiences. It is for such young men that I have written. They may be few, but if they are also fit their influence may reach far.

LIST OF AUTHORITIES CITED IN THE TEXT

Cited as	*Full Title.*
Aberdeen . . .	Balfour, Lady Frances : *The Life of George, Fourth Earl of Aberdeen*. London, 1922.
Acton . . .	Acton, Lord : *Historical Essays and Studies*. London, 1907.
Albin	Albin, Pierre : *D'Agadir à Serajevo*, 1911–14. Paris, 1915.
American Historical Review, January 1918	Goriainov, Serge : *The End of the Alliance of the Emperors*.
A.R.B. *See* Collected Diplomatic Documents	
Asquith . . .	Asquith, Rt. Hon. H. H. : *The Genesis of the War*. London, 1923.
Aust. Docs. . .	*Diplomatische Aktenstücke zur Vorgeschichte des Krieges*, 1914. Wien, 1919. There is an English translation *Austrian Red Book*. London : George Allen & Unwin, Ltd.
B.B.B. *See* Collected Diplomatic Documents	
B.G.B. *See* Collected Diplomatic Documents	
Baker . . .	Baker, Ray Stannard : *Woodrow Wilson and World Settlement*. London, 1923.
Barclay . . .	Barclay, Sir Thomas : *The Turco-Italian War and Its Problems*. London, 1912.
Begbie . . .	Begbie, Harold : *The Vindication of Great Britain*. London, 1916.
Belgian Despatches .	*Zur Europäischen Politik*, 1897–1914. Unveröffentlichte Dokumente in amtlichen Auftrage, herausgegeben unter Leitung von Bernhard Schwertfeger, Berlin, 1919.
Bérard . . .	Bérard, Victor : *L'Affaire Marocaine*. Paris, 1906.

Cited as	Full Title.
Bethmann-Hollweg	Th. von Bethmann-Hollweg : *Betrachtungen zum Weltkriege.* 1. *Theil. Vor dem Kriege.* Berlin, 1919.
Bismarck . . .	Bismarck : *Gedanken und Erinnerungen.* Stuttgart, 1898.
Bland . . .	Bland, J. O. P. : *Recent Events and Policies in China.* London, 1912.
Blunt	Blunt, Wilfrid Scawen : *My Diaries : being a personal narrative of events,* 1888–1914. London, 1921.
Bogitshevich . .	*Causes of the War. An examination into the causes of the European War, with special reference to Russia and Serbia.* London, 1919.
Bourgeois et Pagès .	Bourgeois, E., et Pagès, G. : *Les Origines et les Responsabilités de la grande Guerre.* Paris, 1921.
Brandenburg ● ●	Brandenburg, Erich : *Von Bismarck zum Weltkrieg dargestellt auf Grund der Akten des Auswärtigen Amtes.* Berlin, 1924. This book is of authority, being based on the German Documents, including those not yet published, to which the author had access.
Browne ● ● ●	Browne, Edward G. : 1. *The Persian Revolution of* 1905–9. Cambridge, 1910. 2. *The Persian Crisis of December* 1911. Privately printed. Cambridge University Press. 3. *The Reign of Terror at Tabriz.* Compiled for the use of the Persian Committee, October 1912.
Bülow . . .	Bülow, Fürst von :
1. *Imperial Germany*	1. *Deutsche Politik.* English translation : *Imperial Germany,* 1914, to which I have usually referred.
2. *Erste Stundenschläge*	2. *Die ersten Stundenschläge des Weltkrieges,* 1922.
C.D.D. . . .	Collected Diplomatic Documents relating to the outbreak of the European War. London : Stationery Office, 1915. I. List of the Principal Persons Mentioned.
B.B.B. . . .	II. British Diplomatic Correspondence.
F.Y.B. . . .	III. French Yellow Book.
R.O.B. (*see* also under Romberg and Wegerer)	IV. Russian Orange Book.
B.G.B. . . .	V. Belgian Grey Book.
S.B.B. . . .	VI. Serbian Blue Book.

Cited as	Full Title.
C.D.D.—continued.	
G.W.B. . .	VII. German White Book.
A.R.B. . . .	VIII. Austro-Hungarian Red Book.
	IX. Documents published subsequently.
Cambridge History of British Foreign Policy	Cambridge History of British Foreign Policy, 1783–1919. Ed. by Sir A. W. Ward and G. P. Gooch. 3 vols. Cambridge, 1923.
Campbell-Bannerman	Spender, J. A.: The Life of the Rt. Hon. Sir Henry Campbell-Bannerman. London, 1923.
Caillaux . . .	Caillaux, Joseph: Agadir. Paris, 1919.
Chéradame . .	Chéradame, André: La Question d'Orient— Le chemin de fer de Bagdad. Paris, 1915.
Churchill . . .	Churchill, Rt. Hon. Winston Leonard Spencer: The World Crisis, 1911–14. London, 1923.
Cocks	Cocks, F. Seymour: The Secret Treaties and Undertakings. London, Union of Democratic Control, 1918.
Conrad . . .	Conrad von Hoetzendorf: Aus meiner Dienstzeit, 1906–18. Wien, Berlin, Leipzig, München, 1921–3.
Crispi	Crispi, Francesco: Memoirs. Translated by Mary Prichard-Agnetti. London, 1912.
Darcy . . .	Darcy, Jean: France et Angleterre. Cent Années de Rivalité Coloniale. L'Afrique. Paris, 1904.
Delaisi . . .	Delaisi, Francis: Oil : its Influence on Politics. Trans. by C. L. Leese. London, 1922.
Dilke . . .	Gwynn, Stephen, and Tuckwell, Gertrude: Life of Sir Charles Wentworth Dilke. London, 1917.
Dillon . . .	Dillon, Emile Joseph: The Eclipse of Russia. London, 1918.
Disraeli, Life . .	Monypenny, W. F., and Buckle, G. E.: The Life of Benjamin Disraeli, Earl of Beaconsfield. London, 1910.
Dobrorolski . .	Dobrorolski, General Sergei: Die Mobilmachung der Russischen Armee, 1914. Berlin, 1922.
Drei Konferenzen .	Pokrowski, Prof. M.: Drei Konferenzen zur Vorgeschichte des Krieges—Russische Korrespondenz, 1920.
Earle . . .	Earle, Edward Mead: Turkey, the Great Powers, and the Bagdad Railway. London, 1923.
1. Eckardstein . .	Eckardstein, Hermann Freiherr v.: 1. Lebenserinnerungen und Politische Denkwürdigkeiten. 2 Bde.
2. Eckardstein. Isolierung Deutschlands.	2. Die Isolierung Deutschlands. Leipzig, 1919.

Cited as	Full Title.
Eversley . . .	Eversley, Lord : *The Partitions of Poland.* London, 1915.
F.Y.B. *See* Collected Diplomatic Documents	
Feuvrier . . .	Feuvrier, Docteur: *Trois Ans à la Cour de Perse,* 1889–92.
Fischer . . .	Dr. Eugen Fischer: *Holstein's Grosses Nein. Die Deutsch-Englischen Bündnissverhandlungen von 1898–1901.* Berlin, 1925.
Fisher. . . .	Admiral of the Fleet Lord Fisher : *.Memories.* London, 1919.
Friedjung . .	Friedjung, Heinrich : *Das Zeitalter des Imperialismus,* 1884–1914. 3 Bde. Berlin, 1919–22.
G.W.B. *See* Collected Diplomatic Documents	
Gathorne-Hardy .	Gathorne-Hardy, Alfred Erskine : *Gathorne-Hardy, First Earl of Cranbrook.* London, 1910.
Ger. Docs. . .	*Die Grosse Politik der Europäischen Kabinette,* 1871–1914. Deutsche Verlagsgesellechaft für Politik und Geschichte, Berlin. (Twenty-five volumes published up to date of compilation of this list.)
Giolitti . . .	Giolitti, Giovanni : *Memoirs of My Life.* Trans. by E. Storer. London, 1923.
Gooch . . .	G. P. Gooch : *History of Modern Europe.* London, 1923.
Grey	Viscount Grey of Fallodon : *Twenty-five Years,* 1892–1916. London, 1925. This book was not published until my own was in page proof. It does not adduce any new facts for the years with which I am dealing ; but I have added references where it seemed necessary. Lord Grey endorses fully the main thesis of my book. *See,* e.g.,i. 92, 104, 112, 190; ii. 52, 274 seq.
Guéchoff . . .	Guéchoff, Iv. E.: *L'Alliance Balkanique.* Paris, 1915.
Guyot, Yves . .	Guyot, Yves : *Les causes et les conséquences de la guerre.* First edition.
Haldane . . .	Haldane, Viscount : *Before the War.* London, 1920.
Haller. . . .	Haller, Johannes : *Die Aera Bülow, eine historische-politische Studie.* Berlin, 1922.

Cited as	Full Title.

Hammann . . Hammann, Otto :

1. *Neuer Kurs* . 1. *Der neue kurs.* Berlin, 1918.

2. *Vorgeschichte* . 2. *Zur Vorgeschichte des Weltkriegs. Erinnerungen aus den Jahren* 1897–1906. Berlin, 1919.

3. *Der Missverstandene Bismarck* 3. *Der Missverstandene Bismarck. Zwanzig Jahre Deutscher Weltpolitik.* Berlin, 1921.

4. *Weltpolitik* . 4. *Deutsche Weltpolitik,* 1890–1912. Berlin, 1925.

Hanotaux . . . Hanotaux, Gabriel : *La Guerre des Balkans et l'Europe,* 1912–13. Paris, 1914.

Hayashi . . . Hayashi, Viscount Tadasu : *Secret Memoirs,* ed. by A. M. Pooley. London, 1915.

Helfferich . . . Helfferich, Karl : *Die Vorgeschichte des Weltkrieges.* Berlin, 1919.

Hirst . . . Hirst, F. W. : *The Six Panics and other Essays.* London, 1913.

Hoyos . . . Hoyos, Alexander : *Der Deutsch-Englische Gegensatz und sein Einfluss auf die Balkanpolitik Osterreich-Ungarns.* Berlin and Leipzig, 1922.

Huldermann . . Huldermann, Bernhard : *Albert Ballin.* Oldenburg, 1922. English translation by W. J. Egger. London, 1922. My references are to the English translation.

Is Germany Guilty ?. *Deutschland Schuldig ? Deutsches Weissbuch über die Verantwortlichkeit der Urheber des Krieges.* Berlin, 1919.
My references are to the English translation, *Is Germany Guilty ?* Berlin, 1919.

Isvolski . . . 1. *Der Diplomatische Schriftwechsel Isvolskis* 1911–14, *herausgegeben von Friedrich Stieve,* Deutsche Verlagsgesellschaft für Politik und Geschichte. Bde. 4. Berlin, 1924.

Isvolski, *Memoirs* . 2. *Memoirs of A. Isvolsky,* ed. and trans. by C. L. Seeger. London, 1920.

Jagow . . . Jagow, Gottlieb von :

1. *Ursachen* 1. *Ursachen und Ausbruch des Weltkrieges.* Berlin, 1919.

2. *Remarks* 2. *Remarks on the article of Prince Lichnowski, " My London Mission,"* translated by Munroe Smith, American Association for International Conciliation. No. 127, June 1918.

Jones . . . . Jones, Kennedy : *Fleet Street and Downing Street.* London, 1920.

Kaiser . . . Kaiser Wilhelm II :

1. *Kaiser to Tsar* 1. *The Kaiser's Letters to the Tsar,* ed. by N. F. Grant. London [1920].

Cited as	Full Title.
Kaiser (contd.)	Kaiser Wilhelm II :
2. Memoirs	2. *My Memoirs*.　Ex-Kaiser　William　II. London, 1922.
Kautsky	*Die Deutschen Dokumente zum Kriegsausbruch* 1914 nach gemeinsamen Durchsicht mit Karl Kautsky herausgegeben von Graf Max Montgelas und Prof. Walther Schücking. Bde. 4.　Charlottenburg, 1919. English translation, *Outbreak of the World War*.　Carnegie Endowment for International Peace.　Oxford, 1924. My citations are from the English version.
Kiderlen-Waechter	*Kiderlen-Waechter der Staatsmann und Mensch* herausgegeben von Ernst Jäckh.　Berlin, 1924.
Kriegsschuldfrage	1. *Die Kriegsschuldfrage. Monatsschrift für Internationale Aufklärung*.　Schrift leitung Alfred von Wegerer.　Berlin. A monthly journal, from July 1923 onwards. Contains articles and notices dealing with all new publications bearing on the origins of the war. 2. *Die Kriegsschuldfrage. Ein Verzeichniss der Literatur des In- und Auslandes*.　Leipzig, 1915.
Lichnowski	Prince Lichnowski : *My London Mission*, 1912–1914. The disclosures from Germany.　American Association for International Conciliation.　No. 127.　June 1918.
Livre Noir	*Un Livre Noir.　Diplomatie d'avant-guerre d'après les documents des archives Russes, November 1910–July 1914*.　Librairie de Travail.　Paris.
Loreburn	Loreburn, Earl : *How the War Came*.　London, 1919.
Louis, Georges	Judet, Ernest : *Georges Louis*.　Paris, 1925.
Ludendorff	Ludendorff, Erich :
1. Ludendorff	1. *The General Staff and its Problems*.　Trans. by F. A. Holt.　London, 1920.
2. Ludendorff, Fälschung	2. *Französische Fälschung meiner Denkscrift von 1912*.　Berlin, 1919.
Lyons	Newton, T. W. L. : *Lord Lyons.　A Record of British Diplomacy*.　London, 1913.
McCullagh	McCullagh, Francis : *Italy's War for a Desert*.　London, 1912.
MacKenzie	MacKenzie, F. A. : *The Tragedy of Korea*.　London, 1908.

Cited as	*Full Title.*
MacMurray	MacMurray, J. V. A.: *Treaties and Agreements with and concerning China.* New York, 1921.
de Martens	Martens, Charles de : *Recueil des Traités.*
Martin	Martin, B. Kingsley: *The Triumph of Lord Palmerston.* A study of Public Opinion in England before the Crimean War. London, 1924.
Mijatovich	Mijatovich, Count Chedomille : *The Memoirs of a Balkan Diplomatist.* London, 1917.
Montgelas	Montgelas : Graf Max : *Leitfaden zur Kriegsschuldfrage.* Berlin and Leipzig, 1923. English translation by Constance Vesey, *The Case for the Central Powers,* London, 1925. My references are to the English text.
Morel	Morel, E. D. : *Morocco in Diplomacy.* London, 1912. This contains, in the Appendix, the treaties concerning Morocco, etc.
Morley's *Gladstone*	Morley, John : *The Life of William Ewart Gladstone.* 2 vols., 1908.
Nationalism and War	*Nationalism and War in the Near East.* By a Diplomatist. Ed. by Lord Courtney of Penwith. Oxford, 1915.
Nekludoff	Nekludoff, A. : *Diplomatic Reminiscences before and during the World War,* 1911–17. Translated from the French by Alexander Paget. London, 1920.
Nineteenth Century, December 1917, and January 1918	Articles by J. Y. Simpson on the *Memoirs of Sabouroff.*
Oman	Oman, C. : *The Outbreak of the War of 1914–18.* London, 1919.
Paléologue	Paléologue, Maurice : *La Russie des Tsars pendant la grande guerre.* Paris, 1921. English translation, *An Ambassador's Memoirs,* by F. A. Holt. London, 1923. My references are to the French edition.
Perla	Perla, Leo : *What is National Honour ?* New York, 1918.
Pinon	Pinon, René : *France et l'Allemagne,* 1870–1913. Paris, 1913.
Poincaré	Poincaré, Raymond : *The Origins of the War.* London, 1922.
Pourtalès	Pourtalès, Graf : *Am Scheidewege zwischen Krieg und Frieden.* Berlin, 1919.

Cited as	Full Title.
Pribram . . .	Pribram, Dr. Alfred Francis: 1. *The Secret Treaties of Austria-Hungary*, 1879–1914. Oxford University Press, 1920–1. Two vols.

    I. Texts of the Treaties and Agreements.

    II. Negotiations leading to the Treaties of the Triple Alliance with documentary appendices. English edition by A. C. Coolidge.

    2. *Austria's Foreign Policy*.

R.O.B. *See* Collected Diplomatic Documents

Repington . . Repington, Charles à Court: *The First World War*, 1914–18. London, 1920.

Reventlow . . Reventlow, Graf Ernst zu: *Deutschlands Auswärtige Politik*, 1888–1914.

I have referred to the edition of 1916, unless otherwise mentioned.

Rohrbach . . Rohrbach, Paul: *Die Bagdad bahn*. Berlin, 1911.

Romberg . . Romberg, Baron G. von: *The Falsifications of the Russian Orange Book*. Translated by Major Cyprian Bridge. With a Foreword by G. P. Gooch. London, 1923.

My references are to the translation. See also the fuller edition, by Wegerer.

Roosevelt . . Bishop, J. B.: *Theodore Roosevelt and his time*. London, 1920.

S.B.B. *See* Collected Diplomatic Documents

Salisbury, *Life* . . *Life of Robert, Marquis of Salisbury*, by his daughter, Lady Gwendoline Cecil. London, 1921.

Salvemini . . Salvemini, Gustavo: A series of articles in the Italian Press, to which I have occasionally referred, giving the source.

Sanger & Norton . Sanger, C. P., and Norton, H. T. J.: *England's Guarantee to Belgium and Luxemburg*. London, 1915.

Schoen . . . Schoen, Freiherr von: *The Memoirs of an Ambassador*. Translated by Constance Vesey. London, 1922.

Séché . . . . Séché, Alphonse: *Les Guerres d'Enfer*. Paris, 1919.

Shuster . . . Shuster, W. Morgan: *The Strangling of Persia*. A Record of European Diplomacy and Oriental Intrigue. London, 1920. My references are to that edition.

Cited as	Full Title.

Siebert . . . *Entente Diplomacy and the World.* Translated from the original texts by B. de Siebert, late Secretary of the Imperial Russian Embassy at London. London, 1924. (George Allen & Unwin, Ltd.) These despatches appear to have been forwarded to Berlin from the Russian Embassy in London. *See* Valentin, p. 145, note 1.

Sixte de Bourbon . *Austria's Peace Offer,* 1916–17, ed. by G. de Manteyer, with an introductory letter by Prince Sixte de Bourbon. London, 1921.

Sosnosky . . . Sosnosky, Theodor von : *Die Balkanpolitik Oesterreich-Ungarns seit* 1866. Berlin, 1913–14.

Stanojević . . Stanojević, Stanoje : *Die Ermordung des Erzhezogs Franz Ferdinand.* Frankfort, 1923.

Tages-Aufzeichnungen Der Beginn des Krieges, 1914. Tages-Aufzeichnungen des ehemaligen Russischen Aussenministeriums, mit einem Vorwort von Alfred von Wegerer. Berlin, 1924. English translation, from the Russian, *How the War began in* 1914, translated by Major W. Cyprian Bridge. London, 1925. My references are to the German text.

Tardieu . . . Tardieu, André :
  1. *Algeciras*   1. *La Conférence d'Algeciras,* Paris, 1907.
  2. *Agadir*   2. *Le Mystère d'Agadir.* Paris, 1912.

Tirpitz . . . Tirpitz, A. P. F. von :
  1. *Memoirs*   1. *My Memoirs.* London, 1919.
  2. *Politische Doku-*   2. *Politische Dokumente.* Berlin, 1924.
    mente

Tittoni . . . Tittoni, 1. *Italy's Foreign and Colonial Policy.* London, 1914.
    2. *Italien, der Dreibund und die Balkan-Verträge.* Berlin, 1913.

Untersuchungs-aus-   *Beilagen zu den stenographischen Berichten*
schuss   *über die öffentlichen Verhandlungen des Untersuchungs-ausschusses.* 1. *Unterausschuss.* Deutsche National-versammlung. Berlin, 1920. English translation in *Official German Documents relating to the World War,* vol. i, Carnegie Endowment for International Peace, 1923. My references are to the German text.

Valentin . . . Valentin, Veit von : *Deutschlands Aussenpolitik von Bismarcks Abgang bis zum Ende des Weltkriegs.* Berlin, 1921.

Cited as		*Full Title.*
Waldersee.	. .	Waldersee, Alfred, Graf von : *A Field-Marshal's Memoirs*, condensed and translated by F. Whyte. London, 1924. My references are to this translation, a much shortened but well-selected version of the original.
Wegerer	. . .	*Das Russische Orange-buch von* 1914. Ergänzt durch die inzwischen bekannt gewordenen neuen Dokumente, mit einem Vowort von Alfred v. Wegerer. Berlin, 1925.
Willoughby	. .	Willoughby, W. W. : *Treaties and Foreign Rights and Interests in China.*
Witte.	. . .	Witte, Count Sergei Julievich de : *Memoirs.* Translated by A. Yarmolinsky. London, 1924.
White	. . .	White, A. D. : *Autobiography.* London, 1905.
Woolf	. . .	Woolf, Leonard : *Empire and Commerce in Africa.* A Study in Economic Imperialism. London, 1920.
Yellow Book	. .	*L'Alliance Franco-Russe. Pages d'Histoire,* 1914–18. *Troisième Livre Jaune Français,* Librairie Militaire Berger-Lerrault. Paris, 1918.

INDEX

(Please see page 516 for Addenda to Index.)

ADDENDA